EFFECTIVE SUPERVISION

Preparing for the 21st Century

EFFECTIVE SUPERVISION

Preparing for the 21st Century

Thomas O. Kirkpatrick
University of Montana

Chad T. Lewis
Everett Community College

THE DRYDEN PRESS
Harcourt Brace College Publishers

Fort Worth   Philadelphia   San Diego   New York   Orlando   Austin   San Antonio
Toronto   Montreal   London   Sydney   Tokyo

Acquisitions Editor	Ruth Rominger
Developmental Editor	Traci Keller
Project Editor	Nancy Weaver
Senior Art Director	Brian Salisbury
Senior Production Manager	Mandy Manzano
Photo Editor	Shirley Webster
Senior Product Manager	Lisé Johnson
Marketing Assistant	Sam Stubblefield
Editorial Assistant	Dona Hightower
Director of Editing, Design & Production	Diane Southworth
Publisher	Elizabeth Widdicombe
Copy Editor	Alison Shurtz
Literary Permissions Editor	Steve Lunetta
Compositor	Typographics
Text Type	10/12 Utopia
Cover Image	Murray Kimber
Text Art	Lamberto Alvarez and Lamberto Alvarez III

Address for Editorial Correspondence
The Dryden Press, 301 Commerce Street, Suite 3700, Fort Worth, TX 76102

Address for Orders
The Dryden Press, 6277 Sea Harbor Drive, Orlando, FL 32887
1-800-782-4479, or 1-800-433-0001 (in Florida)

ISBN: 0-03-097663-4

Library of Congress Catalog Card Number: 94-71180

Printed in the United States of America

4 5 6 7 8 9 0 1 2 3 054 10 9 8 7 6 5 4 3 2 1

The Dryden Press
Harcourt Brace College Publishers

To the countless supervisors who practice their craft with skill, who continue to learn, who care for those they direct and their employers, and who enjoy what they are doing.

T.O.K.

To Anna and Murdoc Gordon.

C.T.L.

THE DRYDEN PRESS SERIES IN MANAGEMENT

PREFACE

*Carla Jones is a first-line supervisor. Not only is she trying to carve out her own identity as a supervisor, she is also trying to manage a group of workers, implement new total quality management standards, and maintain the high production output in a Boeing production plant in Everett, Washington. Carla is beginning to face situations that demand the integration of concepts such as **job effectiveness, performance, productivity, quality, motivation, innovation, and teamwork,** not only for employees, but also for herself. In today's dynamic business environment, how will she meet this challenge?*

Never has there been a greater need for cooperative effort among people for solving mutual problems, and this need for cooperation extends to workers and their managers. Management education today must prepare students to meet this challenge by establishing demanding but realistic expectations. How do we face the challenge?

Effective supervision contributes to continuous improvement while appreciating and tolerating individual differences. The purpose of studying supervision is to begin or to continue the preparation process that leads to a career in supervision. Supervision, unlike some disciplines, is always changing, improving, moving. What worked yesterday may not work today. Preparation for the future is essential as new challenges are continuously being presented to today's supervisor. The purpose of this book is to provide the foundation and the skills needed for individuals to incorporate key concepts and skills vital to succeeding in a 21st century organizational environment.

The philosophy of supervisory management that we have expressed in this textbook is based on observation, research, writing, and practice. Having taught both beginners and veteran practitioners, we have learned that some of the most practical advice comes from those who are on the firing line daily. Our intent is to translate theory—where theories exist—into practical applications. You will notice that the chapters contain many references to research or to persons who should receive recognition for their contributions to supervisory practices and literature. In this sense, we are summarizing the best of current knowledge. The examples illustrating supervisory practices are drawn from real-life experiences, and they include a range of organizations from large to small and from for-profit businesses to not-for-profit institutions. Finally, we have tried to write in a style that suggests a dialogue is taking place. We talk with the students, pausing now and then for an answer. We are not lecturing with ultimate wisdom, but we are sharing knowledge gained from our experiences.

Text Overview

Effective Supervision is a book whose structure is based specifically on the activities of a supervisor. The integration of teamwork in each chapter illustrates the authors' understanding and experience in supervision.

The textbook is organized into four parts. The first two of these parts are particularly concerned with concepts, a summary of which follows each chapter. In the remaining two parts, the emphasis is on developing skills. Each chapter in these parts concludes with a series of specific skill-related actions for supervisors to consider.

Part 1 is concerned specifically with the foundations of supervision. As such, the nature and importance of effective supervision are discussed along with major issues facing supervisors today. In Part 2, our attention turns to exploring the work of supervisors, that is, what they do. Here, supervisory functions are described and explained. We include an analysis of the functions supervisors perform: planning, organizing, staffing, leading, and controlling. Because supervisors typically interface with many others in their organizations, we attempt to illustrate the relationships that develop and methods of nurturing those relationships.

Part 3 presents chapters dealing with supervisory skills such as decision making, motivating employees, managing conflict, communicating, performance appraisal, applying discipline, counseling, managing stress, and organizational change. The book concludes with Part 4, which is devoted to special concerns of individual supervisors, namely, using time more effectively and career planning and development.

Text Pedagogy

- **Learning objectives** are provided at the beginning of each chapter to emphasize the key points for the chapter.
- A **continuing vignette** introduces the student to Carla Jones, a first-line supervisor. The situation Carla encounters at the beginning of each chapter focuses the student on the topic for the chapter, and a resolution to the case is presented at the end of the chapter. The case is clearly marked with an icon.
- The **marginal glossary** of key terms in each chapter has been developed to provide the student with an easy reference to unfamiliar terms the first time they are encountered.
- **Boxes,** dealing with everything from productivity to interview questions to quality standards, add information in an interesting form.
- The **chapter summaries** for the first two parts are organized around the major concepts introduced in the chapter. The summaries in the last two parts of the textbook are based on skills and use a list format to clearly check the student's abilities.
- **Review questions** follow the summaries to focus on key concepts. These questions can easily be used as a testing device.
- Two **cases** follow each chapter, complete with discussion questions. These cases are specifically written to illustrate in a real situation the ideas presented in the chapter.
- A full-text **glossary** is included at the end of the book with all terms and definitions from each chapter. Page numbers are included as a ready reference for students and instructors.

Overview of Supplements

Instructor's Manual/Transparency Masters/Test Bank This important text supplement has been developed with the busy instructor in mind. In the Instructor's Manual section, an overview of each chapter, with a teaching outline as well as lecture notes, gives the instructor an immediate reference. The outline is then expanded to include discussion suggestions with transparency annotations. Full answers to the review questions are included, followed by the case discussions.

Case background and discussion notes for the questions make using the cases easy and effective. At least two projects and skill-building exercises per chapter, including role playing, research activities, and interviewing, give the instructor more options in deciding how to teach a particular section.

Finally, the authors have developed extensive supplementary material for most chapters, complete with transparency references and journal citations. This material may expand on a concept in the textbook or be a specific example from the world today. Transparency masters to accompany the text are conveniently located within the instructor's manual. The transparency masters include art from the text as well as new exhibits for use with the supplementary material in the instructor's manual. The test bank is a collection of true/false and multiple-choice questions referenced by page to the textbook. The questions were prepared by the authors and reflect the key concepts from the chapters.

Computerized Test Bank   The ExaMaster computerized test bank system is available to the instructor. This testing program allows questions to be edited or added, arranged in any order, and saved for future use.

RequesTest Service   This phone-in test service is available to all adopters of the textbook. Test masters can be ordered by question number and are mailed or faxed to you within 48 hours.

Videos   The video package includes six 10-minute segments, featuring material on supervision and small business issues. The supervision topics, such as stress management, verbal communication, and discipline, are chosen from popular CRM footage and *Inc.* magazine videos.

Microcomputer Simulation   The popular *Io Enterprises,* by Chad Lewis et al., is available in a customized form for use with this textbook. This computer-assisted classroom activity emphasizes basic organizational and management concepts and applications. In-class simulations offer students challenging opportunities to practice people skills such as dealing with staff problems and building teams. *Io Enterprises* is successfully being used in both traditional classes and training workshops.

Acknowledgments

We would like to thank the following reviewers for sharing their insight and for contributing with valuable suggestions: Barbara Boyington, Brookdale Community College; John J. "Jack" Heinsius, Modesto Junior College; Robert Ash, Rancho Santiago College; Michael J. Miller, Indiana-Purdue University; Charles H. "Terry" Wetmore, California State University, Fresno; John Cox, New Mexico State University, Las Cruces; Jane W. Gibson, Nova University, Southeastern; Sylvia Ong, Scottsdale Community College; Charles M. Vance, Loyola Marymount University; and David W. Murphy, Madisonville Community College.

Colleagues whose interest and assistance have helped us include Dr. Sarah M. Jobs, David Dunning & Company; Dr. Joseph E. Garcia, Western Washington University; Philip C. Lewis, Gemini Innovations, Inc.; Christie Nelson, Everett Community College; Sherry Rosette, faculty secretary, University of Montana; and researchers deluxe, Renee LaCost and Rain Delaney.

We also deeply appreciate the exceptional dedication of The Dryden Press staff, including Ruth E. Rominger, acquisitions editor; Traci Keller, developmental editor; Lisé W. Johnson, senior product manager; Brian Salisbury, senior art director; Nancy Weaver, associate project editor; Alison Shurtz, freelance copyeditor; Mandy Manzano, senior production manager; Steve Lunetta, freelance literary permissions editor; and Shirley Webster, photo permissions editor. All members of the team were consistently competent and professional during our sometimes grueling work together.

A special hats-off goes to Ruth Rominger for her vision and integrity, and Traci Keller and Shirley Webster for their follow-through and commitment. We also extend special recognition to Alison Shurtz for the superb job she did editing the manuscript, and Nancy Weaver for seeing the project through production.

Supervising others is serious business. We, as supervisors, can do a lot of damage if we are not skilled. On the other hand, it can be fun and fulfilling to supervise effectively. And there should be an immense satisfaction in knowing we have done things correctly and better than anyone else.

Shall we go to work?

T.O.K., Missoula, Montana
C.T.L., Everett, Washington
September 1994

ABOUT THE AUTHORS

Tom Kirkpatrick has over 35 years experience in teaching management and marketing. He has published various articles on the subjects of workers' compensation, unemployment insurance, and employment/retention of Native Americans, and has also written and published a textbook on supervision. Tom served as a vice president and member of the board of directors of the American Society of Personnel Administration (ASPA), now known as Society of Human Resource Management (SHRM), and was chair of the Department of Management, School of Business Administration at the University of Montana. He has also taught numerous workshops in supervisory training and business management. Tom has a B.B.A. and an M.B.A. from North Texas State University and a Ph.D. from Ohio State University.

Chad Lewis has been creating educational software and text materials since 1983. He is the coauthor of three microcomputer simulations and two textbooks covering general business, marketing, and management topics. He has published articles in higher education, business education, human resources, and management journals on the subjects of marketing, decision making, conflict, and compensation. Chad has earned two teaching awards during his 15-year tenure at Everett Community College and also serves as an online faculty member for the University of Phoenix. He has a B.A. from The Evergreen State College, an M.Ed. from Western Washington University, and an M.B.A. from the University of Puget Sound.

BRIEF CONTENTS

CONTENTS

EFFECTIVE SUPERVISION

Preparing for the 21st Century

PART 1

Foundations of Supervision

A foundation is the basis on which something stands or is supported. Supervision has a foundation that consists of fundamental concepts about the nature of the activities supervisors perform, supervisors' positioning within organizations, and a variety of issues challenging them including the legal environment and maintaining good employee relations.

CHAPTER 1   What Is Supervision?

What is supervision and what is the work of supervisors? These are questions answered in Chapter 1. Supervision is the first line of management that oversees efforts of workers for the purpose of accomplishing group and organizational objectives. A realistic picture of supervision calls for insight of the challenges faced by supervisors. Characteristics of successful supervisors are considered along with a view of our changing working environment and its impact upon supervisory practices.

CHAPTER 2   Meeting the Performance Challenge

An organization's success is measured in terms of its ability to prepare for the future. In Chapter 2, methods for improving performance are addressed including the topics of improving quality and productivity in the workplace. The chapter includes discussion of total quality management (TQM), obtaining customer satisfaction, motivating employees, and understanding organizational culture.

CHAPTER 3   Meeting the Legal Challenge

Ensuring legal compliance through appropriate supervisory practices is the thrust of Chapter 3. We begin by exploring how laws are developed and enforced including statutory and case law and continue by differentiating between crimes and torts. The major topics include equal employment opportunity laws, adverse impact and treatment, and affirmative action. Various illustrations assist in distinguishing between acceptable and legal practices and those prohibited by law.

CHAPTER 4   Labor Relations

Chapter 4 is concerned with methods for developing and maintaining positive working relationships between supervisors and members of work groups that belong to unions or employee associations. We begin with a brief history of the labor movement in the United States, and we cover the major provisions of management-labor regulations. The chapter includes discussion of collective bargaining and the several stages involved in the organizing process.

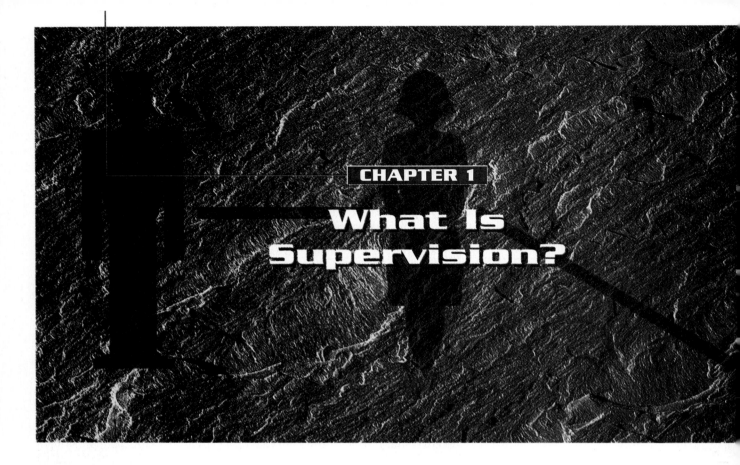

CHAPTER 1

What Is Supervision?

> In academic study, as in social life, an introduction is no more than the first stage in the departure from a state of complete ignorance, leaving much to be learned later, not without constant possibility of surprise.
>
> **Sir Alexander Gray[1]**

LEARNING OBJECTIVES

1. Define supervision and explain the meaning of the management pyramid.
2. Explain the importance of the study of supervision.
3. Differentiate among the concepts of performance, productivity, efficiency, quality, and effectiveness.
4. Give two primary reasons why people desire supervisory jobs.
5. Name the four major attributes of successful supervisors and explain each.
6. Identify the six factors currently challenging supervisors.

Carla Jones sat in her cubicle off a production line at a Boeing production plant in Everett, Washington. She sipped tepid coffee and considered events of the day.

Three of her subordinates had called in sick; she had been chewed out by Larry, her boss; top management had announced a mission to implement something called "total quality management," necessitating endless meetings and visits by consultants; and she still had a production report, performance appraisal reports, and personnel action forms to complete before going home. She would be lucky to get home before sunup.

Carla is a supervisor. The most important part of her job is to successfully supervise people—no easy task in the increasingly competitive, litigious, and confusing times we live in. Supervisors work for a salary rather than for an hourly wage, in accordance with the federal Fair Labor Standards Act (FLSA) of 1938, and therefore Carla could work all night without an increase in her paycheck. No question about it, being a supervisor is a tough way to earn a living.

The challenge of supervision can be compared to the story depicted in Figure 1-1 of a young man who drove his small truck through Pittsburgh, Pennsylvania. At each stoplight, he got out and beat on the truck with a piece of lumber. After several blocks, he came under the surveillance of the local police,

who followed him for several additional blocks and then pulled him to the curb to ask for an explanation of his odd behavior. The perplexed driver answered, "You see, officer, I've got a two-ton limit truck. I'm carrying an overweight load of canaries, so I've got to keep 'em flying." At times, being a supervisor is akin to navigating a two-ton limit truck filled with too many canaries. It calls for creativity, courage, and intelligence.

Supervision: The First Line of Management

supervision
The first line of management that oversees efforts of workers for the purpose of accomplishing group and organizational objectives.

management pyramid
Consists of top, middle, and bottom management with supervisors occupying the bottom or first level of management.

heap reversal theory
Suggests that when employees are promoted to supervisory positions from rank-and-file positions, they may experience anxiety due to their reversal in position from the top of one group (with their coworkers) to the bottom of another (management).

Supervisors work under a variety of job titles, including "basketball coach."

Supervision is the first line of management that oversees efforts of workers for the purpose of accomplishing group and organizational objectives. Effective supervision, then, is the process of intelligently utilizing human and other resources to accomplish these objectives. Supervisors are part of management. They work under a variety of job titles including foreman, administrative assistant, staff manager, assistant chef, lead, warehouse supervisor, sales assistant, office manager, crew leader, department chair, and assistant coach. In a traditional organization, the position of supervisors like Carla is at the bottom of a **management pyramid** comprised of top, middle, and supervisory management (see Figure 1-2).

The experience of many new supervisors is described by the **heap reversal theory.** This theory states that in many instances, supervisors are promoted to their jobs because they were the most competent members of their work groups. As their organization needs new supervisors, they are promoted. Previously, they enjoyed an informal leadership role and high status among their coworkers. Upon promotion, however, they leave the apex of the rank-and-file heap and assume the bottom-of-the-heap position in a new group, management. The resulting new role relationships create an unfamiliar setting with the potential consequences of anxiety and a longing for the old role, as former coworkers become the new supervisor's subordinates. Unsettling, too, is the burning of the bridge back to the previous job. The new supervisor often is quickly replaced in the former group by a new informal leader. For many, there is no return. Becoming a supervisor thus may require extensive adjustments in interpersonal relationships.

Many principles of supervision are universal. Any time you are responsible for supervising the activities of a group, you are practicing supervision. Parents, for example, supervise children; instructors supervise students; team captains supervise teammates. The wide applicability of supervisory principles adds much meaning to study of this subject. As you read this text, stop occasionally and consider how chapter material relates to your day-to-day life.

The difficult job of supervisor is essential in any organization in three important ways: First, competent supervision contributes directly to improving employee performance in terms of productivity and the quality of work processes and output. Second, knowledgeable, ethical, and equitable supervision helps the organization assure compliance with employee-related legal requirements. Third, a supervisor's job is important to the job satisfaction and career aspirations of the individual supervisor. As illustrated in Figure 1-2, it is the first step toward higher-level management positions offering more responsibility, higher pay, and generally, more interesting work.

Figure 1-1 Keep 'Em Flying

| **Figure 1-2** | The Management Pyramid and Heap Reversal Theory |

Source: Carl A. Benson, "New Supervisors: From the Top of the Heap to the Bottom of the Heap," *Personnel Journal* 55, (April 1976): 178.

performance
The productivity and quality of individual or group output.

productivity
The ratio of output (the results of production) to input (the various economic resources used to produce that output).

labor productivity
Typically expressed in terms of the amount of production obtained per hour of labor.

efficiency
Amount of production obtained based upon either a theoretical or practical limit of what can be obtained.

Improving Employee Performance

Improving the performance of individuals and the work teams they are part of is an important objective of all levels of management. **Performance** is defined in terms of the productivity and quality of individual or group output.

Productivity is concerned with the efficiency of production or operations. **Productivity** is a ratio of output (the results of production) to input (the various economic resources used to produce that output). It deals with how much is produced in goods or services by a work force with a given level of resources. **Labor productivity** is typically expressed in terms of production per labor hour. For example, labor productivity is said to increase if more aircraft parts are manufactured with the same level of labor staffing, or if the same number are produced with a reduction in staffing. **Efficiency** is the amount of production obtained based upon either a theoretical or practical limit of what can be obtained.

Other resources can also be brought into productivity calculations. Besides labor hours, managers also assess productivity in terms of the productivity of capital, or the return on invested money and equipment. Supervisors, as part of the management team, are involved in the productivity of capital, but increasing productivity of the work group is their primary concern.

Quality is also important. It is the essential characteristics of something, typically measured in the degree of excellence, value, or worth. A work group could be highly productive and produce increasing numbers of bicycle handlebars, for example, and still fail if their work is shoddy—if customers go flying because the handlebars twist off bicycles! The quality of production or operations is concerned with their **effectiveness.** It is how well, not how much, output is produced or services are rendered. Essentially, effectiveness is the capability of achieving organizational objectives. Quality is concerned with satisfying customers by adding value to goods and services sold or otherwise offered by an organization.

quality
The essential characteristics of something, typically measured in the degree of excellence, value, or worth.

effectiveness
The capability of achieving organizational objectives.

Note that effectiveness and efficiency are related. Many companies have shown that improvements in the effectiveness of manufacturing processes—improvements in quality—lead to higher productivity. The relationship between productivity and quality is discussed in more detail in Chapter 2.

Assuring Legal Compliance

A second purpose of supervision—to help the organization assure legal compliance—is a relatively recent development. The 1960s and early 1970s ushered in an era of increased concern for human rights and workplace safety. It became illegal to discriminate on the basis of age, gender, race, ethnicity, religion, national origin, disability, and so on. Employers also became accountable for maintaining a safe workplace.

Legal reprisal occurs when a prospective or actual employee seeks a remedy through the courts or alternative dispute resolution (mediation or arbitration) for damages based on illegal discrimination, harassment, or injury. A supervisor who pressures his secretary into a dinner date, for example, may be guilty of sexual harassment. His employer could be liable for damages if the secretary's performance is adversely affected, or if she feels compelled to quit or to transfer from her job. An African American may feel she was fired by a supervisor because of her race, rather than because of performance on the job. A diabetic may sue because a supervisor won't reasonably accommodate his meal schedule.

The supervisor plays an important role in helping the organization assure legal compliance. Every supervisory activity—hiring, appraising performance, promoting, compensating, or firing employees—is subject to legal standards and review. Chapter 3 covers the subject of meeting the legal challenge.

It takes more to maintain legal compliance than just understanding the laws or underlying legal issues, however. Supervisors need to understand how to manage equitably and ethically, and should have an understanding of issues associated with managing a diverse work group. This understanding, together with knowledge of legal issues, not only helps to assure legal compliance, but also enhances productivity and product quality. Ethics is covered in more detail later in this chapter.

Job Satisfaction and Career Development

Another purpose of supervision is to serve the individual needs of the supervisor. Most supervision texts do not mention this purpose of supervision. However, if

Supervisors are caught in the middle. An article in the *Harvard Business Review* by Sasser and Leonard illustrated this point well. According to these authors, the supervisor

- may not be informed of management policies, but is still expected to carry out directives based on policy.
- is separate from the work group, but must depend heavily on the work group.
- has relatively little authority to act.

- is expected to maintain high morale, but is forced to spend a large amount of time keeping records and dealing with minor emergencies.
- is asked to have a commitment to management, but may be in a dead-end job.
- often has training, education, and work background that is more compatible with the group he or she is supervising than with the managerial group with whom he or she is supposed to identify.[2]

supervisors become dissatisfied with their jobs, their organization will be in a great deal of trouble. It makes sense for middle and top management to help supervisors achieve satisfaction in their day-to-day work, because an organization needs a motivated cadre of supervisors in order to succeed.

It's no easy task to help supervisors find meaning in their jobs. The work is difficult, the pay is relatively low, and supervisors sometimes feel crushed between demanding middle managers and complaining line workers. Given the inherent difficulty of being a supervisor, one may wonder why people want to be supervisors in the first place.

People move into supervisory positions for two primary reasons. The first reason is that some people like being in charge. They have a strong motivation to lead others. Researchers have identified a legitimate "motivation to manage."[3]

A second reason, related to the first, is that supervisory jobs are the first step on the road to better-paying, more interesting middle or top management jobs. A new supervisor sees this step in the form of a modest pay raise and freedom from punching a time clock.

Chapter 19 discusses the career development of aspiring or practicing supervisors. **Career development** is the process whereby an individual identifies and acquires transferable skills as she or he moves along the management track.

career development
The processes whereby individuals identify and acquire transferable skills as they move along the management track.

Characteristics of Effective Supervisors

The most important resource a supervisor manages is people. Getting results by working with and through people is the essence of effective supervision.

There are few absolute answers to questions involving people and human behavior. However, successful supervisors—those who lead high-performing work groups—possess some common attributes. They tend to be leaders who work with and through people in a systematic, innovative, knowledgeable, and ethical manner.

best-planning managing

Effective Supervisors Are Systematic

Management at all levels should be viewed systematically. Successful supervisors understand this, and also understand the components of a management system. Before proceeding with a discussion of a management system that can be used by supervisors, we will begin with a definition of a system.

A **system** is comprised of a flow of inputs, transformation processes, outputs, and feedback, as illustrated in Figure 1-3. Consider the following examples of systems: registration for classes, the operation of an automobile, baking a batch of chocolate chip cookies, writing a term paper. What are the inputs? Transformation processes? Outputs? Feedback? The list of systems is virtually endless.

A management system includes inputs such as labor (sometimes called human resources), capital, technology, and information; transformation processes that add value to or otherwise use or alter the inputs; resulting in output that is then taken to market or otherwise transmitted to a customer; and feedback that is used to adjust the system to improve effectiveness and efficiency.

Systems are not exclusively comprised of specific tangible processes that result in specific, tangible outputs such as course registration, transportation, cookies, or a term paper. Systems can also be conceptual. For example, we can envision a management system comprised of **managerial functions** that outlines the relationships between managerial inputs (planning, organizing, and staffing); transformation processes (directing); and outputs with feedback (controlling), as depicted in Figure 1-4.

Note the order in Figure 1-4. This example shows that the supervisor should first plan where she is going before she organizes to get there. It shows that the directing function of management, the function concerned with motivating employees, is only one part of supervision. For example, a boss could be a great motivator, but still be a poor supervisor because she leads people in the wrong direction. All the parts of a system are important. The success of all systems is dependent on a logical flow of processes.

Figure 1-4 also illustrates the importance of feedback. **Feedback** occurs whenever information is transmitted back to other parts of a systematic process. (The topic of feedback is also covered in Chapters 8, 11, 13, and 14.) Without feedback

system
A flow of inputs, transformation processes, outputs, and feedback.

managerial functions
Activities performed outlining relationships between managerial inputs (planning, organizing, and staffing); transformation processes (directing); and outputs with feedback (controlling).

feedback
Occurs when information is transmitteed back to other parts of a systematic process.

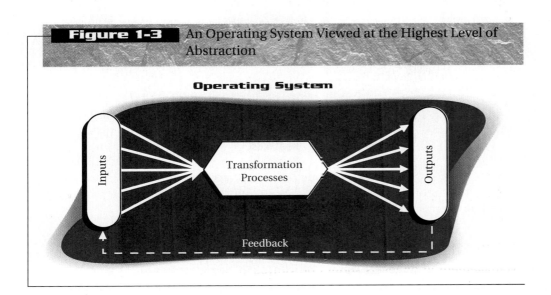

Figure 1-3 An Operating System Viewed at the Highest Level of Abstraction

(the arrow looping backward in Figure 1-4), future supervisory activities lack information, and the individual or work team may fail to get the desired results.

Systems thinking benefits supervisors and other managers in three important ways.[4] The first benefit of systems thinking is that it compels the supervisor to identify and to contend with factors outside of immediate supervisory tasks at hand. A management system such as the one outlined in Figure 1-4 is an **open system**—that is, it is affected by external factors such as government regulation, new technology, the competition, and so forth. Effective supervision within an open system requires that supervisors constantly take environmental change into account. The concept of an open system reminds supervisors of the need to look beyond the supervisory process at hand.

The second benefit of systems thinking is that it helps the supervisor to view his or her goals as being related to a larger set of goals within the organization. Successful supervisors understand not only the goals of their work team, but also how those goals, and the processes required to reach those goals, fit into larger goals and processes for the total organization. The systems approach thus provides a goal- and process-directed backbone for day-to-day operations throughout the organization, at all levels of management.

open system
A type of system affected by external factors such as government regulation, new technology, and competition.

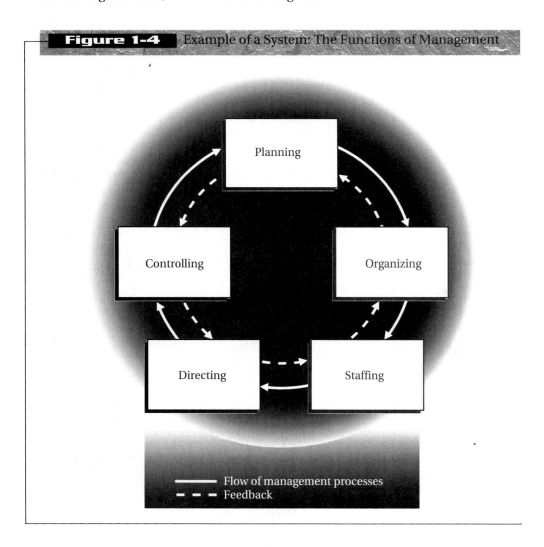

Figure 1-4 Example of a System: The Functions of Management

Planning

Controlling

Organizing

Directing

Staffing

———— Flow of management processes
– – – – Feedback

The third benefit of systems thinking is that it helps managers structure subsystems so they effectively and efficiently serve larger systems. A subsystem is a system that provides outputs necessary to the functioning of a larger system. A performance appraisal review system, for example, provides information regarding employee performance necessary to the larger human resources system in an organization to drive decisions relating to training and development, compensation, and termination. A subsystem works well to the extent that the larger system is well organized and its purpose is understood.

The systems approach is a way of thinking, planning, and problem solving that begins with assessment of what the individual, group, or organization wants to accomplish. This stage includes identifying inputs. The second and third stages involve transformation of inputs for the purpose of creating output. Finally, feedback is used to moderate and improve all steps in the process.

Systems thinking may seem machine-like. Mechanical systems do follow linear, sequential processes based on the system outline shown in Figure 1-3. Mechanical, measurable processes—for example, involving the quantity of red paint needed to cover a Ford Taurus—tend to be relatively predictable. Social systems involving human beings are not as predictable. Consequently, do not fall into the trap of taking systems thinking too literally when human behavior is involved, and particularly when supervising others in a changing world. Systems thinking works best when applied hand-in-hand with an appreciation of the foibles of human behavior and with an accompanying focus on quality and innovation.

Effective Supervisors Are Innovative

The rapid rate of change in the world, and the movement to an information-driven workplace where how well management uses information is as important as how much capital management has to invest, requires contemporary supervisors to innovate. Marvin Weisbord said it well when he noted

> We are in a quantum leap into a workplace . . . shifting from physical manipulation to machine-controlled processes, from doing the work to making sure machines do it right, from routine and predictable sequences to "anything can happen." It is a global society awakening to the interdependence of every living thing.[5]

Innovation is the act of bringing something new into an established process or way of thinking. It is not limited to inventing novel products or processes; it also includes the way supervisors act in their supervisory roles. Innovative supervisors are effective at helping people work together and finding solutions to "people problems" inherent in any organization.[6]

innovation
The act of bringing something new into an established process or way of thinking.

The supervisor plays an important role in establishing a climate where employees innovate effectively. Effective supervisors make employees feel comfortable about offering suggestions for improvement or at ease when collaborating with coworkers.

Creative innovation is closely linked to the productivity of an individual or work group. As William Miller said, "When we are our most creative, concentrated, and expressive selves, we are also our most productive. Creativity is rarely our primary objective, yet it helps us attain our objectives and goals."[7]

Systems thinking, covered in the previous section, and innovation complement one another. In fact, according to management expert Peter Drucker, "creativity is no substitute for [systematic] analysis and knowledge."[8]

The systems approach is sequential and logical. It involves developing a structure within which problems can be defined and solved and opportunities exploited. Innovation, on the other hand, is intuitive and holistic. Solutions are arrived at through inspiration, in a single leap. It is important that supervisors understand and apply both logical, systematic thinking and creative innovation.

An example of an innovative process that can be applied within the context of systematic supervision is **brainstorming.** Brainstorming is generating ideas by permitting nonevaluative presentation of alternatives by group members. A. F. Osborn, an advertising agency executive, developed brainstorming as a way to encourage creativity. A brainstorming group throws out ideas that are then listed on a board by a facilitator during a timed group session. Criticism of ideas is not allowed during this stage.

The purpose of brainstorming is to get out as many ideas as possible for later consideration, regardless of how silly or ineffective the ideas may seem at the time. The subject of brainstorming is covered in more detail in Chapter 10.

Other methods for encouraging innovative, holistic thinking include meditation, invoking images, finding analogies, and dreaming.[9] These approaches can have surprisingly effective outcomes. For example, a group of Gillette executives went through a problem-solving session in which they were called upon to imagine themselves as a shaft of hair. Some participants wanted a gentler shampoo to help them with split ends; others were concerned about having a more concentrated shampoo to help clean dirt near the scalp. The result of this process was Silkience, a top-ten-selling shampoo that adapts itself to the cleaning needs of customers' hair.

Being an innovative supervisor and leading an innovative work group is an essential attribute of successful supervisors. The increasing rate of change; introduction of new technologies; steep challenges from competitors; and declining resources make innovation an essential survival skill for contemporary supervisors and their organizations.

brainstorming
Generating ideas by permitting nonevaluative presentation of alternatives by group members to obtain as many ideas as possible for later evaluation.

Effective Supervisors Are Knowledgeable

Supervisors could manage systematically and innovatively and still fail, if they lack necessary knowledge. You may have worked for a supervisor who did not understand *your* job. You may have seen instances in which a work group was relatively ineffective because the supervisor did not know how to manage. According to the late W. Edwards Deming, a renowned management consultant, only about 15 percent of productivity and quality shortcomings can be blamed on the work force; the other 85 percent can be attributed to ineffective, inefficient work processes developed and overseen by management.[10] Conversely, think of circumstances in which your boss was highly effective. It is very likely he or she had a good understanding of supervisory concepts and applications.

Note the distinction between *concepts* and *applications.* Supervisory concepts are concerned with theoretical knowledge. Conceptual understanding helps supervisors to know *why* a particular approach or work process is effective. This theoretical understanding is important. Still, in the words of Harold Geneen, the legendary chief executive officer of International Telephone and Telegraph (ITT), "you cannot run a business, or anything else, on a theory."[11]

Consequently, it is important that supervisors understand not only why a particular practice is effective, but also how to apply that practice. For example, a supervisor must not only know that participatory decision making is a theoretically sound practice under certain circumstances, he or she must also know how to effectively and efficiently conduct a meeting.

A good education is prerequisite to becoming an effective supervisor.

A wide variety of applications are important to supervisors. Probably the most important among these are **people skills.** These skills, also sometimes referred to as human relations skills, include the ability to get along with and to motivate individuals and work teams. Successfully conducting a review of an employee's work performance, for example, requires effective people skills.

Technical skills are also important. These skills are concerned with job knowledge, including knowledge of work processes of those in the supervisor's work group. For example, a snack bar supervisor should know how to change the tanks of a soda machine or how to clean the grill.

Administrative skills include all skills involved with planning, organizing, and controlling work. For example, a supervisor may need to know how to develop a budget, operate a computer to examine department records, or prepare an organization chart.[12]

You may wonder which of these skills can be effectively taught and learned. It is easier to learn technical skills than to learn people skills. However, conceptual understanding of these skills can contribute to their practice. Therefore, even skills that are difficult to measure or to learn should be discussed. boring

Effective Supervisors Are Ethical

The subject of **ethics** is concerned with justifying behavior pertaining to questions of right and wrong. Behavior is said to be ethical to the extent it is good or right for the larger society or community. The word *ethics* comes from the Greek word *ethos,* which means "pertaining to the character and sentiment of the community."

As you know, it is not always easy to tell right from wrong. There are few absolute standards for assessing the morality of an act. Obviously, overt misrepresentation of a work process in order to get work completed is unethical—or is it? What if the unwanted overtime spent by workers results in saving an important relationship with a customer and, with it, workers' jobs? Does the end justify the means in this situation?

people skills
The ability to get along with and to motivate individuals and work teams.

technical skills
Job knowledge including knowledge of work processes of those in the supervisor's work group.

administrative skills
The ability to plan, organize, and control the work process.

ethics
Is concerned with justifying behavior pertaining to questions of right and wrong; behavior is said to be ethical to the extent it is good or right for the larger community.

Whistleblowing: Is It Worth It?

Pressure to conform with inappropriate organizational decisions is often quite strong. A recent report on whistleblowers—individuals who have publicly revealed information concerning mismanagement and dishonesty in their organizations—indicates that life after whistleblowing is unpleasant.

Whistleblowers have reported feeling isolated from other people in the organization. They frequently cite attempts by their superiors and others to undermine their credibility, to disrupt their personal lives through active harassment and threats, and to damage their careers through demotion. Perhaps most disturbing about these negative effects is the possible loss of good organizational citizens. Whistleblowers typically have long records of successful employment, hold moderate political beliefs, and have faith in the integrity of their superiors in the organization.[13]

Criminal behavior would seem to be clearly unethical. However, what if a supervisor is involved in personnel practices that technically skirt the law? What if the supervisor violates a bad or unimportant law? Should a supervisor override decisions of work group members that could be harmful? Should a construction foreman, for example, allow carpenters to work without safety harnesses when that is their wish?

Clearly, it is not easy to draw the line between ethical and unethical behavior in supervision. One general approach would be simply always to follow the rules, whatever the rules might be. Examples of a rule-bound approach to ethical behavior can be seen in company policies, procedures, and rules; legal statutes; and the Ten Commandments. Another general approach involves making ethical judgments based upon circumstances. The following discussion of ethical standards applies both approaches.

Models of Ethical Behavior. Gerald Cavanagh describes three models for guiding ethical behavior. The first, **utilitarianism,** says an act is ethical if its overall benefit to the greater community outweighs its cost.[14] An example of utilitarianism can be seen in a supervisor's decision to schedule a hazardous waste cleanup because the overall benefit to society of cleaning up the environment outweighs the cost to the individual workers exposed to pollutants. This point of view is situational. It involves weighing the costs and benefits to the larger community of a given action.

Another ethical standard outlined by Cavanagh is concerned with **human rights.**[15] This perspective argues that actions are ethical only if they do not violate individual rights such as the right to safety or the right to privacy. Using this standard, the supervisor would *not* schedule the hazardous waste cleanup because she or he would be violating the safety rights of workers.

The final standard is concerned with **justice.**[16] This ethical perspective calls for fair and consistent behavior on the part of supervisors. It also implies adherence to rules created in the interest of fairness and social justice. The supervisor in the hazardous waste disposal example might schedule the cleanup using justice as a standard if selection of the crew was equitable, work processes were legal, and workers were fully informed and willing to take the risks.

As can be seen in the hazardous waste cleanup example, ethical standards can be contradictory. Here is another example: underpaying workers in female-dominated jobs relative to those working in male-dominated jobs of comparable worth to the employer might be called ethical according to utilitarian standards. The business may earn relatively more profit because its overhead is lower;

utilitarianism
An act is ethical if its overall benefit to the greater community outweighs its cost.

human rights
Actions are ethical only if they do not violate individual rights.

justice
The impartial treatment of employees by organizations through maintaining conditions of fairness and equity.

shareholders may earn higher dividends; and government may receive more tax revenue. However, this pay inequity is hardly fair to the individual worker.

Given the inherent contradictions, how does an individual supervisor select an ethical behavior? While not an easy question to answer, the following three-step process can serve as a guide. Supervisors should

1. Be aware of the ethical standards of utilitarianism, human rights, and justice.
2. Reconcile these standards when making decisions. *Reconciliation* means to bring into agreement or consistency. It often is not easy to reconcile ethical factors. There will be times when you have to choose one standard over another.
3. Model ethical behavior. This is a particularly important aspect of maintaining an ethical work environment. Decisions that benefit society, are just, and respect individual rights do not exist in a vacuum. Decision makers learn ethical behavior from societal institutions such as the family, church, and school; from peer groups and, in the workplace, from the values and behavior of coworkers and supervisors. As a supervisor, you may not be able to affect societal influences, but you can certainly provide a model of appropriate behavior in the workplace. Employees tend to watch and model those above them. Exclaiming "Don't do as I do, do as I say!" will not get a supervisor very far.

Systematic, innovative, knowledgeable, and ethical supervision leads to supervisory success. Recall that success is improving worker performance—leading a work team that is effective and efficient, that is highly productive and produces a high quality product. These characteristics will help the supervisor face the challenges of the changing workplace that are discussed in the following section.

Into the Future

The terms *change* and *transformation* are mentioned several times in this chapter for a good reason.

The environment in which the effective supervisor lives and works is going through a profound transformation. Old patterns of behavior and organizational structures are being challenged and are shifting at an increasing rate. Change has always been a factor in the supervisory world. What is different today is the speed at which the workplace is being transformed by **technology**—the practical application of human knowledge. An example of technological change can be seen in the evolution of computers from the behemoths that weighed tons and filled entire rooms, but lacked the processing power of today's checkbook calculators.

technology
The practical application of human knowledge.

An excellent example of the rise in technology can be seen in Alvin Toffler's book *Future Shock,* a classic dealing with how technological change affects individuals and entire societies. The single most important technological advance affecting the present day is the microprocessor—the computer on a chip. Yet, nowhere in the 491 pages of *Future Shock* did Toffler mention the microprocessor.[17] Why? Because when the book was published in 1970 the microprocessor had not yet been invented!

Change is also being driven by the increasing rate of information creation, changes in the demographic profile of workers, and the economic profile of an increasingly global economy. Following is a discussion of trends that will affect the supervisor of the mid-1990s and beyond.

Kizen

The Information Explosion

The scientific and educational communities crank out new information at an incredible rate. Over 7,000 research articles are published every day.[18] The pool of information is doubling every three to four years. Information, the technologies to which it is contributing, and the technologies required for its management have replaced land, gold, and oil as the new wealth.

Whereas an earlier era saw capital investment in manufacturing technologies as the pathway to prosperity and competitiveness, the future will see capital investment in information management technologies—fiber optics for communications, networked computer systems, communications satellites, and data bases—as the means to be competitive.

During an earlier era, supervisors were concerned with management of production on the factory floor. In the future supervisors will interact more with information and the means to process it. In other words, they will increasingly interact with computers in all their different guises.

A Need for More Education

Activities as simple as typing or using a rudimentary word processor are only a few of a myriad of new technological skills that will be used by the supervisor of the future.

Learning new technologies is tough. In office environments, supervisors are beginning to experience great difficulty in adjusting to the office of the future. Factory supervisors are experiencing comparable difficulty learning how to operate computer-assisted machines. As noted by Stephen Kerr and his associates, "It is becoming all but impossible for foremen to understand fully all the complex equipment and processes for which they are responsible."[19]

Employers are responding to the need for more highly educated leaders by putting a higher proportion of college graduates into supervisory positions. Presently, over 75 percent of new entrants into managerial positions have a college degree and this proportion is expected to increase in the future.[20]

A Move from Manufacturing to Service

The North American economy has moved steadily toward an increased emphasis on services rather than manufacturing. There are two primary reasons for this evolution.

First, in many industries—including steel, automobiles, and consumer electronics—American manufacturers have been unable to keep up with the productivity and quality of foreign competitors. Consequently, manufacturing jobs in the United States have declined because the underlying industries have declined. The number of manufacturing positions has also fallen because American companies have moved manufacturing to other countries to take advantage of cheaper labor. A worker in Juarez, Mexico, for example, may be paid $2 an hour, while the same job costs $13 an hour in Greenville, Tennessee.

An increase in the service sector has picked up much of the slack from lost manufacturing jobs. In fact, as of 1992 more American employees were working for local, state, and federal governments than were employed in manufacturing![21] Services include industries such as banking, insurance, real estate sales, convenience stores, restaurants, hair salons, laundries, and government employment. Service jobs tend to pay less than manufacturing positions.

The decline of smokestack America has meant supervisors will continue to deal with a high proportion of **displaced workers**—workers who have lost jobs in the manufacturing sector and are now working in the lower-paying service sector.

displaced workers
Individuals who have lost their jobs in the manufacturing sector and are now working in the lower-paying service sector.

An Increase in Teamwork

Supervisors will find themselves increasingly involved in collaborative, rather than competitive, work environments. One reason for this trend is the need for improved innovation and problem solving in the workplace in order to increase productivity and quality. Smoothly functioning work teams are able to generate more and better ideas than employees or supervisors working alone. The days of management abuse of managerial privilege and employee resistance and work slowdowns and strikes are ending. Management and workers must either learn to work together more effectively to improve productivity and quality or find themselves unemployed!

Another reason for increased teamwork is the perception of many managers that participative decision making makes a positive contribution to improvements in productivity and quality. Many managers believe that giving workers more opportunity to participate in decisions that affect them is simply good management. We will discuss the role of employee participation in more detail in Chapters 2 and 10. Each chapter in this text dealing with supervisory skills also includes a section concerning the supervisor and the work team.

Changes in Employee Representation

In today's global, competitive environment, it is no surprise that once-influential unions in the United States have been unable to continue to gain wage increases for their members or to maintain their former power with employers. Union membership as a percentage of private nonagricultural workers has declined steadily from its peak of one-third of the work force in the middle 1950s and will probably continue to decline. Supervisors are now less likely to be dealing with employees through union representation.

Labor relations is still an important subject, however. The decline and refocusing in unionism has been paralleled by growth in employee associations, which are similar to unions. Labor is giving more attention today to increased cooperation with management through efforts to raise union member productivity by training, redesigning work, embracing technology, and willingness to assume greater flexibility in job assignments.[22] Also, now more than ever, supervisors need to understand how to cooperate with union representation in organized environments, as well as how to practice effective supervision in non-unionized organizations. (See Chapter 4 for further discussion of labor relations.)

Increased Importance of Legal Issues

The decline of unionism means employees are less able to rely on union contracts and shop stewards to resolve disputes. This factor, together with increased concern for the rights of ethnic minorities, older workers, women, and the disabled will contribute to an increased need for managers to be able to resolve employment-related issues without the necessity of litigation.

Litigation is the process of bringing forth a lawsuit, or claim for damages, in a court of law. Recall from earlier in the chapter that one of the objectives of effective supervision is to assure compliance with legal requirements. Chapter 3 provides more detail on the legal challenges facing supervisors.

litigation
The process of bringing forth a lawsuit, or claim for damages, in a court of law.

Changing Demographics in a Changing World

The effective supervisor deals with an increasingly diverse workplace. The divorce rate has soared to about 50 percent in much of the United States; there are increasing numbers of single-parent families in which the parent puts in a full work day in addition to taking care of children. In two-parent families, often both parents must work to make ends meet. Ethnic minorities and women continue to increase as a percentage of the U.S. work force, a dynamic trend that means supervisors must become more sensitive to diversity and cultural differences.

New and unanticipated global, economic, and health issues are also affecting today's worker. By 1990, the AIDS epidemic hit over 150 nations, with an HIV virus infection rate of 35 percent in some African countries. Global projections predict as many as 40 million carriers of the HIV virus and people with active infections by the turn of the century. While difficult to project, there may be as many as 3 million HIV carriers and active AIDS cases in the United States by the year 2000. Supervisors will continue to be confronted with managing workplace issues and problems associated with AIDS.

Telecommunications have linked the world. Disputes overseas will increasingly affect the day-to-day life of the supervisor and employees.

Persistent economic problems caused by trade imbalances and stiff international competition, deficit government spending, a crumbling infrastructure, and loss of high-paying factory jobs will continue to affect the supervisory climate. In all likelihood, the environment in which the American supervisor operates will become increasingly somber as the world moves into the twenty-first century. New economic challenges will, no doubt, continually arise.

What do world events or personal concerns with health, family, and finances have to do with supervision? Concerns outside of work encroach on performance in the workplace for supervisors and employees alike. The effective supervisor must manage his or her own life and supervise others in an increasingly turbulent environment.

How to Use This Textbook

Each chapter of this book follows the same format. At the beginning of each chapter, the learning objectives list the most important concepts and information to be acquired from the chapter.

Each chapter has a brief case at the beginning and is followed by a conclusion of the case. Material within the chapter assists in arriving at a course of action to take. All of the cases involve the same individual, our friend "Carla."

Each of the first nine chapters ends with a summary section entitled "Focus on Concepts" that reviews the highlights of the chapter. Commencing with Chapter 10, instead of summaries we have included a section titled "Focus on Skills" that cites specific actions for supervisors to take.

Key concepts are defined in the page margins. Frequent referencing will enable you to locate additional information elsewhere in the text. A glossary and an index are included at the end of the book.

Review questions provide an opportunity to test yourself by recalling information covered in the chapter and applying it to real-life situations. The review questions may also be assigned by the instructor for either written homework exercises or preparation for class discussions. For readers interested in obtaining additional information, the "Notes" section following the review questions may be useful.

Finally, two cases are included at the end of each chapter to allow application of concepts previously covered in the chapter and other chapters. They also serve as a setting for class problem-solving discussions.

Each of the chapter sections described is designed to make the learning process easier and more meaningful for you by providing tools to help you master the subject of supervision.

Carla took a last sip of her coffee and kicked back in her chair. She would be listening to early birds, if any had been nearby. It had been a long night!

She thought again about her role at the company. She wasn't a big shot. The work was difficult and rather thankless. Still, she knew her job was vitally important to cost-effectively producing a high-quality aircraft.

The production report she'd completed reflected a significant increase in department productivity over the past three months without a corresponding increase in rejects. Larry, her boss, would like that. She decided not to reprimand Fred for his poor performance during the past month. Something was clearly going on in his life that was affecting his work. Maybe he would talk with her about it, or maybe Fred would benefit from the counseling provided for by the company.

The personnel action form she had completed called for three new lathe operators. She knew the human resources office would want her to be aware of affirmative action issues, because there was only one woman and no person of color working in that position in her department. That was okay with Carla. She liked working for a company that was in touch with the current work force.

Carla stuffed papers in her briefcase, turned out the light, and walked out the door. She would take a nap and return during the second shift.

Summary: Focus on Concepts

Supervision is the first line of management that oversees efforts of workers for the purpose of accomplishing group and organizational objectives. Supervisors are at the bottom of the management pyramid. The essence of successful supervision is the effective supervision of people.

The often difficult job of a supervisor is important in three ways: competent supervision helps the organization to attain productivity and quality goals and to assure compliance with legal requirements, and it helps supervisors to reach personal goals related to individual promotion and satisfaction.

Supervisors strive to lead highly productive work teams that do quality work. *Productivity* is concerned with the efficiency of production and operations—how much of an organization's product (goods and services) is produced with a given amount of resources. *Quality* is concerned with the effectiveness of production or operations.

Supervisors can help an organization to assure legal compliance by making appropriate decisions concerning equal employment opportunity issues and employees' rights.

People often become supervisors to attain personal goals of career progression and job satisfaction.

Effective supervisors—those who lead productive, effective work groups—possess common attributes. They tend to be leaders who are systematic, innovative, knowledgeable, and ethical.

Systematic leaders correctly assess inputs, transformation processes, and outputs and make use of feedback. Innovative supervisors are able to find creative solutions to production and quality problems. Effective supervisors are also knowledgeable and possess people, technical, and administrative skills.

The effective supervisor is also ethical. Managing ethically requires that supervisors balance utilitarian needs with concern for employee rights and justice. Effective supervisors need to be aware of ethical considerations, to reconcile this understanding when making ethical decisions, and to model ethical behavior as an example for others.

The future holds many challenges for supervisors. Supervisors must contend with the information explosion and with technologies necessary for information management. They need to be well educated. They will find themselves increasingly engaged in supervising in a services-rather than manufacturing-based environment, and their role in facilitating productive and effective teamwork will become even more significant.

The union movement in the United States has been declining or refocusing for the past four decades and will probably continue to decline. Although supervisors will increasingly find themselves working in nonunionized environments, maintaining good labor relations will remain an important concern.

The litigation explosion in the United States, driven in part by the civil rights movement and an increased recognition of human rights, is likely to continue. Supervisors need to be aware of the legal implications of their behaviors in the workplace.

Demographic and economic changes in the world will continue to have profound effects on the workplace, adding immeasurably to the supervisory challenge.

Review Questions

1. Define the term *supervision*. What is the management pyramid? What is the heap reversal theory?
2. Give three reasons why the job of a supervisor is important in organizations.
3. Define *performance, productivity, efficiency, quality,* and *effectiveness.*
4. It has been said that supervisors are "caught in the middle." Explain what this means. Is this bad for the supervisor?
5. To be most successful, supervisors should be systematic, innovative, knowledgeable, and ethical. Elaborate upon and give examples of each characteristic.
6. Describe what constitutes a system and list the benefits of systems thinking.
7. Define *brainstorming* and illustrate how it should be carried out. Of what value is it?
8. Describe three skills supervisors should possess.
9. What is ethics? Indicate three models of ethical behavior.
10. What are whistleblowers? Do they have any value either to their organizations or to society? If so, what is their value?
11. List the major changes or forces affecting our society that confront today's supervisors.

Notes

1. A. Gray, *The Development of Economic Doctrine* (London, ENG: Longmans, Green and Company, Ltd., 1931), 5.
2. W. E. Sasser and F. S. Leonard, "Let First-Level Supervisors Do Their Job," *Harvard Business Review* (March–April 1980): 113–121.
3. J. B. Miner, "Twenty Years of Research on Role Motivation Theory of Management Effectiveness," *Personnel Psychology* 31 (1978): 739–760.
4. P. B. Schoderbek, C. G. Schoderbek, and A. G. Kefalas, *Management Systems: Conceptual Considerations,* 3d ed. (Plano, TX: Business Publications Inc., 1985).
5. M. R. Weisbord, *Productive Workplaces: Organizing and Managing for Dignity, Meaning, and Community* (San Francisco: Jossey-Bass, 1987), 177.
6. M. Olivero, "Get Crazy! How to Have a Breakthrough Idea," *Working Woman* (September 1990): 145–147, 222.
7. W. C. Miller, *The Creative Edge* (Reading, MA: Addison-Wesley, 1990), 13.
8. P. Drucker, *Management: Tasks, Responsibilities, Practices* (New York: Harper & Row, 1973), 268.
9. Miller, *The Creative Edge.*
10. M. Walton, *The Deming Management Method* (New York: Putnam Publishing Group, 1986).

11. H. Geneen, *Managing* (Garden City, NY: Doubleday, 1984).

12. Supervisory skills descriptions are based on L. R. Bittle and J. W. Newstrom, *What Every Supervisor Should Know*, 6th ed. (Lake Forest, IL: Glencoe, 1990).

13. M. P. Glazer and P. M. Glazer, "Whistleblowing," *Psychology Today* (August 1986): 36–39, 42–43.

14. G. F. Cavanagh, *American Business Values*, 2d ed. (Englewood Cliffs, NJ: Prentice-Hall, 1984). Utilitarianism is also associated with the philosophical writings of nineteenth-century philosophers John Stuart Mill and Jeremy Bentham.

15. Ibid.

16. Ibid.

17. A. Toffler, *Future Shock* (New York: Random House, 1970). Also see J. Naisbitt and P. Aburdene, *Megatrends 2000: Ten New Directions for the 1990's* (New York: William Morrow and Company, 1990).

18. J. Naisbitt, *Megatrends* (New York: Warner Books, 1982).

19. S. Kerr, K. D. Hill, and L. Broedling, "The First-Line Supervisor: Phasing Out or Here to Stay?" *Academy of Management Review* 11 (1986): 103–117.

20. National Center on Education and the Economy, *America's Choice: High Skills or Low Wages!* The report of the Commission on the Skills of the American Workforce, June, 1990.

21. D. Vobejda, "Government Employs More U.S. Workers Than Manufacturing," L.A. Times News Service, August 30, 1992.

22. D. Hage and R. Knight, "Unions Feel the Heat," *U.S. News and World Report* 116 (January 24, 1994): 61.

Case 1-1

The Smokejumpers' Supervisor

"Before I became crew boss of this unit, I never realized how much responsibility a supervisor really had," said John Marshall, who managed a crew of smokejumpers stationed at the Northern Regional Headquarters of the U.S. Forest Service. The unit, located in Missoula, Montana, was the first established in the United States and dates back to July 12, 1940. Smokejumpers are forest fire fighters. When the terrain is inaccessible to vehicles or fires are distant from trails, they parachute into mountainous areas to contain and extinguish fires.

Marshall was one of eight supervisors located at the Missoula airport and fire depot. He was responsible for 16 of the 128 jumpers stationed at the base. Now in his second year as crew boss, he had previously spent nine summers as a smokejumper. All but 20 of the men were summer employees. Most had other jobs during the remainder of the year. Many were college students and teachers. Some were ski instructors or were unemployed.

For major forest fires—those consuming over 500 acres of timber—the crew bosses often accompanied the fire fighters to the fire sites. For smaller fires, after dropping the jumpers, they returned to the fire depot to direct operations. It was common for crew members to be scattered over 1,000 square miles fighting as many as six or eight fires simultaneously.

Safety of employees was of paramount importance. The work was very hazardous. However, with over 60,000 individual parachute descents, not one person from the Missoula detachment had been killed. Broken legs and other bones, yes. The danger they face is illustrated by a tragedy that occurred in 1949. Thirteen men died in the Mann Gulch forest fire near the Missouri River a few miles from Helena, Montana. A shift in wind direction trapped the men. (The episode is portrayed in a Hollywood movie, *Red Sky Over Montana*, with Richard Widmark playing the role of crew boss.)

Marshall and members of his crew maintained a rigorous training schedule involving physical exercise and conditioning along with developing fire-fighting skills. One of the most critical skills is the ability to guide a parachute with precision.

Technical developments in the design of parachutes now permit extremely accurate landings, although becoming entangled in trees continues to be a major problem for smokejumpers. The period between fighting fires is spent on reconditioning equipment, preparing supplies, repacking parachutes, and on such forest projects as improving trails and campgrounds.

A particularly hot and dry summer was ending with the arrival of rains and cooler weather. The fire danger was over for another year. During the previous 60 days, Marshall and his crew had worked fighting fires continuously with the only time off consumed by sleep and periodic rest breaks. Most of the crew members were leaving for their homes, returning to their other jobs, or going back to college. Although considerable work had yet to be completed in replenishing the supplies consumed during the past summer, renewing and replacing equipment of the unit, and preparing a stack of reports that had been delayed, Marshall took a few minutes to reflect upon the past and the prospective future.

"Am I getting too old to be jumping out of airplanes and climbing up mountains?" he thought to himself. "I've been doing this for 12 years. Each summer seems just a little bit tougher than the previous one. The bruises and muscle strains take longer to heal. But George Cross quit jumping only a few years ago and he was 54." Marshall remembered the movie *North Dallas Forty* and chuckled. "I love jumping. There is an exhilaration and excitement few persons experience. Why, once when I was descending I almost bumped into a bald eagle. Boy, was it surprised."

"And I believe in the work we do. It's important. Still, being responsible for 16 people and their safety is a burden I really don't enjoy at all. We had some close calls this year, too." He considered a gradual change in the jumpers. "While my crew is cooperative and we get along okay, the fellows are more independent now than when I first started. My first boss gave the orders and that was that. No discussions, no explanations of why we were doing something a certain way. We just did it. Now it seems that everyone wants an explanation. The pressures are greater now. There never seems to be enough money to do the things we would like to do. The philosophy is: do more with less. Next year should be interesting, though. I will have the first two women jumpers in the Service. My guys are divided about that prospect. And because of budget cutbacks, there will be two fewer crew members next year. I hope it rains all summer and never gets above 60 degrees."

Marshall looked off toward the nearby mountains south of the fire depot. Then he noticed a lone bald eagle flying up the Bitterroot River. "I wonder if we've met before?"

Questions

1. What motivates people to become smokejumpers and supervisors of smokejumpers?
2. How would you describe the satisfactions and accomplishments of John Marshall? How do you think he determines whether he is successful? What criteria for measuring success would you recommend?
3. What frustrations go with this job?
4. Finally, how would you determine when it is time to hang up your parachute for the last time?

Case 1-2

Personal Philosophies

Personal philosophies guide the thinking and behavior of people. This case describes the philosophies of two recently appointed supervisors, Zen Zaroski and Sylvia Rausch. What is *your* philosophy of being a supervisor?

Zen's Philosophy

Supervision means looking out for your people's interests and their welfare. I came up the ranks and understand how workers feel. Management will always squeeze every drop of sweat out of their workers. I don't see any of the "wheels" having to punch the clocks. They have their own cushiony offices with pretty pictures on the walls, their own parking spaces for their fancy cars, some company-owned at that, and other perks you wouldn't believe.

Funny, now *I'm* a member of management. I just don't squeeze as hard as the other bosses. I know what it is like to walk the picket line and to be laid off when business is bum. Most of the managers and white collar types never even experienced getting their hands dirty. They don't know what work is, that is, the hard physical kind. They ought to come down here and maybe they'd learn something.

When I was a worker, we would tell them something wasn't safe or a piece of equipment needed repairing. Nothing would happen until there was an emergency, an accident, or something broke. Seems they are always concerned with saving money, making bigger profits for the owners. If they spent more time listening to us and taking care of their hourlies, they'd probably make more money. But they don't listen. The sad thing is they probably don't really care.

To me, my workers come first. My job as shift supervisor is to protect them from hassles and to get everything I can get for them. As long as they do their jobs, what more can management expect from them, or me? Of course that doesn't make me the most popular supervisor with the higher-ups. I'm not in a popularity contest with them, though. I would rather be liked by my own employees. They are my friends.

Sure, every now and then one of my workers will bend a rule or two and screw up, but usually I can take care of them without going through the disciplinary business. No need to get others involved and make a federal case out of something that's not that important.

My employees like me, though, and that is important. We get along without problems. In fact, maybe that's what management is all about—getting along.

Sylvia's Philosophy

Supervision does not have to be complicated, if only people would follow instructions and orders. I am used to taking orders and, now, giving them. My father was a career officer in the Air Force. He began his career as a second lieutenant. When he retired after 20 years, he was a brigadier general, not a small accomplishment in peacetime. He earned his promotions by good work and dedication. He knew how to give orders and how to follow them.

And that largely sums up how I feel about supervisors and their responsibilities. They are supposed to give and carry out orders—up and down the chain of command. If people cannot perform their missions and follow orders, they should be replaced immediately. When I am *tasked* (military jargon for receiving a work assignment), my purpose becomes one of achieving the objective, even if someone's feelings get hurt. Their feelings are not my problem. As a member of management in my company, I see that jobs are performed and the mission is accomplished even when the people I supervise dislike it.

I have little patience with complainers. If they are so disenchanted with their work and the company, they should get out. In other words, "don't re-enlist." The purpose of our organization is not primarily to provide them with employment. If we are to achieve our objectives as an organization, then we must set aside our personal goals.

When higher management formulates new policies, my function is to carry them out. I am not running a debating society where we vote on the rightness of each policy. Nor do I tolerate disobedience and violations of the rules. The people I supervise know what to expect from me because I go by the letter of the law and enforce regulations without exceptions.

Life is simpler that way. To me, supervision is creating order out of what otherwise would become chaos. We achieve harmony by each person carrying out his or her job, following orders and ensuring they are executed in a timely manner. I fully expect my subordinates to do what I tell them to do. And when they don't, they answer for it.

Questions

1. Assume one of these supervisors is going to be your boss. Which would you prefer to work for and why?
2. What are the management philosophies of Zen and Sylvia?
3. Which of the two, in your opinion, will be most successful in management? Why?
4. Why do these people hold such divergent views about management? Is this knowledge useful in predicting future behavior of others?
5. If you were Zen's boss and trying to help him develop as a supervisor, what advice or counsel would you give? If you were Sylvia's boss?

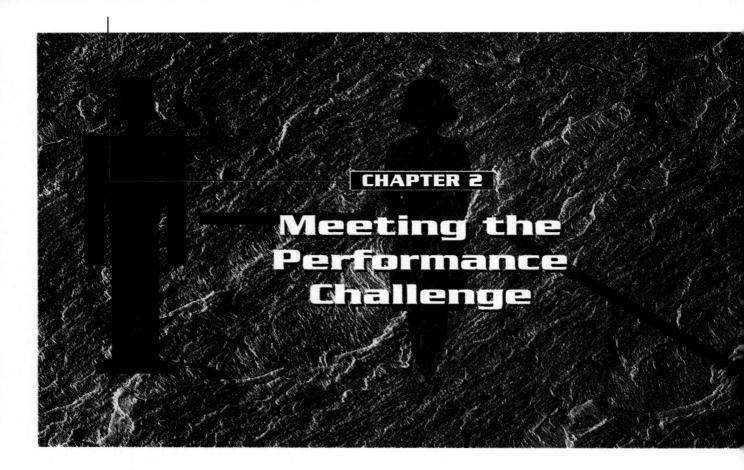

CHAPTER 2

Meeting the Performance Challenge

> Anything that is worth doing at all is worth doing well.
>
> **Lord Chesterfield**

1. Explain how improvements in productivity create higher revenues.
2. Trace the historic development of scientific management, bureaucracy, and human relations and their impact on management practices.
3. Understand the total quality management (TQM) system and its application.
4. Describe a model for improving performance.

Larry: "Carla, I don't understand why you can't get more out of your people. We've talked about this before. Your machines have been calibrated, and you got the latest equipment in the last capital improvement push. Why is productivity of your group down?"

Carla: "Quality is up—our rejects are down 20 percent from last year."

Larry: "Yes, but productivity is flat. Why?"

Carla: "I don't know."

Improving performance—increasing productivity and quality of output with the same or fewer resources—is a deceptively simple goal for two reasons.

First is the issue of quality. It is not enough for a work team to produce more, it is also important that it continuously improve quality. This is difficult to do for many reasons. Quality is in the eye of the beholder, the customer, who may be fickle. New technologies may not work as anticipated. Quality improvements also may not be financially feasible. Market forces outside of the influence of the company can also affect product quality. For example, having the most cost-effective manufacturing process for building buggy whips would hardly be an advantage.

A second major issue affecting performance involves the interplay between the people the supervisor oversees and their environment. No two situations confronted by the supervisor are exactly alike. What increases productivity and quality under one set of circumstances may not work under another set of

circumstances. As mentioned in the previous chapter, the increasing rate of change in the world also adds to the complexity of situations the supervisor confronts.

There is no simple answer to the question of how to lead an effective, efficient work team. As you read this book, keep in mind that effective supervision is very much an art as opposed to an absolute science. Be distrustful of easy solutions to supervisory challenges. An easy solution is a blessing when it occurs, but easy solutions tend to be few and far between!

This chapter breaks down the complexity of the productivity and quality challenge by first looking at the "big picture," then concluding with a framework a supervisor can use to diagnose work group performance.

Improving Efficiency: The Productivity Challenge

In 1965, General Motors, the largest industrial company in the world, earned more profit than the 30 largest Japanese and 30 largest West German companies combined.[1] In 1980, the company suffered its first loss since the Great Depression. Then, during seven financial quarters spanning 1991 and 1992, it lost hundreds of millions of dollars. As a result, in the fall of 1992 General Motors officials announced plans to cut 74,000 jobs and to close 21 plants by 1995.[2]

Sluggish productivity hurt companies like General Motors because increases in profits and wages must be supported by increases in productivity. Without productivity gains, it is impossible for businesses to support wage increases to workers and still maintain satisfactory profits.

income statement
A financial statement that depicts revenues, expenses, and profit or loss for a business enterprise over a period of time.

One way to understand this relationship is to look at scenarios involving an organization's **income statement.** An income statement is a financial statement that depicts revenues, expenses, and profit or loss for a business over a period of time. The income statement formula is as follows: Revenue minus expenses (which include wages) equals profit or loss.

Productivity increases lead to higher revenues because the company is able to produce and sell more products. If productivity gains cause revenues to increase while wage expenses are held constant, company profits will go up: Increased revenue minus constant expenses equals increased profit.

Another way to understand the benefit of productivity increases is to consider a scenario involving production and sales of the same amount of products with less labor cost: Constant revenue minus decreased expenses equals increased profit.

Sluggish productivity makes it difficult for companies to compete. If other companies are relatively more productive, they can reduce prices and still maintain profit margins: Decreased revenue minus decreased expenses can equal a constant profit.

Bear in mind that these examples are simplistic. Other factors besides wages affect productivity and expenses. For example, interest on borrowed money is an expense that reduces profits as interest rates rise independent of wage expense.

General Motors' problems are related to the productivity gains of its competitors. GM's failure to keep up in productivity made it impossible for the company to cut prices to counter competitors' price cuts and still maintain profits. General Motors not only failed to keep up with Japanese automakers, but was outproduced by domestic counterparts as well. In 1992, it took an average of 5.12

The Positive Side of U.S. Productivity

The productivity of U.S. management and workers has been much maligned over the past 20 years. Just as a glass of water presented as "half empty" is also half full, U.S. productivity has a positive aspect. The United States still has the highest productivity in the world. Japan's productivity was surpassed in 1992 not only by the United States, but also by France and Germany in total goods and services produced by the average full-time worker.[3]

Japan is presented by the media as out-producing the world primarily because of the country's skill in selected industries such as automobiles, consumer electronics, and computer chips, and because its *relative gains* in productivity have been high. For example, between 1960 and 1988 U.S. labor productivity grew 1.3 percent per year and German productivity grew 3.1 percent, while productivity growth in Japan averaged 5.3 percent per year.[4]

General Motors line workers to assemble a car, compared to only 3.76 for Chrysler and 3.01 for Ford.[5]

Increasing productivity is also important to nonprofit organizations, which have the same concern for increasing output relative to inputs. Everywhere workers are led by a supervisor, you will find a concern for getting more accomplished with the same or fewer resources.

Improving Productivity: A Historical Perspective

How can one increase productivity? How is it possible to increase output without adding commensurately to expenses such as wages?

There is a lot more to this question than simply getting people to work harder. Many factors affect productivity. Educational levels of workers, technology, quality of tools, and research and development all play a role. Throughout this text, we will focus on what the supervisor can do to improve the productivity of work team members, given whatever level of other factors happens to exist. Throughout history, supervisory methods have contributed to significant productivity improvements. These methods have included scientific management, bureaucracy, and the human relations school.

Scientific Management. The factory system was in full bloom in the United States by the early 1900s. Management theorists of the time promoted managerial practices typified by Frederick Taylor's call for scientific management. **Scientific management,** a management approach that scientifically assesses the best methods for accomplishing work, had five basic objectives:

scientific management
A management approach developed in the early 1900s that scientifically assesses the best methods for accomplishing work.

1. The development of a science of management that would enable managers to identify the one best way to do a job.
2. The scientific selection of workers, so that the best-suited person was hired for each job.
3. The scientific training of each worker, so that he or she knew precisely how to accomplish the work.
4. A high degree of cooperation between labor and management.[6]

Taylor also strongly believed in pay for performance, in other words, that higher worker productivity should be rewarded with higher pay.

Taylor's work led to impressive improvements in productivity. For example, scientific management was used to increase productivity of common laborers

Frederick Taylor's Instructions to a "High-Priced Man"

Scientific management wasn't sentimental, as can be seen in a conversation Taylor cited in his classic, *The Principles of Scientific Management.*

Schmidt was a turn-of-the-century laborer who was very interested in earning a pay raise from $1.15 to $1.85 per day. He was instructed in the following manner by Taylor to obey the orders of his supervisor:

Well, [Schmidt] if you are a high-priced man, you will do exactly as this man [the supervisor] tells you tomorrow, from morning till night. When he tells you to pick up a pig and walk, you pick it up and you walk, and when he tells you to sit down and

rest, you sit down. You do that right straight through the day. And what's more, no back talk. Now a high-priced man does just what he's told to do, and no back talk. Do you understand that? When this man tells you to walk, you walk; when he tells you to sit down, you sit down, and you don't talk back to him. Now you come on to work here tomorrow morning and I'll know before night whether you are really a high-priced man or not.[7]

Taylor believed pig iron handlers should "resemble the mental make-up of an ox."

bureaucracy
An organizational structure characterized by clear lines of responsibility and authority where communication, policies, procedures, and rules flow in a top-down manner from managers to employees.

transporting 92-pound pig iron ingots from $12\frac{1}{2}$ to 47 tons a day. In this situation, management obtained a 400 percent productivity increase and workers received 60 percent more wages!

Productivity gains from scientific management benefited both workers, who received significantly higher wages, and companies, who were able to become more competitive and profitable.

Bureaucracy. At about the time Taylor was popularizing scientific management, Max Weber, a German sociologist, published his views of an ideal organization. Weber supported the notion of the bureaucracy. A **bureaucracy** is defined as an organizational structure characterized by clear lines of responsi-

Scientific management significantly improved productivity, but not the desirability of work.

bility and authority where communication, policies, procedures, and rules flow in a top-down manner from managers to employees. Weber argued that organizations should adhere to five basic bureaucratic principles:

1. Organizational tasks should be divided into highly specialized jobs. Workers should be trained to perform only those tasks required by their jobs.
2. Each task should be performed according to only one set of procedures. This requirement eliminates uncertainty caused by differences in the way individual workers approach a task.
3. Positions within the organization should be ordered into a rigid hierarchy with a clear definition of reporting lines and authority.
4. Supervisors should assume an impersonal attitude when dealing with subordinates to eliminate personal prejudice in supervisory decision making.
5. Initial placement and advancement in an organization should be based on qualifications and merit.[8]

Weber's and Taylor's theories, together with the work of other classic management theorists including Henri Fayol, Henry Gantt, and Frank and Lillian Gilbreth, helped make American productivity the envy of the world. Time and motion studies, improvements in assembly line techniques, training tied to specific jobs, rising wages tied to productivity gains, and clear organizational reporting lines contributed to high productivity and thus to a rising standard of living.

The Human Relations School.   The problem with scientific management and rigid bureaucratic hierarchies, however, was that they dehumanized work. This dehumanization of work contributed to worker boredom and dissatisfaction. These management methods also did not fully utilize worker potential. The typical U.S. organization made decisions in a top-down fashion, and employees were expected to do their jobs and little else.

Taylor's and Weber's theories minimize the social nature of human beings. They do not account for the need for recognition and social interaction possessed by American workers. These needs were identified by Elton Mayo and his associates in 1927–1932 studies at Western Electric's Hawthorne plant in Cicero, Illinois. The most famous of what have become known as the Hawthorne studies involved modifying lighting for a group of female workers. The researchers were not surprised when productivity increased after lighting was improved, but were shocked to find that productivity also increased when illumination was reduced to levels equal to that of moonlight.

The researchers had identified a factor not accounted for by scientific management. In time, this factor came to be known as the Hawthorne effect. The **Hawthorne effect** occurs when people are influenced by recognition to perform at a higher level than they might otherwise. This effect demonstrates that productivity is influenced by factors other than money and training. There is a social, as well as rational, dimension to workplace behavior.

A large number of motivation theories grew out of the discovery of the social side of human performance. (Motivation theories are covered in detail in Chapter 11.) Eventually, these theories coalesced into the **human relations school** of management. This school of thought emphasizes the importance of helping employees meet social and esteem needs associated with work.

It is important to understand that Taylor, Weber, and other early management theorists weren't entirely wrong. There is a need in the workplace for structure, clear goals, training, and compensation tied to performance, but workers also

Hawthorne effect
When recognition influences people to perform at a higher level than they might otherwise, thus indicating that productivity is influenced by factors other than money or training.

human relations school (of management)
A school of thought emphasizing the importance of helping employees meet social and esteem needs associated with work.

have needs that relate to recognition, opportunity to participate in decision making, and opportunity to work meaningfully with others.

The effective supervisor should realize that no one perspective or school of thought is best. As noted at the chapter's beginning, different situations call for different supervisory approaches. Generally, today's approaches—even organizational structures—emphasize the need for flexibility.

Figure 2-1 contrasts "old" thinking influenced by the views of theorists such as Taylor and Weber with "new" thinking influenced by the evolution of the human relations school to the present day. Notice how the ideas supported by scientific management and bureaucratic organization contrast with the modern view that emphasizes importance of individual workers, contributions of teams, and communication among people.

Improving Effectiveness: The Quality Challenge

To reiterate, it is not enough to lead a highly productive work team. It is also necessary that the team continuously improve the quality of what it produces. Returning to an earlier example, even if General Motors had kept up with the productivity gains of competitors, it would still fail if customers were dissatisfied with the quality of GM automobiles and trucks.

Quality and productivity are related. Quality improvements in production processes often improve productivity. For example, the Ford Motor Company gained $400 million in productivity improvements in the development of the Taurus and Sable automobiles through improving the quality of production processes.[9] A company saves money and becomes more productive to the extent its work force and other resources are used to build high-quality products, rather than to fix past mistakes.

Figure 2-1	Old versus New Management Thinking Regarding Effective Organizations

Old Thinking (early 20th century)	New Thinking (late 20th century)
■ Technology first	■ Social/technical systems optimized together
■ People as extensions of machines	■ People complement machines
■ People as spare parts	■ People as scarce resources
■ Narrow tasks, simple skills	■ Multiple, broad skills
■ External control: procedures book	■ Self-control: teams and departments
■ Many levels of organization, autocratic style	■ Flat organization, participative style
■ Competitive	■ Cooperative
■ Organization's purposes only	■ Individual and social purposes included
■ Alienation: "it's only a job"	■ Commitment: "it's *my* job"
■ Low risk-taking	■ Innovation

Source: Adapted from M. R. Weisbord, *Productive Workplaces: Organizing and Managing for Dignity, Meaning, and Community* (San Francisco: Jossey-Bass Publishers, 1987).

The Different Faces of TQM

TQM stands for total quality management. This system is also known by many other labels. Here are a few:

TQM—Total Quality Management
TQA—Total Quality Assessment
TQC—Total Quality Control
CWQC—Company-wide Quality Control
SQM—Strategic Quality Management
QFD—Quality Function Development
CI—Continuous Improvement, or *kaizen*

TQS—Total Quality Systems
QIP—Quality Improvement Program

Organizations practicing TQM are sometimes referred to as "learning organizations," because these organizations continuously apply learning from their past in order to improve their futures. The Japanese use the word *kaizen,* which means "improvement," to refer to the continuous monitoring and improving of a work process.[10]

In the traditional approach to quality control in the United States, manufacturers checked product quality at the end of the production line, reworking or discarding products that were not up to standard. U.S. manufacturers were not directly and systematically improving quality throughout the production process. Prior to the quality revolution in the United States, the typical factory invested up to 25 percent of its operating budget in finding and fixing mistakes and satisfying product warranties.[11]

The Quality Revolution

Traditional approaches to quality improvement might still be in place today in the United States, had it not been for the need to meet the Japanese challenge.

Japanese competition eroded the United States' market position in a wide variety of industries. Since the early 1970s, Japanese products, notably in the automobile, steel, textiles, microprocessor, and electronics industries, earned a well-deserved reputation for quality that devastated the market share and profitability of comparable U.S. industries. Not only were Japanese companies more productive, but their products were of higher quality. A case in point is the performance of the Toyota Motor Company, a leading Japanese auto manufacturer.

By 1982, Toyota could manufacture and ship a subcompact to the United States for significantly less cost than American companies could make a comparable car in the United States. Labor costs were not a factor, for although Japanese labor cost was less, this advantage was offset by shipping costs. Studies determined the Toyota advantage of approximately $1,500 per car over comparable U.S. autos was due to more productive manufacturing methods and better management. The company could produce more automobiles with the same level of resources.[12]

Toyota's quality was also higher; between 80 and 85 percent of Toyotas were manufactured with zero defects, whereas at Ford cars rolled off the production line with seven to eight defects each.[13]

Japanese industry was helped by the late W. Edwards Deming and Joseph Juran, Americans who worked with Japanese industrialists beginning in the early 1950s. The management system promoted by Deming, Juran, and hundreds of other quality consultants has many labels (see box titled "The Different Faces of TQM"), but it is most often known as **total quality management (TQM).** TQM is "the act of managing an entire organization to assure the continuous improvement of its ability to meet and exceed customer needs and expectations."[14] Today, the highest quality award in Japan is titled the Deming Award in honor of W. Edwards Deming.

total quality management
A management system used to assure the continuous improvement of an organization's ability to meet and exceed customer needs and expectations.

[handwritten note: led by Jap taught by Americans!]

In a TQM environment all employees strive to improve product quality, not just the quality control department. Ski manufacturer K2, for example, implemented TQM and was able to decrease the number of its quality control inspectors from 20 to 1 because every K2 employee became involved with quality control. In the words of Director of Marketing Services Charlie Jenkins, "instead of one inspector we have 375 today."[15]

Focus on Data

TQM systems continuously collect data to improve processes that produce goods and services. TQM practitioners use a wide variety of statistical charts and methods to organize and to interpret data. Supervisors are often called on to collect data and to interpret statistical diagrams for the purpose of improving process quality.

Pareto chart
A diagram used to determine priorities by identifying and distinguishing between the important events or activities and the unimportant ones.

The Pareto Chart.   One statistical tool used by TQM practitioners is a **Pareto chart.** A Pareto chart is a diagram used to determine priorities by identifying and distinguishing between the *vital few* and the *trivial many.*

In an 1897 study of wealth and income in Italy, Vilfredo Pareto observed that a large percentage of the total national income was concentrated in a small percentage of the population. It occurred to him that the significant contributors in a given group will usually constitute a small percentage of the group while the majority of group members will have only minor importance as contributors. Pareto's observation caught on, and today is often referred to as the **Pareto principle.**

Pareto principle
Illustrates that often a few items, events, or people will comprise the majority of something, and vice versa.

Interestingly, the relationship Pareto described can be expressed mathematically: roughly 80 percent of a group contributes about 20 percent; the remaining 20 percent of the group contributes approximately 80 percent. For example, about 20 percent of a given floor space receives about 80 percent of the wear and tear; 20 percent of sales personnel account for about 80 percent of sales, with 80 percent of sales personnel accounting for the remaining 20 percent of sales.

Suppose you keep a checklist for a semester on reasons why you are late to class. You end up with a list that looks like this:

Occurrence	Number of Times
Slept late	19
Dawdled over coffee	2
Missed bus	2
Late bus	1
Phone call	1

As can be seen, about 80 percent of the time (19 out of a total of 25 occurrences) your lateness is accounted for by about 20 percent of the reasons (sleeping late—1 of the 5 reasons). Time and attention should now be focused on resolving the problem of sleeping late. Similarly, supervisors and groups can use Pareto charts to define and attend to virtually any kind of problem that arises in the workplace.

Figure 2-2 shows how this list would be graphed as a Pareto chart. As can be seen, Pareto charts graphically prioritize causes. Chapter 5 describes more statistical tools and applications used in TQM.

Figure 2-2   Pareto Chart of Reasons for Being Late to Class

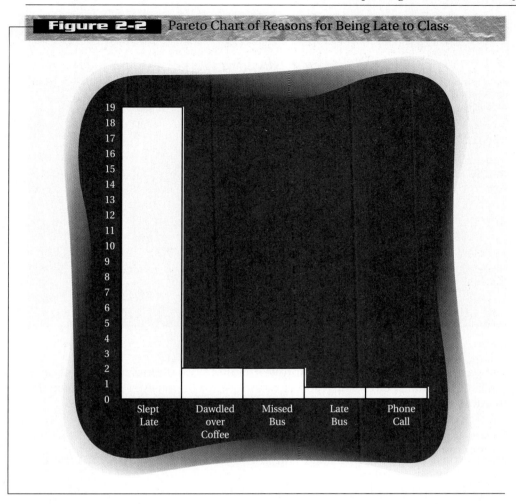

Importance of Teamwork

Supervisors play an important role in both collecting statistical information and bringing a group of workers together as a problem-solving team. TQM requires the effective functioning of teams of committed workers who are empowered to act on their ideas. TQM practitioners use methods designed to free workers so their creative and productive potential is unlocked to solve problems. In TQM, people work together to further department, division, and company-wide productivity and quality goals. Individuals can use the statistical tools discussed in the previous section, but they are primarily designed to help solve problems within a group process.

Many TQM organizations use quality circles. A **quality circle** is a relatively small team of workers who meet periodically to find ways to improve quality of work processes. Quality circles became popular in the late 1970s and continue to play a role in companies practicing TQM.

Quality circles are effective to the extent the organization as a whole, including top management, is committed to improving quality; to the extent groups are truly empowered to act; and when groups are allowed to be ongoing, rather than

quality circle
A relatively small team of workers who meet periodically to find ways to improve the quality of work processes.

An effective supervisor helps a team to pull together.

just part of a one-time effort to improve quality.[16] Too often management does not listen to quality circle suggestions, or the groups themselves are not given the freedom to fully implement needed change.

Focus on the Customer

customer
The recipient of a work team's output, either outside the organization or within the organization.

The purpose of continuous quality improvement is to please the **customer.** A customer is the recipient of the work team's output. For example, within a law firm, a secretarial pool might be responsible for typing briefs to be used by the firm's attorneys. The customers in this example are the attorneys, not their clients. Yet, the productivity and quality of work done by the secretarial pool ultimately affects the quality of service provided by the attorneys to their clients, who are the organization's ultimate customers.

In this way, outcomes of productivity- and quality-minded supervision ripple through an entire organization as one satisfied "customer" satisfies another. The objective is eventually to satisfy the end user of an organization's product mix of goods and services—the ultimate customer.

Total Quality Management and Organizational Culture

Because increasing numbers of supervisors will be involved in TQM and its variations in the years ahead, the effective supervisor should have a good understanding of the theoretical basis of TQM covered in this chapter. As with any new management program, the supervisor should also be aware of potential problems with TQM.

TQM can take years to fully implement. Take another look at Figure 2-1, where new thinking is contrasted with traditional management practices. All elements of new thinking outlined in this figure are part of a successful TQM organization. Consider the significance of the changes called for by this new thinking.

Is 99.9 Percent Quality Okay?

TQM advocates argue that the only acceptable goal is 100 percent quality. No rejects or mistakes! An alternative to perfection is the seemingly acceptable level of 99.9 percent perfection. Yet, if 99.9 percent is "good enough," then,

- Two million documents will be lost by the IRS this year.
- 22,000 checks will be deducted from the wrong bank accounts in the next hour.

- 360 newborn babies will be given to the wrong parents every month.
- Two plane landings every day at O'Hare International Airport in Chicago will be unsafe.
- 20,000 incorrect drug prescriptions will be dispensed during the next year.[17]

Traditional management has a hard time making these changes, particularly in difficult economic times when money for new management approaches is scarce.

TQM requires a significant change in organizational culture. **Organizational culture** refers to the shared beliefs, values, language, history, rituals, and stories held by members of an organization. Changing organizational culture is difficult. See Figure 2-3. It's not easy for old-school production supervisors to change the way they look at input from workers or to change their language. (Chapter 19 discusses related issues in career development.)

Keep in mind that TQM's success in Japan was due, in part, to the compatibility of Japanese culture with TQM theory and practice. Japanese culture emphasizes group cooperation and working together for the common good. The United States, in contrast, has a tradition of conflict between management and labor. Japanese culture places emphasis on the individual satisfying the other person in an interchange, such as the customer. The United States, in contrast, has a tradition of *caveat emptor,* or "let the buyer beware." The Japanese work ethic—influenced by culture and driven by a need to rebuild from the rubble of World War II and to improve per-capita income from a resource-deprived island base—has also been powerful.

The above factors all contributed to Japanese success with TQM. This does not suggest that the American worker is less worthy, but rather that the differing cultures and economic situations explain Japan's success with TQM relative to the experience of the United States.

A final comment regarding TQM and its variations: American management is susceptible to fads.[18] A new management technique seems to comes along every three to five years. Top management jumps on the bandwagon. Middle management, supervisors, and employees are retrained or reoriented, and change is implemented. Future chapters will touch on techniques that started out as popular new methods but were later found wanting. Every new method, including TQM, contains useful, valid information and techniques. Remember, though, that no management method has a corner on truth, despite how good it initially looks.

Regardless of whether an organization fully implements TQM, any supervisor can glean useful ideas from TQM that will improve the productivity and effectiveness of a work group. Supervisors should

1. use objective, specific data to drive decision making, particularly when making important decisions

organizational culture
The shared beliefs, values, language, history, rituals, and stories held by members of an organization.

[handwritten: Jap has narrow culture]

[handwritten: TQM success]

| **Figure 2-3** | The Difficulties of a Changing Organizational Culture |

High above the hushed crowd, Rex tried to remain
focused. Still, he couldn't shake one nagging thought:
He was an old dog and this was a new trick.

Source: THE FAR SIDE © Copyright 1992 Farworks, Inc. Distributed by Universal Press Syndicate.
Reprinted with permission. All rights reserved.

2. make use of statistical graphing techniques such as fishbone or Pareto charts to better understand data
3. look for ways to help workers unlock their creative potential and make contributions to the group effort
4. improve processes continuously _Rizen_
5. emphasize satisfying the customer, keeping in mind that the customer is whoever the individual or group serves _Cust satisfaction_

A Model for Improving Performance

Regardless of what methods or techniques he or she employs, three characteristics—motivation, ability, and environmental factors—affect performance in every situation a supervisor confronts. The supervisor must address these characteristics to optimize individual or group performance.

Motivating Employees

WHY? **Motivation** is a psychological state that compels people to pursue or to avoid certain activities or goals. Motivation is increased to the extent people have clear direction and are energized. (Chapter 11 covers this subject in detail.)

Clear goals contribute powerfully to motivation and ultimate performance. Supervisors therefore contribute to performance to the extent they help individuals or work teams have clear direction. Motivation is also increased to the extent people feel energized or otherwise inspired to move in the desired direction. Many factors contribute to such inspiration. An important contributor is whether or not an activity meets an unmet need. If you are hungry, for example, a banana split will be motivating; if you have just finished a big meal, it will not. Supervisors should be sensitive to the needs of employees and should try to create an environment that satisfies them. Worker needs might include such things as achievement, social interaction, and income.

motivation
A psychological state that compels people to pursue or avoid certain activities or goals.

Improving Employee Ability

A worker could be highly motivated and have clear goals that are compatible with meeting his or her needs, but performance could still be inadequate if this person lacks ability. **Ability** is the actual capacity to carry out specific, job-related tasks. It is developed from all of the training, experience, talent, and aptitude that are necessary to perform well in a given situation.

An important consideration in improving ability is training. **Training** is a systematic attempt to change employee behavior through the learning process in order to improve performance. Each year, American employers spend about $30 billion for training. Unfortunately, this investment is made by only a handful of employers. Only $\frac{1}{2}$ of 1 percent of all American employers account for 90 percent of all training expenditures![19] Training in the typical organization, if it happens at all, tends to involve one worker—typically a supervisor—showing the job to another.

Even if a training budget is unavailable, supervisors should make sure employees know how to do their jobs. This may entail working with employees to help them learn skills on their own. It may involve the supervisor or a coworker acting as a trainer to help an employee learn specific job-related skills, rather than just showing him or her the job. Providing clear direction helps the worker understand *what* to do, but it's also important that employees know *how* to do the work. (Chapter 9 includes more information on the supervisor's role in training.)

ability
The actual capacity to carry out specific, job-related tasks.

training
Is a systematic attempt to change employee behavior through the learning process in order to improve performance.

Confronting Environmental Factors

Whereas motivation and ability deal with intrinsic variables, **environmental factors** are factors affecting performance that are outside the worker, over which the worker has little control. For example, an employee may not have the tools to complete a job. A skilled secretary still needs a computer or word processor to type correspondence. A plumber needs the right wrench.

Environmental factors also include personal matters that affect an employee. An impending divorce or the death of a loved one; a chronic disease such as AIDS or cancer; or even stress incurred during a long vacation all may adversely affect work. People do bring their personal lives to the job. (Stress is discussed in greater depth in Chapter 17.)

environmental factors
Factors affecting performance that are outside the worker, over which the worker has little control.

Supervisors should be mindful of environmental factors and do everything possible to reduce the likelihood these factors will have an adverse effect on the employee's performance. Supervisors should be proactive, anticipating and solving potential problems in the environment before they arise, as opposed to reactive. Sensitivity to employee problems outside of work is good management, although there are no pat answers on how to provide assistance. Sometimes the supervisor's sensitivity and willingness to help are all that is necessary.

Carla scowled at Larry's back as he left her office. The door slammed, and Carla flinched.

"So Larry wants me to improve productivity without lowering quality," Carla thought to herself.

"What shall I do? I think I'll do nothing right now. I'm going home!" Carla left work an hour early.

She drove to her apartment in Edmonds, made a cup of coffee, and settled on her favorite couch. The last conversation with Larry, her boss, continued to haunt her. She picked up a trade magazine that happened to include an article titled "Deming's 14 Points: Pathway to Quality and Productivity" and was intrigued by the article's discussion of statistical quality control.

The following week, Carla and 180 other line supervisors attended the first of a series of weekly training sessions dealing with the company's move to TQM. Within five weeks, her group was using statistical charts to graph progress; within two months, the first cost savings were realized.

Carla also started to look at her work group in terms of environmental factors and the motivation and ability of employees. She realized that two of her charges would benefit from additional training. The company did not have funds available for outside training, so she spent some time training them herself. Their performance improved. Carla also started working with her work team to clarify goals. She was surprised that a few group members had not been aware of what the team was trying to achieve.

Six months after the unpleasant conversation with Larry about productivity, Carla's group was functioning splendidly. Quality and productivity were both significantly improved.

Summary: Focus on Concepts

Supervisors must keep up with constant changes in people, environments, and the interactions of these variables with an eye on improving performance, the productivity and quality of team or individual output.

Productivity is concerned with increasing output relative to expenses. It is a measure of efficiency, or how much is produced by a work group with a given level of resources. One way to assess productivity is to look at its effect on an income statement, a financial statement that accounts for business revenues, expenses, and profit or loss over time. Increased productivity improves profitability of business enterprises in many ways because it contributes to higher revenues, to lower expenses (such as wage expense), or to both.

Historically, scientific management, as first described by Frederick Taylor, and bureaucratic organization, as defined by Max Weber, contributed to significant productivity improvements in the United States. While these practices are still beneficial, research first conducted by Elton Mayo and his associates at the Western Electric Hawthorne plant in Cicero, Illinois, found that workers also have social needs.

The discovery of the social and recognition needs of workers contributed to the development of management practices that complemented and, in some cases, replaced scientific management. New management thinking calls for valuing the individual worker and providing opportunities for advancement and self-fulfillment. It relies on collaborative decision making and empowerment of the worker to act on his or her ideas.

Quality is defined in terms of value added to goods and services so that they satisfy the customer. Quality is concerned with effectiveness, or how well work group output has been produced. Quality improvements can increase productivity because they allow a company to put its resources into building products, rather than into fixing mistakes.

The quality revolution began in Japan. Assisted by American consultants including the late W. Edwards Deming and Joseph Juran, Japanese industry developed a management system called *total quality management (TQM)*. TQM is an organization-wide effort to assure the continuous improvement of products in order to meet and exceed customer needs and expectations.

TQM systems rely on the use of statistical data. An example of a statistical tool used in TQM is a Pareto chart. Teamwork is emphasized. The company benefits from the contributions of committed employees who work together to improve product quality. Organizations practicing TQM sometimes form quality circles, relatively small teams of workers who meet periodically to find ways to improve quality. TQM organizations focus on satisfying the customer. Customers are defined as the recipients of a work group's output, and can be internal or external.

TQM can be difficult to implement. It usually takes many years to change organizational culture to TQM methods. The fact that TQM methods are highly successful in Japan does not guarantee they will be as successful in the United States. Culture and history account for some of the success of TQM in Japan.

A model for improving individual performance was presented that suggests all situations confronted by a supervisor include elements of worker motivation and ability as well as environmental factors.

Motivation is a psychological state that compels people to pursue or to avoid certain activities or goals. Ability is the actual capacity to carry out specific job-related tasks. Training—a systematic attempt to change employee behavior through the learning process in order to improve performance—is an important contributor to improving ability.

Environmental factors are factors outside the worker, over which the worker has little control. Supervisors should be proactive in dealing with environmental factors that affect performance.

Review Questions

1. What is an income statement? Illustrate how productivity increases lead to higher revenues.
2. What is scientific management? State the five basic objectives of scientific management.
3. Would Frederick W. Taylor's approach to scientific management, such as his instructions to a "high-priced man," be appropriate today? Explain.
4. Define *bureaucracy*. Indicate the five basic principles of bureaucracy developed by Max Weber.
5. What is the human relations school of management? The Hawthorne effect?
6. Contrast old and new management thinking.
7. What factors created the quality revolution?
8. What is total quality management (TQM)?
9. Explain the operation of a Pareto chart. Indicate how it can be applied to a management situation.
10. What are quality circles? What is their function?

11. Comment on the following statements: A very acceptable level of quality would be 99.9 percent. At this level, only one reject or error would occur for every 1,000 items or events.
12. How does TQM affect an organization's culture?
13. What can supervisors do to improve productivity and effectiveness of their work groups?
14. Define motivation. Then indicate how ability and environmental factors affect an individual's state of motivation.

Notes

1. H. Lewis and D. Allison, *The Real World War* (New York: Coward, McCann, & Geoghegan, 1982).
2. General Motors statistics from the Prodigy News Service, 10:21 PM, October 16, 1992.
3. "Study Still Ranks U.S. No. 1 in Productivity" (article on a study by the McKinsey Global Institute), *Seattle Post-Intelligencer,* October 13, 1992, B5.
4. W. S. Dietrich, *In the Shadow of the Rising Sun* (University Park, PA: The Pennsylvania State University Press, 1991).
5. Business Section, *Time,* October 11, 1992, 22.
6. F. W. Taylor, *The Principles of Scientific Management* (New York: Norton Company, 1967) (first published in 1911).
7. Ibid., 45–46.
8. M. Weber, *Essays in Sociology* (New York: Oxford, 1946).
9. M. Walton, *The Deming Management Method* (New York: Putnam Publishing Group, 1986).
10. Based on J. Cleveland, "Total Quality Management," *Jackson Area Quality Initiative,* April 9, 1991.
11. "The Push for Quality," *Business Week,* June 8, 1987, 131–143.
12. S. Lohr, "Wanted: Japan's Toyota Know-How," *The Herald* (Everett) (from New York Times News Service), April 1, 1982, D3.
13. Ibid.
14. "TQM," *Michigan Modernization Service,* February 1991, 2.
15. Associated Press, "Ski Maker Reverses Slide," *The Herald* (Everett), August 4, 1992, C1.
16. J. Shonk, *Team-Based Organizations* (Homewood, IL: Business One Irwin, 1992).
17. Adapted from "Is 99.9% Quality Good Enough?" *Nichols Northwest News,* April, 1992, 4.
18. M. Lasden, "Fad In, Fad Out," *Computer Decisions,* May 21, 1985, 74–76, 78–84, 88.
19. National Center on Education and the Economy, "The Education and Training of America's Adult Workers," *America's Choice: High Skills or Low Wages,* June 1990, 49–56.

Case 2-1

The Corporate Day-Care Center

When the idea was first expressed at the weekly staff meeting, those in attendance either smiled or laughed. What began as a brainstorming session for obtaining ideas for better utilization of the wasted space on First National Bank's main floor turned into an animated discussion. Convert the wasted space into a day-care facility for children of the bank's employees.

There is something incongruous about a bunch of youngsters and babies in the midst of serious banking business surrounded by a large number of the bank's customers.

Pamela Coolidge supervised eight tellers at First National Bank. She had a practice of scheduling the final hour of the working week, Friday afternoon from four until five, as a staff meeting. The eight tellers gathered in the bank's employee lounge for their meetings. Not only were the sessions generally productive, they also gave the employees a chance to unwind from the week's work. In one sense, the last hour was also perceived as a reward. If you survived the previous 39 hours, the 40th was free from hassles. During the meetings, information was exchanged about jobs and new procedures or policies. Time was also spent discussing problems experienced during the previous week. Morale was good in Pamela's group, although employee turnover continued to be a problem. Apparently, there was genuine friendship among the tellers.

Teller turnover is a common problem for many banks. Tellers are predominantly young. Many have very young children or are expecting. While some parents prefer employment over staying home, others, by necessity, take jobs separating them from their children during the working days; they need the money. Getting their children to baby-sitters or day-care facilities has always been a problem for many parents, especially when the day-care centers are several miles from where the parents work.

As Pamela began the meeting, she explained that after covering the preliminaries they were going to take up the topic of space utilization on the first floor. As in many large banks, considerable center space is unused on the main floors. The various work areas are concentrated around the four walls. Recently, Pamela received a memo from the operations officer asking for suggestions on how to make better use of the center space. A prize of $100 would be awarded for the best suggestion—the one adopted. When the routine

business was completed, the group turned to the space subject.

Pamela's employees made a number of recommendations. They ranged from the usual comments of "more greenery—foliage," to such ideas as turning a portion of the area into an exhibition space for showing paintings and crafts by community residents, adding more chairs for customers, and creating a small museum with artifacts from the period of the community's early pioneer settlement. Then Louise, the most outspoken member of the group, stated in a resolute voice, "I think we ought to convert the space into a day-care center."

"Out of the nine of us here five have young children, and two more are expecting. We need a day-care center that is more convenient for all of us than the ones we are presently using. And there is plenty of space here. With good soundproofing, there wouldn't be any noise, and it certainly would be a lot more convenient for us. I think we need a day-care center."

Questions

1. What do you think of Louise's idea? Pros? Cons?
2. What types of actions can management take to improve working conditions for employees? Separate your answers into two categories: (a) those things that can be done at a small cost and (b) those that are more expensive.
3. What advantages does the bank derive from increasing employee job satisfaction and motivation? Why would the firm wish to reduce turnover of tellers?
4. What evidence and arguments would you present to support a recommendation to create a day-care center on the first floor of First National Bank? Do you think higher management would give the suggestion of a day-care center serious consideration?

Case 2-2

Dream Homes

Casey Jones retired two months ago. He had worked for a mobile home manufac-

turing company in Indianapolis. For over thirty years, Casey had supervised crews at the firm, initially starting as a carpenter, and rapidly advancing to foreman. He was just about as expert as one could become in building a mobile home.

When he retired, Casey and his wife moved to Mt. Ida, Arkansas, near Lake Ouachita. He planned to spend the rest of his life in leisure, fishing, boating, and loafing. But things didn't work out that way as Casey quickly became bored with the easy life. He was still young at 55 and in good health. Before the end of two months, he was back at work.

Casey was offered and accepted a job with a small manufacturer of precon-structed houses in Mt. Ida, a community with 1,000 people. The company carried the whimsical name, "Dream Homes," and the owner of the business, to say the least, was delighted to have Casey as Dream Homes was rapidly becoming "nightmares." The firm was nearing insolvency. Casey was hired as the production manager of Dream Homes.

Preconstructed houses are typically built in two, more or less equal, sections in a factory-type environment. They are then transported to and erected on the buyer's property after footing and foundations are prepared. Because of factory construction with its production efficiencies, the buildings are usually less expensive than conventional "stick built" houses.

Casey toured the plant and concluded that the construction time in building each house was excessive. They were requiring approximately twice the labor needed to produce similar buildings. Currently, the plant was turning out about two houses per week. It should be producing four, considering the amount of labor being used. Also, quality was low. Some employees did not have enough work. Most were poorly trained or their skills were still primitive. In addition, perhaps 20 percent of materials were wasted. As was the practice at Dream Homes, most employees at one time or another traded jobs and, thus, worked as carpenters, dry wall workers, electricians, plumbers, and painters.

The layout of the main building where construction took place could charitably be called a disaster area. The work processes were confusing, disorganized, and helter-skelter. Still, it was a spacious building.

Employees were from the predominantly rural area in and around Mt. Ida. The owner and many customers described the workers as "good old boys" who did their best. It was apparent to Casey that their best was not going to save Dream

Homes unless changes were made. Most of the workers lacked basic craft skills when they first joined the company. Carpenters, for example, acquired their skills by building their own houses. One of the painters had painted his house once, and so on. Skills could be developed though. The work ethic was alive and well in Mt. Ida. Employees just lacked the training and leadership to become more productive, along with an organized place to work.

Breakeven was estimated at four houses. Casey believed he could implement several changes in the production process immediately and, through training, bring the productivity of the workers up to standard within two months.

Casey had scheduled a meeting in one hour, at 3:45, with the 30 employees to discuss the changes that they would have to make. He prepared an outline of the topics to be discussed, including:

1. We've got problems because we are not efficient or competitive, and quality is too low.
2. We must double production—soon.
3. We need more skill training for everyone.
4. We need to specialize more in job assignment.
5. We should reorganize the plant layout.
6. We must reduce waste by better work methods.
7. We need to reassign work so that each person has a similar amount to do.
8. We must improve safety conditions and work practices.
9. We should implement a comprehensive cost-reduction program.
10. Cover the new policies and rules.

Casey reviewed his list. "How should I go about this?" he thought. "Should I lay it on the line? If we don't get cracking, we aren't going to make it, and everyone will be out of work. Or should I ask for their support and appeal to their pride? We can do better—a lot better."

Questions

1. How should Casey approach talking to the employees for the first time? That is, what should he say and what tone should he set for the meeting?

2. Which items on Casey's agenda are most important and should be covered in detail? Are there any points he missed? Others on the list that could be deleted?

3. How would you handle the following questions and objections raised by members of the group during the meeting?

   a. "We didn't know there were any big problems. No one said anything to us before."

   b. "How can we double production without adding more people?"

   c. "You came from another part of the country. We do things differently here—and seem to get by okay."

   d. "Does this mean that I can't take any scrap lumber and leftovers home anymore?"

   e. "I don't think I want to do just one thing. I like the variety of different jobs, and doing just one job would be boring."

   f. "It's five o'clock. Can we go home now?"

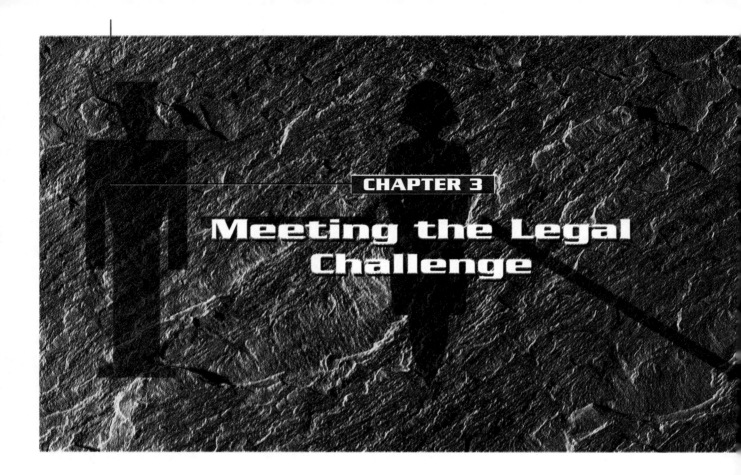

CHAPTER 3

Meeting the Legal Challenge

● Murphy's Law: If anything can go wrong, it will.

LEARNING OBJECTIVES

1. Understand the background of the legal environment in the United States.
2. Define equal employment opportunity and indicate the basic provision of Title VII of the Civil Rights Act of 1964.
3. Relate other equal employment opportunity laws and their basic content.
4. Describe adverse impact and adverse treatment.
5. Explain the concept of validation and the several methods used to achieve validity.
6. Discuss affirmative action and how it is obtained.

Carla sighed. Her incredibly busy schedule had eased; production and quality standards were being met; she finally felt on top of her job. And then the problems started with Alan, a supervisor from another department.

"The guy's a real bother. I wish he'd leave me alone," Carla mused during a solitary lunch in the company cafeteria. Alan had developed an irritating habit of stopping by Carla's desk every morning with a different request for a date. At first, she'd politely rebuffed him. Lately, Carla had told him she was not interested in dating him. Still, he persisted. Lost in thought, she didn't hear the approaching footsteps. But she smelled the cheap cologne. She looked up in irritation.

"Is this seat taken?" It was Alan.

"Look Alan, I'm just finishing up and want to be left alone with my thoughts. Find another seat. There's plenty of space."

"Hey, babe. . . . look, how about you and me tonight at eight o'clock? Dinner at Thirteen Coins. Whad'ya say?" Alan sniggered.

Carla, furious, silently stood, picked up her tray, and walked away.

As stated in the first chapter, helping the organization assure legal compliance is an important objective of effective supervision. The issues involved are complex and not amenable to easy, prescriptive solutions. This chapter will help you understand underlying legal issues, as well as provide you with guidelines for ensuring that the organization and you yourself are in compliance with legal requirements.

Background of the Legal Environment

It is important to first understand some background terms and issues affecting the legal environment in which the contemporary supervisor operates.

Where Does the Law Come From?

Our system of government has three branches: the legislative, judicial, and executive branches.

The legislative branch writes the law. These writings are called laws or statutes. The collection of statutes written by the legislative branch constitutes **statutory law.** Statutes are rules, often referred to as "regulations," that cover a wide range of subjects affecting society. An example of statutes affecting supervision can be found in the federal Civil Rights Act of 1964, which prohibits discrimination in employment based on race, color, sex, religion, or national origin.

The executive branch of government is responsible for enforcing the law. The federal government, for example, requires employers with federal contracts of a certain size to maintain affirmative action programs to assure equal opportunity in employment.

The judicial branch of government interprets the law. The judicial branch is necessary because statutes often tend to be ambiguous and are subject to different interpretations. Statutes only have meaning when they are applied in specific situations and then tested, if necessary, in the courts. There are state and federal courts that interpret state and federal statutes respectively. The highest court in the land is the Supreme Court comprised of nine justices.

Judicial interpretation makes up **case law,** the body of law concerned with precedent. For example, in a case to be discussed later in this chapter, *Griggs v. Duke Power,* the U.S. Supreme Court put the burden of proof on employers to validate employment tests in order to show that employment practices did not adversely affect a protected group.[1] The court's decision and, as importantly, the rationale for their decision, set a precedent that became the basis for understanding and enforcing the law.

A constant give-and-take between the branches of government gives the law its meaning. To summarize, legislators make the law by passing statutes, and judges and the court system interpret the law's meaning based on precedent. New laws are written constantly by the legislative branch to modify existing statutes. New laws are regularly scrutinized by the judicial branch. The executive branch enforces the law. The development of laws is a never-ending process at both state and federal levels.

Crimes and Torts

The judicial branch is called on to interpret statutes relating to crimes and torts. This section defines these terms and covers implications for supervisors.

Supervisors and employees may break statutes in such a way that a crime is committed. A **crime** is an act that violates a statute and implies a penalty. It is a public wrong committed by a party against the state. For example, some state safety and health regulations carry criminal penalties for violators. If a court determines that you, as a supervisor, ordered employees to work without safety

statutory law
The collection of legislative branch writings consisting of rules or regulations covering a wide range of subjects affecting society.

case law
A body of law based upon precedent, that is, something that has occurred before that serves as a guide for future decisions.

crime
A public wrong committed by a person or organization against the state that violates a statute and implies a penalty to be levied.

Effective supervision helps avoid costly litigation.

harnesses despite clear statutory requirements that harnesses be worn, and a worker is seriously injured, you or your employer could pay steep criminal fines and even go to jail.

A **tort** differs from a crime in that it represents a private, or civil, wrong committed by one party against another. A tort involves damage to a person or to a person's property or reputation. For example, the worker injured in the above example could claim damage in the form of lost wages and "pain and suffering" and seek monetary relief through the civil court system.

tort
A private or civil wrong committed by one party against another person or organization or to a person's property or reputation.

The basis of litigation is a claim that a tort has been committed. The United States has the most litigious culture in the developed world. Litigious is pronounced "la-'tij-us," and means "given to engaging in litigation," defined in Chapter 1 as the "process of bringing forth a lawsuit, or claim for damages, in a court of law." The United States, for example, supports 25 times more attorneys than does Japan. The cost of litigation is staggering to American society, ranging as high as 1.8 percent of the U.S. gross domestic product, or about $300 billion annually.[2]

Damages awarded by the court in a civil case may be for actual damages and, sometimes, if the behavior of the defendant is particularly reprehensible, the court may require additional payment for punitive damages.

It is possible for a supervisor to commit both a tort and a crime. The supervisor who commits a crime by ordering employees to work without safety harnesses might be liable for payment of civil damages, as well as for jail time and court-imposed fines if convicted of a crime. It is also possible that the supervisor's employer will be held liable.

It is difficult to avoid prosecution through the court system if a crime is committed. However, civil disputes should be resolved using methods other than civil litigation if at all possible. **Alternative dispute resolution** involving use of processes outside of the court system, such as mediators, arbitrators, in-house ombudspersons, and contractually prescribed grievance proceedings help

alternative dispute resolution
Involves use of processes outside of the court system, such as mediators, arbitrators, in-house ombudspersons, and contractually prescribed grievance proceedings.

individuals and organizations to avoid the expense and nuisance of litigation. These processes typically involve a relatively informal reconciliation of differences using direct communication between concerned parties themselves rather than solely between or among their attorneys.

Effective supervisors need to know the dispute resolution processes that exist in their organizations. Supervisors need to understand not only how to legally conduct themselves, but also why such conduct is legal. It is not enough to simply memorize a list of rules to follow when dealing with certain situations or employees.

The ensuing discussion of laws, Supreme Court decisions, validation processes, and affirmative action will help you understand the legal basis of many personnel practices and ensure legal compliance in your supervisory practices.

Equal Employment Opportunity

Equal employment statutes are written at the municipal (city), state, and federal levels. Federal law requires municipal and state law to be applied first to a claim of illegal discrimination before federal statutes apply. Keep in mind that the state court system parallels the federal system; state court rulings give meaning to state statutes.

Federal equal employment opportunity legislation encompasses a wide variety of variables. It is illegal to discriminate in employment on the basis of age, race, color, religion, national origin, sex, disability, pregnancy, or veteran status. State and city equal employment opportunity laws, besides duplicating federal law, also cover additional factors, often making it illegal to discriminate on the basis of such factors as arrest records, marital status, sickle-cell trait, and sexual preference.

Civil Rights Act of 1964 (Title VII)

Civil Rights Act of 1964 (Title VII)
States that it is illegal for an employer with 15 or more employees in an industry affecting interstate commerce to discriminate on the basis of race, color, religion, sex, or national origin.

Equal Employment Opportunity Commission (EEOC)
The federal agency responsible for establishing guidelines to enforce Title VII of the Civil Rights Act of 1964 and investigating and resolving complaints of illegal discrimination.

The most significant equal employment act passed to date is the federal **Civil Rights Act of 1964.** This act has several sections called titles. Title VII makes it illegal for an employer with 15 or more employees in an industry affecting interstate commerce to discriminate on the basis of race, color, religion, sex, or national origin.

The Civil Rights Act of 1964 included establishment of an agency to enforce provisions of the act. This agency is called the **Equal Employment Opportunity Commission (EEOC).** The EEOC is charged with establishing guidelines for enforcing the act, and with investigating and resolving complaints of illegal discrimination. In 1972, the act was amended to increase the EEOC's enforcement authority. The EEOC can now sue employers on behalf of employees. Civil litigation can be brought against an employer independent of the employee's interest or intent. For example, an employee files a complaint and withdraws it. The EEOC can become a plaintiff against an employer independent of the employee's intent or wishes. Similarly, an incident brought to the EEOC's attention by a person other than the affected employee can lead to an investigation and action by the EEOC. The EEOC, and state and local equal opportunity agencies, seldom, however, get involved in court action. Their primary role is to investigate and resolve complaints of illegal discrimination, not to sue employers.

To deal effectively with issues related to equal employment opportunity, supervisors should, at the very least, have an understanding of the provisions of the 1964 Civil Rights Act. They should understand the types of discrimination that equal employment opportunity law covers. Types of discrimination will be covered shortly. First, though, we will discuss an emerging area of equal employment opportunity regulation that has profound implications for supervisors: sexual harassment.

Sexual Harassment. Confirmation hearings for Supreme Court Justice Clarence Thomas were jolted by Anita Hill's claim that she had been sexually harassed by Mr. Thomas. Ms. Hill's accusations brought the subject of workplace harassment of women to public attention. Sexual harassment is a serious problem.

Sexual harassment is defined by the EEOC as unwelcome sexual advances, requests for sexual favors, or other verbal or physical conduct of a sexual nature associated as a condition of employment, or that otherwise interferes with an employee's job performance.

Numerous surveys show a high proportion of women are harassed at some point in their careers. A recent study indicated that relatively few countries in the world, the United States among them, have sexual harassment laws and that high proportions of women—often over 30 percent of the female work force—eventually experience overt harassment, often leading them to switch jobs.[3] Consultant Michael Rubenstein summarizes the problem this way, "Sexual harassment is one of the most offensive and demeaning experiences an employee can suffer. For those who are its victims, it often produces feelings of revulsion, violation, disgust, anger, and powerlessness."[4]

Supervisors should know they can be held responsible not only by their company, but also by the courts, for sexual harassment committed by employees they supervise.

Supervisors need to be aware of several types of harassment. *Overt harassment* involves lewd comments and unwelcome sexual advances from one employee to another. *Environmental harassment* occurs when the work environment itself is made inherently hostile. For example, allowing nude pinups and a pattern of harassing communication such as off-color jokes or sexist comments around the water cooler or production line can lead to a charge of sexual harassment.

Sexual harassment charges are processed by the same local, state, and federal equal employment opportunity agencies that investigate other claims of illegal discrimination. Most sexual harassment charges involve women being harassed by men. While it does occur, harassment of men by women is rare. Sexual harassment claims can include criminal charges such as assault and battery and even rape.

sexual harassment
Any unwelcomed sexual advances, requests for sexual favors, or other verbal or physical conduct of a sexual nature associated as a condition of employment, or that otherwise interferes with an employee's job performance.

Other Equal Employment Opportunity Laws

Other equal opportunity laws speak to rights pertaining to gender, age, and disabled status.

Equal Pay Act (1963). The **Equal Pay Act of 1963** makes it illegal to discriminate on the basis of sex when paying employees. Prior to the passage of the act, employers often paid men more than women for doing the same work. (Sexist thinking was that men had families to support; women just needed spending money.)

Equal Pay Act of 1963
Makes it illegal to discriminate in pay based on gender.

The Comparable Worth Controversy

A 1974 study conducted by Norman Willis and Associates found that Washington State employees working in female-dominated job classes were paid 20 percent less than employees working in male-dominated job classes of comparable worth. Nevertheless, Washington State was not guilty of violating the Equal Pay Act of 1963. Why? Because this act prohibits gender-based pay discrimination only when employees are working in the same job. No provision existed for correcting pay inequity occurring when people worked in dissimilar jobs of comparable worth to an employer.

The Willis study was the beginning of the comparable worth movement in the United States. Proponents call for equal pay for work of comparable worth to an employer, as opposed to equal pay for equal work. The comparable worth controversy calls for fair pay for people working in female-dominated job classes.[5]

The Equal Pay Act provides for "equal pay for equal work." However, it is legal to discriminate on the basis of just about any other variable (for example, seniority or merit). It is, consequently, very difficult to win a case based on the Equal Pay Act. An employer need only submit a reason for a pay difference that is not related to gender.

Another problem with the Equal Pay Act is it does not account for equal pay for work of comparable value to an employer. People working in female-dominated job classifications tend to be paid much less than people working in male-dominated jobs of comparable worth to an employer (see the box titled "The Comparable Worth Controversy").

Age Discrimination in Employment Act of 1967
Makes it illegal to discriminate on the basis of age for individuals 40 years of age and older.

The Age Discrimination in Employment Act (1967). The **Age Discrimination in Employment Act of 1967,** as amended, makes it illegal to discriminate on the basis of age for individuals 40 years of age and above. This legislation, also overseen by the EEOC and state equal opportunity agencies, was necessary because age was excluded by the 1964 Civil Rights Act.

Like the Equal Pay Act, it is relatively difficult for an individual to win a case based on this legislation. An employer need only come forward with nondiscriminatory reasons other than age for hiring, promotion, or termination decisions. Employers can also discriminate on the basis of age if they prove that age significantly affects work performance.

Supervisors need to be aware that age is not an acceptable reason for a supervisory decision. As a supervisor, you should not give preference or otherwise assign work based on age.

Americans with Disabilities Act of 1990 (ADA)
Extends to all qualified persons with disabilities protection from discrimination in application, hiring, firing, promotion, compensation, training, or any other terms or conditions of employment.

The Rehabilitation Act (1973) and Americans with Disabilities Act (1990). Two acts deal with accommodating disabled people in the workplace. The Rehabilitation Act of 1973 requires that federal agencies and organizations with federal contracts include disabled persons in affirmative action plans and make reasonable efforts to accommodate disabled persons (more on affirmative action later in the chapter).

The **Americans with Disabilities Act of 1990 (ADA)** extends protection to all qualified persons with disabilities from discrimination in application, hiring, firing, promotion, compensation, training, or any other term or condition of employment. The ADA extends the requirements of the Rehabilitation Act of 1973 to the private sector. The act covers all employers with 25 or more employees, and will include all employers with 15 or more employees after 1994.

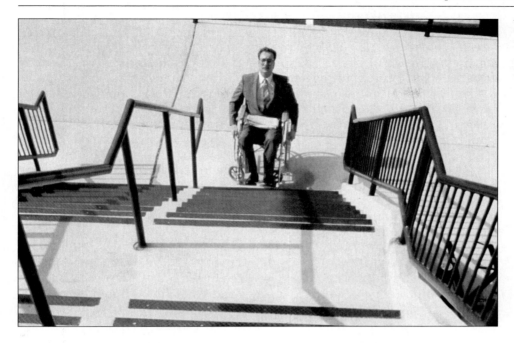

This fellow has not been "reasonably accommodated" by his employer.

Definitions of "disabled status" and "reasonable accommodation" are key components of the ADA. The act defines disability rather loosely. A disabled person is one who:

- Has a physical or mental impairment that substantially limits one or more major life activities.
- Has a record of such an impairment; or
- Is regarded as having such an impairment.

The ADA, like the Rehabilitation Act of 1973, requires that employers make reasonable accommodations for employees covered under the act. These accommodations need not be costly. For example, Greiner Engineering in Irving, Texas, installed lighter-weight doors in a restroom and added height to a drafting table by putting bricks under the table's legs to accommodate an employee who used a wheelchair.[6] Supervisors may find themselves helping their organization find ways to make reasonable accommodations for those with disabilities.

Some people who are covered by the ADA do not have obvious disabilities. For example, people who have a history of alcoholism or drug abuse are considered disabled under the ADA as long as they are no longer using alcohol or drugs. These individuals are considered to have a record of mental impairment. People with AIDS are also covered by the ADA.

Adverse Impact and Adverse Treatment

Equal opportunity legislation forbids illegal discrimination, but it is up to the courts and administrative agencies such as the EEOC to define what is meant by illegal discrimination. Two classifications define illegal discrimination: *adverse impact* and *adverse treatment*.

Adverse Impact

adverse impact
Occurs when an employment practice related to hiring, promoting, training, compensating, or terminating employees has a negative impact on an entire class of employees covered by equal opportunity legislation.

Adverse impact occurs when an employment practice related to hiring, promoting, training, compensating, or terminating employees has a negative impact on an entire class of employees covered by equal opportunity legislation.

Intent to produce this effect does not have to be proven in adverse impact cases, only that the employment practice in question significantly and adversely affected a class of employees. For example, a manufacturer may require that employees speak fluent English. This practice has an adverse impact on those for whom English is a second language, such as Russian immigrants. In this example, Russian immigrants will tend to be underrepresented in the company's work force. If a relatively larger proportion of job-qualified citizens living in the surrounding community are of Russian origin relative to the proportion working for the company, a claim of adverse impact might be made by a Russian immigrant on behalf of the group.

Civil Rights Act of 1991
Clarified the definition of "adverse impact" and its interpretation by the courts, requiring employers to prove the validity of their employment practices.

Two Supreme Court cases, *Griggs v. Duke Power* and *Ward's Cove Packing Co. v. Atonio,* and a new law, the **Civil Rights Act of 1991,** have significantly affected the way adverse impact claims are interpreted by the courts. The Civil Rights Act of 1991 better defined "adverse impact" and codified the requirement that employers prove the validity of their employment practices.

Griggs versus Duke Power.   The *Griggs* case was the first major test of Title VII of the Civil Rights Act of 1964.

A group of black employees at Duke Power, a Louisiana power company, charged the company with employment practices that had adversely impacted the promotion of black workers. For an employee to be promoted, Duke Power required a high school diploma or equivalent and satisfactory scores on the Wonderlic Personnel Test (an intelligence test) and the Bennett Mechanical Aptitude Test. A significantly higher proportion of black employees failed these tests compared to white employees seeking promotion.

This case was eventually decided in a landmark decision by the Supreme Court. The court ruled against Duke Power and, by doing so, established the need for employers to validate employment tests. The *Griggs* case established that the employer, Duke Power, had a responsibility to prove its employment tests were a reasonable measure of job performance. The company, however, was unable to show that a high school diploma and IQ and mechanical aptitude tests related to the promotional opportunities involved, which included jobs such as shoveling coal.

The *Griggs* decision had a widespread effect. It required employers to look at the effect of all personnel practices, even those that seemed relatively benign, and to justify personnel practices showing an adverse impact.

A Challenge to Griggs.   The *Griggs* precedent was overturned in 1989 by another federal Supreme Court decision: *Ward's Cove Packing Co. v. Atonio.*[7] This case involved a claim by Filipino and Native Alaskan fishery workers that Ward's Cove's personnel practices were inherently biased in favor of white employees. Filipino and Native Alaskan workers were limited to unskilled jobs packing fish while a disproportionate number of white workers had higher-paying, skilled, noncannery jobs.

The Supreme Court's ruling in the *Ward's Cove* case meant the burden of proof to show adverse impact would now, under certain circumstances, be the responsibility of the employee, rather than the responsibility of the employer.

Congress then passed new statutes—the Civil Rights Act of 1991—that returned burden-of-proof issues to standards imposed by the *Griggs* decision. It is again up to employers to justify the validity of personnel practices (validity will be covered later in this chapter). Judicial interpretation of the Civil Rights Act of 1991 will further clarify the meaning of the act's language.

The effective supervisor needs to be aware of adverse impact issues. He or she needs to be aware that simply treating all employees the same is insufficient, if equal treatment results in a protected group being underrepresented because practices are inherently biased. Keep in mind that intent to discriminate need not be present for illegal discrimination to occur.

Adverse Treatment

Adverse treatment cases involve intentional discrimination. An adverse treatment charge is a claim by an individual that an employer has committed illegal discrimination. Whereas adverse impact involves discrimination by an employer against an entire class (for example, all blacks or all women), adverse treatment involves only the individual or individuals included in the claim. Adverse treatment cases involve a claim of overt, intentional discrimination.

McDonnell-Douglas v. Green was the first Supreme Court case to establish adverse treatment standards based on the Civil Rights Act of 1964.[8] This 1973 case involved a black employee named Green who was terminated by McDonnell-Douglas in a reduction-in-force.

Green, angered by his termination, participated in an illegal demonstration against the company. (The demonstration blocked traffic by stalling cars at plant entrances.) Later, he saw a newspaper advertisement placed by McDonnell-Douglas advertising positions in his specialty. He applied and was rejected by the company because of his role in the illegal demonstration. Green sued the company under the Civil Rights Act of 1964, claiming his rejection was based on race, and lost.

The burden of proof is much easier for employers to meet in adverse treatment cases. The Green case established that employers can defeat a claim of adverse treatment simply by giving a plausible nondiscriminatory reason for a personnel decision. The reason or reasons need not be objective or statistically validated as in adverse impact cases.

Supervisors need to be mindful of the potential for adverse treatment. Racism, sexism, or other bigotry cannot be tolerated either by supervisors or by those they supervise. It is conceivable that a supervisor could inadvertently contribute to an employee's feeling that he or she has been adversely treated. This situation is less likely when supervisors maintain a high degree of sensitivity to the differences among and needs of all employees. As a matter of practice, supervisors should get to know workers, including learning about their cultures, and establish an environment where all parties feel comfortable with communicating about cultural differences or perceptions.

Validating Supervisory Practices

A key to understanding legal supervisory conduct lies in understanding the term **validity** as it applies to interactions with employees. Valid supervisory practices tend to be legal. Invalid practices tend to be illegal.

adverse treatment
Involves intentional discrimination where a claim is made by an individual that an employer has committed illegal and intentional discrimination.

validity
Is the accuracy of a measurement or test whereby tests measure what they are supposed to and the results are true.

Validity applies to the truth or accuracy of a measure. A test is said to be valid to the extent test items measure what they are supposed to. For example, a geography test would be an invalid measure of students' knowledge of English grammar. Consistency or **reliability** of results is an important prerequisite to validity. However, consistency alone is an insufficient measure of validity. For example, if you get the same score 50 times on a geography test given to test knowledge of English grammar, the test results would be reliable, but they would still be invalid. Valid outcomes must be both consistent (reliable) and accurate. A test used to make employment decisions is valid only if it accurately measures workers' ability to do a particular job.

Once you understand the concept of validity, it is possible to see applications throughout a supervisor's job. It is valid, and therefore legal, to critique an employee's output; but a criticism of "loyalty" or "attitude" may be misinterpreted as a criticism based on gender or race, and may be invalid. It is valid to select or to promote employees based on objective qualifications such as education, years of experience, or job performance, but it is invalid, and illegal, to make these decisions based on race, gender, or age. It is valid to require a medical exam as a condition of employment if it can be documented that the job requires a particular level of physical effort. Consider, for example, the importance and validity of periodically checking the health of pilots responsible for airliners moving 550 miles per hour at 30,000 feet!

Validation of supervisory practices requires objective documentation that shows that hiring, promotion, and termination decisions are valid. This documentation should show that supervisory practices consistently and accurately relate to characteristics of the job and focus on job performance, rather than on personal characteristics of employees.

The following discussion provides general understanding of ways to validate supervisory practices. Keep in mind that assessing the validity of supervisory practices can be complex, involving statistical tests and input from industrial organizational psychologists. Information beyond that covered in this chapter is available in the **Uniform Guidelines on Employee Selection Procedures.** These 1978 federal guidelines describe equal opportunity compliance requirements and include a discussion of validation procedures.

Approaches to Validation. The validation process that is the most difficult to follow because it requires the most empirical support is called **criterion-related validity.** This approach involves predicting employee success (the criterion) on the basis of a performance measure (the predictor). For example, a supervisor may believe workers with a high school diploma are significantly more productive than those without a diploma. The predictor in this example is the high school diploma; the criterion is productivity. If the supervisor, or his or her employer, can statistically establish that a predictor is valid—that those with high school diplomas truly do outperform those without a diploma—then it would be valid and legal to require a high school diploma for a job, or for promotion into a job.

A less rigorous validation approach is called **content validity.** This approach requires that the content of a test and the content of a job logically match. It would be invalid, for example, to require candidates for a bookkeeper's job to be timed in the 40-yard dash. A 40-yard dash is valid, however, if you are a sports franchise interested in hiring a football player. Conversely, a test of mathemati-

"Right" and "Wrong" Questions

You may have heard there are questions that are illegal to ask during an interview or performance review. By now, you should understand such questions are also invalid.

It is usually illegal (and invalid) to ask a job candidate if he or she is married or divorced, or to ask how many children a person has. Why? Because marital status and number of children do not predict success on a job; do not relate to the content of a job; and have no proven relationship to a construct important for success on a job.

What if a person named Terry Jones applies for a job, or is a current employee interested in transfer to your department? Can you ask Terry's gender? The answer to this question is "yes" only if you can establish that a valid relationship exists between gender and the nature of the job—for example, if you were hiring or transferring in a locker room attendant. Under these circumstances, you will have established gender as a bona fide occupational qualification (BFOQ) (see chapter discussion). Otherwise, gender does not predict success on the job; does not relate to the content of the job; and cannot be empirically connected with a construct important to success on the job.

What should you do if you are asked an inappropriate, invalid question during a selection interview, or a supervisor bases a performance review on factors not related to the content of your job? One approach is to tactfully ask the interviewer or boss why the question was asked. See if she or he can tie the question or evaluation criteria to the job.

Invalid interview questions and evaluation criteria are commonplace, particularly in smaller organizations. It is difficult to effectively enforce standards of validity and legal supervisory and personnel practices.

cal ability would be invalid for selecting a football player, but valid for a prospective bookkeeper.

Examples of content validity are present throughout a supervisor's job. It is logical, and valid, to match performance appraisal review questions pertaining to worker behavior and output to the behavior and output requirements of a job. It is logical, and valid, to provide pay bonuses to workers who have met predetermined production requirements.

Construct validity is similar to content validity, but is more abstract. A construct, in psychological terms, is a label applied to an unobservable characteristic. Intelligence, loyalty, team spirit, and mechanical aptitude are examples of constructs. Construct validity exists to the extent a test or assessment accurately measures a construct. For example, if mechanical aptitude is deemed important for a job and if a test can be found that accurately measures such aptitude, then we can say the relationship among the job, the construct, and the test is valid.

construct validity
Exists to the extent a test or assessment accurately captures dimensions of an unobservable characteristic.

One way supervisors can improve construct validity is to use multiple measures of the same construct. In selection or promotion decisions it may be appropriate to ask questions that cover various dimensions of a job and then take the candidate "out on the job" for further assessment of the same dimensions. Interview questions and field assessment of the candidate should yield similar results. For example, an employee who expresses strong commitment to a job during an interview should show a high level of commitment in the field assessment.

If different measures of the same construct diverge, then supervisors should check the validity of the tests. The tests may measure different things, or there may be a problem with the administration of the tests. A factor as simple as low reading ability might cause a job candidate or employee to perform differently on a paper-and-pencil test than in a field assessment.

For the practicing supervisor, an implication of construct validity is that it is important to look at the same construct from several perspectives. For example,

An age restriction for the job of bartender is an example of a bona fide occupational qualification.

consider the construct "worker dissatisfaction." A work group may offer one set of complaints explaining dissatisfaction in a public setting, and an entirely different set in one-on-one meetings with a supervisor.

The Bona Fide Occupational Qualification

bona fide occupational qualification (BFOQ)
Legal discrimination arising from predictors of job success based upon characteristics normally protected by law such as gender, race, religion, age, national origin, or disabled status.

A **bona fide occupational qualification (BFOQ)** exists when an employer legally discriminates on the basis of characteristics normally protected by law, under circumstances in which it is valid to consider predictors such as gender, race, religion, age, national origin, or disabled status. A bona fide occupational qualification is allowed only if discrimination can be justified by the employer. For example, it is legal (and valid) to discriminate on the basis of religion when hiring people to work in a Christian mission; on the basis of age when hiring bartenders; and on the basis of gender when hiring an attendant for a men's restroom. It is valid to disqualify those with poor eyesight from jobs as bus drivers.

Remember, in an adverse impact case, the employer has the burden of defending a personnel practice that adversely affects an entire group. One way to do this is to show the personnel test in question is valid, that it is tied to business necessity. Another way is to establish a BFOQ by demonstrating through validation that a characteristic such as sex, race, or religion is necessary to do the job.

Affirmative Action

[handwritten: Create more jobs for minorities]

A highly controversial area of equal employment opportunity is affirmative action. **Affirmative action** involves systematic employer efforts to provide work-related opportunities to underrepresented groups.

Organizations put together affirmative action plans for many reasons. If the organization does work for the federal government—if it has federal contracts—it is required to maintain an **affirmative action plan,** a document describing the composition of a work force and outlining plans to increase underrepresented groups. This requirement comes from Executive Order 11246, signed by President Lyndon Johnson in 1965. An executive order is an administrative order from the president to federal agencies and to those who have dealings with federal agencies.

[handwritten: for a gov.]

A court may require an organization to have an affirmative action plan to address past discrimination. Organizations may also have voluntary plans because they feel a moral obligation to improve inequity, or because they feel affirmative action is good management.

The Office of Federal Contract Compliance (not the Equal Employment Opportunity Commission) checks federal contractors' compliance with affirmative action. This agency has the power to take government contracts away from organizations making unsatisfactory progress in offering affirmative action.

Affirmative Action Cases

The courts have had a tough time with affirmative action. Supreme Court decisions of the past 20 years suggest general principles, but have not provided definitive remedies to specific affirmative action problems. For example, as ironic as it might sound, a significant problem with affirmative action is the potential for discrimination based on Title VII of the Civil Rights Act of 1964. This situation is referred to as **reverse discrimination,** a situation where a dominant group, such as white males, is excluded from employment or training opportunities because of affirmative action.

Title VII of the Civil Rights Act of 1964 does not refer to specific race or color. The law is "color-blind." Consequently, employers must walk a tight line between using affirmative action to remedy past wrongs and avoiding adverse impact or adverse treatment affecting a dominant group in a particular workplace.

The most famous affirmative action court case is *University of California v. Bakke.*[9] Bakke's application to the University of California at Davis Medical School was rejected. The school had 100 seats available, 16 of which were available only to minority persons. Bakke was rejected despite having objective credentials—grade point average and test scores—higher than some of the minority students admitted under the special program. Bakke sued under the equal protection provisions of the Constitution. His case was eventually heard by the Supreme Court. The court rendered a split decision. The justices ruled that Bakke must be admitted to the Davis Medical School, but also agreed that race could be a factor in an affirmative action program provided it was not applied in a rigid quota-like way.

Weber v. Kaiser Aluminum & Chemical Corporation, a case heard by the Supreme Court the year after *Bakke,* continued to uphold the legality of

affirmative action
Is a systematic attempt by employers to provide work-related opportunities to underrepresented groups.

affirmative action plans
Documents describing the composition of a work force and outlining plans to increase underrepresented groups.

reverse discrimination
Occurs when a dominant group is excluded from emloyment or training opportunities because of affirmative action.

affirmative action.[10] Based on his seniority, Weber would have qualified for a company apprenticeship program leading to a higher-paying job. However, an affirmative action program negotiated between the union and the company required half the spots in the apprenticeship program to go to minorities until an equitable racial balance was achieved. Weber, a white male, would likely not get into the program before retirement. He sued under Title VII.

The Supreme Court ruled against Weber. The court felt it was in the spirit of affirmative action that temporary quotas be allowed. The court felt such practices should not last indefinitely, but should be allowed for as long as necessary to correct past illegal discrimination.

Later Supreme Court rulings during the 1980s supported the legality of hiring individuals from underrepresented groups rather than a dominant group such as white males, if the individuals were qualified for the job in question, and if the action was necessary to bring balance and equity into a work force.

Supervisors need to understand that affirmative action does not mean they are compelled to hire unqualified persons, or that they must tolerate poor work habits. Affirmative action in employment is primarily intended to reverse past discrimination, and should be viewed as a temporary measure. Affirmative action should never extend to employee performance issues, unless performance has been affected by a condition covered by Title VII for which the employer can make a reasonable accommodation. Also, unless part of a court-ordered program, affirmative action is not required if a much better qualified member of the dominant group is available for a job, training program, or promotion.

Some Concluding Thoughts on Legal Issues

Supervisors need to have an understanding of the information covered in this chapter. This understanding will help to assure legal compliance. Keep in mind, though, it is relatively easy for an employee to allege illegal discrimination or to pursue a grievance through a contracted grievance procedure. Supervisors should be prepared for legal challenges revolving around a wide variety of issues that affect day-to-day interactions with employees. As pointed out earlier, we live in litigious times.

Effective supervisors should make sure they understand organizational policies and procedures. They should know to whom they should go with legal questions and concerns. This knowledge, together with ethical, considerate treatment of employees and the information covered in this chapter, will go a long way toward reducing legal entanglements.

Carla thought long and hard about filing a sexual harassment complaint against Alan. She finally decided to talk it over with a company human resources officer, Joyce Carlin. Joyce began, "I understand you've been having some trouble with a fellow worker. What's been happening?"

Carla recounted the story of her constant, annoying run-ins with Alan.

"So," Joyce continued, "you made it clear to Alan that his attention was definitely unwelcome?"

"Yes."

"And, still, his requests for dates continued?"

"Yes."

"Did he ever touch you or threaten in any way?"

"No . . . and that is part of the problem. I realize it is not really sexual harassment unless he 'goes too far.' It has just been this annoying, bothersome irritation that is getting to me. It is affecting my attitude about coming to work and I am having difficulty settling down once I am here. I keep expecting to be interrupted by that leer of his!"

"Carla, Alan's actions are harassment. He does not have to touch you or make obvious comments of a sexual nature. The fact that his attention is unwelcome, that you have made it clear it is unwelcome, and that it is affecting your work is enough for me. We will talk to Alan as soon as possible, and I will get back to you."

Imagine Carla's surprise the next morning when she learned about Alan's termination the previous afternoon. He was even barred from the company's premises! Alan had already received both verbal and written warnings concerning his harassing behavior. Carla's complaint had come on the heels of two other complaints from women about Alan over the past year.

Alan's consequent termination sent a needed message throughout the organization: The company will not tolerate sexual harassment. Sexual harassment is not funny.

Summary: Focus on Concepts

Our system of government has three branches: the legislative, judicial, and executive branches. The legislative branch writes the laws (statutory law); the judicial branch interprets these statutes; and the executive branch enforces the law. The judicial branch's interpretation of written laws constitutes case law. The judicial branch is often asked to interpret statutes relating to crimes and torts.

Equal employment opportunity statutes are written at the federal, state, and municipal levels. Federal EEO laws usually require that local and state agencies be approached first in a discrimination dispute. Federal statutes make it illegal to discriminate in employment on the basis of age, race, color, religion, national origin, sex, disability, pregnancy, and veteran status. State laws sometimes add other variables to this list such as sexual preference, arrest records, and marital status.

The most significant equal employment act passed to date is the Civil Rights Act of 1964. Title VII of this act makes it illegal for an employer with 15 or more employees to discriminate in employment on the basis of race, color, religion, sex, or national origin. This act authorized the formation of the Equal Employment Opportunity Commission (EEOC), a federal agency charged with monitoring and correcting illegal discrimination in the workplace.

Besides the characteristics listed in the Civil Rights Act of 1964, the EEOC also has the responsibility for investigating complaints of discrimination based on age and disability. The EEOC also oversees complaints of sexual harassment, which involves unwelcome sexual advances, requests for sexual favors, and other verbal or physical conduct of a sexual nature.

Other federal legislation includes the Equal Pay Act of 1963 and the Age Discrimination in Employment Act of 1967. The Equal Pay Act mandates equal pay for equal work regardless of gender; the Age Discrimination Act makes it illegal to discriminate on the basis of age for individuals over 40 years of age.

The Americans with Disabilities Act of 1990 added to the Rehabilitation Act of 1973. Taken together, these acts require that all employers reasonably accommodate the needs of disabled persons, and if an employer is a federal contractor, that people with disabilities be included in affirmative action planning.

Determining whether illegal discrimination has occurred involves understanding adverse impact and adverse treatment. Adverse impact occurs when an employer inadvertently discriminates against an entire protected group. Adverse treatment occurs when an employer discriminates against an individual or individuals because of race, color, age, or another protected characteristic.

The Civil Rights Act of 1991 indicates that employers have the burden of justifying employment practices that have an adverse impact. The federal Uniform Guidelines on Employee Selection Procedures outline validation procedures to be used to validate employment practices. These procedures involve determining whether employment procedures or tests predict success on the job (criterion-related validity), pertain to the job itself (content validity), or measure a construct that is important to the job (construct validity).

Employers can legally discriminate on the basis of characteristics normally protected by law if they can establish that discrimination is justifiable based on the nature of the job. This legal discrimination is referred to as a *bona fide occupational qualification.*

Affirmative action is defined as systematic employer efforts to provide work-related opportunities to underrepresented groups. The Office of Federal Contract Compliance monitors adherence to affirmative action requirements for federal contractors, and has the authority to withdraw federal money from noncomplying organizations. While the courts have not provided clear direction, landmark Supreme Court cases have generally supported the legality of affirmative action as a way to redress past discrimination.

Review Questions

1. Where does the law come from? Distinguish between crimes and torts; statutory law and case law.
2. What are the alternative forms of dispute resolution available to those involved in civil disputes?
3. Explain the content of Title VII of the Civil Rights Act of 1964.
4. What is sexual harassment, and what are its two dimensions? Give three examples of each.
5. Cite other Equal Employment Opportunity laws affecting supervisors. For each, show how supervisors can positively respond to the legislation, achieving not only the legal requirements but also the social intent.
6. What is adverse treatment? Give three examples of such treatment.
7. Define the concepts of validity and validation. Then, explain the meaning of criterion-related, content, and construct validity. Which is most appropriate for supervisors in carrying out their jobs?
8. What is a bona fide occupational qualification (BFOQ)? Give five examples of a BFOQ.
9. What is an affirmative action plan?

Notes

1. *Griggs v Duke Power,* 401 US 424 (1971).
2. "Guilty," *Business Week,* April 13, 1992, 61–66.
3. "Few Countries' Laws Define Sexual Harassment," *The Herald* (Everett), December 1, 1992, C6.
4. Ibid.
5. C. T. Lewis, "Assessing the Validity of Job Evaluation," *Public Personnel Management* 19 (1989): 45–63.
6. "Business Has to Find a New Meaning for 'Fairness,'" *Business Week,* April 12, 1993, 72.
7. *Ward's Cove Packing Co. v Atonio,* 109 S. Ct. 2115 (1989).

8. *McDonnell-Douglas v Green,* 411 US 792 (1973).
9. *Regents of University of California v Allan Bakke,* 438 US 265 (1978).
10. *Weber v Kaiser Aluminum & Chemical Corporation,* 443 US 193 (1979).

Case 3-1

"Cooperation" and Permanent Employment

Naomi Bradbeer was completing her sixth month of employment with Mariposa Aircraft Corporation, located in Rosemont, a community near Sacramento, California. Mariposa employed over 5,000 nonunion persons and was a subcontractor for larger aircraft manufacturers. It specialized in producing landing gear and hydraulic systems for commercial and military aircraft. Naomi worked in the "tool cage," where she and other employees issued tools to workers at the beginning of their shifts and checked the tools in at the end of their shifts. She was facing a dilemma and did not know what course of action to take. In two days, her probationary period would end. She would either be retained as a permanent employee at Mariposa or would be terminated.

Naomi placed great importance on her job and the income it provided as she was the sole source of financial support for her family, consisting of her two young children and her widowed mother. Furthermore, jobs were scarce. Where else, she thought, could she earn as much as she did from Mariposa, especially when her formal education was limited?

The job of issuing tools was more complicated than she had initially anticipated. Over 10,000 different types of tools were inventoried, although only a third of that number were frequently used. Consequently, when workers requested tools, they often asked for them by either slang terminology or a technical nomenclature she was slowly mastering. Speed in locating tools and issuing them was critically important as the workers were highly skilled— and highly paid. Time waiting for tools was wasted time with lost production.

During her employment at Mariposa, Naomi's progress was adequate. While she had yet to attain the performance standards for the job, she was making progress. Occasionally, though, she fell behind in her work. At other times, she issued incorrect tools, requiring workers to return to the tool cage for replacements. Naomi viewed her job as a challenge. She enjoyed her work. She wished she had more time to become acquainted with coworkers but her responsibilities at home precluded socializing after working hours. As a result, she had acquired few friends although many acquaintances during the past six months.

The problem was caused by Naomi's supervisor, Russell Morgan. Russell was in charge of the eight day-shift tool cage workers. He was well-liked by his subordinates, treated them with respect, and seemed fair in handling problems. He was also very competent. Russell seemed a devoted family man, married twelve years, and had four children. His work was invariably rated as excellent by his bosses during his annual performance appraisals. In the past four years, several of his employees— both men and women—had been promoted and his employee turnover record was lower than the average for the company. Still, Naomi felt that Russell was pressuring her and considered some of his behavior as sexual harassment. She couldn't prove it, though.

Periodically, Russell made suggestive remarks to Naomi, always away from other employees, that securing a permanent job at Mariposa required "teamwork" and, his favorite expression, "cooperation." Russell understood the importance of Naomi's job to her. He implied that her future with the company was based upon her "cooperation." When queried about what he meant by "cooperation," he invariably responded, "You know what I mean." On other occasions, he placed an arm around her shoulder when explaining some procedure or answering a question. None of her coworkers had observed any of Russell's advances toward Naomi. In fact, his conduct toward her was letter-perfect when other employees were present.

This morning, Russell delivered what she considered the ultimatum. "Naomi, the day after tomorrow I have to turn in my evaluation of your work at Mariposa. Your probationary period will end then. I really don't know what my recommendation will be. I am wondering if you and I might discuss it over a drink tomorrow evening after work."

Questions

1. If you were Naomi, how would you handle this situation?

2. What courses of action, if any, are available to Naomi?

3. How can organizations protect their workers from sexual or other harassment by either supervisors or other employees?

A Woman in the House

"Herbie, Tom's transfer is official. You'll need to start the ball rolling on hiring a replacement," Stu advised. "The sooner you can find someone, the better."

"O.K., boss, I'll let personnel know right away," Herbie Victor replied.

As supervisor of the production planning group, Herbie was responsible for selecting Tom's successor. The three planning positions were traditionally held by men, but Herbie found himself interviewing several women for the position. As the latest female candidate left his office, Ron Bridges, one of the planners, stuck his head in the door. "You've interviewed a bunch of women, Herbie. You really wouldn't do that to us, would you?"

"Do what, Ron?"

"Hire a woman planner. A woman just couldn't do the job."

"Why Ron, I never thought you were a male chauvinist," Herbie kidded. Both men laughed.

A few days later, Herbie did decide to hire a woman—Shirley Edwards, a recent college graduate with a degree in math. When Herbie took her around to meet the others in the department, Ron mumbled, "hello." He said he'd like to talk to Shirley but had a deadline to meet. "I'll drop by later," he added, "after I turn in this job." However, the afternoon found ron working intently on his next project.

Shirley quickly caught on to the work, but Ron's attitude toward her continued to be icy. This bothered Herbie, but he felt that the problem would eventually disappear. Ron would just have to get used to working with a woman.

When Shirley had been in the position about six weeks, Herbie stopped by her desk to see how she felt about the job. "Oh, I'm very pleased," she replied. "This is the kind of work I've always wanted to do."

"Well, good. I've been pleased with your progress. If you keep on, you'll be a real asset to the planning group." As Herbie walked back to his office, he noticed Ron scowling. Ron obviously had overheard his conversation with Shirley.

Thereafter, the situation grew more and more unpleasant. Herbie frequently heard Ron and Shirley arguing. Once he heard the other planner tell Ron to give Shirley a break. "She's really a good worker, Ron," he said. "I don't see why you can't be nice to her." Finally, Stu summoned Herbie to his office to discuss the civil war that was raging in Herbie's department.

Stu told Herbie that the planners' feud had to stop. Because of it, the production planning group had missed two deadlines in the past two weeks. "Shirley seems capable enough, but I'm not sure that having her on staff is worth all this aggravation," Stu concluded.

Herbie didn't know what to do next. He wanted to keep Shirley, not only because she was a good worker, but also because she would have excellent grounds to level a discrimination charge if he fired her. But he just couldn't think of a way to make peace between her and Ron.

Questions

1. What is the employer's legal obligation?

Source: Reprinted, by permission of publisher, from *Supervisory Management,* June 1985 © 1985. American Management Association, New York. All rights reserved.

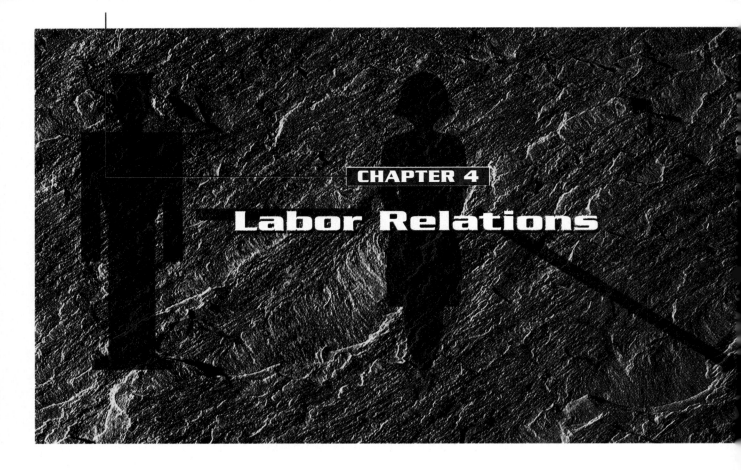

CHAPTER 4
Labor Relations

● My wife and I went to Hawaii for a vacation. When we returned in two weeks, I had a new union at my business.

Owner of a small firm employing 36 persons

LEARNING OBJECTIVES

1. Comprehend why an organization's employees unionize.
2. Appreciate the history of union development in the United States and understand why unions are formed.
3. Indicate the major labor relations acts passed by Congress since the early 1930s and their major provisions.
4. Outline the process of unionization activities leading to an election for representation.
5. Explain the collective bargaining process and the rights of supervisors in the election process.
6. Describe how the supervisor functions in contract maintenance.

Carla sipped a freshly made cup of hot coffee and looked out the window at the shop floor. She couldn't believe it. But still it had happened. Dave Hensley, the best worker in her group, was quitting.

Carla understood Dave's frustration. He had worked hard after coming to work for the company, earning every merit raise possible for a period of six years. Then, the union decided to bargain for a change in the way merit increases were allocated. Two years previously, union negotiators had decided merit pay was unfair; that any future pay raises should go instead to equalize pay across job classifications. Management agreed.

The consequences were devastating to Dave. He had earned his way to the top of the pay scale, and now found himself shut out of cost-of-living pay raises while those below him received healthy increases. Dave resigned from the union in protest, but found he still had to pay the union a representation fee. He kept his mouth shut, but no longer volunteered for overtime or offered quality improvement suggestions.

Carla thought back to her last discussion with Dave.

"It's not right, Carla. I earned every merit increase possible. Now, I find myself running in place while deadbeats and new employees catch up to me. Our esteemed union negotiators had nothing to lose. With seniority, they'd already been at the top for years."

Dave didn't even say goodbye. He quietly found another job, gave two weeks notice, and one day simply wasn't there. His replacement was delighted by the relatively high starting wage now offered by the company.

An outcome of chronically poor management practices, at all levels including supervisory management, is union organizing activity. Workers who are underpaid and otherwise poorly treated will often vote in a union as a remedy for their problems with management. Once in place, a union then bargains to improve pay and working conditions for all workers in a bargaining unit. Individual workers no longer bargain for themselves. A union local can stay in place for decades. Auto, steel, and manufacturing unions have represented workers in the United States for over the past 50 years.

labor unions
Organizations of wage earners formed for the purpose of serving the collective interests of their members through the bargaining process with employers on such issues as employee compensation and working conditions.

Labor unions are organizations of wage earners formed for the purpose of serving the collective interests of their members through the bargaining process with employers on such issues as employee wages and working conditions. A controversial subject for many people, unions are often viewed with emotional fervor by supporters as well as opponents. Historically, this emotional fervor has resulted in violence and, at times, death.

The subject of unions is most appropriately treated by not making a value judgment about their worth. Our interest in unions is twofold. First, supervisors should understand how their behaviors, when adverse to desires of their employees, can encourage the formation of unions within their organizations. Conversely, enlightened managers can behave in a manner that diminishes the need for unions within their organizations. Second, supervisors should know the appropriate protocol in dealing with unionized employees and their representatives. In both instances, supervisors perform a more important role than is generally recognized.

In this chapter we will briefly examine the history of worker-manager relationships leading to the formation of unions, and several important federal laws that govern those relationships. Next, we'll explore the organizing and collective bargaining processes and review day-to-day contract administration. Finally, we shall attempt to forecast the future of union-management relationships.

Understanding Unions

collective bargaining
The process of negotiation between management and a union to arrive at a contract and the process of administering an existing contract.

A union is a legally recognized organization that bargains with management on behalf of the employees it represents. **Collective bargaining** is a term used to describe contract negotiations between management and a union, as well as the process of administering a contract once it has been negotiated.

Legally, collective bargaining requires management and union representatives to "meet at reasonable times, to confer in good faith about certain matters, and to put into writing any agreement reached if requested by either party. The parties must confer in good faith with respect to wages, hours, and other terms or conditions of employment, the negotiation of an agreement, or any question arising under an agreement."[1]

As noted in Chapter 1, union membership is declining in the United States. Membership has fallen from 34 percent of the work force in 1956 to less than 15 percent today.[2] Though in decline, supervisors should not minimize the importance of unions or collective action on the part of employees.

associations
Less formal collectives of employees that periodically meet and confer with management on a wide range of employment issues and negotiate employment contracts, but possess much less bargaining power than unions.

More than just union members are organized. Many employees, particularly those working in the public sector, are members of **associations** rather than unions. For example, approximately 40 percent of government employees in the United States belong to an association. Associations are much less likely than unions to strike and members often behave in a more collegial way with management. Associations do, however, meet and confer with management on a wide range of employment issues and negotiate employment contracts much as a union does.

Also, certain industries in the United States are highly unionized. Labor relations are very important to a supervisor working in a union environment for a U.S. auto manufacturer, but less important to a supervisor in the relatively unorganized microprocessor industry.

History of the Labor Movement in the United States

Until relatively recently in the history of employer-employee relationships, bargaining power resided almost exclusively with the employer and the employer's designated managers and supervisors. Owners of businesses were buyers of labor. Workers had to accept the terms of employment set forth by those owners to be hired. Individual workers possessed very limited power to negotiate because they could be replaced by persons willing to accept the employer's terms. Consequently, there was no balance of power. About 60 years ago, society recognized labor's disadvantage. A series of federal laws designed to redistribute bargaining power were passed.

Conditions Leading to Unionization

To understand why unions exist, we must review a bit of history. Changing social values growing out of the industrial revolution of the late 1700s underlie the beginnings of unions.[3] The organization of work called for the creation of large factories with a movement away from agriculture and small work groups in household industries. The number of people employed in industrial activities greatly increased. Industrialization in the United States picked up momentum after 1865. The mass production required to produce armaments for the Civil War concentrated workers in northern factories, where working conditions were awful.

A personal relationship between the employer and workers was disappearing. It was replaced, in many instances, with absentee owners who lacked concern about the well-being of employees. The issues of employee safety and compensation for injuries or deaths arising from accidents are exemplified by several conditions workers faced in the 1800s and early 1900s.

The first example is a classic. It illustrates the lack of safety measures existing in many if not most industries of the period. The Triangle Waist Company, a New York City garment manufacturer, occupied the eighth through tenth floors of a loft building. A fire, discovered at 5:00 p.m. on Saturday, March 25, 1911, killed 145 workers, mostly women. Large quantities of flammable materials spread the fire while doors by which workers could have escaped were locked. The supervisor who had the keys could not be located.[4]

Another condition that workers had to contend with was the legal system. Under common law, injured employees had to take their cases to court and win them to receive payments for damages suffered in industrial injuries (these payments are called indemnity). Unless injured workers could prove their injuries resulted from negligence of the employer, they had no recourse for compensation. In turn, employers had three defenses against claimants. First, the

There are no winners
when labor relations are
poorly managed.

contributory negligence rule stated that the employer was not liable if the injured worker's accident resulted from that worker's negligence. Second, the *fellow-servant rule* relieved employers from responsibility for injuries to employees arising from negligent acts of other employees. Finally, the *doctrine of assumption of risk* released the employer from responsibility for injuries when the employer fulfilled several requirements for securing the safety of employees. For all practical purposes, though, the inherent dangers of work in many occupations and industries could not be eliminated. Employees assumed the risk of injury as a hazard of the job or condition of employment.[5]

In addition, workers had little job security or protection from the financial panics periodically sweeping the country. The Great Depression of the 1930s, for example, found 25 percent of the American labor force unemployed. Benefits, when they existed, typically were minimal.

American and European business owners' attitude toward organized labor was hostile. One exception, in Scotland, was Robert Owen, an owner of textile mills. Labeled a Utopian Socialist, Owen was progressive in setting standards regarding child labor and working conditions. In the 18th century in Europe, children as young as 10 years old worked in underground coal mines. Early child labor laws limited their working hours to no more than 70 hours per week. Among their assignments was carrying the canary cages in underground coal mines (Figure 4.1). When the bird stopped chirping and fell off its perch, indicating the presence of poisonous fumes, the child suffered as well.

Although organizing efforts in the United States occurred as early as the late 1700s, little headway was realized until the mid-1930s. Even the Sherman Antitrust Act of 1890, designed to prohibit conspiracies and restraint of trade among businesses, was initially interpreted by courts to prohibit union boycotts and strikes against employers. Such actions were considered as restraining trade.

Figure 4-1 Carrying the Canary

In 1869, a group of tailors formed the Knights of Labor in Philadelphia. Membership in the organization quickly spread from garment workers to other crafts and industries. Though its membership approached 700,000 workers by 1885, the Knights of Labor soon declined and died out. The government did not provide any statutory protection for the Knights. The Knights also suffered because their leadership became more interested in political reforms than in promoting the membership's specific concerns regarding wages and working conditions.

Another labor organization, the American Federation of Labor (AFL), formed in 1886 and managed to survive until federal protective legislation was passed in

1932 and 1935 (this legislation will be covered in the following section). The AFL's leadership, first Samuel Gompers and then William Green in 1924, remained focused on the needs of craft workers in its membership. **Craft workers** are those employed in specific trades, such as shoemaking and plumbing.

craft workers
Employees in specific trades such as shoemaking or plumbing.

Another labor organization, the Congress of Industrial Organizations (CIO), was created by 1938 primarily because millions of factory workers, such as those employed in auto manufacturing plants, did not fit into the AFL's craft worker framework. These workers are referred to as **industrial workers** because they are employed within a general industry, such as steel manufacturing, rather than within a specific craft or job. Both the AFL and CIO grew significantly.

industrial workers
Persons employed in a general industry such as steel manufacturing or automobile production.

In 1955, at the peak of union power in the United States, the two organizations merged to form the AFL-CIO. The future looked bright for organized labor, although internal problems plagued the AFL-CIO. The largest single union in the United States, the Teamsters, was even expelled by AFL-CIO leadership in 1957 because of the union's alleged connection to organized crime.

The gradual decline of the labor movement in the United States during the 1960s and 1970s was hastened during the conservative presidential administrations of the 1980s. Economic competition from abroad also weakened the ability of U.S. unions to win large wage increases from employers. In fact, previous gains won by labor were often lost in "rollbacks" of wages and benefits. In spite of this decline, union leadership is trying hard to win new members. Gains in membership in service industries and education are offsetting some of the losses in the "smokestack" industries.

Supervisors can learn an important lesson from the history of the labor movement. It is important to treat employees with dignity and respect. It is important to develop and to support work rules that protect and nourish the career aspirations and interests of workers. To do otherwise invites counterproductive discord. If a union is in place, supervisors and other managers must learn to work well with union representatives. In the absence of a union, responsive supervisors and other managers are less likely to have a union voted in. (More on union elections later in the chapter.)

Management-Labor Legislation

The union movement in the United States would have failed without dedicated effort on the part of union leaders and organizers and assistance from the federal government.

The Norris-LaGuardia Act

Norris-LaGuardia Act of 1932
Permitted the formation of unions as legal entities and prohibited employers from requiring yellow dog contracts.

Prior to passage of the **Norris-LaGuardia Act of 1932,** the courts could rule unions to be illegal monopolies, and employers could use yellow dog contracts to keep out union employees. A **yellow dog contract** is a contract that requires an employee to agree, as a condition of employment, not to join a union or engage in union organizing activity. The Norris-LaGuardia Act outlawed yellow dog contracts and guaranteed employee rights to bargain collectively.

yellow dog contract
Requires an employee to agree as a condition of employment not to join a union or engage in union organizing activity.

The Norris-LaGuardia Act has relatively little impact on supervisors. Nevertheless, unions are legal entities. Supervisors should not discriminate among employees or job applicants on the basis of union membership or support.

The Wagner Act

Three years after passage of the Norris-LaGuardia Act, Congress passed the **Wagner Act of 1935,** also called the National Labor Relations Act of 1935. This act more clearly defined the process for creating a union local. It required that employers bargain with a union in good faith and forbade certain employer practices, such as discriminating against union organizers, that made union formation unduly difficult.

The Wagner Act also formed the **National Labor Relations Board (NLRB),** a government agency charged with policing unfair labor practices and overseeing union elections. The National Labor Relations Board has wide authority, though public employees are usually covered by state boards rather than the NLRB.

The Wagner Act made supervisors and their employers liable for unfair labor practices against union members. It is important that supervisors base discipline on employee performance, not on an employee's standing as a union member. Supervisors should not interfere with legally conducted union organizing activities.

The Taft-Hartley Act

The **Taft-Hartley Act of 1947,** also called the Labor-Management Relations Act, was passed to reduce union excesses. The Taft-Hartley Act more clearly defined employer and employee rights and limited union activities in several significant ways.

Union membership increased significantly after passage of the Wagner Act. With this growth, and in the absence of regulatory control, came abuses on the part of organized labor. The pendulum had swung too far in favor of organized labor. Public pressure mounted to apply a legislative solution to these abuses.

The Taft-Hartley Act limited unions in several important ways. Unions could be charged with unfair labor practices under this act; management could now file charges with the NLRB or local agencies with oversight authority. The rights of employees as union members and those of employers were more clearly specified. Unions could no longer threaten employee jobs, refuse to bargain in good faith with employers, or set excessive union dues. The Taft-Hartley Act also outlawed the "closed shop" and permitted states to pass right-to-work laws (the subjects of closed shops and right-to-work states will be discussed shortly). Passage of the Taft-Hartley Act affirmed that collective bargaining is a give-and-take process involving union members and management.

Passage of the Taft-Hartley Act means supervisors may be called on to assert management rights such as documenting union unfair labor practices that might involve a union representative interfering with a supervisor's responsibilities or undermining a supervisor's authority (for example, calling for an illegal work slowdown or an illegal strike affecting a supervisor's area).

Union Security and Right-to-Work States. The Taft-Hartley Act also deals with the extent of control a union has over its membership. It is possible for an employee to be a member of a **bargaining unit**—the specific group of employees a union must represent—and not be a member of the union. Unions are legally obligated to represent all employees in a bargaining unit (for example, all company electricians or all school district teachers). Under these circumstances, a nonmember could enjoy the benefits of collective bargaining without having to pay the union.

Wagner Act of 1935
Also called the National Labor Relations Act of 1935, it required employers to bargain with unions in good faith and prohibited certain employer practices such as discriminating against union organizers.

National Labor Relations Board (NLRB)
Created by the Wagner Act of 1935, it is a federal government agency that polices unfair labor practices and oversees union elections.

Taft-Hartley Act of 1947
Also called the Labor-Management Relations Act of 1947, it reduced union excesses by defining employer and employee rights, outlawed closed shops, and permitted states to enact right-to-work laws.

bargaining unit
Composed of the specific group of employees a union must represent. Members of a bargaining unit are entitled to representation by the union even if they are not union members.

union security
The amount of control a union exerts over its membership including the right to represent employees and collect dues from members of a bargaining unit.

closed shop
A form of union security that requires that employers hire only union members.

union shop
New employees must join the union within a specified period of time after being hired and must pay dues to the union local.

agency shop
A union security arrangement in which all bargaining unit members must pay dues but do not have to join the union.

open shop
A union security arrangement in which employees are free to determine whether they join the union and do not have to pay union dues if they decide not to join but are still represented by the union.

right-to-work laws
Authorized by the Taft-Hartley Act, state laws permitting prohibition of union and agency shops.

Union leadership would like every member of a bargaining unit to be a dues-paying member of the union. Union leadership wants a high degree of union security. **Union security** is concerned with the right of a union to represent employees and includes the amount of control a union has over dues payments by members of a bargaining unit. There are four general categories of union security: closed shop, union shop, agency shop, and open shop.

A **closed shop** is a type of union security that requires that employers only hire union members. This arrangement represents the highest degree of union security. People must be union members to even apply for a job. The Taft-Hartley Act prohibits closed shops.

A **union shop** is a situation in which a new employee must join the union within a specified period (usually 30 days) after being hired. In a union shop, all members of the bargaining unit are dues-paying members of the union local.

An **agency shop** is a union security arrangement in which all bargaining unit members must pay either union dues or a representation fee. Employees don't have to join the union. This arrangement provides compensation to the union for representing the employees and addresses the problem of nonmembers getting a "free ride." However, recent Supreme Court decisions have required unions to reimburse the portion of payments made by nonmembers that doesn't relate directly to bargaining with management and contract administration. These rulings have reduced union income and flexibility and have significantly increased union bookkeeping and accountability requirements.

An **open shop** is a union security arrangement in which employees can choose whether to be members of the union local. Employees do not have to pay dues or representation fees. However, all employees are still covered by any contract provisions negotiated by the union, and the union must continue to represent nonmembers. An open shop represents the weakest form of union security.

The Taft-Hartley Act makes it possible for states to pass **right-to-work laws.** These state laws make union and agency shops illegal. Unions have little security in states with right-to-work laws (see Figure 4-2). Employees do not have to join unions or pay representation fees in right-to-work states. Many companies choose to locate factories in states with right-to-work laws because by doing so they avoid dealing with a strong union.

People join unions for many reasons, including ineffective management as well as employee needs to have a voice in decisions that affect them. Individual supervisors have little control over higher management decisions that lead employees to unionize and should actively work with union members. As the box titled "Unions and Management Working Together" illustrates, unions and management can cooperate effectively.

The Landrum-Griffin Act

Landrum-Griffin Act of 1959
Called the Labor-Management Reporting and Disclosure Act of 1959, it improved union internal affairs and governance by restricting illegal activities by union leaders and increased union member rights such as voting and dues paying.

The **Landrum-Griffin Act of 1959** (also called the Labor-Management Reporting and Disclosure Act) amended the Taft-Hartley Act. Congress passed this law to improve union internal affairs and governance and to restrict illegal activities by union leaders that included blackmail, arson, election-rigging, and taking payoffs. The Landrum-Griffin Act stipulates that union members have the right to vote in union elections and to vote on proposals to increase union dues and are entitled to a hearing before a union can impose any disciplinary action.

The Landrum-Griffin Act represents a continuation of legislative control over union excesses. Supervisors sometimes learn of possible abuses of the union rank-and-file during conversations with employees. The supervisor should

Figure 4-2   States with Right-to-Work Laws

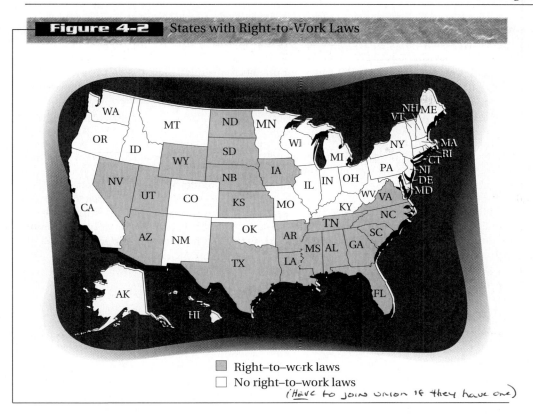

☐ Right–to–work laws
☐ No right–to–work laws
(Have to join union if they have one)

report suspected abuses to her or his immediate boss. Upper management may choose to investigate any problems and bring them to the attention of the appropriate authorities.

The Organizing Process

Why Employees Join Unions

Why do workers join unions? The majority of employees probably join unions for one of two reasons. First, they believe a union will further their own interests or, second, outside forces such as peer pressure are exerted on them. In the first instance, joining a union may be a defensive action related to retaining a job, income, and benefits. Or, joining a union may be a positive method of fulfilling a need for independence or control over one's job, participation, or recognition.

In general, unions are voted into organizations because employees are dissatisfied. The greater the degree of dissatisfaction and the more widespread it is within an organization, the higher the probability that employees will turn to unions for assistance in achieving their goals. Dissatisfaction takes various forms. Traditional areas leading to formation of unions include the "bread-and-butter" issues of wages, benefits, and working conditions. A firm that pays lower wages than the prevailing scale, provides fewer benefits than a competitor, or allows unsafe working conditions to exist is a candidate for being organized. However, other conditions can also contribute to dissatisfaction including poor

Unions and Management Working Together

Historically, management and unions have had an adversarial, "we-versus-they" relationship. In recent years, however, the concept of working effectively together for the benefit of all has taken hold.

General Motors' Fremont, California, plant once had one of the poorest labor relations records in the automotive industry. The plant finally closed in 1982 because of productivity problems caused, in part, by poor relations between management and the United Auto Workers local.

Productivity and labor relations completely turned around, however, after the plant's reopening in 1983. A new car took only 14 labor hours to build, compared to the 22 hours it had taken prior to the plant's closing. This improvement was accomplished with the same workers, in the same plant, and with the cooperation of the United Auto Workers.

Fremont's turnaround can be traced to adaptation of a team management system whereby employees and management work together to solve problems on the factory floor. Besides being given more opportunity to participate in decision making, workers were extensively cross-trained to work in a wide variety of jobs. Executive perks, such as reserved parking places and an executive lunch room, were also eliminated.

Employees were made part of production solutions. Put another way, "The bottom line is that employees must feel a sense of ownership in the company. They have to feel that their decisions will concern substantive issues and that, once made, those decisions will be implemented."[6]

communication between management and employees, promotional inequities, harassment of employees by supervisors and managers, and the inability of employees to participate in decisions affecting their jobs. In many cases, supervisors themselves have been a central reason for employees to seek union representation. Even poor economic conditions or other forces outside of management's control can contribute to unionization.[7]

Stages of the Organization Process

union organizing
The process of forming a union in an organization.

The process of forming a union is called **union organizing.** Typically, the organizational process involves five stages:

1. Initial employee interest in forming a union
2. Signing of authorization cards reflecting employee desire to have union representation
3. Definition of a bargaining unit
4. An election
5. Certification of a bargaining unit when the union wins an election

Figure 4-3 illustrates the sequence of activities typically followed in the organizing process.

The National Labor Relations Board conducts about 8,000 representation elections annually, including decertification elections. Unions now win about 45 percent of those elections, down from 55 percent in 1969.

The organizing process presents several challenges to supervisors. During this period, supervisors need to maintain their composure and minimize emotional behavior. They should exercise caution in what they say to their employees regarding the unionization process, especially to union activists. Even what normally would be considered innocent remarks may lead to charges of unfair labor

Figure 4-3   Sequence of Union Organizing Events

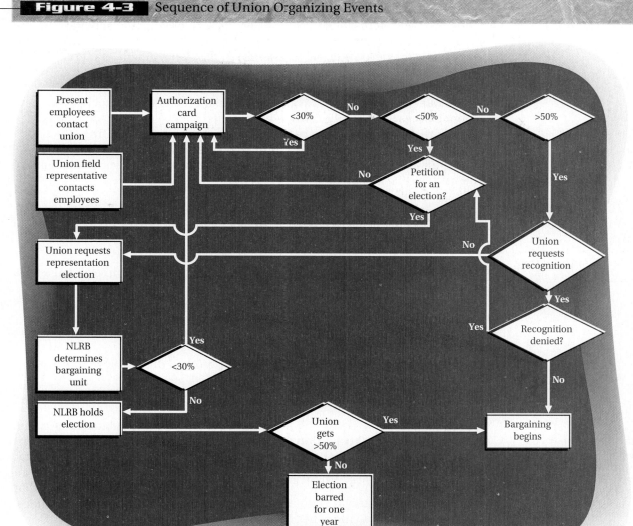

Source: John A. Fossum, *Labor Relations: Development, Structure, Process* (Plano, TX: Business Publications, Inc., 1985), 120.

practices. Supervisors should assist management to counter union organizing efforts by calmly discussing issues with employees, rather than by attacking the union or pro-union employees. This will allow supervisors to continue to work effectively with employees regardless of a campaign's outcome. Don't burn your bridges!

Initial Organizing Activities.   The impetus for organizing workers can come internally from employees themselves, or from outside the organization. In the latter instance, professional union organizers distribute materials promoting the formation of a union, contact individual workers, and hold mass meetings. (The motion picture *Norma Rae* realistically depicts organizing activities in the Southern textile industry.) During this period, certain practices are allowed and others are considered illegal. As members of management, supervisors are legally permitted to

- Point out the potential disadvantages of union membership such as the payment of dues and membership requirements
- Compare the employer's wages and benefits to those of other firms
- Prohibit union literature distribution in work areas during hours of work
- Continue to fairly and consistently enforce work rules and apply disciplinary measures

An employer cannot interfere with the rights of employees to organize unions and bargain collectively or coerce employees exercising these rights. It is illegal for a supervisor to

- Promise an increase in employees' pay or offer promotions in exchange for a vote against union representation
- Spy on or use an informer at union meetings
- Threaten to terminate an employee who lawfully engages in union activities
- Question employees about whether they have signed authorization cards or how they will vote
- Indicate the firm will go out of business or move if the union is approved by the employees
- Make antiunion speeches to workers within 24 hours of the election[8]

Signing Authorization Cards.   A major objective of union organizers is to get employees to sign **authorization cards** indicating an interest in union representation. Usually a minimum of 30 percent of the employees must sign authorization cards before the NLRB will schedule an election. If a majority of an organization's employees sign authorization cards, the union may request that the employer voluntarily recognize the union. Generally, the employer declines. The union will then petition the NLRB to conduct an election.

Employees who sign authorization cards, however, will not necessarily vote for a union. A study found that unions won only 70 percent of 1,174 elections in which over 75 percent of the employees had signed cards.[9] In 1989, the United Auto Workers sent 30 organizers to Nissan's assembly plant in Smyrna, Tennessee. Despite an intense 18-month effort by these organizers, the UAW still lost the representation election by a 1,622 to 711 vote.

Nissan management defeated the union by turning the election campaign into a referendum on participatory management, distributing T-shirts reading "Nissan: Union Free and Proud" and "Keep One Team." As one assembly line worker noted, "The company is giving me everything I need. I get a leased car, they've got an employee recreation center and a swimming pool. They treat me like a movie star. Why do I need a union?"[10]

Determining the Bargaining Unit.   With the exception of a consent election in which management and the unions agree to a mutually defined bargaining unit, the employee composition of a bargaining unit is determined by the NLRB. A number of criteria are used to define bargaining units, including the commonal-

authorization cards
A minimum of 30 percent of employees must sign such cards indicating their desire to form a union to obtain approval of the National Labor Relations Board to conduct a representation election.

ity of member interests in bargaining, employee desires, geographic dispersion of employees, and the degree of functional integration of the work unit.

The Election. The NLRB is responsible for conducting most representation elections. The election process is relatively simple if the election is not contested. Through secret ballots, employees indicate whether they desire union representation. If either the employer or the union contests the request for representation, or if two or more unions seek recognition, the NLRB must resolve the problem. The ballot for the contested election allows employees to vote for one of the unions seeking recognition, vote "no union," or vote "no choice." If "no choice" receives a majority of the total votes cast, a runoff election is required between the two choices receiving the most votes. When the majority votes "no union," there is no bargaining agent for employees and another election cannot be held for a minimum of one year.

Certification. The NLRB must certify the union winning an election. Certification means the union is recognized as the bargaining agent for the group of employees it represents. An employer is then required to bargain in good faith with the union.

Decertification. Union members may also conduct a decertification campaign if they become unhappy with union representation. **Decertification** is the process of removing union representation. As does a representation election, decertification requires that the NLRB or other oversight agency approve an election. A simple majority of bargaining unit members determines whether the union continues to represent employees.

Decertification has become more common in recent years. For example, 2,100 employees of Nordstrom's, a large department store chain, voted out the United Food and Commercial Workers Union (UFCWU) even though they had won a $15 million settlement from Nordstrom's in a lawsuit filed by the union.[11]

Generally, employees decertify unions that they believe have served their purpose or become corrupt or ineffective. As a supervisor, you may be called on to provide information to workers about the benefits of decertification and development of greater cooperation between management and labor.

decertification
The process of removing union representation through an election conducted by the National Labor Relations Board where a simple majority of bargaining unit members determines a union's continued representation.

Collective Bargaining

According to the Wagner Act, management has an obligation to conduct good faith bargaining with a union once it has been approved as a bargaining agent for employees. The Taft-Hartley Act requires that unions, in turn, bargain in good faith with management. **Good faith bargaining** occurs when a party in a contract negotiation makes every reasonable effort to come to agreement with the opposing party.

Parties reach agreement in contract negotiations through a process of give-and-take and compromise. Union and management representatives make offers and counteroffers and eventually agree on issues pertaining to wages, benefits, working conditions, work rules, and sick and vacation leave.

Occasionally, the two parties cannot come to agreement. Employees may then agree to work without a contract while negotiators continue to work out differences. The two sides may also call in a mediator. A **mediator** is a neutral third

good faith bargaining
Occurs when a party in a contract negotiation makes every reasonable effort to reach agreement with the opposing party.

mediator
A neutral third party who is skilled at helping opposing parties resolve differences but who has no authority to impose a solution.

party who is skilled at helping opposing parties to resolve differences. The mediator has no authority to impose a solution, but functions as a concerned counselor.

arbitrator
Functions as a judge in settling disputes and may or may not have authority to make decisions binding on both parties.

Sometimes an arbitrator acceptable to both parties will be brought into the negotiations. An **arbitrator** functions as a judge. His or her involvement is more formal and carries more authority than that of a mediator. The arbitrator makes decisions on issues over which management and the union have been unable to agree. The arbitrator's decisions are usually binding on the two parties. (See Chapter 15 for more about arbitrators and arbitration.)

After management and the union have agreed to contract terms, the contract must be ratified, or approved, by the union membership. Union members ratify a contract by a simple majority. Once ratified, the contract becomes binding to both parties. If the contract is not ratified, the negotiators must go back to bargaining.

Hammering out a labor agreement may be very difficult, especially during the first contract negotiations between the two parties. Supervisors may be asked to provide information to upper management for use in contract negotiations. They may discover employees in their work group are temperamental during this period. Supervisors should hope for a balance in power between management and the union in the negotiations process. A weak management or union position can lead to an unbalanced contract that ultimately dissatisfies both parties and contributes to unproductive conflict and rising employee dissatisfaction.

Administering the Contract

Collective bargaining doesn't end with the negotiation and ratification of a contract. In some respects, the more difficult work has just begun. Management and union members must make the contract work. Supervisors play a vital role in the contract administration process.

Contract language is not always clear. Some sections of labor contracts are also purposefully vague to allow for flexibility in interpretation. Supervisors should understand the contract language that applies to employees under their supervision, and should consult their boss about any significant disagreement with an employee about a contract issue.

union steward
An employee who has been appointed or elected by union members to investigate complaints against management by members of a bargaining unit.

An employee who believes his or her supervisor has violated the terms of the contract may lodge a complaint with the union steward (also sometimes referred to as a shop steward). A **union steward** is an employee who has been appointed or elected by union members to investigate complaints against management by members of the bargaining unit. A union steward might represent an entire local or part of a local (such as the employees in a particular plant or building).

For example, the contract might require that employees receive a break every two hours. A supervisor overseeing a busy production line might tell an employee who takes long restroom breaks in between contractually mandated breaks that the restroom breaks will no longer be allowed. Suppose the supervisor's boss supports the supervisor's action. The employee may then go to the union steward. The steward will meet with the supervisor to learn more about the problem and to negotiate a solution.

grievance
A complaint that has not been solved or settled and is usually viewed as being more serious, often expressed in writing.

If the problem is not worked out with the first line supervisor, the steward, after consulting with union leadership, may decide to file a grievance. A **grievance** is a written union complaint that alleges management has violated a contract. (See Chapter 15 for additional information about grievances.)

The filing of a grievance is the first step in a grievance procedure outlined in the contract. **Grievance procedures** differ among firms, but typically involve a prescribed series of actions between management and union representatives intended to work out differences. If the parties cannot agree on a solution, most contracts provide for binding arbitration.

grievance procedures
A prescribed series of actions between management and employees intended to resolve differences.

In binding arbitration, an arbitrator hears both sides of a grievance during a formal hearing and then decides on a solution. For example, the arbitrator may decide that contract language and past practice in the company allow for impromptu restroom breaks. The arbitrator may support the union in this instance. Conversely, the arbitrator may support management's decision and rule that the contract is clear—a 15-minute break every two hours is provided employees, and no more. In either case, the arbitrator's decision is final.

Supervisors may be asked to provide information to the company's attorneys for use during the arbitration hearing. They may also be called on to testify during the hearing or to give a **deposition,** a statement given under oath to an opposing party's attorney.

deposition
A statement given under oath to an opposing party's attorney.

It is essential that supervisors keep clear, chronological, and accurate written records. A supervisor may be called on to report specific events, including times and dates. It is also important that supervisors understand the questions being asked them during a hearing or deposition, and ask for clarification when in doubt. In any event, supervisors should look for guidance from the company's attorneys or the human resources department when preparing for an arbitration hearing or preparing a deposition.

Tactics Used in Labor Disputes

Unions and management use a variety of tactics to pressure each other. The threat of these tactics is often as persuasive as their actual use.

Tools of the Union

Labor's Tactics. The primary union tactic is the strike. A **strike** occurs when union members voluntarily withhold labor. Normally, the union pays members a portion of their normal wages from a strike fund during a strike, although, this is not always the case. Workers end the strike when management agrees to their demands or when a compromise is worked out between management and union contract negotiators.

strike
Union members voluntarily refuse to work.

Another tactic of labor is the boycott. A **boycott** occurs when union members refuse to use or purchase their employer's products in order to exert financial pressure on the employer. One step further is the **secondary boycott,** in which unions attempt to influence third parties, such as customers and suppliers, to refrain from conducting business with the employer. The Taft-Hartley Act made secondary boycotts illegal.[12]

boycott
Union members refuse to use or purchase their employer's products.

secondary boycott
Union attempt to influence third parties such as suppliers and customers to refrain from conducting business with the employer; made illegal by the Taft-Hartley Act.

Unions may also use **informational pickets** to garner public support for their cause. Here, union members remain working, but picket their employer and provide information supporting their position to people who pass by and to the media.

informational pickets
Union members remain working but picket their employer and provide information supporting their position to people who pass by and to the media.

Management's Tactics. Sometimes unions lose strikes, or boycotts and informational pickets are ineffective, and management refuses union demands. Management might even hire substitute workers to cross union picket lines. Supervisors and other managers may also be called on to work in place of striking employees. Management can also use a lockout to influence union members.

lockout
Management locks the doors of a plant or office building keeping workers out of the workplace until they agree to contract terms.

A **lockout** occurs when management literally locks the doors of a plant or office building and keeps workers out of the workplace until they agree to contract terms. There have been many union losses in recent years that have contributed to union decline, including the UAW strike against Caterpillar, the meatpackers' strike against Hormel, and the air traffic controllers association's illegal strike during the early 1980s.

Strikes and lockouts are divisive strategies, and there is seldom a clear winner when these strategies are used. Charles Bofferding, a union leader at the Boeing Company, when criticized for not being more eager to strike, aptly noted, "We have not been slow to strike. We understand that striking will be ringing a bell that can't be unrung, an action of last resort."[13]

During a strike or lockout supervisors should avoid alienating employees. As noted previously, there is little to be gained from burning bridges with employees who will be returning to the supervisor's work group at the conclusion of a strike or lockout.

The Future of Unions in the United States

Sumner H. Slichter, a prominent labor economist of Harvard University, predicted in 1946,

The growth of unions . . . means that the United States is gradually shifting from a capitalistic community to a laboristic one—that is, to a community in which employees rather than businessmen are the strongest single influence.[14]

That prediction has not come true. Almost every major economic sector has registered a loss of union membership during the past three decades. The percentage of government employees belonging to unions has, however, remained relatively constant.

Although recessions and foreign competition explain some of the decline of union membership, other factors have also contributed. In particular, the historic agenda of union leaders to improve the standard of living and protect the working rights of union members has been preempted by the federal and state governments through legislation enacted during the past 60 years.

As the previous decades have seen an erosion in the power of unions, United States firms have experienced a dramatic increase in the intensity of domestic and foreign competition. The number of business failures has increased. Improvements in productivity and efficiency arising from technological developments have displaced many workers. Meanwhile, the ability to compete is a priority topic for management. Quinn Mills observed:

Collective bargaining procedures and relationships between labor and management must reflect less conflict [and] more cooperation as the Nation's economy struggles to meet international competition and domestic needs.[15]

Figure 4-4 portrays the remarkable reduction of work stoppages in the United States during the past 40 years. In 1950, over 30 million work days were lost to striking employees. By 1990, the number declined to less than 6 million days. More dramatic, though, was the decline in percentage of days lost to strikes

Figure 4-4	Work Stoppages in the United States: 1950–1990			
Year	**Number of Work Stoppages**	**Number of Workers Involved (in thousands)**	**Number of Days Idle (in thousands)**	**Percent of Estimated Working Time Lost**[a]
1950	424	1,698	30,390	0.26
1955	363	2,055	21,180	0.16
1960	222	896	13,250	0.09
1965	268	999	15,140	0.10
1970	381	2,468	57,761	0.29
1975	235	965	17,563	0.09
1980	187	795	20,844	0.09
1985	54	324	7,079	0.03
1990	44	185	5,926	0.02

[a]Agricultural and government employees are included in the total working time; private household, forestry, and fishery employees are excluded.

Source: U.S. Bureau of the Census, *Statistical Abstract of the United States: 1984,* 104th ed. (Washington, D.C.: U.S. Bureau of the Census, 1984), Table 730, p. 441 (for years 1950 through 1980); and U.S. Bureau of the Census, *Statistical Abstract of the United States: 1992,* 112th ed. (Washington, D.C.: U.S. Bureau of the Census, 1992), Table 669, p. 420 (for years 1985 through 1990).

relative to total days worked from 0.26 percent to 0.02 percent (that is, two one-hundredths of one percent). In other words, if the average worker put in 2,000 hours of labor during a year, only 4 hours were lost to being on strike.

The relationship between labor and management has in the past been adversarial. Collective bargaining in the United States has resulted in contractual rules that bind parties and often reduce flexibility and the capacity to change.[16] In the years ahead, we may anticipate greater cooperation between unions and management. Cooperation takes several forms, including companies sharing more information with their employees, greater involvement of workers in decision making affecting their individual jobs, and a shared concern for their relationship of mutual dependency.

Carla's unit missed Dave's contributions. The new hire, Julie Anderson, was not as effective or as efficient as Dave had been, in spite of the high starting wage she earned. Carla decided to talk with Julie.

"Julie, you've been with us now for two months. I'm afraid that after a great start you've slowed down quite a bit. What's happening?"

"I do my job. I'm here on time. The cuttings are being processed. Quality is satisfactory."

"I know. But what I'm getting at is it seems you're not going much beyond just doing the job. . . ."

Julie interrupted, "I was just hired to do the job! What's in it for me if I do more? Also, the shop steward made it clear to me that other people don't like it when new people overwork."

Carla sat silently. It was going to be tough to motivate Julie. What should she do?

"Carla, what's the problem? I'm meeting the contract to the letter. My probation will be up next month, and I should be approved for permanent employment. You don't have a leg to stand on. I don't want to file a grievance, but I don't appreciate being reprimanded!"

Carla sputtered, "What? I'm not reprimanding you! This is just a conversation. You're not in trouble."

"Well, that's good. Say, can I go now? It's time for my break."

"Sure."

Summary: Focus on Concepts

Wage earners form labor unions to serve their interests by collectively bargaining with employers on such issues as employee wages and working conditions. Collective bargaining is the term used to describe the contract negotiation and administration process that exists between management and the union.

The union movement in the United States got its start after the Civil War when factory workers began to organize in response to poor working conditions and low pay. The American Federation of Labor (AFL) was formed in 1886 and managed to survive the years before federal protective legislation was passed in 1932 and 1935. The AFL served craft workers—people who worked in specific trades. The Congress of Industrial Organizations (CIO) formed in 1938 primarily to represent industrial workers—employees who lacked specific skills or a trade and worked in a general industry. The AFL and CIO merged in 1955, becoming the AFL-CIO.

A number of federal acts support or restrain the union movement. The Norris-LaGuardia Act of 1932 guaranteed employee rights to collective bargaining; the Wagner Act of 1935 defined employer unfair labor practices, established the National Labor Relations Board (NLRB), and defined the representation election process for establishing a union local; and the Taft-Hartley Act of 1947—passed to reduce union excesses—more precisely defined employer and employee rights, limited union activities by outlawing closed shops and allowing right-to-work legislation at the state level, and required unions to bargain in good faith with employers.

Unions may have different degrees of security within an organization. A "closed shop" allows only union members to apply for jobs; a "union shop" requires new employees to join the union after hire; an "agency shop" allows workers to pay a representation fee rather than union dues, but they don't have to join the union; and an "open shop" allows workers to choose whether to join the union and pay dues.

The Landrum-Griffin Act of 1959 was passed to improve internal union affairs and to restrict illegal activities by union leaders that included blackmail, arson, election-rigging, and taking payoffs.

Unions are formed through a process requiring approval by the NLRB or state oversight agency to conduct a representation election. The NLRB will approve an election if it receives authorization cards signed by at least 30 percent of employees. A simple majority can vote in a union. Unions can also be decertified by workers through a similar election process.

After a union has been approved, contract negotiations take place. If management and union negotiators cannot agree to terms, a mediator or arbitrator may be called in. A mediator has little authority and functions as a counselor. His or her role is to bring the two sides together. Arbitrators have significant authority; they function as a judge, hearing both sides and then making a binding decision. Once a contract has been negotiated, it must be ratified by the union membership, or else negotiators go back to bargaining.

Administering a contract is a process of give-and-take between management and union representatives. Problems should be resolved at the lowest level possible. As the lowest level of management, supervisors, consequently, play an important part in maintaining good labor-management relations.

If a solution is not found with a supervisor, dissatisfied employees may take their complaints to the union steward, who will attempt to work out differences with the supervisor. When a solution isn't found, the grievance procedure will expand to higher levels. If the two sides remain apart, an arbitrator is often called in to deliver a binding judgement.

Unions use strikes, boycotts, and informational pickets and management uses lockouts as collective bargaining tactics. These strategies are divisive and should only be used as a last resort. Ideally, parties to a collective bargaining agreement can successfully resolve differences as they arise without stopping production or involving the media or outside community.

Review Questions

1. Are unions good or bad for an organization? Explain management's view and organized labor's view.
2. What conditions create an environment for unions to be formed? Consider the historical perspective.
3. Differentiate among the various kinds of unions including craft and industrial unions and associations.
4. Indicate the major features of the following laws: Norris-LaGuardia Act of 1932, Wagner Act of 1935, Taft-Hartley Act of 1947, Landrum-Griffin Act of 1959. What conclusion do you draw from these legislative acts?
5. What is a yellow dog contract? Is it legal today?
6. What is an authorization card? What percentage of employees must sign such cards before the NLRB approves an election?
7. Describe the stages of a campaign to organize a firm.
8. What actions are legally available to management to avoid having their employees form a union? What can they not do? Similarly, what are the rights and responsibilities of labor?
9. What should supervisors do during the organizing process?
10. Contrast the functions of mediators and arbitrators.
11. What is a grievance procedure?
12. Explain the terms *strike, boycott, secondary boycott, informational picket,* and *lockout.*

Notes

1. General Counsel, National Labor Relations Board, *A Guide to Basic Law and Procedures under the National Labor Relations Act* (Washington, DC: Government Printing Office, 1993).
2. R. B. Freeman and J. L. Medoff, *What Do Unions Do?* (New York: Basic Books, 1984).
3. See T. O. Kirkpatrick, "Workers' Compensation in Montana," *Montana Business Quarterly* 15 (Spring 1977): 5–18.
4. G. F. Michelbacher and T. M. Nial, *Workmen's Compensation Insurance* (New York: McGraw-Hill Book Company, 1925), 8–9.
5. D. H. Van Doren, *Workmen's Compensation Insurance* (New York: Moffat, Yard and Company, 1918), 3–19.
6. "Making Work into Teamwork," *Utne Reader,* March/April 1992, 82–83.
7. H. J. Churden and A. W. Sherman, Jr., *Managing Human Resources,* 7th ed. (Cincinnati, OH: South-Western Publishing Company, 1981), 330. Also see W. L. French, *The Personnel Management Process: Human Resource Administration and Development,* 5th ed. (Boston: Houghton Mifflin Company, 1982), 514–515.
8. R. L. Mathis and J. H. Jackson, *Personnel: Human Resource Management,* 5th ed. (St. Paul, MN: West Publishing Company, 1985), 573.
9. M. H. Sandover, "The Validity of Union Authorization Cards as a Predictor of Success in NLRB Certification Elections," *Labor Law Journal* 28 (1977): 698–701.
10. "Making Work into Teamwork," *Utne Reader,* 83.

11. "Nordstrom to Pay Millions in Class-Action Suit Settlement," *Seattle Post-Intelligencer,* January 12, 1993, A1.

12. R. W. Mondy and R. M. Noe, *Human Resource Management,* 4th ed. (Boston: Allyn and Bacon, 1990), 617.

13. K. Anderson, "SPEEA Strike's Impact on Boeing Seen as Muted," *The Herald* (Everett), January 10, 1993, D4.

14. J. Hoerr, "Beyond Unions: A Revolution in Employee Rights Is in the Making," *Business Week,* July 8, 1985, 72.

15. D. Q. Mills, "Reforming the U.S. System of Collective Bargaining," *Monthly Labor Review* 106 (March 1983): 19.

16. Ibid.

A Union in Just Two Weeks

Rod Robertson and his wife, Cathy, had just returned to Cincinnati from two weeks of vacation in Hawaii. In mid-January the weather was cold, cloudy, and dreary. But if the weather was depressing, it was a portent of events yet to come.

Robertson owned and managed a relatively small steel-fabrication firm that employed three dozen workers. The business was highly cyclical and closely followed the business patterns of the construction industry. Good times were very profitable. Bad times were terrible. One consequence of the business cycle was the destabilizing effect upon the work force. Over the previous 10 years, Robertson had employed as many as 75 workers and as few as 15. Lately, though, the employment level had been relatively stable.

Upon entering his place of business, Robertson was greeted by his senior supervisor, C. J. Higgins.

"We've got a union!" Higgins exclaimed to his boss. "While you've been gone, they got authorization cards and a majority of the workers signed them. They want an election to get American Bridge to represent them. And the guy that's behind it is Charles Brown. I told you before, we should've fired Charlie. He has been a troublemaker as long as he's been here."

"Wait a minute," Robertson responded. "Start at the beginning and tell me what has been going on. I know we have had some problems in the past because of turnover and layoffs. A few accidents in the shop certainly haven't helped either. But how can we get a union in only two weeks?"

For the next two hours, Higgins provided details of the previous two weeks. From the information, Robertson realized he had serious trouble with his employees and that there was a high probability that unfair labor charges would be filed by his workers. Several actions by Higgins particularly disturbed Robertson.

Higgins had threatened to "punch Charlie's lights out" if he did not quit talking about the union and encouraging other workers to join. He threatened Charlie in front of other employees and indicated to them that if they joined a union, they would be replaced. He also said the company could not afford a union, that it would shut down if a union was formed, or it would move across the river and start over with nonunion personnel. To compound the problem, Higgins threw a union organizer off the company's property, asked every employee whether he planned to vote for the union, and suggested that the promised pay raise due in February would be canceled if an election was held.

As events developed over the next several months, 45 unfair labor practice charges were filed with the NLRB. During this period, Robertson was required to attend six hearings along with providing numerous documents. In May, the NLRB conducted a representation election, which the union won by a substantial majority.

Questions

1. How could this situation have been prevented?

2. Describe the specific practices of Higgins that were illegal or, at least, questionable.

3. Considering the future, when Robertson negotiates with union representatives on a labor contract, what advice and strategy do you recommend?

Unions

Morrison, Schneider, and Marchant is a labor law firm in Seattle. They conducted workshops to train supervisors and small business owners in how to avoid unionization. For a fee of $750 each, participants attended a two-day training program. During a recent session conducted by Sam Marchant, a junior partner in the firm, supervisors were asked to state their philosophies about organized labor and unions in general. Marchant prepared a list of their comments:

1. "I guess I am rather neutral about unions in general. While they certainly have done some good, we don't need them where I work. We pay competitive wages, have the full range of fringe benefits, and in general, employees seem happy. I don't see where a union would help them."

2. "I hate unions. They take away management's rights to run a business. I don't want to share decision making with any union member. If my employees want a union, then let them start their own businesses and make the decisions."

3. "Unions are often corrupt. Read the newspaper or watch television news and learn which union leader is being sent to prison this week."

4. "I check up on persons before hiring them. One of the things I look into is whether they favor joining a union. If they do, then I won't hire them."

5. "There are ways of getting around unfair labor charges. Just don't put things in writing or talk to others about what you're doing. Then you can always deny it."

6. "Companies that get unions usually deserve them."

7. "Sometimes there are conditions such as inflation and intense competition that can cause labor unrest and bring about a union. We can't control these outside conditions."

8. "Often, it seems, many employees don't want to join a union but are forced into it by their fellow workers who do want union representation. Then there's the NLRB. It has tended over the years to side with labor on most grievance issues."

9. "If we had a right-to-work law, all of our problems would be solved."

10. "I favor unions, for my competitors."

Questions

1. Evaluate the comments on the basis of their merit and accuracy, as you perceive them.

2. If you presently belong to a union or have in the past, what do you consider the benefits and disadvantages of membership?

The Supervisor as a Manager

In Part 1, we established the foundations of supervision, namely, understanding the work of supervisors and how they attempt to meet the performance challenge of obtaining high levels of productivity and quality from those they supervise. The legal challenges they face along with maintaining positive labor relations were also discussed.

In Part 2, we consider the functions performed by supervisors, such as planning, controlling, organizing, leading, staffing (human resources), and directing (orientation and training).

CHAPTER 5 Planning and Controlling for Productivity

Planning is the process of determining the supervisor's work objectives and the activities that are performed to achieve them. We learn how to apply planning components such as objectives, policies, rules, procedures, and performance standards to develop plans. The concept of systems is discussed along with management by objectives. In addition, more recent developments in benchmarking and reengineering are introduced. The discussion of controlling includes examples of financial and physical controls and TQM.

CHAPTER 6 Principles of Organizing

Organizing is the function of creating the structure of working relationships, designing facility layouts, balancing workloads, and scheduling work to be performed. Organization structure, including the departmentation process, is examined. Team-based forms of organizations, growing in popularity, are considered in addition to using authority effectively and developing and maintaining positive line and staff relationships. Major principles of organization are offered. The chapter ends with a discussion of scheduling and methods for obtaining coordination of work.

CHAPTER 7 The Supervisor as a Leader

The characteristics of competent leaders are explored in Chapter 7. Here, the development of leadership theory leads to current perspectives, including the contingency model, path-goal theory, situational leadership, and leader decision theory. The chapter concludes with a discussion of the leader as a role model and developing the ability to manage diversity.

CHAPTER 8 Human Resources Management and the Supervisor

The purpose of Chapter 8 is to delineate the relationships between supervisors and the organization staff responsible for human resources management. Both the role of supervisors and effective practices are considered in the process of recruitment and selection. Especially, consideration is given to the interviewing process, maintaining a safe workplace, and compensating employees fairly.

CHAPTER 9 Orientation and Training

We learn about new employee orientation in Chapter 9, then concentrate on the employee training process and methods for improving its effectiveness. The chapter ends with consideration of the directing function of giving orders and instructions.

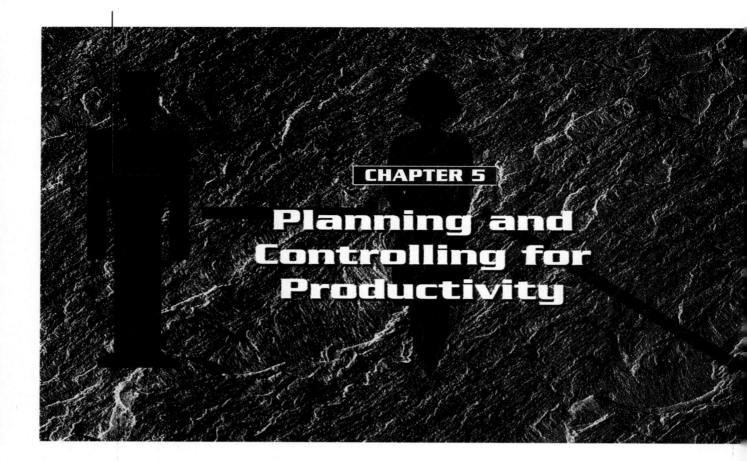

CHAPTER 5

Planning and Controlling for Productivity

● Never insult an alligator until after you have crossed the river.

Betty White

LEARNING OBJECTIVES

1. Define planning and indicate the major components of plans.
2. Discuss three planning situations supervisors encounter.
3. Indicate the meaning of strategic and tactical planning.
4. Discuss how supervisors can analyze the value of a plan and determine the probability of its successful execution.
5. Explain the following basic concepts used in planning: objectives, policies, work rules, procedures, and performance standards.
6. Identify several planning tools including systems and Management by Objectives (MBO).
7. Understand the concepts of benchmarking and reengineering.
8. Define the function of controlling and indicate two major components of controlling.
9. Understand and be able to apply several types of financial and physical controls including operating budgets, Gantt project planning charts, fishbone diagrams, flow charts, and run charts.

"When I arrived at Boeing four years ago, Larry was my boss. I replaced him as supervisor and he continued to be my boss," Carla related to a newly appointed supervisor, Henry Smith, who had come to Carla for advice. "Although I have a job description indicating my duties and there have been training sessions for supervisors, I still haven't been able to figure out all that I need to know about planning. Most of the training sessions seem to be about interpersonal relationships—touchy-feely stuff. In staff meetings, we often talk about budgets and the necessity for keeping costs down and productivity up."

It was evident that Carla was frustrated. "For all practical purposes, learning my job has been on-the-job training. The bosses use terms I don't understand and they seem too busy to explain. Why, once I thought a mission statement had religious connotations. You know, friars and the Spanish missions."

"Oh?" said Henry.

Planning and controlling are two sides of the same managerial coin. Planning helps supervisors to know where they and their work teams are heading; controlling determines whether they got there. In other words, we must specify in a

plan how results can be measured and forms of corrective actions to take when deviations occur so outcomes can be compared to the plan's goals.

What Is Planning?

"I'm too busy to plan. Planning is a luxury we just don't have time for." "How can I plan in my job when every day is different from the previous one?" These comments should sound familiar. Each has been made many times by supervisors. They could serve as epitaphs on organizational tombstones when the consequences of poor planning or the lack of planning has produced adverse outcomes.

planning
The process of determining what objectives to pursue and what activities to perform to achieve them.

Planning is the process of determining what objectives to pursue and what activities to perform to achieve them. Planning identifies the results we want to obtain and sets forth a blueprint or guideline to follow. Blueprints, by the way, are one form of plans and are vitally important to contractors. A well-crafted set of prints can provide the basis for a well-constructed building. A builder who once constructed a multi-level recreational and lodging structure had all of the plans in his mind, but none appeared on paper. He intended to create a building with three levels. When finished, the building had four levels, and the pipes extended twelve inches from the interior walls. While a handsome building on the outside, the interior was not quite right. A set of blueprints would have helped the builder turn his ideas into the structure he had in mind.

Common sense suggests that we should plan our actions. Sometimes, though, we undertake projects without adequately determining what we wish to accomplish or how we are going to arrive at our desired results. Lewis Carroll in *Alice in Wonderland* observed, "If you don't know where you are going, it doesn't make much difference which road you take." The consequences of inadequate planning are found in wasted resources, including people and time. Poor planning also affects the well-being of those responsible for carrying out the plans. Goals, by themselves, are powerful incentives for workers. (See the discussion on goal-setting as a motivator in Chapter 11.)

In the following pages, we explore the supervisor's role in planning, how to prioritize in planning and to predict the probability of successful completion of plans, planning tools including the process of Management by Objectives, and new concepts of benchmarking and reengineering. The latter part of this chapter considers responsibilities supervisors have in the functional area of controlling.

The Supervisor's Role in Planning

Time Spans of Planning

A major area of planning for many supervisors is scheduling the work of their subordinates. Consequently, they are planning for relatively brief periods such as today's work or the schedule for next week or month. Figure 5-1 illustrates time spans for planning at various levels of management. Note that 78 percent of

Figure 5-1 Time Spans for Planning at Various Management Levels

	Today	1 Week Ahead	1 Month Ahead	3 to 6 Months Ahead	1 Year Ahead	2 Years Ahead	3 to 4 Years Ahead	5 to 10 Years Ahead
President	1%	2%	5%	10%	15%	27%	30%	10%
Executive Vice President	2%	4%	10%	29%	20%	18%	13%	4%
Vice President of Functional Area	4%	8%	15%	35%	20%	10%	5%	3%
General Manager of a Major Division	2%	5%	15%	30%	20%	12%	12%	4%
Department Manager	10%	10%	24%	39%	10%	5%	1%	1%
Section Supervisor	15%	20%	25%	37%	3%			
Group Supervisor	38%	40%	15%	5%	2%			

Source: George A. Steiner, *Top Management Planning* (New York: Macmillan Publishing Company, Inc., 1969), 26.

supervisory planning is for a period of one week or less. Only 7 percent exceeds three months or longer into the future. By contrast, company presidents might spend only 3 percent of their time planning for periods of one week or less.

Some supervisory jobs require large amounts of planning, others do not. Many supervisors would, however, benefit from more planning. The hectic work schedules and pressures supervisors face often cause them to postpone planning.

Three Planning Situations

Newly appointed supervisors will encounter one of three situations: They will work with existing plans developed by others, modify existing plans, or develop entirely new plans. We will discuss the best methods for handling each situation.

Working with Existing Plans. Usually, a new supervisor will be expected to operate with existing plans. However, to manage effectively, the supervisor still needs to obtain information about several areas of operations. A substantial amount of learning may be required. As a supervisor, you need information to answer such questions as:

1. What are the goals expressed in the plans of the work unit and how are results measured?
2. Are the goals presently being met?
3. Do the stated formal plans correspond with the way the organization actually operates and how people are held accountable? Plans reflect an ideal state of what is to be accomplished, but they may not be followed in performing work to achieve objectives.
4. How do the plans actually operate? Who does what, when, how, where, and why?
5. Do your boss and subordinates support continuing the present plans?

Modifying Existing Plans.   Sometimes plans have to be modified because the environment has changed since plans were first drafted or because initial plans were inadequate. Before making changes, answer the following questions:

1. Why is the modification required? Are goals being achieved? Are existing plans causing problems? If so, what are the problems?
2. Do your supervisor and members of your work group support making changes?
3. Who developed the plans initially? Does this person still have responsibilities over them and if so, what reaction would be obtained if the plans were changed? (Some people may have a vested interest in existing plans and resent any efforts toward revision. Here is an example of understanding the organizational climate. They may view their past efforts as sacred and not to be touched.)
4. Is there a consensus toward the general direction in which the changes should be made?
5. What resources are needed for the changes, and are they available?
6. Which resources presently used in carrying out the plans can be applied to the modified plans?

Developing New Plans.   The need to develop totally new plans usually arises when the old plans are so ineffective it is better to start over than attempt to modify them. Perhaps the old plans are obsolete or circumstances make them inappropriate. For example, objectives of an organization may change, causing the supervisor to revise work team plans. When little of value can be salvaged from the old plans, it is more appropriate to create entirely new plans rather than to redesign the old. Building a new house may be superior to remodeling the old one. So it is with plans.

In each of these three situations, the supervisor needs information about the existing plans and the environment in which he or she will operate. The process of acquiring information requires the supervisor to become a researcher or, in some instances, a detective, to learn about past operations of the work unit. The more complete and accurate the supervisor's knowledge about a situation, the greater the probability of achieving the desired results.

Strategic and Tactical Planning

While senior level managers are involved in what is called strategic planning, supervisors typically are more concerned with tactical planning and control activities. **Strategic planning** is "defined as a continuous, interactive process aimed at keeping an organization as a whole appropriately matched to its environment."[1] Strategic planning includes

> developing a business mission, identifying an organization's external opportunities and threats, determining internal strengths and weaknesses, establishing long-term objectives, generating alternative strategies, and choosing particular strategies to pursue.[2]

(A mission is the purpose of an organization that differentiates it from other organizations and, in the process, delineates its scope of operations.) One of the benefits of strategic planning is that it reveals uncertainties about the future to limit destructive surprises.[3]

Tactical planning concentrates on implementing the strategic plans. It emphasizes the current and short-term activities required to achieve the objectives of the strategic plans.[4] The deployment of resources is an important part of tactical planning.[5] In other words, strategic planning specifies what is to be done, and tactical planning specifies how to do it.

The result of planning is, of course, a plan. A **plan** is a course of action designed to produce some specific result or outcome. It consists of objectives and the major methods to be used to attain them. Not all planning, of course, concludes in a written document. However, important plans should be committed to paper. A written document aids in communicating a plan. Also, mental plans are often incomplete and disorganized, and if the person preparing a mental plan is unavailable, there is no trail for others to follow. Those responsible to carry out the plan should also be involved to some degree in its construction.[6]

Programs.   As a supervisor, you may be responsible for carrying out a program. A **program** is a comprehensive plan that includes objectives to be attained, specification of resources required, and stages of work to be performed. The designation of a plan as a program may be limited to those major activities that require a large commitment of resources, a high degree of detail including a monetary budget, activities that are ongoing or will continue for long periods, and methods for measuring performance. Programs may be submitted to an arena of debate with other supervisors and their superiors to compete for limited funding within an organization.

Planning is a form of organized thinking. It requires application of logic and systematic analysis. (Systems are discussed in Chapter 1 and later in this chapter.) In addition, planners build into good plans the methods by which their effectiveness can be evaluated. Before developing a plan, consider the following questions:

- What is our goal?
- Why did we choose this method to reach our goal?
- Who said we should be doing this?
- If we did not do this, what would happen? Is that bad?
- Can we do this better, that is, achieve the same or superior results with fewer resources and in a shorter period of time?

strategic planning
A continuous, interactive process aimed at keeping an organization as a whole appropriately matched to its environment.

tactical planning
Emphasizes current and short-term activities to achieve the objectives of strategic plans.

plan
A course of action designed to produce some specific result or outcome.

program
A comprehensive plan that includes objectives to be attained, specification of resources required, and stages of work to be performed.

Considerations in Planning

Planners frequently overlook two critical considerations in the effective utilization of organizational resources. The first consideration pertains to the choice of subject areas in which planning can occur. Those areas promising the largest payoffs should be selected first and those with the smallest benefits dealt with last, if at all. The second consideration is a realistic appraisal of whether the organization can successfully carry out the plan. If a plan is unlikely to succeed, it should be changed. The following discussion presents models for measuring the relative value of a plan and for estimating the probability of successfully implementing a plan.

Measuring the Value of a Plan

The cost of planning should not exceed its benefits. Supervisors need to determine rather quickly the importance of the alternatives available to them. The following four criteria are useful in evaluating a plan:

1. *Payoff.* The result supervisors are attempting to achieve is the payoff. The larger the payoff, the greater the value of the plan.
2. *Repeatability.* What is the probability of using the plan more than one time? Plans that are repeated in operation for longer periods generally justify more careful development. Usually, they should be more comprehensive.
3. *Risk.* Consider the types of risks encountered and the potential losses or consequences if things turn out badly. The greater the risk and potential loss, the larger the need for more careful analysis and the greater the weight given to this criterion.
4. *Duration of effects.* How long will the effects of a plan, if carried out, be felt? Are all of the outcomes positive? Some of the results usually are realized initially while others could continue for a long period or indefinitely. Plans with the potential for producing long-term or irreversible effects require more careful analysis and even testing before implementation.

Figure 5-2 is a model for determining the value or utility of a plan. A plan with a low value probably does not merit pursuing; a plan with a higher value deserves greater consideration and analysis. (The model produces a maximum numerical value of 100.) The purpose of the model is to assist in determining how much time to commit to developing a plan and how to prioritize among competing planning situations. For example, if you are confronted with several planning situations, which should you select as your first priority? Which should be skipped?

The following scenario illustrates how the model is applied. Suppose you are an office supervisor and are considering changing your office layout. A preliminary analysis prepared by one of your organization's engineers indicates the conversion of the existing open space into private offices will cost $20,000, and a potential increase of employee productivity worth $5,000 per year will be realized. At the same time, you can also increase the efficiency of heating and air conditioning by reducing the amount of window space. The savings in energy costs are estimated to be $500 annually. Thus, the total annual payoff is projected at $5,500, along with greater privacy for your employees—something most members of your group have requested. These considerations might lead you to assign

Figure 5-2   A Model for Determining the Value of a Plan

Instructions: Circle the appropriate number for each of the four elements below. At the bottom of the figure enter each number and multiply.

Payoff: Determine the importance of the results of the plan if carried out, that is, the estimated amount of payoff. Calculate the cost of resources and the potential gains and savings, if any. Where possible, use dollars or develop a common denominator.

Small Payoff				Large Payoff
1	2	3	4	5

Repeatability: How often will the plan be used? Is it a single-time plan or one that will be repeated in the future?

One Time	Multiple Use
1	2

Risk: What is the risk and what are the chances of a loss occurring? Consider, also, the interrelationships with other organizational activities and the dependency of others upon the output of the plan.

Little Risk			Large Risk
1	2	3	4

Duration of Effects: Consider the time-frame during which the effects of the plan will occur. Will they be short in duration or last indefinitely?

Short Term			Long Term
1.0	1.5	2.0	2.5

(   ) × (   ) × (   ) × (   ) =   Plan Value

---

a payoff value of 4 to the plan. It is a one-time plan and will not be repeated in the near future. The repetition value, therefore, is 1. Risks are difficult to determine but are identified as (1) employees may change their minds toward the privacy factors and (2) the company may sell the building within the next three years, thus wasting some of the investment. Few, if any, anticipated negative effects upon your group's operations or those of other departments would result from the change. You might therefore assign a risk value of 2. Finally, effects of the new layout are expected to last indefinitely, so the value assigned to duration of effects would be 2.5. The total value of this plan, if carried out, is 20 ($4 \times 1 \times 2 \times 2.5$) out of the 100 points possible. The plan, therefore, has a relatively low value.

Let us change the variables to demonstrate how the plan's value could increase. Consider what would happen if the risk factor of 2 became 4, perhaps because your employees do not want private offices but are being forced to work in the new layout situation. Because of the potential for conflict, the total value of the plan under this new condition doubles to 40 ($4 \times 1 \times 4 \times 2.5$). Adding one other change, the assumption that several additional offices in the organization would be redesigned if your plan is successful, the value of 1 for repeatability becomes 2. The plan's value now doubles again to 80 ($4 \times 2 \times 4 \times 2.5$). The increased score reflects the greater importance of the plan to the organization.

Estimating the Probability of a Plan's Successful Execution

Effective supervisors think before acting. They look before they leap.

The folklore of management is filled with marvelous observations. For example, "never undertake projects doomed to failure." Yet, sometimes supervisors are involved in carrying out plans that, if not doomed to failure, certainly produce results of minimal value. Lack of experience or perceptiveness, or even an undue degree of loyalty to one's superior, may contribute to this problem. Think before acting on a plan.

Figure 5-3 is a model for assessing the probability of a plan producing positive results if implemented. Three major criteria are considered: (1) the availability of resources, (2) sufficient time to carry out the plan, and (3) an acceptable amount of risk.

The maximum numerical score of this model is 100. Plans with high scores have greater probabilities of achieving their goals than those with lower scores. Plans with a low likelihood of success should not be implemented. For example, a score of 70 could be chosen as a cutoff point below which the plan would not be implemented in its present form. However, modification of the plan by reducing risks or increasing resources could increase the probability of success.

Figure 5-3 A Model for Determining the Probability of a Plan's Successful Execution

Instructions: Circle the appropriate number for each of the three factors below. At the bottom of the figure, enter each number and multiply.

Availability of Resources: Are the following available: (a) people with needed skills; (b) space and suitable working environment; (c) equipment, tools, and supplies; and (d) working capital?

Low Resource Availability				High Resource Availability
1	2	3	4	5

Time: (a) Is sufficient time available to obtain the desired results? (b) What is the best method for determining the amount of time required to achieve the results? (c) Can the time required for obtaining results be reduced, if needed, and what are the costs associated with different time frames?

Limited Time Available			Sufficient Time Available
1	2	3	4

Risk: (a) Describe the types of risks surrounding the plan. (b) Measure the potential size of losses and the probability of their occurrence (using tools from Chapter 4). (c) Determine the methods available to either eliminate or reduce the risks and the costs of these methods.

Great Risks				Minimum Risks
1	2	3	4	5

(   ) × (   ) × (   ) =   Plan Success

Each of these two models is a useful tool in the planning process. They give the supervisor a basis for determining the relative value of plans and assessing the probability of a plan's successful execution. The supervisor can then allocate planning time primarily to those areas producing the largest payoffs.

Basic Planning Concepts

Previously, we said a plan consists of objectives and methods for their achievement. The elements of a plan include objectives, policies, work rules, procedures, and performance standards.Writers, instructors, and supervisors may define these terms differently. Yet, precision is required in applying these concepts. As a supervisor, you need to understand how others in your organization define and use these concepts. Caution is especially needed in use of the terms *goals* and *objectives,* which may be defined in several conflicting ways.[7]

Objectives

Every plan must have at least one objective. If we are taking a trip, for example, but do not know where we are going, how will we select the best travel route? An **objective** or **goal** is any value a person, firm. or organization desires to acquire, and in the acquisition process, is willing and able to make the necessary sacrifice of time, money, or effort.[8]

Sometimes we establish unrealistic objectives. How many New Year's resolutions—personal objectives—have you kept? Let us take a closer look at the components of an objective: value, desire, and ability. *Value* means the worth, usefulness, or importance of something to someone who either possesses or wishes to acquire it. *Desire* refers to a person's motivation to pursue the object of value. Motivation may be strong or weak. Finally, *ability* means possession of or the ability to acquire the necessary resources to translate the desire into an accomplished event. Achieving objectives is a value exchange process: To acquire something of value, first we must give up something of value.

In developing objectives or goals, you may be able to apply the acronym *SMAC.* Objectives or goals should be (1) specific, (2) measurable, (3) achievable, and (4) clear.

As an illustration of a personal objective, consider the pursuit of a college education or taking a course in supervisory management. To acquire knowledge, you have sacrificed or exchanged something of value to you: financial resources, time, and effort. There is also an opportunity cost: Selecting the pursuit of one objective means you have foregone, at least temporarily, seeking other goals such as entertainment or monetary gain which, in the short term, could have greater utility for you. Think about the last time you crammed all night in preparation for an important exam. In pursuing your objective, you exchanged something of value, foregone sleep, for knowledge and a high grade.

Objectives are expressed in several dimensions. For example, they have a time dimension, which may be short or long term. The former are accomplished quickly, within a few hours, days, or months, while the latter may take years.

The dimension of importance gives rise to the classifications of major and minor objectives. Major objectives are those that must be accomplished because they affect the success and survival of organizations. A major objective could be

objective/goal
Any value a person, firm, or organization desires to acquire, and in the acquisition process, is willing and able to make the necessary sacrifice of time, money, or effort.

the development of a new product line or a manufacturing process leading to lower production costs. A minor objective, on the other hand, could be landscaping corporate headquarters by the end of the summer. Failure to achieve this goal may evoke derisive comments from our competitors, but it is not organizationally life-threatening. Dented pride and flourishing crabgrass we can live with, at least for a while.

Objectives also vary by degree of specificity. They can be nonquantifiable or quantifiable. The former are often more philosophical or express general values to be attained, and the latter indicate the quantity of something we want to acquire. In practice, although some objectives are considered nonquantifiable, they do not become operational until they are translated into quantifiable terms. Quantifiable objectives allow people more responsibility for achieving goals, establish a basis for holding people accountable, indicate when they are to be completed, and allow a more factual basis for distributing rewards or assessing penalties for the outcomes achieved.

Policies

policy
A guideline consisting of a principle and a rule governing the behavior of employees in an organization.

Often, plans are developed with a listing of restrictions governing how they will be carried out. These restrictions are called *policies*. A **policy** is a guideline governing the behavior of employees in an organization. An effective policy consists of two elements: (1) principles illustrating cause-and-effect relationships or basic truths and (2) rules governing the behavior of persons in organizations. Objectives set forth the results we wish to obtain, and policies prescribe how people should behave or act while pursuing those objectives. In other words, policies indicate what employees should or should not do in a given circumstance.

As an example of a policy, consider disciplinary action in a company in which employees are unionized. The union contract prohibits supervisors from unilaterally discharging employees. They must follow the disciplinary process set forth in the collective bargaining agreement. In this case, they must first consult with the human resources department and the union shop steward before taking more severe forms of corrective action. The principle is illustrated by the necessity to promote a positive relationship between the union and management. The rule in this case specifies that all supervisors are to abide by contract provisions regarding disciplinary action. Policies have several purposes. They guide the behavior of people striving to achieve organizational objectives. They assist in making decisions by establishing the boundaries within which employees act. Policies also allow greater delegation of authority, reduce and/or define risks, provide faster decision making, and produce more uniform and predictable results. Although some persons believe policies are oppressive and reduce their personal freedom, policies can also increase opportunities for exercising initiative. Those areas not covered by policy provide freedom for individuals to exercise self-determination.[9] On the other hand, in some highly bureaucratic organizations, the pursuit of policy compliance has replaced goal attainment.

Work Rules

work rule
Specific statement governing the behavior of employees while on the job.

Work rules are specific statements governing the behavior of employees while on the job. They are basically policies that do not need stated principles because the practice described in the work rule is so widely accepted by employees as reasonable and useful that no justification is needed. For example, the necessity for coming to work as a prerequisite of holding a job needs no explanation.

Here are some examples of work rules: "The hours of work shall be from 8:00 AM until 5:00 PM with one hour taken for lunch between noon and 1:00 PM. Employees shall be ready to start work at 8:00 AM and not leave their work stations until 5:00 PM." "No smoking is allowed except in areas designated with 'Smoking Permitted' signs." "An employee who is ill and unable to report for work should call the human resources office at least two hours prior to the start of her/his shift."

Work rules, like policies, are designed to produce uniform behavior to limit risk, conserve time, and reduce conflict. Remember, though, rules should be justifiable and not arbitrary. If the desired result can reasonably be obtained without a rule, do not introduce a rule. Unnecessary rules detract from a supportive and trusting work environment, and many people resent unnecessary restrictions. Finally, policies and rules that cannot be sensibly enforced are invitations for organizational warfare. Casualties, yes. Winners? Probably none.

Procedures

We have described what planners wish to accomplish as objectives and the guidelines of behavior within which decisions are made as policies. Yet, how is work actually performed? For many people, a large part of work done is accomplished by following procedures.

A **procedure** is a specific method followed in performing a task or following a policy. In decision making, for example, the steps taken to identify a problem and solve it represent a procedure. A procedure should reflect the best method for completing a task. For example, going to class involves walking or driving a specific route. Although you could travel countless directions and eventually arrive at class, one path is most productive in getting there on time.

procedure
Specific method followed in performing a task or following a policy.

Procedures are usually repeated many times because they are the most efficient and productive methods for obtaining the desired outcome. They will be performed either until superseded by better procedures or until goals are changed and the procedures are no longer needed.

Procedures are valuable because they reduce the time required to complete tasks, increase efficiency, minimize risk, and reduce waste. By applying standard procedures, we do not constantly "reinvent the wheel," so to speak. On the other hand, learning a new routine when appropriate may increase employees' productivity.

Performance Standards

Performance standards are management's expectations of what persons should do in their jobs and how well they should perform. These standards should be explicit. In other words, our subordinates should know the standards by which their performance is appraised. Standards should be developed in the planning process. They are then applied in the controlling process to be described later in this chapter.

performance standard
Management's expectations of what persons should do in their jobs and how well they should perform.

Consider an example of a performance standard for a production worker operating a plastic blow-molding machine making laundry baskets. A standard would be "to produce an average of one basket per minute with a daily scrap rate not exceeding 2 percent."

ISO 9000

Founded in 1947, the International Organization for Standardization is a nonprofit group that comprises industrial standard-setting bodies from 92 countries (the U.S. is represented by the American National Standards Institute). The organization sets but does not enforce international norms for everything from paper sizes to screw threads to film speeds.

But ISO 9000's biggest virtue, its universality, is also its greatest vice. By setting norms that are attainable across a broad range of industries and cultures, ISO 9000 falls far short of the quality that world-class corporations demand of themselves and their suppliers.[10]

Performance standards should be communicated to employees frequently. For example, standards may be conveyed with the initial hiring of an employee, during the orientation process, in training sessions, and at the periodic performance appraisal interview. Supervisors are, by far, the most important link in communicating to their subordinates the organization's performance standards.[11]

ISO 9000
An international set of standards that provide a framework for showing customers how a firm tests products, trains employees, keeps records, and fixes defects.

ISO 9000 is a rapidly spreading guideline of standards. Your organization may be one of its future adherents, if not so already. **ISO 9000** is an international set of standards that "provide a framework for showing customers how you test products, train employees, keep records, and fix defects. Think of ISO 9000 not as another variant of total quality management but as a set of generally accepted accounting principles for documenting quality procedures."[12]

Planning Tools

Systems

Several methods are available to help supervisors plan. In recent years the terms *systems* and *models* have become common in organizations. In Chapter 1, a system is defined as being comprised of a flow of inputs, transformation processes, outputs, and feedback. In other words, a system is a set of integrated components designed to achieve an objective. The concept of systems is widely applied in organizations today. An organization itself is a system. Mercy Hospital in Kansas City; Fitzgerald's Supermarket in Burbank; Everett Community College in Everett, Washington; and the city government of Dallas are all examples of systems. So are General Motors, Intel, and Motorola. Each of these is, in turn, composed of many subsystems that are linked together in the larger whole of the organization.

Supervisors can utilize the concept of systems in their planning by viewing their units as one of several organizational subsystems. In linking one subsystem to another, supervisors should consider the goals of each unit and how goals are interrelated, roles of individuals and groups, and communication networks. Diagramming these relationships in a model helps in understanding how systems operate. A **model** is a representation of a real world event, process, object, or system.

model
A representation of a real world event, process, object, or system.

Management by Objectives

Management by objectives (MBO) is a collaborative setting of goals between a supervisor and his or her superior and a determination of the criteria to be used for evaluating that supervisor's performance in achieving those goals. Or, the collaboration may be between a supervisor and a subordinate or a group of employees. MBO first appeared in 1954, was promoted by Peter Drucker, and since then has been the subject of countless articles in management literature. (Chapter 14 tells how to apply MBO to performance appraisal.)

For the supervisor, the opportunity to participate in framing objectives upon which her or his performance will be evaluated can provide an important stimulus for pursuing the objectives. The supervisor may feel, "I am the master of my job destiny." In MBO, emphasis is placed on attaining goals with, perhaps, greater freedom in how they are achieved. Once again, we see the importance of employee empowerment. MBO requires a flexible environment in which employees have some control over resources and how they are applied. The major steps in the MBO process are illustrated in Figure 5-4 on page 104.

The conditions leading to successful MBO implementation are (1) a supervisor must have control over resources needed to achieve the goals, (2) senior management must have a strong commitment to implement and master the operational requirements of MBO, (3) goal achievement must be measurable and usually involve quantitative objectives, and (4) the organization must deliver the rewards when they are earned. If these conditions are present, an organization is likely to succeed in using MBO. A good MBO program is valuable and the risks often are worth taking to make it work. However, very careful planning is required.

management by objectives (MBO)
A collaborative setting of goals between a supervisor and his or her superior and a determination of the criteria to be used for evaluating that supervisor's performance in achieving those goals.

Benchmarking and Reengineering

As progressive organizations implement total quality management (TQM) to survive and, for many, to excel, they are turning to new methods of operations. Successful TQM permeates the organizational structure from top to bottom, and that includes supervisors who ultimately will carry out the changes necessary for improving an organization's competitive effectiveness. Two of the most exciting developments in recent years are known as benchmarking and reengineering.

Benchmarking

Benchmarking is a part of total quality management. (See Chapter 2 for a discussion of TQM.) The Xerox Corporation defines **benchmarking** as

> the continuous process of measuring products, services, and practices against the toughest competitors or those companies recognized as industry leaders. . . . Benchmarking has become a common component of the many Total Quality Management programs adopted by large companies since benchmarking was introduced to the U.S.—by Xerox—in 1979.[13]

benchmarking
The continuous process of measuring products, services, and practices against the toughest competitors or those organizations recognized as industry leaders.

Figure 5-4 An MBO Planning Process

1. **Job Review and Agreement.** The employee and the superior review the job description and key activities comprising the employee's job. The focus of this phase is for the employee and the superior to agree on the exact components and functions of the employee's job. Included in this phase is the determination of the most important activities the employee performs.

2. **Development of Performance Standards.** Specific standards of performance must be mutually developed. This phase specifies a satisfactory level of performance. The standard is specific and definite and is established for each of the main activities agreed upon in the first step. For example, a salesperson's quota to sell five cars per month may be an appropriate performance standard. Selling that number of cars can be measured and constitutes a satisfactory level of performance. Standards should be clearly established for each managerial or employee position and should be revised as economic conditions or other variables change.

3. **Guided Objective Setting.** Objectives are established by the employee in conjunction with, and guided by, the superior. The important factor in this phase is that the employee plays the major role in setting the targets, instead of having them set by the superior as with the other methods. Continuing the example of the automobile salesperson, an objective might be set to challenge the employee to improve performance; the salesperson might set a new objective of selling six cars per month. Notice that the objective set may be different from the performance standard. Objectives should be set so that attainment is realistically possible.

4. **Ongoing Performance Discussion.** The employee and the superior use the objectives as bases for continuing discussions about the employee's performance. While a formal review session may be scheduled, the employee and the manager do not necessarily wait until the appointed time for performance discussions. Objectives are mutually modified and progress is discussed during the period.

Source: Robert L. Mathis and John H. Jackson, *Personnel: Contemporary Perspectives and Applications,* 4th ed. (St. Paul: West Publishing Company, 1979), 309.

Benchmarking frequently involves observing, on site, the operations of non-competing firms that are recognized as being industry leaders. Reciprocity is expected when they or other firms participate in exchange visits. The payoff of benchmarking is measured in quantum improvements in operations—not a 2 or 4 percent reduction in costs, for example, but an improvement of 20 or 40 percent.

Reengineering

reengineering
The search for and implementation of radical change in business core processes to achieve breakthrough results.

Reengineering has been described as follows:

Business Process Engineering (BPE)—and by extension, reengineering—involves redesigning (generally simplifying) the work tasks performed to conduct any activity.

Reengineering is a process innovation and core process redesign in the search for and implementation of radical change in business processes to achieve break-through results. Its chief tool is a clean sheet of paper.[14]

Essentially, reengineering is starting over. It involves questions of "What if." How would we do things differently if we were to start over? Reengineering works toward the present and future. Intermediate improvements are skipped and discarded. The intent is to reconfigure the organization to match the future.[15]

Financial and Physical Controls

Planning becomes meaningful only when it is translated into action. Periodic measurements are required to determine whether the plan is on track and objectives are being achieved. To accomplish this end, controlling is required.

"If I can't measure it, I can't control it," is a good summation of the need for clear direction provided by the planning function of management. Without clear objectives, it is not possible to know if you, as a supervisor, are leading a productive work team.

The function of management that assesses whether objectives have been or are being accomplished is termed *controlling*. **Controlling** is the process of comparing results to objectives and taking corrective action when deviation from objectives occurs. The performance standards developed in planning are applied to the controlling process.

controlling
The process of comparing results to objectives and taking corrective action when deviation from objectives occurs.

Controlling has two major components: (1) measuring performance and comparing that performance to some standard or objective and (2) making corrections or taking actions when results deviate from these standards or objectives.[16]

In the initial stage of controlling, the effective supervisor compares outcomes (which can be the results of a process or the behavior of persons) to standards (which can be objectives, policies, work rules, or performance standards). In the action stage of controlling, the supervisor then attempts to correct problems or bring results back into line with objectives.

The organization's objectives largely determine the types of controls applied. Supervisors derive a number of benefits from exercising various types of controls. For example, controls may be used to

- *Achieve uniform performance and results.* Standardization of work and processes should increase productivity and efficiency. Uniform results, furthermore, make it easier to predict outcomes and reduce risks. The types of controls used to achieve uniform performance include written procedures, policies, production schedules, budgets, and inspections.
- *Obtain uniform quality of production.* The work of a group or the products of an organization should attain a consistent level of utility or produce a desired outcome. In the case of the final product, the level of quality required reflects customers' expectations. Quality control methods include developing product specifications and performance standards and conducting inspections of products.
- *Measure employee performance.* Daily or weekly measurements of performance provide a timely source of information about short-term operations. Types of controls include quotas, audits, time reports, and output

Supervisors often play an important role in forecasting and budgeting.

reports. In the long term, performance appraisals are made to increase job effectiveness, recognize and reward good performance, and motivate employees. Performance appraisals are usually made by the employee's supervisor. (The subject of performance appraisals is discussed at length in Chapter 14.)

- *Designate the extent of formal authority.* Through the process of delegating authority, accountability is established. The person receiving the authority has a range of alternatives he or she may implement without approval from higher management. Policies, work rules, and procedures are all examples of controls that provide a supervisor with guidance.

- *Protect organizational assets from misuse.* Theft and waste of corporate assets are two examples of misuse of assets. Methods of controlling the use of assets include separation of accounting activities (including audits), defining individual responsibilities, record-keeping, and authorization systems.[17]

Examples of Financial and Physical Controls

budget
A formal quantitative expression of management plans.

Budgets. An example of a financial control is a budget. A **budget** "is a formal quantitative expression of management plans."[18] It is derived from the planning process and represents a projection of the results to be achieved during a specific period of time. Many supervisors either receive or prepare budgets covering the operations of their work units.

operating budgets
Project the amount of income to be received or expenses of a supervisor's unit during a given period such as a year, quarter, or month.

Operating budgets are commonly used. These budgets project the amount of income to be received or the expenses of a supervisor's unit during a given period such as a year, quarter, or month. Expense items are listed as *line items* recurring from one budget period to the next. A typical budget period is one year. A supervisor's ability to hire personnel and purchase supplies or other resources is limited by the availability of funds and the operating procedures of the organization. Supervisors often spend a considerable amount of time managing operating budgets.

Gantt project planning chart
Illustrates when the various stages of work must start to complete a project by the deadline.

Gantt Project Planning Charts. A **Gantt chart** is an excellent physical control used to track project activities across time. There are several kinds of Gantt charts. For example, a project planning chart is used in mapping detailed plans to show when the various stages of work must start to complete a project by the deadline. A sample project planning chart is shown in Figure 5-5. Note that progress to date is indicated by the heavy bottom lines. In this example, because materials procurement is one week behind schedule, the fabrication processes of parts 9 and 10 have been delayed.

Physical Controls within TQM. The current day emphasis on total quality management (TQM) to improve quality has led to the development of a wide variety of physical controls, including the Pareto chart, fishbone diagram, flow chart, and run chart. The Pareto chart, discussed in Chapter 2, helps supervisors to identify the "vital few" and the "trivial many" factors of work processes.

fishbone diagram
A statistical method that systematically assesses relationships between cause and effect.

A **fishbone diagram** is a statistical method that systematically assesses relationships between cause and effect. An effect is an outcome of a system of causes. For example, suppose you get together with your spouse and use a fishbone diagram (Figure 5-6) to assess why you are constantly late to work. This diagram shows that causes related to people, materials, methods, and machines lead to the undesirable effect of late attendance. Notice how complex even a simple matter, such as going to work, can be! Advantages of using a fishbone diagram are that it helps to break down complex relationships into manageable, identifiable parts, keeps discussion focused on the problem at hand, and results in an active search for a cause or causes.

Preparing a flow chart is an excellent way to understand differences between how a process works and how it should work. A **flow chart** is a diagram that graphically depicts the sequence of steps in a process. It can be used to help a work group or individual understand how a process actually runs, as opposed to how they think it runs. Figure 5-7 shows the steps involved in getting to a morning class on time. Before studying this figure, briefly consider what steps are

flow chart
A diagram that graphically depicts the sequence of steps in a process.

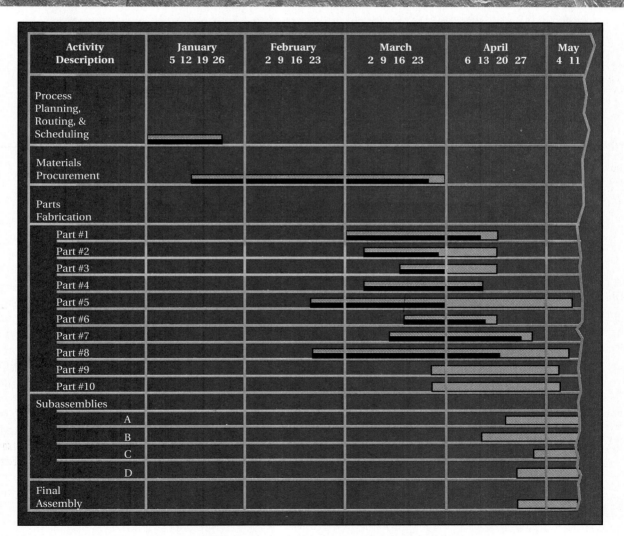

Figure 5-5 A Gantt Project Planning Chart

Activity Description	January 5 12 19 26	February 2 9 16 23	March 2 9 16 23	April 6 13 20 27	May 4 11
Process Planning, Routing, & Scheduling	▬				
Materials Procurement	▬▬▬	▬▬▬▬			
Parts Fabrication					
Part #1			▬▬▬▬		
Part #2			▬▬		
Part #3			▬▬		
Part #4			▬▬		
Part #5			▬▬▬▬		
Part #6			▬▬		
Part #7			▬▬▬		
Part #8		▬▬▬▬▬			
Part #9			▬▬		
Part #10				▬▬	
Subassemblies					
A				▬▬	
B				▬▬	
C					▬
D					▬
Final Assembly					▬

Source: Elwood S. Buffa, *Modern Production Management,* 3rd ed. (New York: John Wiley & Sons, 1969), 436.

Figure 5-6 A Fishbone Diagram

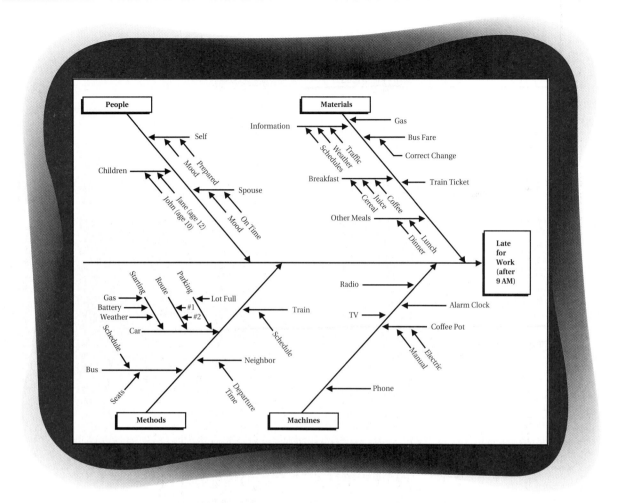

Source: M. Walton, *The Deming Management Method* (New York: Perigee Books, 1986).

normally involved. Then, compare your impression to the figure. Did you complete any steps out of sequence or leave any steps out?

run chart
A common TQM statistical tool that tracks trends.

One of the most common TQM statistical tools is a **run chart.** A run chart tracks trends. For example, the time it takes you to get to class could be tracked on a daily basis for a month (see Figure 5-8). You might determine from this charting that Mondays are particularly bad days in terms of timeliness. This analysis could lead you to look at Mondays in much more detail. In the workplace, supervisors employed by organizations practicing TQM collect information pertaining to any aspect of production or the provision of services.

Planning becomes meaningful only when it is translated into action. In turn, that action must be continuously monitored through the controlling process to ensure results obtained lead to achieving work team objectives. In the following chapter, we continue our study of the functions of supervision by examining how the effective supervisor organizes work.

Figure 5-7   A Flow Chart

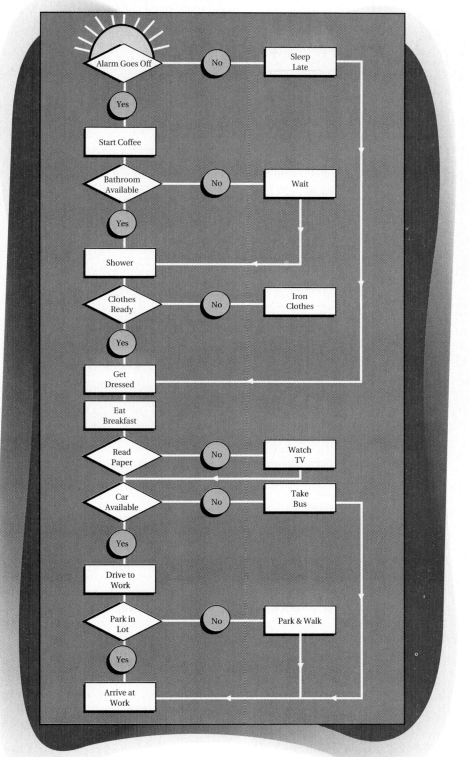

Source: M. Walton, *The Deming Management Method* (New York: Perigee Books, 1986).

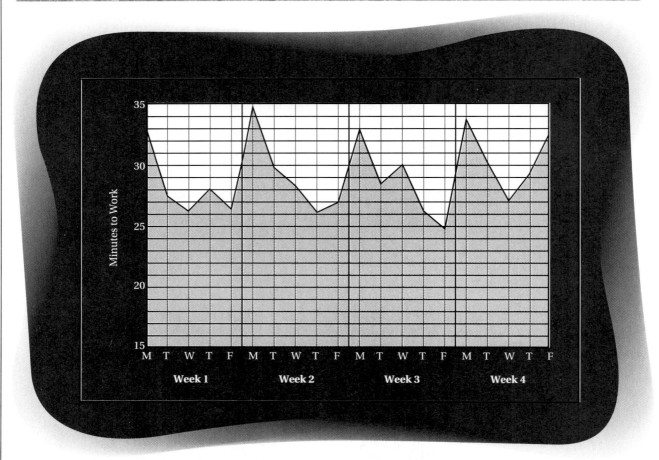

Figure 5-8 A Run Chart

Source: M. Walton, *The Deming Management Method* (New York: Perigee Books, 1986).

"Several times I have tried to put together plans, other than work schedules, and either haven't been able to carry them out because Larry, my boss, says we don't have time to try them or I'm just not that confident that they would work. Maybe I should come to you for advice, Henry," Carla related to the new supervisor. "I read an article about the planning process last night. It seems I really need to develop my planning skills if I'm ever to get another promotion in this company."

After Henry departed, Carla, with pencil in hand, began to prepare a list of specific things she could do to learn more about planning:

1. Bring the issue up in staff meetings and ask for explanations of unfamiliar terms.
2. Talk to other supervisors for their input. How do they go about planning?
3. Suggest to the company that training sessions on planning be offered.
4. Take a night course on planning at a local community college if one is offered.

"I need to do something, and now is the time to get started. What I need is a plan," Carla concluded.

Summary: Focus on Concepts

Planning is the process of determining objectives to be pursued and the activities necessary to achieve them. The end product of planning is a plan, a course of action designed to produce some specific result.

Planning is a dynamic activity. Although supervisors have planning responsibilities, they spend less time planning than do managers at higher organizational levels. Supervisors are more concerned with plans implemented within short periods such as one week or less in the future. Typically, their plans are oriented toward determining work assignments and schedules for their work teams.

Supervisors may work with plans previously developed by others, modify those plans, or develop entirely new ones. In each planning situation they need to acquire information about the work unit including its objectives, problems, and operational characteristics.

Senior managers are involved in what is called strategic planning, and supervisors typically are more concerned with tactical planning and control activities. Strategic planning is a continuous, interactive process aimed at keeping an organization as a whole appropriately matched to its environment. Tactical planning concentrates on implementing strategic plans and entails the implementation of current and short-term activities required to achieve the objectives of the strategic plan.

Two models assist the supervisor in analyzing the relative values of planning alternatives and determining the probability of plans' successful execution.

Important concepts in developing plans include establishing objectives and the application of policies, work rules, procedures, and performance standards.

An objective is any value a person, firm, or organization desires to acquire, and in the acquisition process, is willing and able to make the necessary sacrifice of time, money, or effort. A policy is a guideline governing the behavior of persons in an organization. Work rules are specific statements governing the behavior of employees on the job. A procedure is a specific method for performing a task or following a policy. Performance standards are management's expectations of what persons should do in their jobs and how well they should perform.

Systems and models are planning tools. A system is comprised of a flow of inputs, transformation processes, outputs, and feedback. Models are often used to describe the operations of systems.

Benchmarking is a part of Total Quality Management (TQM). It is the continuous process of measuring products, services, and practices against those of the toughest competitors or of companies recognized as industry leaders.

Reengineering involves redesigning (generally simplifying) the work tasks performed to conduct any organizational activities.

Controlling is the process of comparing results obtained to objectives and taking corrective action when deviation from the planned direction occurs. Financial controls include using budgets. Physical controls include application of Gantt project charts, fishbone diagrams, flow charts, and run charts.

Review Questions

1. Define the function of planning and explain why good planning is important.
2. What is the supervisor's traditional role in planning? For what periods of time does the supervisor usually plan?
3. Three types of planning situations confront supervisors when they are assigned to work teams. What are the three situations? What advice do you have for supervisors in each of the three?
4. Differentiate between strategic and tactical planning. Which of the two is the supervisor most concerned with?
5. Explain what a program is and give its characteristics.
6. State the criteria for determining the quantitative value of a given plan. What are the criteria for determining the probability of a plan's successful execution?

7. Define the terms *objectives* and *goals,* and list their major components.
8. It was suggested that objectives could be expressed several ways, including by time dimension, importance, and degree of specificity. Explain the meaning of each.
9. Why is attaining an objective considered a value exchange process?
10. Define the term *policy.* What are principles and rules? Why is it useful to include a principle as a part of a policy statement?
11. Define the term *work rules.* Indicate why we use them. Why is it not practical to transform work rules into policy statements?
12. What are procedures and how are they helpful to supervisors?
13. What are performance standards? Of what value are they to supervisors?
14. What is ISO 9000? Although the administering organization was established over 40 years ago, it is receiving attention today. Why is its virtue also considered its vice?
15. What is a system? How can supervisors utilize the systems concept? How do models apply to the concept of systems?
16. Define Management by Objectives (MBO) and explain how MBO operates successfully.
17. Explain the concepts of benchmarking and reengineering and how supervisors are affected by them.
18. Define *controlling.* What are its two major components?
19. Why do we utilize controls in organizations? What are the benefits of effective controls?
20. What is a budget? How are supervisors affected by the use of operating budgets?
21. Describe the application of Gantt project planning charts.
22. What is a fishbone chart? What is its purpose and how is it used? Give an example.
23. Prepare a flow chart.
24. Describe the use of a run chart.

Notes

1. S. C. Certo and J. P. Peter, *Strategic Management: A Focus on Process* (Homewood, IL: Austen Press, 1993), 5.
2. F. R. Davis, *Strategic Management,* 2d ed. (New York: Macmillan Publishing Company, 1993), 5.
3. P. C. Haas and W. B. Wemple, "Planning for a Change in Banking," *The Bankers Magazine,* November/December 1986, 55.
4. J. D. Hunger and T. L. Wheelen, *Strategic Management,* 4th ed. (Reading, MA: Addison-Wesley Publishing Company, 1993), 299.
5. L. E. Boone and D. L. Kurtz, *Contemporary Marketing,* 7th ed. (Fort Worth, TX: The Dryden Press, 1992), 119.
6. R. E. Brooker, Jr., "Orchestrating the Planning Process," *Journal of Business Strategy* 12 (July/August 1991): 4.
7. Thirty years ago, objectives were considered nonquantifiable and goals were expressed in quantitative terms. In most management literature today, it is just the opposite.
8. R. C. Davis, *The Fundamentals of Top Management* (New York: Harper and Brothers, 1951), 90–116.
9. Ibid, 172–201.
10. "The Hot New Seal of Quality," *Fortune,* June 28, 1993, 116–117.
11. An excellent discussion of the role expectations and performance standards of employees is found in M. H. Dunahee and L. A. Wangler, "The Psychological Contract: A Conceptual Structure for Management/Employee Relations," *Personnel Journal* 53 (July 1974): 518.
12. "The Hot New Seal of Quality."
13. H. Rothman, "You Need Not Be Big to Benchmark," *Nation's Business,* December 1992, 2.

14. "Reengineering: The Hot New Management Tool," *Fortune*, August 21, 1993, 41.

15. Also, see R. Cafasso, "Rethinking Re-engineering," *Computer World*, March 15, 1993, 102; M. Schwartz, "Re-engineering: The 90s Buzzword," *National Underwriters Life Health-Financial Services Edition*, October 5, 1992, 32.

16. Many writers include setting standards as the first step in controlling. We believe, however, that standards should be developed during the planning stage, not after the fact in controlling.

17. L. E. Boone and D. L. Kurtz, *Principles of Management* (New York: Random House, 1981), 282.

18. C. T. Horngren and G. L. Sundem, *Introduction to Management Accounting*, 7th ed. (Englewood Cliffs, NJ: Prentice-Hall, Inc., 1987), 154.

Group Ten

Josephine Brookshire, age 26, supervised a group of 10 bookkeeping and clerical workers in the accounting department of a large bank in Columbus, Ohio. She had recently replaced Gladys Goodman, who was promoted to an assistant cashier's job in another of the firm's banks. Gladys was well-liked, even admired, by her employees. They called themselves "Group Ten." On a scale of 1 to 10, they considered themselves to be 10s.

The overall work performance of the group was considered outstanding by both Gladys and higher bank management. In fact, she had recently received a commendation from the operations vice president. Because of their good work, Gladys reciprocated with small favors such as bending rules on the length of breaks, and if someone was a few minutes late in the morning or needed to leave a little early in the afternoon, she did not mind as long as the work was completed on time. Her management philosophy was to build teamwork and minimize the use of controls over workers. Because of this style, her employees were appreciative and loyal. They were also apprehensive when she left.

Josephine worked for the bank at a branch in another Ohio city. She had joined the bank three years earlier. Her work was always considered excellent. Therefore, when the vacancy developed in Columbus, she was offered the promotion and took the new job. By the time Josephine arrived, Gladys had already left. Whereas Gladys was flexible in applying work rules, the new supervisor advised her employees that they must be ready for work at the starting time of eight in the morning and that breaks must not exceed the allotted time of 15 minutes. When three workers showed up for work 15 minutes late, Josephine called all of the members of the group together, reviewed the rules, and informed them the next time this happened, they would be suspended for the rest of the day without pay.

On the following morning, all 10 employees reported for work one-half hour late. Subsequently, Josephine told each to leave for the remainder of the day. They were suspended without pay, she advised them, and they should plan to be at work on time tomorrow or more serious discipline faced them.

Soon after the last person departed, Josephine's manager came into her office and inquired, "Where are your folks?"

"I've sent them all home," Josephine replied. "I warned them to follow the rules but they did not obey me. I had to show them I was the boss."

"I guess you know we have a big problem," her superior commented with rising anger. "Who is going to do the records work today? In all of my years at this bank, this has got to be the dumbest thing I have ever seen."

During the next 12 months, both morale and productivity of the group declined precipitously. Most of the members either quit or transferred to other departments. The last to leave was Josephine Brookshire, who resigned one year to the day after assuming command of Group Ten.

Questions

1. What went wrong? Who is responsible for what occurred in Group Ten?

2. If you were Josephine, how would you have handled the situation upon assuming leadership of the group?

3. Does Josephine's boss have any responsibilities in this case? If so, what should her boss have done, and when?

4. The irony of the case is that one supervisor permitted employees to break rules and was rewarded while the other enforced work rules and was penalized. How do you explain this?

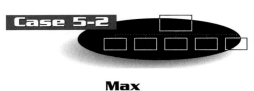

Case 5-2

Max

Not a doubt about it. Maximilian Q. Fisher was bright, bright as a summer day is long. A self-educated man, Max completed only his second year of high school before quitting and going to work at age 16 as a security person at a regional shopping mall. Too busy to get married or have a family, by the time Max was 20, he had organized his own security force business, Fisher Security, Inc., serving a variety of client firms within the metropolitan Chicago area. At age 28 he employed over 200 security personnel along with 4 assistants who supervised the others. In addition, Max had a bookkeeper.

The only records Max kept were those required by government and state agencies, primarily business statements for tax purposes, licensing and bonding documents, and payroll information. There were few policies, rules, or other guidelines for employees. Company policies and work rules were verbally communicated to his supervisors, who passed them on to the security personnel. No one in the organization was familiar with his short- or long-range goals or business plans.

During the past three years his business had grown rapidly, expanding geographically to the Minneapolis area to the north-west, Indianapolis to the east, and St. Louis to the south. While the majority of clients were large regional shopping centers, others included office buildings and factories. He had yet to incorporate. Max believed within the next three years the security force would grow to 500 members. Sometime during this period, he thought, he should incorporate the business. The majority of his employees were retired military personnel, mostly male, whose ages ranged from 42 to 55 years. Many were previously in the security branch of the armed forces.

Max personally interviewed each person he hired. His criteria for employment were few. An applicant had to be in good physical condition, have previous experience in security work, and pass a polygraph test. The four supervisors and Max were kept busy traveling to the various locations where Fisher Security operated. They not only visited each employee at least weekly, but they also were in frequent contact with client organizations. To date, the business was highly successful. Clients were satisfied with Fisher Security because they could depend upon the service it provided to be both effective and cost efficient. Labor turnover was low. Employees generally indicated satisfaction with their work. They considered Max and the supervisors as tough but fair bosses. The future looked bright, indeed, for both Max and Fisher Security.

On Memorial Day, 1994, Maximilian Q. Fisher died instantly in an automobile accident on the Chicago toll road north of O'Hare Airport.

Questions

1. Excluding the tragic accident, what are the values of planning in this type of organization?
2. Give examples of planning elements that would be appropriate for an overall comprehensive plan for this type of business. Namely, develop (a) objectives, (b) policies, (c) work rules, (d) procedures. Be as realistic as you can.
3. What are the values of having plans formalized, that is, in written (and available) form? Consider the potential outcomes to the organization as the result of Max Fisher's death.

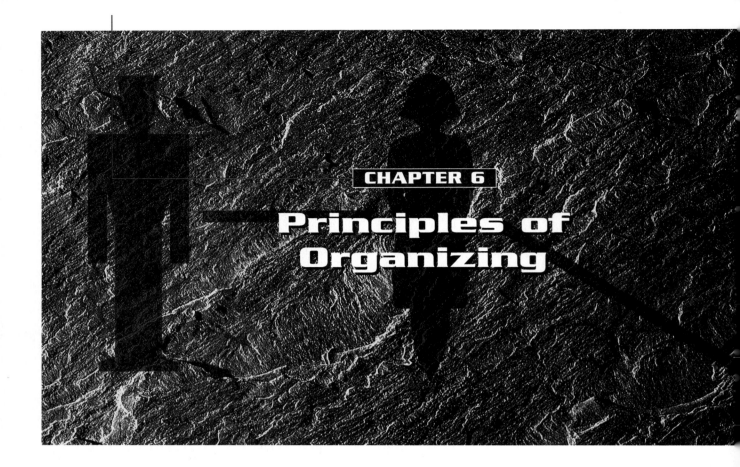

CHAPTER 6
Principles of Organizing

• The Spare Parts Principle: The accessibility, during recovery, of small parts which fall from the work bench, varies directly with the size of the part . . . and inversely with its importance to the completion of the work under way.[1]

LEARNING OBJECTIVES

1. Define the function of organizing and explain what kinds of work are involved in the organizing process.
2. Explain how work is organized through departmentation and indicate the several major types of organizational structures.
3. Describe the concept of team-based organizations and the characteristics of four types of teams.
4. Provide guidelines for the effective use of authority.
5. Indicate the meanings of line and staff functions.
6. Explain the following principles of organization: the parity principle, exception principle, scalar principle, unity of command, and span of supervision.
7. Define scheduling.
8. Explain the meaning of coordination and cite several guidelines for improving coordination.

Carla was sitting in her office, by herself. Overtime. Some workers love it, others hate it. The problem facing Carla was matching her employees' preferences and skills with organizational needs. In addition, she continuously faced the need to fill in for absent workers. Her boss, Larry, did not understand that she could not predict who would be ill with the flu, attending a funeral of a loved one, or had a date tonight. Several times a month, Carla had to perform the work of a missing employee. On more than one occasion her boss had known days in advance that overtime would be required, but told her only at the last minute. Frustrated, she reflected, "How can I ever plan a schedule and enjoy its implementation? It seems that the harder I try, at times, the poorer the results."

Organizing

Organizing is the function of creating the structure of working relationships, designing facility layouts, balancing workloads, and scheduling work to be performed. We have defined planning as determining objectives to attain and identifying the activities necessary to achieve those objectives. Organizing is putting the tasks that must be performed together in an orderly and structured whole. In this chapter we will discuss the basic principles of organizing. (In Chapter 18 we shall illustrate a number of ways by which you can improve upon the productive use of your time.)

organizing
The function of creating the structure of working relationships, designing facility layouts, balancing workloads, and scheduling work to be performed.

The organizing process, when properly carried out, contributes greatly toward increasing productivity and efficiency. When it is poorly performed, resources are wasted, deadlines are missed, sleep is lost, and performance appraisal ratings decline.

Although the emphasis in the following discussion is on organizing people and the work they perform, organizing also includes how resources such as equipment, raw materials, supplies, and work space are used.

Organizing is challenging work. In one sense, it is similar to assembling the pieces of a jigsaw puzzle. Only when the last piece is in place is the picture complete. Good organizers in our society are in both scarce supply and profound demand.

Organizing consists of several interrelated steps. The major activities performed and the sequence in which they occur are as follows:

1. Analyze the organization setting. What is the organization's culture? What resources are available? What is feasible?
2. Identify the types of work that have to be performed.
3. List the skills of each member of your work unit and consider the level of skill each member possesses.
4. Apply performance standards and standard times for tasks.
5. Divide the total amount of work to be performed into balanced jobs for individual workers.
6. Schedule work by determining when it will be performed.
7. Coordinate work with that of other units.

In addition to these activities, organizing involves acquiring the tools, equipment, machinery, materials, supplies, and working space required to complete tasks; delegating the necessary authority to members of your group so they can perform their jobs; and measuring the effectiveness of the organizing process, itself, as well as developing methods for identifying problems.

In the following pages, we consider how organizations are put together, that is, how people are organized and the types of organizational structures found in modern organizations, including team forms of organizing. Next, the subject of using authority intelligently is considered with an emphasis on the process of delegating authority. A discussion of line and staff relationships follows. The chapter concludes with a discussion of important supervisor responsibilities of scheduling work and coordinating the efforts of group members.

Organizational Structure

organizational structure
The configuration of interpersonal and authority relationships within a work unit and among other organizational work units.

Organizational structure is the configuration of interpersonal and authority relationships within a work unit. Organizational structure, in a broader sense, also includes relationships of work units with other organizational units. Initially, organizational structure is concerned with how work is organized. The list in Figure 6-1 indicates key factors and conditions affecting an organization's structure.

As organizations are created, decisions must be made about what goals to pursue, what work has to be performed, and who will perform that work. Authority relationships are established to maintain a coherence among personnel, minimize confusion, use resources intelligently, and concentrate everyone's atten-

| **Figure 6-1** | Factors and Conditions Affecting Organizational Structure |

1. Is there an up-to-date job description for each position in my department? Does it depict the actual work to be done?
2. Does each employee of my department report to and receive directions from only one supervisor?
3. Does each employee know specifically to whom he or she reports and is responsible?
4. Are personnel homogeneously assigned?
5. Are related operations and tasks grouped together?
6. Is authority delegated commensurate with responsibility?
7. Do I have more people reporting to me than I can effectively coordinate and direct?
8. Are responsibilities decentralized to the lowest possible level?
9. Is span of control considered for: (1) time, (2) distance, and (3) numbers?
10. Does each employee understand the organizational structure and the relationships of his or her particular segment to all parts of the organization?

Source: James E. Morgan, Jr., *Principles of Administrative and Supervisory Management* (Englewood Cliffs, NJ: Prentice-Hall, Inc., 1973), 183.

tion toward achieving the organization's objectives. This activity is called organization design.

Organization design is a process of determining the division of work and establishing the formal authority relationships among members of an organization. "The *design* or *structure* of an organization is the . . . set of formally defined working relationships among the members of an organization."[2] The perspectives of managers and supervisors about organization design are influenced by their positions within the management hierarchy. While the chief operating officer is making decisions affecting the entire organization, supervisors make decisions relating to their work teams.

organization design
A process of determining the division of work and establishing formal authority relationships among members of an organization.

The Departmentation Process

When the number of employees working within a typical firm and the great amount of work that is performed are considered, it makes sense to organize people and their work. In other words, the tasks that must be performed are arranged into individual jobs and persons performing those jobs are organized into work groups or teams. This is known as differentiation. **Differentiation** is the process of dividing the total amount of work that has to be performed into meaningful categories of tasks and workers.

differentiation
The process of dividing the total amount of work that has to be performed into meaningful categories of tasks and workers.

Departmentation. Differentiation, in turn, leads to departmentation. **Departmentation** is the process of creating organizational units of a manageable structure, composition of activities, and number of personnel.[3] Organizational units created by departmentation have various names. A few examples include branch, division, territory, squadron, department, product line, church diocese,

departmentation
The process of creating organizational units of a manageable structure, composition of activities, and number of personnel.

precinct, and team. Large units are divided into smaller ones. Thus, an army is divided into smaller units beginning with corps, divisions, regiments, battalions, companies, platoons, and ending with squads. A state government agency may consist of departments, divisions, bureaus, and sections. An educational institution such as a college may have schools divided further into departments.

Organization Charts. Departmentation is graphically pictured by creating an organization chart. An **organization chart** symbolically illustrates the organizational units and the formal authority relationships among personnel (see Figure 6-2). Such charts are useful in allowing you to visualize how functions and tasks are grouped. Furthermore, charts illustrate how the pieces fit together by designating the flow of formal authority. More elaborate charts present the management levels within organizations and the subordinates who report to each manager and supervisor.

organization chart
A symbolical illustration of organizational units and the formal authority relationships among personnel.

Note that charts are organizational maps. "A map is invaluable for finding towns and their connecting roads, but it tells us nothing about the economic and social relationships of the regions."[4] So, too, are organization charts. They are one method for understanding complex relationships and the general organization of work. Keep in mind, though, that they are limited. For example, organization charts do not indicate information about informal authority relationships. Furthermore, they lack information about communication networks, that is, the methods people follow in communicating with one another.

Types of Departmentation

The most common forms of departmentation are characterized by the presence of formal authority relationships in which employees know specifically to whom they report. The more conventional organizational structures include the functional structure and those organized by types of products, geographic areas, customers served, and process or equipment utilized.

functional structure
The most common form of organization structure, based upon similarity of related jobs grouped together into units reflecting these similarities.

Functional Structures. The most common type of organizational structure is the **functional structure.** When people have similar or related jobs, their work is organized into units reflecting these similarities. Functional structures are particularly suitable for smaller organizations, those operating in only one geographic area or under one roof, and where the firm has a single product line. Three major functions found in all types of businesses and many nonprofit organizations are production, marketing, and finance. Figure 6-2 is an example of a functional structure.

product organization structure
Shaped by the products or services produced, often used by firms having several types of products with different quality, image characteristics, or markets.

Product Organization Structures. The **product organization structure** is shaped by the products or services produced. It is often appropriate when a firm produces several types of products that have different quality, image characteristics, or markets. Thus, a company making products going to industrial markets, consumer goods markets, and the defense industries would organize using product divisions with different brand names, production technologies, and channels of distribution.

geographic organization structure
Organized by geographic territories, when facilities or markets are physically dispersed throughout the country or the entire world.

Geographic Organization Structures. In the **geographic organization structure,** territories are established and geographic areas serve as the basis for departmentation. This structure is commonly used when facilities are physically dispersed or when markets cover the entire country or the world. Frequently, larger

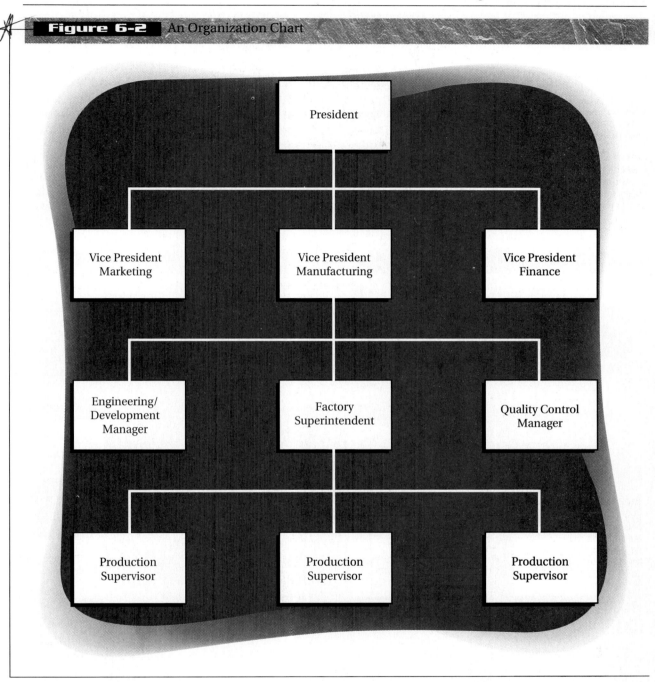

Figure 6-2 An Organization Chart

organizations are departmentized geographically in addition to employing other types of structures.

Customer Organization Structures. An organization that attempts to satisfy the needs and interests of different groups of customers or clients may use a **customer organization structure.** This structure is particularly applicable when the categories of customers have important differences in needs and are served more

customer organization structure
Satisfaction of different needs of specific customer groups determines the structure.

effectively or efficiently if separated into different groups. For example, a commercial bank may be organized into departments such as commercial accounts for business customers and personal accounts for consumers.

process or equipment organization structure
Organization is based upon the major processes or types of equipment used in making products.

Process or Equipment Organization Structures. Departmentation is based upon the major processes or types of equipment used in making products in the **process or equipment organization structure.** For example, a food processing plant could have separate departments for receiving produce, washing and grading, cooking and mixing ingredients, packaging, and shipping.

matrix structure
A mixture of the functional organization structure and project management.

Matrix Structures. The **matrix structure** (Figure 6-3) is a mixture of the functional organization structure and project management. The matrix structure has special applications to highly dynamic organizations in which technology is

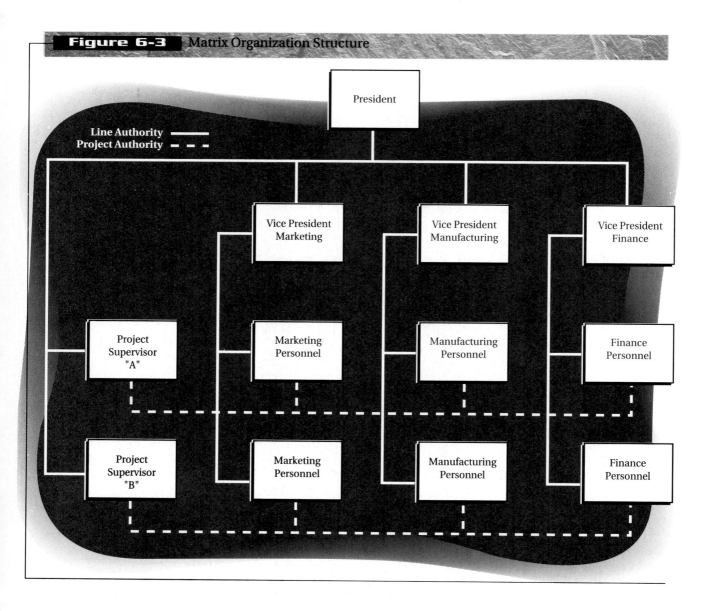

Figure 6-3 Matrix Organization Structure

rapidly changing, frequent and prompt communication is required, and the need to implement continuous changes calls for a maximum of flexibility.

A major value of matrix structure is the ability for vertical and horizontal communication among supervisors and other employees. As a result, a high degree of flexibility in interactions is possible. The vertical structure of the organization (solid line in Figure 6-3) reflects the traditional line authority exercised by the functional manager over subordinates. However, the matrix structure also has a horizontal flow of project authority (broken line in Figure 6-3). This horizontal flow violates several principles of organization to be covered shortly and increases the potential for conflict arising from subordinates and their supervisors having two bosses. Coordination and cooperation among supervisors and managers are therefore vital if the matrix form of structure is to be effective.

Team-Based Organizations

Are you going to supervise people making "Edsels or new car models? Typewriters or word processors? LP records or compact disks? Hoola Hoops or video games?"[5] Methods used for organizing and controlling in the past often are no longer suitable today. Traditional structures for organizations typically included departmental or functional designs. Yet, consider the contrast between working environments in the American culture of 30 years ago and those of today:[6]

30 Years Ago	Today
White male work force	Ethnically diverse male/female work force
Conformity	Multiple life styles
Blue collar	White collar
Manufacturing	Services
Domestic competition	International competition

Many organizations have experienced conditions in which employees lacked a work commitment and quality of production declined. In dealing with these issues, an increasing number of organizations have experimented with new forms of organizing work, including using teams.[7] (See Chapters 2 and 10 for additional information about work teams.)

A **team** consists of "two or more people who must coordinate their activities to accomplish a common goal."[8] A team is collaborative when members are empowered to exchange information and participate in decision making. Members share common goals, strive to achieve a high level of coordination, and often are self-directed. Several types of teams exist, determined in large part by the degree of autonomy the team possesses, as illustrated in Figure 6-4.[9] **Suggestion teams** have low team autonomy. Some are tasked to focus on a single issue and have a temporary life, others are ongoing. Usually, suggestion teams have little authority for making or implementing decisions. Rather, they make recommendations.

team
Consists of two or more people who must coordinate their activities to accomplish a common goal; empowered to exchange information and participate in decision making.

suggestion teams
Having low team autonomy with little authority for making or implementing decisions, they make only recommendations.

Teamwork in the
Information Age.

**problem-solving
teams**
Having no decision
making authority and
serving in a fact-finding or
advisory capacity, they
concentrate on finding
solutions to work-related
problems.

task force
Serving in a fact-finding
or advisory capacity, a
team of management and
nonmanagement
personnel who have been
assigned to a specific
problem or issue.

quality circle
A relatively small team of
workers who meet
periodically to find ways
to improve quality of work
processes.

Problem-solving teams concentrate on finding solutions to work-related problems. Usually such teams consist of a supervisor with five, and as many as eight, employees having common interests in the problem areas. Task forces and quality circles are examples of problem-solving teams. A **task force** is a team of management and nonmanagement personnel who have been assigned to a specific problem or issue. They usually do not have decision-making authority but rather serve in a fact-finding or advisory capacity. A task force may consist of cross-functional and multilevel participants. Often, their output is in the form of recommendations.[10] A **quality circle** is a small team of workers who meet periodically to find ways to improve quality of work processes.[11] (See Chapter 2 for additional information on quality circles.)

Figure 6-4	Team Autonomy

Low Autonomy◄─────────────────────────────────►High Autonomy

Suggestion Teams	**Problem-Solving Teams**	**Semiautonomous Teams**	**Self-managing Teams**
Advisory committees Suggestion teams	Quality circles Interfunctional teams Total system task forces	Business unit teams Work unit teams	Business unit teams Autonomous work teams

Source: James H. Shonk, *Team-Based Organization: Developing a Successful Team Environment* (Homewood, IL: Business One Irwin, 1992), 27.

Semiautonomous teams, headed by a supervisor, are extensively involved in their day-to-day work team activities through performance of the functions of planning, organizing, and controlling. Semiautonomous teams participate in formulating goals of their work units, provide information for team plans, identify and make recommendations to solve problems, and make substantial contributions by either providing information or by making operating decisions.

Self-managing teams manage their own work. Their activities include[12]

- Team goal setting, based upon organization goals, or having considerable input to team goals
- Planning how goals will be accomplished
- Identifying and solving problems within the work area
- Making daily operating decisions within their defined level of authority
- Recommending solutions to external problems—that is, problems caused by factors or influences outside the team's control and affecting the team's performance
- Scheduling work
- Hiring team members[13]

The self-managed team form of organization permits teams to operate the daily activities of their units. Supervisors function as facilitators for the members by acquiring needed resources and providing general directions.

Using Authority Effectively

As management determines how the total work of an organization will be divided into individual units, it is also sorting out the necessary authority relationships. **Authority** is the right or power to command performance, require obedience, or make decisions. (See Chapter 7 for additional information about authority.)

The degree of authority supervisors possess is governed by the amount of influence they have acquired either through their position within an organization or through their recognized leadership skills. **Influence** is the ability to affect the thoughts and behavior of others. It often consists of an indirect or intangible ability. To illustrate, you may consider someone you know to have great influence, yet find it difficult to identify the single cause of that influence.

Rensis Likert has determined that the degree of influence supervisors have with their superiors will, in turn, largely determine the results those supervisors will obtain from their subordinates. He states:

> To function effectively, a supervisor must have sufficient influence with his own superior to be able to affect the superior's decisions when required. Subordinates expect their supervisors to be able to exercise influence upward in dealing with problems on the job and handling problems which affect them and their well-being.[14]

Delegating Authority

Delegation is a process of transferring authority from a member of management at a higher level to a person at a lower organizational level. Positional or formal

semiautonomous teams
Led by a supervisor and extensively involved in day-to-day work team activities, they perform the functions of planning, organizing, and controlling and may participate in setting goals for their work units along with providing information or making operating decisions.

self-managing teams
Well-trained and informed individuals working together as a group who manage their own work by setting goals, planning how goals will be accomplished, solving problems, making daily operating decisions, scheduling work, and hiring team members.

authority
The right or power to command performance, require obedience, or make decisions.

influence
The ability to affect the thoughts and behavior of others.

delegation
A process of transferring authority from a member of management at a higher level to a person at a lower organizational level.

authority is always delegated downward. When relatively large amounts of authority are delegated, authority is decentralized. Conditions supporting decentralization include availability of personnel trained to make decisions, a need to make decisions quickly, risks that are relatively small, and potential losses that are containable if realized. When these conditions are reversed—when a high degree of uniformity is required in making decisions and risks are very large—then centralization of authority is favored.

Guidelines for Delegation

Delegation allows the more routine decisions to be made at the lowest organizational levels. By delegating to their subordinates, supervisors can concentrate their time on more important activities. Still, in some organizations, the "dirty hands" syndrome prevails:

dirty hands syndrome
The belief of some higher level managers that supervisors should regularly participate in nonmanagement tasks.

> Anyone who has worked in industry or business for any length of time has probably heard some executive say, 'I want a supervisor or manager who is not afraid to get his hands dirty.' The statement is typical of executives afflicted with the **dirty hands syndrome,** and reflects the misguided belief that managers should regularly participate in nonmanagement tasks.[15]

Although there may be highly justifiable reasons for not delegating, sometimes a refusal to delegate is a sign of more serious problems residing either with the supervisor or within the work team. Common reasons for not delegating include a lack of confidence in the abilities of subordinates, a belief that the job is done better by the supervisor, fear of antagonizing employees with additional work, and the enjoyment of performing nonmanagement work rather than supervising.[16] Some supervisors believe that delegation jeopardizes their jobs. In other words, they believe that if they delegate they are giving up their authority or they will lose control of their employees. If they are correct in these assumptions, they do have problems, but delegation is not the cause of these problems, only the symptom.

As general rules, the following observations about delegation are warranted: First, responsibility for results of actions taken by a manager's subordinates cannot be delegated to those subordinates. The manager cannot "pass the buck" for actions taken in the name of his or her general area of responsibility to those below. Second, making "everyone" responsible for a particular job means that no one is responsible. Hence, attempting to share responsibility is a bad practice in general.[17]

Alice Rowe suggests the following actions in effective delegation: First, communicate to the employee how much responsibility is being given to him or her. Second, tell the employee how much discretion is allowable without prior consultation with the supervisor. Third, establish the time frame for task completion. Finally, plan to follow up to ensure the action has been taken and measure its success. If successful, consider praising the employee.[18]

Line and Staff Relationships

Another dimension of authority relationships exists between line and staff organization functions. Every organization has a line function. Many also have staff functions. The **line organization** creates products or services that are sold or distributed to customers or clients. The **staff organization** assists the line and other staff units by providing specialized services, expertise, or control over activities when the staff possesses functional authority. Figure 6-5 is an example of an organization consisting of both line and staff units. The most reliable method for determining whether an employee belongs to the line or staff organization is to analyze the employee's job. Line personnel directly contribute to creation or marketing of an organization's products. Staff personnel, on the other hand, provide advice. Even experts occasionally have difficulty differentiating between line and staff jobs.

One additional meaning given to line authority should be mentioned. All supervisors, whether line or staff, possess line authority over the employees they supervise. The supervisor has positional authority, the authority of command.

line organization
Creates products or services that are sold or distributed to customers or clients.

staff organization
Assists the line and other staff units by providing specialized services, expertise, or control over activities when the staff possesses functional authority.

Figure 6-5 A Line and Staff Organization Structure

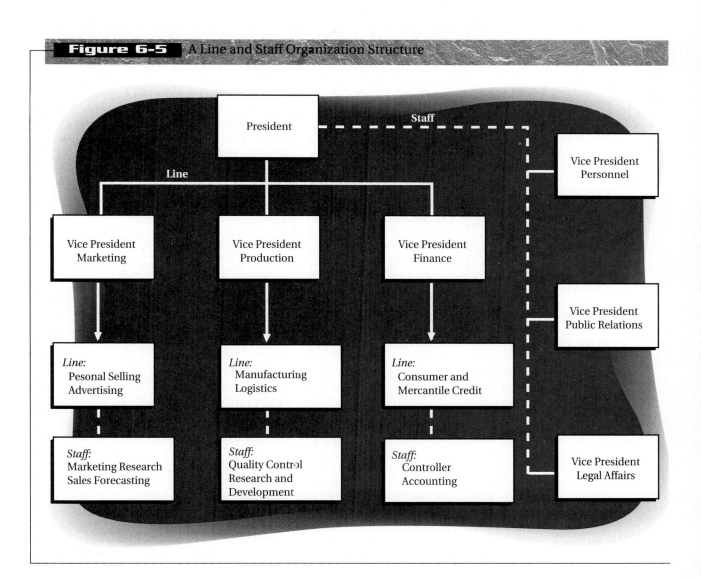

Years ago, staffs served primarily in an advisory capacity to line and other staff units. Excluding functional authority, the line organization could perform the work handled by staffs. Then why do organizations have staffs? Primarily, staffs are justified when they perform activities more effectively and efficiently than the line. For example, where the volume of work is large, specialization occurs along with economies of scale. Consequently, a professional staff of human resources technicians may perform most of the recruitment and selection activities in acquiring new employees rather than having each manager and supervisor perform these tasks. The organization should benefit in the long run by obtaining more qualified employees at a lower cost.

More recently, in larger organizations, several types of staffs possessing functional authority have been created to add a dimension of control. While some staffs with functional authority have existed for many years, others are relatively modern in origin. For example, the following staffs commonly have functional authority today:

- *Accounting and finance staff.* This staff maintains responsibilities for budget oversight, prepares tax information and reports for government agencies, and authorizes expenditures made by supervisors and managers.
- *Legal staff.* The legal staff prepares and monitors contracts to ensure compliance and periodically reviews the legal consequences of proposed decisions.
- *Human resources staff.* The human resources or industrial relations staff has authority in the areas of labor relations including contract negotiations, contract maintenance, and day-to-day contract interpretations with unions. Human resources also enforces federal and state laws pertaining to equal employment opportunities, monitors worker safety and health, and internally enforces other federal and state regulations pertaining to labor.
- *Quality assurance staff.* The quality assurance staff maintains control over product quality through a variety of inspection, sampling, and testing activities. This unit may have the authority to halt production when tolerances or production standards are not maintained.

Principles of Organization

From the preceding discussion about organizing, organizational structures, authority relationships, and line and staff relationships, several principles of organization can be developed to guide supervisors in making decisions. These principles include the parity principle, exception principle, scalar principle and unity of command, and principles regarding the span of supervision.

The Parity Principle

parity principle
The amount of formal authority should be commensurate with the amount of responsibility a supervisor possesses.

A dilemma that supervisors may encounter is an imbalance between their responsibilities and the amount of authority they possess, with their responsibilities exceeding their authority. The **parity principle** states that the amount of formal authority should be commensurate with the amount of responsibility a supervisor possesses. In other words, an employee's power to act (authority) should equal his or her obligation to act or perform (responsibility). To illustrate the need for this principle, envision a situation in which you are responsible for another person, but do not have the authority to discipline or otherwise compel that person to act.

Problems arise when responsibilities exceed the authority given to achieve the desired results. For example, a supervisor may be responsible for achieving production objectives while two vacancies exist in the work team that management is unwilling to fill.

The "authority gap" problem often is less acute in smaller organizations, but in larger ones, "the lines of responsibility and authority often become unclear."[19] As a general rule, the following observation is warranted: "An individual should not be held responsible for a particular action unless he or she has the authority to carry out the action."[20]

The Exception Principle

Policies, work rules, and procedures facilitate the delegation of authority when the exception principle is applied. The **exception principle** states that only exceptions to policies, rules, and procedures must be referred to higher management for action. Thus, a supervisor is delegated authority to handle a variety of decisions. When decisions are required outside of the guidelines and scope of authority possessed by the supervisor, such decisions are referred to the supervisor's boss or higher management. For example, a consumer loan officer in a credit union may be authorized to make loans up to $5,000 but must refer all requests exceeding this amount to the loan committee.

exception principle
Only exceptions to policies, rules, and procedures must be referred to higher management for action.

The Scalar Principle and Unity of Command

The **scalar principle** states that there is a chain of command within an organization and authority flows from the top of the management hierarchy to the bottom. When this principle is observed, lines of authority are more clearly defined.

Unity of command is a relationship established in organizations in which members know to whom they are accountable. Originally the concept implied that every person had only one supervisor and accountability was required only to that individual. However, over the years, the concept has been modified with the growth of staffs holding functional authority and the realization that many employees, by organizational necessity, work for two or more superiors.

Ideally, each employee should have just one boss. However, in some instances they have more than one. For example, in the field of public accounting, accountants may work for and be appraised by several senior managers or partners. Or a secretary may be accountable to several superiors. Problems can arise, though, when the secretary's bosses simultaneously make requests that their work be performed first. Another problem arises when these bosses give conflicting orders. The simplest solution to these problems is for one of the supervisors to be designated the primary boss to whom the employee is ultimately responsible.

Organizations can apply the scalar principle and unity of command to assist in building and maintaining good working relationships among supervisors and their employees. The benefits include more effective communication, improved coordination, less conflict, and a more orderly execution of orders. The scalar principle, furthermore, provides a blueprint guiding the flow of authority and directing the communication process. The concept is applicable to organizations of various types and sizes and is not limited to large ones.

scalar principle
There is a chain of command within an organization and authority flows from the top of the management hierarchy to the bottom.

unity of command
A relationship established in organizations in which members know to whom they are accountable.

Although the capacity for maintaining control is one goal of the exception principle, delegation must be made with a realistic assessment of the situation. For example, Edward Teller, "father of the H-bomb," during a lecture, presented a scenario of Earth's colonization of a planet 40 light years away, perhaps in the year 2200.

Earth reserved the right to render certain decisions and others were within the scope of the colonists. Eventually, a problem developed at the new colony and a message was transmitted to Earth calling for a decision because the colonists lacked the authority to make it.

It was Teller's belief that the settlers, needing an answer, would not be able to wait 80 or more years for the message to return from Earth, but would opt for self-administration with local decision making thereafter.[21]

There are limits to applying the exception principle as this example illustrates. The inability to control events must be considered in delegating authority.

To illustrate, when employees bypass the chain of command, problems occur. In these instances, subordinates go around their bosses to contact others in higher management. While there are certainly circumstances that may justify the practice—such as a very ineffective or unfair boss, or a superior engaged in unethical or illegal activities—the practice is usually counterproductive. An employee who circumvents the chain of command reduces the effectiveness of the working relationship with his or her boss. Future communication is impaired and trust is reduced.

Managers should not apply the scalar principle and unity of command based upon rigid rules. Rather, they may need to modify the rules periodically to reflect their organizations' unique situations. What is correct, obviously, is what works best, regardless of theory.

Span of Supervision

span of supervision
The total number of people for whom a supervisor is responsible; the ideal span is the number that can be supervised effectively.

Span of supervision (or span of control) is the total number of people for whom a supervisor is responsible. An ideal span is the number that can be supervised effectively. How many people should a supervisor oversee? Spans vary in size from only one or two people to as many as 100. An Air Force missile capsule commander supervises one person, the deputy commander. Meanwhile at Lincoln Electric Company in Cleveland, a supervisor routinely oversees up to 100 workers. The number of people who can be supervised effectively is influenced by the following factors and conditions:

- *The amount of time available for supervising others.* A supervisor who has other tasks in addition to supervision cannot spend as much time in overseeing a work team as those with full-time supervisory responsibilities. Thus, the span would be smaller.
- *Physical concentration of employees and place of work.* The span of supervision can be increased when employees work in the same general physical area. If employees are dispersed, the span would be smaller because more time is consumed in traveling to various work sites.
- *Competency and skills of the supervisor and employees.* As a general rule, the greater the skills of both the supervisor and workers, the broader the span of supervision. Thus, a convincing argument exists for sufficiently training employees and their supervisors: The better the training, the broader the span of supervision.

4 ■ *Similarity of work performed by employees.* The more similar the tasks are among members of a work team, the broader the span of supervision. The reverse is also true. If tasks performed are substantially different among employees, more time is consumed giving instructions and reviewing work for each member of the group.

5 ■ *The amount of formality in the organization.* Formality includes the number of policies, rules, standards, and procedures. The more numerous and specific they are, the greater the degree of formalization. Up to some point, greater formality permits broader spans of supervision since employees have a greater understanding of what they should be doing.

6 ■ *Predictability of the future and risk containment.* A supervisor should be capable of handling more employees when an organization's operations are stable, accurate prediction of the future is possible, and risks accompanying potential losses are known.

7 ■ *Interrelationships with other units.* Spans of supervision tend to be related to the degree of task interdependency between a supervisor's work team and other organizational units. The more interdependency, the smaller the span. Where there are numerous interactions with other departments and personnel, a supervisor necessarily devotes more time to planning and coordinating.

We have considered the process of creating organizational structures, the application of authority, line and staff relationships, and several principles of organization. Next, we turn to a major area of importance for many supervisors, namely, how to go about scheduling and coordinating the activities of a work unit.

Scheduling

Scheduling is the process of specifying the activities of a plan, the sequence for performing these activities, the time frames for completion of each phase of work, and a deadline for accomplishment of the plan. The formal result of scheduling is a **schedule,** that is, a plan specifying the sequence of work to be performed.

Several conditions or factors influence the scheduling process. Key factors include deadlines, availability of resources, and the logical development of products or stages of work.

Many, if not most, supervisors continuously face deadlines for completing work assignments. One method for handling the work is to complete each project before beginning the next. Frequently, though, this method is impractical or inefficient because some personnel or equipment are idle while awaiting the next project. Another method of scheduling is to undertake several projects simultaneously, although each is in a different stage of completion.

Scheduling is also affected by the availability of resources. There are limits to personnel, machinery, equipment, personal computers, and available space.

Finally, the nature of the work process influences the stages of production. Some activities must be performed sequentially because completion of one stage depends upon completion of the previous ones.

scheduling
The process of specifying the activities of a plan, the sequence for performing these activities, the time frames for completion of each phase of work, and a deadline for accomplishment of the plan.

schedule
A plan specifying the sequence of work to be performed.

Coordination

coordination
A condition wherein harmonious actions result from individual and group efforts.

Coordination is a condition wherein harmonious actions result from individual and group efforts. In other words, the results obtained are appropriate or pleasing. "To coordinate is to develop unity of action in common purposes."[22] Coordination does not mean the same thing as cooperation. Cooperation implies persons working to achieve a common goal. A cooperative attitude does not guarantee the actions taken will be coordinated. Although cooperation is helpful in attaining coordination, and the absence of cooperation reduces the probability of achieving coordination, other factors also affect coordination.

First, coordination is not a fixed entity that either does or does not exist. Rather, it varies in degrees. Second, a united work effort reflects integration and orderliness. Poor coordination is exemplified by confusion. Third, in coordinated work the efforts of individuals are harmoniously integrated and the timing of activities varies by individual circumstances.[23]

Several guidelines for improving coordination are as follows:[24]

- *Coordination starts in the planning process.* Chances are greater that you will obtain the desired results if the people affected by your actions participate in the planning phase. Not only will they be better informed about what is going on, but they also will have the opportunity to share information that may be useful in developing the plan. Questions such as "Who does what?" and "When do we do it?" can be answered in the planning stage.
- *Focus on organizational and work unit objectives.* Each member of the supervisor's group should understand the objectives of the organization and the work unit, as well as how the unit's goals are integrated into the organization's. This is important for understanding the interrelationships of each person's job. It is not uncommon in organizations for individuals and groups to consider their work more important than that of others. Consequently, the lack of team effort reduces effectiveness.
- *Develop a cooperative attitude.* Cooperation is a genuine willingness of people to help one another. Persons displaying a cooperative attitude have assumed a secondary responsibility for the well-being of others. David Schwartz observed:

Unfortunately, in all organizations there are examples —some very obvious—of individuals who do not project a cooperative attitude. Jealousy, pettiness, bickering, and other examples of psychological sabotage within organizations are very common.[25]

Schwartz continues with several examples of psychological sabotage:

Secretary:	"She didn't help me when we had that big project last month, so why should I help her?"
Production foreman:	"I'm not going to hurry up production. That customer can wait another ten days."
Senior executive:	"Clark [another senior executive] embarrassed me badly last week at the meeting. I'll figure out a way to put a hold on his budget request."[26]

Although we may be unable to mandate cooperative attitudes, we can provide examples to our employees of shared mutual interests. Psychological sabotage rebounds detrimentally against its originator. Logic suggests that self-interest is fostered, in the long run, through cooperation.

- *Communicate frequently and clearly.* Effective communication is directed to the appropriate persons in understandable language and in a timely manner, that is, before the event occurs to which the information is related.

Good coordination is not a substitute for good plans and well-trained personnel. It complements them. It must be very discouraging to individuals who have failed to achieve substantive objectives because of coordination problems. In the 1972 Olympics, for example, two American track athletes who were expected to win gold and silver medals missed their race because they were inadvertently given the wrong starting time. How many years of preparation were wasted by this lack of coordination?

You probably have experienced the pleasure of participating in or viewing well-coordinated activities at work, in school, or during athletic contests or concerts. Everything was "right." Harmony pervaded the activities, and the results were spectacular. Not only did the participants achieve their goals, but they probably immensely enjoyed what they were doing. They knew they were successful.

There's an underlying reason why good organizing and coordination are so satisfying. As a supervisor, you are complimenting others when you organize and coordinate intelligently. The message you are sending is, "I think you are important. I am not going to waste your skills. Rather, let's obtain the most we can from them."

In the following chapter, we show how to apply the principles of effective leadership to enhance the successful application of the functions of planning and organizing.

Still sitting in her office, alone and thinking about the day's events, Carla continued to reflect about organizing and scheduling work for members of her team. Remembering a joke she had heard a trainer tell at a seminar—"Fix what you can fix and delegate what you can't fix to someone else"—she began to realize organizing and scheduling problems were caused by several parties. "Until now, I have been blaming myself. I need to get more people involved. My workers need to assume more responsibility and so do other folks including my boss, Larry."

After pouring another cup of coffee, Carla returned to the subject. "Empowerment is a big issue today. Maybe one of the ways I can develop better schedules is to have my workers participate in developing them. It is going to be harder to change Larry's behavior. Still, I can keep reminding him to let me know about overtime that is coming up. When my unit looks good, he does too."

Summary: Focus on Concepts

Organizing is the function of creating the structure of working relationships, designing facility layouts, balancing workloads, and scheduling work to be performed. Organizing involves arranging resources systematically to obtain maximum benefits from them.

Organizational structure is the configuration of interpersonal and authority relationships within a work unit. It also includes relationships of work units with other organizational units.

Organization design is a process for determining the division of work and establishing the formal authority relationships among members of an organization. The design is a set of formally defined working relationships among the members of an organization.

Differentiation is the process of dividing the total amount of work to be performed into meaningful categories of tasks and workers. Differentiation leads to departmentation, the process of creating manageably structured organizational units.

Departmentation is graphically pictured in an organization chart. Organization charts symbolically illustrate the organizational units and the formal authority relationships among personnel.

The most common forms of departmentation are characterized by formal authority relationships in which employees know specifically to whom they report. The more common types of organization structure are determined by functions performed, products produced, geographic areas of operations, customers served, and processes or equipment used.

A matrix structure is a mixture of the functional organization structure and project management. This structure is most commonly found in organizations that need to make rapid changes in operations, communicate quickly, and have resources available rapidly without lengthy consultations with members of higher management.

A newer form of organization is one based on teams. A team consists of two or more people who coordinate their activities to accomplish a common goal. There are several types of teams, largely based upon the degree of autonomy the team possesses, including suggestion teams, problem-solving teams, semiautonomous teams, and self-managing teams.

Authority is the right or power to command performance, require obedience, or make decisions. The degree of authority supervisors possess is governed by the amount of influence and power they have acquired either because of their position within an organization or because of their recognized leadership. Influence is the capacity to affect the thoughts and behavior of others.

Every organization has a line function. Many also have staff functions. The line organization creates products or services that are sold or distributed to customers or clients. The staff organization assists the line and other staff units by providing specialized services, expertise, or control over line and staff activities.

Several principles of organization affect the supervisor's operations. The parity principle states that the amount of formal authority a supervisor has should be commensurate with his or her responsibility. The exception principle states that only exceptions to policies, rules, and procedures must be referred to higher management for action. The scalar principle states that there is a chain of command within an organization and authority flows from the top of the management hierarchy to the bottom. Unity of command is a relationship established in organizations in which members know to whom they are accountable. Span of supervision is the total number of people a supervisor is responsible for or manages. The ideal span is the number that can be supervised effectively.

Supervisors are often responsible for scheduling and coordinating the activities of their work teams. Scheduling is the process of specifying the activities of a plan, the sequence for performing tasks, the time frames for completion of each phase of work, and a deadline for accomplishment of the plan. The formal result of scheduling is a schedule.

Coordination is a condition wherein harmonious actions result from individual and work team efforts. For effective coordination, start coordination in the planning process, focus on organizational and work unit objectives, develop a cooperative attitude, and communicate frequently and clearly.

Review Questions

1. What is organizing? What are the steps or activities performed in the organizing process?
2. What is an organizational structure? Organization design?
3. Explain the meanings of differentiation and departmentation.
4. How can departmentation be graphically illustrated?

5. Indicate the uses and limitations of organization charts.

6. Describe the structures of functional, product, geographic, customer, process or equipment, and matrix organizations.

7. What is a team-based form of organization? Why are they growing in importance today?

8. Cite the four types of team-based organizations as based upon the degree of autonomy present in the work situation.

9. What is authority? Indicate the conditions supporting decentralization of authority.

10. Indicate the guidelines for delegating authority.

11. Define and differentiate between line and staff organizations. Why do organizations have staffs? Give examples of line and staff activities.

12. Explain each of the following organization principles: parity principle, exception principle, scalar principle, unity of command, and span of supervision.

13. Comment on the following statement. "The ideal span of supervision is 10 employees." What factors and conditions determine the span of supervision?

14. What is scheduling? A schedule?

15. Define the concept of coordination. Does it mean the same thing as cooperation?

16. Give guidelines for improving coordination.

Notes

1. B. Weisz, *The Philosophy Memos* (Schaumburg, IL: Motorola University Press, 1993), 28.

2. R. Albanese, *Managing: Toward Accountability for Performance,* 3d ed. (Homewood, IL: Richard D. Irwin, 1981), 558.

3. Ibid., 564.

4. H. Mintzberg, *The Structuring of Organizations* (Englewood Cliffs, NJ: Prentice-Hall, 1979), 37.

5. P. M. Van Auken, "Control vs. Development: Up-to-Date or Out-of-Date as a Supervisor?" *Supervision* 53 (December 1992): 17.

6. Ibid.

7. J. H. Shonk, *Team-Based Organizations* (Homewood, IL: Business One Irwin, 1992), vii.

8. M. Plovnick, R. Fry, and I. Rubin, "New Developments in O.D. Technology: Programmed Team Development," *Training and Development Journal,* April 4, 1975.

9. The discussion is based on Shonk, *Team-Based Organizations,* 27.

10. R. Kreitner, *Management,* 5th ed. (Boston, MA: Houghton Mifflin Company, 1992), 365.

11. Ibid., 404.

12. Shonk, *Team-Based Organizations,* 29.

13. For additional information about team building and the operations of teams see G. E. Huszczo, "Training for Team Building," *Training and Development Journal* 44 (February 1990): 37–45; E. A. Kazemek, "Ten Criteria for Effective Team Building," *Healthcare Financial Management* 45 (September 1991): 15; R. S. Wellins, "Building a Self-Directed Work Team," *Training and Development Journal* 46 (December 1992): 24–28; and K. Matthes, "Team Building: Help Employees Change from Me to We," *HR Focus* 69 (September 1992): 6.

14. R. Likert, *New Patterns of Management* (New York: McGraw-Hill, 1961), 94.

15. E. R. Archer, "Delegation and the 'Dirty Hands Syndrome.'" *Supervisory Management* 22 (November 1977): 31.

16. Ibid., 32.

17. D. A. Tansik and others, *Management: A Life Cycle Approach* (Homewood, IL: Richard D. Irwin, 1980), 87.

18. See A. Row, Row and Associates, uncirculated paper (Everett: Row and Associates, 1993), 2.

19. Tansik, *Management: A Life Cycle Approach,* 87.

20. Ibid.

21. Lecture by Edward Teller, Texas A&M University, 1958.
22. D. E. McFarland, *Management: Foundations and Practices*, 5th ed. (New York: Macmillan Publishing Co., 1979), 186.
23. Ibid.
24. D. Schwartz, *Introduction to Management: Principles, Practices, and Processes* (New York: Harcourt Brace Jovanovich, 1980), 223.
25. Ibid., 225.
26. Ibid., 226.

Case 6-1

Tootsie, Tootsie, Bye-Bye

"I wish you wouldn't call me that!" Carl Jenkins emphatically exclaimed to his coworker, Denise Nakamura. "Tootsie may be a humorous endearment and you are just kidding, but my workers have picked up on it and are now starting to call me Tootsie. Like Rodney Dangerfield, I'll get no respect around here."

Carl and Denise were supervisors of the day-shift nurses at Cleveland Memorial Hospital. Carl was in a field that was nontraditional for men. He had begun his nursing career ten years earlier, after his graduation from Cuyahoga Community College and certification as a Registered Nurse. Carl supervised 24 RN's and was in "perpetual motion." Thus, the comment "Tootsie, tootsie, bye-bye," was often made as he whizzed from one area to another.

Denise, on the other hand, was relatively new to Cleveland, arriving from Detroit the previous year. She managed an even dozen nurses. With the exception of Carl, all of the RNs at Cleveland Memorial were women. Both supervisors were well-received by their employees, although Carl's nurses found it difficult to stop him long enough for any conversations other than those pertaining to the immediate health care of patients. Denise was in charge of nurses in the recovery room and intensive care unit, and Carl was responsible for most other nursing specialties including surgery, obstetrics, pediatrics, internal medicine, and the emergency room.

"My major worry," Carl continued, changing the subject, "is that I can't keep on top of everything my nurses are doing—or should be doing. Most of them, at least three-fourths, are experienced and know the ropes. It is the other quarter that concerns me. Some are fresh out of school and have almost no experience other than their practicums. We can't just turn them loose without checking all of their procedures until we know how they will handle situations, especially the emergencies that always seem to occur when you least expect them."

"Why don't you talk to the hospital administrator and see if she can't split your group and maybe give me several," Denise commented. "I think the emergency room nurses belong in my area anyway." Denise thought to herself that Carl was the major source of his own problem. He equated the number of nurses he supervised with power and his concept of self-importance.

"We've been through this before," Carl responded. "I don't mind the number of nurses, just getting ones that are inexperienced and having to spend the time in training and familiarizing them with our routines. If they assigned me people who knew what was going on, I'd have no problems. Besides, I don't even get to interview the new nurses. The administrator hires them and then assigns them to me. Consequently, I'm stuck sometimes and can't do anything about it."

Questions

1. What do you consider the most relevant issues in this case? In addition to identifying the problems, rank them in importance.
2. Look at the possible motives Carl and Denise have in the span of supervision each maintains. What are the implications you draw?
3. How would you determine the optimum span for each?
4. What changes, if any, do you recommend? Why?

Case 6-2

Peaches, Inc.

Line authority tends to be absolute unless restricted by functional authority, but staff authority typically is advisory: The person receiving staff advice can take it or leave it. Because of this, conflicts do occur between line and staff personnel, especially when staff employees are perceived as overstepping the boundaries of their authority.

Martin Mobry returned to his office after a very frank discussion with his boss about the relationships of his unit with others at Peaches, Inc., a manufacturer of software used by cities and counties for planning highway transportation systems. Located in the southeastern part of Atlanta on Martin Luther King Jr. Drive, Peaches, Inc., employed over 750 people. The majority of employees were either programmers or systems analysts—known in the industry to be independent types, often desiring to be left alone to "do their thing." The company had grown rapidly during the past decade.

Mobry was in charge of a staff support team that provided liaison assistance to programmers and analysts in monitoring projects with clients and solving problems when they occurred. In that sense, his work team consisted of in-house consultants. His boss, Marilou Henson, was unhappy with several recent complaints received from programmers and others about their relationships with Martin's staff personnel. Henson decreed: "I want you to prepare a plan to improve those working relationships with the line and deliver a report to me no later than next Friday. The plan should reflect guidelines for improving the working relationships between line and staff personnel, including staff conduct in working with line personnel and vice versa."

"Conceivably, there is an unsolvable natural antagonism between staff and line people," Mobry thought. "The line thinks, 'We are the ones who really do the important work around here.' 'They frequently don't take our advice after all of our careful planning and assistance,' responds the staff. Conflict, if it occurs, may be partially explained by the different objectives of the two groups and the pressures they face from higher management."

Questions

1. Why does friction develop between line and staff groups?
2. Develop several principles of appropriate staff conduct in working with line personnel.
3. What would you consider appropriate behavior of line groups toward staff personnel?

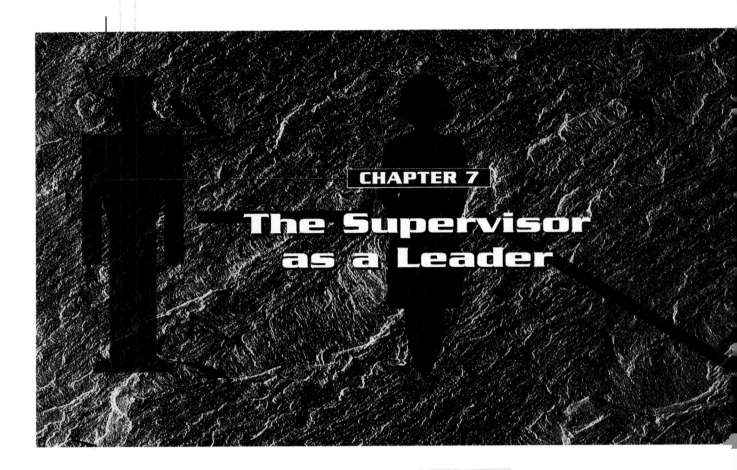

CHAPTER 7

The Supervisor as a Leader

● Going to church on Sunday no more makes one a Christian, than going into a garage makes one an automobile.

Billy Sunday, Evangelist

LEARNING OBJECTIVES

1. Describe the concept of leadership and the bases of power leaders have.
2. Differentiate between formal and informal leaders.
3. Explain the several concepts of situational leadership.
4. Understand the supervisor's role model responsibilities.
5. Indicate the importance of understanding and managing diversity of people in today's organizations.

Members of Carla's work group were constantly late. It drove Carla nuts. Admonishing them had little effect, and they always managed to skirt serious lateness problems that would have subjected them to the company's progressive discipline policy. What should she do?

Carla considered the old adage that it's easier to trap flies with honey than with vinegar. "A little positive reinforcement might do the trick," Carla thought. An idea for a contest came to her.

The next day, Carla convinced her staff to agree to a program in which a late arrival would have to donate $3 to a kitty. At the end of the month, Carla would spend the money on a plant for the work area or take three employees drawn by lot to lunch at the Buzz-Inn Steakhouse.

The program started. The kitty grew quickly, then tapered off. The program appeared to be working. After six weeks, $30 had collected. Carla announced to the team at a morning briefing that it was time for lunch. She started to ask for names for the drawing when she noticed that normally cheerful group members were sullen. Something was wrong.

Leadership affects all aspects of a supervisor's job. It also touches all members of an organization. Any time you influence others to accomplish tasks you are practicing leadership.

Many challenges are associated with effectively leading a work group. Supervisors must contend with the ambiguity of the environment. They must

reconcile their characteristics to those of followers and the constantly shifting demands of the situation.

The ambiguity of the leadership challenge has made it tough to teach effective leadership. One might even ask whether effective leaders are born leaders, or whether they can be made through education. Personal characteristics are important. Still, although it is difficult to train people to lead more productive groups, it can be done. This chapter provides a framework for effectively applying the concepts and skills that contribute to effective leadership.

What Is Leadership?

leadership
The process whereby an individual influences a group of followers to attain goals deemed important by the leader.

Leadership is the process whereby an individual influences a group of followers to attain goals deemed important by the leader. Ideally, these goals are also important to the organization and to the group being led.

Bases of Power

bases of power
Leaders influence followers in many ways including sources of power that are legitimate, expert, referent, reward, and coercive.

Leaders influence followers in many ways. Researchers Raven and French identified five different **bases of power:** legitimate, expert, referent, reward, and coercive power.[1]

Leader influence is, understandably, applied by people who are formally and officially entitled to exercise authority. A Cub Scout packmaster, a chief executive officer, a football coach, and a supervisor in a manufacturing facility all exercise formal authority that accrues to them because of their position in an organization. This type of power is referred to as *legitimate power.*

People also possess influence because of their expertise (*expert power*) or the respect in which they are held (*referent power*) or because of their ability to reward (*reward power*), or to punish others (*coercive power*).

These bases of power often overlap. A supervisor exercises legitimate power when she asks an employee to do a job; she uses expert power when she trains the employee to do a task or steps in to help with a complex problem. The supervisor may be highly respected by members of the work group. This respect contributes to referent power. A supervisor's ability to give overtime pay as a reward, or to dock pay for tardiness, are examples of reward and coercive power, respectively. Figure 7-1 shows a humorous example of coercive power.

Which base of power is best or has the most influence? Studies of different power bases have shown that use of expert and referent power leads to higher levels of follower performance and member satisfaction, and lower absenteeism and job turnover.[2] In other words, supervisors tend to be more successful when their power stems from the respect and admiration of others, rather than from their position in the organization. Successful supervisors' power is conveyed upon them by followers rather than by an organization.

Interestingly, all power bases, except coercion, will contribute significantly to employee satisfaction and commitment if a supervisor takes the time and effort to explain the reason for his or her actions. Employees greatly prefer being given a rational explanation for complying with a supervisor's request.[3]

In short, simply being in charge and ordering employees about is not enough to successfully influence a group. (Refer to the epigram at the beginning of this chapter.) Ralph Stayer, the chief executive of a successful family-owned business, said it well when he observed, "Real power is getting people committed.

First-Line Supervisors in the 21st Century

Work is changing. Computers and automated production processes have proliferated into nearly every nook and cranny of the modern organization. The work force is more highly educated. Competition in the marketplace is fierce. Organizations increasingly recognize the importance of human resources to their bottom lines. How will these trends affect the first-line supervisor's job?

Some researchers predict that first-line supervisors will become more involved in counseling, nurturing, and group facilitation in a workplace characterized by more worker participation, work group self-direction, access to information, and staff specialist involvement. There will also be fewer first-line supervisors.[4] These changes mean the directing or leading function of management will be more important to the everyday work of a 21st century supervisor.

The first-line supervisor will not vanish. Instead, the job will change from one of controlling work processes to a more consultive human relations role.

Real power comes from giving it up to others who are in a better position to do things than you are. Control is an illusion. The only control you can possibly have comes when people are controlling themselves."[5]

The effective supervisor realizes that influencing others through application of legitimate position power is inadequate. Employees should *want* to follow the leader.

Formal and Informal Leaders

The supervisor who is in charge of a work group is the *formal leader*. As mentioned previously, legitimate power resides in the formal, appointed leader of a

Figure 7-1 Coercive Power

THE WALL STREET JOURNAL

—Baloo

"This firm is just one big happy family, Pemberton, and if you don't get your sales total up, I'm going to spank the living daylights out of you!"

Source: From *The Wall Street Journal.* Permission, Cartoon Features Syndicate.

group. However, other group members can also have influence by virtue of their expertise or the respect in which they are held. In fact, a group member can even have more power to influence others than the formally appointed leader! An *informal leader* such as this may arise in a group that is poorly led. A competent supervisor may also allow an informal leader to take the lead in an area in which he or she has more expertise than the supervisor. There is nothing wrong with letting others in the work group take the lead in an area of their expertise.

By competently exercising his or her authority as a formal leader, and by recognizing the contributions of informal leaders in a work group, a supervisor can lead a highly productive work group. **Effective leadership**—the ability to lead a highly productive work group—is an important objective of effective supervision.

effective leadership
The ability to lead a highly productive work group.

Effective Leadership: Traits or Behaviors?

For well over 100 years researchers felt that effective leadership could be defined solely in terms of the personality characteristics or traits of the leader. This intuitively appealing view was first articulated by Thomas Carlyle in 1841.[6] In other words, researchers believed effective leaders possess a universal set of common characteristics such as high intelligence and compassion. This approach, called by various names including the **trait approach** and Great Man Theory, simply did not prove true.[7]

trait approach
An erroneous belief that effective leaders possess a universal set of common characteristics such as intelligence or compassion.

Researchers found that leader traits effective in one situation did not apply or were ineffective in another situation. A supervisor who is effective in leading a logging crew, for example, may be ineffective in leading office staff involved in the administration of a logging operation.

Focus on Behavior

The focus in research shifted from trait approaches (who effective leaders *are*) to consideration for how leaders behave (what effective leaders *do*).

In the mid-1950s, researchers at Ohio State University discovered that leader behavior could be described in terms of either initiation of structure or consideration for others.[8] During the same period, researchers at Michigan State University identified job-centered and employee-centered leadership styles.[9] In other words, leaders tend to focus upon either task or people.

These studies were inconclusive regarding the most effective leader behavior. The Ohio State University researchers, for example, placed emphasis on using factor analysis (a relatively sophisticated statistical technique) to find the most prominent categories of leader behavior. They left it to other researchers to develop and test theories pertaining to the appropriateness of leader behavior. The search for the most effective or best set of leader behaviors was on.

The Managerial Grid.   A school of thought that evolved from the Ohio State and Michigan studies contends that the most appropriate leader behavior is to be high on both task and structure behaviors. Robert Blake and Jane Mouton, for example, believe that effective leadership always involves leader behavior that is high in concern for people and concern for production.[10]

Blake and Mouton arrayed concern for people and task along a nine-point scale on a managerial grid (see Figure 7-2). The ideal leader, according to these theorists, is the 9,9 leader who believes that work should be accomplished

Figure 7-2 Blake and Mouton's Grid Model

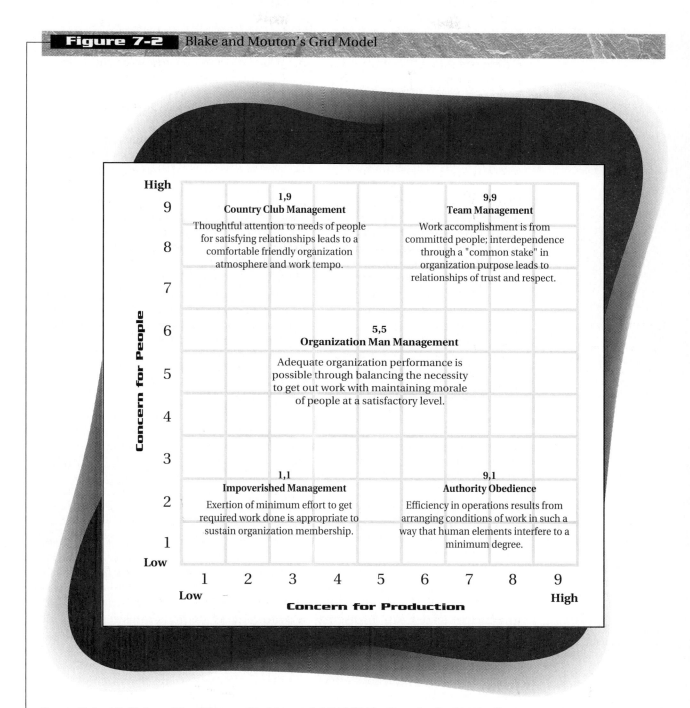

Source: Robert R. Blake and Jane Mouton, *The Managerial Grid III: The Key to Leadership Excellence* (Houston, TX: Gulf Publishing Company, 1985), 12.

team management
A task-motivated leadership approach that includes the full participation of followers.

through **team management,** defined as a "task-motivated leadership approach that includes the full participation of followers." The 9,9 leader has maximum concern for both people and production and leads a group of committed, motivated followers who share in decision making and are focused upon task. A 1,1 leader, on the other hand, leads an uncommitted group that accomplishes very little work.

Some experienced managers believe a 9,9 leadership approach works.[11] However, research that tests Blake and Mouton's theory using an organizational index of productivity as a dependent variable is lacking. Asking managers if they believe an approach is effective isn't as convincing as finding objective data that empirically demonstrate effectiveness. Sometimes intuitive perceptions of what seems right or effective can be inaccurate.

Moreover, there are situations in which it is very difficult for an effective leader to be high on both people and task. For example, a supervisor dropped into a situation characterized by low trust between leaders and followers and difficult working conditions may be more effective using a behavioral focus that emphasizes task. Imagine yourself supervising a crew of unruly teenagers who are raking rocks in 100-degree heat! It may not be realistically possible to focus on the needs of people in this setting. Under these circumstances, an emphasis on both people and task might even be contradictory. It would be impossible to let your crew sit in the shade and sip lemonade and still get the work accomplished.

Despite these criticisms, Blake and Mouton's theory represents an important application of earlier research. These theorists brought research out of the laboratory and into the workplace. Their framework is also important because it recognizes that effective leadership involves a focus on both people and task, even if the degree of focus on either people or task varies in a given situation.

A Situational Perspective

Although some consultants, researchers, and human resources professionals believe it is possible to define the one right set of leader behaviors for every situation, the dominant point of view today is that effective leadership is situational. It depends on characteristics of the environment, the leader, and followers.

The Contingency Model

contingency model
A theory that leader effectiveness is determined by the fit between the leader's personality and the amount of situational control or predictability in the leadership situation.

The first research that confirmed the importance of a situational perspective, published in the middle 1960s, was Fred Fiedler's **contingency model.** This theory holds that leader effectiveness is determined by the fit between the leader's personality and the amount of situational control or predictability in the leadership situation.[12] The contingency model acknowledges there is no one best road to effective leadership. A discussion of the theory demonstrates the inherent complexity of the leadership situation, and shows that simplistic behavioral approaches to understanding and practicing leadership are inadequate.

Fiedler and his associates found that group productivity—the most significant variable for defining leader effectiveness—is affected by the personality of the leader and the amount of control the leader has over a situation. The leader's personality is defined in the theory as being either task or relationship motivated. Situational control is defined by leader-member relations, task structure, and the position power of the leader as follows:

In this situation, task-motivated supervision will be most effective. Leader effectiveness depends on the leader's personality, the characteristics of followers, and the nature of the situation.

Leader-member relations —the degree to which the leader and group members get along with each other

Task structure —the degree to which the task can be organized into an orderly sequence or pattern

Position power —the degree to which the leader has formal recognition and legitimate authority from the organization

According to Fiedler, situational control improves for the leader as leader-member relations improve, task structure becomes better defined, and position power increases.

The contingency model predicts that task-motivated leaders will have effective groups under conditions of either high or low situational control. Groups led by relationship-motivated leaders will be more productive under conditions of moderate situational control (see Figure 7-3). This prediction is supported in a number of studies.[13]

The contingency model indicates that ineffective leadership is caused by a poor match between the leader and the situation. To improve group productivity, leaders must change the situation to match their styles rather than try to change their personalities.[14] For example, a task-motivated leader in a moderate control situation could improve the situation by setting goals with followers. A relationship-motivated leader in a low control situation might improve the situation by conducting weekly meetings with followers in a social setting, such as the leader's home or a local restaurant.

A primary limitation of the contingency model is that it does not effectively rationalize the effectiveness of leaders who have balanced relationship and task motivations. These leaders may conceivably perform well across a wide range of situations.[15] Another limitation of the contingency model is its basic proposition that it is more effective to change the situation than the behavior of the leader.

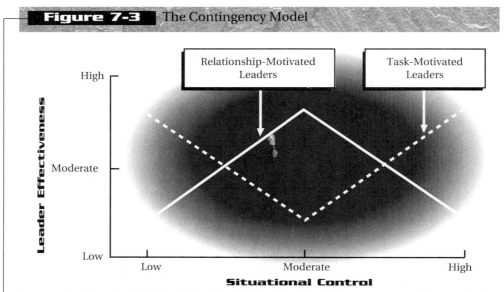

Figure 7-3 The Contingency Model

Source: Based on F. E. Fiedler, "The Contingency Model and the Dynamics of the Leadership Process," in *Advances in Experimental Social Psychology,* 2 vols., ed. L. Berkowitz (New York: Academic Press, 1978), vol. II. Copyright © 1990 by Allyn and Bacon.

Sometimes even subtle modifications in leader behavior can significantly improve group productivity, and these changes may not be as difficult as Fiedler's theory suggests.

In the final analysis, the contingency model is useful as a diagnostic tool. If you find yourself in a leadership situation that is not going well, take a look at the match between your style and the situation. Then consider how to change the situation to make it more compatible to your style.

Path-Goal Theory

path-goal theory ✗
A follower-driven theory of leadership that defines effective leadership in terms of leader behavior that enables followers to achieve satisfaction by accomplishing their goals.

Another situational leadership theory is **path-goal theory.** Path-goal theory is a follower-driven theory of leadership in that it defines effective leadership in terms of leader behavior that enables followers to achieve satisfaction by accomplishing *their* goals.

Path-goal theory states that effective leaders show consideration toward subordinates, initiate structure by clarifying paths to goals important to subordinates, and make rewards contingent upon goal achievement.[16] Path-goal theory was modified by Robert House and Terence Mitchell, who provided more detail regarding the fit between specific leader behaviors and specific follower needs.[17] Generally, the validity of House and Mitchell's predictions has continued to be supported.[18]

Path-goal theory, as developed by House and Mitchell, predicts supportive leader behaviors are most effective when followers are involved in boring, repetitive, or stressful tasks. Directive leadership is effective when the task seems ambiguous to followers who are relatively unskilled. Participative leader behavior is effective with followers who have a high need for achievement and for control of the task. Finally, an achievement-oriented leader sets goals and expects subordinates to perform at a high level. Achievement-oriented leader behavior is indicated when followers can reasonably be expected to work with little supervision doing relatively unstructured work.

For example, a supervisor leading a group of bored, highly stressed assembly line workers should be supportive. When leading a group of untrained, poorly focused workers, a supervisor should be directive. (See Figure 7-4.) Participative leadership will be effective if a supervisor leads a group of engineers with a strong need for involvement in redesigning a new product feature. Achievement-oriented leadership will also tend to work with this group, particularly if the engineers have a good understanding of their jobs.

Situational Leadership

One leadership theory is so tied to the importance of the situation that it is called **situational leadership.** This theory, developed by Paul Hersey and Ken Blanchard, holds that leaders should modify their behavior based on the maturity of followers.[19] Maturity is defined in the theory as "the ability and willingness of people to take responsibility for directing their own behavior" with regard to a specific task or set of responsibilities.

Maturity, in this sense, does not refer to whether people are generally mature or immature; rather, it refers to follower maturity in terms of a specific situation. For example, when employees are unwilling and unable to do a job, the theory classifies them as immature, even though they might be models of maturity in everyday life. Here are descriptions of different levels of maturity:

Low maturity (M1)	—Employees are unwilling and unable to take responsibility to do a job.
Low to moderate maturity (M2)	—Employees are unable but willing to take responsibility.
Moderate to high maturity (M3)	—Employees are able but unwilling to take responsibility.
High maturity (M4)	—Employees are both able and willing to take responsibility.

Figure 7-5 shows how the leader should change his or her task and relationship behavior based on the maturity of followers. Task behavior is the leader's

situational leadership
A theory of leadership that states leaders should modify their behavior based on the maturity of followers.

Figure 7-4   The Mail Must Go Through

Source: King Features Syndicate.

efforts to direct work toward accomplishing specific goals; relationship behavior is the leader's efforts to establish good rapport, trust, and friendship with employees.

After determining employee maturity levels, you can simply draw a line up to the appropriate spot on the bell-shaped curve to determine the best leadership style for the situation. For example, a supervisor leading a group of highly motivated, well-trained electricians leads a group with high maturity. As can be seen in Figure 7-5, delegating is the most appropriate leadership style for these highly mature employees.

Conversely, suppose the supervisor leads a cleanup crew of day laborers. These employees are able to do the work, but are unwilling—they would rather be anywhere but cleaning up garbage in the hot sun. Here, a selling strategy on the part of the supervisor involving a strong emphasis on both completing the work and building a good relationship is indicated.

Hersey and Blanchard's situational leadership theory is consistent with path-goal theory because it requires the leader to diagnose a situation and pick an appropriate strategy for leading a group. The theories are also consistent with each other in terms of recommended leader behaviors.

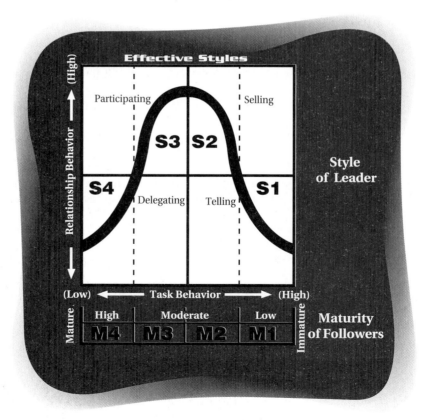

Figure 7-5 Situational Leadership

Source: Paul Hersey and Ken Blanchard, *Management of Organization Behavior: Utilizing Human Resources,* 4th ed. (Englewood Cliffs, NJ: Prentice-Hall, 1982), 205.

Leader Decision Theory

Leader decision theory, developed initially by Victor Vroom and Philip Yetton, is concerned with the role and extent of follower participation in leader decision making.[20] This theory is concerned with decision making as well as leadership. It is also covered further in Chapter 10.

According to Vroom and Yetton, follower involvement in decision making should be dependent upon two primary criteria: quality and acceptance. Employees should participate in decision making to the extent their contribution improves the quality of the decision and to the extent follower acceptance of the decision is necessary (participation in decision making leads to follower acceptance).

The extent of employees' involvement in decision making has two elements: the source of information for the decision and responsibility for the final decision. From these elements, Vroom and Yetton developed a set of decision methods which range from extremely autocratic, where the leader has the information and makes the decision alone, to extremely participative, where information and ultimate decision making reside with the group (see Figure 7-6).

The validity of leader decision theory has been supported by other research.[21] This theory has made a significant contribution to understanding leadership and decision making. The primary implication of leader decision theory is that

leader decision theory
Is concerned with the role and extent of follower participation in leader decision making; employees should participate if their contribution improves the quality of the decision and when follower acceptance of the decision is necessary.

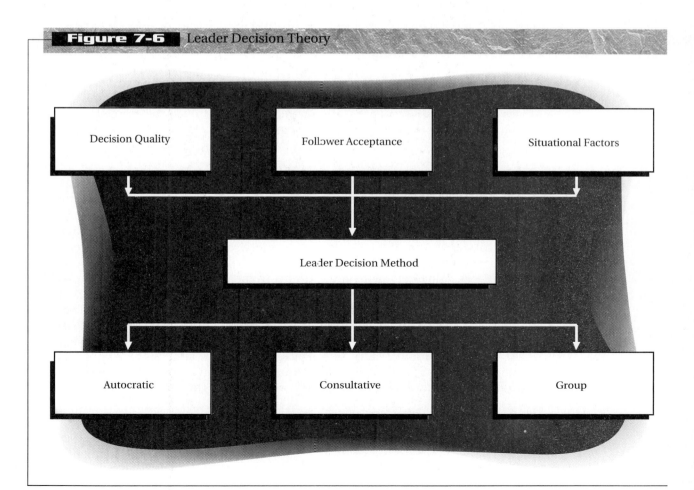

Figure 7-6 Leader Decision Theory

leaders should consider decision quality, follower acceptance, and situational factors when deciding who to include in decision making.

The idea that employees should be involved in all decision making, a proposition that some supervisors might think enlightened, is misdirected. Vroom and Yetton's theory suggests that employees should be involved in decision making only if they have information that will improve the quality of the decision or if participation will improve their acceptance of the decision. Sometimes it is all right for the supervisor to make a decision alone or with a minimum of consultation.

The Leader as a Role Model

A good conceptual understanding of leadership, and the theories and applications discussed to this point, is useful, but it is important that supervisors also practice what they preach. Supervisors, as leaders, should model the behavior and performance they are trying to encourage in employees.[22] It is important to keep in mind that employees tend to do as supervisors do, not as supervisors say. Supervisors serve as role models. **Role models** are persons who by virtue of their position influence the behavior and performance of those around them.

role models
Persons who by virtue of their position influence the behavior and performance of those around them.

The tendency to follow a role model is well documented in the literature on human development and learning. Much human behavior stems from learning by observation.[23] This learning does not have to be formal or planned. Observations seep into the consciousness of the observer and become part of the observer's future behavior.

If you want employees to work hard, then you as a supervisor need to work hard. If you want people to report to work on time, then don't be late yourself. If you want an employee to learn a tough, demanding job, then show your willingness to learn the job yourself, and provide assistance when the employee needs it. In short, effective leaders lead by example.

Understanding and Managing Diversity

Effective leaders understand and are sensitive to issues associated with leading a diverse work group. The contemporary supervisor faces a workplace of increasing diversity.

By 1990, 75 percent of all new entrants to the workplace—people most likely to be reporting to a first-line supervisor—were either women or ethnic minorities.[24] Los Angeles has a larger Mexican population than any city in Mexico, except for Mexico City. Two-thirds of Miami citizens are Cuban. Political disruption in the world led to a large influx to the United States of Southeast Asians in the 1970s, and then Eastern Europeans in the 1980s and 1990s. Women have entered the workplace in significant numbers. Today, it is not uncommon for both husbands and their wives to work, that is, to be gainfully employed.

Stereotyping and Attributional Bias

Effective leaders are sensitive to cultural and gender differences. Sensitivity is an important prerequisite to working well with a diverse group of employees, but it must be preceded by understanding.

The Honeywell Company in Minneapolis conducted sensitivity training a few years ago and discovered that "managers didn't know what to do with their new-found awareness of the existence of diversity."[25] In an attempt to be sensitive to differences, managers started to lump people into groups, such as all Asians or all African-Americans. In trying to be sensitive, managers were guilty of **stereotyp-ing,** the classification of individual behavior on the basis of a group standard. Stereotyping is an oversimplified opinion or belief about someone often not supported by facts.

Understanding **attributional bias** (also discussed in Chapter 14) that leads to stereotyping helps supervisors to avoid mistakes in leading a diverse work group. Attributional bias occurs when people try to interpret a person or a situation based on available information. The more incomplete or inaccurate the information, the more likely it is the person will make an erroneous attribution. Attributions are influenced by a wide variety of cultural, social, and contextual factors. Attributions of other people's behavior are often formed from just a small sample of observations. The mind filters these observations selectively, forms a prototype based on them, then fills in the gaps of the prototype where necessary.[26] This process forms the basis of stereotyping.

Attributional bias and stereotyping are a natural part of human perception. Effective leaders understand this. They also understand that every employee brings a different set of cultural biases to the workplace. The idea is not to eliminate bias. Rather, it is to understand the process by which bias occurs to reduce the negative effects and misunderstandings it causes. With an understanding of the nature of attributional bias comes meaningful sensitivity to the needs of others.

The effective supervisor needs to walk a fine line between understanding needs characteristic of an ethnic group and treating members of that group as individuals. For example, supervisors should not assume, just because many Asian cultures are group oriented, that an individual Japanese-American worker will want to work in a group. Supervisors seldom go wrong if they ask questions of employees before making such assumptions.

stereotyping
The classification of individual behavior made on the basis of a group standard; an oversimplified opinion or belief about someone often not supported by facts.

attributional bias
Occurs when people try to interpret a person or situation based on available, sometimes incomplete or inaccurate, information.

English as a Second Language

Cultural sensitivity and understanding are necessary when supervising employees who speak English as a second language. Don't make the classic attributional mistake of thinking people who speak English poorly are unintelligent!

Following are some strategies for supervising people who have a relatively poor understanding of English:

- Do not get angry or impatient.
- Put requests in writing whenever possible. Provide enough time for the employee to absorb the communication and get clarification, if necessary.
- Use standard English. Avoid slang. Keep in mind that many English expressions don't make sense when translated literally (for example, "they don't cut any corners," "look sharp," or "make sure all the bases are covered").
- Show a genuine interest in learning about the employee's culture. But also get to know the person as an individual.
- Put yourself in the employee's shoes. Imagine what it is like to understand little of the verbal and written communication taking place around you. If you have traveled in a foreign country, you know how it feels to be immersed in a different culture.

Avoid making statements such as "I am not prejudiced" or "I never stereotype." Many, if not most, human beings carry prejudices and are influenced by stereotypes. With sensitivity and understanding, supervisors can lessen the negative effects of this reality. We can all learn to not only understand and be sensitive to differences, but to celebrate them in our everyday lives.

"What's wrong? Doesn't anyone want to go out to lunch?"

The group stared back at Carla.

Finally, Al spoke up. "Carla, you've been late to work five times in the past month. Where's your contribution to the kitty?"

Carla gasped. She slapped her forehead and groaned. As a supervisor, Carla didn't punch a time clock. She sometimes came in late, but more often than not, she worked long past first shift. Of course, her work group did not see this part of Carla's schedule. They did notice her morning lateness, however!

"I'm really sorry. It just never occurred to me. . . . I'm not on a schedule like you folks. I guess that's not a very good excuse. I do work late."

"It's okay, Carla," Al replied, unconvinced.

Three team members and Carla had a great lunch. During lunch, Carla told the others she planned to end the contest. She privately resolved to instead come to work every morning at the beginning of the day shift.

The lateness problems with Carla's work group tapered off and soon ended.

Summary: Focus on Concepts

Leadership, the process whereby an individual influences a group of followers to attain goals deemed important by the leader, is a broad concept that touches all members of an organization. Effective leadership cannot be easily taught or learned.

Leaders influence others through the use of power. There are several bases of power: legitimate, expert, referent, reward, and coercive power. Formal leaders have influence because of their position within the organization. Informal leaders do not possess legitimate power, but influence others through use of other power bases. Bases of power often overlap. A leader can exercise any or all types of power. Studies have shown that expert and referent power lead to the highest levels of follower performance and member satisfaction, and lower absenteeism and turnover. All types of power, however, except coercion, will contribute to employee commitment and satisfaction if the supervisor explains his or her actions.

Research on leader traits and behaviors does not identify ideal traits or behaviors possessed or practiced by all successful leaders under all circumstances. The idea that effective leaders are always high on both people and task dimensions fails to account for circumstances in which such an emphasis is counterproductive or even contradictory.

The dominant point of view today is that effective leadership is situational. It depends on characteristics of the leader, the environment, and followers. These characteristics constantly shift. Therefore, solutions to the leadership challenge are elusive.

The first research that confirmed the importance of a situational perspective was published by Fred Fiedler in the mid-1960s. Fiedler's contingency model indicates that effective leadership is a function of leader-situation match. Task-motivated leaders tend to do best in either low or high control situations; relationship-motivated leaders do best in moderate control situations.

Path-goal theory, as developed by House and Mitchell, is a follower-driven theory of leadership. It contends that effective leaders clarify pathways to goals desired by followers. Supportive leadership is most effective when work is boring, repetitive, or stressful;

directive leadership is effective when tasks seem ambiguous to relatively unskilled followers; participative leadership works well with followers who have high achievement needs; and achievement-oriented leadership is indicated when followers can reasonably be expected to work with little supervision while doing unstructured work.

Situational leadership, developed by Hersey and Blanchard, holds that leaders should modify their behavior based on the maturity of followers. Maturity is the ability and willingness of employees to take responsibility for directing their own behavior.

Leader-decision theory by Vroom and Yetton indicates that leaders should include employees in decision making to the extent participation improves the quality of a decision or employee support is needed for implementation of a decision. If an employee has little to offer to the decision process or employee acceptance is already a given or is unimportant, then the supervisor should make the decision alone or with a minimum of consultation.

Effective leaders serve as good role models to followers. A significant amount of learning is socially derived from observation. Consequently, supervisors should model the behavior they expect in employees. Employees tend to be influenced more by what a supervisor does than by what a supervisor says.

Understanding and managing diversity is an increasingly important part of a supervisor's job and is an important part of the leadership challenge. Women and ethnic minorities make up the majority of new entrants to the labor market. Supervisors need to both understand and be sensitive to differences among people. Understanding the nature of attributional bias and stereotyping helps supervisors to treat employees with dignity and respect.

Review Questions

1. How is the nature of a supervisor's job changing? Is the supervisor becoming the dinosaur of the 21st century?
2. Explain the concept of leadership. Upon assuming the position of supervisor, does an individual automatically become a leader?
3. Cite and explain the five bases of power.
4. Which base of power is the best? Why?
5. What are formal and informal leaders?
6. Is the trait approach to defining leaders valid today? Explain.
7. Indicate the meanings of initiation of structure and consideration for others in the behavioral approach.
8. How does the managerial grid function?
9. What is situational leadership?
10. Within a situational approach to leadership, explain the contingency model, path-goal theory, and leader decision theory.
11. What is a role model? Of what significance is the concept of role models to supervisors?
12. Why has the management of diversity increased in importance in the United States?
13. Indicate several strategies available to supervisors in charge of employees who have a relatively poor understanding of English.

Notes

1. J. R. French Jr. and B. Raven, "The Bases of Social Power," in *Studies in Social Power*, ed. D. Cartwright (Ann Arbor, MI: Institute for Social Research), 1959.
2. G. A. Yukl, *Leadership in Organizations* (Englewood Cliffs, NJ: Prentice-Hall, 1981).
3. T. R. Hinkin and C. A. Schriesheim, "Power and Influence: the View from Below," *Personnel*, May 1988, 47–50.
4. S. Kerr, K. D. Hill, and L. Broedling, "The First-Line Supervisor: Phasing Out or Here to Stay?" *Academy of Management Review* 11 (1986): 103–117.
5. T. A. Stewart, "New Ways to Exercise Power," *Fortune*, November 6, 1989, 52–64.
6. T. Carlyle, *Heroes and Hero Worship* (Boston: Adams, 1907).

7. B. M. Bass, *Stogdill's Handbook of Leadership: A Survey of Theory and Research* (New York: Free Press, 1981).

8. A. Korman, "'Consideration,' 'Initiating Structure,' and Organizational Criteria—a Review," *Personnel Psychology* 19 (1969): 349–362.

9. A. D. Szilagyi and M. Wallace, *Organizational Behavior and Performance* (Santa Monica, CA: Goodyear Publishing Co., 1980).

10. R. R. Blake and J. S. Mouton, *The Managerial Grid III: The Key to Leadership Excellence* (Houston, TX: Gulf, 1985).

11. R. R. Blake and J. S. Mouton, "Theory and Research for Developing a Science of Leadership," *Journal of Applied Behavioral Science* 18 (1982): 275–291.

12. F. E. Fiedler, *A Theory of Leadership Effectiveness* (New York: McGraw-Hill, 1967).

13. M. J. Strube and J. E. Garcia, "A Meta-Analytic Investigation of Fiedler's Contingency Model of Leadership Effectiveness," *Psychological Bulletin* 90 (1981): 307–321. Also, L. H. Peters, D. D. Hartke, and J. T. Pohlman, "Fiedler's Contingency Theory of Leadership: An Application of the Meta-Analysis Procedure of Schmidt and Hunter," *Psychological Bulletin* 97 (1985): 274–285.

14. F. E. Fiedler and M. M. Chemers, *Improving Leadership Effectiveness: The Leader Match Concept,* 2d ed. (New York: John Wiley & Sons, 1984).

15. J. K. Kennedy, "Middle LPC Leaders and the Contingency Model of Leadership Effectiveness," *Organizational Behavior and Human Performance* 39 (1982): 1–14.

16. M. G. Evans, "The Effects of Supervisory Behavior on the Path-Goal Relationship," *Organizational Behavior and Human Performance* 55 (1977): 277–298.

17. R. J. House and T. R. Mitchell, "Path-Goal Theory of Leadership," *Journal of Contemporary Business* 3 (1974): 81–97. Also, R. J. House, "A Path-Goal Theory of Leader Effectiveness," *Administrative Science Quarterly* 16 (1971): 321–338.

18. J. Indvik, "Path-Goal Theory of Leadership: A Meta Analysis." in *Academy of Management Best Papers Proceedings,* ed. J. A. Pearce and R. B. Robinson, Jr. (Chicago, IL: Academy of Management, 1986).

19. P. Hersey and K. Blanchard, *Management of Organizational Behavior* (Englewood Cliffs, NJ: Prentice-Hall, 1982).

20. V. H. Vroom and P. W. Yetton, *Leadership and Decision Making* (Pittsburgh, PA: University of Pittsburgh Press, 1973). Also, see V. H. Vroom and A. G. Jago, *The New Leadership: Managing Participation in Organizations* (Englewood Cliffs, NJ: Prentice-Hall, 1988).

21. R. H. Field, "A Test of the Vroom-Yetton Normative Model of Leadership," *Journal of Applied Psychology* 67 (1982): 523–532.

22. "Peak Performance—It Can be Learned. And Taught," *Management Solutions,* June 1986, 27.

23. A. Bandura, *Social Learning Theory* (Englewood Cliffs, NJ: Prentice-Hall, 1977).

24. L. Copeland, "Valuing Workplace Diversity," *Personnel Administrator* 33 (November 1988): 38–40.

25. S. Overman, "Managing the Diverse Workforce," *HR Magazine,* April 1991, 32–36.

26. J. M. Feldman, "Beyond Attribution Theory: Cognitive Processes in Performance Appraisal," *Journal of Applied Psychology* 66 (1981): 127–148.

Case 7-1

The Memorable Memorandum

The following memorandum was delivered to 47 employees of a state agency. As you read the memo, assume you are one of these employees—a supervisor of eight people. Your boss, Renshaw, has been the administrator for about one year.

DEPARTMENT OF TRANSPORTATION—DIVISION OF RIGHT-OF-WAYS

MEMORANDUM   December 24, 1994

TO: Division Staff
FROM: Melissa Renshaw, Administrator
        Division of Right-of-Ways

SUBJECT: CONDUCT ON THE JOB OR FIRST ANNUAL WOODSHED AWARD

I cannot stress strongly enough to each of you the importance of maintaining a sense of dignity and professionalism on the job. The Division of Right-of-Ways is directly responsible to the Director of the Department of Transportation, and far more than any other Division, the manner in which we conduct ourselves directly reflects on the Director's office.

We have critically important jobs to do; our only concerns should involve getting those jobs accomplished. Our goal is to facilitate operational and programmatic improvements in the Department, working in cooperation with all existing Departmental resources.

Our assignments require full-time commitments. I suggest that consultation with people within and without the Department, during the work day, be on a scheduled basis. I want to see the general bull sessions reduced to a minimum. I am not suggesting the *total* elimination of informal communication; I am requiring diligent attention to Divisional responsibilities.

Finally, I will say in writing what I have expressed in person many times. Change *in this Department* requires cooperation, understanding, compromise, and conciliation. We have changes to be implemented; therefore, we will not be involved in any internal intrigue that does not promote a positive response to change and progress. Any staff member who cannot abide by this philosophy will need to seek employment elsewhere.

This memorandum is sent to document a Divisional philosophy. For the most part, I have never had the privilege of working with a group of people I respect more than I respect the staff in this Division. You are a joy to work with. This memorandum is a reminder of the visible position we each maintain as members of the Division and as staff of the Department of Transportation.

Melissa Renshaw
_____
Melissa Renshaw

MR/job

Questions

1. How would you feel after reading the memorandum? What are your initial thoughts and reactions? What are the potential effects in the long run?
2. What organizational climate factors are implied by this memorandum?
3. What leadership style does this memo suggest Renshaw follows?
4. How would you, as a supervisor, carry out the action requested in the memo as it pertains to your employees?
5. Can you think of more effective methods for dealing with the problem? If so, what are they?

The Shakedown

The air conditioning was not working. It was hot and the room was stuffy, the air pungent with the odor of sweat. The thermometer registered 98 degrees—5 degrees hotter than half an hour ago when McKenzie McBride had entered the room. The August heat made life very uncomfortable for the eight men occupying that small room. Today's training exercise was about to conclude.

Five of the eight men were trainees. The other three were their trainer, who was also the director of training; his assistant; and McBride, soon to be the supervisor of the five men undergoing the training.

For the past several hours, the trainees had been indoctrinated about their new jobs and the organization for which they were now working—a state prison in the upper Midwest. The trainees were called correctional officers, and would be guarding inmates. After tomorrow, their fifth and final day of training, they would be assigned to their regular guard duties. McBride, as their supervisor, was a First Lieutenant. He had begun working as a guard seven years ago. His most recent promotion was two years ago. He had stopped by to observe how his new employees were performing in their training. This was his usual practice on the fourth day.

The afternoon's exercise was called "The Shakedown." In popular slang, a shakedown is a form of extortion or blackmail. However, another meaning, and the one applicable here, is a thorough search of either a place or person. The purpose of the shakedown is to determine if an inmate possesses items prohibited during his or her incarceration. These items are called "contraband." Possessing contraband is considered bad behavior. If contraband items are found on an inmate or in the living quarters, the inmate is usually punished by loss of privileges or more severe discipline. Guns and knives are viewed most dimly by correctional personnel, as are drugs and alcoholic beverages. Many different types of contraband make up the list of forbidden items.

The shakedown exercise began with all trainees leaving the room. Real contraband was then hidden on the training assistant, who assumed the role of inmate. One by one, the trainees entered the room to conduct their searches of the "inmate" suspected of possessing contraband. Items found were replaced and the trainee sat to observe the next person. Eventually, all five completed their searches.

The next step was for each trainee to make a presentation of the correct procedure for conducting a body search of an inmate in the quest for contraband. One trainee found three items of contraband, another located four, two of the trainees discovered five, and the last detected seven. This last trainee had a smile on his face, reflecting his perceived achievement relative to his peer officers.

The smile faded as the "inmate" began removing contraband items from his pockets and began stripping to reveal objects taped to various and assorted body parts. Included in the undetected booty were two prison-fashioned guns and five knives. In all, over 50 pieces of contraband were hidden, and were placed upon the desk at the front of the room. All five of the men in the simulation exercise could have been killed in an actual shakedown. Their performance, while most inadequate, was typical of trainees during their first practice shakedown.

McBride stood up, walked to the front of the room, turned toward the men and exploded. "You have got to be the dumbest bunch I have ever *not had* the privilege of working with. Not only are you stupid, but your hearing isn't any good. Don't you remember what your instructor told you? When you find more than a couple of contraband on a person, you get help and don't continue the search by yourself.

"Now maybe you are tired of living and you're looking for a fast way of dying or your wives are going to be rich in collecting your insurance, but I am not ready to die yet. If I have to depend upon you, then someone is going to get hurt badly or killed because you surely are the sorriest specimens imitating correctional officers I have ever seen. I could get better results with trained monkeys. At least they know where the bananas are hidden.

"I bet you think I am unhappy, don't you? Well you don't know how unhappy I can get. When I'm unhappy, *everyone* around me feels the same way.

"You know what your problem is, don't you? It's not because you're stupid after all. You can't help that. Your problem is you just don't give a damn about other people. You think this job is one easy pushover and you get dressed up like soldiers and be big shots. You think you're tough, don't you? Well, let me tell you this. I'll be back tomorrow. If you don't get it right by then, I'll personally escort you to the main tower gate and kick you out of here. You're not going to get me killed or my friends either. I'm never going to call your mothers or wives and tell them their stupid son or husband got himself killed. Shape up, pretty boys. You really disgust me. You don't even sweat good!"

With the final remark, McBride turned toward the front of the room, winked at the Director of Training, slammed the door, and plowed his way through the crowd of off-duty personnel that had assembled over an hour ago in the hall.

Questions

1. What kind of leader do you think McBride is?
2. What style of leadership is he reflecting? Would you anticipate he is capable of any other style?
3. If you were to estimate the trainees' performances tomorrow, do you forecast any improvement?

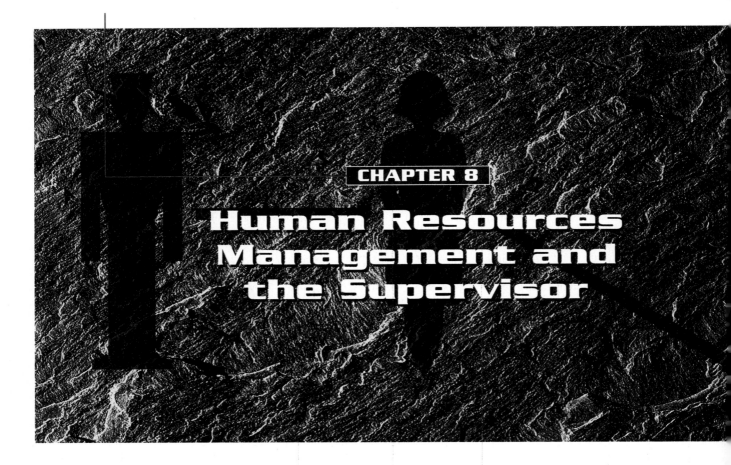

CHAPTER 8

Human Resources Management and the Supervisor

● When all else fails, read the instructions.

Allen's Axiom

LEARNING OBJECTIVES

1. Describe the supervisor's role in human resources management.
2. Understand the growing importance of HRM and the causes of its elevation.
3. Outline the recruitment and selection process including the tools and methods utilized.
4. Indicate the impediments detracting from the validity of interviewing including the psychological barriers and interviewing errors.
5. Describe methods for improving the validity of selection.
6. Apply the concepts of the realistic job preview and the psychological contract.
7. Indicate actions supervisors can take to improve employee workplace safety.
8. Explain the concepts of pay equity and pay adequacy and compensation trends.

"George, I don't get it. I *was* being fair. I recommended both you and Al for the same pay raise. Your pay and his are equitable. I don't see what the problem is."

George glared at Carla.

Carla continued. "Let's go back again to the issue. It's about how much you are being paid, right?

"Yes, but . . . "

Carla cut in. "I don't get it! You're one of the highest paid machinists in the company."

"It's not entirely about how much I'm getting paid."

"Then you're angry because your pay is not fair? How can that be? You and Al are paid the same."

"That is what isn't fair!"

Human resources management (sometimes referred to as human resources development) covers staffing, compensation, performance appraisal, worker safety, training and development, and, sometimes, labor relations functions in an organization. Human resources management is an outgrowth of the traditional personnel function.

Traditional personnel office workers did paperwork related to staffing. Or, as a former President of the Society for Human Resources Management (SHRM) put

human resources management
A variety of organizational functions related to human resources, including staffing, compensation, performance appraisal, worker safety, training and development, and, sometimes, labor relations.

it, "The head of personnel was the one who carried the watermelon to the annual company picnic."[1] The office's main purpose was to find people to fill job vacancies. The personnel manager tended to have a low rank in the organizational hierarchy. Because the personnel office operated in a support role, it was often underfunded.

In the past 20 years, prompted in part by exponential growth in job-related litigation and the competitive challenge from other countries, a new perspective—that of human resources management—emerged. Organizations began to place more importance on human resources functions because enlightened managers realized that hiring the right people, training them to work productively, compensating adequately and equitably, keeping the workplace safe, and providing useful feedback through performance appraisal was essential to organizational success.

Enlightened organizations also realized that potentially costly and divisive legal problems could only be reduced by having an expert, professional human resources manager overseeing organizational compliance with equal opportunity, worker safety, and job-related federal and state regulations.

We have covered legal issues in Chapter 3 and labor relations in Chapter 4. The subject of performance appraisal is addressed in Chapter 14. In this chapter, the topics of employee recruitment and selection, worker safety, and compensation are explored. Training, including new employee orientation, is included in the following chapter.

Effective supervisors play an important part in human resources management. They make employee selection decisions, conduct performance appraisals, recommend employees for promotion, conduct training, and recommend candidates for training programs. Supervisors are further involved in some compensation-related decisions including recommending employees for pay raises and scheduling work, and serve as the first line in creating a legally compliant, dignified working environment for employees. Figure 8-1 illustrates a typical division of responsibilities in the staffing area between the human resources staff and the individual supervisor.

Job Analysis: The Starting Point

job analysis
The systematic investigation of a job in order to identify its essential characteristics and to translate these characteristics into a written job description.

job description
Describes all work activities associated with a position.

job specification
Lists the minimum qualifications necessary to perform adequately in a specific position.

A supervisor can provide the human resources office with an accurate description of a job to be filled. The best way to develop a valid job description is to conduct job analysis. (See the discussion of validity in Chapter 3.) **Job analysis** is a systematic investigation of a job in order to identify its essential characteristics and to translate these characteristics into a written job description. Figure 8-2 indicates the importance of job analysis.

Some organizations have full-time job analysts who systematically observe jobs and write a job description and job specification for each position. A **job description** describes all work activities associated with a position. A **job specification** lists the minimum qualifications necessary to perform adequately in a specific position. In other organizations, the supervisor conducts the job analysis and participates in preparing job descriptions and specifications.

Job analysis, leading to a current job description and job specification, is an important starting point for hiring the right person for a job. Supervisors, or anyone else who systematically analyzes work, should not attempt to conduct job analysis from the comfort of an office. Work needs to be carefully observed. Job

Figure 8-1	The Supervisor's Role in Staffing Activities		

	Responsibility	
Staffing Activities	**Human Resources**	**Supervisor**
Preparation		
Job analysis (job descriptions and job specifications)	secondary	primary
Labor forecasting	primary	secondary
Acquiring Employees		
Recruitment	primary	secondary
Selection methods		
Application forms	primary	secondary
Testing	primary	—
Reference checks	primary	—
Interviewing	shared	shared
Hiring decision	—	primary
Maintenance of the Work Force[a]		
Promotions	shared	shared
Transfers	shared	shared
Separations	shared	shared

[a]Decisions shared with affected supervisors, managers, and employees

incumbents need to be interviewed to determine what they actually do on the job. If the job analysis is faulty, all else—from the job description and specification, to recruiting methods and interview questions—will be faulty, with repercussions that ripple through the organization.

Employee Recruitment and Selection

A typical recruitment and selection procedure involves several steps or stages of activities and follows job analysis and preparation of job descriptions and job specifications. Figure 8-3 illustrates these steps involved in obtaining new employees. If a job applicant does not meet organizational selection criteria, the procedure can be terminated for that applicant.

Recruitment

Recruitment is the process of acquiring employees to fill job positions. Although the majority of activities in recruiting new employees will be performed by the human resources staff, we will review briefly the work of that staff as background for a supervisor's participation in the process.

New employees come from outside the organization. Either a firm attempts to attract job applicants through its own communication efforts or applicants come

recruitment
The process of acquiring employees to fill job positions.

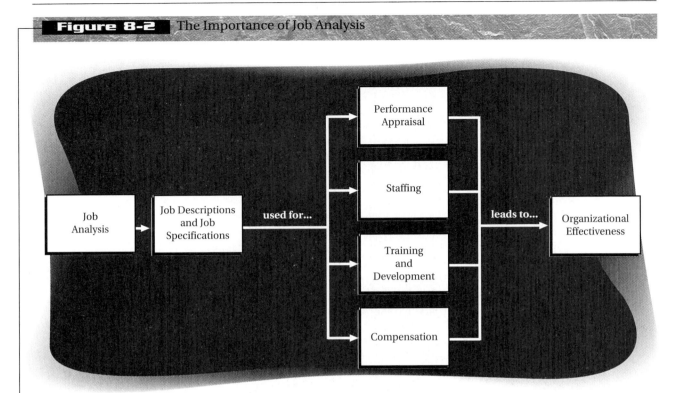

Figure 8-2 The Importance of Job Analysis

to the firm. The human resources office works with management to write a position announcement, which they then advertise outside the organization, often in classified newspaper ads. In metropolitan areas they may also use television and radio. Other methods include recruiting at educational institutions, public and private employment agencies, and operation of an employment office within the organization.

In addition, some organizations encourage their employees to recommend friends and relatives to apply for jobs. Informal word-of-mouth communication about jobs is extremely important in attracting job applicants. Studies indicate over one-half of blue-collar workers learned about employment opportunities by word-of-mouth from friends and relatives working for the employing organization.[2]

Increasing in importance for many employers is the use of internships in which potential permanent employees work while going to school. Job posting is also practiced in many larger organizations, permitting employees to bid on job vacancies. Posting is particularly common in government agencies and among employers who have union contracts.

Selection

Employee selection is the process of hiring the right person for a job by screening the various job candidates through the use of tools such as application blanks, personal interviews, tests, and reference checks. A poorly conceived, poorly implemented selection process is expensive. It costs between $5,000 and

employee selection
The process of hiring the right person for a job by screening the various job candidates through the use of tools such as application blanks, personal interviews, tests, and reference checks.

Figure 8-3   Steps in the Recruitment and Selection Process

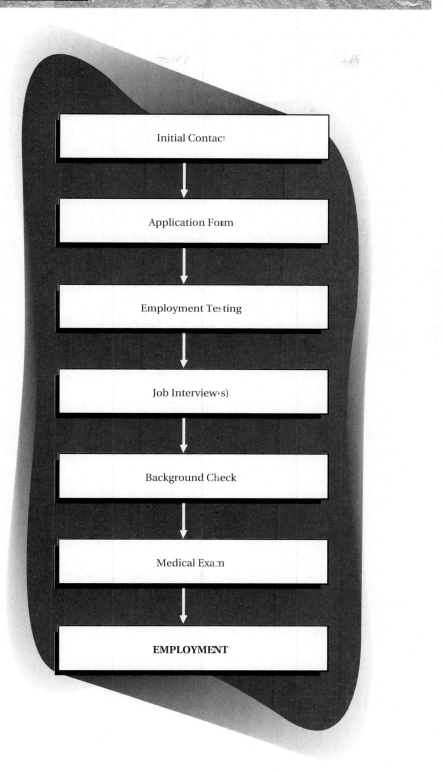

$2(,000 to train each new line worker.[3] The real costs can be much greater when lost productivity and the stress of employing a poorly performing employee are factored in.

The right person for a job is the individual exhibiting the greatest probability of being successful on the job. The human resources office and the individual supervisor play important, though different, roles in hiring employees. In addition to recruiting, the human resources department usually performs a preliminary screening of job applicants. **Screening** is a process designed to eliminate from further consideration those persons who do not possess the minimum requirements set forth in the job specification. Based on attributes and characteristics stated in the job specification, the human resources department usually screens out all but the best three to five applicants. Supervisors enter the selection process to interview the finalists and make a hiring decision.

Any method followed to screen applicants should be valid. (See Chapter 3 for more information on validity.) The information required from applicants or used in differentiating among them should be correlated to the probability of the person's success in performing a job. If supervisors ask questions having no valid relationship to the probability of job success, the questions are not predictors. Asking such questions might also be illegal. Be cautious asking questions that do not have verified validity. Even a friendly and casually asked question such as, "Are you married?" can create profound problems because it is illegal to require this information in the employment selection process.

Tools and methods utilized in the selection process include review of completed application blanks, preliminary interviews, tests, reference checks, and physical examinations. The supervisor, sometimes together with other members of the management team, usually makes the actual selection, with the approval of the organization's equal employment opportunity officer to ensure the selection process meets requirements of federal and state laws.

Of all the selection tools, two are of particular importance to supervisors: review and analysis of application forms and personal interviews. We will explore the mechanics of these, along with employment testing, and conclude this section by suggesting a more appropriate method for the modern supervisor, the realistic job preview. Each of these has flaws that, to some extent, may be overcome with diligence.

screening
A process designed to eliminate from further consideration those persons who do not possess the minimum requirements set forth in the job specifications.

An effective supervisor hires the right person for the job. Hiring the wrong person wastes time and training dollars.

Application Forms

Almost all organizations with more than two or three employees rely upon application forms to acquire preliminary information about job applicants. As a screening device, they allow a rapid determination of whether an applicant possesses minimum qualifications for a job. When minimum qualifications are absent, the screening process is terminated. For persons subsequently hired, the application form frequently becomes a part of the employee's permanent record.

Equal Employment Opportunity (EEO) legislation has caused many firms to revise and shorten their application forms. Application forms should not request data prohibited by legislation unless it is a bona fide occupational qualification (BFOQ) for employment. (See Chapter 3 for a discussion of BFOQs.) The first function of the application form is to provide a tool for preliminary screening; the second is to supply an information base for personal interviews of the most promising applicants. The most useful information on an application form typically pertains to the following:

- *Career goals.* What are the applicants' short- and long-term career objectives? What types of jobs are they most interested in performing?
- *Educational background.* What institutions did they attend and what were their major areas of study, grades earned, awards received, and participatory activities?
- *Previous employment history.* Who were their former employers and what were the periods of employment, jobs held or types of work performed, and reasons for leaving previous employment?
- *References.* Who are the persons listed as references and what types of references are provided?

As you review the credentials of applicants, compare the information given to the job specification and performance standards or criteria established for the job they would perform if hired. Not infrequently, the qualifications may be excellent, but not relevant to the job for which the person has applied. Some organizations have developed evaluation forms to assist you in your review. Otherwise, create your own system. Weight the informational categories from the most important to the least to obtain a numerical ranking, or spread, among the applicants. The evaluation process should not be too mechanical, however. Otherwise, you may screen out applicants who deserve closer inspection.

Evaluating information calls for "reading between the lines." You may form a picture of the applicant different from what was suggested by individual pieces of information. What was said? How was it stated? What was not said, but should have been? A job applicant who listed under experience, his military service during the Vietnam war wrote, "Pilot, bomber, four-engine, 25 combat missions." What did he communicate? First, he likely was a skilled pilot and a brave person. Second, his ego may have kept him aloft, at times.

In another instance, an applicant for a business school dean's position submitted the names (but not the addresses) of 102 references, beginning with the president of the United States. Although he probably intended to impress the potential employer with whom he knew—unsuccessfully—it would have been interesting to write the president for a recommendation of the applicant.

The more important points to reference analysis are the types of references and their comments. Among the references should be previous supervisors, who have the best knowledge of the applicant's past employment history including working habits and abilities. If the applicant includes only the names of family members and friends, you probably should be suspicious. Recommendations that "damn by faint praise" are also suspect. Here, the reference acknowledges the applicant's existence but gives no substantive information.

Some job applicants may falsify information on the application form. If something looks strange to you, ask the applicant to explain during the interview. At least, review the application form very carefully before you interview the applicant. In the final analysis, many employers probably use application forms primarily in order to have evidence in terminating an employee who has falsified information and turns out to be a poor worker.

Employment Testing

Applicants passing the preliminary screening of the application form, and perhaps a first personal interview, may then be tested in one or more areas. A variety of tests are used in the selection process. One study of 2,500 firms of varying sizes found that almost one-half of the firms used tests in hiring new employees.

Where Do You Put Time Spent in the Bastille?

One of the authors taught courses at a state prison. One of the student inmates asked, "Where do I put my time spent in prison?" A lively class discussion produced several suggestions including placement of prison time either in the education or the experience section. Some students realized the necessity to account for the time spent in prison. To leave it off the application blank could be grounds for dismissal when their former incarceration was discovered. Yet, to include the time might mean not obtaining the job in the first place.

Is there any way to solve this dilemma?

Another study suggests the percentage of firms testing applicants has declined rather significantly in recent years.[4] EEO laws and enforcement of the Equal Employment Opportunity Commission's guidelines on testing have caused this decline, because of the real or imagined difficulties of firms in validating their tests. (See Chapter 3 for additional information about validity and the legal implications of employer hiring practices.)

The most common types of tests are:

- Interest tests, which measure a person's motivation toward something
- Aptitude tests, which measure a person's potential ability to perform a task
- Personality tests, which measure the behavioral, temperamental, emotional, and mental traits a person possesses
- Intelligence tests, which measure a person's general mental abilities or specific intellectual capabilities
- Achievement tests, which measure a person's present ability or knowledge of something.

For many jobs, a physical exam is also required. This exam may take place either before or after hiring, although the trend has been toward requiring an examination before a hire decision is made.

Interviewing

Interviewers usually place great stock in talking with job candidates. Yet, the selection interview is notoriously flawed. In the words of researcher Wayne Cascio, "The record of the employment interview as a selection device over the years has been dismal."[5] Three major studies conducted since the turn of the century show that the selection interview, as typically conducted, is riddled with problems. Although this may be true, supervisors still must know how to handle interviews.

After the human resources department has narrowed the number of applicants to the finalists, supervisors should not only interview the finalists but also make the hire decision. There are several logical reasons why supervisors should have the hiring authority, with the organization's EEO officer's prior approval.

1. Because supervisors are responsible for the performance of the employees in their work units, they should have the right to determine over whom they are responsible.
2. The right to hire supports the formal authority base of the supervisor. The supervisor can say, "I hired you. You owe me some degree of loyalty." If the hire decision is made by some other person, the new employee may demonstrate less allegiance toward the supervisor.

3. Supervisors are in the best position to determine how applicants would fit into their work groups. They have a more intimate knowledge of the group dynamics of their subordinates.

4. Interviewing as an activity is an important dimension of management training. Interviewing skills developed in the hiring process can be applied to other interviewing situations such as performance appraisals, counseling, and taking corrective actions.

5. Supervisors are also in the best position to know the intricacies or details of the job. The inquisitive applicant will want more information about the job than is contained in the job description or the human resources staff interviewer can provide. The supervisor is in the best position to answer specific questions.

The process of interviewing applicants has a unique set of interpersonal dynamics. It is affected by the interviewing environment, emotional states of participants, and techniques applied to elicit information. Elements influencing an interview also include psychological barriers, interviewer errors, nonverbal behavior, and interviewing techniques.

Psychological Barriers. Inherent limitations of the interviewing process, called *psychological barriers,* can place an applicant at a disadvantage and reduce the validity and fairness of an interview. Psychological barriers include unequal power, phony behavior, and questions without answers.[6]

Unequal power exists between the applicant and the supervisor conducting the interview. Applicants generally are very interested in obtaining the job. However, to the supervisor, interviewing is only one part of a larger picture and, perhaps, a very small portion of the day-to-day routine. Therefore, applicants may suffer stress while the interviewer is relaxed and comfortable.

Job candidates may use phony behavior to project an image they perceive as the type of person the organization is seeking. To obtain the job,

> . . . many applicants seem to feel, one must be perceived as sociable, highly intelligent, considerate, and so on. They love to "work with people," never have problems with superiors, and are universally liked, they are seeking a job with challenge, responsibility and an opportunity to prove themselves. . . .
>
> The preponderance of phony behavior can cause an applicant with the virtues of a saint to be rejected as unreal, while the wolf in sheep's clothing is allowed into the flock.[7]

Some questions defy good answers. They can cause an applicant to become uncertain as to what the interviewer wants to know. Examples include, "Tell me about yourself." "What are your life's goals and where do you want to be 5 years or 25 years from now?" In the first instance, the applicant ponders which of several responses would reflect what the interviewer is searching for. "Should I be modest, aggressive, or demonstrate self-confidence?" "Should my answers be brief or thorough?" Referring to the life goals, many young applicants probably have not mastered the present, let alone contended with thoughts about what they want to be doing 5 or 25 years into the future. The "right" answer at Procter & Gamble might be the "wrong" one at IBM. This may cause the interviewer to make an incorrect analysis of a dishonest answer from a tense and uncomfortable applicant.[8]

Interviewing Errors. Interviewers are fallible. Recognizing the potential for errors is a means by which supervisors can minimize them. Some of the errors also exist in other kinds of interview situations.[9] (Refer to Chapter 14 for additional information about measurement errors.) Common interviewing errors are as follows:

- *Previous information bias.* The difficult-to-control previous information bias arises when we allow our opinion to be influenced by what others tell us about the applicant. We may subconsciously view a person more or less favorably depending on whether we have heard supportive or critical comments about him or her.
- *First impression error.* First impressions can be formed quickly and last for a long time. They may reflect nonverbal behavior. Because the interviewer usually has only a brief encounter with an applicant—from a half-hour to a few hours—first impressions become very important. Unfortunately, they may be inaccurate and therefore misleading.
- *Halo effect.* The halo effect occurs when an interviewer forms an opinion based on only one or two characteristics of an applicant. For example, an applicant who arrives at the interview two minutes late may be viewed less favorably because punctuality is of major importance to the supervisor, even though the candidate possesses a long list of job virtues. The reverse could occur when an applicant who is on time, although possessing far fewer qualifications, is rated more highly by the interviewer.
- *Stereotyping.* A stereotype is an oversimplified opinion or belief about someone that often is not borne out by facts. Stereotyping can hurt people because the belief is not an accurate representation of the individual or because it is not relevant to the job situation.
- *Personal biases.* Personal biases probably arise from prior culturation and learning experiences, and have great persistence or staying power. For example, one of the authors interviewed a human resources director who believed that blonde females were poor employees, and never hired them. Although it is difficult to apply Title VII of the Civil Rights Act of 1964 to this case, personal bias, like stereotyping, is unfair to job applicants.
- *Similar-to-me effect.* We may react more favorably to persons similar to ourselves than those who are different. The range of similarity covers personalities, avocational interests, and demographic characteristics such as age, sex, physical size, and religion. Notice, for example, how people who share similarities break into smaller, unique flocks at social events.
- *Asking leading questions.* When interviewers attempt to obtain agreement from applicants to questions, they are asking leading questions. "You think we should continue using the ZYX process which I support, don't you?" and "Wouldn't you agree that our company would be a good one to work for?" are leading questions. Applicants tend to answer these questions as the interviewer is prompting them to in the questions themselves.

Nonverbal Cues. Until now, we have concentrated on the verbal aspects of interviewing. Yet, nonverbal communication can have an important influence on how the interviewer perceives an applicant or vice versa. (The topics of proxemics and body language are discussed in Chapter 13.) The total communication process is affected by nonverbal communication in two ways. First, interviewers often place more meaning on nonverbal factors than on an applicant's verbal messages. Second, when the interviewer receives nonverbal information that conflicts with the verbal, he or she relies more heavily on the nonverbal communication.

Types of Interviews. Several interviewing formats are available for evaluating job applicants. Each method has its own style for obtaining information. The four basic types of interviews are structured, unstructured, problem-solving, and stress interviews.

In structured (or patterned) interviews, the interviewer follows a systematic form of questioning. The same list of questions is asked each applicant and their answers are recorded. In unstructured (or unpatterned) interviews, the interviewer varies the questions. The interview is free flowing and conversational in character. Questions are tailored to each applicant, although they may cover the same general topic areas. Probing for additional information is a feature of this type of interview.

In problem-solving interviews, questioning takes the form of presenting either hypothetical or real-life problems. Applicants are asked for their solutions or how they would handle the situations. In stress interviews, the applicant is placed in a pressured or stressful situation. The purpose is to determine the applicant's ability to retain composure and to think clearly under stress.

The type of interview to use is determined by what you wish to learn about the applicant. Probably the majority of interviews are unpatterned. Usually, the highest validity is obtained from either patterned or problem-solving interviews.

The Realistic Job Preview

A **realistic job preview** (RJP) is one way to inform candidates about the working environment and nature of a job. An RJP occurs when the hiring organization arranges for a candidate to experience the work environment before being employed. The RJP represents a creative and often useful approach to improving the selection process and reducing later employee turnover. An example of an RJP best illustrates the use of this method.

Procter and Gamble (P&G), the packaged consumer goods giant, interviews and tests prospects for sales positions. If candidates pass an initial screening, they go out for a day on the job with a P&G sales manager. The candidates observe the type and pace of work as they visit 10 or 12 stores in an eight-hour period, stopping for a quick burger for lunch. This experience provides a frame of reference when the candidates and company representatives later discuss employment.

RJPs are particularly useful if applicants can be selective about accepting a job offer (if other employment opportunities exist or the candidate is not dependent on employment income). They are also helpful if the candidate has unrealistic job expectations and would have difficulty coping with the job without benefit of an RJP. For example, the P&G prospect may learn he is unable to build store displays because of the lifting involved.[10]

Although company policy may keep supervisors from conducting formal RJPs, they should still try to communicate an accurate picture of a job to prospective employees. This step can improve subsequent employee satisfaction and reduce costly turnover.

The Psychological Contract

A **psychological contract** may develop between the supervisor (or other interviewer) and the applicant during the interviewing process when each party

realistic job preview
Occurs when the hiring organization arranges for a job candidate to experience the work environment before being employed.

psychological contract
Expectations formed during the interviewing process by a job applicant and the employer about the other's future behavior if the applicant is hired.

Some years ago, one of our students who was about to graduate was interviewed for a job with Electronic Data Services (EDS). The student was puzzled about the presence of a man who quietly sat during the interview without ever participating. The man never smiled but maintained a serious expression along with a disconcerting degree of eye contact.

Following the interview, after the quiet man had departed, the student asked the chief interviewer who the man was.

"Why that's Mr. Perot—Ross Perot. He owns the company and he often attends these interviews," was the answer.

formulates expectations of the other's future behavior. However, the "contract" may disintegrate if one person believes the other has not delivered the expected rewards.[11] Therefore, the supervisor must convey to the applicant as accurately and thoroughly as possible just what the job involves and what the organization is like. He or she must give what in communication theory is called a *"two-sided message,"* relating both the positive and negative aspects of the organization, the job, and the future relationship the applicant may expect if hired. This is also called **leveling,** or being realistic about the job.

leveling
Communication activity where two parties relate both negative as well as positive aspects about a job and themselves.

Workplace Safety

Safety contributes to effective and efficient production. However, workplaces often are unsafe. The **Occupational Safety and Health Act of 1970** was passed in response to the need to improve workplace safety. This act regulates safety and health conditions in most workplaces. Government, agricultural, and mining environments are either excluded from this legislation or are covered by other regulatory agencies.

Occupational Safety and Health Act of 1970
Act regulating safety and health conditions in most workplaces, excluding government, agricultural, and mining operations.

The Occupational Safety and Health Act authorized the creation of the **Occupational Safety and Health Administration (OSHA),** a federal agency charged with setting safety standards and monitoring compliance with safety and health standards in the workplace. In some states, compliance with regulations is monitored by state OSHA offices.

Occupational Safety and Health Administration (OSHA)
A federal agency created by the Occupational Safety and Health Act of 1970 to establish safety and health standards and monitor compliance in the workplace.

OSHA is relatively ineffective. There are so few inspectors and so many potentially dangerous workplaces to inspect that conscientious employers and supervisors cannot rely on either state or federal OSHA offices to ensure safety.[12] Safe and healthy workplaces should instead be regarded as the responsibility of each employer and each supervisor overseeing employees engaged in potentially dangerous work. Supervisors should, however, be aware that violations of some state safety and health statutes can lead to criminal prosecution.[13]

The Supervisor's Role in Promoting Safety

A safe working environment is a primary responsibility of the supervisor and each individual employee. Although there is no simple prescription for keeping the work environment safe, Lester Bittle offers the following good advice for supervisors:

- Instill in employees the belief that they are the most important source of accident prevention.

Several years ago one of the authors experienced an event indicating that even classrooms may be unsafe. As one of his students closed a classroom door, the door opener, a metal cylinder weighing eight pounds, came loose from the external frame, swung down on its hanger, and smashed through the glass window, showering broken glass on the woman.

The classroom was deathly quiet for a few seconds as students craned their necks to see what had happened.

The student's first words were, "I didn't mean to do it."

"Are you hurt?" the instructor asked.

"No," she responded.

The author learned from this incident that he as an instructor and the custodians and maintenance personnel had a shared responsibility for maintaining a safe and healthy instructional environment.

Safety and high performance go well together.

- Train employees in how to develop and practice safe work habits. Demonstrate safe work practices, observe employee performance, and provide feedback.
- When training in workplace safety, be specific. General warnings such as "work smart" are insufficient. It is necessary to train employees in what "smart work" entails, such as wearing safety goggles, putting the lids back on containers, and so on.
- Set a good example. If supervisors bend the rules, so will employees.
- Enforce safety standards. Follow progressive discipline with employees who break safety rules. (See Chapter 15 for a discussion of progressive discipline.) Safety is not something to be taken lightly.[14]

Compensating Employees

Compensation helps organizations to recruit, retain, and motivate employees. **Compensation** includes pay and benefits such as vacation and sick leave, health insurance, and employer pension contributions. Supervisors are usually not involved in designing an organization-wide compensation system, but must still understand and explain compensation to employees and monitor parts of a compensation system. For example, supervisors sometimes have the authority to offer overtime pay, and usually have to complete paperwork when an employee calls in sick or wishes to take time off. The recommendations a supervisor makes to upper management also help to determine employee pay raises.

compensation
The pay and benefits employees receive, such as vacation and sick leave, health insurance, and employer pension contributions.

Pay Adequacy and Pay Equity

Compensation's role in motivating employees is highly complex. The same compensation level can affect two similar employees differently. Much of compensation's role as a motivator depends on the basic sustenance needs of employees and their perceptions of fairness.[15] The following discussion focuses on pay, though the principles to be covered can be extended to compensation in general.

Pay must first be adequate for an employee. **Pay adequacy** means the pay level allows an employee to meet basic needs and to achieve a standard of living that is minimally acceptable to the employee. A wide variety of socioeconomic, psychological, and physiological variables influence an individual's perception whether compensation is adequate. Beverly Hills physicians and unskilled

pay adequacy
A pay level that allows an employee to meet basic needs and to achieve a standard of living that is minimally acceptable to the employee.

laborers who grew up in poor families usually have very different pay adequacy boundaries. Pay adequacy boundaries can change, however. People very quickly become accustomed to different standards of living and can come to define those standards as being minimally acceptable.

pay equity
A pay level that is fair.

Once pay adequacy needs have been met, **pay equity** has influence as a motivator. Pay equity is concerned with the fairness of pay. Because many employees in the North American work force have already met pay adequacy needs, fairness of compensation takes on increased importance. It is not surprising that studies of compensation as a motivator find employees rating fair pay as being more important than high pay.[16]

external pay equity
Pay and other compensation deemed fair by employees when comparing their jobs to comparable jobs in other organizations.

There are different levels of pay equity to consider. **External pay equity** means that pay and other compensation is deemed fair by the employee when comparing his or her job to comparable jobs in other organizations. **Internal pay equity** is concerned with perceived fairness when an employee compares compensation for his or her job with other comparable jobs within an organization. **Individual pay equity** deals with the employee's perception of fairness when comparing his or her individual pay and effort, education, training, and other inputs to a job with those of others in an organization.

internal pay equity
Concerned with perceived fairness when employees compare compensation for their jobs with other comparable jobs within an organization.

Employee dissatisfaction with either pay adequacy or equity will result in counterproductive behavior, such as job avoidance (for example, calling in sick) or job attraction (a search for a new job).

If employees are not meeting pay adequacy needs through pay or other resources, then striving to maintain fair pay is irrelevant.

individual pay equity
Employees' perceptions of fairness when comparing their individual pay and effort, education, training, and other inputs to a job with those of others in their organization.

The effective supervisor should be sensitive to the pay needs of members of his or her work team. If supervising low paid employees, it is important to be sensitive to pay adequacy needs. A few extra hours of overtime or scheduled work may mean an employee can pay bills as well as buy needed shoes for a child. Scheduling of work hours, under such circumstances, should be done carefully, following well-defined criteria.

Even if pay is adequate, pay equity is not easy to maintain. Supervisors should consider the effect a reward provided to one employee (such as additional hours or favorable daytime working hours) has on the morale of others. Every effort should be made to keep pay and other rewards equitable. This does not mean that pay has to be equal. If one employee works harder than another, or is otherwise clearly more deserving of a particular reward, then it is not counterproductive to compensate that person differently.

Compensation Trends

Improving employee performance in terms of productivity and quality of output has become increasingly important in today's competitive world. This need is coupled with pressure to reduce wages and other forms of compensation as U.S. manufacturers compete with stiff domestic and foreign competition. The question that arises is how to increase employee performance while holding wages and other compensation costs down.

pay-for-performance
Compensation programs that tie pay raises or bonuses to employee performance.

Many U.S. businesses and other organizations have responded to this question by developing **pay-for-performance** programs. These compensation programs tie pay raises or bonuses to employee performance. For example, an employer might distribute a percentage of net profit to employees or might pay a bonus based on cost reductions in a particular work unit. In this way, an employer can justify additional compensation expense and encourage employees to improve their performance. The supervisor's role in a pay-for-performance program is to monitor and report on employee progress.

Another compensation trend is a movement toward allowing employees to choose their benefits. Many employers now offer **cafeteria plans,** benefit programs in which employees can choose among a wide variety of benefit packages including sick leave, vacation leave, and insurance benefits.[17] The movement to cafeteria benefit plans was prompted, in part, by the increasing diversity of the work force. The days of the husband working as sole earner for a family of four are gone. His wife may also be working full time and the couple may wish to use the life insurance program at one employer and the health program at another. Supervisors may find themselves explaining benefit program options to employees, though this is usually the responsibility of the human resources office.

There has been a continuing movement to reduce pay differences between those working in female-dominated and male-dominated job classes. As mentioned in Chapter 3, a trend toward establishing **comparable worth** in compensation started in the United States in the mid-1970s and continues to this day. Comparable worth is concerned with providing equal pay for jobs of comparable value or worth.

Job evaluation, a method for quantifying the content of different jobs in terms of their relative value to the employer, has been extensively used to compare pay for male-dominated and female-dominated job classes. The conclusion of these comparable worth studies has invariably been that men tend to be paid more than women even when jobs are of comparable worth.[18]

The goal of the comparable worth movement is to bring about social justice rather than to improve employee performance or profitability. Some critics of the comparable worth movement argue it would harm the American economy. Implementing comparable worth could mean a 20 percent pay increase for employees working in female-dominated job classifications such as nurses, secretaries, and grade school teachers.

Even if job evaluation and comparable worth are required, pay equity might still be elusive. One study that controlled all variables associated with job evaluation (for example, the job description and job evaluation method), except the gender of the job holder, found that evaluators awarded significantly more job value points to a job when they thought it was held by a male. Interestingly, both male and female job evaluation raters granted more points when they thought a man held the job![19]

cafeteria plans
Compensation programs that allow employees to choose the mix of their benefits.

comparable worth
Providing equal pay for jobs of comparable value or worth.

job evaluation
Method for quantifying the content of different jobs in terms of their relative value to the employer for the purpose of establishing wage and salary structures.

George slammed the door behind him as he stomped back to work. Carla sat at her desk with a puzzled look. Then, she remembered a comment her mom used to make, that she had to treat Carla and her brothers and sisters *differently* in order to be fair. It finally made sense.

Summary: Focus on Concepts

Human resources management covers staffing, compensation, performance appraisal, worker safety, training and development and, sometimes, labor relations in organizations. This chapter discussed staff recruitment and selection, training, worker safety, and compensation. Today's human resources management evolved from the traditional personnel office function that was primarily concerned with staffing. This evolution occurred because organizations realized they needed to do a better job of increasing the performance of human resources and dealing with job-related legal issues.

The contemporary supervisor plays an important role in human resources management. He or she makes selection decisions, recommends employees for promotion, conducts training, makes pay raise decisions, and facilitates work scheduling, and generally helps to create a legally compliant, dignified work environment for employees.

Employee selection, the process of hiring the right person for a job, involves collaboration between the human resources office and the supervisor. The human resources office usually recruits, tests, and screens candidates. Employment tests relate to the job for which the candidate has applied (for example, a typing test may be required for office workers). The supervisor, sometimes together with other members of the management team, makes the final selection after interviewing candidates.

There can be significant problems with traditional staffing processes. The typical employment interview is often a poor way to pick the right person for a job. Letters of recommendation also tend to be invalid. The consequences of making a poor selection are significant.

There is much a supervisor can do to improve the selection process. He or she can make sure the human resources office has an accurate job description for the job opening. A job description (describing the duties of the job) and job specifications (listing the minimum qualifications) should be developed through job analysis. Conducted by the supervisor or a specialist, job analysis is a process that involves measuring and recording a job's work activities.

A structured selection interview, in which all applicants are asked the same questions based on job content, and a realistic job preview can improve the selection process. A realistic job preview (RJP) allows a job candidate to experience a job before being hired.

Overseeing and maintaining workplace safety is an important supervisory responsibility. The Occupational Safety and Health Act of 1970, legislation that regulates safety and health conditions in most workplaces, created the Occupational Safety and Health Administration (OSHA). The act and the agency it created are unable to fully cover safety issues confronted by supervisors and employees. That responsibility is up to the individual supervisor and each individual in the work team. Supervisors should instill this responsibility in their employees; provide specific training and feedback in safe work habits and procedures; set a good example; and enforce safety standards.

Employee compensation includes pay and benefits. The individual supervisor, although he or she has little influence on overall organizational compensation policies and procedures, does influence scheduling of overtime and make recommendations concerning pay raises.

Supervisors should strive to maintain pay adequacy and pay equity within their work teams. Pay adequacy is concerned with minimum compensation sufficient to meet basic needs; pay equity is concerned with the fairness of pay. External, internal, and individual pay equity represent different levels of fairness that concern employees.

The need to increase employee performance has led to development of pay-for-performance compensation programs. These programs tie pay raises or bonuses to employee performance. Cafeteria plans—programs in which employees can choose from a variety of benefit packages—represent another recent trend in compensation.

Another trend in compensation is the comparable worth movement. This movement is concerned that people working in male-dominated job classes are paid more than those working in female-dominated job classes. Comparable worth proponents support making pay adjustments on the basis of job evaluation, a method for measuring and quantifying the content of different jobs in terms of their value to an employer.

Review Questions

1. What is human resource management (HRM)?
2. Why has the importance of HRM increased during the past 20 years?
3. Differentiate between the roles of the HRM office and the supervisor in the recruitment and selection process.

4. Almost all organizations use application forms in the selection process. Why? What types of information should be acquired on these forms? What should not?

5. Why should supervisors, with the concurrence of the EEO officer of an organization, have the right to make the selection decision?

6. Identify and explain the psychological barriers job applicants face in the interviewing process. What methods would you use to control them? Give examples.

7. State the four types of interview formats. Overall, which is superior and why?

8. Indicate four methods by which the selection process can be improved.

9. What is the realistic job preview (RJP)? The psychological contract? Why are they useful to supervisors?

10. How can the supervisor improve safety in the work environment?

11. Explain the meaning and importance of maintaining pay adequacy and pay equity in an organization. What are the three levels of pay equity to consider?

12. Considering compensation trends, what are cafeteria plans and comparable worth?

Notes

1. The Society for Human Resources Management (SHRM) is the major HRM professional national organization. Previously, it was known as the American Society for Personnel Administration (ASPA).

2. See J. P. Wanous, *Organizational Entry: Recruitment, Selection, and Socialization of Newcomers* (Reading, MA: Addison-Wesley, 1980), 24.

3. See "Employment Testing and Selection Procedures—Where Are They Headed?" *Personnel Management: Policies and Practices* (Englewood Cliffs, NJ: Prentice-Hall, 1975), 658. Also see Bureau of National Affairs, *Bulletin to Management*, No. 1727, May 5, 1981.

4. L. R. Bittle and J. W. Newstrom, *What Every Supervisor Should Know*, 7th ed. (Lake Forest, IL: Glencoe, 1991).

5. W. Cascio, *Applied Psychology in Personnel Management* (Englewood Cliffs, NJ: Prentice-Hall Inc., 1987).

6. R. G. Nehrbass, "Psychological Barriers to Effective Employment Interviewing," *Personnel Journal* 56 (February 1977): 60.

7. Ibid., 60-62.

8. Ibid., 60.

9. Interviewing errors also occur in performance appraisal and in counseling.

10. J. A. Breaugh, "Realistic Job Previews: A Critical Appraisal and Future Research Directions," *Academy of Management Review* 8 (1983).

11. M. Dunahee and W. A. Wangler, "The Psychological Contract: A Conceptual Structure for Management/Employee Relations," *Personnel Journal* 53 (July 1974): 518.

12. D. Nelkin and M. S. Brown, *Workers at Risk* (Chicago, IL: University of Chicago Press, 1984).

13. S. Garland, "This Safety Ruling Could Be Hazardous to Employer's Health," *Business Week*, February 20, 1989.

14. L. R. Bittle and J. W. Newstrom, *What Every Supervisor Should Know*, 7th ed. (Lake Forest, IL: Glencoe, 1991).

15. C. T. Lewis, "Assessing the Validity of Job Evaluation," *Public Personnel Management* 18 (1989): 45-63.

16. E. E. Lawler, *Pay and Organizational Development* (Reading, MA: Addison-Wesley, 1983).

17. L. L. Byars and L. W. Rue, *Human Resource Management*, 2d ed. (Homewood, IL: Irwin, 1987), 363.

18. C. T. Lewis, "Assessing the Validity of Job Evaluation," *Public Personnel Management* 18 (1989): 45-63.

19. C. T. Lewis and C. K. Stevens, "An Analysis of Job Evaluation and Job Holder Gender Effects on Job Evaluation," *Public Personnel Management* 19 (1990): 271-278.

Show and Tell

It was the final day of an intensive week of training for a group of 15 supervisors representing a number of businesses and nonprofit organizations. The class was about evenly divided between men and women of varied ages. The trainer began the session by distributing 8" × 10" lined cards to members of the class with the following instructions:

> One of the responsibilities of being a supervisor is hiring new employees. Some of you have many years of experience while others are just getting started. Those from larger organizations have personnel departments to help you out. Still, much of the information you obtain to help you make your hiring decision is from an application form and the interview you conduct with the job candidate.
>
> I want you to list all of the things you look for in hiring a new employee, that is, the evidence you receive from the applicant and your subsequent impressions. On one side of the card, record those things you believe are good features and predict good job performance. On the other side, list the ones that suggest the person probably would not work out as one of your employees. Unless they are obvious, you might also briefly give your reasons. Please write legibly. We will take five minutes, so if there are no questions, go ahead and begin.

The trainer collected the cards a few minutes later, thumbed through them, and wrote several of the comments on a chalk board:

The Positive Indicators

1. I like neatly prepared application blanks and resumés.
2. Veterans make good employees. Besides, we owe them something.
3. I look for people that have prepared for the meeting and know something about the company's business.
4. Believe it or not, I look for clean fingernails.
5. How long their reference letters are. Usually, if they are more than a couple of paragraphs, that indicates someone cared enough about them to spend the time helping them get a job.
6. Past work experience. For young people, not necessarily the importance of any particular job; rather it is a sign they are not afraid to work.
7. Being on time for the interview. If hired, they probably also will get to work on time.
8. For guys, being married helps. Married men are a lot more dependable.
9. Let's face it. As a guy I admit if a woman is young and pretty it doesn't hurt.
10. The right amount of ambition. Not too much, though.
11. Someone who comes across as "hungry" and needs the job badly. I look for hunger in their eyes.

The Negative Indicators

1. Young women. Especially if they are very pretty. They either leave to get married shortly after we get them trained, or they are a distraction in the office.
2. Ex-cons. You can't trust them.
3. Questions from an applicant early in the interview about our company retirement plan.
4. People who get too close to me. They tend to be pushy.
5. Men with long hair, especially when it looks unwashed.
6. People who smoke.
7. In our kind of business, someone who is a Republican.
8. Misspelled words on the application form and poor grammar during the interview.
9. People who are new to the area rather than having lived here for a long time. Signs of "roots" are important.
10. The serious types who don't smile or have a sense of humor. They tend to be the nervous ones.

Questions

1. Which, if any, of the "indicators" likely has validity as a predictor of job success?
2. Are there any stereotypes in the list? Which ones?
3. Recommend a more analytical approach to evaluating job applicants during the selection process.

Case 8-2

Demotivation

When Susan Howard first began working for Carolina Supreme Printers in Charleston, South Carolina, her hopes were high for a career leading to progressively better positions within the company. That was in 1968. Her employer was a major supplier of checks, drafts, and other printed forms to commercial banking and financial institutions throughout the southeastern region of the United States and Latin America.

Susan had worked for the company for over 25 years. In fact, it was the only employer she had known since graduating from a community college in Columbia, South Carolina. Although she had several attractive job offers with other employers at the time, she chose Supreme Printers as the one holding the most promise. Her goals were not realized though. Initially, while being interviewed for the job, she was led to believe she would enter a junior management program and, upon completion, assume a supervisory position within a year or two.

Whereas Susan was not a dynamic person, she was an excellent worker—bright and conscientious. Still, she probably was the type that is overlooked or taken for granted. Those who really foul up or have a gimmick attract the attention of the bosses. The "steady Eddies" are lost in the crowd, so it seems at times.

At first, Susan felt frustration. The promise of the training program from her supervisor never materialized. Meanwhile, she had foregone other good job prospects. Be patient, she was told by her bosses. There were no openings available. Wait and prepare for the opportunity. So she waited. She even began taking night classes at a local college. After six years, she received her bachelor's degree in management. Still, no training program and no major advancements either.

For the first several years, Susan *did* try with her best abilities. But after awhile her frustrations, first with herself for getting into the situation and later with her supervisors for not helping her get out of it, led to less communication with her coworkers and less cooperation with her bosses. She was transferred to several jobs within the company over the years. In more recent years, her work was described as "barely adequate." She performed at the level of getting by—no more, no less. With her 25th anniversary at Carolina Supreme Printers in 1993, she looked toward retirement in 1998. Bare survival was now her goal. The spark of incentive had long ago died out.

Questions

1. What are the risks of supervisors promising something they cannot or do not deliver?
2. What are the responsibilities of Susan's bosses? Why do you suppose they overlooked her needs and goals?
3. What should Susan have done many years ago? What might she do now?
4. How would you prevent this type of situation from occurring in the future?

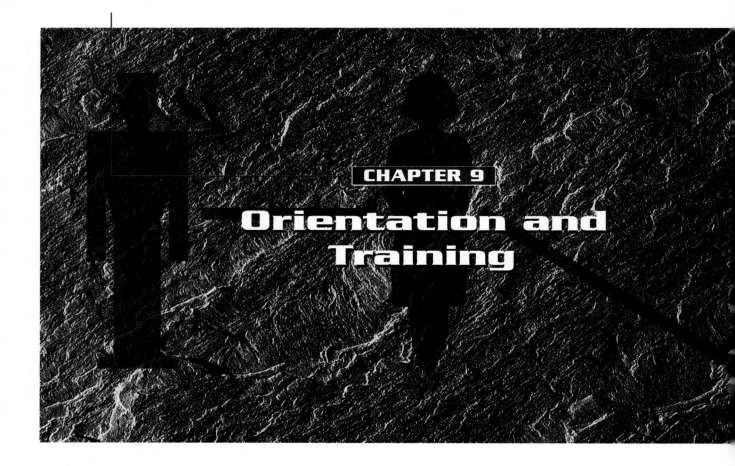

CHAPTER 9

Orientation and Training

● "When I told the three young men they could go home after finishing the work detail, how did I know they would go all the way to Alabama?" a sergeant exclaimed during the court-martial at Ft. Bliss.

Circa 1950s

LEARNING OBJECTIVES

1. Understand and apply the components of an effective employee orientation program.
2. Explain the concepts of task analysis and person analysis.
3. Give the structure of a training plan.
4. Discuss six types of training programs.
5. Understand the terms *orders* and *instructions,* and illustrate appropriate methods for carrying out each.

Carla had a problem. In her office at the Boeing plant in Everett, Washington, toward the end of her shift, she reflected on recent events. "When I started working here, I was overwhelmed with the amount of information the company gave me during the first couple of days. The training continued to the end of the week, and I probably forgot more than I learned. Most of the people who worked with me were nice, but they were very busy. If I asked them to repeat something, I could tell it was stressing them to do it. It was hard to adjust to the pace of Boeing, even though I am used to big-city life.

"And that's where my problem comes from. Several of my recent hires quit the company after only a month or two. One fellow left after his first week on the job, and he had a lot of promise. We are so big and, at times, impersonal, that folks from a rural background have their wits scared out of them."

Carla remembered touring Washington, D.C., when she was in eighth grade. One of the many places she and her parents visited was the Pentagon, the headquarters of the U.S. military establishment. "You parked here, walked three blocks, were given a map of the internal workings of the building, and you were on your own. If you got lost, we'll see you next year." There weren't any guides to tell you where to park or where to go to find your destination.

"And that's what is happening to some of my new people. "They don't know where to park or how to find their way to our working area. They don't know their

way around the city or have any friends here. They are unhappy and scared—I can see it in their faces. So they quit and go home.

"What do I do? I start over in replacing them. I feel sorry for them. It's also a big waste of time. There has got to be a better system."

In this chapter, we consider the critically important supervisory activities of employee orientation and training. A new, promoted, or transferred employee needs to learn how to perform his or her job and how to continue to do work well in a constantly changing work environment.

The importance of training is illustrated by the U.S. Air Force's investment in training new pilots. Training, alone, can require an expenditure of $1.5 million over two years, and the new pilot is subsequently entrusted with the lives of other persons in an airplane costing from $50 million to over $200 million. Training *is* serious business.

Employee Orientation

You have hired the best person for the job. What then? One of the authors, while visiting a large electronic goods retailer in the Midwest, observed a staff member sitting at a desk, hands neatly folded, glancing nervously about. On making small talk, he learned she was in the throes of her first day on the job; her boss wasn't in, and she didn't know what to do. The phone rang. This flustered individual was unable to transfer the call because she had not yet been briefed on how to operate the phone! She needed an **orientation,** a process whereby a new employee is introduced to the organization and to the specific requirements of the job.

orientation
A process whereby a new employee is introduced to the organization and to the specific requirements of the job.

Most new employee orientations are conducted more competently than the situation described above. However, we are reminded of a major state agency that provides orientation only once or twice a year for new hires. Still, too often, employees report for that scary first day and receive little more than a pat on the back, a "welcome aboard," and a brief overview of their job. The supervisor is often given responsibility for orienting the new employee, but usually no provision has been made for the supervisor to take time away from normal duties to provide the new employee with assistance. Employee orientation can be a low organizational priority.

Good orientation reduces labor turnover. It also has the potential for increasing loyalty toward employers. Robert Hollmann describes four kinds of deficient orientation programs:[1]

- *The paperwork design.* After a fast welcome by the human resources office, new employees complete a variety of paperwork and then are sent to their new supervisors, who may or may not complete the orientation.
- *The social Darwinism design.* As the name suggests, the Darwinian approach leads to survival of the fittest. New employees are given a few details about the company. Then they are immediately put to work.
- *The Mickey Mouse design.* Menial tasks are assigned to new employees, or they are given tasks that, otherwise, tend not to be done because they are low priority.
- *The overload design.* Although the employer has good intentions, new employees are so overwhelmed with information that it exceeds the human capacity for absorption. It is just too much knowledge in too brief a period.

Elevators?

A few years ago, one of the authors checked into a new resort to attend a meeting. The following conversation occurred at the reception desk:

"Sir, you are in room 353, and you will need to take the elevator," the reception clerk said.

"Where are the elevators?"

"I don't know," was the response. "I just started working here two hours ago."

An employee orientation program should provide new members, quickly and humanely, with information they need to adjust to their new working environment. Some employees adjust rapidly. Others can experience frustration and anxiety. Perhaps you can recall anxious feelings you experienced as a new employee or as a student starting your freshman year in college.

Anxieties of New Employees and Their Supervisors

Anxiety is a feeling of uneasiness or apprehension that arises from an uncertainty about the future. New employees and their supervisors may experience anxiety during the employee's initial stage of employment. The degree of anxiety is correlated to the magnitude of difference between the organizational culture and setting and the employee's previous cultural experiences. The employee experiences **cultural shock** when the new environment is radically foreign to that he or she previously enjoyed and friends or family are absent. The greater the differences in behavior patterns, beliefs, institutions, and artifacts in the new environment, the larger the cultural shock. For example, a young person moving from a rural setting to a large city or going from a small business with 10 or fewer employees to a factory employing 10,000 or more may experience cultural shock.

New employees' anxieties may be intensified with initiation rituals practiced by coworkers. For example, when one of the authors began working as a roustabout in a West Texas natural gas plant, his boss and members of the work crew would send him to the maintenance shops for nonexistent tools and supplies, such as left-handed monkey wrenches, sky hooks, and striped paint. Coworkers immensely enjoyed his return empty-handed. While he had reservations about the existence of such articles, others made convincing cases of their authenticity. The only time he refused to obey a "fetch" order was for an item known as "fish tape." That was a big mistake. "No sir," he told his boss, "I'm not going to get it because there isn't such a thing." Well, as it turned out, there is something called fish tape (used to pull wire through conduits).

Some rituals are a form of "paying one's dues" before admission into the work team. A junior management trainee at a savings and loan headquarters was required to water the exterior greenery, sweep the sidewalks, and shovel snow—chores he considered a bit below what a management trainee should be doing. Eventually the trainee became a manager, and assigned his former chores to a new management trainee. Dues-paying is part of the social price for admission into the work group and can contribute to group cohesiveness.

Supervisors also may experience anxiety caused by a new employee. The new person may be perceived as a threat, especially when the employee is better educated than the supervisor. The supervisor may fear that the new employee will eventually obtain the supervisor's job or will cause him or her to appear less

anxiety
A feeling of uneasiness or apprehension arising from an uncertainty about the future.

cultural shock
Describes the feelings a person may experience when placed in a foreign environment where friends and family are absent.

competent in the eyes of subordinates or the supervisor's boss. *This threat is very real.* A strategy some supervisors use to reduce this risk is not hiring such applicants in the first place. More than one applicant with superior abilities has, we suspect, been rejected in the screening process by a supervisor for this reason. The effective supervisor should deal with this risk by keeping current in his or her job.

Contents of a Job Orientation Program

Without creating an excessively time-consuming or costly program, let's consider the kinds of information new employees need. Figure 9-1 is an outline of topics that should be covered in orientation. As they share orientation responsibilities with the human resources staff, supervisors convey performance standards and assist the new employee in becoming established in the work group. Human resources provides information about employee benefits and work rules. The orientation should include preparation, welcome, background information, introduction to coworkers, performance expectations, policies and employee benefits, and a follow-up of the trainee's progress.

Preparation.   Preparation involves ensuring the new employee has a place to work and the needed tools and equipment. Scrounging work space, locating tools and other equipment at the last moment, and procuring supplies haphazardly after the employee arrives communicates to that person that she or he is a low priority or that we are unorganized.

Welcome.   The supervisor or staff from human resources should greet the new employee. Often in large organizations new employees are forced to fumble around on their own when they first arrive, their confusion increasing by the minute.

   The timing of a new employee's arrival may be important. It should be scheduled at some time other than the busiest part of the work day. At the beginning of the day, supervisors often are busy instructing employees on details of their assignments. A new employee is left to stand around idly, often uncomfortable and in the way, observing the heightened level of activity. A bank teller supervisor suggested her strategy for handling this situation: "My employees begin working at eight in the morning, but new employees are instructed to arrive at ten o'clock on their first day. Now I have sufficient time to greet them properly."

Background Information.   It is helpful to acquaint a new employee with the history of the organization, its objectives, goals of the work unit, and where the new employee fits in the total picture. When an organization has a meritorious past, a bit of history-telling can develop feelings of pride in affiliation.

   A tour of facilities provides the new employee with an understanding of the physical parts of the organization's operations. Three areas should be included: One is the production processes used to create the organization's products. Some white-collar workers probably have never been on a factory floor to observe how their company's products are manufactured. The second consists of auxiliary services including offices, maintenance shops, and service units. The final area consists of facilities important to employees such as the lunchroom, parking facilities, restrooms, first aid stations, and employee locker areas.

Orienting new employees is an essential part of a supervisor's job.

Figure 9-1	A New Employee Orientation Program

1. **Prepare for the New Employee**
   - Review application form, resumé, and job description.
   - Prepare the work area: desk, tools, equipment, and supplies.

2. **Welcome the New Employee**
   - The employee's supervisor or a member of personnel should be ready to meet the new employee at a designated place.
   - Greet the new employee; review background and interests.

3. **Provide Background Information about Organization and Work Unit**
   - Provide the organization's history, mission, and major objectives.
   - Give information about the goals of the work unit and how the unit fits into the overall operations.
   - Tour facilities, including office or factory layout and special areas of interest to the employee, such as lunchroom or cafeteria, parking facilities, restrooms, dispensary, and so forth.
   - Show how the employee's job fits into the total picture.

4. **Introduce Employee to Coworkers**
   - Introduce to coworkers, giving their names and duties.
   - Take the new employee to lunch the first day.

5. **Outline Performance Expectations**
   - Stress the performance standards of the organization relative to the employee's job.
   - Provide a copy of the employee's job description and any other information about our expectations.
   - Indicate how performance is evaluated, by whom, and the frequency of evaluations.

6. **Review Working Conditions, Policies, Rules, and Benefits**
   - Hours of work and use of time sheets or time clocks, if used.
   - Parking areas and arrangement such as permits.
   - Lunch periods and rest periods or breaks.
   - Use of telephone for personal calls; use of corporate property and services such as vehicles, photocopying equipment, supplies, and mail
   - Vacations: when taken and length
   - Sick leave benefits
   - Union affairs, if applicable
   - Attendance and punctuality requirements
   - General appearance and job behavior
   - Pay periods and procedures required for being paid
   - Maintaining confidentiality of job information
   - People to contact for specific problems
   - Safety: wearing of protective equipment and clothing, what to do if an accident occurs, and reporting procedures after an accident
   - Smoking: when and where permitted
   - Reporting procedures when employee is sick

7. **Follow Up**
   - Review of employee's progress
   - Identify problems and courses of action

Introduction to Coworkers. Appropriate introductions to an employee's co-workers include recitation of both first and last names and the job title or work performed by each team member. When appropriate, take new employees to lunch the first day. New employees often come to work without lunch plans, and may become uncomfortable when everyone else goes to lunch. One of our students summed it up by stating, "The supervisor should have the new employee for lunch the first day."

Performance Expectations. Convey the performance standards you expect the new employee to attain. If there is a probationary period, describe it, and explain how and when the employee's performance will be evaluated. Give information about the reward systems for good performance and about what will happen if performance or behavior is below expectations. Don't avoid the subject of discipline. Lay it on the line in understandable terms.

Policies and Employee Benefits. Information about company policies and benefits is primarily conveyed by the human resources department or in an employee handbook. It is also important, however, to help new employees to learn the informal culture of an organization, which is not covered by these sources and probably differs from the mandated culture. For example, a government administrator who managed a department with over 1,000 employees was immensely annoyed by a new employee who took the most convenient unassigned parking space—the one the administrator considered his. The new employee was the first to arrive at work each day. Therefore, he parked in the space nearest to the front door. Subsequently, the administrator had his personal reserved parking sign erected, surrounded by four disabled personnel parking space signs. From then on, the new employee came to work at the same time as everyone else.

Follow-up. Supervisors should talk to trainees after the second or third week to find out how much information from orientation they recall, and repeat information as needed.

patron
A person who supports people in adjusting to their jobs and organizations by providing friendship and information about the organization and community.

In larger organizations, patrons or sponsors are sometimes used. A **patron** is a person who supports another person. Patrons help new employees adjust to their jobs and organizations as they extend friendship and serve as a source of information, not only about their company and its informal culture, but also about the community. The frequency of contacts declines from daily the first week to once or twice a week thereafter. A coworker in the supervisor's work team may serve in this role. Essentially, a patron is viewed as a friend, source of information, and problem solver.

mentor
An individual who systematically develops a subordinate's abilities through intensive tutoring, coaching, and guidance.

In some instances, a supervisor may become a **mentor** to a new employee. "A mentor is an individual who systematically develops a subordinate's abilities through intensive tutoring, coaching, and guidance."[2] Over a longer term, the mentor relationship usually is between a member of management higher in the organizational hierarchy and a junior member of management—such as a supervisor.[3]

Identifying Special Employee Needs. Some new employees have personal needs requiring special treatment. Physically disabled persons may require modification of work areas to enable them to perform their jobs. The supervisor may need to learn what to do if an employee with epilepsy has a seizure. Not uncommonly, a new employee is financially impoverished or lacks transportation. In this case, the supervisor should be proactive, solving anticipated problems before they arise.

The orientation should be viewed as a process that takes place over a period of days or weeks, as opposed to a one-day briefing. Supervisors should emphasize that they are available to the new employee when questions, problems, or concerns arise. An appropriate orientation has the potential for reducing labor costs and the length of the adjustment period. Orientation is a pragmatic approach to assimilating new employees into the organization.

Employee Training

As first defined in Chapter 2, training is "any systematic attempt to change employee behavior through the learning process in order to improve performance." The current emphasis on employee empowerment, Total Quality Management (TQM), team-based decision making, and job rotation has given employee training new importance. More than ever, effective supervisors need to lead well-trained work groups. The days of an employee doing the same limited job every day, with little involvement in work processes outside his or her area, are rapidly coming to an end. Also, all employees, not just new hires, increasingly need to be trained to keep up with changing technologies.

Unfortunately, training programs receive little attention from many American employers. As mentioned in Chapter 2, U.S. companies spend an enormous amount of money on training each year—some $30 billion. Most of the investment, however, is made by a relatively few companies. In fact, less than 200 U.S. companies spend more than 2 percent of their annual payrolls on training.[4] The training that does occur tends to exclude front-line workers. The work force led by supervisors receives only 23 percent of total training dollars.[5]

The reality is that supervisors must usually serve as trainers for employees under their supervision. Supervisors often cannot depend on the human resources office or upper management to provide training resources.

A Training Framework

Work team training should be tied to organization-wide goals.[6] This makes training more relevant for the employee and will help the supervisor sell training activities to his or her boss. Two steps are required before an effective training program can be designed: task analysis and person analysis.

Task analysis includes definition of the tasks involved in doing a job; definition of knowledge, skills, and abilities required to perform the tasks; and development of training objectives.[7] It is essential that task analysis begin with a valid job description. It does not make sense to define tasks involved in a job without first having an accurate description of the job. (See Chapter 8 for more about job descriptions.)

Person analysis involves determination of the training needs of individual employees. Employees' training needs can be assessed by the supervisor or the human resources office. (New employees always require some type of training based on an assessment of their skills, even if training is nothing more than an introduction to the organization and its mission.) Person analysis can also be conducted through performance appraisal. (See Chapter 14 for a discussion of this topic.) Ongoing performance appraisal results can be used to identify individual employee needs and to develop training opportunities accordingly.

task analysis
The definition of tasks involved in performing a job; definition of knowledge, skills, and abilities required to perform the tasks; and development of training objectives.

person analysis
The determination of training needs of individual employees.

training plan
The integration of person and task analysis into a plan of action that includes specifying training objectives, training program design, time frames, and employees to be trained.

training program
The portion of a training plan that actually delivers instruction or otherwise facilitates learning.

classroom training
A form of training where employees go to a classroom to hear lectures, watch films, and do exercises.

vestibule training
A form of training involving employees practicing the work processes and tools in a separate training area called a vestibule.

programmed instruction
A form of training where employees study standardized printed instructions and take tests after completing sections of the program.

computer-assisted instruction
Similar to programmed instruction except that computers are used to deliver training material and track employee progress.

job rotation
A form of cross training where employees are trained to do several jobs.

on-the-job training (OJT)
A form of training employees while they are doing the actual job or some parts of it.

After tasks and individual needs have been defined, a training plan needs to be developed. This plan integrates person and task analysis into a plan for action. A **training plan** should specify training objectives, training program design, time frame, and employees to be trained. A **training program** involves that part of a training plan that actually delivers instruction or otherwise facilitates learning, and can cover individual employees, an entire work group, or both.

Training plans should also include systematic evaluation that assesses the training program's success in meeting its objectives. Evaluation should feed back into person and task analysis. Supervisors should constantly assess training programs to make sure their content is current with the dictates of the job and the needs of employees. Figure 9-2 shows how training plan components, whether for a group or for an individual, fit together.

Supervisors should consult with their bosses and human resources personnel before designing a training plan. As a supervisor, you may find yourself simply following a plan imposed by your boss or by the human resources department. If you have more flexibility, consider developing an individual training plan for each member of your work team. You can also incorporate employees' success with training into the performance appraisal process.

Performance appraisal, then, not only helps with person analysis, but can also be used to track the progress of a training plan. For this to hold true it is important that performance appraisal focus on employee behaviors or output, rather than on employee traits or characteristics. It is possible to design a training plan to help an employee behave more courteously with customers or to work more productively; it is not possible to design a program that makes an employee more "cheerful" or a better "team player."

Training Programs

There are many different ways to facilitate learning.

Classroom training is a popular form of training in which employees go to a classroom to hear lectures, watch films, and do exercises. Classroom training is used for presenting theoretical material. In **vestibule training,** employees practice using work processes and tools in a separate training area called a *vestibule.*

In **programmed instruction,** employees study standardized printed instructions and take tests after completing sections of the program. Expert assistance is usually available from the training facilitator. **Computer-assisted instruction** (CAI) is similar to programmed instruction except that computers are used to deliver training material and to track employee progress. Some CAI programs include videotaped instruction.

In **job rotation,** or cross training, employees are trained to do several jobs. **On-the-job training** (OJT) occurs when the employee learns the job, or changes in the job, while employed doing the job or some parts of it.

Supervisors are most likely to be involved with training programs that use OJT or job rotation. Teaching the employee on the job, with little support from human resources or from higher management, is the rule rather than the exception in today's workplace.

Implementing OJT

The first step in implementing OJT is to prepare the employee to learn. Whether a new employee or an incumbent, it is important that a person wants to be

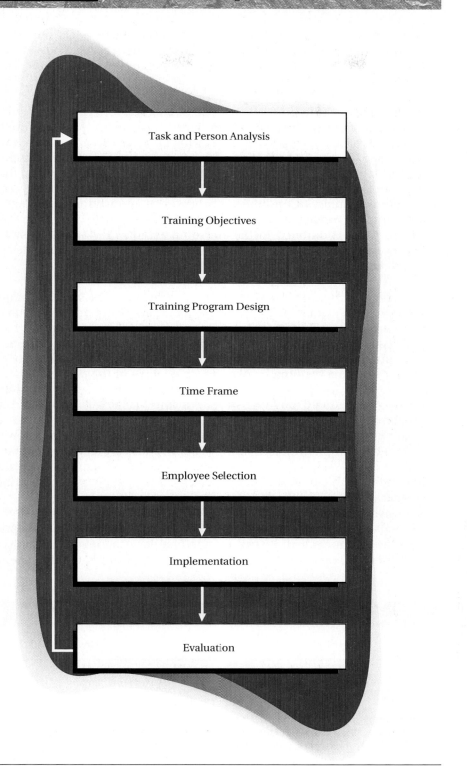

Figure 9-2 Structure of a Training Plan

Task and Person Analysis

Training Objectives

Training Program Design

Time Frame

Employee Selection

Implementation

Evaluation

trained. One way to facilitate the employee's desire to learn is to explain the reasons for and specific objectives of the training program.

Covering the "why" and "what" of training increases the employee's acceptance of training. It also tends to reduce his or her anxiety. It is less threatening to know what one will be confronting and why training is necessary. It is important when discussing training to make the trainee feel at ease. Supervisors should remember that tasks now done easily by them were not always so simple to complete.[8]

The next step is to break the tasks to be learned down into sequential components and demonstrate proper technique for each part. After any questions are answered, have the employee repeat what he or she observed and provide feedback. (See Chapters 11, 13, and 14 for further discussion of the importance of feedback.) Feedback occurs during two-way communication when the receiver of a message responds to the sender. Frequent, accurate feedback is essential to the learning process. Continue this process of demonstration, practice, and feedback until the employee masters the technique or job.

This process outlined in the above paragraph may appear easy to master. However, the supervisor must contend with a number of issues in designing and practicing effective OJT.

Breaking Training into Manageable Parts. How should a job or technique be presented? As a whole? In parts? Or sequentially, with one part building onto another? Figure 9-3 shows three ways to divide training into units.

whole training
Involves covering demonstration, practice, and feedback in one training session.

pure-part training
Involves teaching each of the parts separately, with a final session that puts the parts together.

progressive-part training
Involves training in gradually building steps with previous learning reviewed during each session before new tasks are learned.

As can be seen from Figure 9-3, **whole training** involves covering demonstration, practice, and feedback in one session. The training task is covered all at once. **Pure-part training** involves teaching each of the parts separately, with a final session that puts the parts together. **Progressive-part training** involves training in gradually building steps. Previous learning is reviewed during each session before new tasks are learned.

Generally, whole training is best when doing OJT for complex, interrelated tasks. For example, whole training is appropriate for teaching a person how to drive a car. It makes little sense to teach how to press on the accelerator or to operate windshield wipers independently. The tasks to be accomplished in driving a car are too interdependent to be separated in training.

Conversely, breaking training into parts is best when teaching a job involving a string of relatively independent tasks. For example, OJT for a receptionist can be offered in meaningful parts. On the first day, the new receptionist could be shown how to operate the phone and intercom systems. On the second day, he

Figure 9-3 Size of the Unit to Be Learned	Phase I	Phase II	Phase III	Phase IV
Whole Training	A + B + C	A + B + C	A + B + C	A + B + C
Pure-Part Training	A	B	C	A + B + C
Progressive-Part Training	A	A + B	A + B + C	A + B + C

Source: K. N. Wexley and G. P. Latham, *Developing and Training Human Resources in Organizations,* 2d ed. (New York: Harper Collins, 1991).

or she could be taught how the filing system works and on the third, how to operate the organization's e-mail system. Each of these tasks can be taught and learned separately using pure-part training.

Progressive-part training is effective when tasks are relatively independent, as in the example of the receptionist, but previous learning helps facilitate new learning. In this case, the receptionist might be shown how information is organized on the hard drive of the computer, then taught how to use word processing software, then learn how to format company memos. The learning of each of these tasks facilitates learning the next task.

Distribution of Training Sessions.   As a supervisor, you should provide enough time for employees to learn a new job or technique. Conducting OJT over time can result in better learning than trying to pack training sessions in as short a time as possible.

Distributed practice provides an opportunity for learning to sink in. New employees, in particular, may feel overwhelmed by all the new organizational policies, procedures, and rules with which they are being confronted. Distributing practice over time also provides more opportunity for the employee to reflect on what has been learned, develop insights, and prepare questions to ask the supervisor. (By the way, new or experienced employees should never be made to feel uneasy about asking questions of their supervisor.) Too often, employees are quickly shown a job and then expected to either "sink or swim," as in the Darwinian approach to orientation. Distributed practice and a climate of ongoing OJT help employees to learn and to be productive.

Overlearning.   As a supervisor, you may occasionally deal with an employee who learns and practices a new technique very well during training, but fails when called on to perform on the job. This is similar to an athlete or musician having difficulty when asked to perform in front of people.

This phenomenon can be overcome if a supervisor does not put high pressure on the employee to perform and if the supervisor helps to facilitate overlearning in the trainee. **Overlearning** involves learning and practicing a task far beyond the point at which the task has been successfully learned.[9] Overlearning makes success possible despite environmental pressure.

overlearning
Consists of learning and practicing a task far beyond the point at which the task has been successfully learned.

Appreciating Differences

The proposals covered in this section on training are flexible and can accommodate many different types of people and training situations. Still, to be successful, the effective supervisor should develop OJT or other training approaches with individual differences in mind. For example, some people are better at learning from manuals; others learn better through observation.

There is no single way to accommodate individual differences in training, although using multiple training methods for teaching the same task is one way to respond to differences. For example, a supervisor could provide employees with manuals to read as well as conduct workplace demonstrations of work procedures. In any event, it is important to be flexible. To illustrate, you may find yourself training people who cannot read manuals written in English. Try to assess individual differences and be prepared to modify a training plan by changing the training program or, perhaps, by extending time to complete training.

The Role of Self-Management

Managers must realize that skill retention is largely self-managed. While the organization may reward the outcome (better supervisory skills), the lengthy process of learning a skill is often largely a covert and lonely experience. While a dieter may be rewarded with compliments for a better appearance, he must go unapplauded for resisting an urge to snack at midnight.[10]

You may also wish to encourage such employees to learn English in evening school and be very supportive of their progress.

Giving Orders and Instructions

Supervisors give orders and instructions in orienting and training employees, as well as in the day-to-day conduct of other supervisory activities. The terms *orders* and *instructions* are closely related.

order
A command to someone to do something or to refrain from doing something.

An **order** is a command to someone to do something or to refrain from doing something. It is based upon the authority of the person giving orders that gives him or her the right to obtain obedience from others. **Instructions,** on the other hand, are the transmission of information to a person performing work about the methods required for carrying out an order. Typically, an order is a part of the instruction-giving process. The order is the command to perform and instructions indicate how, when, and where the work should be done.

instruction
The transmission of information to a person performing work about the methods required for carrying out an order.

When employees are well-trained and experienced, they are expected to perform their jobs with a minimum of orders and instructions. In fact, they would probably resent frequent direction of what to do and how to do it. Many

A tongue lashing by a supervisor may lead to counterproductive malicious obedience by an employee.

employees receive very few day-to-day orders or instructions; once they master their duties, they continue to operate under standing orders and follow the same instructions. Other jobs require constant direction, with new orders and instructions continuously conveyed by supervisors.

Orders. In transmitting orders, supervisors expect those receiving them to carry them out. Still, how they express orders may create either favorable or unfavorable attitudes about the order-giver and affect how the recipient performs tasks. We will consider two points: first, the authority relationships with those supervised and, second, the effective management of symbols and meanings conveyed.

Orders can be stated authoritatively or democratically. Which approach is most appropriate is determined by such conditions as timing and urgency of action, workers' experience, and the group members' acceptance of the supervisor as the team leader. (See Chapter 7 concerning the appropriateness of leadership styles.) Generally, it is more effective to frame orders as requests for compliance, perhaps preceded with a "please" and ended with a "thank you." We are not suggesting workers debate or vote on orders and whether they will obey them. We are advising, though, minimizing the appearance of formal authority in giving orders. Once again, this is a way of empowering workers.

Instructions. Good instructions consist of five stages or elements. As you give orders to your team members, consider the following:

1. *Planning.* Determine the specific work objectives to be attained and the actions necessary to attain them. Indicate when the work should begin and when the tasks should be completed.
2. *Communication.* Transmit the order with the most appropriate medium (face to face, by telephone, by memo, and so forth). If instructions are given orally, consider the use of appropriate words, gestures, tone of voice, and facial expressions. Also, consider the effects upon communication caused by the surroundings, such as noise and interruptions.
3. *Verification.* Obtain feedback that the order and instructions were understood and the methods for executing them are understood and suitable.
4. *Action.* The order should be carried out in a timely manner and within the guidelines of organizational policies and procedures.
5. *Follow-up.* Check to verify the order was carried out and the desired results were obtained. If they were not, investigate promptly.

Giving instructions calls for precision and clarity to reduce misunderstandings and mistakes. Also consider the capabilities of the person performing tasks. Sometimes where orders and instructions appear to have the necessary precision, something goes wrong. It is important to formulate alternatives in case this happens. Problems may also arise when a supervisor and employee have a poor working relationship that results in malicious obedience.

Malicious Obedience. Occasionally an individual reverts to a childish form of behavior with the intent to inflict pain or punish others. Perhaps you recall the child running away from home to punish the parents. Poor working relationships invite **malicious obedience,** wherein the employee carries out an order and instructions literally, but not in accordance with the supervisor's intent. When instructions lack precision, the result can be an embarrassment to the supervisor

malicious obedience
A form of employee behavior occurring when an imprecise order or instruction is given, and the employee carries out the order or instructions literally to embarrass the supervisor.

and a self-inflicted wound to the employee. Several examples illustrate the harm caused by malicious obedience.

The epigraph at the beginning of the chapter was taken from an incident in which an army sergeant, who was roundly disliked by his soldiers, was testifying at a court-martial. Toward the end of the fourth week of basic infantry training, the sergeant had selected three trainees for a day-long work detail. At the end of the day, he told the three young men they could "go home." He meant to their living quarters a block away. Instead of returning to their army home, the three went to their homes in Alabama. Subsequently, they were brought back to Ft. Bliss for trial but were acquitted. They had followed an order. The sergeant, in this instance, was the loser and became a private.

In another example of malicious obedience, a director of a small industrial laboratory reprimanded a lab technician about sloppy conditions of the facility, instructing the technician to "get rid of" a box under one of the work tables. Several days later, the director asked the technician the whereabouts of certain instruments valued at $10,000. "I threw them away," the technician responded. "You told me to throw them away." "I did no such thing," the director said with great agitation. "You surely did," answered the technician. "You said to get rid of the box under the table, and that's where the instruments were stored. You didn't ask me if anything was in the box." Both people lost their jobs.

In a final example, a bureau chief of a large state agency experienced periodic problems with a state legislator who chaired the legislative committee responsible for funding the chief's bureau. As the bureau chief left his office for lunch one day, his secretary asked what she should do if the legislator called during his absence. The chief's response was, "Tell him I said he can go to hell," never thinking the secretary would transmit such a message. However, the chairman called and the secretary relayed the chief's comments verbatim. In a matter of weeks, the bureau received the first management audit ever conducted in the state's government, and the bureau chief retired.

In conclusion, good working relationships as well as precision in order and instruction giving are important. Instructions should be clear and require feedback to make sure those carrying them out did so according to your intent.

This concludes Part 2, The Supervisor as a Manager, in which we emphasize the functions supervisors perform. In Part 3, we focus upon the skills competent supervisors must acquire to perform their jobs effectively.

While exercising at the company's recently completed employees' sports spa facility, Carla recalled her concern about turnover of recently hired workers.

"I probably waste a lot of time training people who quit after just a few weeks. I've got to find a way to salvage them. It is hurting them, too. I can appreciate some of their pain in being in a culturally foreign location without any anchors.

"I was talking with another supervisor who suggested finding them a friend. She said the first thing to do with a new hire is to determine if they know anyone in the area, family or otherwise. If they don't, get someone in your group who would like to help them out for the first few weeks—socialize with them, help them get located, show them the ropes. And you know what, she said they usually become good friends. I'm going to try this and, at my next meeting with my people, ask who wants to volunteer for 'Project Welcome.'"

Summary: Focus on Concepts

Employee orientation is a process whereby a new employee is introduced to the organization and to the specific requirements of the job. Supervisors are often given the responsibility for providing orientation for new employees or share this responsibility with the human resources staff.

Several types of orientation programs are deficient. They include the paperwork design, the social Darwinism design, the Mickey Mouse design, and the overload design.

An effective orientation program includes preparing for and welcoming the new employee, providing background information, making introductions to coworkers, relating performance expectations, explaining policies and employee benefits, and follow-up.

In larger organizations, patrons or mentors are sometimes used. A patron is a person who supports another person by providing friendship and is a source of information about the company and the community. A mentor is an individual who systematically develops a subordinate's abilities through intensive tutoring, coaching, and guidance.

Training involves any systematic attempt to change employee behavior through the learning process in order to improve performance. All employees need to be involved in training to keep up with changing technologies.

Training at the work-team level should be tied to organization-wide goals. Two steps are required before an effective training program can be designed. The first step includes performing a task analysis, which includes defining the tasks involved in doing a job; defining knowledge, skills, and abilities required to perform the tasks; and developing training objectives. The second step involves determining the training needs of individual employees.

The more common training methods include classroom training, vestibule training, programmed instruction, computer assisted instruction, job rotation, and on-the-job training (OJT). OJT occurs when the employee learns the job, or changes in the job, while employed doing the job or some parts of it. Supervisors are most likely to be involved in training programs that use OJT or job rotation.

Breaking training into manageable parts entails selection of the most appropriate format, which can include whole training, pure-part training, or progressive-part training.

Supervisors give orders and instructions to team members as a part of their overall duties. An order is a command to someone to do something or to refrain from doing something. Instructions are the transmission of information to a person performing work about the methods required for carrying out an order. Good instructions consist of five elements: planning, communication, verification, action, and follow-up.

When orders or instructions are deficient and a poor working relationship exists between the supervisor and the employee, malicious obedience may take place. Malicious obedience exists when an employee carries out a defective order or instructions literally with the intent to harm the supervisor. Good working relationships along with precision in order and instruction giving are important.

Review Questions

1. What is employee orientation?
2. Indicate four deficient orientation programs and explain why they are lacking.
3. What is anxiety, and why do new employees experience anxiety?
4. Indicate the elements comprising a new employee orientation program and explain the actions taken in each.
5. What is a patron or sponsor? How can they help new employees?
6. Define *training*. What is task analysis and person analysis?
7. Give the structure of a training plan. What is a training program?
8. Describe six types of training. Which are especially used by supervisors?
9. One way to facilitate an employee's desire to learn is to cover the "why" and "what" of a training program. Explain.

10. Training can be presented in several formats including whole, pure-part, and progressive-part training. Illustrate each with an example.
11. What is overlearning?
12. Select an example to illustrate the supervisor's need to appreciate differences in people that call for application of different training methods.
13. Define the terms *orders* and *instructions*.
14. Good instructions consist of five elements. Identify these elements and then prepare an order and the set of instructions required to carry it out which reflect them.
15. What is malicious obedience? Under what conditions does it arise? How can supervisors avoid it?

Notes

1. R. W. Hollmann, "Let's Not Forget about New Employee Orientation," *Personnel Journal* 55 (May 1976): 244–245.
2. R. Kreitner, *Management*, 5th ed. (Boston, MA: Houghton Mifflin Company, 1992), 472.
3. Also see J. L. Mendelson, A. K. Barnes, and G. Horn, "The Guiding Light to Corporate Culture," *Personnel Administrator* 34 (July 1989): 70–72.
4. "The Education and Training of America's Adult Workers," *America's Choice: High Skills or Low Wages*, National Center on Education and the Economy, June 1990, 49–56.
5. Ibid.
6. M. Markowich, "Every Manager a Trainer," *Supervision* 50 (1989): 3–5.
7. K. N. Wexley and G. P. Latham, *Developing and Training Human Resources in Organizations*, 2d ed. (New York: Harper Collins, 1991).
8. C. E. Kozoll, "Delegation, Instruction, and First-Time Understanding," *Supervision* 45 (1983): 8–10.
9. Wexley and Latham, *Developing and Training Human Resources in Organizations*.
10. R. D. Marx, "Self-Managed Skill Retention," *Training and Development Journal* 40 (January 1986): 55.

Case 9-1

Henry McFerrin

Henry McFerrin was a miner, a fifth generation underground coal miner. Born in Terrance, Kentucky, Henry was 32 years old. Since the age of 18, he had worked off and on in the coal fields around Terrance. More off than on, it seemed, as the work was sporadic. Times had been tough in Appalachia for as long as he could remember. Henry had not worked the mines for over two years even though he was a very fine worker. Henry was married and had three children ranging from 2 to 12 years of age. His wife, Cleo, was his high-school sweetheart. The farthest they had traveled from Terrance was to Nashville once, to attend the Grand Ole Opry.

Times were bordering on desperate for the McFerrins, as they had almost no money. Henry had to locate work. It was during this period that he saw a newspaper, the *Houston Post*, with countless help-wanted ads. He and Cleo reluctantly decided he should drive to Houston to find work. If he was successful, Henry's family would join him in Houston in the months ahead. Early on a November morning, he departed for the big city.

Two days later, Henry arrived in Houston in his decrepit 1975 Chevrolet. He had $7.27 in his pocket. For several days, Henry stopped at the employment offices of numerous Houston companies, each time unsuccessfully. By the time he arrived at American Rotary Bit Company, his money was gone. American Rotary was a large manufacturer of rotary bits used to drill oil wells.

"My name is Henry McFerrin. I want a job—now," he said, with more than a touch of desperation in his voice and the appearance of something a cat dragged in.

American Rotary hired Henry McFerrin. After spending his first day completing a variety of forms and documents and receiving indoctrination about the company from the personnel staff, he was taken to the shipping department and introduced to his new supervisor, Mo Miller. His real name was Nosmo King Miller. His father had named him after a "No Smoking" sign he observed from the waiting room while Miller was being born. Mo was a big, gruff man, and no one hassled him. Henry was assigned to Miller as a packer who placed the finished rotary bits into boxes, stapled them shut, and loaded them onto a wooden pallet to be moved later by a fork lift truck.

"You've got to have safety shoes," Miller told Henry.

"I can't afford them until payday and that's two weeks away," Henry said.

"That's your problem," said the supervisor. "Everyone around here has to wear safety shoes. Come on, I'll show you around, let you meet the fellows, and tell you about your job."

During the next few minutes, Henry was introduced to members of his group, most of whom were busy with their jobs. They smiled or grunted and returned to work. Miller then led Henry to a conveyor system on which the finished rotary bits arrived at Henry's work station. After a few minutes of instructions, Miller advised Henry to acquire the safety shoes and report back to work the following day at 7:00 a.m. when his shift started.

Henry left the plant, walked to the parking lot, got into his old car, and slowly drove away. For the past week, he had literally lived in his car, parking it at night in some out-of-the-way place. His immediate problem, though, was acquiring a pair of safety shoes. So he sold the car for $25 and, at a second-hand store, purchased a pair of very used safety shoes for $20. The remainder of his money had to last for food for the next two weeks. With his suitcase, he returned to the area near the plant and, on the south bayou, established his camp. He bathed in the bayou as the sun set.

For the next several days, Henry walked to work. Several times he was a few minutes late, having overslept. His supervisor, Miller, in no unmistakable terms, "read the riot act" to Henry on these occasions. He also was critical of Henry for being too slow to keep up with the packing process, as bits periodically backed up on the line. Other employees paid little attention.

Returning to his camp site after his fourth day at work, Henry discovered his suitcase was missing. Someone had stolen it while he was at work. Now he had no change of clothing.

Friday morning, Henry again was several minutes late. Miller observed him very carefully during the morning. Henry was slower than ever packing bits. When he dropped one on the floor, damaging the bit severely, Miller walked up to him. "McFerrin, I've had it with you. I haven't figured out whether you are stupid or lazy, or maybe both. You're fired. Why personnel ever hired you, I don't know. I'm calling them now to have your check made out. You're finished at American Rotary."

Henry entered the personnel office a few minutes later and inquired about his check. "Mr. McFerrin, I'm sorry things didn't work out for you," said a personnel clerk. "Here's your paycheck for this week's work. By the way, you really should get some new safety shoes," the clerk said as Henry was leaving.

Henry walked several miles to the downtown Houston area. On the way, he stopped to cash his check and buy a hamburger. He was last seen at a bus station. "One ticket one-way to Terrance, Kentucky," he said with a slight smile.

Questions

1. If you interviewed Henry, would you treat him any differently from other applicants? Would factors such as his appearance affect your decision?
2. Describe the negative points of the orientation described in this case. Outline your methods for a more effective orientation.
3. What are the costs to the organization resulting from the turnover of Henry McFerrin?
4. Under the conditions of a good orientation program, could Henry have been "saved"?

When You're in the Swamp with Alligators

Raymon Garcia was completing his fourth year with the Noxon Rapids Machine Tool Company of Barrington, Massachusetts. Ray was the company's quality control supervisor and was responsible for a group of five technicians and engineers.

Noxon Rapids began operations in 1902. It was still controlled by the founding family, although three generations removed. The company manufactured high-speed packaging equipment, usually on a custom-designed basis. Billions of boxes of detergent and small boxes of food products had been packaged by the company's machines over the years. Noxon Rapids had earned an international reputation for producing high-quality packaging equipment and machines. Although the reputation was deserved and still intact, the company was barely profitable. Times had changed and there were problems.

A little history is warranted. The majority of the employees at Noxon Rapids were highly skilled metal workers. Their training required over four years of apprenticeship before an employee became a journeyman. During the past two decades, a shortage of metal workers had developed in the United States. Occupations within metal working were viewed by many younger people as not very glamorous. The training period was too long and complicated. Persons with adequate educational backgrounds in mathematics and computer skills such as CAD—Computer Assisted Design—were scarce or unwilling to undergo the lengthy training periods required. As a result, fewer qualified people were attracted to these jobs. Although several of the more recent arrivals came from vocational-technical schools where they had received preliminary training, the company had also been recruiting people without any metal working knowledge.

Wages and salaries were high, but so was employee turnover. Management estimated that after four years of training a worker, the company had an investment of $150,000 in him or her. When employees quit after the first year but before the end of the second year, they usually dropped out of the metal-working crafts, never to return.

Training was frustrating for the new employees as well as for their supervisors. All of the training was provided by supervisors on the job. In fact, all of the company's supervisors had started as apprentices and worked their way up, with the exception of Ray Garcia, who possessed a mechanical engineering degree. He had worked at a similar manufacturing company for several years before joining Noxon Rapids. Circumstances creating anxiety for trainees included the great amount of supervision and instruction required, the slowness of completing an assignment (a trainee averaged slightly over 25 percent of the productivity of a skilled worker), the large amount of defective work—which was viewed as demotivating—and periodic feelings of inferiority when it appeared a particular problem or task could not be mastered.

Where turnover was high in a supervisor's group, over 50 percent of that supervisor's time typically was spent training apprentices, so the reduction of turnover had great importance.

Martin Powell was the plant superintendent for Noxon Rapids. He was in charge of 13 supervisors, including Ray Garcia. Powell developed the practice of holding a two-hour staff meeting with all of his supervisors the last two hours of work on the last Friday of each month. The general format of the meeting was to spend the first hour discussing problems, relating information about new company plans and policies, explaining new federal and state regulations affecting operations, and determining how his supervisors were doing.

The second hour was usually consumed in a rather novel way. Each month, one of the supervisors was assigned the responsibility for presenting a topic of interest to other members of the supervisor staff. The presentation rotated so each year every supervisor except one made a presentation to the group.

Powell asked Ray to assume the responsibility for next month's topic, "Improving

Training Effectiveness at Noxon Rapids." Powell said he had selected Ray because of his knowledge about quality control and his overview of Noxon Rapid's manufacturing operations. Ray accepted the assignment with mixed feelings. The supervisors were experts who knew metal working from top to bottom. Their skills for training others, however, were more limited.

Later in the day, one of the supervisors kidded Ray about his assignment for next month's meeting. "You'd better be careful, Ray. When you are in the swamp with us alligators, you might forget your initial mission."

Questions

1. You are Ray Garcia. Prepare an outline of your presentation indicating the most important points you wish to cover.

2. What types of information would make your presentation more effective?

3. How would you motivate your colleagues to want to learn more about improving training at Noxon Rapids?

4. What is the best way to muzzle the alligators? In other words, what problems might you encounter in your presentation? What steps could you take to avoid coming into conflict with your peers?

Supervisory Skills

Part 3 presents chapters dealing with supervisory skills—the ability to utilize knowledge in making decisions effectively and in performing the work of supervision. Chapter topics include decision making, motivating employees, managing conflict, communicating, performance appraisal, applying discipline, counseling, managing stress, and organizational change.

Whereas the first two parts of this textbook are particularly concerned with *concepts* summarized at the end of each chapter, in Part 3 and 4, our emphasis is on *skills*. Each chapter concludes with a series of specific skill-related actions for supervisors to apply or consider.

CHAPTER 10   Decision Making

The decision-making process within the context of its dynamic nature is the central issue of Chapter 10. Our emphasis is on the process of making decisions, that is, the steps followed in identifying problems and rendering decisions. Considered in this chapter are programmed and nonprogrammed types of decisions, making decisions within the work team, decision rules for group decision making, and group dynamics.

CHAPTER 11   Motivating Employees

Several theories are valuable for explaining the motivation of employees. An understanding of how these theories operate gives us knowledge of the motivational tools required to guide employee behavior. In Chapter 11, we review the major motivation theories and their application, consider behavior modification techniques, and explore motivation methods within work teams.

CHAPTER 12   Managing Conflict

Conflict is often considered a negative element in organizations. It has value, however, when channeled in the right direction. Our goal is not to eliminate all conflict, but to manage it. The causes of conflict are presented along with several conflict management strategies. Negotiation, the basis for collaboration, is considered along with managing conflict within work teams.

CHAPTER 13   Communicating Effectively

Interpersonal relationships exist largely through the communication process: what we say to one another (or do not say) and how we say it. Formal and informal methods of communication are covered in Chapter 13. Topics include interpersonal communication, reducing defensiveness, nonverbal communication, and improving the communication process within the work team.

CHAPTER 14   Appraising Performance

Performance appraisal is the periodic assessment of employee job performance and behavior. It is an important aspect of organizational life, and supervisors are a particularly meaningful part of a performance appraisal review system. In Chapter 14, we consider several appraisal methods, the performance review, supervisory training for performance appraisal, and methods of applying appraisals within the work team.

CHAPTER 15   Organizational Justice and Discipline

Organizational justice is the impartial treatment of employees by organizations through maintaining conditions of fairness and equity. Organizational discipline is a form of training to produce a desired type of behavior when deviations from the norm occur. Chapter 15 considers the causes of employee misconduct, tests to determine the reasonableness of disciplinary action, types of discipline, stages in the disciplinary process, nonpunitive discipline, characteristics of effective grievance procedures, and how to conduct correctional interviews.

CHAPTER 16   Counseling

Counseling is intended to help individuals to achieve their personal goals or to function more effectively. Supervisors have a responsibility for counseling their employees. That responsibility takes several directions including corrective/remedial, informational, developmental, and referral for therapeutic counseling. The major forms of counseling are treated in Chapter 16, including interactive counseling skills.

CHAPTER 17   Managing Stress and Organizational Change

Stress is experienced whenever a person is confronted with a demand or challenge that threatens his or her ability to attain valued outcomes. Job stress is an outcome of situations where factors cause an individual to undergo a psychological and physiological change from a normal state of functioning. We consider several causes of stress and practical means for reducing their harmful consequences. Chapter 17 concludes with a discussion of organizational change, the change reaction process, and principles to apply in making successful transitions in the change process.

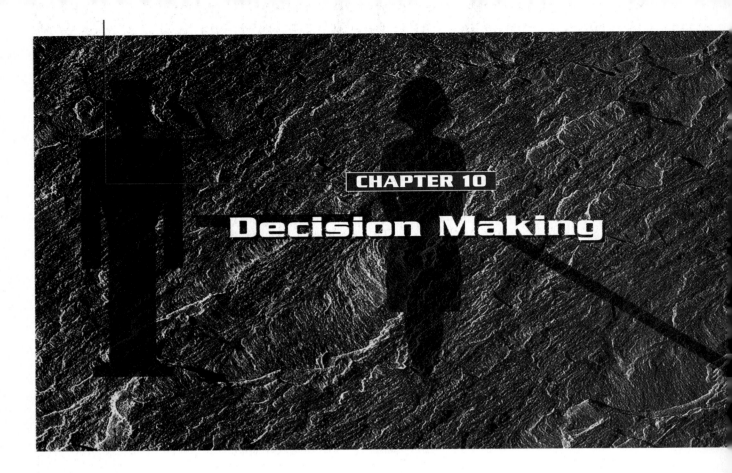

CHAPTER 10

Decision Making

● Decision makers sometimes lean upon statistics for the same reasons drunks lean upon lampposts—for support rather than illumination.

LEARNING OBJECTIVES

1. Understand the dynamics of the decision making process and the nature of decisions.
2. Indicate the stages of the decision making process.
3. State the advantages and disadvantages of group decision making.
4. Demonstrate the application of decision rules in group and consensus decision making.
5. Explain the nominal group technique.
6. Understand group dynamics.

"Carla, can we end this meeting? I've only got a few minutes to get out and set up!" Al's impatience spread over the group.

"Sure, Al. We're almost finished. Just one more quick thing. . . ."

"Like what, Carla?" Judy interjected with a flourish. "None of the things we've been talking about at these twice-weekly team meetings really affects us, including the things we've talked about this morning. I don't like coming in 30 minutes early. I could use the extra sleep!"

"Don't you all want to participate in decision making?" Carla was surprised. She had thought her group would love the mini-meetings she'd started up after reading Tom Peters' latest book. He'd said that empowered workers *wanted* to be included in decision making!

"Really Carla, a lot of these issues on the budget and the company's strategic plan do not affect us." Al spoke in a quietly determined voice. "You did fine handling these things before. We trust you. Why waste our time now?"

We make decisions all day long, from the trivial—what clothes to wear, what to eat for breakfast, where to park after arriving at work—to the important—getting married, buying a house, taking a job. Even *not* making a decision is making a decision. (See Figure 10-1.)

Figure 10-1   Decisions, Decisions . . .

Source: B. C. Cartoon, 6/4/82. Reprinted by permission of Johnny Hart and Creators Syndicate, Inc.

What Is Decision Making?

Decision Making and Problem Solving

The effective supervisor makes all kinds of decisions daily. A **decision** is a conscious choice of one alternative from a set of several alternatives. The process of making the selection is known as **decision making.** All decisions have three elements: choice, alternatives, and objectives.

Choice implies a person has the right to choose among things or alternatives in making a decision. In practice, however, conditions often restrict choice. The amount of time available to make a decision, the ability of the person making the decision, the resources available (such as labor, equipment, or facilities), and organizational policies and rules may limit the options readily available to the decision maker.

Alternatives are the types of actions that may be taken. All decisions have two or more alternatives. When there is only one alternative, there is no choice, and no decision. In most cases, though, there are more alternatives than the decision maker has identified.

The final component of a decision is an **objective,** or value to be obtained or maintained. People make decisions to achieve one or more objectives. The purpose of decision making is to select an alternative that has the highest probability of attaining the objectives.[1]

Another way to understand decision making within the supervisor's job is to view decision making as problem solving. A **problem** exists whenever there is a difference between a real and an ideal situation. For example, if inadequate staff are available to complete a task, or if an essential machine breaks down, decisions must be made to change the situation back to what it should be. Of course not all decisions are made in response to problems. By analyzing the nature of a problem, we can determine how best to handle it.

Classes of Decisions

The word *unique* means the only one of its kind. The uniqueness of a problem is determined by whether we have encountered the problem before, its frequency

decision
A conscious choice of one alternative from a set of several alternatives.

decision making
The process of making the selection of an alternative from several possible courses of action.

choice
The right to choose among things or alternatives in making a decision.

alternatives
The types of actions that may be taken.

objective
Any value a person, firm, or organization desires to acquire, and in the process, is willing and able to make the necessary sacrifice of time, money, or effort.

problem
When there is a difference in results obtained and what was targeted to be achieved in objectives.

of occurrence, and our ability to handle it satisfactorily.[2] The degree of uniqueness of a problem determines how supervisors should treat it, that is, whether to go through a formal decision-making or problem-solving analysis or to implement a previously developed routine for handling the situation. The former are classified as **nonprogrammed decisions,** and the latter are called **programmed decisions.** Whenever possible, it is desirable to change nonprogrammed decisions into programmed ones. Programmed decisions usually can be made faster, use fewer resources, and reduce risks.

Nonprogrammed Decisions.　Decisions that have not been made before or concern problems that have not been solved or treated satisfactorily are called nonprogrammed decisions. Examples include an abnormally high turnover of labor, a series of unsolved thefts, a malfunctioning machine, or an increasing amount of product damaged in shipments to customers. Nonprogrammed decisions are treated by following a series of steps (explained in the following pages) to arrive at a solution. Each time we must make a nonprogrammed decision, we should go through this decision-making process.

Programmed Decisions.　When people repeatedly encounter certain types of problems or decision areas and treat them satisfactorily using a policy or procedure, they are making programmed decisions. Examples of programmed decisions include invoking policies, procedures, work rules, performance standards, tolerance limits, and sets of decision rules. All of these are useful tools in decision making. (Several were covered in the planning section of Chapter 5.) Illustrations of programmed decisions include the following areas:

- *Accepting gifts.* A policy statement prohibits employees from receiving gifts from customers and suppliers, to maintain honesty and reduce potential conflicts of interest.
- *Reordering supplies.* A procedure outlines the steps for determining when to reorder supplies and the quantity to order.
- *Appraising employee performance.* Performance standards indicate the quantity and quality of output to be produced by an employee.

The Challenge of Decision Making

Decision making is not an easy skill to learn, nor is it an easy skill to practice. The study of decision making has led to few conclusions regarding how to make the right decisions. The supervisor, employees, environment, and nature of the decision or decisions to be made all affect the decision-making process. For example, allowing employees to participate in decision making is often good because it leads to employee satisfaction. Under certain circumstances, however, supervisors should make decisions themselves. (This point will be discussed later in the chapter.) Keep in mind that the suggestions offered in this chapter are general guidelines for decision making, rather than inviolable rules.

Also, decision makers are not always rational. Even if hard-and-fast decision rules existed, people often would not follow them. People are not machines. Rational models of decision making look good on paper, but in practice supervisors and other managers often rely on intuition. A classic study, contrasting the way managers should behave with the way they actually do behave, found that most managers make decisions quickly and unsystematically, relying on "soft" information and intuition.[3]

nonprogrammed decisions
Decisions that have not been made before or problems that have not been solved or treated satisfactorily.

programmed decisions
Types of problems or decisions repeatedly encountered with solutions codified into methods for handling them such as policies, procedures, work rules, performance standards, tolerance limits, and sets of decision rules.

One of the reasons supervisors should learn to make decisions systematically and rationally is to reduce mistakes associated with only relying on intuition. At the same time, intuition is not always bad or wrong. Again, it depends on circumstances and the nature of the problem or problems to be solved.

The Decision-Making Process

decision-making process
A systematic process applied to making decisions including definition of the problem or the goal to be attained through consideration of alternatives, selection of an alternative, implementation, and evaluation.

A simple, systematic process exists that can be applied to all types of decisions. This **decision-making process** includes definition of the problem or goal to be attained to solve the problem; consideration of alternatives; selection of an alternative; implementation; and evaluation. (See Figure 10-2.)

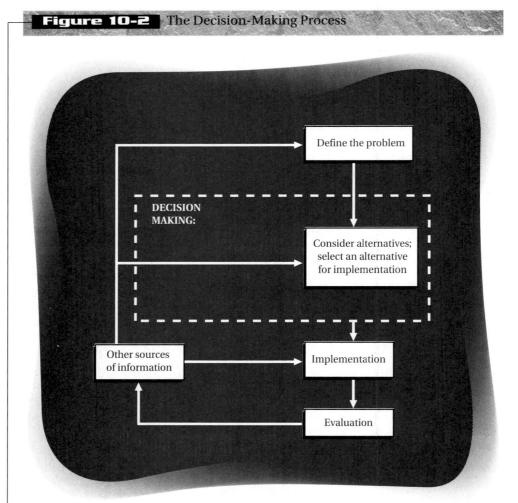

Figure 10-2 The Decision-Making Process

Source: C. T. Lewis, J. E. Garcia, and S. M. Jobs, *Managerial Skills in Organizations* (Boston, MA: Allyn and Bacon, 1990), 191.

The decision-making process follows the systems approach introduced in Chapter 1. Recall that the systems approach is a way of thinking, planning, and problem solving that involves inputs, transformation processes, outputs, and feedback.

In the decision-making process, inputs are information necessary for defining the problem and alternatives; the transformation process occurs when an alternative is selected and the decision is implemented; and output is reviewed during the evaluation phase. Subsequent evaluation addresses the question, How successful was the decision? Information from evaluation then feeds back into future decision making.

The Nature of Decisions

It is very important that steps in the decision-making process be followed in order if the decision maker is trying to solve an important problem. Individuals and groups often make the common mistake of trying to define a problem without gathering information or trying to solve a problem without defining it first. People occasionally select the first alternative that comes to mind rather than searching for a better way to solve a problem. These errors are caused by a failure to work through the decision-making process in an orderly fashion. Learn the steps in the decision-making process outlined in Figure 10-2, and cover the steps in sequence when making and following through on important decisions.

Some decisions are more important than others and require a systematic, information-driven approach. It is not necessary to "haul out the heavy artillery of careful, hard analysis for decisions of minor importance."[4] A decision to eat pizza rather than tofu, for example, does not require a systematic decision-making process.

The decision strategy to use depends in part on the environment and characteristics of the decision. You should use the formal decision-making process, and rely on accurate data, when decisions are irreversible, when they are important, when time and other resources are available, and when the decision maker is highly accountable.[5] Careful, systematic decision making is also called for as decision characteristics become less familiar, more ambiguous, complex, and unstable.[6]

There is, however, a need for balance in decision making. Intuitive decision making is fine for many everyday decisions. As a supervisor, you should use the decision-making process when, for example, making a significant change in the overtime pay you allow your work group to earn, or when changing a work schedule. Intuition will serve you just fine, though, when it comes to deciding what color to paint your office walls or how to arrange the office-supplies cabinet.

The focus of the rest of this section is on the steps to take in making relatively important decisions: defining the problem, considering and selecting an alternative, implementing the decision, and evaluating the decision.

Step One: Define the Problem

Defining the problem is the most important step in the decision-making process, from which all else in the process flows. The famous philosopher, John Dewey, once regretted the problem of "indefiniteness of meaning"—in other words, failure to define the problem, commenting,

> A constant source of misunderstanding and mistake is indefiniteness of meaning. Because of vagueness of meaning we misunderstand other people, things, and

ourselves. . . . It is the aboriginal logical sin—the source from which flow most bad intellectual consequences.[7]

The Importance of Information.   One way to promote clear problem definition is to use the best information possible. All steps in the decision-making process benefit from the use of relevant, valid information. If you put good information into the decision loop, your chances of making a good decision improve. Conversely, if you put garbage in (bad information) you will get garbage out (a bad decision). To the extent information is invalid, problem definition is usually also invalid, and the remaining steps in the decision-making process suffer accordingly.

It is also important to check out assumptions. Sometimes decision making is flawed because the decision maker assumes information to be valid rather than seeking to verify it. It is not possible to gather all information relating to a particular problem, nor is it possible to eliminate all assumptions. However, a responsible decision maker uses the best information he or she can gather to define a problem.

Step Two: Consider and Select an Alternative

Once the problem has been defined, the decision maker should consider alternatives—prospective courses of action for solving the problem.

bounded rationality model

Consideration of alternatives is constrained by the limited capability of humans to assimilate and store data, thus causing decision makers to focus on only a few alternatives in making decisions.

Consideration and selection of an alternative would seem to be a straightforward proposition: simply consider all alternatives and implement the alternative that best solves the problem. In reality, there is a significant difference between the way people should behave when selecting an alternative and the way they actually do behave.

Herbert Simon stated that consideration of alternatives is bounded by the limited capability of human beings to assimilate and store data.[8] His **bounded rationality model** asserts that it is impossible for decision makers to consider all

An effective supervisor checks out assumptions.

The Information Industry

Decision making should be guided by the best information a decision maker can find. This basic principle is well understood by American business managers. U.S. expenditures on commercial market research now exceed $2 billion a year. Usually the research helps; sometimes it doesn't. Sometimes the wrong information is collected, information is misinterpreted, or some factor beyond the control of the decision maker affects decision quality.

For example, Coca-Cola conducted exhaustive taste tests in developing Coke II, but failed to assess one crucial factor: brand loyalty. The unveiling of Coke II was a major marketing flop, standing next to the Ford Edsel. The Edsel fiasco involved another product that had been extensively researched. *Star Wars,* one of the most successful films ever, would not have reached the theaters if film director George Lucas had listened to market researchers.

It is hard to find good, reliable data. Several businesses, for example, have hired University of Arizona anthropology professor William Rathje to rummage through consumers' garbage. A major problem, according to Rathje, is that "dogs and cats sometimes eat our data."[9]

alternatives. Instead, people tend to focus on only a few alternatives, and ultimately select an alternative that is minimally sufficient to address the problem. In short, decision makers tend to choose the first alternative that looks as though it will work.

This is an understandable human tendency. Decision makers seldom have access to perfect information. Moreover, overworking a problem can result in **analysis paralysis,** or inaction by the decision maker. Decision makers can only do their best to carefully consider as many alternatives as possible. It is therefore a good idea to force yourself to consider just a few more alternatives, even when you think you have identified a workable solution.

analysis paralysis
A state of inaction in decision making arising from overworking a problem.

A Quantitative Approach.　One fairly simple and effective way to organize and evaluate alternatives quantitatively is by using a decision tree. A **decision tree** shows the expected value of several possible alternatives. Graphing a decision tree allows a decision maker to consider several probabilities associated with a given alternative. Values are often assigned from previous experience.

decision tree
Illustrates the expected quantitative value of several possible alternatives and the probabilities of their occurrence.

Figure 10-3 outlines a decision tree justifying a supervisor's decision to work late for a week to meet a production goal (for example, to prepare a report for her boss). As you can see, in this example, there is about a 90 percent chance of meeting the goal if the supervisor works late each day, and about a 10 percent chance of failure. In contrast, if the supervisor does not put in the extra hours she will only have about a 30 percent chance of getting the report finished on time, and about a 70 percent chance of failing.

The supervisor weighs the attractiveness of meeting the production goal versus the attractiveness of failing on a five-point scale. Suppose she decides that meeting the goal is slightly more attractive (+3 for success versus +2 for failure). By using this analytic decision process, she determines that the expected value of working late is higher than that of not working late (expected value of working late = 2.90; of not working late = 2.30). Consequently, she works extra hours all week and gets the report in on time.

In constructing decision trees, keep in mind that measures of attractiveness can be monetary amounts or can be expressed as a scale as in the example in Figure 10-3. Also, do not confuse the expected value determination with your *actual* return based on the option chosen. If the five-point attractiveness scale used in Figure 10-3 had been stated in dollars, the actual "return" might have

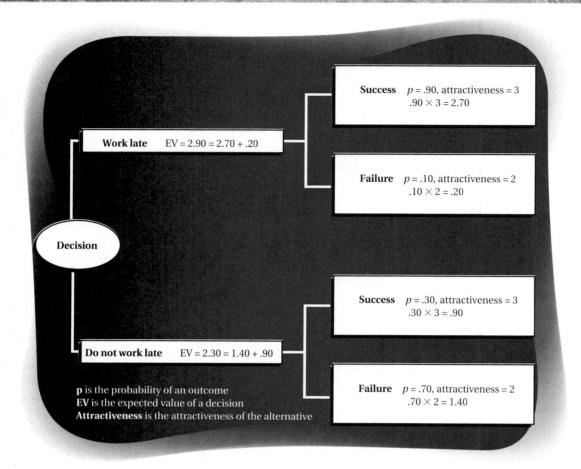

Figure 10-3 A Decision Tree

Success p = .90, attractiveness = 3
.90 × 3 = 2.70

Work late   EV = 2.90 = 2.70 + .20

Failure p = .10, attractiveness = 2
.10 × 2 = .20

Decision

Success p = .30, attractiveness = 3
.30 × 3 = .90

Do not work late   EV = 2.30 = 1.40 + .90

Failure p = .70, attractiveness = 2
.70 × 2 = 1.40

p is the probability of an outcome
EV is the expected value of a decision
Attractiveness is the attractiveness of the alternative

Source: Adapted from J. E. Garcia, C. T. Lewis, and F. E. Fiedler, *Instructor's Manual for People, Management, and Productivity* (Boston: Allyn and Bacon, 1986), 198.

been $2.70 (work late and succeed); $.20 (work late and fail); $.90 (not work late and succeed), *or* $1.40 (not work late and fail). The expected value computation is used to estimate the value of one alternative relative to another; it does not predict the value of the action to be taken. To summarize, despite the tendency of decision makers to choose the first acceptable alternative, most decision making is improved by systematic consideration of alternatives. A quantitative tool such as a decision tree may be helpful even though all weighting schemes involving human judgement are subjective to some degree. The idea is not to eliminate subjectivity, but to reduce problems associated with excessive subjectivity. Figure 10-4 summarizes the range of rationality in decision making. Some decisions are made based upon personal judgements, intuition, and hunches. Others involve the application of common sense and logic. As noted previously, the most important ones, though, should entail careful, rational analysis.

Step Three: Implement the Decision

The bridge between making a decision and evaluating the results is the **implementation** phase of the decision making process. In evaluating the success or failure of any decision, the evaluator should question whether outcomes can be attributed to the quality of the decision or to the quality of execution. Good decisions are sometimes poorly implemented.

Beyond this comment, we will simply note that although implementation is an important part of the decision making process, the topic of how to best carry out a decision is beyond the purpose of this chapter. Implementation is an important part of all the supervisory functions covered throughout this book.

implementation
The actions taken after making a decision, followed by an evaluation of the results obtained.

Step Four: Evaluate the Results of the Decision

The importance of assessing the success or failure of a decision cannot be overstated. We have discussed the importance of using good information to formulate problem definition. **Evaluation** of past decisions should drive future decision making as part of an ongoing decision-making loop as illustrated in Figure 10-2.

Evaluation is sometimes compromised by **rationalization.** Rationalization leads decision makers to imagine benefit from a past decision. For example, a person might fail at a job selling advertising space for a local newspaper, yet justify the decision to work for the newspaper based upon the perceived quality of sales training that he received. Because the real reason for failure (for example, poor selling skills) is not acknowledged, this unfortunate person might next try his hand at another sales job without solving the problem.

One reason for rationalization can be found in **dissonance balancing.** Dissonance is the difference between a person's image of something and the actual characteristics of that thing. People tend to try to explain away or balance dissonance they feel when things don't go as well as planned. In the hypothetical

evaluation
A review process of the outcome obtained from a decision.

rationalization
A process that compromises evaluation when decision makers attempt to cause outcomes to appear reasonable even though actual results suggest a different interpretation.

dissonance balancing
Occurs when a person's image of something and the actual characteristics of that thing are rationalized when events do not go as well as planned.

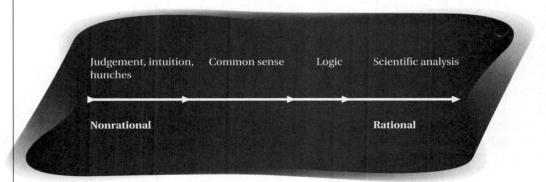

Figure 10-4 The Range of Rationality in Decision Making

Judgement, intuition, hunches   Common sense   Logic   Scientific analysis

Nonrational   Rational

Source: Robert Albanese, *Management: Toward Accountability for Performance* (Homewood, IL: Richard D. Irwin, 1981), 156. © Copyright, 1981. Reprinted with permission from Richard D. Irwin, Inc.

situation described above, perceiving benefit in failure balanced the dissonance felt by the salesperson—the difference between the salesperson's self-image and his actual performance.

Dissonance balancing causes people to remain committed to losing causes, particularly if the decision maker is highly responsible for a previous poor decision.[10] The example of the ineffective advertising salesperson cited previously shows this tendency. Maintaining an unprofitable product line, retaining an unproductive employee, and following an ineffective procedure are other examples of this tendency.

To summarize, the need to balance dissonance means that decision makers often compound past mistakes by continuing to act on poor decisions. The negative effects of dissonance balancing can be reduced by having other informed people, with less at stake in terms of responsibility for the decision, involved in evaluating the outcome of past decisions.

Supervisors should consult those they trust from time to time about outcomes of their decisions. An excellent source of information is employees in the supervisor's work team. Employees often have a valid perspective on past decisions, which they will share if asked.

Making Decisions within the Work Team

Systematic decision making as outlined in Figure 10-2 also works well with teams, although, as you will see, group decision making is more complex than individual decision making. Managing this complexity requires that team members understand and practice good conflict management and communication skills. (See Chapters 12 and 13.)

self-managed teams
Well-trained and informed individuals working as a group who manage their own work by setting goals, planning how goals will be accomplished, solving problems, making daily operating decisions, scheduling work, and hiring team members.

Group decision making has taken on increased importance in recent years because of an increased interest in using **self-managed teams** to accomplish work in organizations. (See Chapter 2 for a discussion of "new management thinking" and Chapter 6 for more about teams.) Self-managed teams are ideally comprised of empowered individuals who are well trained and well versed in the organization's mission.[11] Instead of having tasks dictated to them from above by a supervisor, self-managed teams typically determine their own work objectives and schedules. Supervisors function more as facilitators and coworkers than as traditional bosses. Even when functioning as a facilitator within a self-managed team, a supervisor can do much to help a team to function smoothly. There are also times when a supervisor can best function alone—when group input is relatively inefficient or ineffective. The next few sections discuss advantages and disadvantages of using groups; when to use groups for decision making; and how to plan a meeting.

Advantages and Disadvantages of Group Decision Making

There are many advantages and disadvantages associated with group decision making.[12] Groups accumulate more knowledge and facts; they often consider more alternatives; participation in group decision making usually leads to higher member satisfaction, rather than feelings of exclusion; and a group process is an effective communications and political device in its own right. Also, a team can call on the resources represented by each of its members.

Characteristics of a Successful Team Leader

The qualifications of a successful team leader are listed below in priority order:

- Is recognized as competent in present job
- Is committed, enthusiastic, and believes in the philosophies of a team-based organization
- Is viewed as impartial and able to work with unions, employees, and management

- Has good interpersonal and communications skills
- Has good analytic and problem-solving skills
- Is able to identify issues and take constructive action with minimal direction
- Has group facilitation skills and knowledge of how to bring about change[13]

On the other hand, groups make decisions more slowly than individuals; groups may compromise and, consequently, not make optimal decisions; a "squeaky wheel" in the group may dominate discussions and overly influence results; and overdependence on group decision making can compromise a supervisor's flexibility. Generally, work teams make decisions less efficiently than individuals.[14]

Leader Decision Theory

Leader decision theory as developed by Vroom and Yetton provides insight into when a supervisor should use group decision making and when the supervisor should make a decision alone.[15] (This theory is also covered in Chapter 7.)

Vroom and Yetton identified two concerns affecting whether a manager should rely on a group when making a decision: is there enough information to make a good decision, and is acceptance of the decision by subordinates important for effective implementation of the decision? These concerns can be expressed as the **quality rule** and the **acceptance rule.**

More participative strategies should be used when the supervisor needs information from group members to improve decision quality and/or when acceptance of the decision by subordinates is important to the success of implementation. (Participation improves member acceptance because, as noted, it leads to greater member satisfaction.) Participative strategies also require that the goals of employees be compatible with the goals of the supervisor's department or work unit.

Supervisors do not always have to include employees when making decisions. If trust levels are relatively high and the relationship between supervisors and work groups is good, supervisors may find they can make many decisions on their own. Of course, if decisions begin to adversely affect employees, it may become necessary to involve employees in decision making more frequently.

quality rule
Participative strategies should be used when the supervisor needs information from group members to improve decision quality.

acceptance rule
Participative strategies should be used when acceptance of a decision by subordinates is important to the success of implementation.

Planning the Meeting

An important part of planning a meeting is preparation of an agenda. The **agenda** states the purpose of a meeting and the items to be considered. Supervisors should make sure the purpose of the meeting is clear to all team members. Supervisors should also make sure that participants understand the decision rule to be employed (to be discussed); specify meeting characteristics (physical setting, time, group size); and select participants based upon quality and acceptance rules discussed previously.[16] Most group decision making is conducted around a table. (Also see Chapter 18, "Using Time Effectively.")

agenda
An outline or plan for a meeting including a statement of the meeting's purpose and items to be discussed.

The Abilene Paradox

An unusual illustration of group dynamics in decision making, given by Jerry Harvey, is the **Abilene paradox.**[17] On a July afternoon some years ago, Harvey and several members of his wife's family were playing dominoes in the small west Texas town of Coleman. The summer temperature was 104 degrees. Harvey's father-in-law suggested driving to Abilene for dinner at a cafeteria. All agreed the idea "sounded good," and they loaded into an old Buick that did not have air conditioning. After four hours and 106 dusty miles, they arrived back in Coleman hot, tired, and dirty. Even the dinner had been second rate.

Upon returning, Harvey discovered that no one had wished to undertake the trip in the first place. Even his father-in-law had not wanted to go, although he suggested the trip. He was concerned that the other family members might be bored playing dominoes and wished to be hospitable to his visiting family. In this situation, everyone agreed with a decision no one wanted.

> The Abilene Paradox can be stated succinctly as follows: Organizations frequently take actions in contradiction to the data they have for dealing with problems and, as a result, compound their problems rather than solve them. Like all paradoxes, the Abilene Paradox deals with absurdity.[18]

The moral of the story: Even when agreement is unanimous, decisions do not always reflect the true feelings of those affected by them. (See Sarge's dilemma in Figure 10-5.)

Abilene paradox
A situation where everyone agrees with a decision that no one wants.

The points outlined in the previous paragraph may seem obvious. However, in practice, decision making is often attempted without an agenda and participant selection is often questionable in terms of quality of contribution, representativeness, or number of participants. Meetings often drag on too long. This problem is exacerbated when the agenda or decision rules are not clear.

Decision Rules for Team Decision Making

decision rules
Procedural guidelines that direct, and tend to improve, a group decision-making process.

Group decision making is benefited by the understanding and practice of **decision rules** that guide the team decision-making process. Decision rules are procedural guidelines that direct, and tend to improve, a group decision-making process. Untrained decision-making groups tend to be ineffective as well as inefficient.[19]

Decision rules can be used to facilitate different parts of the decision-making process outlined in Figure 10-2 or, in the case of consensus decision making, can be used for all steps in the process. Following is a discussion of rules for brainstorming, consensus decision making, and nominal grouping.

Brainstorming

brainstorming
Generating ideas by permitting nonevaluative presentation of alternatives by group members to obtain as many ideas as possible for later evaluation.

As mentioned in Chapter 1, A. F. Osborn, an advertising agency executive, was concerned about encouraging group creativity. Osborn developed **brainstorming** as a way to encourage a decision-making group to consider many alternatives.

The purpose of brainstorming is to get as many ideas out for consideration as possible, regardless of how silly and ineffective the ideas may seem at the time. Here are the rules for brainstorming:

1. The group engages in free-wheeling—group members are encouraged to offer suggestions as they occur to them. The facilitator lists alternatives as people speak.
2. Group members will not criticize alternatives as they are being generated.

Figure 10-5   "I Concur Too."

Source: King Features Syndicate, 1987.

3. Quantity of alternatives is encouraged. Get all the ideas on the board!
4. Combination of and improvement on previously suggested alternatives is sought, without criticism.

Brainstorming focuses on generating ideas rather than on choosing an alternative. It is a good technique to use after a problem has been defined when alternatives need to be generated. Brainstorming can also be used to identify a problem in the first place.

Consensus Decision Making

Consensus is defined as a "collective opinion." Consensus is reached when all group members are able to accept a group decision on the basis of logic and feasibility. The rules for **consensus decision making** include the following:

1. Viewing differences of opinion as being natural and expected.
2. Not assuming that there must be winners and losers when discussion bogs

consensus decision making
The process of finding a collective opinion wherein all group members are able to accept a group decision on the basis of logic and feasibility.

Anyone for a Mouse Toaster?

Some years ago, a manufacturer of small household appliances conducted a brainstorming session to improve the design of the company's toasters. Suggestions were recorded and evaluated at a later time. One of the suggestions was to "make the toaster mouse proof." The individual who made the suggestion had the following comment, "Mice eat toast crumbs. If the rodent gets into a toaster and cannot escape, a toasted mouse results." Brainstorming may generate strange ideas.

down. Instead, group members should continue to search for acceptable alternatives.
3. Avoiding conflict-reducing techniques such as voting or averaging.
4. Avoiding argument for its own sake.
5. Not changing one's mind simply to avoid conflict and to reach agreement. Allowing decisions that are acceptable at least in part.[20]

Consensus decision making can be applied to most parts of the decision-making process. Groups can reach consensus on defining the problem, selecting an alternative to implement, and analyzing the outcome of a decision.

Consensus decision making is usually more effective than is unstructured decision making.[21] Consensus, however, is often not easy to reach. It is a time-consuming process and cannot be effectively used to make immediate decisions. Also, as an interactive process, consensus decision making does not entirely eliminate problems associated with interacting groups (such as domination of the group by one person). Moreover, effective consensus decision making requires trained or otherwise knowledgeable group members. Team members need to possess communication and conflict management skills, as well as have an understanding of the rules of consensus decision making.[22]

As with other decision rules, it is important that the group know the rules. Supervisors should spend time making sure that group members have a shared

A clear agenda and decision rules understood and practiced by all help even large groups make decisions, eventually.

understanding of the decision-making process being used. Other training, for example in communication or conflict management skills, may be necessary to improve the quality of consensus decision making.

Nominal Grouping

A nominal group is a group in name only. A group using the **nominal group technique (NGT)** does not interact directly.[23] As with brainstorming, members are asked to generate ideas without direct comment. The idea generation phase of NGT is more confined than that of brainstorming—group members take turns presenting ideas in a round robin, rather than through free-wheeling. After idea generation, group members vote upon or rank the ideas that have been generated. The final decision is mathematically derived from this ranking. Following is a summary of steps in the NGT process:[24]

nominal group technique (NGT)
A form of "group" decision making in which the members do not interact directly, rather they record, rank, and vote on alternatives to arrive at the decision.

1. Group members silently record ideas on notepads.
2. Group members take turns giving ideas. The facilitator records the ideas on a flipchart or blackboard.
3. Each recorded idea is discussed in turn. This step clarifies ideas and provides group members with the opportunity to agree or disagree with an idea. The primary purpose of this step is clarification of ideas, not argumentation.
4. A preliminary vote is then conducted. Delbecq and associates recommend that NGT groups conduct a preliminary vote to be followed by a final vote. A typical NGT group will identify 12 to 18 ideas. Use of a preliminary vote allows the group to reduce this number to about five for the final vote. The facilitator asks each member in the group to choose the five most important ideas and rank them in order of importance. The facilitator then uses the rankings to mathematically determine the most important ideas. The group then discusses these ideas to clarify them.
5. The final vote is conducted among the most important ideas. This last step determines the decision of the group, provides a sense of closure and accomplishment, and documents the group's judgement.

NGT is useful for defining problems and for considering and selecting alternatives. This technique controls for problems of interacting groups. For example, one member cannot dominate the group. It is also very efficient. NGT groups can make decisions more quickly than groups using consensus decision making. Problems with NGT are associated with the rigidity of the process and the restriction of interaction. NGT sometimes does not work well with complex problems within organizations.[25]

NGT should be used as special circumstances dictate—for example, at a planning workshop or with an ad hoc committee working on a well-defined task. Day-to-day group decision making between supervisor and work team is usually better handled by using consensus or other approaches such as the leader making the decision alone or the work group voting on the decision.

This coverage of decision rules is by no means complete. *Robert's Rules of Order,* a parliamentary system of group decision making, is another example of a workable set of decision rules. Groups can also come up with their own rules and procedures, or modify the methods discussed here.

Regardless of the decision rules employed, it is important that teams use decision rules as guideposts for deliberations. A supervisor should take the lead in establishing guidelines for group decision making if tradition and the experience of group members does not provide direction. A supervisor should help improve whatever process the group currently uses.

Group Dynamics: Problems and Considerations

group dynamics
Reflect how interaction among individuals comprising a group affects the group decision-making process.

Decision-making groups must contend with group dynamics that directly affect the quality of the decision-making process. **Group dynamics** are concerned with how interaction among individuals comprising a group affects the group process. For example, a group member may be reticent to offer an opinion because he or she thinks it would be unpopular with other group members, or go along with a group decision because he or she does not want to create division in the group.

Group decision making always involves group dynamics. Supervisors should understand potential problems in order to reduce their adverse effects upon decision quality. Following is a discussion of problems and considerations associated with group dynamics.

Groupthink

groupthink
Describes the breakdown in critical thinking that occurs within highly cohesive decision-making groups in which members strive for conformity.

Sometimes groups can be too compatible. **Groupthink** describes the breakdown in critical thinking that occurs within highly cohesive decision-making groups in which members strive for conformity. (See Chapter 12 for further discussion of group cohesiveness.)

Cohesive decision-making groups experiencing groupthink are guilty of (1) an illusion of invulnerability, (2) a belief in the morality of the group, (3) collective rationalization, (4) stereotyping, (5) self-censorship, (6) an illusion of unanimity, (7) applying direct pressure to dissenters, and (8) the emergence of self-appointed mind guards who protect the group from outside information.[26] A lesson to be learned from studying the groupthink phenomenon is that conformity itself does not improve the quality of group decisions.

Janis developed his ideas after reviewing historical fiascoes and successes, such as the attack on Pearl Harbor that brought the United States into World War II and the Cuban missile crisis during the Kennedy administration that pulled the superpowers from the brink of nuclear war.

Groupthink can be avoided if groups follow decision rules such as consensus, brainstorming, or NGT that provide for relatively open expression of contrary opinions. Also, groups should keep information channels open. Even bad news will improve decision quality if it is not ignored.

devil's advocate
A method for countering groupthink when an individual argues against the group's preferred course of action.

Finally, the appointment or the recognition of a **devil's advocate** effectively counters groupthink. (Devil's advocates were originally appointed by Catholic church officials to argue against sainthood for candidates being considered for canonization.) If a highly cohesive group lacks a devil's advocate, then the supervisor could play that role.

squeaky wheel
Slang term implying an overly dominant team member who can compromise the quality of a group's decision by overparticipation.

Squeaky Wheels and Social Loafers

A **squeaky wheel** (to be covered in Chapter 13) is an overly dominant team member who can compromise the quality of a group's decision. Team members have an unfortunate tendency to equate the quantity of participation by a group member with the quality of the presentation.[27] Team members who are valuable resources may be overlooked because they do not or cannot speak up.

social loafing
Occurs when group members put in less effort believing their individual contributions cannot be assessed.

Sometimes people do not fully participate in a group because of **social loafing** (to be discussed in Chapter 11). Group members have a tendency to put in less effort when they believe their individual contributions cannot be assessed.[28] You may have experienced this phenomenon while participating in a group activity in which individual effort could not be monitored or demonstrated.

Supervisors should seek balanced participation from group members to reduce the negative effects of squeaky wheels and social loafers. They should slow down the squeaky wheels and make loafing group members accountable for participating in deliberations. Using decision rules helps in doing this.

The Group Polarization Effect

Group discussion tends to cause group members to shift farther toward the end of an issue they already favor (for example, a risky or conservative decision).[29] This tendency, called the **group polarization effect,** leads, in turn, to a more extreme posture for the group as a whole, particularly when several group members share the same initial view of a problem.

Risky (or conservative) decisions are not always bad. However, when teams make decisions, they should do so because the situation merits the decision, not because they are being overly influenced by a group dynamic. In this regard, a devil's advocate can prove useful by questioning individual and group direction toward a risky or conservative decision.

The leader's initial instructions to a group also have a significant effect on the group's decision.[30] This situation is analogous to the instructions a judge gives to a jury. In providing instructions, the judge should try to avoid biasing the jury's verdict. The verdict of a jury, like the decision of any group involved in analytic decision making, should stand on its own merit. Supervisors need to be careful not to inadvertently bias a work group toward a particular position because of their own initial position on a subject.

group polarization effect
Occurs when group members shift toward either a risky or conservative decision creating a more extreme posture for the group as a whole.

The meeting broke up. Carla walked to her cubicle with a puzzled look. "They don't want to be included in decision making? I don't get it!"

That afternoon, at her boss Larry's request, Carla sat in on a division meeting. Larry wanted to broaden Carla's horizons and was starting to show her different company operations. The meeting agenda included an informational briefing by the finance department on changes in the company's buy/lease decision criteria. Summaries were to be distributed at a later date, and implications of the change were already well understood by most middle-managers.

"This meeting is boring," Carla thought. "I've nothing to contribute and Larry handles these things pretty well anyway."

That night, Carla attended a neighborhood block meeting. She snoozed through the discussions on providing better play areas for children (Carla has no children). When the agenda moved to a city program to hang flower baskets on street signs, Carla politely excused herself.

At the next group mini-meeting, Carla served coffee and donuts to her group. She told a couple of truly funny jokes. Then Carla informed the group that, although they would have meetings as necessary in the future, the early morning regime of scheduled meetings was over.

A cheer bubbled up from the group. Carla smiled.

Summary: Focus on Skills

At the individual and group level, decision making is defined as, "working toward a goal by choosing among alternative courses of action." The decision-making process adds to this definition the implementation of an alternative and evaluation of results.

Following are 14 suggestions to help supervisors improve the quality of individual and group decision making:

1. Learn the steps in the decision-making process (define the problem, consider alternatives, select and implement an alternative, and evaluate the outcome), and follow these steps in sequence when making important decisions.
2. Realize that not all decisions require the use of a systematic decision-making process. The decision strategy to use depends, in part, upon the decision environment (for example, the accountability of the decision maker and resource constraints) and decision characteristics such as ambiguity and complexity.
3. Define a problem before trying to solve it.
4. Avoid the "garbage in–garbage out" syndrome by using the best information available and checking out assumptions whenever possible.
5. Systematically consider multiple alternatives.
6. Even if using a quantitative approach to consider alternatives (such as a decision tree), remember that the idea is not to eliminate subjectivity. Rather, it is to have better control over what is an inherently subjective process.
7. Consider whether a decision was successful or unsuccessful because of the quality of the decision or because of the manner in which it was implemented. Good ideas are sometimes poorly implemented.
8. Try to include other people who have less at stake in the evaluation of past decisions. Learn from and accept the lessons of past mistakes, even though it may be difficult to accept failure.
9. Plan the deliberations! Prepare an agenda, determine decision rules, set a time, location, and length for the meeting. Select participants based upon the need for representativeness (acceptance) and/or information (quality).
10. Learn and apply the rules for brainstorming, consensus decision making, and nominal grouping when working with your team. Also, understand the advantages and disadvantages associated with the use of these approaches.
11. Know that the most appropriate decision rule to use depends upon the situation. Keep in mind that consensus decision making and brainstorming used together are appropriate much of the time.
12. Encourage the participation of a devil's advocate within the group. Take on this role yourself if necessary.
13. Encourage balanced participation from group members. Call on or give assignments to social loafers or to others who are reticent about participating in deliberations. Slow down squeaky wheels by soliciting input from other group members and by applying appropriate decision rules.
14. Reduce the tendency of groups to make extreme decisions by giving balanced instructions and guidance to the group, and use a devil's advocate to reduce the group polarization effect.

Review Questions

1. What is a *problem?*
2. Define the concepts of decision making and problem solving.
3. Differentiate between nonprogrammed and programmed decisions. Briefly explain each. Which are usually the most desirable to make in organizations and why?
4. What are the steps or stages of decision making?
5. Explain the meanings of *bounded rationality* and *analysis paralysis.*
6. How can you apply quantitative methods in making decisions? Give three examples.
7. Define *dissonance balancing.*
8. Describe the dynamics of decision making within the work team. Indicate the advantages and disadvantages of group decision making.
9. What is leader decision theory? How is it applied?
10. Explain decision rules that can be applied to group decision making.

11. What is consensus decision making?
12. Characterize the nominal group technique and how it operates.
13. Is groupthink a bad thing? Explain.

Notes

1. See R. Albanese, *Managing: Toward Accountability for Performance*, 3d ed. (Homewood, IL: Richard D. Irwin, 1981), 145–146.
2. See H. A. Simon, *The New Science of Management Decisions* (New York: Harper & Row, 1960), 5–6.
3. T. R. Mintzberg, "The Manager's Job: Folklore and Fact," *Harvard Business Review* July–August 1975, 49–61.
4. L. R. Beach and T. R. Mitchell, "Individual and Group Decision Making," in J. E. Garcia, C. T. Lewis, and F. E. Fiedler, *People, Management, and Productivity* (Boston, MA: Allyn & Bacon, 1986), 57.
5. L. R. Beach and T. R. Mitchell, "A Contingency Model for the Selection of Decision Strategies," *Academy of Management Review* 3 (1978): 439–449.
6. Ibid.
7. J. Dewey, *How We Think* (Boston, MA: D.C. Heath and Company, 1910), 159.
8. H. A. Simon, *Models of Man* (New York: Wiley, 1957).
9. A. Miller and D. Tsiantar, "A Test for Market Research," *Newsweek*, December 28, 1987, 32–33.
10. B. M. Staw, "The Escalation of Commitment to a Course of Action," *Academy of Management Review* 6 (1981): 557–578. Also, B. M. Staw, "Knee Deep in the Big Muddy: A Study of Escalating Commitment to a Chosen Course of Action," *Organizational Behavior and Human Performance* 16 (1976): 27–44.
11. J. H. Shonk, *Team-Based Organizations* (Homewood, IL: Business One Irwin, 1992).
12. N. R. F. Maier, "Assets and Liabilities in Group Problem Solving: The Need for an Integrative Function," *Psychological Review* 47 (1967): 239–249.
13. Shonk, *Team-Based Organizations*, 152.
14. E. A. Locke and D. M. Schweiger, "Participation in Decision Making: One More Look" in *Research in Organizational Behavior*, ed. B. M. Staw (Greenwich, CT: JAI Press, 1979), vol. 1.
15. V. Vroom and P. W. Yetton, *Leadership and Decision Making* (Pittsburgh, PA: University of Pittsburgh Press, 1973). Also, V. Vroom and A. G. Jago, "On the Validity of the Vroom-Yetton Model," *Journal of Applied Psychology* 63 (1978): 151–162.
16. S. A. Stumpf, D. E. Zand, and R. D. Freeman, "Designing Groups for Judgmental Decisions," *Academy of Management Review* 4 (1979): 589–600.
17. J. B. Harvey, "The Abilene Paradox: The Management of Agreement," *Organizational Dynamics* 3 (Summer 1974): 63–80.
18. Ibid., 69.
19. J. Hall, "Decisions, Decisions, Decisions," *Psychology Today*, November 1971, 51–88.
20. Ibid.
21. Ibid.
22. B. H. Drake and D. Hansen, "Enhancing Group Decision Making: Re-examining Process Losses," paper presented at the Western Academy of Management meeting, Big Sky, MT, 1988.
23. A. Van de Ven and A. L. Delbecq, "The Effectiveness of Nominal, Delphi, and Interacting Group Decision Making Processes," *Academy of Management Journal* 17 (1974): 605–621. Also, A. Van de Ven and A. L. Delbecq, "Nominal versus Interacting Group Processes for Committee Decision-Making," *Academy of Management Journal* 14 (1971): 203–214.
24. A. Delbecq, A. Van de Ven, and D. Gustafson, "Guidelines for Conducting NGT Meetings," *Group Techniques for Program Planning* (Glenview, IL: Scott Foresman and Company, 1975).

25. J. K. Murningham, "Group Decision Making: What Strategies Should You Use?" *Management Review* 70 (1981): 55–62.

26. I. Janis, *Groupthink: Psychological Studies of Policy Decisions and Fiascoes* (Boston, MA: Houghton Mifflin, 1982).

27. E. Haynes and L. Meltzer, "Interpersonal Judgments Based on Talkativeness: Fact or Artifact?" *Sociometry* 35 (1972): 538–561. Also, J. E. Baird and S. B. Weinberg, *Communication: The Essence of Group Synergy* (Dubuque, IA: Wm. C. Brown, 1977); and R. M. Sorrentino and R. G. Boutillier, "The Effect of Quality and Quantity of Verbal Interaction on Ratings of Leadership Ability," *Journal of Experimental Social Psychology* 11 (1975): 403–411.

28. B. Latane, K. Williams, and S. Harkins, "Many Hands Make Light Work: The Causes and Consequences of Social Loafing," *Journal of Personality and Social Psychology* 37 (1979): 822–832.

29. J. McGrath and D. A. Kravitz, "Group Research," *Annual Review of Psychology* 33 (1982): 195–230.

30. J. B. Miner, *Organizational Behavior: Performance and Productivity* (New York: Random House, 1988).

Case 10-1

False Alarms: Bugs or Burglars?

Charlene Washington was the branch manager of Thrifty People's Saving and Loan Association in San Jose, California, one of 15 branches operated by Thrifty People's, which was headquartered in Oakland. Eight employees reported to Charlene, each of whom was cross-trained to perform a wide range of duties. As a result, they had extensive knowledge about operations of the business. The eight had worked for the company an average of four years. The most experienced employee had nine years service and the newest was in her probationary period, having been hired a little over four weeks ago. Employee morale was descending.

Thrifty People's S&L was located in an older building in downtown San Jose. The building, constructed in 1917, had been extensively remodeled several times, most recently a year ago following an earthquake and resultant fire that damaged a portion of the building. Adjacent to the S&L was a large commercial bank, San Jose Commerce Bank and Trust Company.

Washington had become branch manager four years ago. She was highly competent and valued by her boss in Oakland.

However, her upcoming performance review would reflect the events she was currently experiencing and was unable to control. Charlene was increasingly concerned about the mystery that was going on at her branch.

The problem had begun two weeks ago when the security system started to be repeatedly triggered at times shortly after sunset and just before sunrise. Repeated checks failed to identify what was causing the firm's silent alarm system, which was activated by movement, to go off.

The silent alarm system notified both the security maintenance company that operated the equipment and the San Jose police department. During the past two weeks, Charlene had been informed 10 times by telephone that the alarm was tripped and had made 10 emergency journeys to the S&L, arriving shortly after the police. Because of the false alarms, law enforcement personnel were becoming less convinced of the system's reliability.

Charlene reviewed several facts that might have a bearing on the cause of the problem:

1. The problem began two weeks ago.
2. The most recent employee was hired four weeks ago.
3. An earthquake and fire occurred a year earlier.
4. No money was ever missing nor were any other abnormal conditions observed.

5. The security system was checked and rechecked without disclosing the source of the problem.
6. The police department was becoming convinced the security system was unreliable.
7. Notices in the San Jose daily newspaper reported the security problem. Customers were calling and some were closing their accounts. Others made jokes about the problem, such as "Thrifty People's recently installed an all-night coffee machine for the convenience of the police department."

"What is going on?" Charlene wondered, after being awakened at 5 AM with another tripped alarm. "We cannot continue this way. What can I do?"

Questions

1. Although you are not given sufficient information to solve the problem, what do you think is causing it?
2. What approach would you use to solve the problem? What additional information do you need?
3. If the problem is not solved, what outcomes do you foresee?

Case 10-2

Vacations

Ever since Traci Myers started her business in 1970, the subject of vacations had been a source of conflict. Traci's firm, Big Sky Jerky, produces a product called jerky—a snack item consisting of strips of beef that are sliced, spicily seasoned, and dry cured. Jerky is sold in grocery stores, supermarkets, and sporting goods outlets and is popular with hikers and campers. Sales are stable throughout the year. Currently, Traci oversees her 20 employees without assistance. Because most of the jobs are not complicated, employees are capable of performing one another's tasks, with the exception of sales and accounting.

A continuing problem is the issue of when employees take their vacations. There are only two criteria for determining when vacations are taken and by whom. First, only one person at a time can be on vacation. Second, preferences for vacation dates are determined entirely by seniority. Workers may trade vacation periods with one another, but the person with the most seniority has first preference. Only the employees with the greatest seniority are satisfied with the system. Older workers, who have accumulated an average of three weeks vacation time, usually take the summer periods, and the younger employees

(with school-age children) often have only one week that must be taken during a non-summer period. Those left with winter periods often find their vacations considerably less rewarding. However, a few love the winter sports.

Although few like the present method of determining vacation schedules, Traci has been unable to invent a better system. She is frustrated, and resentment and hostility over the vacation issue is a continuing problem. Almost constantly during the year, one member of the organization is on vacation, therefore, employees are continuously reminded of the problem.

Traci thinks, "This is really dumb. Paid vacations are a benefit to employees. A benefit is something that should promote well-being, yet the only feeling being created here is ill will. I've got to find a solution to this problem."

Questions

1. This case poses an interesting source of conflict—competition for a scarce resource, vacation time. What method or methods for problem solving/decision making would you apply?
2. How would you resolve the problem? Should employees be involved in the decision? If so, how would you obtain their meaningful participation?
3. How does the concept of equity apply to the vacation problem?
4. What other examples can you think of in which benefits create conflict situations?

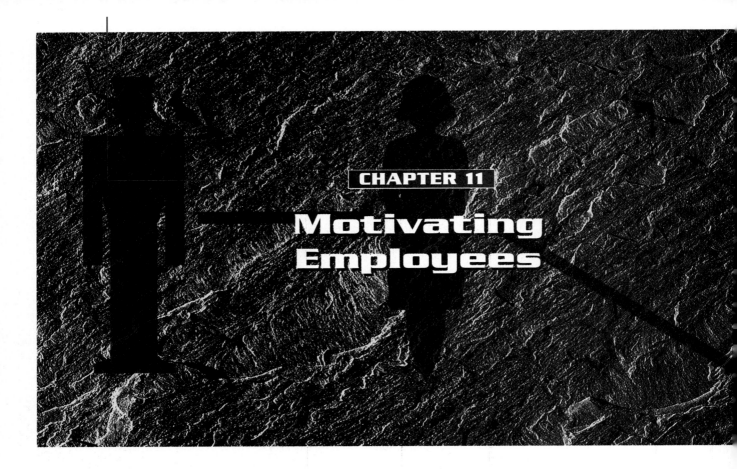

CHAPTER 11

Motivating Employees

● From the past: "The most self-actualization I have observed in a factory was the graffiti in the washroom."[1]

LEARNING
OBJECTIVES

1. Define motivation and illustrate its major components, energy and direction.
2. Describe how unmet needs serve as motivators.
3. Describe Maslow's hierarchy of needs and Herzberg's two-factor theory along with the validity of the concepts.
4. Explain the concepts of job enrichment, job redesign, and employee empowerment.
5. Understand the operation and application of expectancy theory and goal setting theory.
6. Relate the theory of behavior modification and how it is achieved.

"Larry, I'm telling you we can get more out of Al if we change his job! He needs more responsibility and opportunity to grow in his work."

Carla's boss looked unconvinced.

"What do you mean 'grow in his work'? Carla, Al's a machine operator—where's the growth there?"

"We can do more for the job and more for Al!"

"I don't agree. I think you should just crack down on the guy. Tell him to do things your way or find another job."

"No, don't get me wrong. I'm not saying Al's doing a poor job. His performance is fine. I just think he's capable of so much more."

"You're saying his performance is fine, but you still want to change his job? Well, go ahead. Just make sure you get his approval before proceeding. I don't think you'll get very far."

"Thank you, Larry. I'll try it. I'm sure he will love the ideas I have in mind."

The next day, Carla talked with Al. Imagine her amazement when Al told her he wanted his job to stay exactly the same!

What are the secrets to motivating others, particularly in the work environment? As you will see, the answers to this question are complex. This chapter will help you better understand the nature of motivation and how supervisors can successfully motivate employees.

Motivation: More Than Just Being Energized

Motivation is a psychological state that predisposes people to pursue or to avoid certain activities and goals, as discussed previously in Chapter 2. Both energy and direction are essential components of motivation (see Figure 11-1). A person may be energized, but may not be constructively motivated because he or she lacks direction. Alternatively, a person with clear direction may show interest in a goal, but may not put forth the effort needed to reach the goal because he or she lacks the requisite energy.

The effective supervisor needs to consider both energy and direction when motivating others. Giving a motivational pep talk is insufficient. An employee might perform well for a brief time after the talk, but if direction is unclear or unmeaningful to the employee, motivation and productivity will decline or return to the status quo.

It is also insufficient to only make sure that goals are clear. If the goals are not meaningful to the employee or if the employee is insufficiently energized, motivation will be compromised.

Remember also from Chapter 2 that even if energy and direction are strong and clear (in other words, if motivation is strong), performance may still be compromised if employees lack ability or if situational factors make it difficult to work. This chapter is concerned only with the motivation part of the performance equation covered in Chapter 2.

Supervisors can improve employee motivation by recognizing and responding to employee needs; providing fair compensation and other rewards; setting clear, achievable, and acceptable goals; and offering incentives valued by employees. This chapter addresses each of these topics, as well as other considerations pertaining to motivation.

Unmet Needs as Motivators

Supervisors frequently describe their most difficult problem as one of motivating an individual employee in a work group. "Why is it that I just can't get Joe or Alice to show a little enthusiasm?" is an often-heard lament. An understanding of how Joe or Alice's needs tie into motivation could help the supervisor develop strategies to improve motivation and subsequent performance.

What Are Needs?

need
The lack of something requisite, desirable, or useful which, if met, will satisfy an individual.

want
The recognition of a need.

People have a variety of needs. A **need** is the lack of something requisite, desirable, or useful which, if fulfilled, will satisfy an individual. A **want** is the recognition of a need. Needs for food, water, shelter, friendship, recognition, and self-expression are examples of common needs. Motivational theories that address the role of needs agree that unmet needs activate behavior—unmet needs energize people.

A hungry person, for example, spends time and energy searching for food. Think of your behavior when you experience hunger. You probably find your way into the kitchen, check out the refrigerator or investigate the cookie jar. When you are lonely you might call up a friend or a member of your family. You might go out to a common meeting place, perhaps the gym or coffee house. You would

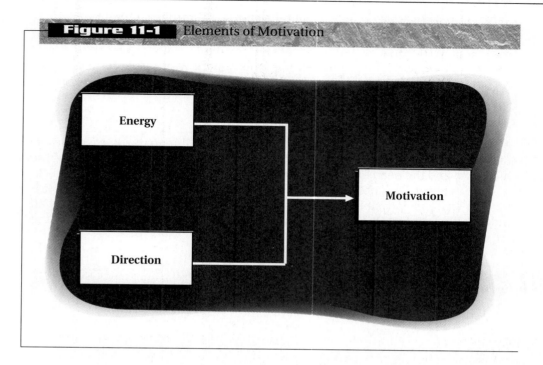

Figure 11-1 Elements of Motivation

not spend the time looking for a cookie jar or going to a friend's house unless an unmet need activated that behavior. The notion that unmet needs motivate is a primary consideration in the need-based theories of David McClelland, Abraham Maslow, and Frederick Herzberg.

The Need for Achievement

David McClelland has studied a cluster of human needs that influence work motivation and leadership. Building on earlier work in personality theory, McClelland established several important work-related needs including the need for affiliation, the need for power, and the **need for achievement,** which is the need to exceed a performance standard.[2]

Studies have demonstrated that people with a high need for achievement tend to concentrate more on personal accomplishments compared to people with a low need for achievement. They generally assume more responsibility for tasks, seek task-relevant feedback, and prefer moderate risk situations. Challenging tasks motivate people who have a high need for achievement.[3]

McClelland's research findings show that need achievement training can improve motivation.[4] McClelland's training program taught people to think in achievement-oriented terms; to set high goals; and to develop self-awareness. Business people trained in this program had more success in creating new businesses than an equivalent control group; a group of people living at the poverty level increased their standard of living; and a group of managers improved their effectiveness.[5]

These studies suggest that performance can be improved if supervisors teach employees to concentrate on results. McClelland's training program succeeded because it enabled individuals to focus their motivation. It enabled people with a high need for achievement to see a path to meeting this need. The components

need for achievement
The need to exceed a performance standard such as a personal accomplishment.

of this training can be applied to everyday life in organizations. Supervisors can remind or even train employees to think in terms of achievement, to set high goals, and to be sensitive to the effect of efforts upon results. Supervisors should also match those with a high need for achievement with results-oriented jobs such as sales or production jobs whenever possible.

The Hierarchy of Needs

hierarchy of needs
A vertical arrangement of needs with the most basic physiological needs at the first level and the most complex self-actualization needs at the highest level.

According to Abraham Maslow's **hierarchy of needs,** human needs exist in a vertical structure with basic needs such as hunger and thirst at the bottom of the hierarchy and the need for esteem toward the top of the scale.[6] (See Figure 11-2.)

Only as lower-level needs are satisfied do higher-level needs become motivating. For example, physiological needs, such as hunger, motivate to the extent an individual is hungry. Once fed, safety needs become motivators (for example, the

Figure 11-2 Maslow's Need Hierarchy

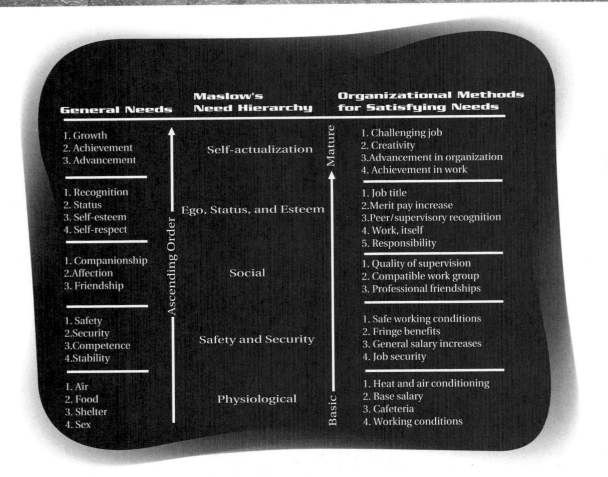

General Needs	Maslow's Need Hierarchy	Organizational Methods for Satisfying Needs
1. Growth 2. Achievement 3. Advancement	Self-actualization	1. Challenging job 2. Creativity 3. Advancement in organization 4. Achievement in work
1. Recognition 2. Status 3. Self-esteem 4. Self-respect	Ego, Status, and Esteem	1. Job title 2. Merit pay increase 3. Peer/supervisory recognition 4. Work, itself 5. Responsibility
1. Companionship 2. Affection 3. Friendship	Social	1. Quality of supervision 2. Compatible work group 3. Professional friendships
1. Safety 2. Security 3. Competence 4. Stability	Safety and Security	1. Safe working conditions 2. Fringe benefits 3. General salary increases 4. Job security
1. Air 2. Food 3. Shelter 4. Sex	Physiological	1. Heat and air conditioning 2. Base salary 3. Cafeteria 4. Working conditions

Ascending Order

Mature — Basic

Source: John M. Ivancevich, Andrew D. Szilagyi, Jr., and Mark J. Wallace, Jr., *Organizational Behavior and Performance* (Santa Monica, CA: Goodyear Publishing Company, 1977), 105.

need for adequate shelter). Following safety needs in Maslow's hierarchy are belongingness needs (the need for meaningful social interaction with others), and esteem needs (the need for recognition). The need to self-actualize, or to become all that one is capable of becoming, is at the highest level of Maslow's hierarchy. The unmet need to self-actualize motivates behavior only if all lower needs have been satisfied.

Maslow believed most citizens in an affluent society will have satisfied lower-order needs such as physiological needs and the need for safety. Consequently, unmet higher-order needs usually have greater motivational value in the North American workplace.

An exception to this premise involves individuals who have experienced negative events such as job loss, rising financial obligations, or personal stress. Lower-order needs serve as the primary source of motivation for people who have had such experiences. For example, a striking worker may be motivated to cross a picket line to meet physiological needs. Social needs, met by solidarity with fellow strikers, become unimportant in the face of lower-order needs to eat and to pay the rent. Essentially, under these circumstances, people tend to move down the hierarchy of needs.

Maslow's theory is often discussed when the topic of motivation is covered. Sometimes, Maslow's theory is offered by trainers or instructors as the primary explanation for motivation. Maslow's hierarchy of needs is, however, imprecise, simplistic, and difficult to empirically test.[7] Several studies have failed to support the theory. The theory's popularity in spite of the problems probably emanates from two sources: First, there is an intuitive attractiveness to Maslow's needs hierarchy. Many people can recall personal experiences or those of others that tend to support it. Second, a modified version of Maslow's hierarchy using only two levels of needs, lower-level security needs at the bottom and higher-level needs on top, has received some verification by research.[8]

For supervisors, the main thing to take from Maslow's theory is that most employees are motivated by unmet higher-order needs. Therefore, supervisors should recognize good performance rather than noticing employees only when they make mistakes, and should not minimize the importance of social interaction in the workplace. Also, supervisors should keep in mind that the importance of a particular need varies with circumstances. What motivates an employee on payday, for example, may not motivate the same individual on some other day.

An effective supervisor recognizes employees when they do something right.

Two-Factor Theory

According to Frederick Herzberg's **two-factor theory,** needs are satisfied by two types of job factors: hygiene factors and motivators.[9]

Hygiene factors have to do with the work environment and satisfy lower-level needs as identified by Maslow. These extrinsic factors include job security, company policies, quality of supervision, working conditions, and pay. Motivators, in contrast, are intrinsic to work and have to do with the employee as a person. They serve to fulfill higher-level needs. Motivators exist in jobs that provide opportunities for achievement, recognition, responsibility, and advancement.

Herzberg believed that hygiene factors and motivators affect workers differently. The presence of hygiene factors, at best, only reduces job dissatisfaction. The presence of motivators, on the other hand, improves job satisfaction and work motivation. Herzberg claimed that motivation and productivity problems are a result of managers relying too heavily on hygiene factors and underestimating the power of motivators.[10]

two-factor theory
Needs are satisfied by two types of factors: hygiene factors that are related to the work environment and capable of reducing job dissatisfaction; and motivators that are intrinsic to work and an individual and can improve job satisfaction and motivation.

What Do Workers Want from Their Jobs?

A survey of members by the American Productivity and Quality Center found that employees rated having challenging work as the most important motivating factor on their jobs. Following on the list in order were having your opinion matter, being recognized for a good job, and having pay reflect performance.[11] (Also see Chapter 19, "Career Planning and Development.")

What is your most important motivator? And why?

The results of research evaluating two-factor theory have not always supported the theory.[12] For example, two-factor theory regards pay as a hygiene factor, despite pay's usefulness as recognition for achievement. Nevertheless, two-factor theory was the first theory to tie job conditions and outcomes with motivation and job satisfaction. In contrast to Maslow's theory, two-factor theory effectively put into operational terms those variables that lead directly to motivation in the workplace.

An important idea supervisors can obtain from Herzberg's theory is that most employees need more than just adequate pay, sensible work rules, and a good work environment in order to be highly motivated. They also need to be recognized for their achievements and generally offered the opportunity to meet higher-order unmet needs as defined by Maslow.

Job Enrichment and Job Redesign

job enrichment
The process of increasing motivation factors in jobs by giving employees more control over their work.

Frederick Herzberg did not stop at developing a theory of work motivation. He carried his theory into practice by developing the concept of job enrichment. **Job enrichment** involves building motivational factors into jobs. The essence of job enrichment is to give employees more control over their jobs, more freedom in their everyday work. Herzberg felt that the nature of work itself needed to change in order to make it more intrinsically motivating.

job redesign
A part of the job characteristics model to increase motivation by adding skill variety, task identity, task significance, autonomy, and job feedback.

Herzberg's theory of job enrichment was extended by Richard Hackman and Greg Oldham's job characteristic model to incorporate the concept of **job redesign.**[13] According to Hackman and Oldham's theory, jobs should be redesigned with a high degree of skill variety, task identity, task significance, autonomy, and job feedback. This redesign will increase the motivation for employees who have high growth needs.[14] Following is a description of each of the factors of job redesign:

- *Skill variety*—The degree to which a job requires a variety of different activities involving different employee skills and talents.
- *Task identity*—The degree to which a job requires completion of a whole and identifiable piece of work. That is, doing a job from beginning to end with a visible outcome.
- *Task significance*—The degree to which a job has a substantial impact on the lives of other people, whether in the immediate organization or in the world at large.
- *Autonomy*—The degree to which a job provides substantial freedom, independence, and discretion to an individual to schedule work and to determine procedures to be used in carrying it out.
- *Job feedback*—The degree to which carrying out work activities provides an individual with direct and clear information about the effectiveness of his or her performance.[15]

Going beyond Pay

There is no question that rewards other than pay influence employee motivation. Some of these rewards cost the organization little, if anything.

SEA Inc., a Seattle-area marine radio manufacturer, has come up with a wide variety of fringe benefits to tell employees that the company cares about them: Service awards include a silver 1-year pin; a silver and garnet 3-year pin; a gold and sapphire 5-year pin that comes with a letter from the company president, balloons, and a plaque; a gold and diamond 10-year pin that comes with a special personalized gift; and a gold and ruby 15-year pin.

Other incentives include free coffee, tea, cocoa, and soup daily; doughnuts every other day; a flower fund; cash awards to employees wearing service pins at unannounced times; $25 to any employee who recruits a friend to work for the company; $50 to any employee who guesses the company's monthly profit; an Employee of the Quarter plaque with a $250 award; tickets to sporting events; three SEA-labeled T-shirts for each employee; a Christmas party and raffle; a picnic and raffle; a semiformal dinner dance; and a "fiscal Friday" once a month that includes mementos, decorations, snacks, and beverages including free domestic and imported beer.[16]

Increasing the motivating potential of work will increase motivation of high growth-need employees if periodic feedback is provided to employees; if employees have adequate knowledge and skill to do their jobs; and if context variables, such as pay, job security, and relations with coworkers, do not interfere with satisfaction.[17]

An Example of Job Redesign and Its Limitations. A supervisor could redesign the work of typists, for example, by having them complete documents in their entirety for specific departments or individuals as opposed to a typical arrangement in which sections of documents are assigned among several typists.

These typists would experience the entire piece of work (facilitating task identity), and would understand the effect of their work on others (facilitating task significance). The typists should also be given considerable latitude in scheduling their work (facilitating autonomy) and be given the option of using different software (facilitating skill variety).

In this hypothetical situation, the supervisors would also have to provide sufficient feedback to the typists. The typists would have to be adequately trained. There should also be no contextual problems to compromise satisfaction, such as inadequate pay.

Job enrichment and job redesign are idealistic concepts. There are several potential threats to success of which the effective supervisor should be aware. First, not every employee has high growth needs. If a supervisor gives more responsibility to employees who have low growth needs, the employees might even get angry. They might feel the supervisor is just trying to get them to do more work. Don't assume that all employees are ambitious! Some employees simply do not have strong unmet esteem needs. (See Figure 11-3.)

Furthermore, redesigning jobs is not as simple as it might appear. Any change in the design of work affects other jobs in the work group or organization.[18] For example, adding more autonomy to a typist's job might reduce the supervisor's responsibility for overseeing this employee's work. It might also reduce the supervisor's decision-making authority. Redesigning work may also turn out to be impractical and expensive, particularly if the organization has invested large sums of money in equipment or in developing a specific work process. Supervisors might not even have the authority to redesign jobs.

Figure 11-3 Different Strokes for Different Folks

Calvin and Hobbes by Bill Watterson

Job redesign is most likely to be successful for jobs that can be successfully modified within the context of the organization; for jobs in which high growth-need employees will hold the redesigned jobs; and in situations in which supervisors and employees accept job redesign as a method for making work more satisfying and motivating.[19]

Empowering Employees

employee empowerment
Expanding the power employees have over their jobs by increasing planning responsibilities, autonomy in making decisions, and so forth.

A new addition to the concept of job enrichment and redesign is the idea of **employee empowerment.** This approach involves employees having more power in the conduct of their everyday work lives—more power to shape their destiny on the job (which is similar to job enrichment's objective of giving workers more freedom and job redesign's call for building more autonomy into work). The idea is to help employees see the organization's objectives as *their* challenges.[20]

Employee empowerment is not just something that a supervisor gives a worker. The employee has to also feel free to exercise that power. To be effective, employee empowerment needs to ripple throughout the organization: managers at the highest level in the company need to empower middle management; middle managers need to empower supervisors; and supervisors need to empower employees. All organizational members need to feel it is all right to exercise their freedom to act.

Redesigning work to give employees more interesting work and more power in its conduct is compatible with contemporary total quality management (TQM) methods that require each employee to take responsibility for the quality and efficiency of his or her contribution to the group's and organization's efforts. (TQM is covered in Chapter 2.)

In short, the contemporary supervisor ideally leads a team of empowered workers who are driven by intrinsic, growth-related motivation. For this ideal to happen it is important that the overall organization provide an empowering climate. An individual supervisor, however, usually has little control over directing resources to improve an entire organization's climate.

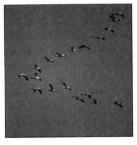

Empowered employees head in the same direction, take turns leading, and adjust their structure to accommodate a task.

The supervisor can strive to hire employees for his or her work group who appear to have high growth needs. (Chapter 8 discusses employee selection in more detail.) The success of employee empowerment programs, as that of job enrichment and job redesign, requires that employees have a desire to grow in their jobs and want to do more than just put in time.

The Difference between Buffaloes and Geese

Traditional employees in highly bureaucratic organizations tend to behave like buffaloes. Buffaloes follow the leader and become disoriented and directionless if the leader is confused or gets lost. If the leader is removed, the herd mills around waiting for someone to take charge.

Truly empowered employees, however, are like geese. Geese fly together in a "V" formation of individuals who know the common goal, take turns leading, and adjust their structure to the task at hand (for example, they fly in a wedge, but land in waves). Most importantly, each individual bird is responsible for its own performance.[21]

Going beyond Unmet Needs

There is a group of motivational theories that go beyond consideration of unmet needs of employees to include factors that affect the process of motivation. Two such theories are expectancy theory and goal setting.

Expectancy Theory

An alternative to need-based theories is the belief that motivation is largely determined by individual choice based on environmental factors. Expectancy theory embraces this view.

Expectancy theory states that the force of motivation is a function of an individual's perception that effort will lead to a required level of performance *(expectancy)*; the likelihood that performance will lead to an outcome *(instrumentality)*; and the overall attractiveness of the outcome *(valence)*.[22] Expectancy theory is related to path-goal theory discussed in Chapter 7. Path-goal theory covers specific leader behaviors that are motivating in different situations; expectancy theory explains why this leader behavior is motivating.

Motivation is maximized to the extent all three components of expectancy theory are high. For example, people will work hard if they feel a task can be accomplished, believe accomplishing the task will lead to a particular outcome, and value the outcome. Alternatively, the force of motivation is diminished if any one or more of these components is compromised.

For example, you might work for a fair boss who provides rewards you value highly. In this instance, instrumentality and valence are high—you know that preparing a report will lead to recognition that you value highly. However, if expectancy is low—if you doubt you can actually prepare the technical report required by your boss—motivation will be low. No matter how consistent and fair your boss is, no matter how much you value recognition or pay as rewards, your inability to do the work will considerably reduce your work motivation.

Here is another example, using a mathematical estimate of motivation: Suppose you strongly believe you can perform well on a test by studying hard (perhaps on a scale of zero to 1.0 your belief is .85), strongly believe your performance will be rewarded with a grade of "A" (.95), and place a high value on earning an "A" (.99). The force of your motivation to study hard for a test will be high $(.85 \times .95 \times .99 = .80)$. If you assign a value of zero to any of these factors, however, the theory says the force of your motivation will still be zero regardless of how high the other values might be.

An obvious criticism of expectancy theory is that it treats people as rational calculating machines. People tend to be nonrational and human motivation is not as simple as it might seem from the theory.[23] Also, the processes described

expectancy theory
The force of motivation is a function of an individual's perception that effort will lead to a required level of performance (expectancy), the likelihood that performance will lead to an outcome (instrumentality), and the relative attractiveness of the outcome (valence).

by expectancy theory operate at the cognitive level and cannot be easily measured or quantified. The use of numerical values in the above example was intended to illustrate the relationships. Pinpointing real numerical values to fill into the equation would be difficult to do.

Despite the limitations of expectancy theory, it is an excellent diagnostic tool and motivational framework for supervisors. Rather than deal with the sometimes vague notion of helping employees meet unmet needs, supervisors can systematically compare environmental factors and supervisory methods against each part of the theory. Based on this assessment, supervisors can make specific workplace changes that will positively affect employee motivation.

For example, expectancy—belief that effort will lead to performance—is reduced if employees are inadequately trained, are unsure of their job duties, or are ill-equipped. Instrumentality—belief that performance will lead to an outcome—is compromised if employees are treated inconsistently. Valence—the value of the outcome to the employee—is lessened if the reward lacks meaning to the particular employee. The effective supervisor needs to make sure that employees are well trained and equipped, know their specific job duties, are treated in a consistent fashion, and are provided with meaningful rewards.

The usefulness of expectancy theory is well summarized by Walter Newsom:

> Exposure of the expectancy theory to many levels of people . . . proves that the reaction of supervisors of high- and low-skill workers, professionals, students, parents, and clericals has been unanimously positive. These people [supervisors] say the theory is a powerful diagnostic tool in determining why the individuals they supervised have or haven't been motivated.[24]

Goal Setting Theory

goal setting theory
The process of setting specific and difficult, but achievable goals provides direction toward accomplishing a task and leads to high levels of motivation and performance.

Clarifying direction is also central to the **goal setting theory** of Edwin Locke and Gary Latham.[25] The process of setting a goal provides direction toward accomplishing a task. Specific and difficult, but still achievable, goals have been demonstrated to lead to high levels of motivation and performance.[26] Telling an employee to "do her best" or to "give it the old college try" is not as effective as having a specific goal to increase sales by 15 percent by the next month. Moreover, a 15 percent sales increase, assuming it is achievable, will lead to greater motivation than a goal of a 5 percent increase.

Effective goal setting requires goal commitment from employees. Setting a goal has little effect on motivation if an employee does not accept the goal. Individual participation in setting goals may lead to the adoption of more difficult goals and greater goal commitment. However, employee participation is not necessary for goal acceptance. Assigned goals, if accepted by followers, also lead to improved motivation and performance.[27]

In practice, deciding whether to use participation in goal setting depends upon the relationship between the supervisor and employees and the supervisor's need for employee involvement. When employees trust a supervisor's judgement and the supervisor has adequate information upon which to make decisions, employee participation in goal setting is often not necessary. This concept can be related to Vroom and Yetton's leader decision theory covered in Chapters 7 and 10.

Goal setting's success as a motivator requires the provision of feedback. Feedback in goal setting provides information about progress toward the goal, which improves performance by permitting individuals to adjust performance on the basis of goal-relevant information.[28] (See Chapters 1, 8, 13, and 14 for further discussion of the importance of feedback.)

Goal setting theory is consistent with Management by Objectives (MBO), in which goals are mutually set between employees and management using time lines to direct the efforts of individuals or groups. MBO is applicable as both a productivity enhancement tool and as a performance appraisal method. (See Chapters 5 and 14 for further discussion of MBO.)

Supervisors gain a powerful motivational tool when they adopt and apply goal setting with individuals and work groups. One advantage of goal setting is that it often does not require approval from middle or top management to implement. And, properly implemented, goal setting is unquestionably one of the most important steps a supervisor can take to improve individual and group productivity. Goal setting does not require trying to determine employees' unmet needs; nor is the success of goal setting entirely dependent on what other areas of the organization may be doing. The setting of difficult but achievable, measurable goals for a specific time frame is a straightforward and usually effective process for a supervisor and employees.

Behavior Modification

There is a school of thought that believes present behavior is driven by the consequences of past behavior. Put another way, the theory of **behavior modification** contends that consequences of past behavior lead to, inhibit, or otherwise shape future behavior.[29]

This perspective, to the extent it is rigidly adhered to, is limiting when applied to human behavior. More than just the consequences of past behavior operate when people make decisions to act in certain ways. Humans have the capacity to "look before they leap," to think before they act. Human behavior should not be explained just by the consequences of past actions. (For example, "Past leaps were fun. I'll do it again!" Or, "I broke my leg the last time I jumped. I surely won't do that again!")

Still, as with other theories of motivation, behavior modification provides some answers. Knowing when and how to reward (or if you should punish) employees is a significant addition to understanding and improving employee motivation.

Reinforcement and Punishment

Behavior is modified through operant conditioning.[30] **Operant conditioning** means to change behavior of others through application of positive or negative reinforcement, punishment, or extinction.

Reinforcing Behavior. Reinforcement increases the likelihood of a type of behavior occurring in the future. A reinforcer can be positive or negative. **Positive reinforcement** occurs when an attractive consequence is presented to an individual as a result of behaving in the desired manner. Common positive reinforcers in the workplace include pay, praise, improved working conditions, and greater responsibility.

Negative reinforcement occurs when a disliked condition is removed or avoided as a result of an individual's behavior. An example of negative

behavior modification
Contends that consequences of past behavior lead to, inhibit, or otherwise shape future behavior.

operant conditioning
Behavior is changed through application of positive or negative reinforcement, punishment, or extinction.

positive reinforcement
Occurs when an attractive consequence is presented to an individual as a result of behaving in the desired manner.

negative reinforcement
Occurs when a disliked condition is removed or avoided as a result of an individual's behavior.

reinforcement is illustrated by the domineering supervisor who stops nagging when a report is submitted on time. To reiterate, reinforcement, whether negative or positive, is intended to increase the occurrence of a desired form of behavior in the future.

Punishment and Extinction. Negative reinforcement is not punishment. **Punishment** occurs when an unpleasant consequence is delivered to a person after a behavior occurs. Punishment, as opposed to reinforcement, is intended to reduce the occurrence of an undesirable form of behavior in the future.

punishment
Occurs when an unpleasant consequence is delivered to a person after exhibiting an undesirable form of behavior.

Interestingly, supervisors can find themselves in an escalating cycle of punishment and negative reinforcement. For example, a supervisor can be negatively reinforced for punishing an employee whose work station is untidy. The punishment (scolding the employee) leads to the reward (a clean desk that is attractive to the supervisor). Under these circumstances, the supervisor will probably resort to punishment as a control mechanism in the future. This means the work environment will probably become rather unpleasant, as an escalating cycle of destructive conflict between unhappy employees and a highly stressed supervisor takes hold.

Promotive strategies, involving positive reinforcement and extinction, are usually more effective in the workplace than are negative strategies involving negative reinforcement and punishment.

extinction
Involves not reinforcing a pattern of behavior one is trying to reduce in another person.

Extinction involves *not* reinforcing a pattern of behavior one is trying to reduce in another person. A supervisor, for example, might choose to ignore irritating memos sent by a particular employee. Eventually, the memos will stop. If the employee instead discusses the problem personally with the supervisor—a behavior the supervisor is trying to encourage—the supervisor can positively reinforce that behavior by offering coffee and being a good listener. In this example, extinguishing the memo-writing behavior, coupled with positive reinforcement during the office visit, leads to a better future relationship between supervisor and employee.

On the other hand, if the supervisor engages in a "memo war" with the employee, more memos will be forthcoming because the behavior of memo-writing is being rewarded by the supervisor's replies. Eventually, the supervisor may get angry and punish the employee, reducing memos from the employee, but also resulting in the cycle of negative reinforcement and punishment described previously.

The application of positive control strategies can have pronounced positive effects on productivity. A widely cited example of success occurred at Emery Air Freight. The company significantly improved customer service through a program of positive reinforcement. Emery supervisors and other managers began to reinforce desired employee behavior and provided feedback of results. Performance improved from 30 percent to 90 percent of a standard for responding to customer queries regarding service and schedules. This improvement resulted in an estimated savings of $650,000 per year for the company![31]

Motivation within the Work Team

Many of the principles discussed thus far for motivating individuals can also be applied to groups, particularly work teams led by a supervisor. The supervisor must take care, though, to consider the effect of group dynamics on motivational processes, discussed in Chapter 10. Motivating a team, as opposed to an individual, calls for carefully attending to relationships involving the contributions of group members and rewards. It requires finding ways to connect individual efforts and responsibilities to group results.

Setting Team Goals

Goal setting, discussed previously, is also effective when used with an entire work group. In this situation, the group must work together to accomplish a shared goal or goals.

Supervisors should be careful when administering rewards for goal attainment within an **interdependent group**—one in which team members must rely on one another to attain a group goal. It is more constructive in terms of member perceptions of fairness to work with group rather than individual goals and to evenly distribute compensation.[32]

A general rule is that supervisors should establish individually assigned goals only if they can truly and objectively separate out individual contributions to a group effort, and if subsequent rewards, such as pay, are judged by other group members to be fair (more on the importance of fairness later in this chapter). Rewarding people differently when individual contributions to the attainment of group goals cannot be readily determined can destroy team cohesiveness.

interdependent group
A work group in which team members must rely on one another to attain a team goal.

Social Loafing

A significant threat to productivity within groups is social loafing.[33] Social loafing, discussed in Chapter 10, is the reduction of individual effort that occurs in a group setting when an individual's contribution cannot be distinguished.

Social loafing has been demonstrated in a number of tasks including brainstorming, rope pulling, and evaluating essays.[34] People put more effort into accomplishing a task when told they might have to later explain their ratings.[35] Individuals also put forth more effort when told their ratings would be the only ratings used by the researchers. From a supervisor's perspective, these results highlight the importance of making individual group members accountable for results. The problem of social loafing will be reduced if individual group members have clear assignments and if a strong group norm is established that team members do their share of the work.

Equity Theory

Fair treatment of work group members is an essential part of the effective supervisor's job. Equity theory strongly supports the importance of treating employees fairly. (See Chapters 8 and 14 for further discussion of equity theory.)

Equity theory states that individuals compare the ratio of their inputs (such as education and experience) to outcomes (such as pay and recognition) to the ratio of inputs to outcomes for a "comparison other."[36] (See Figure 11-4.) Equity exists when these ratios are equal. People tend to be more satisfied when relationships with others are perceived to be fair and equitable.[37]

Employees are motivated to restore equity when these ratios are unequal. When undercompensated, salaried individuals tend to reduce the quantity and quality of work. Employees working on a piece rate system are also more likely to reduce the quantity of output. Undercompensated employees tend to be absent from work more frequently.[38]

equity theory
Individuals compare the ratio of their own inputs to the outcomes they receive to others' ratio of inputs to outcomes they receive.

Figure 11-4	Equity Theory

Work Inputs	Work Outcomes
Effort	Money
Time	Authority
Responsibility	Freedom
Work experience	Status
Skill	Travel
Business connections	Company fringe benefits (car, health club)
Aptitude	Stock options
Attitude	Retirement package
Previous training/academic degree	Recognition
Certification or license	

Studies of how overcompensated individuals restore equity provide mixed results. According to the theory, employees should work harder and produce more if overcompensated relative to a comparison other. Increases in output do occur in laboratory settings. However, in a real-world environment, overcompensated people do not tend to restore equity by working harder or producing more.[39] Instead, people have a tendency to rationalize overcompensation by inflating their self-worth.[40]

The primary implication of equity theory for supervisors is, Be fair! Remember, employee perceptions of fairness are based on relative rather than absolute rewards. For example, you could give an employee a huge pay increase or special attention and praise and he or she might still be dissatisfied if a less productive "comparison other" receives the same reward.

Supervisors must also contend with equity comparisons not only within a group and an organization, but also between organizations. A member of your work group might be dissatisfied because of what others in a comparable job earn working in another organization (more on this subject in Chapter 8).

"I don't get it, Al. The changes we're talking about will only make your job more interesting."

"Yeah, maybe for you."

"I don't understand."

"Carla, I don't want more interesting work. I just want to punch in, do my job, and punch out. The truth is that I'm much more interested in coaching my son's little league team and building model airplanes. I work to live, I don't live to work."

"You don't want more responsibility?" Carla still could not believe it.

"No. I just want to do my job. I will be happy to help you out with overtime if you get in a bind. Otherwise, just let me know if I'm doing something wrong. If I'm doing all right, I would appreciate being let alone."

That night while driving home, Carla realized that not every employee wants to move up. She realized she had attributed her own strong desire for growth in the job to Al. She would have to communicate more closely with Al in the future to find out more about what *he* wanted out of work. Maybe she could not expect to do more to improve Al's performance than was already being done.

Summary: Focus on Skills

Motivation is a psychological state that predisposes people to pursue or to avoid certain activities or goals. Energy and direction are essential components of motivation.

Following are 12 suggestions to help supervisors improve motivation of employees within the work team:

1. Remind employees to think in terms of achievement, to set high goals, and to be aware of the effect of their efforts upon results. Match employees with a high need for achievement with results-oriented jobs whenever possible.
2. Help employees to meet unmet needs. Realize that most unmet needs in the workplace are higher-order needs for belongingness and esteem.
3. Be sensitive to individual differences in needs. What motivates one employee may not motivate another, or even the same employee at another time.
4. Consider employee growth needs when enriching or redesigning jobs. Employees with high growth needs are more receptive to job enrichment and job redesign than are those with low growth needs.
5. Apply job redesign for jobs that can be successfully modified within the context of the organization; for jobs where high growth-need employees will benefit from the redesign; and in situations in which both supervisor and employees accept job redesign as a method for making work more satisfying and motivating.
6. Try to hire employees who will benefit from empowerment programs.
7. Use coaching and training to increase employee belief that effort will lead to successful performance (to increase expectancy); ensure clear and consistent relationships between employee performance and work outcomes (to increase instrumentality); and provide outcomes that are valued by employees (to increase valence).
8. Be sure that employee-acceptable, specific, difficult-but-achievable goals are in place, and provide feedback to employees regarding progress and goal attainment.
9. Reinforce appropriate employee behavior with rewards such as praise, recognition, pay, and better working conditions. Avoid the escalating cycle of conflict caused by punishment and negative reinforcement.
10. Use group goals and evenly distribute rewards when leading an interdependent work group. Reward individual contributions to group efforts only if individual efforts can be objectively separated and if individual rewards are deemed fair by group members.
11. Combat social loafing by making individual group members accountable for their contributions to the group effort.
12. Be fair. Remember that employee perceptions of fair treatment are based upon relative rather than absolute comparisons of treatment.

Review Questions

1. What is motivation? Describe how energy and direction are essential components of motivation.
2. What is a need? A want? How do unmet needs energize people?
3. Need-based theories include those of McClelland, Maslow, and Herzberg. For each, indicate the operational characteristics, how they are applied by supervisors, and their validity.
4. What are job enrichment and job redesign? Indicate the elements to consider in the job redesign process.
5. Do all employees want enriched jobs? Explain.
6. Employee empowerment is a popular term today. What does it mean? How can supervisors empower their team members?
7. Describe the content of expectancy theory and goal setting theory. Cite several illustrations of how these theories can be applied to motivate employees.
8. What are behavior modification and operant conditioning?

9. Reinforcement increases the likelihood of a behavior occurring in the future and can be either positive or negative. Mention several examples of each.
10. Under what conditions should a supervisor apply interdependent group goals rather than individually assigned goals for work teams and their members?
11. Explain the meaning of *social loafing*.
12. What is equity theory? What are the implications of equity theory for supervisors?

Notes

1. R. Schrank, "Work in America: What Do Workers Really Want?" *Current* 196 (October 1974): 41.
2. H. A. Murray, *Explorations in Personality* (New York: Oxford University Press, 1938). Also D. C. McClelland, *Assessing Human Motivation* (New York: General Learning Press, 1971); and D. C. McClelland, J. W. Atkinson, R. A. Clark, and E. L. Lowell, *The Achievement Motive* (New York: Appleton-Century-Crofts, 1953).
3. D. C. McClelland, *The Achieving Society* (Princeton, NJ: Van Nostrand, 1961).
4. D. C. McClelland, "Managing Motivation to Expand Human Freedom," *American Psychologist* 33 (1978): 201–210.
5. Ibid.
6. A. H. Maslow, *Motivation and Personality* (New York: Harper & Row, 1954). Also see J. M. Ivancevich, A. D. Szilagyi, Jr., and M. J. Wallace, Jr., *Organizational Behavior and Performance* (Santa Monica, CA: Goodyear Publishing Company, 1975), 105.
7. M. Wahba and L. Bridwell, "Maslow Reconsidered: A Review of Research on the Need Hierarchy Theory," *Organizational Behavior and Human Development* 15 (1976): 212–240.
8. G. Dessler, *Organization and Management* (Reston, VA: Reston Publishing Company, 1982), 303–304.
9. F. Herzberg, *Work and the Nature of Man* (Cleveland, OH: World Publishing, 1966).
10. F. Herzberg, "One More Time: How Do You Motivate Employees?" *Harvard Business Review* 46 (1968): 53–62.
11. *The Wall Street Journal,* August 16, 1988.
12. V. M. Bockman, "The Herzberg Controversy," *Personnel Psychology* 24 (1971): 155–189.
13. J. R. Hackman and G. R. Oldham, *Job Redesign* (Reading, MA: Addison-Wesley, 1980).
14. W. H. Glick, G. D. Jenkins, Jr., and N. Gupta, "Method versus Substance: How Strong are Underlying Relationships between Job Characteristics and Attitudinal Outcomes?" *Academy of Management Journal* 29 (1986): 441–464.
15. Hackman and Oldham, *Job Redesign.*
16. "At SEA Inc. You Could Call Them 'Beyond-the-Fringe' Benefits," *The Herald,* (Everett) February 21, 1993, D4.
17. Hackman and Oldham, *Job Redesign.*
18. "At SEA Inc.," D4.
19. Ibid.
20. P. Kizilos, "Crazy about Empowerment?" *Training,* December 1988, 47–56. Also, P. Block, *The Empowered Manager* (San Francisco, CA: Jossey-Bass, 1987).
21. R. Stayer, "How I Learned to Let My Workers Lead," *Harvard Business Review,* November-December 1990, reprint 90610.
22. V. H. Vroom, *Work and Motivation* (New York: John Wiley & Sons, 1964).
23. Ibid. Also D. R. Ilgen, D. M. Nebeker, and R. D. Pritchard, "Expectancy Theory Measures: An Empirical Comparison in an Experimental Simulation," *Organizational Behavior and Human Performance* 28 (1981): 189–223; and T. R. Mitchell, "Expectancy Models of Job Satisfaction, Occupational Preference, and Effort: A Theoretical Methodological, and Empirical Appraisal," *Psychological Bulletin* 81 (1974): 1053–1077.

24. W. B. Newsom, "Motivate, Now!" *Personnel Journal* 69 (1990): 51–55.
25. E. A. Locke, "Toward a Theory of Task Motivation and Incentives," *Organizational Behavior and Human Performance* 3 (1968): 157–189. Also see E. A. Locke and G. P. Latham, *Goal-Setting: A Motivational Technique That Works!* (Englewood Cliffs, NJ: Prentice-Hall, 1984).
26. E. A. Locke, K. N. Shaw, L. M. Saari, and G. P. Latham, "Goal Setting and Task Performance 1969–1980." *Psychological Bulletin* 90 (1981): 125–152.
27. Ibid.
28. M. E. Tubbs, "Goal Setting: A Meta-Analytic Examination of the Empirical Evidence," *Journal of Applied Psychology* 71 (1986): 474–483.
29. B. F. Skinner, *Contingencies of Reinforcement: A Theoretical Analysis* (Englewood Cliffs, NJ: Prentice-Hall, 1969).
30. Ibid.
31. "At Emery Air Freight Positive Reinforcement Boosts Performance," *Organizational Dynamics* 1 (1973): 41–50.
32. L. Miller and R. Hamblin, "Interdependence, Differential Rewarding and Productivity," *American Sociological Review* 28 (1963): 768–778.
33. B. Latane, K. Williams, and S. Harkins, "Many Hands Make Light the Work: The Causes and Consequences of Social Loafing," *Journal of Personality and Social Psychology* 37: 822–832.
34. G. Bartis, K. Szymanski, and S. G. Harkins, "Evaluation and Performance: A Two-Edged Knife," *Personality and Social Psychology Bulletin* 14 (1988): 242–251.
35. E. Weldon and G. G. Gargano, "Cognitive Loafing: The Effects of Accountability and Shared Responsibility on Cognitive Effort," *Personality and Social Psychology Bulletin* 14 (1988): 159–171.
36. J. S. Adams, "Equity in Social Exchange," in *Advances in Experimental Social Psychology,* ed. L. Berkowitz (New York: Academic Press, 1965), Vol. 2.
37. E. H. Walster, G. W. Walster, and E. Berscheid, *Equity: Theory and Research* (Boston, MA: Allyn & Bacon, 1978).
38. P. S. Goodman and R. S. Atkins, *Absenteeism* (San Francisco, CA: Jossey-Bass, 1984).
39. Walster, *Equity: Theory and Research.*
40. R. T. Mowday, "Equity Theory Predictions of Behavior in Organizations," in *Motivation and Work Behavior,* 4th ed., eds. R. M. Steers and L. W. Porter (New York: McGraw-Hill, 1987).

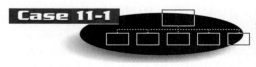

Case 11-1

Too Much, Too Often

Managing a trade association, thought Anthony Califano, was great work. Sure, there were times when he became frustrated but, overall, the good aspects of the job outweighed the bad. Tony was the executive secretary of a League of Credit Unions in the Southwest. He and his staff of 12 were responsible for administering to the needs of 135 credit unions. They provided advice on problem solving to members requesting help. They carried on lobbying activities for passage of favored legislation by the state legislature and testified against bills unfavorable to the League members. In addition, the League staff carried on a series of informational and training programs, including arranging the annual meetings of League members.

Tony was an "easy" boss. A deeply moral man, he almost invariably identified the good in people and overlooked their shortcomings. Gossip was not in his vocabulary. It was reported several years ago that Tony had expressed a "dog-gone-it" when agitated. That was the known extent of his temper, at least as recorded in the annals of the League offices.

Tony Califano constantly praised the work of his staff, both to them personally and to others. If a secretary typed a letter for him, it was "beautifully done." A report submitted by a subordinate would never receive less than a "great work." The custodian always produced an "immaculate" job with floors so clean "we could eat off them." People always "looked great." Tomorrow would be a "fantastic" day.

The annual meeting involved more of the same. Without exception, he spent the first ten minutes of his address to members of the League in listing the virtues of his staff. The tributes were profuse. He covered every member of his staff with praise. His assistants could recite from memory the glowing comments. Occasionally they were embarrassed with the extensiveness of his public pronouncements of their organizational value. "No one can be that good," one member of his staff whispered to another after listening to Tony lay it on. Still, Tony was sincere in his belief of having an outstanding group of employees. Over time, though, the frequency and extensiveness of his recognition of their work lost much of its motivational value. It was just too much, too often.

Questions

1. What is your opinion about employee recognition? Can it be overdone? What is the "correct" amount of recognition? How do you know the right amount?
2. Would you consider the average employee suffers from the problem of too much recognition or praise? Explain.
3. Give counsel to Tony about other strategies for motivating. How should he implement such changes without creating morale problems?

Case 11-2

Vang Toua

In the final days of the American presence in Vietnam and for several years thereafter, hundreds of thousands of Asians from Vietnam and surrounding countries fled their homes, many immigrating to the United States. Some of the people seeking refuge in the United States had supported the U.S. involvement during the war and faced harsh terms if they remained in their native homelands. Among the refugees were mountain tribespeople of Laos, the Laotian Hmongs. Vang Toua was a Hmong.

Vang fought against the communist forces in Laos. Although recovering from a serious wound, he lost a leg. Several of his relatives, including a brother and uncle, were killed in the fighting. Vang, his wife, and two children came to the United States in the 1970s. Initially, they settled in Western Montana, partially because of the presence of General Chu Xiong who formerly led the Hmongs in Laos and because the mountains reminded them of home, at least in the opinion of U.S. government relocation experts. At one time, almost 600 Hmongs lived in Missoula, Montana, and adjoining valleys. In the years following their arrival, they began moving to other cities. So it was with Vang when he and his family relocated in Minneapolis.

After a year's search for work, Vang found employment with an electronics manufacturing company. His new boss was Shirley Gordon. Of the several applicants Shirley interviewed, Vang was her first choice. She was somewhat concerned, though, about the reactions of other members of the group he would be working in. She had overheard comments expressing resentment about "foreigners" who obtained jobs that would otherwise go to "Americans." Three of her workers had husbands or wives who had lost their jobs during the recession of the early 1990s. Unemployment was a painful subject for them. While discrimination was not unknown to newcomers to the United States, as well as to citizens who were born here, it still was unpleasant to encounter it. In tough economic times, the problem often became worse.

Shirley contemplated the integration of Vang into her group. He would begin working in a few days. In the meantime, she reflected on what she could do to assist his assimilation into the group. She supervised 15 women who soldered electronic components on "boards" that became modules for the firm's electronic products. Critical skills or abilities used in building the modules were manual dexterity and patience, since the work was highly repetitive. Vang appeared to have both. Still, she wondered how he would fit into her work group and what she should do to motivate her employees to accept him.

Questions

1. If you were Shirley, how would you ease the integration of Vang as a new group member?
2. Would your answer differ if the group was primarily male or predominantly female? If it had members of various ethnic minorities?
3. Although this chapter stresses motivation directed toward increasing production by workers and quality of their work, how can you apply motivation theory toward gaining employee acceptance of a new member?
4. What evidence would you look for to determine if Vang was being accepted by the others?

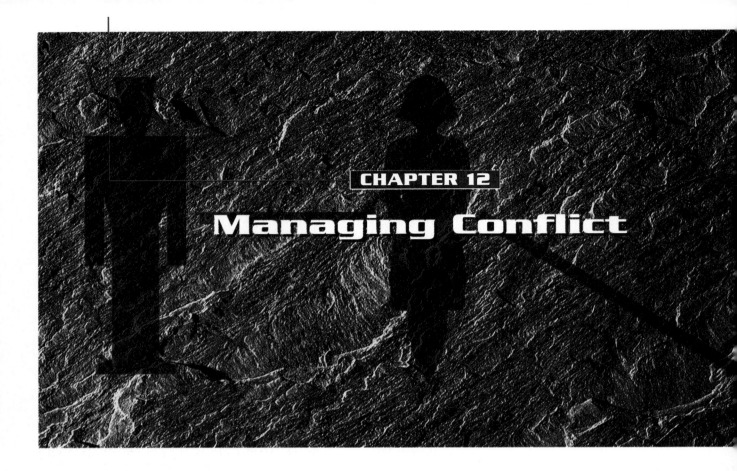

CHAPTER 12

Managing Conflict

● Rule No. 1 is, don't sweat the small stuff, Rule No. 2 is, it's all small stuff. And if you can't flee, flow.[1]

"Carla, I can't keep covering for George! He's a deadbeat. The guy's never there for me or the company!"

Carla sighed. One of the employees in her group constantly called in sick. He even took days off without pay. His ailments were all rather vague. Too bad, too. George had been a highly productive worker.

"Al, I'm sorry about George. But he's entitled to sick leave and company policy says he can take days off without pay."

"What's his problem!?"

"Well, he's entitled to privacy regarding his problem."

"But what about *my* right to do just *my* job!"

"Well, I'll talk to George. We'll get to the bottom of what's happening to him. For now, though, please calm down. Blowing your stack isn't making things easier or better."

"I'm not going to calm down! I want this situation fixed. Now!"

"Okay, okay. I'll see what I can do."

With a terse "Thank you," Al walked out the door.

Carla sighed again.

Conflict, a lack of fit in the goal-directed behavior of interdependent parties, is common in organizations because it occurs whenever and wherever people gather. The ability to effectively manage conflict is an essential supervisory skill.

conflict
Situations when one party actually or potentially disrupts the goal-directed behavior of another party.

Up to 20 percent of a manager's time is spent actively managing conflict.[2] **Conflict** occurs when one party actually or potentially disrupts the goal-directed behavior of another party. Notice the use of the term *party*. Conflict occurs between or among groups as well as between individual people.

Conflict can occur even if differences aren't real. Invalid perceptions can be as important as reality. If you think someone is angry with you, it may affect your behavior regardless of the other person's true feelings. Conflict often occurs because of mistaken impressions or misinterpretations of what are otherwise benign actions or communications on the part of another.

Conflict Management versus Conflict Resolution

Attempts to resolve *all* conflict in an interdependent relationship can actually be counterproductive. For example, a conflict resolution strategy that calls for warring parties to "shake hands and stop fighting" might be a quick fix that does not provide for an understanding of issues necessary to long-term management of an interdependent relationship.

Although some conflict can be effectively resolved, supervisors should try to maintain a balance between too much conflict, which is inherently destructive, and too little, which is counterproductive. The idea is to manage conflict rather than always try to resolve it.[3] This conflict management view is contrasted with the traditional conflict resolution perspective in Figure 12-2 on page 246.[4]

Positive Effects of Conflict

Most of us have been socialized to believe that conflict is bad (See Figure 12-1). Yet, there are several reasons why well-managed conflict is beneficial. An important benefit of conflict is it signals a need for supervisory attention and possible intervention. Conflict brings concerns into the open. Divergent views offered during decision making sharpen participants' understanding of problem complexities and can lead to better outcomes, as suggested by the old adage, "Two heads are better than one."

Figure 12-1 It Was a Dark and Stormy Night

Source: Peanuts, 11/19/81. Reprinted by permission of UFS, Inc.

Trainer Patricia Link has had success helping supervisors to manage conflict by recommending they use a checklist to help warring parties to work out differences. Employees are asked to answer the following set of questions to be used during a mediation session with a supervisor or other mediator.

1. What is it you want or need?
2. Why do you feel frustrated in this situation?
3. What do you think the other person wants or needs?
4. Why do you think he/she feels frustrated in this situation?
5. Do you and the other party differ over facts? Goals? Methods? Roles?
6. What are the major outcomes of this conflict to date?
7. What could you lose if the conflict continues or escalates?
8. What aspects of this issue are you unwilling to negotiate?
9. What might you trade off (compromise) to achieve your primary goal?
10. Who could best help you get what you want or need?
11. What common hopes do you and the other person have in regard to this matter?
12. If you decide to collaborate to help resolve this conflict, what are the first steps you might take?[5]

Conflict generally challenges individuals, heightens attention, increases the likelihood of innovation, provides for more careful consideration of new ideas, and encourages parties to monitor behavior more closely than they would under normal circumstances.[6] Well-managed conflict sharpens focus and is stimulating and motivating.

The motivating aspects of conflict are pervasive and familiar. You have probably argued with a family member or friend over a historical or factual point and felt a strong desire to go to an encyclopedia or other reference to look up the correct answer to prove your point. You may have spent half a night solving a problem just to prove you could do it after being challenged by an instructor. In the work setting, well-managed conflict can provide the same kind of motivation and desire to prove oneself and to achieve.

Conflict Management Strategies

There are several ways to manage conflict, some more effective than others. The essence of effective conflict management "is not the masterful utilization of any particular technique. Rather effectiveness results from using whatever approach is most appropriate for a given set of circumstances."[7]

Figure 12-3, on page 247, shows a variety of **conflict management strategies** classified on the basis of assertiveness (behaviors intended to satisfy one's own concerns) and cooperativeness (behaviors intended to satisfy the concerns of others).[8] It arrays the conflict management approaches of avoidance, competitiveness, compromise, collaboration, and accommodation along these dimensions of assertiveness and cooperativeness.

What Is the Best Approach? Which approach best manages conflict? **Collaboration** is usually the best approach because it is high on both assertiveness and cooperativeness: all parties have their interests represented by a collaborative solution. The problem with this simplistic view, however, is that collaboration is effective primarily when interdependent parties are willing to ignore power issues, have open-minded attitudes, and are mutually aware of the

conflict management strategies
Approaches to managing conflict situations based on assertiveness (behaviors intended to satisfy one's own concerns) and cooperativeness (behaviors intended to satisfy the concerns of others).

collaboration
A form of conflict management in which all parties work together to find a solution.

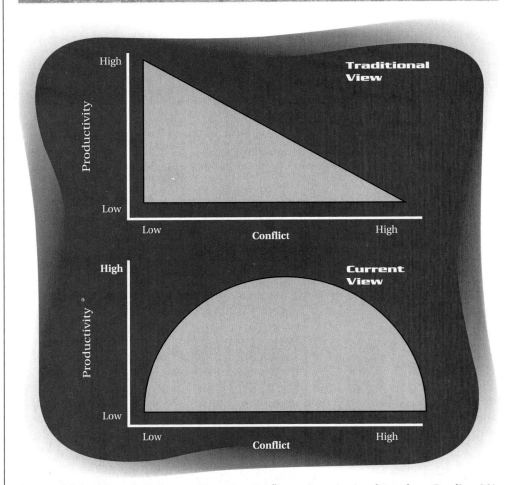

Figure 12-2 Traditional and Current Views of Conflict

Source: Adapted from L. D. Brown, *Managing Conflict at Organizational Interfaces* (Reading, MA: Addison-Wesley, 1983); and J. L. Gray and F. A. Starke, *Organizational Behavior,* 4th ed. (Columbus, OH: Merrill Publishing Company, 1988).

potential for conflict between or among parties.[9] Supervisors are often confronted by conflict situations in which only some or none of these elements exist. Under these circumstances, other conflict management approaches must be used.

Accommodation and **avoidance** are effective in handling temporary situations. In accommodation, one party is willing to indulge the behavior of another in handling temporary or unimportant situations. You may choose to accommodate the rudeness of a temporary employee or a rude waiter at a restaurant because spending time and energy on a fleeting problem is not worth the trouble. A supervisor may choose to accommodate a union steward on a relatively small point because it is not worth contesting.

Avoidance is a good way to temporarily handle the anger of another person or group. Heated exchanges tend to obscure substantive issues. Allowing people to cool off by temporarily avoiding confrontation usually improves the quality of a

accommodation
A form of conflict management in which one party is willing to indulge the behavior of another.

avoidance
A form of conflict management in which one party evades or circumvents another.

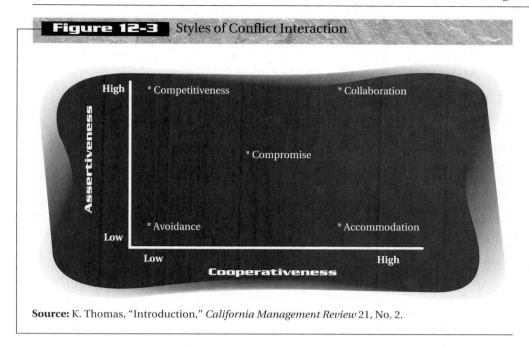

Figure 12-3 Styles of Conflict Interaction

Source: K. Thomas, "Introduction," *California Management Review* 21, No. 2.

future exchange. Wise supervisors know when to push an issue and when to back off and let some time pass.

Avoidance is an excellent long-term conflict management strategy only if the relationship between the parties is, or can become, independent. There is no point in experiencing potentially destructive or counterproductive conflict if you can completely separate yourself from another party. Unfortunately, the option of bailing out does not always exist. It may be necessary to maintain interdependence for a variety of reasons—for example, when supervising an employee protected by a strong labor contract; or because of financial ties in a business partnership; the need to maintain relations with a key supplier or customer; or obligations inherent in international politics and business.

Competition, or a win-lose strategy, should be used when a supervisor faces an important issue, the other party is uncooperative and will not budge, and the supervisor needs to win.[10] **Compromise** has merit as a conflict management strategy in that it can be the "lesser of two (or several) conflict management evils." Compromise requires each party to make concessions to arrive at a solution. In a given situation, compromise may be more constructive than ignoring, accommodating, or trying to defeat an opponent.

In summary, no conflict management approach is 100 percent effective under all circumstances. Ideally, a supervisor will be in a position in which conflicting employees have relatively similar values and where differences are not grounded in personal beliefs, values, or in the expectation that survival of any party is at stake. Ideally, there will be sufficient trust and commitment to work group goals among members of a work group to encourage collaborative solutions.

competition
A form of conflict management in which one party wins and the other loses.

compromise
A form of conflict management in which each party is willing to make concessions to arrive at a solution.

More on Collaboration

Collaboration leads to win-win outcomes that satisfy the needs of all those in conflict. Collaboration also helps to maintain a mutually satisfying relationship which, in turn, facilitates the future management of conflict. Collaboration does require confrontation. It is not necessarily an orderly or rational approach. In the end, though, effective collaboration results in meeting the needs of all parties in conflict.

There's a classic story that describes two people fighting unnecessarily over an orange. Had these people explored mutual needs they would have determined that one wanted the orange peel for baking; the other wanted the fruit to eat. A power struggle could have been avoided and a win-win solution found. Don't assume that different needs or goals mean that mutual gain is impossible.

From a practical perspective, a supervisor should always try collaborating with employees. It may take a lot of work, but supervisors need to be concerned not just with managing conflict today, but also with reducing the likelihood of destructive conflict in the future. View collaboration as the starting point in most conflict situations. Fall back to other conflict management strategies only if you must.

Negotiation: The Basis of Collaboration

This section focuses on how to successfully collaborate with another party. We will first consider how to lay the groundwork for successful collaboration. It's important that attitudes be positive on the part of all involved—including the supervisor—before trying a collaborative conflict management strategy. People have to want to work together to find a mutually beneficial solution. (See Figure 12-4.)

Creating a Collaborative Environment

The first prerequisite to creating a favorable environment for collaboration is for supervisors to do a good job of managing all aspects of the supervisory challenge.

All parties eventually lose when conflict is poorly managed.

Figure 12-4 How Not to Resolve Conflicts

"Well, Craigmeyer, I see we wasted our money sending you to that workshop on turning confrontations into constructive stepping stones for resolving conflict."

Source: Reprinted by permission of Tribune Media Services.

Chapters in this text that cover communication, motivation, decision making, performance appraisal, counseling, and progressive discipline describe supervisory practices that will also help supervisors to manage conflict. As noted earlier in this chapter, the existence of conflict signals a need for supervisory attention. Good management can head off a lot of conflict.

Another way to lay the groundwork for effective collaboration is to do attitudinal restructuring. **Attitudinal restructuring** builds bonds between individuals or groups by favorably influencing the attitudes of participants toward one another.[11] For example, one party might unilaterally concede a point to give the other party evidence of good will. A supervisor might let an employee stay out on break for an extra 15 minutes simply as a sign of trust in the employee, or may give him or her a day off with pay to attend to a family emergency.

Employees, particularly in unionized environments, may regard the boss as an enemy. Attitudinal restructuring is intended to change this perspective so that employees regard the supervisor in a favorable, trusting light before, during, and after any conflict management that happens to take place.

attitudinal restructuring
The attempt to favorably influence the attitudes of participants toward one another by such actions as unilaterally conceding a point to give the other party evidence of good will.

Principled Negotiation

Assuming that employees are receptive to collaboration, supervisors can benefit through the use of **principled negotiation.** Fisher and Ury, the authors of this approach, describe it this way:

principled negotiation
Deciding issues on their merits rather than through a haggling process.

The method of principled negotiation developed at the Harvard Negotiation Project is to decide issues on their merits rather than through a haggling process focused on what each side says it will and won't do. It suggests that you look for mutual gains wherever possible, and that where your interests conflict, you should insist that the result be based on some fair standards independent of the will of either side. The method of principled negotiation . . . employs no tricks and no posturing. Principled negotiation shows you how to obtain what you are entitled to and still be decent. . . .[12]

Principled negotiation has the following basic tenets:

- Separate the people from the problem.
- Focus on interests, not positions.
- Invent options for mutual gain.
- Use objective criteria.

Separate the People from the Problem. People sometimes allow personalities and personal issues to get tangled up with substantive issues under consideration. In the workplace, rather than attack problems, supervisors and employees sometimes attack each other. This tactic not only compromises finding win-win solutions, but interferes with the maintenance of a healthy long-term relationship. As mentioned previously, maintaining a good working relationship after conflict has been managed facilitates the future management of conflict.

Try to reframe personal attacks against you during a confrontation as an attack upon the problem. For example, suppose an employee accuses a supervisor of being insensitive because she will not let him have next Friday off. Rather than go on the attack, the supervisor might respond by saying, "Throckmorton, despite your contention that I'm insensitive, the fact remains that we're short-staffed. We need you here this Friday."

The problem in this situation is not the supervisor's insensitivity—it's the fact there is a lack of staff. In any event, try to be, in Fisher and Ury's words, "hard on the problem, but soft on people."

Focus on Interests, Not Positions. Collaboration stalls when people focus on positions (figuratively, when negotiators draw lines in the sand by taking an unwavering stand on an issue) rather than on interests.

Consider a potential conflict between a supervisor and work group concerning vacation leave. Employees want to plan vacation breaks around when their children will be out of school; the supervisor wants to make sure she's not short-staffed. The supervisor could announce her concern and, in the interest of fairness, put together a schedule that randomly assigns vacation days among employees. The supervisor's intractable position is sure to negatively impact some employees.

If the supervisor had instead announced her concern and then worked with employees to find a mutually beneficial solution, a lot of negative conflict could have been avoided. Perhaps, childless employees would have coordinated vacation schedules so the supervisor's needs for adequate staff coverage and parent needs to vacation with kids could both have been met.

Supervisors should try to avoid taking an intractable position in managing conflict. If conflict exists with an employee who has taken a seemingly intractable position, look behind his or her position to try to determine underlying interests. Then respond to those interests in framing replies.

Invent Options for Mutual Gain. After identifying interests, it's necessary to create options that provide mutual gain.

Inventing options for mutual gain is not easy, as the story of vacation leave for employees suggests. People fear criticism of their ideas, exposure, being taken advantage of, and looking foolish. Sometimes, conflict cannot be managed so that all parties are winners. However, at the very least, a supervisor's sincere attempt to reconcile interests by working with employees to invent options for mutual gain will improve the likelihood of effective conflict management in the future.

Brainstorming is one strategy a negotiator can use to create options for mutual gain (see Chapters 1 and 10 for more discussion of this technique). Brainstorming allows participants to freely propose alternatives for solving a problem. The key to effective brainstorming is separating the act of inventing options from critical evaluation of those options. Brainstormers must be able to suggest any option— regardless of how crazy it might seem.

Look for dovetailing interests once all possible options have been placed on the table. Different needs do not in themselves mean that mutual gain is impossible, particularly if you find that your adversary only wants the "orange peel," and all you really want is the "fruit."

Supervisors can use brainstorming to find a mutually beneficial option either with an entire work group or one-on-one with an employee. For example, "Fred, I understand your needs. Why don't you and I take a few moments to brainstorm some solutions?"

Use Objective Criteria. How would you determine the right price for a house you were planning to buy? Would you accept the realtor's word that a particular house is a good deal? Probably not. You would look at several houses and compare price versus amenities. You would also look for hidden costs such as costs associated with repairing a leaky roof, exterminating termites, or paying off liens against the property. You would hunt for a low-interest loan. In short, you would not be satisfied you had a good deal until you had assessed a prospective purchase against a set of objective criteria.

Supervisors should evaluate differences against a set of objective criteria that seem fair and reasonable to all parties. Use of objective criteria allows the supervisor to bring external data to bear upon solving problems; problems and solutions can be better understood by all parties. The use of objective criteria gives a position more legitimacy. It's far more constructive for a supervisor to show production data that supports a particular work schedule than it is for the supervisor to announce a schedule that simply "looks good." A further advantage of focusing on objective criteria is that the data often lead to a solution much like a key unlocking a door.

When Principled Negotiation Does Not Work

Unfortunately, there are times when win-win negotiation is difficult or impossible. Sometimes a party simply doesn't want to cooperate.

Fisher and Ury recommend that negotiators use **negotiation jujitsu** when dealing with a difficult opponent. That is, when your opponent pushes you, don't push back. Instead, ask questions. Seek clarification. Reframe an attack upon you as an attack upon the problem. If absolutely necessary make use of a **BATNA (best alternative to a negotiated agreement).** It is a warning of the action you will take if the other party refuses to negotiate. The more potent your BATNA, the

An effective supervisor uses negotiation jujitsu when confronting a difficult employee. When the opponent pushes, the supervisor doesn't push back.

negotiation jujitsu
Applied in dealing with a difficult opponent by responding to a challenge through questions and requests for clarification rather than hostility.

BATNA (best alternative to a negotiated agreement)
The most powerful and influential alternative one party has in negotiating with another to arrive at an agreement or solution to a problem.

better your bargaining leverage when dealing with a recalcitrant opponent. Examples of BATNAs include going on strike, quitting your job, and, quite literally, going to war. Supervisors can threaten to fire an employee as a BATNA.

What to Do When Someone Is Yelling

To this point, conflict management, including negotiation, has been presented as a controlled, rational process. Unfortunately, supervisors are sometimes in situations in which they face an angry customer or employee. It is difficult to avoid the situation to allow people to cool off; the conflict must be handled immediately. And, the conflict appears to be out of control, even dangerous.

The most important initial factor to consider is your safety and the safety of those around you. A supervisor should immediately contact security or the police if he or she feels a situation is potentially dangerous. This contact should be made before walking out to confront the angry party. If a supervisor must give bad news to a potentially explosive employee at an appointed time, the supervisor should consider asking security to be in the area at that time, out of sight but ready to move in if necessary.

Many of the communication skills discussed in Chapter 13 help to calm down a yelling employee or customer. Try to move the angry person to a private setting, such as your office. Don't begin by offering opinions or indicating that you cannot help. Instead, paraphrase what you hear the other person saying (paraphrasing is discussed in Chapter 13). Make sure you understand the source of their anger. Ask lots of questions—it is more difficult to remain angry while answering questions. You will find if you have been using a quiet voice, the yeller will naturally lower his or her voice as well. But if he or she hasn't stopped screaming, ask the person to please lower his or her voice. Keep the angry person talking while you listen.

Using this method, you may eventually gain a good understanding of the problem. Restate the problem and get the employee or customer's confirmation. Once you understand why the person is angry, either go into problem solving, or refer the person to another party or department if his or her problem is outside of your domain. A good starting point is to ask the other person, "What do you think should be done about this problem?"[13]

If you do not or cannot gain a good understanding of the issues because of a lack of information, schedule an appointment for later when the information will be available or, if you can't help, refer the individual to another office or individual where help might be available. Also, indicate if help is *not* available elsewhere. Upset people particularly hate to get the "run-around."

Occasionally, supervisors must deal with difficult people who will not back off an issue or a point. A useful communication technique to apply under these circumstances is **broken record.** This technique involves sticking to a position or response regardless of another person's attempts to move you off the subject. For example, a supervisor will continue to tell Alice she cannot have next Thursday off, regardless of Alice's attempts to attack the supervisor's position from different directions: "But this is the first time all year there has been enough snow for skiing! . . . I came in early last week to help you with the inventory! . . . I'll trade vacation leave with Ralph!" The supervisor uses broken record by replying, "Yes, Alice, I hear your concern about skiing (or coming in early, or trading vacation leave), and I am sorry, but you must come to work this Thursday."

Broken record is a win-lose strategy that should be employed when the supervisor doesn't wish to collaborate or negotiate, and wants to end a confrontation.

broken record
A communication technique in conflict resolution characterized by adhering to a position or response regardless of another person's attempt to change the subject.

Conflict within the Work Team

It is possible for a supervisor to have a good, collaborative relationship with individuals in his or her work team, yet have conflict-related problems whenever the group gets together.

Norms and Roles

Conflict occurs when the behavior of an individual differs from the behavioral standards, or norms, of the group. **Norms** are standards of behavior expected for an individual within a group.[14] For example, a new employee might work late, volunteer for every committee possible, and skip scheduled breaks to do more work. This employee may be puzzled by the conflict his hard work has created with less energetic fellow employees. After all, he is doing a good job! His relationship with the supervisor is great. He is exceeding all performance standards. Nevertheless, the conflict between this person and other group members is just as real as conflict that occurs for any other reason. He has violated a group norm limiting work effort.

norms
Standards of behavior expected for an individual within a group.

As you might expect, work teams have different norms. The above example could be reversed; an unambitious employee could end up in a group with high production norms. Supervisors should try to understand the norms of the work team they are leading, and encourage establishment of norms that promote high productivity. We say "encourage" because norms are established by the group, not imposed by the supervisor. New employees should be helped to learn norms by including work group members in new employee orientation (discussed in Chapter 9).

Standards of behavior expected for individuals within a given position are called **roles.** For example, by virtue of their position, mail sorters working in a mail room are expected to behave differently from members of top management. Role expectations of a supervisor and chief executive officer are usually different.

roles
Standards of behavior expected for individuals within a given position.

Role conflict occurs when expectations from different roles are incompatible. For example, a single parent employed in a full-time job experiences role conflict to the extent there is conflict between the roles of "parent" and "employee." To whom (family or work) does this person give his or her time and loyalty? Another example of role conflict occurs when you attempt to be both a friend and a boss. This example is particularly difficult for supervisors who come up the ranks and find themselves managing friends.

role conflict
Occurs when expectations from different roles are incompatible.

Though some conflict should be expected in any role, supervisors can reduce role conflict by clearly defining jobs and outlining expectations for employees, including those who are friends. Such clarification helps people to reconcile conflicting roles because roles, and accompanying expectations, can be better understood.

Group Cohesiveness

Group cohesiveness is the atmosphere of closeness that results in a group from common beliefs, attitudes, and goal directedness.[15] In other words, cohesiveness is the glue that bonds members of a group. High cohesiveness within a work team is generally positive because member satisfaction is high. Figure 12-5 presents several cohesiveness factors present in determining whether a group ranks high or low in cohesiveness.

group cohesiveness
The atmosphere of closeness that results in a group from common beliefs, attitudes, and goal directedness.

Figure 12-5 Determinants of Group Cohesiveness

Cohesiveness Factor	High Cohesiveness	Low Cohesiveness
Homogeneity	Homogeneous	Heterogeneous
Group size	Few members	Many members
Opportunities to communicate within group	Frequent opportunity to communicate	Very limited opportunities to communicate
Group isolation	Isolated from other groups	Frequent contact with members of other groups
External threat	Major threat perceived by members	No external threat perceived by members
Group success	Highly successful in achieving goals	Unsuccessful in achieving goals
Individual mobility	Low turnover of members	High turnover of members
Membership in other groups	Members have few other group affiliations	Members have many affiliations in other groups
Availability of effective leadership	Strong informal leadership present	Weak or nonexistent informal leadership

Source: Adapted from J. Clifton Williams, *Human Behavior in Organizations*, 2d ed. (Cincinnati, OH: South-Western Publishing Company, 1982), 138–141.

Other factors that increase group cohesiveness include agreement on group goals, frequency of interaction, personal attractiveness of group members to each other, intergroup competition (battling a common enemy makes a group more cohesive), and favorable evaluation of the group by an outside party.[16]

Factors that decrease cohesiveness include disagreement over goals, anything that decreases interaction of group members (for example, physical location of members), fighting within the group, and domination of the group by one member or a clique.[17] A supervisor can use this understanding of factors that increase or decrease group cohesiveness to improve cohesiveness or head off potentially unproductive group conflict.

A poorly performing team can be turned around if group cohesiveness and performance standards improve.[18] Note that high cohesiveness by itself does not mean a team will be more productive or will make better decisions. (See Chapter 10 on "groupthink" decisions.) For example, the output of a highly cohesive group engaged in sabotage will counter organizational objectives, as will a highly cohesive group whose goal is to relax and to do as little work as possible.

superordinate goals
Higher-order goals that transcend differences between groups and compel them to work together to solve common problems.

Superordinate Goals

Establishing superordinate goals, besides enhancing group cohesiveness, also improves relations between groups. **Superordinate goals** are higher-order goals that transcend differences between groups and compel them to work together to solve a common problem. (See Figure 12-6.)

Figure 12-6   Superordinate Goals: The Common Enemy

Source: FOR BETTER OR WORSE, 1988. © Copyright Lynn Johnston Prod., Inc. Reprinted with permission of Universal Press Syndicate.

Solidarity is increased within a work team when attention is focused upon overcoming an external problem, such as a common enemy. In a classic study of superordinate goals, the Robber's Cave experiment, Sherif and associates found that after the seeds of intergroup conflict were sown, once a common enemy was recognized, competing groups invariably pulled together.[19]

Sherif's experiment manipulated two gangs of 11- and 12-year-old boys—the "rattlers" and the "eagles." Initially, the researchers promoted conflict between the groups by awarding prizes each time a group won a contest (a treasure hunt, tug-of-war, and so forth). Fighting and name calling between opposing group members became common. Later, the researchers introduced situations in which cooperation was necessary to attain a goal important to both groups. For example, both groups were told the camp could not afford to rent a movie for both eagles and rattlers. Unless the two groups could agree on a film there would be no entertainment. By the end of the experiment, the introduction of superordinate goals led to a cooperative climate between the groups.

Sherif's experiment suggests that supervisors can reduce conflict within and between groups by establishing superordinate goals—by getting people to work together for the common good, rather than squabble. The process of identifying the "common good" can be incorporated into goal setting. It is important that employees understand *why* goals are significant to their work team. Developing superordinate goals not only serves to promote harmony in the present, but can also result in better future working relationships within a work team.

"George, how are you today?" Carla looked across at the gaunt, feverish-looking young man sitting in her office.

"I'm doing okay, Carla. As well as can be expected."

"Are you sure? I mean you haven't been making it to work regularly. I'm getting complaints." No response from George. Carla continued, "I mean if there's anything I can do to help . . ."

"There really isn't, Carla. I'm . . . I'm suffering from a terminal illness. I didn't really want to bother you with my problems."

Suddenly, the door pushed open. Al stood at the doorway glaring down at George. "Sorry to interrupt, Carla, but I knew you and George were talking and I have some things to say!"

Carla quietly replied, "Al, please lower your voice."

Pause. Al shuffled nervously. "Ah . . . sorry. But I'm really annoyed!"

"Look, Al, let me talk to George. I'll get back to you later."

"Shouldn't I be part of this conversation?"

"Al, you're certainly part of the team, and will have the opportunity to comment later. But you're not part of this particular conversation. I will get back to you. I promise."

Al nodded, "Well, okay. Sorry to barge in." He stepped out, shutting the door behind him.

Carla returned to her conversation with George.

Over the course of the next hour Carla learned that conflict has many different faces, ranging from the overt, dramatic conflict she had correctly handled with Al, to the quiet, agonizing conflict she subsequently experienced with George.

George was dying from AIDS. The conflict between his physical incapacities and the company's needs would never be resolved. Carla and George could only work together to manage the conflict, keeping George's dignity and need for privacy intact, until the day, soon thereafter, when George eventually left work.

Summary: Focus on Skills

Conflict is defined as a lack of fit in the goal-directed behavior of interdependent parties. Following are 18 suggestions to help supervisors improve the quality of their conflict management:

1. Recognize that conflict is a natural part of day-to-day interactions among people.
2. Realize that conflict can be beneficial. Conflict signals the need for attention to a problem. Conflict also leads to sharpened attention and can contribute to higher levels of follower motivation.
3. Manage conflict, as opposed to always trying to resolve it.
4. Practice collaboration as a conflict management strategy whenever possible. Collaboration is high on assertiveness and cooperativeness. It leads to win-win solutions.
5. Avoid conflict only as a short-term tactic preceding an attempt to use a collaborative strategy.
6. Accommodate conflict when politically or practically expedient.
7. Use a competitive strategy only when necessary. Win-lose propositions are not conducive to maintenance of long-term relationships.
8. Although compromise is never ideal, it can, however, be employed when collaboration is not possible and can be more effective than avoidance, accommodation, or competitive strategies.
9. Lay the groundwork for effective collaboration by being an effective manager.
10. Use attitudinal restructuring with employees in order to facilitate good relations and to build trust.
11. Follow the basic tenets of principled negotiation when collaborating: separate people from the problem; focus upon interests, not positions; invent options for mutual gain; and use objective criteria.
12. When dealing with a difficult opponent, employ "negotiation jujitsu" and have a BATNA (best alternative to a negotiated agreement) ready if negotiations break down. If your opponent pushes you, don't push back. Ask questions. Seek clarifica-

tion. Look behind your opponent's position for underlying interests. If negotiations fail, employ your BATNA.

13. If facing an extremely angry adversary, keep safety in mind; respond in an even, quiet voice; use good communication techniques. Try to move the confrontation to a private office. Do not begin your communication by saying you cannot help. Ask a lot of questions. Try to help the person if possible, either at that time or later when more information is available, or refer the person to someone who can help.

14. Practice broken record with difficult individuals you must firmly confront with an unyielding position.

15. Try to understand the norms (standards of behavior expected of an individual working within a group) of the team being led. Encourage establishment of norms that promote high productivity.

16. Help reduce role conflict by clearly defining jobs and outlining expectations for subordinates.

17. Know that a poorly performing team can be turned around if both group cohesiveness and performance standards are improved.

18. Establish superordinate goals in order to build cohesiveness within your own team, to effectively manage conflict between groups, and to promote harmony with competing groups in the future.

Review Questions

1. Define the term *conflict*.
2. Should conflict always be considered as something negative to be avoided, if possible? Explain.
3. Contrast the traditional versus current views regarding conflict and its management.
4. If you were to develop a checklist to help conflicting parties work out their differences, what questions would you ask?
5. If there are any values to having conflict occur in organizations, what are they?
6. There are several approaches to conflict management including collaboration, accommodation, avoidance, and competition. Briefly explain the nature of each. Finally, which is the best approach? Why so?
7. What is attitudinal restructuring? What is principled negotiation?
8. You should separate people from the problem in resolving conflict. What does this mean?
9. Cite and explain several methods supervisors can apply in the negotiation process.
10. How do work team norms and roles create conflicts?
11. What is group cohesiveness? How can group cohesiveness reduce conflicts within a work team?
12. What are superordinate goals and how can they be used to reduce conflict?

Notes

1. University of Nebraska cardiologist Robert Eliot on how to cope with stress, as reported by C. Wallis, "Stress: Can We Cope?" *Time*, June 6, 1983, 48.
2. K. W. Thomas, "Conflict and Conflict Management," in *Handbook of Industrial and Organizational Psychology*, ed. M. D. Dunnette (Chicago: Rand McNally, 1976).
3. P. M. Buhler, "Power and Conflict in the Workplace," *Supervision* 49 (1988): 13–21.
4. A. C. Robbins, "Conflict Management and Conflict Resolution Are Not Synonymous Terms," *California Management Review* 21 (1978): 67–75. Also, L. D. Brown, *Managing Conflict at Organizational Interfaces* (Reading, MA: Addison-Wesley, 1983).

5. P. B. Link, "How to Cope with Conflict between the People Who Work for You," *Supervision* 51 (1990): 7–9.

6. R. A. Baron, *Behavior in Organizations* (Boston, MA: Allyn & Bacon, 1986).

7. B. D. Debois and C. D. Pringle, "Choosing a Conflict Management Technique," *Supervision* 50 (1989): 12.

8. T. L. Ruble and T. L. Thomas, "Support for a Two Dimensional Model of Conflict Behavior," *Organizational Behavior and Human Performance* 16 (1976): 143–155.

9. C. B. Derr, "Managing Organizational Conflict: Collaboration, Bargaining, and Power Approaches," *California Management Review* 21 (1978): 76–90.

10. Ibid.

11. R. E. Walton and R. B. McKersie, *Behavioral Theory of Labor Relations* (New York: McGraw-Hill, 1965).

12. R. Fisher and W. Ury, *Getting to Yes* (New York: Viking Penguin Inc., 1981).

13. C. Conley, "What to Do When Someone's Yelling," *Supervisory Management* 35 (1990): 6–7.

14. D. C. Feldman, "The Development and Enforcement of Group Norms," *Academy of Management Review* 9 (1984): 47–53.

15. C. A. O'Rielly and O. F. Caldwell, "The Impact of Normative Social Influence and Cohesiveness on Task Perceptions and Attitudes: A Social Information Processing Approach," *Journal of Occupational Psychology* 58 (1985): 193–206.

16. A. J. Lott and B. E. Lott, "Group Cohesiveness as Interpersonal Attraction: A Review of Relationships with Antecedent and Consequent Variables," *Psychological Bulletin*, October 1965, 259–309.

17. S. Seashore, *Group Cohesiveness in the Industrial Work Group* (Ann Arbor, MI: University of Michigan Institute for Social Research, 1954).

18. S. Schachter, N. Ellertson, D. McBride, and D. Gregory, "An Experimental Study of Cohesiveness and Productivity," *Human Relations* 3 (1954): 229–238.

19. M. Sherif and C. W. Sherif, "The Robber's Cave Study," *An Outline of Social Psychology* (New York: Harper & Row, 1956).

Case 12-1

Debits and Credits

As sensible adults we would expect a rather high intelligence level and mature behavior in a public accounting firm—large or small. That expectation would be particularly applicable to one of the largest public accounting firms in the country. Exceptions do occur, though, as the following story testifies.

Swearingen, Swearingen, and Steinberg (SSS), headquartered in St. Louis, was founded in the early 1900s by Amos Swearingen. Three generations later, not only were the Swearingens still represented in the firm, but the firm itself had steadily grown. Today, it ranked among the 20 largest public accounting firms in the United States. SSS employed over 400 accountants along with another 200 supporting staff personnel. It operated from branch offices in fifteen cities located throughout the midcontinent states.

The St. Louis office was the largest. Some 175 accountants and 60 support employees worked there, plus half of the firm's 30 partners.

A common practice in public accounting is for the most successful accountants to be offered partnerships within 10 years or so after entering their firms, that is, being hired. Success is measured not only in competent work and good production rates, but also the ability to attract new business to the firm or expand existing client billings. The practice at SSS was similar to other major public accounting firms. If an accountant had not made partner by the end of 10 years, he or she could anticipate a rather limited future career—Christmas bonuses excepted. All of the accountants at SSS were CPAs, with the exception of those who had passed their examinations but had not yet accumulated the necessary practical experience to be certified.

This brings us to the first of our two principal characters, Margaret Hurley. Hurley supervised one of the three headquarters T/DP (typing/data processing) sections. She was finishing her tenth year with the firm. Highly competent, she came close to being labeled a perfectionist. In addition, once she formed an opinion about something or somebody, it rarely changed. Although Hurley could hold a grudge, she could conceal it through her competency. In other words, she could make situations appear reasonable or correct and in her favor even when the facts disputed her position. Four typists, four terminal operators, a stenographer, and a reproductions clerk comprised Hurley's group. All of them, including Hurley, were called "staff support" personnel.

Some antagonism existed between staff support personnel and the accountants, who were known as the "professional staff." One wit suggested if there is a professional staff, then the other should be known as the "unprofessional staff." Status was part of the problem. In the pecking order at SSS, support personnel were a couple of pecks below the accountants. Then, some of the accountants lacked tact. Their submissions of materials for typing or processing were presented more as commands than requests. Finally, the business cycle of the firm reflected the importance of tax work. Soon after the first of each year and continuing until April 15, overtime hours were the norm, creating pressure, stress, and conflict.

The second party to our story is G. William Dobbs, IV. Dobbs had been with the firm for eight years. He supervised six accountants. He had not yet attained partnership status although he believed that he was nearing the threshold of entering the select group. Dobbs was recognized throughout the headquarters as one of its brightest members—perhaps, *the* brightest. And he was a brilliant and creative accountant. His capacity for work was legendary. In fact, his work was almost unequaled in the firm. However, Dobbs suffered a major flaw. His abrasive personality frequently offended those with whom he worked. Out of his range of hearing, others often called him "Little Napoleon." Fortunately, he had not antagonized any major clients of the firm. As a taskmaster, he drove his junior accountants with exhortations for high production levels with zero defects. Still, his abrasiveness was holding him back.

Recently, Hurley's group was assigned the work of Dobbs and his staff. He had outlived his welcome from a supervisor of another T/DP section who emphatically stated "either Dobbs goes or I will!" To maintain organizational peace, the senior partner of the firm who supervised Dobbs arranged transfer of Dobbs's secretarial and processing work to Hurley's unit. During the next two months, working relationships between Hurley and Dobbs were professional and largely cordial. Perhaps the high standards they set for their employees became a common, if temporary, bond. The honeymoon ended shortly thereafter.

What precipitated the deterioration was a minor event in retrospect. Dobbs requested priority treatment for a particular account. Hurley replied "no" because the work was handled on a FIFO (first in, first out) basis. All of her employees were busy at the time. Dobbs then appealed to his boss who, in turn, asked Hurley if she would make an exception this once. She agreed. Subsequently, though, the work for Dobbs coming out of Hurley's unit took progressively longer and longer to complete. The delays were beginning to create problems for Dobbs in meeting his work deadlines for clients. You see, Dobbs was quite dependent upon the T/DP personnel.

During the following weeks, the working relationship between Hurley and Dobbs declined rapidly. Delays became longer. Ultimately, the two refused to speak to one another. They communicated by memos and intermediaries. Some event—its value not great because no one recalls exactly what it was—sent Dobbs storming into Hurley's office.

"I've really put up with this silly business long enough," Dobbs yelled. "If you were a man, I'd ask you to step outside and we'd settle this once and for all."

"Why Mr. Dobbs," Hurley responded with a smile, "if you *were* a man, I would give you that opportunity."

Questions

1. What factors and conditions created this conflict situation?
2. Realistically, could the situation have been prevented?
3. At this stage of development in the working relationship between Dobbs and Hurley, how would you attempt to solve the problem?
4. If the problem cannot be resolved without terminating one of the two principals, which one should go? Why?

Case 12-2

Weather Report

It was late September when Harley Talarzik arrived for his appointment with Professor Morton Adamowitz. During the past summer, Harley had spent three months working at an Ontario, Canada, manufacturing plant that produced auto parts such as plastic moldings found in the interiors of passenger cars and trucks. Harley's internship had been arranged by his Toronto college, and for the report he submitted he could earn 12 credits. Among his several summer assignments was to prepare, administer, and evaluate an employee attitude survey. Over 300 questionnaires were anonymously completed by employees at the plant. The response rate for the survey was 92 percent. Not too bad.

Harley had tabulated the questionnaire data. Following several weeks of analyzing the findings, he had written a report and submitted it to his summer boss, the company's human resources manager. He gave another copy of his report to Professor Adamowitz, who had circled a number of comments he wished to discuss with Harley. Negative comments made by employees outnumbered the positive about ten to one. The following reflect the range of employee attitudes about their company:

"I have worked for this supervisor for three years now and he has never given me any compliments about my work. Before he came, my old supervisor let me know how I was doing and thought my work was excellent."

"We are just getting used to a new work rule when you change it or put two in its place. Most of them are disputed and end up going to the union-management griev-ance committee for resolution. I don't think you trust us."

"I am really ticked off about the compensation system here. I have worked for the company over ten years and recently you hired a new person and pay her the same as me. That isn't fair in my book."

"I'd like to know more about where the company is headed. What are our objectives and are we going to open a new factory in London? Some workers are saying this plant is going to be closed and the jobs will move to the States now that NAFTA is in effect."

"I made over a half-dozen suggestions this past year and haven't heard anything about any of them yet. Are you serious about the suggestion program or not?"

"The day you promote a woman to be my supervisor is the day I quit. I've never had a woman boss in my 30 years of working here and I don't plan to start now."

"It seems everyone here is busy protecting his rear. Always get it in writing. No wonder we are so slow in getting things done. We are constantly bickering and fighting."

"I used to think a union wouldn't do us any good. Lately, I've had second thoughts. The company has too many rules covering everything we do. I don't have any freedom."

"I wish somebody would tell me why only the college kids get the good jobs. I know a lot of people here that have never gone to college and they could do the work. Probably even better."

"The jobs of my work group are really dependent upon other groups and what they send us. If they are behind schedule, we end up getting the blame because we are late."

"Who do you think you are fooling in doing this survey? The young guy you've got doing it is probably a management spy."

"My priorities here are my work group and its well-being. The company comes second, and sometimes, not at all."

Questions

1. How would you describe the organization's climate? What areas of the climate appear particularly deficient?

2. How much confidence would you place in an employee attitude survey?

3. If you were the supervisor of these employees, how would you react to their comments? What are the sources of these conflicts and potential conflict management strategies?

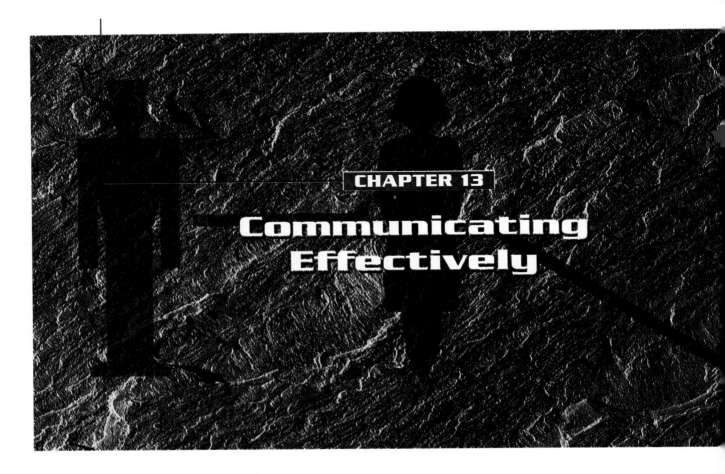

CHAPTER 13

Communicating Effectively

● Don't call me "darling" in front of the police with your dead husband on the floor.

Dialogue from the movie *The Cheap Detective*

LEARNING
OBJECTIVES

1. Describe the communication process and what makes it effective.
2. Indicate how the field of experience influences communication.
3. Explain how paraphrasing and perception checking are applied to improve the quality of feedback.
4. Suggest methods for reducing defensiveness in the communication process.
5. Illustrate the impact of nonverbal forms of communication and how supervisors can apply knowledge about kinesics and proxemics.
6. Understand the dynamics of group behavior upon the communication process.

Carla felt enormous pride in the report.

It had taken four weeks to compile data justifying an approach for her department's implementation of TQM. She included a summary of TQM methods because she wanted her boss, Larry, to know she understood the subject. She also felt he should understand the probable reaction of each employee to TQM. So, Carla provided an individual work history for each of her charges.

The report ended up 21 pages long. Four pages of color pie charts and schedules added to the length.

A week after submitting the report Carla saw Larry walking quickly out to the parking lot.

"Larry! Wait up!"

Larry turned impatiently. "Carla, I'd love to talk, but I've got to go."

"Hey, this'll just take a second. . . . Like the report? Do you think we should go with run charts? Do you like the schedule? What do you think of moving Sheila to another department? She's not exactly a team player . . . "

"Carla, send me a summary of your ideas. I'd be happy to go over it with you when I've got more time. I've got to go! Sorry."

"Summary? . . . But, what about my report?"

Larry was already out the door.

Facilitating effective communication is an essential part of a supervisor's success. Supervisors and other managers spend up to 80 percent of their day communicating.[1] In a recent survey, 85 percent of 700 middle managers noted it was a subordinate's communication skills that determined success or failure in critical situations.[2] Effective communication is a necessary requirement for many parts of a supervisor's job—performance appraisal, conflict management, motivation of subordinates, decision making, and leadership.

Unfortunately, complaints about communication are common in all types of organizations across all organizational levels. For example, supervisors and subordinates often do not agree on whether they even met during the week![3] Up to 95 percent of high-ranking managers report believing they have a good grasp of employee problems. In contrast, only about 30 percent of subordinates agree that this is so![4]

What Is Communication?

Communication problems are understandable in light of the difficulty of even simple transmissions of information. There is a lot more to communication than just talking. (See Figure 13-1.)

communication
A process whereby symbols generated by people are received and responded to by other people.

Communication is a "process whereby symbols generated by people are received and responded to by other people."[5] Communication includes verbal, nonverbal, and written transmissions of information to the individuals and groups within an organization. Communication is effective between a supervisor and an employee to the extent that meaning is achieved. Are the sender and the receiver of a message "on the same page" in terms of having the same understanding of what was communicated?

There is a virtually unlimited set of reasons why supervisors want to achieve meaning with employees.[6] There are many reasons for communication: to have fun, to persuade, to describe, and to inform are just a few. The primary reason why supervisors wish to achieve meaning in communication is to improve individual and team performance.

The Spiritual Child Metaphor

Regardless of purpose, the spiritual child metaphor demonstrates that communication is a reciprocal process—with all parties responsible for creating and maintaining a unique, shared meaning. John Stewart describes the metaphor this way:

> Whenever you encounter someone, the two of you together create a spiritual child—*your relationship*. Unlike the creation of physical children, there are no contraceptives available for spiritual children; when two people meet, they always create a relationship of some sort. Also, unlike physical children, the spiritual child lives as long as at least one person lives. . . . The spiritual child can change drastically, but it can't be killed. . . .
>
> If the (spiritual) child is born in a meeting characterized by manipulation, deceit, and exploitation, it will be deformed and ugly. If it's raised in that same atmosphere it can never be healthy. Often it can be nurtured back to health, but it takes a heavy commitment from both parents. On the other hand, if it's born and raised in an open caring atmosphere, it will grow healthy and strong. . . .
>
> I hope the spiritual child metaphor is useful for you. What it does for me is to give me another way to look at the relationship . . . between the persons. As a child, you

Figure 13-1 Communication and the Long Distance Call

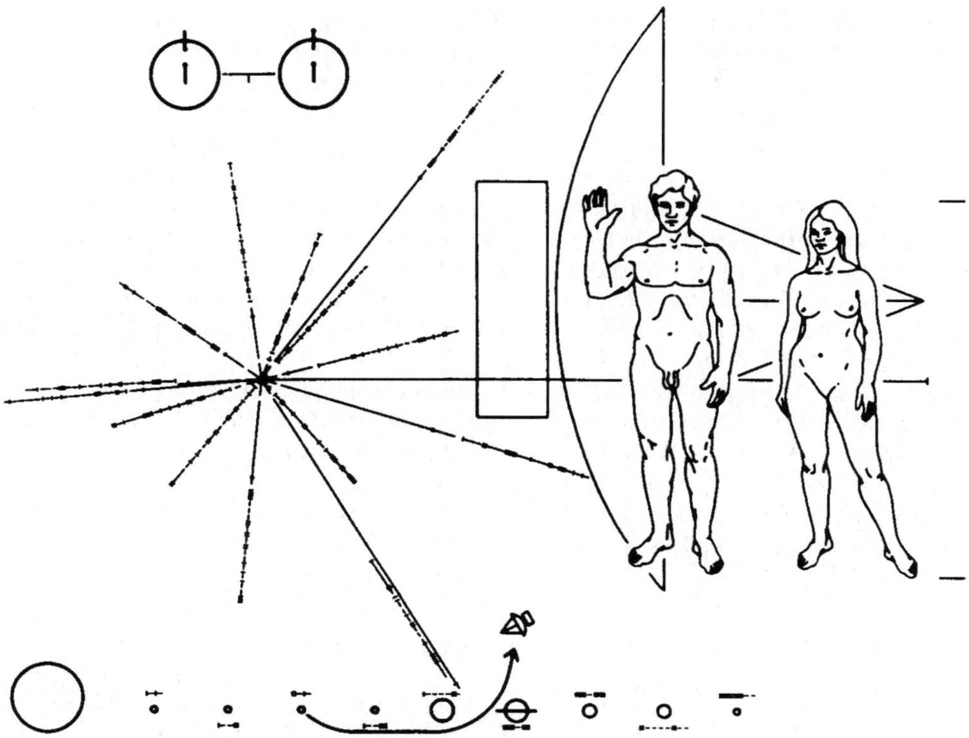

On June 13, 1983, the Pioneer 10 spacecraft became the first human-designed object to leave our solar system. Along with its sistership Pioneer 11, it carried the gold-anodized aluminum plaque pictured above, designed by Carl and Linda Sagan and Frank Drake. The plaque consists of various inscriptions about the planet earth that intelligent life elsewhere could understand including the location of the solar system and earth within the system, dominant life found on earth (the man and woman), and the element hydrogen, among other information. According to astronomer Sagan, "This is the first time that something associated with life and intelligence has left [the solar system]."

Pioneer 10 was launched in 1972 to photograph the planet Jupiter and its moons. Conceivably, the vehicle will still be traveling 100 billion years from now, long after the sun dies along with the planet Earth in five billion years.

When departing the solar system to become our first "star ship," the vehicle was traveling 30,558 miles per hour. Radio messages from Pioneer 10 required over four hours and twenty minutes to travel the 2.8 billion miles from the sun—truly a long distance call.

Source: Suggested by the work of David A. Tansik and others, *Management: A Life Cycle Approach* (Homewood, IL: Richard D. Irwin, 1980), 138.

are neither of your parents, but the result of their meeting, their contact. Similarly, the spiritual child who is born whenever two people communicate is an entity that emerges *between* them.[7]

As can be seen from the spiritual child metaphor, good communication between a supervisor and employee or work team requires more than just following rules, or being a good listener. It begins with understanding that effective communication does not reside with one communicator or the other —it exists *between* people. Just as both parents are responsible for the health of their child, so too all communicators are responsible for the health of communication. This suggests supervisors need to work to clarify meaning and what others are trying to get across. This is a constant process (just as raising a child is!). We'll be covering several techniques for keeping communication healthy in this chapter.

Although there are general guidelines for improving the quality of interpersonal communication, there are no hard-and-fast rules. Every communication situation is different, just as every child-raising situation is different.

There *are* communication guidelines—equivalent to telling children not to play on the freeway—that are effective most of the time. Nevertheless, every individual and group represents a unique communications situation. Strategies discussed in this chapter may not always be effective or even relevant in a given situation involving a supervisor and employee. Knowing when an exception to a general communications rule is necessary is the art of becoming an effective communicator.

It is impossible to not communicate (just as it is impossible to be "a little bit pregnant"). It is impossible to avoid communicating in the presence of another person. Everything you say, do (or don't do), or *are* communicates.

interpersonal communication
The communication between two people.

The next section covers **interpersonal communication**—communication between two individuals. The quality of interpersonal communication is the foundation of a supervisor's relationship with individual workers.

Interpersonal Communication

Wendell Johnson's classic article, "The Fateful Process of Mr. A talking to Mr. B," concludes with the comment that people are a "noisy lot; and of what gets said among us, far more goes unheard and unheeded than seems possible. We have yet to learn on a grand scale how to use the wonders of speaking and listening in our own best interests and for the good of all our fellows. It is the finest art still to be mastered by men."[8]

As suggested by Professor Johnson, interpersonal communication is surprisingly complex. This complexity often contributes to a failure to achieve meaning.

The Sender-Receiver Model

sender-receiver model
A representation of the communication process with several elements or stages beginning with the encoding of messages by the sender, message transmission, decoding by the receiver, and response or feedback.

Figure 13-2 outlines the **sender-receiver model,** a popular model depicting the interpersonal communication process. This model only covers communication transactions between two people, such as the communication that occurs between a supervisor and an individual worker. The complexity of communication (and potential for failure to achieve meaning) usually increases as more people participate in the process (such as communication between the supervisor and the entire work group).

The interpersonal communication process begins when one person wishes to transmit information to another person. This desire to transmit information need not be conscious, rational, or even eventually expressed using verbal or written language. A scowl, a smile, and a puzzled look are as much communication as is a five-page memo or the Gettysburg Address.

Regardless of the communication vehicle used, the interpersonal communication process begins with a perception (a thought or a feeling) which must be encoded before it can be transmitted. (*Encoding* literally means to put a message

Figure 13-2 The Sender-Receiver Model

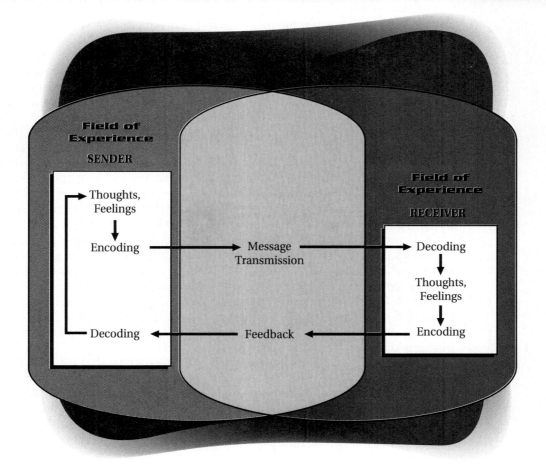

Source: Developed from discussion of communication models in Ernest G. Bormann, *Communication Theory* (New York: Holt, Rinehart and Winston, 1980).

into code.) As noted, a sender can put a message into code using verbal, nonverbal, and written means.

After transmission, the receiver must decode the message. ("I wonder what that scowl means?" "What is this five-page memo really saying?" "Was the Gettysburg Address really about soldiers dying for freedom, or soldiers dying for economic prosperity?") After decoding, the message is then transformed into a perception on the part of the receiver. The entire process is repeated when the receiver provides feedback. Feedback occurs during two-way communication when a receiver responds to the original sender of a message. (Feedback is also covered later in this chapter and in Chapters 1, 8, 11, and 14.)

In reviewing this model, it should be apparent that even very simple communication can be hampered because many parts of the communication process are private and not shared (thoughts and feelings, encoding, decoding). Only the actual verbal, nonverbal, or written transmission of a message is received.

Besides the inherent complexity of the communication process, the field of experience of communicators influences the achievement of meaning. **Field of**

field of experience
Factors and conditions influencing the communication process including perceptions, values, culture, attitudes, and opinions derived from previous experiences by the various communication participants.

The cultural setting and other aspects of a field of experience significantly influence interpersonal communication.

experience is broadly defined here to include perceptions, values, culture, attitudes, and opinions derived from previous experience.

For example, if you think another person is angry with you, you may perceive an angry message, even if the person is not really angry. Communication breakdowns also occur because of difficulty understanding another person's culture or language. For example, the Japanese language expression for "yes" can, depending on the context, actually mean "no." You may find yourself communicating differently in one setting than in another. Communication in a court of law, for example, differs from communication on a basketball court because people know from experience that these audiences are very different. You may communicate differently in a quiet restaurant than in a noisy bus station.

Supervisors need to be sensitive to the field of experience of employees. As a supervisor, you may be busily explaining a procedure or communicating top management's policy changes, and be amazed by the lack of understanding on the part of followers. Employees may not share your enthusiasm about procedural or policy changes. They may be thinking of their bowling league, upcoming PTA meeting, or vacation at Disneyland while you are speaking.

In an increasingly diverse workplace, employees may speak English as a second language, or be accustomed to using slang different than that of the supervisor. Sometimes communication fails because of language difficulties on the part of either supervisor or employee. As one writer noted in communication breakdowns, "It could be that 9 out of 10 business managers and supervisors are more interested in their *own expressions* than on their *impressions* on others—particularly on those who work for them. Solving this problem is the key to all good business communications."[9]

To summarize, the sender-receiver model is useful in that it presents interpersonal communication as a multidimensional process involving many steps to better understand communication breakdowns. It also helps us to appreciate the complexity associated with the sending and receiving of even simple messages.

Conversely, the sender-receiver model does not capture the full richness of interpersonal communication, nor does it account for all threats to the achievement of meaning. Simply understanding the complexity of communication will not make a supervisor a better communicator. Understanding must be coupled with the use of techniques, such as those discussed in the next section, that help to break down communication barriers.

Active Listening and Feedback

active listening
Provision of timely and appropriate feedback that improves the understanding between persons who are communicating.

Active listening involves the timely and appropriate provision of feedback that improves the achievement of meaning between communicators. Imagine a situation involving one-way communication between a supervisor and work group where you, as a member of the group, can only receive information from the supervisor without being allowed to ask questions or to provide feedback. You would not be able to add to other group members' understanding of the topic being discussed. Suppose you do not understand the material being covered. There is no way to communicate your lack of understanding to the supervisor, and the supervisor would be completely unaware of your lack of understanding. Providing for feedback is the key to resolving these communication difficulties.

Two-way communication provides for feedback, which improves the accuracy of communication. This is true because with feedback there is opportunity to correct or to otherwise refine communication, leading to mutual understanding and agreement. An added advantage to two-way communication is that it is more satisfying to communicators, who may feel stifled by one-way communication.

A lack of feedback significantly affects the quality of communication, unless the communication is very simple and feedback is unnecessary. Problems with the communication *process* can interfere with interpretation of communication *content*. Supervisors improve communication accuracy by encouraging two-way communication, and should actively solicit feedback from and provide feedback to subordinates.

Paraphrasing and Perception Checking.

Two communication techniques that improve the quality of feedback are **paraphrasing** and **perception checking.**

Paraphrasing and perception checking are active listening skills.[10] *Active listening* is an appropriate term, because active listening skills supplement and enhance basic listening for the purpose of clarifying meaning. Paraphrasing and perception checking involve communication that helps the sender and receiver of a message to clarify communication or intent.

Paraphrasing involves repeating back in your own words what you thought you heard the sender say. Noise and the symbols used in a communication sometimes make it hard to understand a message, particularly a long and/or complex communication. **Noise** is anything that detracts from the transmission quality of messages or anything that prevents the communication process from being completed. The objective of paraphrasing is to ensure that the receiver got the message the sender actually sent.

Perception checking is similar to paraphrasing. Here, however, the focus is on checking out what you perceive to be the intent of another person's communication. Here, the concern is not with *what* the person communicated as much as it is with what the other person *means.* (See Figure 13-3 on the next page.)

For example, an employee might be consistently late to work. The supervisor might assume from this communication that the employee does not care much about his or her job. However, the supervisor might learn, on checking out this perception, that the employee is usually extremely punctual and cares a great deal about his or her job, and that the problem was a temporary one associated with late arrival of buses.

Paraphrasing and perception checking work well together. Lincoln's Gettysburg Address could have been paraphrased as: "President Lincoln, did I hear you say that the founders of our country expressed the belief 78 years ago that all people are created equal, and the Battle of Gettysburg was fought, and thousands of lives were lost to keep that ideal alive?"

President Lincoln might have stroked his beard, thought for a moment and then replied, "Yes, this is essentially what I said. However, 'four score and seven years ago' was 87, not 78, years ago."

Satisfied that you had accurately received the message, you could then proceed to verify the message's meaning, "Because of the way your address tied a definition of 'freedom' to the lives lost at Gettysburg, it seems you did not intend to eulogize the 20,000 Confederate soldiers who died in this battle. Is this so? Also, was it your intent to include women in your statement that 'all men are created equal?' As you know, women are not allowed to vote or to own property." (This was true in 1863.)

President Lincoln would then have had the opportunity to respond.

Put It in Writing and KISS.

Other approaches that improve clarity of communication and feedback between a supervisor and employee are to express responses in writing and to follow the **KISS principle.**

paraphrasing
An active listening skill involving repeating back in your own words what you thought you heard the sender say.

perception checking
Verifying what you perceive to be the intent of another person's communication message.

noise
Anything that detracts from the transmission quality of messages or anything that prevents the communication process from being completed.

KISS principle
Acronym for designing communication messages stating: "keep it short and simple."

Figure 13-3	Semantics and Perception Checking

Source: Peanuts, 11/5/73. PEANUTS reprinted by permission of UFS, Inc.

Written communication has the important advantage of being open to close review and analysis. You may not understand what the sender meant, but there can be no doubt about the words (symbols) that were actually sent.

All forms of communication benefit when the KISS principle is applied. There are several versions of the underlying meaning of this acronym. The one we particularly like is "keep it short and simple."[11] Organizational psychologist Bob Baron sums up advantages of the KISS principle this way:

> If we are exposed to more facts, ideas, or concepts than we can comfortably handle at a given time, much of this information is lost. In addition, the experience of having one's "cognitive circuits" overloaded is quite unpleasant. For these reasons, communicators who present too much (either by words or written comments) run the dual risk of failing to get their message across *and* annoying their audience. Thus, the moral for all would-be communicators is straight forward: avoid cramming too much information into written or verbal messages; doing so can be disastrous![12]

Reducing Defensiveness

Sometimes neutral, or even positive, messages are communicated in such a way that they sound negative. How many times have you heard the old adage, "It's not what you said that angers me, it's how you said it!"

Poor delivery leads to defensiveness on the part of the recipient. Defensiveness, in turn, puts up barriers to achievement of meaning. It is as though supervisors and employees put up walls or put on suits of armor, making it difficult for messages to get through.

supportive communication techniques
Methods for reducing defensiveness in communication by applying positive rather than negative messages.

Supportive communication techniques reduce defensiveness.[13] Supportive communication tends to be descriptive rather than evaluative. Rather than say to an employee, "You're always late to work!" a supportive supervisor might say "I've noticed you've been late the last three days." Both messages say the same thing, but delivery is much different.

Supportive communication also reinforces the idea that the supervisor and employee are on the same team. The employee is not a subordinate who works *for* a supervisor as much as he or she is a team member who works *with* a supervisor. Supportive communication also tends to be tentative rather than absolute. It's generally more supportive to say "it appears" or "it seems" rather than "it is."

Constructive communication between supervisor and employee is usually invited. This means a person offering a criticism or an idea to another is doing so by invitation, or by virtue of his or her position within the organization. We tend to be defensive when suggestions are offered by those who appear to lack expertise or are not appropriately positioned in the organization to offer advice. Consequently, when in doubt, check out whether or not communication is invited. Even if you are the boss, it's a good idea to make sure your comments are welcomed before providing feedback. This tactic is similar to phoning a friend at dinner time and asking if it's okay to talk.

Constructive communication is also timely. As a supervisor, you should try to avoid holding back adverse information, or feelings, and then "dumping" this information during a later conversation. On the other hand, sometimes it is constructive to let some time pass before providing feedback or advice. Waiting might allow you or an angry individual the time needed to cool off. An angry response from another person may have nothing to do with content of your communication, but rather may be a function of bad timing.

Finally, reduce defensiveness by being "soft on people and hard on the problem."[14] Try to attack the problem, not the person. If the person *is* the problem, the suggestions we offer for improving the quality of communication should still be used. You may not always succeed in having constructive dialogue with another person, but using these techniques will improve your chances.

Nonverbal Communication: Kinesics and Proxemics

Kinesics, or body language, includes the whole range of nonverbal cues: eye contact, body posture, handshakes, facial expression, gestures, and body movement. **Proxemics** (distances) is the study of the way people use space. Kinesics and proxemics are interesting and important parts of understanding nonverbal communication.

Kinesics

Kinesics is a highly speculative field. Even Julius Fast, author of a popular trade book titled *Body Language,* noted, "Unfortunately, something like kinesics, related facts on the way to becoming a science, also runs the risk of being exploited. For example, just how much can we really tell from crossed legs?"[15]

Although the topic of body language may be difficult to define and to understand, there is no question about its importance. The way a message is *sent* is often more relevant than what is *said.*

Only a small portion of interpersonal communication is expressed in words. Most of our messages are expressed by facial expressions and posture (about 55 percent) and vocal intonation and inflection (38 percent). Only about 7 percent of communication is verbal.[16] Judgments from visual cues are often more valid than judgments from vocal communication. When verbal and nonverbal messages differ, we tend to believe the nonverbal.[17] Judgments from visual cues in the environment are more accurate than are judgments based upon vocal cues.[18] It is more difficult to fool people nonverbally.

The importance of nonverbal communication cannot be overemphasized. Positive nonverbal behavior has a significant, positive effect upon perceptions of

kinesics
Another term for body language that includes nonverbal cues such as eye contact, body posture, handshakes, facial expression, gestures, and body movement influencing the validity of the communication process.

proxemics
The study of the way people use space.

observers relative to negative nonverbal behavior. It is relatively easy to build a convincing case for the importance of nonverbal communication. Describing positive nonverbal behavior in general terms is also simple. The difficulty lies in being specific about which nonverbal behavior is effective under which set of circumstances.

Take eye contact, for example. Under most circumstances making eye contact with another is perceived as a positive nonverbal form of behavior. However, too much eye contact can make another person uneasy. Indeed, to fix someone with a "cold stare" is usually a sign of hostility. In certain cultures, eye contact acceptable by Western standards might be perceived as being rude (for example, in Japanese culture). The same thing can be said with regard to certain gestures.

Body language usually plays a more important role in interpersonal communication than do the words that are spoken because it is impossible to avoid communication. Everything you say, or do, or *are* sends a message. The key to effective nonverbal communication is sensitivity to one's environment.

sensitivity audit
A personal evaluation by an individual of the effects of her or his nonverbal behavior upon other persons.

Supervisors should conduct a periodic personal **sensitivity audit** to ascertain what their nonverbal communication is saying to others.[19] For example, when giving a presentation, notice if your audience is fidgeting or looking bored. Is the audience nodding their heads with approval? In the process of conducting this sensitivity audit, consider whether your verbal and nonverbal communication is appropriate. Work toward connection between verbal and nonverbal communication.

Also, observe the nonverbal communication of others. Be sure to use active listening skills (discussed previously) to check out nonverbal cues emanating from those around you. For example, if an employee with whom you are communicating obviously yawns, don't get angry. Instead, check out the yawn: "I notice your yawning, Ralph. What's the matter?" Ralph might respond by telling you that he stayed up all night in anticipation of your meeting. Ralph isn't bored, he's tired!

Proxemics

Some of the most meaningful communication in life is nonverbal.

Edward T. Hall defined four distinct distances of which people are aware: intimate, personal, social, and public distances.[20] These distances range from skin contact up to 18 inches for intimate encounters to 12 feet and beyond for public distance.

Most communication in business meetings uses social distance, which ranges from 4 to 12 feet. Personal distance, 18 inches to 4 feet, is often employed in interpersonal communication.

As with other nonverbal communication, it is difficult to set rules for maintaining personal space. The effect of personal distance should be included in the sensitivity audit described previously. For example, ask yourself, "Am I too close? Should I back off? Is personal distance appropriate in *this setting* with *this person?*"

A related concern pertains to touch. Touching, outside of incidental contact and handshakes (as part of a mutually understood greeting ritual) is always intimate. Sometimes it is appropriate to slap another on the back or touch an arm to emphasize a point. For the most part, however, at least in Western culture, supervisors should avoid extensive touching as part of their interpersonal communication repertoire. In fact, today touching may be interpreted by some as a form of sexual harassment.

Another application of proxemics concerns open versus closed office design, the manner in which office furniture is laid out. An office with an

Communication in the Electronic Era

Electronic bulletin boards involving communication transmitted by computer modem have become increasingly popular. E-mail ("electronic mail") is now widely used within organizations.

Unfortunately, electronic, or on-line, communication lacks the usual compensatory methods people use to check out meaning. It's not easy to figure out precisely what another person means in an on-line message, or to elaborate on a particular point that is potentially vexing. It is difficult to smile or set another at ease with a reassuring touch. It is difficult to understand what another person may be feeling when you cannot assess nonverbal communication. Words themselves have greater power in on-line communication. Still, words are slippery.

Sometimes people misinterpret on-line communication, get angry, and fire off a reply that is both surprising and insulting. On-line communicators refer to this type of communication as *flaming*—defined by *The Hacker's Dictionary* as "to speak incessantly and/or rabidly on some relatively uninteresting subject or with a patently ridiculous attitude."[21]

open office design typically has the desk and chairs aligned so there are no physical barriers between those sitting in the office. Conversely, offices with **closed office designs** typically place a desk or other office furniture between people.

Studies indicate that people feel more welcome and comfortable in offices with an open design compared to offices with closed designs. Also, people tend to view the occupants of offices with an open design as being friendlier and more helpful.[22]

An open office design should be used by people in the helping professions (for example, counselors or professors). The question of whether this statement extends to supervisors is debatable. We tend to favor open office design for most supervisors because this design facilitates interpersonal communication, which is an important part of an effective supervisor's job.

open office design
Typically has the desk and chairs aligned so that there are no physical barriers between those sitting in the office.

closed office design
Typically places a desk or other office furniture between people.

Communication within the Work Team

Everything discussed to this point can be applied to communication within a work team. Skills that help improve the quality of interpersonal communication should be applied within a group process.

Participation within a team does not mean that **group communication** is taking place. Indeed, when two people pass notes or whisper with each other during a team meeting, group communication skills are not being practiced. Instead, interpersonal communication within a group is occurring. One could also make the point that group communication skills are being poorly practiced.

Much of the literature concerning group communication is primarily concerned with decision making.[23] The focus of the following discussion of group communication is on how to improve group communication. (Decision making within a work team is covered in detail in Chapter 10.) Group communication involves a problem solving and/or decision making group comprised of three or more persons "who are interacting with one another in such a manner that each person influences and is influenced by each other person."[24]

Communication among members of a work group takes place for a wide variety of reasons that may be formal or informal. The emphasis of this section,

group communication
Occurs when all members of a group are actively communicating within the context of the group.

Positive Body Language

- Be physically alert.
- Maintain eye contact.
- Use an open, relaxed body posture.

- Minimize gestures and random movement.
- Reinforce the speaker—for example, give head nods and other cues that communicate you are listening.[25]

formal group
A group composed of members brought together for the purpose of making decisions or solving problems, often a work group.

however, is placed on communication among members of a **formal group,** such as a work team. A formal group is comprised of members brought together for the sole purpose of making decisions or solving problems.

Group Size and Communication

The question of optimum group size is related to why a group has been created in the first place. For example, information can be effectively communicated to very large groups convened to passively receive one-way communication (from several hundred students sitting in a lecture hall, to millions of people sitting in front of television sets across the country). Effective two-way interaction among group members requires a smaller group size. Smaller groups (three to seven people) provide for more active information exchange relative to large groups.

Five to seven people is an effective size for a problem solving/decision making group. Groups of four tend to set two pairs of people against each other, and a group of three tends to allow one person to slide from one position to another.[26] A group of five people is "probably the smallest number in which the psychological forces tend to foster cooperation instead of setting the stage for contention."[27] A group of five to seven persons is large enough to bring in a variety of ideas and small enough to function efficiently.

Five to seven members is an ideal for which to strive. Supervisors can't always work with a team of five to seven employees, however. Sometimes the most important consideration in putting a group together is not group size but, rather, the expertise and/or personal characteristics of group members.

Beware of Squeaky Wheels!

The more a person verbally contributes to a group, the greater the likelihood that he or she will be perceived as being the leader. (This point is also discussed in Chapter 7.) This is true regardless of the quality of what the talkative group member communicates.[28] Squeaky wheels—talkative group members—do "get the grease."

This phenomenon has a limit, however. Domination of verbal communication in a group can eventually lead to a reduction in the perceived leadership of the dominant person.[29] Essentially, as in the story of the boy who cried wolf, group members grow weary of listening to a dominant member.

The implications of the squeaky wheel phenomenon are straightforward. The *extent* of contribution by a group member should not be confused with the *quality* of contribution. Supervisors should actively solicit input from less talkative group members. This task is a particularly important part of the supervisor's job when working with a group.

listening
An accurate receipt and interpretation of communication wherein a person hears and pays attention to something or someone.

Listening

Probably the most important communications skill, whether in terms of interpersonal or group communication, is listening. **Listening** is a skill that involves the accurate receipt and interpretation of communication wherein a person hears and pays attention to something or someone. Poor listening skills are sometimes less apparent, and more of a problem, in a group process than when two people are communicating verbally because there tends to be less accountability in a group.

There is a difference between hearing and listening. Hearing is concerned only with the ability to hear transmitted information, not with the person's capacity to understand the message that was sent. A person with a finely developed sense of hearing can be a poor listener, whereas a person with a hearing impairment can be an excellent listener.

A key impediment to effective listening lies in the difference between the speeds at which we can talk and comprehend the spoken word. People think much faster than they can talk. Unfortunately, people have a tendency to fill up this cognitive spare time by daydreaming or otherwise thinking about subjects other than those being communicated by a speaker at a given moment. Recall the example earlier in the chapter in which employees were thinking about bowling leagues, PTA meetings, and vacation opportunities while a supervisor was communicating. A key to more effective listening is to use this "spare time" to better understand what the speaker is communicating.[30]

Supervisors would benefit from following these recommendations when communicating with a work team:

1. Fully understand a question or statement of a fellow discussant before framing a reply. Try to avoid leaping to conclusions. Remember, you cannot both listen to your own internal dialogue as you think of what to say and truly listen to what another person is saying.
2. Avoid becoming focused upon irrelevancies and distractions that do not relate to what the speaker is saying. Don't let the setting of a meeting or mannerisms of a group member distract from the content of a presentation.
3. Do not become overly emotional or ego-involved.
4. Stay on the topic! Groups easily become sidetracked. If sidetracking occurs, bring the group back to the topic.
5. Keep listening, and keep using active listening skills, even if you disagree with a team member. You cannot effectively and constructively refute a position if you do not understand its basic tenets.[31]

We might also add, the use of humor in communicating should be appropriate to the situation as depicted in Figure 13-4 on page 277.

Communication Rules

Supervisors will be well served by approaching group communication from the standpoint of communication rules. **Communication rules** define the communication process to be used by group members. If a relatively complex decision must be made, then a decentralized, consensus group communication process should be used. If the problem or the group's purpose is well defined, then a more centralized process using *Robert's Rules of Order* may be more effective. (See Chapter 10 for further discussion of group decision making.)

Group communication using Robert's rules is more centralized because it is channeled through a chairperson such as the supervisor. In consensus decision making, group members communicate directly without going through a chairperson. This distinction between Robert's rules and consensus is one of degree. Group members communicate with each other regardless of the communication rule employed. The difference lies in the amount of control exercised in the

communication rules
Define the communication process to be used by group members.

Listening: A Lost Art?

Good, old-fashioned listening is an important part of effective communication. Yet, how often do we actually listen to what is being said by a speaker? And, if we are not listening, what are we thinking about? An answer to this question was presented at an American Psychological Association meeting in 1968 by Paul Cameron, then an assistant professor of psychology at Wayne State University.

Professor Cameron collected the thoughts of his students at 21 random intervals during the course of a nine-week quarter. He discovered that at any given time,

- 20 percent of his students were pursuing erotic thoughts
- 20 percent were reminiscing about something
- about 40 percent were daydreaming or thinking about food or religion
- only 20 percent were paying attention to the lecture, and of this percentage only about half were actively listening—only 12 percent of the entire class!

group communication process by the chairperson. Robert's rules of order, or a comparable set of rules, is *relatively* more centralized compared to consensus decision making.

In any event, it is important that communication rules —whether Robert's rules, consensus, or some other approach—be clear to all group members at the outset of a meeting. It is also important that the group have an agenda. (Chapter 10 also discusses this point.) Agenda means literally "things to be done"; it is a list of items to be covered in a meeting. Clear understanding of communication rules, together with an agenda, improve the group communication process. Communication rules help with the flow of information and an agenda provides direction.

Encouraging Upward Communication

mum effect
The tendency of subordinates to hesitate to pass bad or threatening news up the chain of command.

Most people don't like to pass on bad news. Employees often avoid giving bad news to supervisors. Supervisors, in turn, don't like to pass bad news on to their bosses, and so forth all the way up the management pyramid. As a result of this tendency, known as the **mum effect,** a work team could be on the verge of disaster and the supervisor not know until it was too late![32]

Interestingly, the responsibility for reducing the mum effect is the supervisor's, not the employee's. Supervisors need to make it clear to employees that even though bad news is never welcome, the messenger who delivers it will not be harmed.[33] In short, don't "shoot" the messenger!

Informal Communication

informal organization
The organization dynamics portraying the status, power, politics, friendship ties, and proximity of organization members; not represented by an organization chart.

grapevine
The informal communication channel that connects the informal organization.

Besides the formal relationships drawn up in an organization chart, there is also an **informal organization.** No company document portrays the informal organization, which is defined by the status, power, politics, friendship ties, and proximity of organization members.

The informal communication channel that connects the informal organization is called the **grapevine.** The grapevine exists in all organizations and stems from the need of people to understand what is happening around them. It acts as an escape valve for employee tensions and is usually quite active in organizations undergoing change. The grapevine is surprisingly accurate. One study found that about 80 percent of the information transmitted through the grapevine was cor-

---

| **Figure 13-4** | "How Do We Get Down Off This Rock?" |

B.C.

Source: B.C., 7/12/93. Reprinted by permission of Johnny Hart and Creators Syndicate, Inc.

rect.[34] Problems occur, however, because of the 20 percent of grapevine information that is inaccurate, and because even if accurate, information may not be understood in context.

The grapevine is the communication channel that carries all rumors. It is difficult to combat rumors. Supervisors can combat rumors by providing accurate information, discrediting the source of a rumor, or helping employees to recall facts or experiences of their own that are contrary to the rumor.

Carla cooled off.

Larry was not the world's best manager, but he could not really be blamed. He had asked for a one-page summary. Carla had given him 21 pages. She had heard what he wanted, but had not actually *listened.*

His nonverbal behavior had clearly said he was in a hurry, heading out to the parking lot at a walking trot to make an appointment. She had held him up outside the door. Bad timing and location.

She thought about times in the past when she had missed what others said by either their words or behavior.

Later that week, Carla presented Larry with a one-page executive summary of her report. It summarized key points and recommendations and was designed to go on page one of the 21-page report. She got credit for extra work, but Larry also got the summary he'd requested.

Carla and Larry then had a productive conversation about her recommendations at a mutually agreeable time in the privacy of Larry's office.

Summary: Focus on Skills

Communication is defined as a "process whereby symbols generated by people are received and responded to by other people." The intent of interpersonal, group, and organizational communication is to achieve meaning for the purpose of improving individual, group, and organizational productivity.

Following are 19 suggestions to help supervisors improve communication with employees within the work team.

1. Keep in mind that communication is pervasive. It includes all nonverbal and written, as well as verbal, attempts to achieve meaning.

2. Actively solicit feedback from others. Ongoing feedback helps supervisors to improve and otherwise assess the quality of their communications.

3. Learn and practice active listening skills such as paraphrasing and perception checking.

4. Understand that written communication plays an important role in clarifying communications.

5. Practice the KISS principle in written and verbal communications.

6. Describe the behavior of others, rather than critically evaluating the behavior.

7. Reinforce the idea that you and the employee are on the same team.

8. Be tentative in comments to other people. For example, it is usually more constructive to say, "I believe . . ." than it is to say "I know . . ."

9. Remember that constructive communication is usually invited, timely, and "soft on people and hard on the problem."

10. Conduct a periodic personal sensitivity audit. Ascertain the extent to which your verbal and nonverbal communication is congruent, and the way your communication is being perceived.

11. Identify discrepancies perceived in the verbal and nonverbal communication of others. Recognize nonverbal cues of others whenever there are doubts or questions about their meaning.

12. Be sensitive to the importance of personal space. Do not inappropriately violate the personal space of others.

13. Use an open office design to facilitate interpersonal communication.

14. Try to keep the size of problem-solving or decision-making groups manageable. Five to seven members is usually an effective range.

15. Beware of squeaky wheels. Do not confuse the extent of contribution by a group member with the quality of the contribution.

16. Understand a communication from another group member before framing a reply; avoid focusing upon irrelevancies and distractions; do not become overemotional or let ego get in the way; stay on the topic; and keep using active listening skills regardless of disagreement with a speaker.

17. Be sure to clarify communication rules for group members. Set an agenda for meetings. Communication rules facilitate the flow of information, and an agenda provides direction for communication within the group.

18. Encourage upward communication from employees, even if the news is bad.

19. Don't forget the grapevine! Combat rumors carried by the grapevine by providing accurate information, discrediting the source of a rumor, or encouraging subordinates to recall facts or experiences of their own that are contrary to the rumor.

Review Questions

1. Define *communication*. What makes communication effective? Ineffective?

2. Explain the meaning of the spiritual child metaphor. Provide an example of the negative and positive outcomes experienced by persons within the spiritual child context.

3. Indicate the elements and processes involved in the sender-receiver model of communication.

4. What is the field of experience in communication and how is it applied?

5. Define *listening*. How can supervisors apply techniques such as paraphrasing and perception checking?

6. What does KISS mean?

7. How can defensiveness in communication be reduced?

8. Kinesics and proxemics are forms of nonverbal communication. Define each and indicate their impact in the communication process.

9. Only a small portion of interpersonal communication is actually expressed by words. How significant is nonverbal behavior relative to the verbal portion? Explain.

10. What is a sensitivity audit?

11. How does group size affect the communication process? Is there an ideal group size for effective problem solving or decision making? Explain.

12. What is the difference between hearing and listening in the communication process?
13. Indicate six strategies for improving communication within a work team.
14. What is a grapevine? Is it good or bad within an organization? Why so?

Notes

1. T. R. Mintzberg, *The Nature of Managerial Work* (New York: Harper and Row, 1973).
2. C. Downs and C. A. Conrad, "A Critical Incident Study of Effective Subordinancy," *Journal of Business Communication* 19 (1982): 27–28.
3. C. A. Conrad, *Strategic Organizational Communication* (New York: Holt, Rinehart and Winston, 1985).
4. R. Likert, "Motivational Approach to Management Development," *Harvard Business Review,* July–August 1959, 75–82.
5. S. W. King, "The Nature of Communication," in *Small Group Communication,* eds. R. S. Cathcart and L. A. Samovar (Dubuque, IA: Wm. C. Brown, 1988).
6. W. G. Scott and T. R. Mitchell, *Organizational Theory: A Structural and Behavioral Analysis* (Homewood, IL: Irwin, 1976).
7. Citation from J. Stewart, *Bridges Not Walls,* 2d ed. (Reading, MA: Addison-Wesley, 1977), 23–24. The spiritual child metaphor was developed by John Keltner and Loraine Halfen.
8. W. Johnson, "The Fateful Process of Mr. A Talking to Mr. B," *Harvard Business Review,* January–February 1953, 56.
9. R. Wilkinson, "Do You Speak Obscuranta?" *Supervision* 49 (1988): 3–5.
10. C. R. Rodgers, *On Becoming a Person* (Boston, MA: Houghton Mifflin, 1961).
11. E. Borman, *Interpersonal Communication in the Modern Organization,* 2d ed. (Englewood Cliffs, NJ: Prentice-Hall, 1982).
12. R. A. Baron, "Communication," in *People, Management, and Productivity,* eds. J. E. Garcia, C. T. Lewis, and F. Fiedler (Boston, MA: Allyn & Bacon, 1986), 34.
13. J. R. Gibb, "Defensive Communication," *Journal of Communication* 11 (1961): 141–148.
14. R. Fisher and W. Ury, *Getting to Yes: Negotiating Agreement Without Giving In* (Boston, MA: Houghton-Mifflin, 1981).
15. J. Fast, *Body Language* (New York: Pocket Books, 1970), 146.
16. A. Mehrabian, *Tactics of Social Influence* (Englewood Cliffs, NJ: Prentice-Hall, 1972).
17. P. Ekman, *Telling Lies: Clues to Deceit in the Marketplace, Politics, and Marriage* (New York: Norton, 1985).
18. K. L. Burns and E. G. Beier, "Significance of Vocal and Visual Channels in the Decoding of Emotional Meaning," *The Journal of Communication* 23 (1973): 118–130.
19. C. T. Lewis, J. E. Garcia, and S. M. Jobs, *Managerial Skills in Organizations* (Boston, MA: Allyn and Bacon, 1990).
20. E. T. Hall, *The Hidden Dimension* (New York: Doubleday, 1966).
21. G. L. Steele, *The Hacker's Dictionary* (New York: Harper & Row, 1983).
22. P. C. Morrow and J. C. McElron, "Interior Office Design and Visitor Responses: A Constructive Replication," *The Journal of Applied Psychology* 66 (1981): 646–650.
23. R. Y. Hirokawa and R. Pace, "A Descriptive Investigation of the Possible Communication-Based Reasons for Effective and Ineffective Group Decision Making," *Communication Monographs,* 1983, 362–379.
24. M. E. Shaw, *Group Dynamics: The Psychology of Small Group Behavior,* 3d ed. (New York: McGraw-Hill, 1981).
25. Adapted from J. Brownell, *Building Active Listening Skills* (Englewood Cliffs, NJ: Prentice-Hall, 1986), 249.
26. T. M. Scheidel and L. Crowell, *Discussing and Deciding* (New York: Macmillan, 1979).
27. Ibid., 12.
28. E. Haynes and L. Meltzer, "Interpersonal Judgments Based On Talkativeness: Fact or Artifact?" *Sociometry* 35 (1972): 538–561.
29. J. E. Baird and S. B. Weinberg, *Communication: The Essence of Group Synergy* (Dubuque, IA: Wm. C. Brown, 1977).

30. R. B. Adler and N. Towne, *Looking Out/Looking In* (New York: Holt, Rinehart and Winston, 1987).

31. J. K. Brilhart, *Effective Group Discussion* (Dubuque, IA: Wm. C. Brown, 1982).

32. S. Rosen, R. J. Grandison, and J. E. Stewart, "Discriminatory Buckpassing: Delegating Transmission of Bad News," *Organizational Behavior and Human Performance* 12 (1974): 249–263.

33. W. J. Lynott, "The Upward Communication Barrier," *Supervision* 45 (1983): 14–16.

34. E. Walton, "How Efficient is the Grapevine?" *Personnel* 28 (1961): 45–49.

Dear Fellow Employees

MEMORANDUM

FROM: *Harper W. Jones, President*
TO: *All Employees, Montfort Valve Company*
SUBJECT: *Money*
DATE: *December 2, 1993*

Dear Fellow Employees:

I am taking this means of posting this memo on all of our bulletin boards at Montfort Valve Company. For some time now, it has been apparent to me that many of you are not aware of, or do not read, the bulletin boards.

Therefore, I am going to test the system. At 5 p.m. tomorrow, Dec. 3, I will be in the company cafeteria and will distribute $5,000 in cash to be divided by the number of persons attending. Since there are 200 of us working here, the distribution of money could range from $5,000 (if I am the only one there) to $25 per employee if everyone is there.

You are welcome to tell your fellow workers who did not read this notice, or to keep the information to yourself and take home more money. I figure it will cost you a minimum of $25 for everyone you tell. On the other hand, you might make a lot of money tomorrow. See you then.

Questions

1. Is the memo a legitimate method for testing the effectiveness of the company's bulletin boards? Why?

2. If you were one of Montfort's employees and noticed the memo, would you tell a friend?

3. Does this form of communication check have any long-range values? If so, what benefits?

4. Suggest other procedures for testing the effectiveness of organizational communication systems.

C*O*M*M*U*N*I*C*A*T*I*O*N

The Synergistic Communication Systems workers had just completed the final phase of the new telephone system for Rorvick products, a manufacturer of medical supplies. Rorvick was a major U.S. producer of catgut sutures used to close surgical incisions. It was a subsidiary of a larger, well-known medical and consumer products company headquartered in the eastern part of the United States. The new plant, located entirely underground for sanitary reasons, was just getting into full production. Three hundred employees worked within the immaculate confines of the new facility.

Edward Anthony was the general manager of the new plant. In operation for less than a year, the plant was now achieving its projected production level. However, costs exceeded what was expected and some quality control problems had not yet been solved.

He spent a few minutes reading a telephone installation brochure that gave instructions for operating his new telephone. The unit possessed several features including a direct line to the company's headquarters, lines to the three department managers, a desk speaker system that amplified telephone calls so anyone in the room could hear, and a plant-wide intercommunication system that allowed him to make announcements to all employees. Over his new phone, Anthony called one of his department managers, Nancy Wiggins, to arrange a staff meeting in an hour in his office. Wiggins was in charge of the manufacturing department. Anthony requested Wiggins to bring her five supervisors to the meeting as the subject involved her department.

During the next hour, Anthony reviewed the latest production data, made a phone call to headquarters, and was just completing dictation of a letter via his phone to a recording unit in his secretary's office when the production manager and her supervisors entered his office. He pushed a couple of buttons on the phone to end the recording of the letter, motioned for everyone to sit down, informed his secretary that under no circumstances did he want to be interrupted, and began talking to his staff.

"I'm glad everyone could make it on such short notice. The reason I've called this meeting is to discuss some of the problems we are having in the manufacturing department and how we might solve them. It's no secret that there are some problems, as the grapevine has been active lately. What I'd like to know from each of you is exactly what you think is causing the production delays, why our scrappage is 25 percent higher than it should be, and any practical ideas you have about solutions. Then I want each of you to go down the list of your employees one by one. Tell me the best of the lot and the poorest, because one of our options is to cut back on our employment roster, perhaps by as much as 20 percent. I want you to be up front with me and lay it out as you see it."

For the following hour, Wiggins and her supervisors recited their opinions of the production problems, talked about the strengths and weaknesses of over 100 employees, and presented a number of alternatives for solving the problems. The discussion, at times, was very frank.

Finally, Anthony indicated that he had a good picture of what they were saying. During the session, he made numerous notes. He was about to summarize his thoughts to the group when he noticed, for the first time, that one of the red lights on his new telephone console was on. With eyes transfixed upon the light, he slowly extended his finger to the light and then to the inscription beside it which read Company Intercom System. For an instant, his corporate life flashed by, including past commendations and promotions. It was several minutes before he raised his eyes from the telephone to those of his managers.

"I think I may have created a problem for you," were his initial words, remembered until this day by all in the room.

Questions

1. What would/could the supervisors say to their own employees? How should they handle the matter?
2. What are the possible reactions of employees when they receive such sensitive and personal information?
3. Can you identify any parallel types of situations occurring in organizations?
4. Any ideas about the company's future grapevine operations?

CHAPTER 14
Appraising Performance

● The best evidence of merit is the cordial recognition of it whenever and wherever it may be found.

Christian Bovee[1]

LEARNING OBJECTIVES

1. Define performance appraisal and its purpose in organizations.
2. Indicate appropriate performance appraisal criteria along with problems associated with use of personal criteria.
3. Explain the Management by Objectives method as it applies to performance appraisal.
4. Discuss how to conduct the performance review, including the importance of providing employee feedback.
5. Know the types of rating errors that can occur in the performance appraisal process and how to control them.
6. Understand the dynamics of the appraisal process within work teams.

"Hi, Carla."

"Hi, Larry."

"Please sit down. Let's get down to it. I hate these performance reviews."

"I do too. But you know, Larry, I could really use some constructive feedback."

"Yeah . . . well, here's the thing, Carla. You do a good job, but I'd still like you to try harder. Be a little easier on your people and try to show a little more team spirit."

"Good job? Try harder? Be easier? . . . What are you talking about?"

"It's really not a big deal, Carla. Look, I'll tell you what. Why don't you complete the appraisal form for me. Evaluate yourself as though you were me, and I'll sign it. How's that sound?" Larry grinned.

Carla and Larry shared meaningless pleasantries for a few more minutes. Carla grabbed the appraisal form and walked out the door.

"Have that to me by this Monday!"

Performance appraisal is an important part of organizational life regardless of organization type. For example, parents evaluate their children, teachers evaluate students, friends evaluate each other, and supervisors evaluate members of their work teams.

Supervisors are a particularly important part of a performance appraisal review system. Performance appraisal is usually conducted by an employee's

immediate supervisor. About 93 percent of performance appraisal programs require immediate supervisors to take responsibility for evaluating their employees' performance.[2] Feedback provided by supervisors during performance appraisal is typically the employees' primary source of information about their performance. Feedback helps workers know how to improve productivity. (See Chapters 1, 8, 11, and 13 for more discussion of feedback.)

What Is Performance Appraisal?

performance appraisal
The periodic assessment of employee job performance and behavior.

Performance appraisal is the periodic assessment of employee job performance and behavior. If conducted well, performance appraisal is an important part of improving performance. It also helps the organization to assure legal compliance in employment-related areas.

Performance appraisal directly affects performance through feedback provided to employees. People perform better if they know how well they are doing. Information from performance appraisal also influences other human resource management areas affecting productivity. These areas include compensation, training and development, and staffing. It is more productive to reward, promote, transfer, and terminate employees based on an assessment of their performance. Performance appraisal is the mechanism that provides for this assessment.

Performance appraisal is affected by legal issues and requirements. In today's litigious environment, supervisors need to understand legal requirements and issues pertaining to performance appraisal and the human resources areas it affects. The proper application of performance appraisal helps protect the organization from legal reprisals.

Getting Started

A good starting place for supervisors when improving performance appraisal is a careful assessment of the organization's existing appraisal system. The effective supervisor should read company or organization policies and procedures manuals pertaining to performance appraisal to gain a thorough understanding of whatever system is already in place.

The next step is defining the performance to be appraised. This may sound simple, but it often is not. Many organizations do not have up-to-date job descriptions outlining all work activities associated with an employee's position. (Preparation of job descriptions is discussed in more detail in Chapter 8.) A supervisor needs to obtain an accurate description of each job in his or her work group.

Evaluation Criteria

evaluation criteria
Standards against which to assess an employee's attributes, motivation, abilities, skills, knowledge, or behaviors.

The primary reason for having accurate job descriptions is to establish valid evaluation criteria. **Evaluation criteria** are standards against which to assess an employee's attributes, motivation, abilities, skills, knowledge, or behaviors.[3] (Chapter 3's discussion of validity and validation provides insight into what valid evaluation criteria might be.) To summarize, valid evaluation criteria are criteria that predict employee success; match the content of the job; or capture the essence of the job being appraised.

Performance appraisal is part of everyday life—whether informal, or a formal appraisal on the road, in the workplace, or elsewhere.

Supervisors sometimes encounter a situation in which the organization's performance appraisal instrument doesn't include the evaluation criteria that should be covered. Most instruments provide for open-ended comments, however. Consequently, a supervisor who has accurately determined evaluation criteria can usually incorporate this understanding into an appraisal.

There has been considerable debate regarding which evaluation criteria are best. Some supervisors prefer performance appraisals that employ definable, observable evaluation criteria based on employee behavior or output. These evaluation criteria are referred to as **performance criteria.** Typing speed and production output are examples of performance criteria.

Many supervisors like the ease of use and simplicity of appraisals based upon the use of **personal criteria.** Personal criteria are based upon traits or innate characteristics of employees. Examples of personal criteria include personality traits such as dependability, loyalty, team play, and initiative.

Performance Appraisal Methods

Figure 14–1 illustrates a **graphic rating scale** that makes use of personal criteria. Graphic rating scales display either a continuum or separate categories of potential performance for each job dimension. These scales are often organized using adjectives (as in Figure 14-1), numbers (for example, a scale of 1 to 5), or descriptions of behavior.

Problems with Personal Criteria

Performance appraisal methods that use personal criteria lead to vague feedback. It is especially difficult to provide specific, meaningful feedback on personality traits, which the employee usually cannot change. Moreover, performance feedback that does occur is compromised because actual behavior or performance is only described in general terms (for example, Bob's work performance was "fair"). *Specific* feedback is an important part of performance appraisal because it contributes to employee development and increased productivity.[4] (See Figure 14-2.)

performance criteria
Evaluation standards based on employee behavior or output that are definable and observable.

personal criteria
Evaluation standards based upon traits or innate characteristics of employees such as personality traits of dependability, loyalty, team play, and initiative.

graphic rating scale
A personal criteria appraisal instrument that describes employee performance by using adjectives, numbers, or descriptions of behavior.

| **Figure 14-1** | A Graphic Rating Scale Using Personal Criteria |

	Excellent	Good	Fair	Poor
Name _____		Date _____		
Rater _____		Department _____		
1. Team play	____	____	____	____
2. Dependability	____	____	____	____
3. Cooperation	____	____	____	____
4. Quality of work	____	____	____	____
Overall Performance	____	____	____	____

Another problem with using personal evaluation criteria concerns potential legal challenges based upon the results of performance appraisal. Subjective performance appraisal methods have not been well received by the courts. In *Albermarle Paper Company v. Moody*, the U.S. Supreme Court determined that performance appraisal ratings were legally tests, and found that Albermarle Paper Company's rating procedures were too vague and overly influenced by individual interpretation to be valid.[5] In *Rowe v. General Motors* the Fifth Circuit Court of Appeals found that subjective determinations of "ability, merit, and capacity" had an adverse impact on black employees.[6]

Performance appraisal that evaluates observable, measurable behavior or output associated with a job, based upon the dictates of a job description developed through job analysis, stands on firmer legal ground than does appraisal that focuses on personal characteristics of the employee.

Performance appraisal that emphasizes personal criteria is also more dissatisfying to employees than is appraisal that emphasizes employee behavior and performance.[7] In this situation, employees may understandably feel that their personality is being criticized, rather than their work performance. It is also more difficult to train supervisors when personal criteria are used. Supervisors can be trained to observe performance, but not to accurately observe and record a personality trait such as loyalty.

The primary advantage of building personal criteria into an appraisal instrument is that it makes instruments easy to design, understand, and use. These advantages may be illusionary, however, if performance is reduced and legal challenges occur.

Figure 14-2 "Keep Up the Good Work . . ."

"Keep up the good work, whatever it is, whoever you are."

Source: Drawing by Stevenson; © 1988 The New Yorker Magazine, Inc.

Less Subjective Appraisal Methods

A less subjective way to design rating scales is to use specific, observable employee behavior.

We use the term *less subjective* to emphasize the fact that all performance appraisal involves some subjective judgment. Evaluating performance is not cut and dried. Ultimately, supervisors must make judgments about individual employees. The supervisor is not just a passive recorder of information, but functions as an evaluator-judge.[8]

BARS and BOS.   Two less subjective modifications of the basic graphic rating scale format are **behaviorally anchored rating scales (BARS)** and **behavior observation scales (BOS).** BARS and BOS focus upon evaluating specific behaviors rather than traits or characteristics.[9]

BARS requires that supervisors assess behaviors associated with a dimension of a job. In contrast to BARS, BOS requires that supervisors indicate the *frequency* that different behaviors occur, and must respond to *all* behaviors associated with a position. Note the differences between BARS and BOS in Figure 14-3.

Personal criteria are not explicitly included in these instruments. This does not mean that personal criteria are excluded as evaluation criteria altogether. However, rather than frame a scale item in terms of an innate characteristic such as an employee's attitude, BARS and BOS instruments allow supervisors to rate observable behaviors and output levels which employees with "good" (or "bad" or "indifferent") attitudes normally exhibit.

BARS and BOS emphasize observable, measurable behavior. In other words, these instruments focus upon what employees do, rather than on who employees are. Constructive criticism can then be provided by the supervisor, if needed. The critique focuses upon job behavior rather than on characteristics of the person such as personality traits. Besides increasing employee satisfaction, this advantage plays an important role in increasing productivity because, as noted previously, specific feedback tied to goal performance improves productivity. (This concept is also discussed in Chapter 7.)

The primary problem with BARS and BOS is that these methods are relatively costly to develop and to maintain. A different instrument may be required for each position because behavioral requirements usually differ by position. Of course, if behaviors are the same across a class of jobs, one instrument will suffice.

Management by Objectives.   Management by objectives (MBO) is a collaborative setting of goals between a supervisor and his or her superior (or the supervisor and members of the work team) and a joint determination of the criteria to be used for evaluating that supervisor's performance in achieving those goals. MBO also becomes a performance appraisal method that focuses on results, using employee goal attainment as the evaluation criterion. (For more information about MBO, refer to Chapter 5.)

A crucial element to the success of MBO is the setting of goals that are hard, but achievable and that are specific, measurable, and have a definite time frame for accomplishment. Employees benefit from having clear targets. Vague goals are little better than having no goals at all. (See Chapter 11's discussion of goal setting for further discussion of this point.)

The distinction between MBO and behavioral performance appraisal methods (such as BARS or BOS) is not as great as you might think. Both appraisal approaches use performance evaluation criteria. The primary difference between MBO and behaviorally oriented performance appraisal is that MBO

An effective supervisor functions much like a fair and impartial judge when he or she appraises employee performance.

behaviorally anchored rating scales (BARS)
A graphic performance rating scale requiring behavioral assessment associated with a job.

behavior observation scales (BOS)
A graphic performance rating scale similar to BARS but requiring measurement of the frequency of occurrence of types of various job related behaviors.

Figure 14-3 Less Subjective Appraisal Methods: BARS and BOS Scales

An example of a behaviorally anchored rating scale (BARS):

Leadership—The Demonstrated Ability to Motivate Others

7 — This employee leads work groups that consistently exceed stated performance goals. Criticisms of leadership style by subordinates are exceedingly rare regardless of circumstances.

5 — Work groups usually exceed performance goals. Criticisms of leadership style would not be expected under normal circumstances.

3 — Performance of work groups is often less than established standards. Criticisms of leadership style are sometimes heard by management. Group performance is occasionally impeded by conflict with the leader. Formal grievances may have been filed.

1 — Group performance is deficient. Goals are seldom met. Criticisms of leadership style occur at frequent intervals. Formal grievances can be expected to have been filed.

An example of a behavior observation scale (BOS):

Leadership—The Demonstrated Ability to Motivate Others

Maintains composure under stress.

| Almost Never | 1 | 2 | 3 | 4 | 5 | Almost Always |

Deals effectively with employee problems (listens, takes action, follows through).

| Almost Never | 1 | 2 | 3 | 4 | 5 | Almost Always |

Treats workers fairly (assigns job evenly, plays no favorites).

| Almost Never | 1 | 2 | 3 | 4 | 5 | Almost Always |

Represents subordinates fairly to upper management levels (e.g., investigates problems, backs subordinates up where appropriate, protects subordinates from inappropriate pressure).

| Almost Never | 1 | 2 | 3 | 4 | 5 | Almost Always |

Maintains cooperation with other foremen (e.g., shares information, leaves area in good shape for next shift).

| Almost Never | 1 | 2 | 3 | 4 | 5 | Almost Always |

Total = _____

Source: C. T. Lewis, J. E. Garcia, and S. M. Jobs, *Managerial Skills in Organizations* (Boston, MA: Allyn and Bacon, 1990), 156.

---

does not explicitly define the behaviors that drive performance. MBO defines performance in terms of goal attainment, rather than in terms of the productive behaviors *leading* to achieving goals.

Other Performance Appraisal Methods

MBO and graphic rating scale formats are used by most organizations. These methods are easy for managers to understand and are relatively inexpensive to maintain.

A wide range of other performance appraisal methods are available, aside from MBO, BARS, BOS, and graphic rating scales. The following is a representative list of alternative appraisal methods:

Weighted checklists: A list of adjectives is provided for each position and points are awarded for each favorable adjective the rater checks.

Critical incidents: Successful performance is based upon practice of behavior deemed critical to success on the job. The standards for determining critical behavior are derived from supervisors, and sometimes employees. The evaluation requires writing incidents of an employee's past job behavior that describe effective and ineffective performance.

Ranking techniques: Here, employees are evaluated on a relative, rather than absolute, standard. Employees are compared to each other and ranked by performance.

Assessment centers: Job candidates are evaluated through systematic interviewing, tests, exercises, and simulation. (This method was first used to select officers by the German high command during World War II.)

The Performance Review: Feedback

In **performance review,** a supervisor and an employee periodically discuss performance appraisal results. Performance reviews are effective to the extent they are specific, timely, impersonal, noticeable, and frequent.[10]

Specific feedback involves relaying to employees precisely what they did well or did not do well. Speaking in general terms, such as "Well, Bob, you did a good job on the Anderson account, but you could have done better with the Higgins account," fails to tell Bob how his performance could have been improved. What is meant by "good" or "bad"? Specific behavior or performance measures are much more informative, and more likely to help Bob improve his performance in the future. For example, "Bob, you completed executive summaries for all meetings with Mr. Anderson" or "Bob, you were late to all four meetings with Mr. Higgins."

Performance reviews should be timely. With timely reviews, deviations from preferred behavior and performance can be corrected so that individual or group objectives can be reached. Performance is increased to the extent deviations from standards are corrected in a timely manner.

Feedback should be relatively impersonal. This does not mean the supervisor should be cold. Rather, as noted previously, feedback based upon personality traits leads to employee dissatisfaction. Performance appraisal based on behavior and/or output eliminates this problem to a large extent. Even if the performance appraisal does emphasize personal criteria, supervisors should still try to stress that they are critiquing performance on the job, rather than innate characteristics of the employee.

Feedback needs to be noticeable. Obviously, if feedback is to improve productivity, it must be acknowledged by the employee. Carroll and Schneier suggest that employees might be encouraged to test their own performance and give themselves feedback. For example, employees could establish production goals and compare their performance to those goals. Or have employees write an

performance review
A periodic meeting between a supervisor and employee to discuss the employee's performance appraisal results.

acknowledgement to supervisors based upon the results of a performance review. The acknowledgement might take the form of a personal action plan describing steps to correct deficiencies and ways to build upon past success.

Frequent performance review can contribute significantly to the success of a performance appraisal system. Frequent feedback is not the same thing as "close supervision." Performance review sessions should be planned, and carried out in locations providing privacy between employee and supervisor. Frequent reviews tell employees that management is committed to performance appraisal and is not simply paying lip service to a management fad. Frequent reviews also provide for timely corrective action. Several studies indicate that frequent feedback contributes to higher employee satisfaction with supervisors.

"Frequent performance review" is a relative term. What is frequent (and necessary) for one employee may not be for another. One approach suggests that the timing of reviews should depend primarily upon the results of past appraisal. High performers should be reviewed less frequently than employees who are having difficulty.[11]

Beware of Negative Feedback!

Negative feedback often reduces productivity. In a classic study, Meyer, Kay, and French reported that employees who "received an above-average number of criticisms . . . generally showed *less* goal achievement 10 to 12 weeks later than those who had received fewer criticisms."[12] These findings are consistent with our earlier discussion of increased employee dissatisfaction resulting from negative feedback.

How should a supervisor deliver negative feedback? Clearly, avoiding feedback is not the solution to this problem. At the same time, the primary purpose of a performance appraisal system is to improve performance, and the study cited above indicates that negative feedback may hurt performance. How can the problem of conveying negative feedback be reconciled?

It is difficult to constructively criticize performance. Nevertheless, employees are more receptive to negative feedback if they are allowed to participate in the performance review, plans and objectives are discussed, and they are evaluated on factors relevant to their work.[13] Supervisors need to carefully separate criticism of the person as an employee from criticism of the employee as a person. (Conflict management and communication skills covered in Chapters 12 and 13 can be effective in improving the delivery of bad news.)

Supervisory Training for Performance Appraisal

Rater Errors

rater errors
A systematic recording of invalid impressions by a rater.

contrast effect errors
When comparisons between employees are not explicitly intended but still affect appraisal outcomes.

An otherwise well-conceived appraisal system will still fail if supervisors are not adequately trained. Our discussion of training begins with a review of rating errors. **Rater errors** involve a systematic recording of invalid impressions by a rater. Common errors include contrast effects, leniency, central tendency, severity, halo errors, and attributional biases.

An employee could be doing a good job, and still receive a poor evaluation because his or her performance was implicitly compared with the superior performance of another employee doing comparable work. **Contrast effect errors** occur when comparisons between employees are not explicitly intended, but still affect appraisal outcomes. For example, instructors who promise to grade students on the basis of a standard scale, rather than on a curve, should not be influenced by overall class performance when grading an individual student.

Is a student "above average" if he or she earns a grade point average of over 3.0? You might think so. A letter grade of "B" (or 3.0) usually indicates above-average performance. Unfortunately, average grades at many colleges and universities run above 3.0! "Grade inflation" is one example of **leniency errors.** Leniency errors result when a supervisor consistently and inaccurately evaluates employees near the top of a scale. Evaluations can also be consistently in the middle or at the bottom of a scale. Psychologists refer to these as **central tendency errors** and **severity errors,** respectively.

Leniency errors in performance appraisal are common. Sixty-two percent of 267 corporations surveyed mentioned inflated ratings as their most severe performance appraisal problem.[14] Probably the main reason for inflated ratings is that supervisors don't like to be harbingers of bad news. Still, it is important that supervisors work through this hesitation. Legal problems—and the payment of large settlements by the employer—occur when fired employees later show favorable appraisals to the court. Also, employee performance is compromised if problems are not noted and corrected.

Individuals in a work group sometimes all do poor, average, or excellent work. Individual ratings that reflect this consistency are *not* invalid. Under such circumstances it is more accurate to speak of a "leniency effect," rather than a "leniency error."[15] (Refer to Chapter 3 and the discussion of validity.)

Halo effects occur when a rater overgeneralizes from one aspect of an employee's performance to all other aspects of his or her performance. The receptionist who does a good job of "meeting the public" might be rated as doing a good job of record-keeping when his performance has, in fact, been poor.

Finally, employees may receive differential treatment because of the attributional bias of a rater. (See Chapter 7 for further discussion of attributional bias.) For example, Bob might be deemed successful because he is a hard worker and might be promoted. Alice, employed in the same job and doing the same quality and quantity of work, might be perceived to be simply lucky and denied a promotion. The search for attributions typically occurs when people are unable to clearly categorize observed behavior. Because we live in a complex world characterized by imperfect information, attributions are a daily fact of life.

Inaccurate attributions in performance appraisal can often be traced to inadequate or otherwise incomplete information about an employee. Under these circumstances, the supervisor's personality plays an important role in filling in missing information. Because of this, performance ratings are often as much a function of the personality of the rater as they are a function of the performance of the person being rated![16] Supervisors should be aware of the potential for attributional bias and avoid it whenever they can, although some bias probably is inevitable.

Reducing Rater Error

Training programs are systematic, structured attempts to improve the validity of ratings by training raters so that rater error is reduced. (See Chapter 9 for further discussions of training.) One of the most important considerations in training raters is to focus training on what to observe, rather than on how to or how not to rate.[17]

---

leniency errors
Consistent and inaccurate evaluation of employees wherein all are considered near the top of a scale.

central tendency errors
Inaccurate evaluation of employees wherein all are consistently considered to be in the middle of a scale.

severity errors
Inaccurate evaluation of employees wherein all are consistently considered to be at the bottom of a scale.

halo effects
Occur when a rater overgeneralizes from one aspect of an employee's performance to all other aspects of his or her performance.

The "Lake Wobegon Effect"

All kinds of tests are subject to rating errors.

According to Chester E. Finn, past Assistant Secretary for Educational Research and Improvement, parents and children are being fooled by standardized achievement tests in which most students' scores are declared above average. Finn labeled this phenomenon the Lake Wobegon Effect, because in the mythical town of Lake Wobegon (invented by author and radio personality Garrison Keillor), "All of the women are strong, all of the men are good-looking, and all of the children are above average."[18]

For example, a training program that teaches supervisors how to rate performance by avoiding leniency could result in highly invalid ratings if a particular group of employees all exhibit superior performance. If the performance of a particular group of employees does not approximate a normal distribution of performance, teaching raters how to evaluate by requiring that ratings fall within a bell-shaped curve will be invalid.

Supervisors instead should be trained to concentrate on observable behavior and output and to ignore factors that do not relate to the job.[19] A focus on teaching supervisors to correctly observe behavior is critical to increasing rater accuracy.[20] With this consideration, it is obvious that performance appraisal based on performance criteria is much more amenable to rater training than is appraisal based upon personal criteria, such as personality traits.

Traits such as enthusiasm and intelligence are difficult to explicitly observe. Consequently, the supervisor must overly rely on subjective judgment of what constitutes enthusiasm and intelligence. An overemphasis on subjective judgment contributes to rater error, particularly attributional bias. On the other hand, enthusiastic and intelligent behaviors can be defined and supervisors can be trained to observe their occurrence in the job setting.

The preceding discussion covered how you, as a supervisor, should be trained to rate employees. Supervisors usually have little control over the content of performance appraisal training programs, however, so what is the point of this discussion? Simply put, having an understanding of training outcomes will either help you assess the quality of training you receive or, because few organizations actually offer performance appraisal training, will alert you to what to look for when assessing performance. (Refer to Chapters 2 and 9 for more information about training.)

Performance Appraisal within the Work Team

The focus of performance appraisal is on the interplay between the supervisor and individual employee. Still, some considerations involve groups.

peer evaluation
A form of performance appraisal in which members of a work team evaluate each other's performance.

Peer Evaluation

Peer evaluation is a form of performance appraisal in which members of a work team evaluate each other's performance. It is uncommon despite favorable reviews regarding the validity and resistance to bias of this method.[21]

Peers usually have a good understanding of work requirements and are often in a better position to observe work performance than are supervisors. Problems with peer assessment include friendship bias and the adverse effect of negative feedback upon employees. Also, coworkers often dislike being accountable for evaluating peers.

Cascio has noted that friendship bias, and the counterproductive effect of negative feedback by peers, might be significantly reduced if performance criteria are clearly specified.[22] Peer assessment should be avoided within highly competitive work groups, however, because of possible self-serving manipulation of results.

In any event, peer evaluation should be used in conjunction with other rating efforts or self ratings by the employee. Peer evaluation should be viewed as a way to validate performance appraisal results from other sources, rather than as a sole means of evaluation.

Obtain approval from the human resources office or your boss if you, as a supervisor, decide to implement peer evaluation. Otherwise, you may inadvertently violate an agreement that exists between management and a union or employee association.

Group Objectives

Management by Objectives (MBO) also works with group objectives. As the name implies, **group objectives** are goals set for the entire work team. Team objectives are effective with interdependent work groups. An interdependent work team is one in which it is difficult or impossible to separate individual effort or results. The team either succeeds or fails as a group.

Group objectives are also useful with temporary work groups or project teams in work environments characterized by rapid change. Group measures also tend to be effective when used with employees motivated by affiliation with coworkers, that is, where individual employees have a strong desire to be accepted by a work group.[23]

group objectives
Goals set for an entire work team, effective with interdependent work groups in which it is impossible to separate individual effort or results within the team.

Equity Theory

An ongoing challenge for the effective supervisor is the need to be fair. It is not easy to balance rewards within a work group. Perceptions of employees about the fairness of rewards are not always accurate. Unfortunately, the *perception* of fairness counts more than the reality.

Equity theory (also covered in Chapter 11) provides a conceptual framework for understanding fairness in the workplace. This theory holds that employees compare the ratio of their inputs into a job (such as education, experience, or effort) and outcomes from a job (such as praise from a supervisor or promotion) with the ratio of inputs and outcomes of "comparison others."[24] That is, the standard used by employees for judging fairness is relative rather than absolute. For example, an employee could be dissatisfied with a good performance appraisal rating if a less productive coworker also receives a good rating.

How do supervisors conduct fair performance appraisal? Basing evaluation criteria on job descriptions, emphasizing performance measures based on employee behavior and outcomes, and conducting constructive performance reviews all contribute to improving employee perceptions of fair performance appraisal. Employee perceptions of fairness should be regarded as a by-product, rather than as the objective, of effective performance appraisal. Supervisors should place themselves in employees' shoes and try to understand and maintain fairness from the employees' perspective.

Carla completed her appraisal form for Larry. That Monday, she stood before him in his office with form in hand.

"Well, here it is, boss. I give myself all 5s. I'm the best employee in the division."

"Well, that's okay by me. These appraisals are just a waste of time anyway."

"Larry, how would you feel if I evaluated my team the way you evaluated me?"

"That's different, Carla. You've got to stay on top of the worker bees."

"You mean by telling each of them to 'work harder' and to be a better 'team player'? Don't you feel that's too vague?"

"Yeah, but that's the way it is . . ."

"Hey, Larry," Carla abruptly interrupted, "You know, you really should dress better."

"What do you mean by that, Carla?"

"Figure it out yourself," Carla replied with a grin, dropping her appraisal form on Larry's desk with a flourish.

Summary: Focus on Skills

Performance appraisal is the periodic assessment of employee performance and behavior. The primary purpose of performance appraisal is to improve productivity and quality of goods and services produced by individuals and groups within an organization. A secondary purpose is to assure the organization is in compliance with employment-related legal requirements.

Following are 11 suggestions to help supervisors conduct effective, valid performance appraisals:

1. As much as possible, employ evaluation criteria that define performance in terms of behavior and output (performance criteria), rather than in terms of individual personality or traits (personal criteria).
2. Translate personal criteria into behaviorally defined scales when possible. If this is difficult or impossible to do, consider using an MBO format.
3. When using MBO, establish goals that are "hard, but achievable," specific, measurable, and state a specific time period for attainment.
4. Provide feedback to employees that is specific, timely, impersonal, noticeable, and frequent.
5. Be aware of and try to avoid rating errors and biases such as the contrast effect, leniency, central tendency, severity, halo effect, and attributional biases.
6. Learn what to observe in performance appraisal, rather than how to or how not to rate.
7. Learn communication and conflict management skills in order to improve the quality of performance reviews.
8. Consider incorporating peer evaluations from work team members into performance appraisal as one source (not the only source) of information.
9. Consider using an MBO format, with group objectives, when working with a highly interdependent work team.
10. Realize that group performance is best supported if team members believe performance appraisal is fair.
11. Remember that employee views of fairness are relative, not absolute, and are based on perceptions, not necessarily on reality.

Review Questions

1. Define performance appraisal.
2. What are evaluation criteria? Valid criteria?
3. Indicate the problems associated with using personal criteria.
4. Why are less subjective appraisal methods such as BARS and BOS superior?
5. How can Management by Objectives be applied to performance appraisal?
6. Cite the four major characteristics found in effective performance appraisal reviews. Briefly explain each.
7. Why should supervisors be cautious in giving employees negative feedback?
8. Indicate and explain the meaning of the six forms of errors and biases that can reduce the effectiveness of performance appraisal.
9. Explain the meaning of the following: "One of the most important considerations in training raters is to focus training upon *what* to observe, rather than how to or how not to rate."
10. What is peer evaluation? Suggest the problems related to such evaluations. Under what conditions can they be effective, and when should they not be used?

Notes

1. Bill Weisz, *The Philosophy Memos: Articles, Speeches and Quotations* (Schaumburg, IL: Motorola University Press, 1993), 42.
2. N. J. Bernadin and R. W. Beatty, *Performance Appraisal: Assessing Human Behavior at Work* (Boston, MA: Kent, 1984).
3. P. C. Smith, "Behaviors, Results, and Organizational Effectiveness: The Problem of Criteria," in *Handbook of Industrial and Occupational Psychology*, ed. M. D. Dunnette (Chicago, IL: Rand McNally, 1976).
4. E. A. Locke, "Toward a Theory of Task Motivation and Incentives," *Organizational Behavior and Human Performance* 3 (1968): 157–189. Also, E. A. Locke and C. P. Latham, *Goal-Setting: A Motivational Technique That Works!* (Englewood Cliffs, NJ: Prentice-Hall, 1984).
5. *Albermarle Paper Company v. Moody* (1975), U.S. Supreme Court Nos. 74–389 and 74–428, 10 FEP Cases 1181.
6. *Rowe v. General Motors* (1972), 4 FEP 445.
7. R. J. Burke, W. Weitzel, and T. Weir, "Characteristics of Effective Employee Performance Review and Development Interviews: Replication and Extension," *Personnel Psychology* 31 (1978): 903–919.
8. B. R. Nathan and R. A. Alexander, "The Role of Inferential Accuracy in Performance Rating," *Academy of Management Review* 10 (1985): 109–115.
9. S. J. Carroll and C. E. Schneier, *Performance Appraisal and Review Systems* (Glenview, IL: Scott, Foresman and Company, 1982).
10. Also, see S. J. Carroll and H. L. Tosi, "Goal Characteristics and Personality Factors in a Management by Objective Program," *Administrative Science Quarterly* 15 (1970): 295–305.
11. L. L. Cummings and D. P. Schwab, *Performance in Organizations: Determinants and Appraisal* (Glenview, IL: Scott, Foresman and Company, 1973).
12. H. Meyer, E. Kay and J. R. P. French, "Split Roles in Performance Appraisal," *Harvard Business Review* 43 (1965): 123–129.
13. R. L. Dipboye and R. Pontbriand, "Correlates of Employee Reactions to Performance Appraisals and Appraisal Systems," *Journal of Applied Psychology (Short Notes)* 66 (1981): 248–251.
14. "Performance Appraisals—Reappraised," *Management Review* 72 (1983): 5–6.
15. M. D. Hakel, "An Appraisal of Performance Appraisal: Sniping with a Shotgun," paper presented at Scientist-Practitioner Conference in IO Psychology, Virginia Beach, VA,

1980. Also, W. F. Cascio, *Applied Psychology in Personnel Management*, 3d ed. (Englewood Cliffs, NJ: Prentice-Hall, 1987).

16. M. D. Hakel, "Normative Personality Factors Recovered from Ratings of Personality Descriptors: The Beholder's Eye," *Personnel Psychology* 27 (1974): 409–421.

17. H. J. Bernadin and E. C. Pence, "Effects of Rater Training: Creating New Response Sets and Decreasing Accuracy," *Journal of Applied Psychology* 65 (1980): 60–66.

18. "Norms above Average in Standardized Tests," *The Everett Herald*, Everett, WA, February 10, 1988, 1.

19. C. H. Fay and G. P. Latham, "Effects of Training and Rating Scales on Rating Errors," *Personnel Psychology* 35 (1982): 105–116.

20. J. W. Hedge and M. J. Kavanaugh, "Improving the Accuracy of Performance Evaluations: Comparison of Three Methods of Performance Appraiser Training," *Journal of Applied Psychology* 73 (1988): 68–73.

21. Cascio, *Applied Psychology in Personnel Management*.

22. Ibid.

23. Carroll and Schneier, *Performance Appraisal and Review Systems*.

24. J. S. Adams, "Inequity in Social Exchange," in *Advances in Experimental Social Psychology*, ed. L. Berkowitz (New York: Academic Press, 1965).

Nancy Partin

During the past 18 years, Nancy Partin has owned and managed a women's sportswear store in Houston, Texas. Starting in the basement of her house, Partin has moved several times over the years from small shopping centers to larger ones until now her store occupies a prominent location in one of Houston's newest and largest regional shopping centers. Partin employs 12 people, evenly divided between full- and part-time employees.

Recently, Partin attended a three-day management development program in Cincinnati, Ohio. Three topics of the meeting especially interested her. One pertained to employee performance appraisal. She learned that *all* employees should receive periodical appraisals and feedback, regardless of the size of operation of the employer. The second pertained to employee motivation. How do you motivate employees in small businesses?

The third topic considered employee empowerment. Until attending the meeting, Partin had never seriously considered the concept of empowerment as it would be applied to her employees. She thought with so few employees and such frequent contact with them, appraising, motivating, and empowering them would be a waste of time. Partin wondered if these subjects had *any* application to her business.

Questions

1. Does Partin really need to be concerned about performance appraisal, motivating, and empowering her employees in such a small business?

2. What methods would be most appropriate for conducting performance appraisals? Explain.

3. What are the opportunities and limitations for establishing methods for motivating employees in a small business? Describe the methods for motivating you would suggest applying.

4. How can you empower employees in small businesses? First, consider the meaning of empowerment and, then, consider the means/methods to utilize.

The Resident Assistant

A feature of many college campuses is the presence of student housing consisting of dormitories and graduate-student quarters. A Director of Student Housing is in charge. The director's job calls for a person who can work with younger people and who will provide much of the dormitory staffing by hiring resident assistants (RAs). In turn, the capacity of the RAs to implement college policies and rules, and still maintain some semblance of harmony among dorm residents, is critically important. Otherwise, anarchy can result. RAs need to get along with and obtain the confidence of dorm residents. It is not an easy task by any means. Good RAs probably possess many of the characteristics and the temperaments of effective supervisors.

Each school year, the director and staff select new RAs to replace those graduating or those who are casualties of the previous year's dormitory wars. The head RA for each dorm will have one or more assistants for each floor, but with large dorms, another level of administration is often created. It is not uncommon for half, or more, of a head RA's group to be new to the job.

RAs spend their on-duty time performing a variety of activities such as lowering the noise level of Room 612, talking with a distraught student who has just flunked a calculus exam or broken up with a very close friend, assisting a dorm resident in locating his room, or just checking to see how the residents are doing. RAs are available for duty during several daylight hours and usually during the early night periods. They also attend periodic staff meetings. To some extent, they work with other RAs or call upon them when problems arise such as quelling a riot. The opportunity for group cohesiveness to develop varies among institutions. In some, close relationships form while in others RAs function more as independent contractors to be undisturbed except in emergencies.

In conclusion, RAs typically have the responsibility of maintaining dormitory law and order with a low profile of formal authority. Those who are successful are accepted and, to some degree, obeyed by their residents. Those who are not successful yearn—with a passion—for graduation to arrive.

Questions

1. Assume that you are a head resident assistant of a dormitory. You are in charge of the building, responsible for its occupants and what goes on in the building. How would you evaluate the performance of your RAs?
2. How would you proceed to create an effective group of RAs?
3. Describe the behavior of your RA staff members if you and they are successful. What situations would indicate they were encountering problems? What could you do to help them?

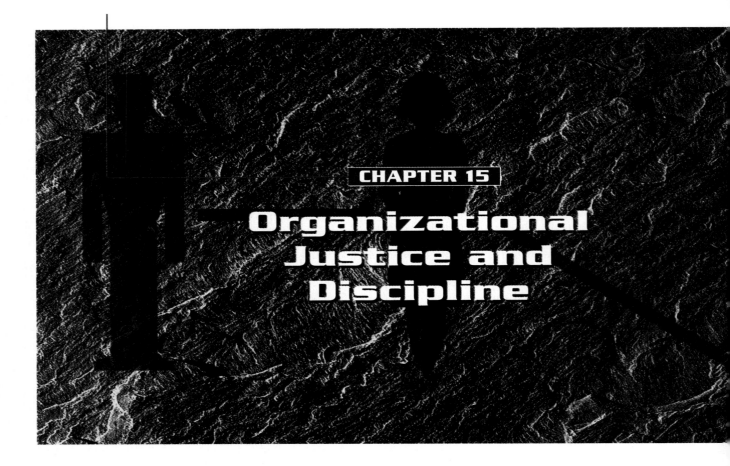

CHAPTER 15

Organizational Justice and Discipline

● I was fired the same way I was hired—with enthusiasm.

Clark Kerr[1]
Former President of the University of California

LEARNING OBJECTIVES

1. Define organizational justice and explain its two major components, descriptive justice and corrective justice.
2. Differentiate between the terms *complaints* and *grievances.*
3. Describe the concept of silent grievers and indicate the several types of silent grievers.
4. Define organizational discipline and give the reasons why supervisors may not apply discipline.
5. Demonstrate how to test the reasonableness of disciplinary actions.
6. Explain the several types of disciplinary action including the application of progressive discipline and the hot stove rule analogy.
7. Indicate the meaning of nonpunitive discipline and how it operates.
8. Describe the characteristics of an effective grievance procedure.
9. Discuss the principles applied to conducting a correctional interview.

During the previous 10 minutes or so, Carla had been talking with Jerry Morrison, a newly designated shop steward for the union representing Carla's group of workers.

"Probably the thing I like least about my job is having to take disciplinary action against one of my employees," Carla related to Jerry. "There seems to be a philosophy in my division of not 'rocking the boat' and 'if there is pain, make it go away'—at least that is the way I understand it. My boss, Larry, is afraid of the unions and has told me several times, grievances filed by members of my unit can make my management career very short. I'm supposed to solve my employee problems. In the past, I've had a couple of bad experiences in trying to take disciplinary actions. One was probably a minor incident, but I think it called for some kind of sanction and support from Larry. One of my people appeared to be under the influence of drugs or had been drinking when he came to work. It was the first time it had happened with this guy. Larry said, 'skip it.' The other was a 'big deal,' in my opinion. I noticed the fellow had brought a handgun to work. Larry backed me up, but to settle the incident took six months, two dozen meetings, several gallons of sweat—mine —and more than a few nights of lost sleep. There are just too many incidents, like the postal service horror stories—10 or 11 rampages in the last decade—to let this one go by."

"Is it worth it to try to discipline workers?" Jerry inquired.

"Who really knows," she responded. "At least there should be a merit point or two for trying."

Sometimes organizations make mistakes, and sometimes they treat employees unfairly. In other cases, employees are to blame where their performance is lacking or their behavior isn't conducive to maintaining a positive working environment. We begin this chapter by looking at the issue of preserving organizational justice and complete it by examining the supervisor's role in maintaining discipline.

If we are to judge the behavior of others and, in some instances, take corrective actions, then our behavior should be appropriate. Each topic has importance. First of all, unfair treatment may also be illegal. Recall from Chapter 3, the importance of validating personnel practices and following laws governing the treatment of employees. Second, most people prefer working in organizations that treat all their employees fairly. Still, when members misbehave, in order to maintain organizational justice, supervisors must apply some form of progressive discipline. Employees need to realize that good deeds lead to rewards. Misdeeds lead to corrective actions and, ultimately, separation from the clan.

Organizational Justice

organizational justice
The impartial treatment of employees by organizations through maintaining conditions of fairness and equity.

Organizational justice is the impartial treatment of employees by organizations through maintaining conditions of fairness and equity. (See Chapter 1 about ethics and Chapter 11 for a discussion of equity theory.) The integral parts of justice are impartiality, which means unbiased treatment, and equity, which is the quality of being fair in transactions. As a result, rewards and corrective actions are based upon what each person deserves. There are two major components of organizational justice: distributive justice and corrective justice.

distributive justice
The impartial allocation of rewards and penalties based upon merit when each person's contribution to achieving organizational objectives is calculated in determining the appropriate distribution.

Distributive justice is the impartial allocation of rewards and penalties based upon merit, that is, each person's contribution to achieving organizational objectives is calculated in determining the appropriate distribution. Thus, the disbursement of rewards is determined by the relative contribution of each person. The greater the contribution, the greater the reward. The larger the offense, the more severe the penalty.

corrective justice
The means by which employees who have been treated unfairly may seek and receive redress from the organization.

Corrective justice is the means by which employees who have been treated unfairly may seek and receive redress from the organization. Grievance procedures provide them with their "day in court" in obtaining justice. Corrective justice deals with organizational processes for maintaining equity.

Neither distributive nor corrective justice means *equality* in the sense of equal portions or exactly the same measure or identical amounts. Rather, they mean attainment of equitable treatment, that is, fair treatment impartially practiced toward all employees. For example, an equal distribution of rewards such as compensation or recognition could be very unfair when some persons are more deserving than others. The relative contribution of each person ideally determines the amount of rewards each receives. Similarly, in applying corrective justice or disciplinary penalties, we must evaluate the facts surrounding each case to determine the appropriate discipline. Perhaps you remember an occasion during grade school when one member of your class misbehaved, causing the teacher to keep you and other members of the class after school. You were punished for something you did not do. That may be equal treatment—everyone was punished—but it certainly was not equitable treatment to punish all for the mischief of one person (although it may place peer group pressure on the offender the next day).

The Organization's Responsibility for Maintaining Equity

The ultimate state of equity within any organization is attained when there is no inequitable treatment of any member. The quest for perfection is utopian. Still, we should pursue the highest level of equity obtainable. This goal is socially correct and personally honorable.

First, the quest for equity is supported by logic and by objective behavior. In the long run, attaining a high level of justice contributes to creating a stronger organization, one better equipped to achieve its mission and sustain adverse conditions. Second, employees continuously observe the treatment of others. (See Chapter 11 for more about equity theory.) Employees relate the treatment of others to themselves, how they are treated and may expect to be treated. Third, fairness conserves resources, including time. The effort consumed in defending an unfair action by making it appear socially acceptable (called "putting a spin on it") is made available for more productive uses when one acts fairly. Equitable behavior requires no justification. Finally, when an organization strives to maintain equity, it protects all of its members. Some persons do not know when they have been treated unfairly. Another group, the silent grievers, do not openly complain. Where inequities are permitted to exist, these groups suffer and so does their productivity.

While many circumstances have equity implications, an organization has particular responsibilities in the following areas:

- *Staffing practices.* Illegal discrimination should be prohibited.
- *Employee on-the-job conduct.* Sexual harassment is outlawed.
- *Safe working conditions.* All employees share in responsibility for a safe and healthy working environment and they are trained to understand the hazards of the workplace.
- *Work loads and responsibilities.* Work loads are balanced and no one is held accountable for results without having adequate authority and control over required resources.

Periodic reviews of policies and practices may also disclose the state of organizational justice. Although a comprehensive investigation remains for others to pursue, supervisors can review their own practices. Questions to ask include "Who am I hiring and who is rejected? Are there any patterns of discrimination?" "Who is promoted and which persons are denied promotions? Are my decisions always based upon employee merit and ability?" Grievance procedures—the methods or steps taken when employees feel they have been unfairly treated—and the formal disciplinary process applied in discipline can increase organizational justice. We'll talk about grievance procedures later in the chapter.

In the following discussion, we begin by considering how employee complaints and grievances can lead to more serious morale problems if they are not handled skillfully. Next, we review the disciplinary process commencing with the most prevalent methods for applying discipline and ending with a newer form that is nonpunitive.

Complaints and Grievances

A **complaint** is a verbal expression of a person's feelings reflecting pain, dissatisfaction, resentment, or discontent. A complaint is usually viewed more

complaint
A verbal expression of a person's feelings reflecting pain, dissatisfaction, resentment, or discontent.

grievance
A complaint that has not been solved or settled and is usually viewed as being more serious, often expressed in writing.

informally than a grievance. If the complaint is not resolved, labor-management contracts typically require the complaint to be submitted in writing, the next stage of the grievance process. At this point, the complaint becomes a grievance. A **grievance** is a complaint that has not been solved or settled and is usually viewed as being more serious. The subject of complaints is considered here because if they are not treated, they can develop into grievances, with the potential for greater adverse consequences in the future. (More on grievances later.)

According to Wendell French, "Many grievances stem from perceived injustices or injured feelings rather than contract violations on the part of supervisors."[2] Complaints against supervisors can be grouped into three forms of dissatisfaction as follows:

1. *Discipline.* The supervisor is perceived as not liking the employee or "picks" on him or her; the employee's mistakes are seen by the employee as being caused by inadequate instructions or insufficient training; or the employee believes the organization is out to get her or him because of union activities.
2. *Dislike for a particular supervisor.* The supervisor is viewed as playing favorites or ignores complaints of the employee.
3. *Dislike of supervision methods.* The supervisor is regarded as "snooping," or there are too many rules to follow. Close supervision is viewed as "bird dogging" by employees when supervisors are continuously watching and correcting subordinates.

Most, if not all, union-management contracts have grievance procedures; yet only 10 to 20 percent of nonunionized organizations have formal grievance procedures or include a final step for arbitration in handling grievances.[3] (See Chapter 4 about unions.) An example of the formal grievance process in a unionized setting is given in Figure 15-1. *Every* organization should have a systematic grievance process allowing employees with complaints to express them through a formal grievance procedure that, ultimately, could lead to arbitration. Complaints may or may not be substantiated by the facts of a case. That complaints are voiced by an employee does not mean that the organization or its management has in fact treated the employee unfairly. It does mean the employee believes he or she received unfair treatment.

People with complaints should be recognized as people with problems worth hearing. As a supervisor, if you encourage an open door policy, you have created a channel for your employees to talk with you. An **open door policy** exists when individuals are encouraged to bring their problems or concerns to their supervisor or other manager. The king of Saudi Arabia, for example, permits any citizen of the country to address him directly at a weekly Friday morning audience.

open door policy
When individuals are encouraged to bring their problems or concerns to their supervisor or managers.

The open door policy may have complications, of course. Habitual complainers overuse an open door practice for resolution of their problems. You may want to modify the open door or discount complaints from chronic complainers. (See Figure 15-2 on page 305.) Occasionally, an employee will take advantage of the supervisor who has announced a willingness to help solve each and every problem of the employee no matter how small. Be cautious making such statements, because you may encourage someone to take you up on it. For you this is business, but for such an employee, it is a form of entertainment.[4]

An employee with a complaint or grievance expects a fair hearing. The meeting with this employee should be held in private, conducted with impartiality, and confidentiality should be maintained. This last point, confidentiality, is important. You can make a universal assumption here that anything you ever tell

Figure 15-1 General Process Followed in a Union Grievance Procedure

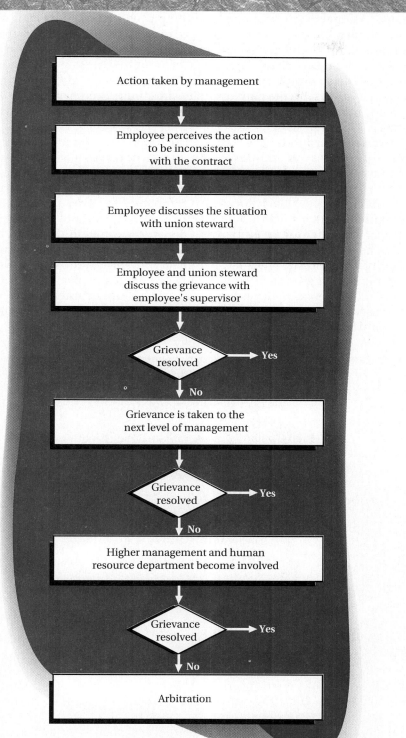

Source: Lloyd L. Byers and Leslie W. Rue, *Human Resource Management*, 2d ed. (Homewood, IL: Irwin, 1987), 445.

anyone else about the meeting will ultimately return to the person who confided in you in the first place. Are you willing to risk this?

Supervisors should listen to what an employee says and to what he or she means.[5] A supervisor's listening to an employee's complaints can be of therapeutic value to the employee. During the discussion, the employee may identify a solution to the problem. Just being able to talk to someone who is sympathetic or will listen can be valuable. When you are required to make a decision, though, you should do so promptly, except when the issues are highly emotional. If your decision is adverse to the employee's desires, there are several ways of expressing *no*.[6] "I don't agree with you," for example, is more positive than, "You're wrong."

ombudsperson

A person appointed by senior management to investigate employee complaints, report findings, and make recommendations leading to equitable settlements of grievances.

Several organizations have instituted an ombudsperson to assist employees to resolve grievances. An **ombudsperson,** in the context of business organizations, is a person appointed by senior management to investigate employee complaints, report findings, and make recommendations leading to equitable settlements of grievances.[7] Such successful companies as Xerox and General Electric have ombudspersons. The function of the corporate ombudsperson is to "assure an impartial outlet for an employee's dissatisfaction with decisions adverse to him [or her]."[8] Powers and duties vary considerably, but frequently they have the authority to investigate any grievance given to them as well as the power to reject any complaint or grievance, subject only to a written explanation for the denial. They can function as policy interpreters or decision recommenders, and, in the latter case, make recommendations in favor of either the aggrieved employee or the organization.[9]

An effective supervisor is a careful and attentive listener.

Figure 15-2 A Modified Open Door Policy

Silent Grievers

Organizations may have a few employees who harbor quiet grievances without overt expression of feelings of actual or imagined unfair treatment. Maintenance of organizational justice requires an attempt to locate these **silent grievers** and act upon the problems offending them. Within reason, supervisors should respond to all complaints employees bring to their attention. Still, there must be an upper limit to concern about the things offending employees. Beyond some point, they must be on their own. They may be offended by life, in general, or by aspects of employment that we cannot control.

silent grievers
Persons having quiet grievances without overt expression of feelings of actual or imagined unfair treatment.

Usually, the "squeaky wheel" complainer is the most evident and the first to be "greased." The problem is that silent grievers do not complain. (Refer to Chapter 13 for details about improving communication.) However, some of them have legitimate complaints. There may be some observable signs of dissatisfactions that alert us to their problems. For example, a reduction in the positive behavior of an employee or even a decline in the normal level of griping may indicate that something is amiss. Other indicators include a lack of cooperativeness, refusal to communicate beyond the minimum communication required, increased absenteeism and tardiness, and scowling or impassive facial expression. Check for nonverbal clues.

Why do some persons silently grieve? We believe several possible explanations exist. They include the following:

- *Negative reactions from coworkers.* Complaining is perceived by some employees as inviting an adverse response from other members of their group. This arises from group norms and resulting peer pressures.
- *Negative reactions from supervisors.* In the past, when a person complained, her or his supervisor responded negatively. The complainer either received no assistance in solving the problem or was punished.
- *Temporary cause of dissatisfaction.* The source of dissatisfaction is viewed as temporary and, with its removal, the complaint disappears.
- *High tolerance for pain.* Some individuals have a greater capacity for enduring pain or frustration than others.
- *Martyr syndrome.* Some persons have the ability to endure great suffering for the principles to which they adhere.
- *The masochist.* A masochist may actually derive pleasure from the perceived source of dissatisfaction, and the removal of the cause may even lead to pain for them. Such behavior likely operates at the subconscious level.
- *Organizational hell.* A few persons feel that the distress they suffer is God's punishment for their past sins. Thus, the organization becomes their "hell."

It's important for supervisors to identify why persons silently grieve. This should affect the methods applied to solve complaints as well as the importance attached to each person's problem. Treatment of a silent griever who fears adverse reactions from coworkers will differ, for example, from the approach taken to solve the problem of the masochist. You can only go so far, though, in psychoanalyzing others. Creating an atmosphere in which people are willing to talk may be the best way to reduce the number of silent grievers. After all, the silent griever may have a legitimate complaint that is concealed by silence but ultimately adversely affects job performance.

Discipline

Probably most supervisors have at least one employee who creates a problem.[10] The ultimate discipline goal of a supervisor is to have no disciplinary problems. This goal is not unrealistic, at least over a period of time. When supervisors enter a work group, they have not selected the people working for them, or participated in the development of their organizational behavior. Therefore, in the short run, supervisors are responsible for conditions they did not create. In the long run, though, they may be able to create working relationships with their employees that are largely free from disciplinary problems. The style with which supervisors exercise discipline and the methods adopted are important for reducing negative effects of the disciplinary process.

Organizational discipline is a form of training to produce a desired type of behavior when deviations from the norm occur. The purpose of taking corrective action and applying discipline is to modify behavior. The intent is not to punish someone in the sense of inflicting pain, but rather to change behavior to a state appropriate within an organization. The ideal situation is for each person to exercise self-discipline, that is, self-control. The majority of disciplinary actions are penalties or forms of negative reinforcement varying in severity. We may be surprised to learn that "punishment may not have inherent magical reform qualities."[11]

Discipline is a major corporate concern in America today. Between one-fourth and one-third of all arbitration cases dealing with a specific issue (as contrasted to general contract issues) pertain to disciplinary matters. **Arbitration** involves the use of a third party to resolve an issue based upon the merits of evidence introduced by each side. The decision of the arbitrator usually is binding for the two parties. (See Chapters 3 and 4 for more details about arbitration.) The ability of an organization to attain its goals is considerably reduced when it is unable to control its employees. Extensive disciplinary problems imply a conflict-oriented working environment, probably accompanied by low morale, low productivity, and a wasting of resources in resolving disciplinary cases rather than concentrating on achieving the goals of the organization.

Why would supervisors hesitate in taking disciplinary actions when situations clearly warranted them? (See Figure 15-3.) Reasons vary, but they may be grouped into two categories. First, there are factors largely outside of the supervisor's control. These include potential union problems, the threat of legal actions against the company and supervisor, and company policies. Working in a union environment requires special care in the disciplinary process. The collective bargaining agreement reflects a contractual arrangement, and violations of the terms bring sanctions or penalties. The law also restricts supervisors' authority with many federal and state laws enacted during the past half century

organizational discipline
A form of training to produce a desired type of behavior when deviations from the norm occur; the intent is to modify behavior.

arbitration
The use of a third party to resolve an issue based upon the merits of evidence introduced by each side.

The purpose of organizational discipline is to assist employees in modifying their behavior, not to inflict pain.

Figure 15-3 Factors Restricting a Supervisor's Ability to Discipline Effectively	
Factors External to the Supervisor	**Factors within the Supervisor's Control**
Union reactions	Dislike for hurting feelings of others
Legal limitations	Insufficient time to take action because of length of grievance process
Court involvement and litigation	Inadequate records to substantiate charges
Company policies	Feeling of indebtedness to others for past favors
	Fear of blackmail

Source: External factors adapted from Alfred W. Travers, *Supervision: Techniques and Dimensions* (Englewood Cliffs, NJ: Prentice Hall, 1988), 266–269.

Secret Taping of Conversations

The Wall Street Journal reports that labor lawyers say secret taping of supervisors by employees is on the rise, spurred by employees' efforts to protect their jobs in a tight labor market and aided by the availability of cheap miniature recorders.[12]

to ensure a variety of employee rights. The courts also often step in to provide additional employee protection. Finally, corporate policies and culture may either support supervisors in disciplining employees or discourage them from acting.[13] (Chapters 3 and 4 provide additional material about the legal and union environments facing supervisors.)

The second reason why supervisors hesitate to take disciplinary actions is that personal considerations prevail. Several motives may explain their reticence to discipline, including a genuine dislike for hurting another person's feelings, insufficient time to take corrective action because the grievance process can be lengthy, lack of adequate records and evidence to back up their charges, a feeling of indebtedness to others for past favors, or a fear of blackmail because their own past behavior violated organization policies or was not exemplary.

Usually, disciplinary actions result from violation of work rules or organizational policies rather than from substandard performance and the quantity or quality of work. The most common infractions leading to disciplinary actions are

- Absence without permission
- Dishonesty, deception, or fraud
- Drunkenness or possession of liquor on the job
- Deliberate damage of material or property
- Fighting or dangerous horseplay on the job
- Gambling
- Use of drugs
- Stealing
- Failure to meet work standards
- Falsifying records
- Smoking in prohibited areas
- Abusive, threatening, or profane language
- Insubordination
- Repeated tardiness
- Carrying concealed weapons
- Immoral conduct
- Sleeping on duty
- Failure to comply with safety rules[14]

To this list, we can add offenses reflecting inattention to laws governing job conduct such as sexual harassment and forms of illegal discrimination actions.

Causes of Employee Misconduct

Employee misconduct that results in a disciplinary problem is caused by either the employee, the employee's supervisor, or the organization.[15]

The Employee as the Cause. Insufficient job knowledge, unsuitability for the job, personal problems, and external factors can contribute to creating employee behavior that requires disciplinary action. For example, when employees lack the necessary job knowledge, they either fail to perform their assigned tasks or they perform them incorrectly.

> An example of this situation is the . . . collision of the Coast Guard cutter *Cuyahoga* with a freighter in Chesapeake Bay. The cause of the accident appeared to be the lookout, who had not alerted the bridge of the collision course because he didn't understand his duties or the lights used in sailing.[16]

The solution to this type of problem is additional training to raise employees' skills to levels needed to carry out assigned tasks.

After hiring employees, we may discover they are unsuitable for their jobs. An employee may understand what is expected in the job, but may be unable to complete assignments because of insufficient ability. Initially, the cause of the problem was poor selection and placement. The solution could take the form of a reassignment or termination of the employee.

External factors also cause disciplinary problems. When employees experience family problems, they often bring the emotional residue to work. A case of insubordination may result from frustrations felt by an employee but derived outside the organization. Supervisors who understand the personal conflicts of employees are better able to prevent personal problems from becoming disciplinary ones.

The Supervisor as the Cause.   Supervisors can contribute to disciplinary problems. As an example, the leadership style they exercise may adversely affect an employee's behavior. An authoritarian approach to managing someone who prefers a more participative treatment increases the potential for disciplinary problems on the employee's part. An unreasonable work assignment or unsafe working conditions can result in employee misconduct.

The Organization as the Cause.   Excessive and unnecessary policies and work rules invite disciplinary problems. So does an unfair organization. Before invoking discipline, investigate to find out whether the causes of the problem are not controllable by the employee. Attempt to answer the following questions:

1. Are there circumstances beyond the employee's control that cause the misconduct? One supervisor had to warn an operator again and again against keeping a can of solvent under his machine, which was against safety regulations. Finally, the supervisor investigated and discovered that other workers were engaging in horseplay by swiping the solvent and hiding it. The operator was keeping it under his machine to keep it out of their reach. He was enduring warnings from his supervisor rather than "squeal" on his fellow workers.
2. Are extenuating factors involved? A supervisor may suddenly decide to crack down on tardiness, but if a late employee is accustomed to seeing others arrive late with impunity, he's sure to resent being singled out for discipline.
3. Has an employee suddenly become physically or mentally incapable of meeting the requirements of his or her job? A sudden reduction in performance or apparent "goofing off" might be caused by such things as illness or emotional strain.[17]

Testing the Reasonableness of Disciplinary Actions

One of the most meaningful tests of whether a type of disciplinary action is appropriate is to consider whether the action would be approved of if the case went to arbitration. Would an arbitrator sustain the company and the disciplinary action taken? Arbitrators apply several criteria in making their judgments. John Tobin studied over 1,100 arbitration cases and concluded that several criteria appear in most of the cases.[18] Although the cases he studied involved disciplinary actions resulting in discharges, the "tests" are probably applicable to other forms of discipline. The following criteria can be applied to gauge the reasonableness of disciplinary action:

- *Reasonableness of rules.* Rules and standards used to justify discipline should be reasonable depending upon the circumstances present in each case. This is a test of common sense.
- *Communication and understanding of rules.* Work rules and policies should be communicated to employees, they should be understood by them, and employees should be informed about the penalties to be applied for violations. Only in those situations involving gross misconduct is it unnecessary to refer to specific rules before taking disciplinary action. Yet, even in cases of gross misconduct there is a risk that employees may not know these infractions can lead to discharge.
- *Length of service and past work record.* Both the length of prior service and an employee's past work record determine the appropriate form of discipline. Thus, the same offense may be viewed less severely because of an exemplary past work record, or more severely because of a poor record. A history of disciplinary problems may lead to discharge even though the most recent one, by itself, does not justify discharge. An incident may be "the straw that broke the camel's back."
- *Consistency in applying discipline.* The disciplinary action should not be arbitrary, inconsistent in application, or illegally discriminatory. If two employees commit the same offense, all other factors being equal or unchanged (*ceteris paribus*), the discipline applied should also be consistent between the two. But consistency requires consideration of the various backgrounds of each case. If the two persons have each been tardy four times during the past two weeks, but one person has been with the organization for 20 years and has a spotless work record and the other arrived six weeks ago and has proven to be a poor worker, the former deserves less censure.
- *Proof of violations.* Facts should prevail in determining the outcome of disciplinary action, not someone's opinions. This means acquiring sufficient and relevant evidence of the violation of a rule or policy. Furthermore, the employer has the responsibility of proving guilt, rather than the defendant-employee proving innocence. The more evidence obtained, the more relevant the evidence is to the case, and the greater the verification—the stronger the case.[19]
- *Due process is followed.* Investigation and verification of charges should precede disciplinary actions. In addition, there should be a due process procedure in which the employee's rights are protected. **Due process** is "systematic, orderly procedures, including individuals' rights to controvert [raise objections to the charges] and to be heard concerning actions pending against them."[20]
- *Equate discipline to the offense.* Corrective actions should fit the offense committed. Although some activities such as setting a fire in the factory, punching one's supervisor, or stealing the new 20-ton lathe warrant immediate dismissal, other, less serious offenses such as taking five minutes extra

due process
Systematic, orderly procedures, including individuals' rights to raise objections to the charges and to be heard concerning actions pending against them.

time for a break, parking in the general superintendent's reserved space, or picking corporate marigolds out of season require less severe discipline, if any at all. The supervisor's judgment is required to determine the seriousness of the organizational "sin."

If the proposed disciplinary actions satisfy these criteria, the discipline applied is likely to be appropriate for the offense.

Types of Disciplinary Actions

In reviewing types of disciplinary actions available to the supervisor, consider the following points: (1) the nature of the offense, (2) the range of disciplinary actions available, including the severity of discipline, and (3) any mitigating circumstances that should reduce the severity of the penalty.

Applying discipline should be analogous to the burn received when touching a hot stove. Often referred to the **hot stove rule,** this approach emphasizes that discipline should be directed against the act rather than the person. Other key points of the hot stove rule are: immediacy, advance warning, consistency, and impersonality.[21]

hot stove rule
Discipline should be directed against the act rather than the person.

For example, employees should know in advance the consequences of specific offenses. When disciplining, supervisors should apply those consequences immediately and consistently, regardless of which employee has committed a violation.[22]

In increasing order of severity of discipline, the process should begin with a verbal warning or reprimand, followed by a written warning, then suspension without pay, and finally, discharge. Each organization is unique, but there should be common procedures for handling discipline. Still, some organizations are more lenient than others.

Several examples of violations leading to discipline illustrate the range of discipline sanctions. We start with the most severe first, proceeding to the least severe.

Immediate Discharge Offenses.   Types of activities that should result in immediate discharge are theft, refusal to work, gross insubordination, fighting, intoxication or drug use, extended absenteeism without notification, falsifying time cards, intentional destruction of property, and providing false information when initially applying for the job.

Warning Followed by Discharge.   For some actions, an employee should receive a written warning for the first offense and be discharged after the second. This type of discipline should be used for infractions such as sleeping on the job, failure to comply with a rule, giving confidential information to others without obtaining authorization, gambling, absenteeism of a shorter duration without prior notification, and negligent use of company property.

Multiple Warnings Followed by Discharge.   For other actions, the sequence is an oral first warning, a written second warning, and finally, discharge. This type of discipline is used for offenses such as tardiness, uncivil conduct, negligence or incompetency in carrying out tasks, and smoking in unauthorized areas.[23]

Stages in the Disciplinary Process

Except for incidences in which misconduct is very serious and results in immediate discharge, the usual procedure is to increase the severity of the penalty each

progressive discipline
The practice of increasing the severity of disciplinary penalties each time an employee is disciplined.

oral reprimand
The first stage of the progressive disciplinary process when an employee is orally informed with precisely stated facts that an offense has occurred.

written reprimand
The second step in progressive discipline wherein the alleged offense is committed to a written form and becomes a matter of record.

suspension
The disciplinary action of temporarily laying off an employee without pay.

discharge
Permanent termination of an employee arising from disciplinary actions.

time an employee is disciplined. This practice, called **progressive discipline,** is illustrated in Figure 15-4.

One reason for applying progressive discipline is that it is accepted by arbitrators in deciding cases. Progressive discipline has become a common industrial practice in the United States,[24] and it passes the test of fairness.

The mildest form of corrective action is the **oral reprimand.** An employee is informed with precisely stated facts that an offense has occurred. At this stage of discipline, the supervisor should emphasize identifying the cause of the misconduct and prepare a plan for preventing its repetition. Supervisors should make a record of the facts surrounding the incident: what the offense was, when it happened, who was involved, when the oral warning was given, where it was given, what was said by each party, and how the incident was to be resolved. The written information does not become a part of the employee's record at this time, but it is important if a repeat offense occurs within the near future (not years from now). Supervisors should record the facts soon after an incident takes place. A single error can substantially reduce the credibility of the supervisor and cause the case to be lost in arbitration.

A **written reprimand** is the second step in progressive discipline. The written reprimand is the first formalized stage in the disciplinary/grievance procedure wherein the alleged offense is committed to a written document. "Psychologically, it has a greater effect on the employee, since the misconduct is now a matter of record. People in general appear to take matters more seriously when put in writing."[25] The written warning can be used later as evidence supporting charges against an employee in the event that subsequent and more severe discipline is required, or if the case goes to arbitration. The purpose of a written warning is to record the facts. The employee is given an opportunity to respond either by introducing written evidence or by indicating that he or she has received notification that discipline is to be rendered by the organization. The letter of reprimand should contain information about the specific incident of misconduct, the rule or policy violated, any previous counseling, oral reprimands given, the disciplinary action taken, and future actions to be taken by the organization in event of any recurrence.

The step just before discharge is suspension of the employee. A **suspension** is the temporary layoff of an employee without pay. Financial pain and loss of status are constraints imposed at this stage. However, in some cases a suspension is viewed by an employee as an unpaid vacation.

The final step is **discharge,** a permanent termination. Sometimes referred to as "industrial capital punishment," discharges are often a mixed experience for both the organization and employee. When jobs are scarce, the deterrent value of threatened termination would be far greater than when jobs are plentiful. Still, a terminated employee might find it more difficult to obtain another job because of being fired. The organization is faced with the costs of replacing the terminated employee.[26]

At every stage in progressive discipline, accurate and complete records are vital, not only because they require supervisors to consider what they are doing in terms of logic and fairness, but also because they later serve as evidence in cases going to arbitration.

There is an increasing interest in exploring other disciplinary methods as alternatives to the customary approach just described. One method is called *nonpunitive discipline.*

Figure 15-4 Progressive Discipline

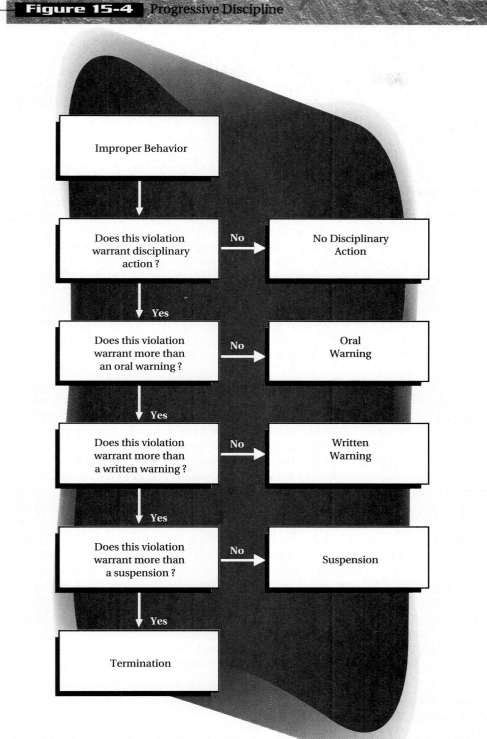

Source: From Mondy, R. Wayne and Noe, Robert M., *Human Resource Management.* Copyright © 1993 by Allyn and Bacon. Reprinted by permission.

Disciplinary Memos

A disciplinary memo that begins with words of praise sends the employee a contradictory message: "If I'm so good, why am I being punished?" Instead, the introduction should state what action is being taken and what caused the need for discipline. This introduction should be followed by a supporting paragraph documenting the incident causing the action. Following the facts with a direct quotation from the union contract or a rephrasing of company policy tells the employee that the manager or supervisor is not acting on a personal whim. The conclusion of the memo should focus on the future, noting any review period imposed and how the employee will be dealt with if the misconduct continues.[27]

The Nonpunitive Discipline Approach

nonpunitive discipline
A method for bringing employee behavior into compliance through a process of counseling in which the employee's future conduct is emphasized.

The traditional method of discipline commencing with an oral warning followed by a written warning, suspension, and discharge is being replaced in some organizations with an emphasis on counseling. **Nonpunitive discipline** is a method for bringing employee behavior into compliance through a process of counseling in which the employee's *future* conduct is emphasized.[28] The traditional and nonpunitive disciplinary processes are pictured in Figure 15-5.

Whereas traditional disciplinary actions often use punishment to change employee behavior, the nonpunitive process attempts to obtain compliance without intimidation. The process of retaining competent employees subject to discipline requires the supervisor and employee to resolve problems by working together.

The emphasis of nonpunitive systems involves counseling directed toward the employee's behavior. Consequently the employee is not considered a problem but rather a person who *has* a problem. However, caution is required in separating the focus from employee to behavior. Don't make excuses for the employee, for example, by glossing over unacceptable performance and giving him or her a performance appraisal rating higher than earned. Why not? First, too much separation allows the employee to relax and not feel the urgency of resolving the problem. Second, in the litigious period of today, if the employee is ultimately discharged, she or he may use past favorable appraisals to support an unfair discharge claim.

Under the traditional method of implementing discipline, the relationship of supervisor to employee is a vertical parent-child relationship. Formal authority becomes the basis for exercising discipline. The nonpunitive form of discipline, on the other hand, relies on a horizontal relationship in which each party is treated as an adult. This collegial atmosphere may have greater effectiveness in changing employee behavior, especially in the growing quest for employee empowerment.

Next, we consider the formal process by which employee complaints and disciplinary actions are resolved, namely, application of grievance procedures.

Characteristics of Effective Grievance Procedures

grievance procedure
A prescribed series of actions between management and employees intended to resolve differences.

Regardless of whether an organization's employees are union members, every organization should have a **grievance procedure** to allow for an orderly handling of employee complaints and disciplinary matters.[29] The grievance procedure is a chance for employees who believe they have been unfairly treated to have their

Does Your Discipline Program Allow Reprimanded Employees to Feel like Victims?

Suspending an employee without pay is like sending a child to bed without supper. The hungry child becomes angry and resentful at the parents, forgetting the reason he or she was punished in the first place. The same is true of the employee suspended without pay. The pain of loss of pay allows the employee to feel victimized and powerless, to cogitate on the unfair treatment just received rather than the negative effect on the workplace of the employee's earlier behavior.

By contrast, the last step in a nonpunitive discipline system is a decision day. That is, the employee receives a day off, usually with pay, to think about whether he or she can make a sincere and purposeful commitment to continued employment with the company. An employee given time off with pay realizes the urgency of the situation, but cannot logically feel like a victim. For what the employer has done, at no expense to the employee, is to give the employee control over his or her own career.[30]

complaints heard and settled, and for the employer to take disciplinary actions, if warranted. Even small organizations with only a few employees should have a formal grievance procedure. In the following discussion, we review the major elements of an effective grievance procedure.

- *Full disclosure.* All rules, policies, standards, and the grievance procedure are in written form, and each employee receives a copy. Discussion among supervisors and employees should cover the grievance process including how it operates within the organization and what the potential outcomes might be if applied to an employee.
- *Early settlement.* The majority of grievances should be settled at the lowest organizational level, that is, between the supervisor and employee. In cases of unionized employees, the shop steward or other union representative would participate in the process at this stage as well as in subsequent stages if the grievance is not resolved.
- *Distinct steps.* The procedure is divided into distinct steps. The sequence, furthermore, requires exhausting the remedies for grievance and disciplinary matters at one stage before going on to the next.

Figure 15-5 Nonpunitive Discipline: An Alternative

	Traditional Systems	Nonpunitive Systems
Methods of discipline:	Retribution (oral warning, written warning, suspension, discharge)	Informal counseling, formal counseling, decision day
Focus of discipline:	Employee's prior conduct	Employee's future conduct
Object of discipline:	The employee	The employee's behavior
Direction of discipline:	Parent-child orientation (bad boy, bad girl)	Adult to adult (mature people)

Source: Adapted from Jonathan A. Segal, "Did the Marquis de Sade Design Your Discipline Program?" *HRM Magazine* 35 (September 1990): 90–95.

- *Specific time frame.* Each stage has a specific time frame for completion. There are a limited number of days within which action must occur or a decision be made.
- *Written records.* Written records are maintained at each stage. Copies of the records may be exchanged between the two parties.
- *Arbitration stage.* The final stage of a grievance procedure is arbitration, that is, the use of a third party to resolve the issue based upon evidence introduced by each side. (Chapter 3 discusses the role of the arbitrator.) Obviously, it is neither reasonable nor desirable to have many grievances go to arbitration. Organizational paralysis would result. Alternatives to arbitration include an organization grievance committee composed of members of management and nonmanagement personnel or the utilization of a corporate ombudsperson.

A sound grievance procedure, from management's standpoint, provides a method for addressing problems on a timely and systematic basis. From the employee's perspective, it is a method for ensuring a fair hearing and justice. Organizational justice, like its civil counterpart, can become bogged down in delays, appeals, and red tape. Under these conditions, the supervisor may find it more convenient or less traumatic to forego taking corrective action on minor matters rather than to pursue a lengthy litigative action. In one sense, this is pragmatic behavior; in another, it may be cowardice. Organizations with good grievance/disciplinary procedures protect the rights of all employees, including their supervisors.

The Correctional Interview

When an employee receives discipline, the usual practice is to conduct a correctional interview, that is, to hold a meeting with the employee to discuss the disciplinary problem.[31] If the correctional interview is handled properly, the potential is greater for resolving the problem at its earliest stage. When correctional actions are poorly administered, settlement takes longer, the methods for bringing about change are less effective, and the parties may harbor ill-will long after the affair has ended.

The correctional interview is not meant to be a profound experience for either employee or supervisor. And it certainly should not be patterned after the Spanish Inquisition. If you do it right the first few times, you may not have to repeat the exercise as often. (The correctional interview is covered in greater detail in Chapter 16.)

In the following chapter, we consider the supervisor's role in the counseling process, various forms of counseling, and suggest several techniques for increasing counseling skills.

Upon arriving back at her apartment in Edmonds, Carla put a TV dinner in the microwave oven. She contemplated what was happening in society today. Some of her thoughts grew out of her youth and family. Her parents were almost always supportive of her endeavors and goals. When she wanted to do something they did not approve, they typically said she could go ahead, but she had to assume the responsibility for her actions. Carla had acquired most of her parents' values during a period of increasing social turmoil.

They had shared with her their philosophies of life and work. "My parents strongly believed in tackling problems when they occurred and not postponing or covering them up. They thought that problems only became worse when their solutions were delayed." She reflected on the BBC television series, "Fawlty Towers," and Basil Fawlty (John Clease of Monty Python fame), who would tell a small lie, followed by progressively larger ones to cover up the previous prevarications.

"And my folks also believed that a failure to respond was either cowardly or stupid. They liked a good argument, part of which was a form of family entertainment.

"I don't think what I did in taking disciplinary actions with these guys was either unwarranted or unimportant. I don't like wasting time on these incidents. But again, I don't believe in 'selective policy obedience' either—one person says this policy is okay and I will follow it and another says it's for the birds and ignores it. In fact, three members of my group talked to me after the recent disciplinary issue was settled and they thanked me for what I did. They appreciated my attempts to maintain 'law and order' and fairness in our unit."

The microwave's buzzer rang. Dinner was ready.

Summary: Focus on Skills

Organizational justice is the impartial treatment of employees by organizations through maintaining conditions of fairness and equity. Employee complaints are verbal expressions of a person's feelings reflecting pain, dissatisfaction, resentment, or discontent. When complaints are submitted in writing they become grievances. Organizational discipline is a form of training to produce a desired type of behavior when deviations from the norm occur.

Following are 17 suggestions to help supervisors improve or maintain the state of justice within organizations and apply progressive discipline:

1. Understand that equitable treatment of employees does not mean the same thing as equal treatment.
2. Adhere to the collective bargaining contract when taking disciplinary actions with employees. Consequently, at times supervisors may have to treat people inequitably to conform to contract provisions.
3. Respond quickly to complaints to reduce the number and severity of grievances filed.
4. Maintain confidentiality with those bringing complaints or grievances to you.
5. Attempt to identify silent grievers, discover the causes of their problems, and help them find solutions.
6. Set a goal of having no disciplinary problems, although attaining it may require a period of time.
7. View organizational discipline as a form of training and counseling and not as punishment.
8. Identify the causes of employee misconduct and, when feasible, the methods for eliminating those causes.
9. Apply progressive discipline and the hot stove rule in disciplinary situations.
10. Ensure that rules and standards you use to justify discipline are reasonable.
11. Communicate work rules and policies to employees and obtain feedback indicating they understand them.
12. Consider employees' length of service and past work records in taking corrective actions.
13. Be consistent in applying discipline.
14. Maintain accurate written evidence of violations.
15. Follow a due process approach in investigating and verifying charges of violations.
16. Equate discipline to the offense—namely, the greater the offense, the more severe the discipline.

17. Apply the nonpunitive approach to disciplinary problems with those employees indicating greatest potential for responding to it.

Review Questions

1. What is organizational justice? Cite and explain its two major components.
2. Give two reasons why maintaining organizational justice is important.
3. If we treat all persons in our work group equally, are we treating all fairly or equitably? Explain.
4. Differentiate between complaints and grievances. Which are more serious? Explain.
5. If an organization is not unionized, should it have a grievance process? Explain.
6. What is an ombudsperson?
7. What are silent grievers? Why do they grieve silently? If they do not make their problems known, should they be of concern to supervisors? Why or why not?
8. Define *organizational discipline.*
9. What factors restrict a supervisor's ability to discipline effectively?
10. Explain the causes of employee misconduct; give several examples to illustrate those causes.
11. How can you test the reasonableness of disciplinary actions? What difference does it make whether a particular form of discipline is reasonable or not?
12. Indicate several forms of disciplinary measures. Which type of disciplinary action is usually applied to each of the following offenses: tardiness, theft, incompetency in carrying out tasks, smoking in an unauthorized area, absenteeism without notification, and sleeping on the job?
13. How would you treat the worker in a Cadillac assembly plant who stole an entire automobile, piece by piece, over a 20-year period?
14. Define *progressive discipline.* What are its major values?
15. Define and describe the operation of the nonpunitive approach to discipline. Why might it be more effective than traditional approaches?

Notes

1. C. Kerr, Address before the American Society for Personnel Administration, Salt Lake City, June 1980.
2. W. L. French, *The Personnel Management Process* (Boston, MA: Houghton Mifflin Company, 1978), 522.
3. Ibid. Also see W. G. Scott, *The Management of Conflict: Systems in Organizations* (Homewood, IL: Richard D. Irwin, 1965), 56–61.
4. See L. L. Byars and L. W. Rue, *Human Resource Management,* 2d ed. (Homewood, IL: Irwin, 1987), 445.
5. R. S. Dreyer, "Take a Tip from Herbert Spencer," *Supervision* 54 (May 1993): 22.
6. M. H. Murray, "Can You Say 'No' Without Twisting the Knife?" *Supervisory Management* 19 (November 1974): 16–20.
7. See R. W. Monday, and R. M. Noe, *Human Resource Management,* 4th ed. (Boston, MA: Allyn and Bacon, 1990), 647.
8. I. Silver, "The Corporate Ombudsman," *Harvard Business Review* 45 (June 1967): 77.
9. Ibid., 77–78.
10. P. Buchler, "Are You Really a Motivator?" *Supervision* 52 (March 1991): 24.
11. G. S. Booker, "Behavioral Aspects of Disciplinary Actions," *Personnel Journal* 48 (November 1974): 529.
12. W. E. Lissy, "Secret Taping of Supervisors," *Supervision* 54 (May 1993): 20.
13. See A. W. Travers, *Supervision: Techniques and New Dimensions* (Englewood Cliffs, NJ: Prentice Hall, 1988), 265–269; and M. P. Norris, "Limitations on an Employer's Ability to Discipline Free Speech," *Employee Relations Law Journal* 17 (Winter 1991–92): 473.

14. L. Stessin, *Employee Discipline* (Washington, DC: The Bureau of National Affairs, 1960), 25–26. Also see R. L. Oberle, "Administering Disciplinary Actions," *Personnel Journal* 57 (January 1978): 29–31.

15. The discussion of causes of misconduct is adapted from an article by L. D. Boncarosky, "Guidelines to Corrective Discipline," *Personnel Journal* 58 (October 1979): 698–702.

16. Ibid.

17. I. H. McMaster, "Unusual Aspects of Discipline," *Supervision* 36 (April 1974): 19.

18. J. E. Tobin, "How Arbitrators Decide to Reject or Uphold an Employee Discharge," *Supervisory Management* 21 (June 1976): 20–23.

19. C. C. Caskey, "Constructive Discipline," *Supervision* 52 (October 1991): 11; W. E. Lissy, "Necessity of Documentation to Support Discipline," *Supervision* 50 (January 1989): 20–24; and M. Wold, "Two Heads are Better," *Progressive Grocer* 71 (June 1992): 10.

20. French, *Personnel Management Process,* 137. Also, see M. Shershin, Jr, and W. R. Boxx, "Due Process in Discipline and Dismissal," *Supervisory Management* 21 (November 1976): 2.

21. L. W. Rue and L. L. Byars, *Supervision: Key Link to Productivity,* 2d ed. (Homewood, IL: Irwin, 1992), 223.

22. Theo Haimann and Raymond L. Hilgert, *Supervision: Concepts and Practices of Management,* 4th ed. (Cincinnati, OH: South-Western Publishing Company, 1987), 375.

23. Oberle, "Administering Disciplinary Actions," 20.

24. Boncarosky, "Guidelines to Corrective Discipline," 699.

25. Ibid., 700.

26. Ibid., 699–700.

27. W. E. Lissy, "Disciplinary Memos," *Supervision* 52 (November 1991): 19.

28. J. A. Segal, "Did the Marquis de Sade Design Your Discipline Program?" *HRM Magazine* 35 (September 1990): 90–95.

29. K. B. Krinke, "Five Steps for Handling Contract Grievances," *Supervisory Management* 22 (September 1977): 14–20. Also, see L. S. Mosher, "Grievance Procedures," *Supervisory Management* 21 (August 1976): 20–26.

30. Segal, "Did the Marquis de Sade Design Your Discipline Program?" 90–92. Also see E. Friley, "Correcting Problems without Correcting People," *Supervision* 54 (June 1993): 3.

31. In the event the employee is being discharged, Douglas Scott proposes a ten-step process for handling the matter. See D. O. Scott, "An Effective Method for Discharging an Employee," *Supervision* 50 (January 1989): 10–12.

Case 15-1

And the Board's Decision Is . . .

"I've called this special meeting of the board to discuss a serious problem that has just come to my attention," Marsha Mitchell began. "Frankly, we have got to do something, but I don't know what we should do."

Going back some four months, in the same board room, Bob Cameron had pre-sented his monthly budget projection of revenues and expenses to the six directors of the Clairmont City Credit Union, located in a community of the same name in upstate New York. A credit union is a financial institution owned by its members. It is a type of cooperative. As a not-for-profit organization, the purposes of credit unions are to encourage savings and make loans to members. The board of directors sets policy and reviews operations during the past month along with considering the manager's recommendations requiring board action. Members of the board meet monthly without compensation for their services.

Because of the continuing growth of the Clairmont City Credit Union, Bob Cameron, the 38-year-old manager, had recommended hiring another teller, which would bring his staff to nine employees. Presently, he supervised four tellers, one bookkeeper, two loan officers, and one collections officer. The board considered Bob's recommendation and approved it. The subsequent events grew directly out of that decision.

Cameron interviewed a number of applicants before hiring the one he considered the best. Her name was Susan Wollensky. She was in her early thirties. To make a long story short, within the month, the two began a not-so-secret romance, one that continues until this day. There are several complicating factors, namely, both Bob and Susan are married but not to one another. In addition, employees of the credit union began noticing the relationship in the office was more than employer-employee. They thought Susan received preferential treatment in assignments. Several resented the special considerations while others were offended by the moral implications of the relationship. What had been a highly motivated group was rapidly disintegrating. Gossip now occupied more employee time as they speculated about the outcome of the affair.

And Bob Cameron seemed to be oblivious to the remarks of others. You could see he was in love. He spent less time managing and more time thinking about Susan. Bob had worked at the credit union since he graduated from college 16 years earlier. He began working as a teller. His appointment to the manager's position was eight years ago. Until recent months, his performance had been considered outstanding. Members of the board increased his salary frequently to reward him for his work. They were also concerned that he would take a higher-paying job at another credit union. He received frequent offers to work elsewhere.

The employees' discontent increased until one of the tellers was selected to represent the group in talking with Marsha Mitchell, the board's president. That was earlier this morning, the day of the special board meeting.

Questions

1. Assume the role of a board member. How can the board maintain proper control?
2. What should the board do to resolve the problem?
3. What corrective action should be taken? Explain your recommendation.
4. What are the potential problems created by this situation; both internal, to the credit union, and external, to the client-members and public?

The Sisters of Charity

"I think we have a serious problem," began Sister Margaret Rose in her opening comment to the Mother Superior. Sister Margaret Rose was the business manager of a retirement home operated by the Order of Charity for retired nuns of the Order. "Our formal annual audit in the business office indicated we were almost $4,000 short in the benevolent fund. When I asked Robert about it, he immediately confessed to taking the money—a few hundred dollars at a time—during the past year. I had no earthly idea it was Robert when I asked him about the matter. I just wanted to determine how we might figure out what had happened. Among his several duties, he was responsible for the gifts we receive. He has always been such a reliable and trustworthy person. Well educated, with a CPA. During his eight years here, we have never had any problems. His work was always excellent."

"I just don't understand it," said the Mother Superior. "We have all known that Robert has had a very rough time during the past year. Since his wife died, he has been trying to take care of his children and work too. One of his children has been very ill during this past year. What I don't understand, though, is why he did not come to us for help if he needed money. We could have done something. After all, we *are* the Sisters of Charity."

Questions

1. What could the Sisters have done? Especially, what responsibility does Sister Margaret Rose have?

2. How would you monitor employees experiencing unusually stressful events in their lives? When is intervention appropriate in these cases?

3. What should be done about Robert?

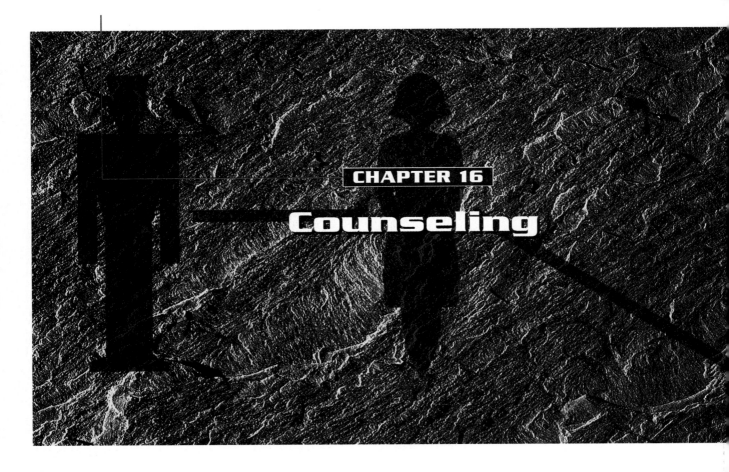

● I'm alone in a world of weirdos.

Miss Piggy

1. Describe the concept of counseling, indicating the supervisor's role in the counseling process.
2. Indicate the values of counseling both to the individual receiving it and to the employer.
3. Relate four major types of counseling and give examples of counseling in each area.
4. Cite two major counseling formats and explain how the supervisor should perform in each.
5. Describe the operation of a company's Employee Assistance Program (EAP).
6. Trace the counseling process and the skills required at each stage.

Carla swung by the company's Employee Assistance Program (EAP) offices to keep an appointment with one of the counselors, Marsha Manning, with whom she had talked on a previous occasion. While Carla's workday was finished, Manning's was just beginning. After several pleasantries, they got down to business.

"What's on your mind, Carla?" Marsha began. "How are things going?"

"Okay, I guess," Carla answered. "But Marsha, at times my job just gets to me. It seems so many of my workers have personal problems and they bring them to the job and I can't solve most of them.

"Several supervisors I know have a philosophy about employees and their personal problems," Carla mused. "They view personal and family problems as not being relevant to their employees' working lives. They expect their employees to turn their personal problems off like a faucet when they come to work. It's their opinion that when employees enter company property, their personal problems are not our concern and we shouldn't waste time on them.

"In fact, they don't have much faith in counseling. People either should be ready for work or find something else to do for a living. Right now, I'm not sure at times that they're not right. It seems that I spend too much time trying to help people in my group solve their personal problems. Still, I believe that when they feel emotional pain away from the job, they bring it to work with them and share the pain with me."

In the past, the corporate response to persons with serious emotional or mental problems typically followed one of two alternatives: deny the problem existed, or terminate the employee. In the enlightened era of today, though, a more conscientious effort toward salvaging troubled employees is expanding. The interest in assisting workers is not entirely altruistic. It makes good business sense to help them solve their problems.

Counseling is popular today, with prospects for additional interest during today's supervisors' management careers.

> More and more, supervisors and managers have begun to realize that their role in motivating their work team expands beyond the basic managerial functions. . . . They know that they must recognize the psychological factors that influence worker performance and that counseling is the most effective way in which to deal with these psychological factors.[1]

Few people would deny the potential value of counseling to improve employee performance. Yet, only within the last two decades have supervisory texts offered more than a few paragraphs about the issue. However, counseling is an activity fraught with risks. It is relatively simple to give advice when requested or even volunteer our opinions. The value of the advice is another matter. Ideally, competent counseling produces good results and, at worst, is not harmful. Poor counseling, on the other hand, can result in substantial damage to the person who receives it and follows the advice.

Therefore, we should be very cautious in our counseling endeavors—particularly in those areas traditionally handled by trained professionals. The typical supervisor is not a professional counselor. Still, supervisors have a legitimate responsibility for providing counseling in several areas. With some training in counseling skills, they should be able to obtain good results.

We begin our discussion of counseling by developing the concept of what counseling is—and is not. We look at the supervisor's role. Then, the values of good counseling are explored. How does the individual gain? The organization? The supervisor? Next, we review four types of counseling situations commonly found in the working environment, followed by a discussion of Employee Assistance Programs (EAPs) and the major techniques utilized in counseling. The chapter concludes with the introduction of several procedures for you to apply in sharpening your counseling skills.

Counseling Defined

counseling
A concentrated form of interpersonal communication with the purpose of assisting normal individuals in achieving their personal goals or functioning more effectively.

interviewing
An information-gathering process wherein facts are obtained, usually through questioning the other person.

Counseling is a concentrated form of interpersonal communication with the purpose of assisting normal individuals in achieving their personal goals or functioning more effectively.[2] The counseling process involves a knowledgeable person supplying advice or guidance to a person who needs or seeks it.

Several concepts are related to the counseling process including helping, interviewing, and psychotherapy. Helping another person is giving aid or assistance of some type, but it does not include a problem-solving orientation or the more concentrated forms of assistance found in counseling. Thus, the supervisor who helps someone perform a task is not counseling that person.

Interviewing is an information-gathering process wherein facts are obtained, usually through questioning the other person. From interviewing, we anticipate

acquiring information for offering advice and making decisions. Skillful interviewing facilitates the counseling process.

Last, **psychotherapy** is a longer process than counseling; it is greater in depth and analysis and is "concerned with reconstruction of the person and larger changes in personality structure."[3] Normally, psychotherapy is applied when a person has a severe problem, although it is not necessarily limited to pathological problems of mental diseases, disorders, or injuries. Supervisors should not attempt psychotherapy.

Counseling excludes most casual conversations—those occurring by chance, unpremeditated, and unplanned—along with many forms of interpersonal communication not related to assisting employees' resolution of personal problems. There is a nebulous line, though, between casual or work-related conversation and counseling. What began as a noncounseling event could easily shift to the counseling arena.

Initiatives for counseling can come from either a supervisor or subordinate. The counseling process may involve a single session or several meetings covering weeks or months. The amount of time consumed could be a few minutes or, cumulatively, could consume many hours.

psychotherapy
A longer and in greater depth process and analysis than counseling; concerned with reconstruction of the person and larger changes in personality structure.

The Supervisor's Role in Counseling

At a minimum, supervisors should be sensitive to the counseling needs of their employees.

Understanding how to identify and help resolve human problems in the workplace is a sensitive and complex task. It is not surprising that many supervisors prefer to ignore subordinates' personal problems, as if to say "that's not my problem"—when, in fact, it is. For if these problems are left unattended, [productivity can decline] for the organization as a whole.[4]

domino theory
Untreated personal problems arising outside of the job have a tendency to spill over into the workplace.

Ignorance about the counseling needs of employees is illustrated in the **domino theory** of personal problems. Untreated personal problems arising outside of the job have a tendency to spill over into the workplace. And the problems expand. (See Figure 16-1.) In other words, there are individuals we can and should help in counseling and others we should refer to professionals or agencies for assistance. First, though, we must be aware of employees with problems and the concerns they have regarding counseling.

Many of us dislike situations containing conflict or hearing about the personal problems of others. As a result, we may avoid tackling issues of personal or job-related problems when they arise even if they affect us. It is probably normal and healthy that we do have an aversion for listening to the personal misery experienced by someone else. And, decisions leading to corrective action can be painful for both parties. Yet in spite of this aversion the effective supervisor should respond to situations calling for action to improve the situation.

range of sensitivity
The appropriate degree of awareness a supervisor should maintain of personal and job problems of employees.

Supervisors, however, need a balance of perspective along with basic counseling skills before attempting to counsel others. The balance is the ability to be aware of the counseling needs of others and the degree of intervention that is appropriate. Figure 16-2 portrays a **range of sensitivity.** Insensitivity allows employee problems to grow more serious. Overinvolvement in counseling wastes time, may infringe on employee privacy and lead to future legal problems, and could indicate certain emotional problems of the counselor who derives pleasure from listening to the problems of others.

What are the values of counseling? To some extent, the payoffs determine the amount and types of resources we commit to counseling.

Values of Counseling

Earlier, we said that counseling benefited three parties: the organization, employees receiving the counseling, and their supervisors. When effective, the following values are obtained:

Figure 16-1	The Domino Theory of Personal Problems in the Workplace	
Personal Pain	**Individual Pain in the Workplace**	**Organizational Pain**
Family	Absenteeism	Increased production costs
Financial	Alcohol use	High personnel turnover
Marital	Long lunch breaks	Interstaff conflicts
Legal	Poor job performance	Low morale
Sexual	Poor staff relations	

Source: Adapted from John H. Meyer and Teresa C. Meyer, "How to Help the Distressed Employee," *Management Review*, April 1982, 45.

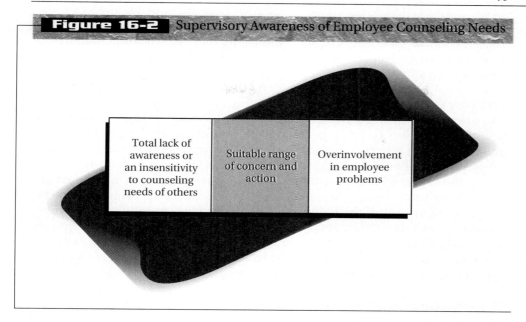

Figure 16-2 Supervisory Awareness of Employee Counseling Needs

| Total lack of awareness or an insensitivity to counseling needs of others | Suitable range of concern and action | Overinvolvement in employee problems |

- *Lower labor turnover and absenteeism.* Employment stability results when counseling prevents employee problems from becoming so severe an employee quits or is discharged. As an example, counseling may identify causes of an employee's absenteeism problem and point out alternatives for solving it.
- *Improved dispositions and moods.* An employee's customary emotional response and temperament are reflected in her or his disposition. **Disposition** is a person's typical manner of behavior or way of acting in given situations. **Moods** are a person's temporary state of mind or feelings. In both disposition and moods, counseling may help the employee identify the problem and methods for resolving it.
- *Reduced anxiety.* When people worry about the future or experience anxiety about the uncertainties it holds, counseling may provide information to reduce fears. Information obtained from counseling can reduce distress or place employees' fears into a more realistic context.
- *Improved role relationships.* Counseling may improve the ability of employees to interact with one another more productively and cooperatively. One of the important relationships to benefit is that between employee and supervisor.
- *Increasingly friendly coworker relationships.* Counseling directed toward team-building can increase friendships by fostering trust among workers. Sharing information and identification of common goals and problems can be facilitated through counseling.

disposition
A person's typical manner of behavior or way of acting in a given situation.

moods
A person's temporary state of mind or feelings.

Types of Counseling

The different types of counseling can be organized into four major categories: (1) corrective and remedial, (2) informational, (3) developmental, and (4) therapeutic.

Corrective and Remedial Counseling

corrective counseling
A form of counseling designed to identify conditions creating employee attitudes that cause undesirable behavior and disciplinary problems.

The goal of **corrective** and **remedial counseling** is to identify the conditions creating the attitudes that are causing the undesirable behavior or substandard performance.

Corrective Counseling. The disciplinary process was discussed in Chapter 15. The discussion included causes of employee behavior leading to disciplinary actions and the forms of discipline applied. The information exchange in communicating with people receiving discipline is a form of counseling. The counseling process should be designed to reflect the following points: (1) identify duties and expected employee behavior, (2) appeal to a commonly shared goal between the subordinate and supervisor, (3) focus on the job rather than directing accusations toward the individual's personality, (4) react to people by concentrating on them rather than on the emotional element, (5) deal with the behavioral effects rather than being judgmental, and (6) encourage the employee to identify the problem and recommend solutions. Disciplinary counseling is important, although the person so disciplined may not believe this.

remedial counseling
A form of counseling of employees whose performance is not up to par or whose behavior, such as careless work, disinterest in the job, or chronic absence or tardiness, is not acceptable to the organization.

Remedial Counseling. Of course, not all corrective counseling involves disciplinary problems:

> At one time or another, every supervisor ... faces the problem of an employee whose performance is not up to par or whose behavior is not acceptable to the organization. The employee may be careless in his work, uninterested in his job, or chronically absent or late.[5]

There is a difference between corrective counseling applied in disciplinary cases and counseling workers lacking competence. The distinction is important.

> The *incompetent worker* is one who attempts to discharge his responsibilities but lacks the capacity to perform to standard. He differs, obviously, from the *careless worker* who possesses the skill and ability to carry out his job duties, but through indifference or other causes, disregards his obligation.[6]

A supervisor should *not* discipline the incompetent worker. Nor should a supervisor discipline an employee experiencing emotional problems.[7] Arbitrators and the courts are finding in favor of such employees who have been discharged. Here, counseling is of a remedial nature rather than corrective. However, before confronting a subordinate whose performance is lacking as evidenced in producing poor results, violating policies, or deviating from standards, supervisors must make sure the employee understands the policies and standards and monitor the employee's future behavior. Work standards become important for establishing a plan and schedule for improvements reflecting those expectations.[8]

Remedial counseling may take several forms. One problem experienced by supervisors is dealing with the slow employee where the goal is to improve performance either by speeding up the individual or taking some other action such as transfer or discharge. The character of Bennie on the television series "L.A. Law" demonstrates a person properly placed for the duties he performs. Although Bennie has diminished mental ability, he is capable of performing the required tasks of his job, thus not only accomplishing a needed service to his law firm employer, but also maintaining his economic independence and feeling of

William Jay

Convincing others that we are right and they are wrong will be about as productive at times as the rightness of the late motorist, William Jay:

Here lies the body of William Jay
He died maintaining his right of way
He was right, dead right
As he sped along
But he is just as dead as if he'd been wrong.[9]

self-worth. Were he placed in a more complicated position, he would be a prime candidate for remedial counseling.

An employee may have a physical disability that restricts mobility and rate of work. In some cases, the limitations may be correctable through devices such as glasses, hearing aids, or work modification. Thus, a normal performance is obtained from a formerly poor one. Modifications of the work area could reduce the severity of the disability's effect upon the work process.[10]

Informational Counseling

Informational counseling is often performed to prevent problems from occurring. By providing information about issues of importance to workers, we keep them informed. Previously, we stressed the value of communicating information affecting the employee's well-being. Counseling is one method of communication. **Informational counseling** may involve exchanging ideas or information between the supervisor and employees or may be used to relate information necessary for workers to perform their jobs. Providing information to employees is another form of sharing power with them, or empowerment.

> By virtue of the hierarchical advantage, managers typically have access to both a greater variety and greater depth of information than their subordinates. This situation can become a barrier to personal and organizational success if key information is not fed back to those who are in a better position to do something about it.[11]

informational counseling
A form of counseling involving exchange of ideas and information between the supervisor and employees or relating information necessary for workers to perform their jobs.

Developmental Counseling

The primary goals of **developmental counseling** are to help employees make the best use of their abilities in achieving their potential, and to identify the goals and capabilities of those employees. "One of the nebulous but important duties [of supervisors] is aiding and encouraging subordinates in their professional development."[12] Another benefit of helping employees to develop their careers or prepare themselves for promotional opportunities is that it enables companies to conform to federal and state government regulations that mandate upgrading of job opportunities and skills for minorities and women to higher-level positions within organizations. Then, **cross training**—in which employees are prepared to perform more than one job—increases organizational flexibility and expands the opportunities of employees. Finally, for many employees, the achievement need

developmental counseling
A form of counseling used to assist employees in making the best use of their abilities in achieving their potential and to identify the goals and capabilities of those employees.

cross training
Preparation of employees to perform more than one job.

> has been shown to be a powerful motive which is learned in early childhood and adolescence.... Thus, it behooves managers and supervisors to be both aware of its existence and be able to counsel employees to help them satisfy it.[13]

Disabilities Are in the Eyes of the Beholder

Gopal Patti observes, "There is no such thing as 'handicapped' people, only people with varied abilities. Disability must not be confused with inability."[14] One of our students with cerebral palsy commented, "I know what my disability is. Many persons do not know what theirs are."

There is a transition area between those persons who have visible evidence of physical limitations and those not perceived as having a disability per se. For example, a person may not be physically attractive and, consequently, encounter discrimination. Others have differences measured in their stature or weight. A student of ours graduated from college with a degree in elementary education. Her professional goal was to teach kindergarten and first grade. She was a small person, however, and experienced discrimination from school boards and principals because of her height. She was told, "We can't hire you because you are shorter than your students and they wouldn't respect you." One administrator commented, "Your students need fresh air in the classroom and you are too short to open the windows."

Counseling is an important activity in helping employees to realize their achievement needs. Problems may result when an individual feels prevented from satisfying that need.

> People who are severely frustrated in a given situation may also try to escape or withdraw, seeking gratification outside of work. Other individuals may become fixated in attaining the thwarted goal. That is, the more they are thwarted, the more energy they may expend fruitlessly to attain the goal.[15]

Subsequently, responses of employees seeking unmet development opportunities may range from apathy to frustration and aggression.

Essentially, developmental counseling is oriented toward assisting employees in continuously preparing for their organizational careers. (See Chapter 19 for more information about career planning.) A career development program—in which supervisors are an important component—could take the following steps:

First, encourage employee self-selection in vocational choices of jobs. Small group sessions have been found useful in exploring the choices available within an organization.

Second, apply modeling in order for employees to learn how other people actually perform those jobs in which they have interests. The more realistically jobs are presented, the more valid the judgment of employees about congruence, that is, whether the characteristics and interests they possess are matched by the requirements of the jobs.

Employee development counseling may lead to the realization for some employees that there are no congruent or harmonious matches of job opportunities with their interests within the organization. Here are two cautions: First development or job enrichment may be a psychologically gratifying experience for some persons, but they may also expect extra compensation for the increased complexity, responsibility, and discretion now experienced in their enriched jobs.[16] **Encapsulated development** occurs when we raise employee expectations through training and development activities but are not able to produce work opportunities for utilizing the new skills. This can result in frustration for employees.[17] Second, some individuals perform well and are content with their present jobs. Consequently, they are not interested in development and, in some cases, forced development could have adverse effects.

encapsulated development
A situation in which employee expectations are raised through training and development activities, but the organization is not able to produce work opportunities for utilizing the new skills.

Therapeutic Counseling

The intent of **therapeutic counseling** is to diagnose personal problems and help employees, through trained third parties, overcome them or cope with them more successfully. Therapeutic means "healing." Therapeutic counseling is substantially different from corrective, remedial, informational, and developmental counseling, in which the supervisor plays an active role in helping employees resolve problems. Therapeutic counseling often calls for professional assistance. And that assistance may take the form of an Employee Assistance Program (EAP).

therapeutic counseling
A form of counseling to diagnose personal problems and help employees, through trained third parties, overcome them or cope with them more successfully.

Employee Assistance Programs

An increasing number of organizations are instituting **employee assistance programs (EAPs)** to handle such problems as alcoholism, drug abuse, emotional illness, personal crises, and stress. It is estimated that over 8,000 EAP programs currently are in operation in the United States.[18] In the following chapter, we will examine the problem of stress in detail. Although companies apply numerous techniques for handling employees experiencing personal problems of this nature, "consultations with supervisors and referrals to outside agencies are the most appropriate approaches, regardless of the type of problem."[19]

employee assistance programs (EAPs)
Organization programs designed to help employees handle such problems as alcoholism, drug abuse, emotional illness, personal crises, and stress.

> To assist supervisors in dealing with troubled employees, most companies provide some combination of training, policy guidance, and opportunities to consult with specialized counseling or medical staff. Policy statements or written suggestions and lists of outside referral agencies are the most frequent forms of such assistance, regardless of the type of problem involved.[20]

The supervisor's role is limited to identifying signs of employees suffering personal problems and referring them to either trained EAP staff counselors or to outside agencies. With training, though, supervisors may provide some of the initial counseling. The more severe problems have to be handled elsewhere. Still, the supervisor performs a valuable role by encouraging distressed employees to seek treatment, monitoring progress during treatment, and operating as a support resource. Recovery should be faster when employees receive support and encouragement from their supervisors.

We will consider several types of personal problems. First, we look at those of an addictive quality, then consider mental and emotional problems, and conclude with some examples of personal problems that are often overlooked.

Addictive and Dependency Problems. Many, if not most, employers strive to maintain a drug-free workplace.[21] The social and economic costs of addictive and dependency problems are immense. For example, the National Council on Alcoholism and Drug Dependence states that untreated substance and alcohol abuse annually costs U.S. employers $165 billion, of which $65 billion results from lower productivity and $100 billion is in increased health-care expenses.[22]

Commonly, people suffering from alcoholism and other drug addictions refuse to admit they have a problem or, if they do, they attempt to minimize its seriousness. Only in the later stages of progressive deterioration in their functioning do they acknowledge they have a problem and need help.

Alcoholism costs American employers billions of dollars each year.

substance addiction
A physiological
dependency condition
that also has social and
psychological
consequences.

In **substance addiction,** the dependency is a physiological condition. It also has social and psychological consequences that can be severe. Between 5 to 10 percent of the typical organization's employees will suffer from alcoholism. Another 10 percent or so take illegal drugs while at work.[23] The degree of impairment in their ability to perform varies, but a majority of those who are alcoholics maintain enough capacity to continue working.

> There is no environment in which the individual is under closer scrutiny than his place of work. His sick record, time-keeping and efficiency are all monitored. Discerning management can identify deteriorating patterns which may have significance. For these reasons, industry can have a major role to play in the identification and help of those with drinking problems.[24]

Signs of substance addiction vary depending on the form of addiction, but often a declining work record is indicative of a problem. Changes in the quantity and quality of production along with unsatisfactory explanation of absences are indicators of problems. Erratic behavior characterized by periods of "ups" and "downs" frequently accompanies the development of addictions. In addition, withdrawal and the loss of friends or more secretive behavior occurs. Supporting addictions, especially those involving illegal drugs, becomes expensive, with employees resorting to embezzlement or theft of company property. The family life of the addict deteriorates, divorces are common, estrangement from children occurs, and problems with the law result from driving under the influence of alcohol or drugs or writing bad checks.

Probably the best-known public organization offering help for the alcoholic is Alcoholics Anonymous (AA). Most communities with over 1,000 residents support one or more AA groups. AA programs have enjoyed a relatively high success rate but it varies with community. A number of private clinics treat alcoholics and others suffering drug dependencies. The majority of states operate programs, often as adjuncts to their mental hospital systems. Federal programs such as those found in Veterans Administration (VA) hospitals offer treatment. For some VA hospitals, the majority of patients are alcoholics.

Often today, treatment of addiction and other dependency problems calls for an integrative approach. More than one problem may be present, and solutions need to incorporate the multiple problems. For example, an alcohol/drug dependency problem could also be related to a financial problem and family difficulties. Consequently, solutions must consider the related problems and the various parties that are affected by the employee's behavior. Successful treatment recognizes the linkage.[25]

compulsive gambling
A psychological addiction.

In more recent years, a drugless addiction, gambling, is being recognized as a problem. In 1992, between 80 to 90 million people in the United States legally wagered $330 billion.[26] **Compulsive gambling** is a psychological addiction. Between 8 to 12 million people are considered compulsive gamblers.[27] Gambling stimulates compulsive gamblers. They experience a "high" from it when they win and also withdrawal symptoms during the withdrawal phase. Usually, it "takes from five to twenty years to develop into a confirmed gambler. To reverse the habit . . . can require as much as two years . . . of therapy and follow-up counseling."[28] (See box, "Identifying the Compulsive Gambler Employee.")

To date, although research is limited, it appears that treatment of compulsive gamblers is only about 50 percent successful, although with more facilities and trained personnel, it is believed the cure rate could be increased to over 90 percent.[29]

Identifying the Compulsive Gambler Employee

How can supervisors identify the person whose gambling is out of control, so they can do something about it? Generally speaking, managers should be on the lookout for employees who have any personal problems and refer them to the EAP. The following signs often are associated with compulsive gambling, however:

- Decreased productivity
- Excessive use of the telephone
- Mood swings

- Borrowing money, often from people on the job
- Frequent absences, often for just part of the day
- Big spending and generosity
- Bragging about gambling
- Rumors of problems at home

These are the warning signs you may see in the workplace. They may not mean your employee is a compulsive gambler, however—they may be simply the signs of some other difficulty.[30]

Mental and Emotional Problems.   There are many different types of mental and emotional problems people experience. Some are deadly serious while others largely permit individuals to continue functioning. The most significant include the following:[31]

Anxiety is an aroused state in which a person experiences a feeling of being upset, frequently accompanied with an undefined feeling that something bad will happen. Many therapists believe anxiety is the most important element of psychological disorders. A very high anxiety level leading to difficulties in functioning is called **neurosis.**

Paranoia is a form of thinking disorder in which the individual experiences delusions, such as false beliefs of persecution or exaggerated personal importance (grandeur). **Psychosis** consists of a large number of serious mental disorders where individuals have extreme distortions in how they think and perceive the world. Their behavior is often bizarre.

Depression is characterized by a dejected mood, dismal or dreary feeling, loss of motivation, and a feeling that few things are important and attempting to change things is useless. Loss of a loved one leads to intense grief, dejection, and depression. In this instance, depression, painful as it is, is a normal condition. It is experienced by many persons who have suffered a major loss of someone or something. Normal depression goes away over time; the individual recovers to normal moods and activities, although there can be residual scars. Abnormal depression, however, occurs when the condition is long-lasting, deep, or acute, and is not directly attributed to conditions or experiences of a loss. Then it can become a psychological problem. Severe depression can even lead to suicide (see box on page 334, titled "Suicide: Popular Misconceptions.")

Personal Problems that May Be Overlooked.   A variety of other situations also require counseling. Individuals with a potential need for counseling include

- Men going through a midlife crisis.
- Individuals of any minority who exhibit "shy" behaviors within a working environment of nonminority persons, or those working in a radically different environment from what they have previously experienced.
- Women reentering the employment market after years of absence.
- Military veterans from past wars.
- Employees being terminated because of technological job displacement.

anxiety
An aroused state in which a person experiences a feeling of being upset, frequently accompanied with an undefined feeling that something bad will happen.

neurosis
A very high anxiety level leading to difficulties in functioning.

paranoia
A form of thinking disorder in which the individual experiences delusions, such as false beliefs of persecution or exaggerated personal importance (grandeur).

psychosis
Consists of a large number of serious mental disorders where individuals have extreme distortions in how they think and perceive the world.

depression
A mental and emotional problem characterized by a dejected mood, dismal or dreary feeling, loss of motivation, and a feeling that few things are important and attempting to change things is useless.

There are many popular misconceptions about suicide, including the following:

1. *If a person talks about killing her- or himself, he or she won't really do it.* This is incorrect. The suicidal person usually gives warnings of his or her intent and talks about it with other people, often in a joking way.
2. *Suicide is a form of psychosis.* The person who commits suicide may be severely depressed, but he or she is not necessarily psychotic or mentally ill.
3. *If the attempt is unsuccessful, the person really did not mean it and had no real intention of killing him- or*

herself. If a suicide attempt fails, the person will probably keep trying. They do mean it.

4. *Suicide is stimulated by changes in the moon cycles.* There is no evidence for that belief.
5. *When a depressed, apparently suicidal person's mood improves, the danger of suicide is over.* This is not necessarily true. Many depressed people do not attempt suicide until after they seem to improve somewhat. A lifting of spirits or mood should not be automatically interpreted as a decrease in suicidal risk.[32]

- Persons who are HIV positive or have AIDS or other terminal diseases.
- Persons who have served jail and prison sentences.
- Employees who are facing retirement in the near future but who are not looking forward to it.

Counseling Formats

Two principal formats for counseling are directive and nondirective counseling. (See Chapter 12 about managing conflict and Chapter 13 about communicating effectively for additional information.)

Directive Counseling

directive counseling
A form of counseling following a structured format or plan wherein the supervisor carries a substantial amount of the conversation by answering questions and giving advice.

Directive counseling typically follows a structured format or plan. The counseling session is largely controlled by the supervisor, who carries a substantial amount of the conversation. The employee asks questions and the supervisor responds with answers and directives. The method requires listening to the subordinate's problems and telling him or her what action to take. Giving advice is an important feature of directive counseling, although it can also be used for motivating, communicating, reassuring, and providing emotional release of feelings.[33]

Unfortunately, although it's relatively easy to give advice to others, often they don't follow the advice even when it is sound. Another criticism of the method is that the supervisor may not fully understand the employee's problem or how it could be solved.

The emotional release of discussing one's problems has potential therapeutic value when the supervisor is a good listener. During counseling, subordinates may clarify their thoughts and communication improves. Often, there is value in reassuring an employee and building the courage required for taking a prescribed course of action.

Nondirective Counseling

nondirective counseling
A form of counseling wherein the supervisor functions in a supportive role as a listener.

In **nondirective counseling,** the supervisor functions more in a supportive role as a listener. Through skillful listening and asking probing questions, the supervisor encourages the employee to explain what the problem is, what is causing the problem, and outline a course of action to solve the problem. The person receiving the counseling is the focus of the meeting, rather than the supervisor as was the case in directive counseling. In fact, the supervisor should avoid appearing in the role of a judge or adviser. Judgments appearing as either criticism or praise are withheld because they could block the employee's true feelings. Those feelings, when expressed, are accepted—not judged.

Nondirective approaches are more time-consuming than are directive ones. In many instances, the nature of problems treated will require trained counselors. Of course, for the method to be successful, the employee must be dedicated to solving the problem.

The advantages of nondirective counseling include a greater opportunity for the employee to experience emotional release, better clarification of his or her thinking, reorientation of the employee's thinking, and an improvement in communication between the supervisor and employee. The method also is effective in dealing with the person in the context of the problem rather than just with the immediate problem itself.[34]

Which approach is most suitable? Generally, the nondirective method is preferable for most counseling situations, especially when problems are not yet thoroughly defined or solutions mapped out. On the other hand, when supervisors know the problem and have identified a best alternative, the directive approach may be more appropriate. The counseling skill of the supervisor also has a bearing on the approach used. The nondirective method requires a higher level of counseling skill.

Improving Counseling Skills

Prior to a counseling session, supervisors should prepare the physical environment. An important factor is ensuring privacy. No interruptions from other people walking in or the telephone ringing should be tolerated. The message conveyed to someone in counseling when interrupted by the telephone is "The telephone call is more important than you." Furthermore, interruptions disrupt rapport and the focus on the problem. A supervisor who is shuffling through the morning mail while an employee is trying to discuss a problem with him or her is also sending the wrong message.

The location of the meeting should be suitable. Many are held in the supervisor's office. However, if the employee also has an office, that location may be preferable because it is more familiar to the employee and, perhaps, less formidable.

Timing is another consideration. The supervisor must judge what is the most appropriate time. When is the best time is influenced by what is mutually convenient and the seriousness of the problem. Mental alertness is another factor. People tend to be tired toward the end of the working day, so perhaps an earlier meeting may be more suitable. However, the employee may prefer a meeting later in the day so he or she will not have to return to work after the session is completed. Serious problems may call for an immediate response.

Supervisors need to maintain confidentiality in counseling. "Confidentiality within the counseling setting has its genesis in the physician-patient relationship."[35] You may occasionally hear things that seem outrageous or even humorous. Keep them to yourself. Otherwise, you assume the risk, as stated before, of the information returning to the person you are counseling and your credibility being destroyed. Confidentiality is essential to mutual trust.

Ten Interactive Counseling Skills

Richard Walsh suggests ten interactive counseling skills as particularly useful.[36] (See Figure 16-3.) By interactive, we mean the setting in which the supervisor is counseling an employee face-to-face. The first four skills pertain to developing rapport with the person you are counseling. They are projecting an attending attitude, becoming an active listener, providing supportive responses, and asking proper questions. The next two skills concern acquiring the other person's frame of reference or perspective by reflecting his or her feelings and meaning. Helping the other person identify the problem is attained in the following two skills, summarizing the feelings and content of what was said along with providing an interpretation of the meaning.

Figure 16-3 Ten Interactive Counseling Skills

Counseling Skill	Supervisor Actions
Developing rapport:	
1. Attending behavior	Put the other person at ease physically and emotionally
2. Active listening	Concentrate on what the other person says; give feedback
3. Support responding	Provide sympathetic understanding with nonverbal methods and verbal comments
4. Proper questioning	Ask appropriate questions that are open-ended
Developing a frame of reference:	
5. Reflection of feelings	See the problem from the other person's perspective using questions and responses
6. Reflection of content or meaning	Derive meanings from the feelings of the other person and the content of what he or she is saying
Identifying the problem:	
7. Summarize feeling and content	Use deductive reasoning to arrive at the specific issue
8. Interpretation responding	Provide answers to why the other person feels a certain way
Arriving at a solution:	
9. Rendering advice	Ideally, the other person arrives at a solution; supervisor may offer alternatives
10. Gaining commitment	Supervisor and other person mutually agree on a course of action and each person's responsibilities

Source: Adapted from Richard J. Walsh, "Ten Basic Counseling Skills," *Supervisory Management* 22 (July 1977): 2–9.

Finally, the last two skills involve arriving at a solution—which may involve rendering advice—and acquiring a commitment of some type of action from the other person. (See Chapter 13, "Communicating Effectively," for more information.)

Attending Behavior.   The word *attend* means to take care of or listen to another person. The supervisor displays attending behavior by putting the other person at ease both emotionally (if possible) and physically through the seating arrangement. Good eye contact also conveys an attending attitude.

Active Listening.   The supervisor establishes mutual trust through active listening including provision of feedback. (See Chapter 13.) This means concentrating on what the other person is saying. The supervisor must not daydream even if the other person speaks slowly, with frequent pauses or breaks in the conversation. It may be helpful periodically to paraphrase what the other person is saying. For example:

> **Employee:** "No one seems to understand my feelings about things."
> **Supervisor:** "You're saying that others are insensitive to your needs?"

By repeating what the other person is saying, the supervisor is indicating communication on the subordinate's same "frequency."

Support Responding.   The supervisor conveys a sympathetic understanding of what the other is saying and experiencing through verbal and nonverbal cues. Head nods and positive facial expressions carry nonverbal messages of understanding and concern. Verbal comments appropriately placed in the conversation can help. Such comments include: "Please go on." "I think I know how you feel." "It has happened to me too." "I see." Supportive nonverbal cues and comments encourage the other person to continue speaking.

Proper Questioning.   The supervisor builds rapport and acquires information by asking appropriate questions. Open-ended questions that are not answerable with one or two words are more effective in allowing the other person to reveal thoughts and emotions.

Reflection of Feelings.   At this stage, the supervisor is continuing to see the problem from the subordinate's perspective. The subordinate's feelings are identified. He or she may say: "The other members of my group leave the dirty work for me to clean up." The supervisor responds: "You feel angry because they have not treated you fairly in sharing the chores?" The subordinate can agree with the observation or clarify it further.

Reflection of Content or Meaning.   While the previous skill focused on feelings and the emotional dimension of what the other person is saying, this skill gets at content or the meaning of the message. For example,

> **Employee:** "Working with Jan is frustrating. Sometimes she concentrates on what we are doing and at other times her mind is somewhere else and we are late finishing our work."
> **Supervisor:** "What I hear you saying is that sometimes Jan is unreliable in helping you complete the work on time."

To clarify an employee's problem, it is necessary to derive meanings from both feelings and content. If only feelings are considered, the fallacy of solving symptoms rather than problems may occur. When supervisors attack the issue of content as the cause of the problem, they can anticipate the negative feelings will subside.

Summarizing Feeling and Content. Objectivity in understanding what is being said is aided by summarizing feelings and content. Deductive reasoning is applied to arrive at the specific issue or problem.

Interpretation Responding. The counseling supervisor then interprets what the subordinate has been saying. Previously, the emphasis was on deriving the meaning from the employee's perspective. Ideally, the supervisor now presents a perspective that is a more functional way for the employee to view the problem. The interpretation skill is the supervisor's answer explaining *why* the employee feels a certain way. The supervisor might respond, "From what I hear you saying, you are angry or frustrated because Jan sometimes causes your work to be finished late. And you get blamed for something that is not your fault."

Rendering Advice. Usually, it is better for the person being counseled to arrive at the solution. The supervisor may suggest alternatives along with pros and cons of each. The other person will feel a greater responsibility if he or she determines the solution, though.

Gaining Commitment. The ultimate success of the counseling process is neither a solution nor a commitment, but rather the implementation of the solution and attaining the desired results. The commitment may include stated obligations from both parties. The supervisor may agree to take certain actions, and the employee also accepts certain responsibilities. Specific dates for action to occur or results to be obtained are desirable. Follow-up is required to track progress made toward achieving the agreed-upon objective.

Good counseling is more than a casual process of assisting others achieve their goals. It is a serious endeavor in which a supervisor has the responsibility of helping subordinates solve their personal problems. In some situations, the supervisor's contribution is an awareness of the problem and assistance in helping the employee solve it including, when necessary, locating professional help.

The meeting with Marsha was about to end. "During the past year," Carla recalled, "almost all of the people in my group have received some type of counseling from me other than the annual performance appraisals when I sit down and talk to each person. It seems most cases are concerned with personal problems rather than on-the-job issues. Most of the time I don't tell them what to do other than help them lay out alternatives. Sometimes it seems that just listening to them helps."

Marsha asked, "Okay. But how does this affect you?"

"I end up taking on their problems. Monkey transference. Here's an example: Yesterday, just before the end of the shift, Mary Beth, who has been with the company 10 years, stopped by my office and said she wanted to talk if I had time. So we talked. She began by saying things were not going well at home. She has three children, all of whom are grown and have left home. Her husband periodically mistreats her physically and emotionally. He is usually drunk when he abuses her. It sounded like her marriage was about to end. She was one unhappy person.

"I asked Mary Beth what I could do to help. Do you know what she told me? She said just listening helped. Then, when she was leaving, she said it was her birthday and it wouldn't be quite as bad if someone in her family had remembered. I almost cried.

"Then I remembered our EAP staff could give her a hand. She will be calling your office for an appointment within a day or two. By the way, listening does help."

"And so does not assuming all of the world's problems," the counselor responded.

Summary: Focus on Skills

Counseling is a concentrated form of interpersonal communication with the purpose of assisting normal individuals achieve their personal goals or function more effectively. Following are 19 suggestions to help supervisors in counseling employees:

1. Be sensitive to what is going on in your employees' lives.
2. Understand the meaning of the domino theory of employee personal problems. When personal problems arise outside of the job, they have a tendency to create other problems in the workplace.
3. Refrain from becoming overinvolved in counseling. There is a range of awareness of employee counseling needs. Usually the most appropriate posture is in the middle of that range.
4. Set goals for counseling. Examples include reducing turnover and absenteeism, improving disposition and moods, reducing anxieties, improving role relationships, and increasing friendly coworker relationships.
5. In corrective or remedial counseling identify duties and expected employee behavior.
6. Appeal to commonly shared goals.
7. Focus on the job rather than directing accusations toward the individual's personality.
8. React to people by concentrating on them rather than on the emotional content of what they say.
9. Deal with behavioral effects rather than being judgmental.
10. Encourage the employee to identify the problem and recommend solutions.
11. Do not discipline incompetent workers. Remedial counseling calls for identifying the cause of poor performance, which may be of a mental or physical nature.
12. Keep employees informed by providing information about company issues of importance to them.
13. Identify the goals and capabilities of employees and assist in providing appropriate developmental opportunities.
14. Do not oversell development where its benefits cannot realistically be used by the organization; otherwise, encapsulated development can occur.
15. Where feasible, encourage employee self-selection in vocational choices of jobs.
16. Follow up employees to ensure they are getting the assistance they need when referred to others for counseling or treatment.
17. Understand the two principle counseling formats: directive and nondirective counseling. Usually, use the nondirective format except in taking corrective actions.
18. Ensure more beneficial counseling results by providing privacy of meeting, no interruptions, and appropriate timing.
19. Finally, develop the following effective counseling skills: attending behavior, active listening, support responding, proper questioning, reflection of feelings, reflection of content or meaning, summarizing feeling and content, interpretation responding, rendering advice, and gaining commitment.

Review Questions

1. What is counseling? How does it differ from other forms of interpersonal communication?
2. How would you describe the supervisor's role in counseling? What problems should a supervisor handle? Which should be referred to professionals and why?
3. What is the domino theory of personal problems?
4. What are the values of counseling: to the person receiving it, to the organization, and to the supervisor?
5. Four types of counseling were discussed. Explain the purpose of each type; then give three examples of each.
6. What is an Employee Assistance Program? Indicate the scope of such a program.
7. What should supervisors do if they believe one of their employees is an alcoholic? Addicted to drugs? Suicidal?
8. Distinguish between directive and nondirective counseling. When would you recommend using one or the other?
9. Describe the proper counseling setting and then give the ten counseling skills.

Notes

1. G. L. Frunzi and J. R. Dunn, "Counseling Subordinates: It's up to You," *Supervisory Management* 19 (August 1974): 2.
2. See A. E. Iven and L. Simek-Downing, *Counseling and Psychotherapy: Skills, Theories, and Practice* (Englewood Cliffs, NJ: Prentice-Hall, 1980), 13.
3. Ibid., 13–14.
4. J. H. Meyer and T. C. Meyer, "The Supervisor as a Counselor—How to Help the Distressed Employee," *Management Review* 7 (April 1982): 44.
5. J. J. Walker, "Counseling Sessions that Do Some Good," *Supervisory Management* 21 (November 1976): 10.
6. G. S. White, "Past and Current Trends in Negligence and Incompetence Arbitration," *Personnel Journal* 58 (November 1979): 796.
7. W. E. Lissy, "Emotionally Troubled Employees," *Supervision* 54 (January 1993): 20.
8. See P. Muniz and R. Chasnoff, "Counseling the Marginal Performer," *Supervisory Management* 27 (May 1982): 29.
9. G. P. Cross, "How to Overcome Defensive Communications," *Personnel Journal* 57 (August 1978): 48.
10. See A. W. Farrant, "Speeding the Slow Employee," *Supervision* 37 (March 1975): 29.
11. R. K. Kreitner, "People Are Systems, Too: Filling the Feedback Vacuum," *Business Horizons* 28 (November 1977): 56.
12. H. Hellwig, "How to Counsel a Promising Subordinate," *Supervisory Management* 20 (January 1975): 32. Also see J. W. Gilley and H. L. Moore, "Managers as Career Enhancers," *Personnel Administrator,* March 1986, 51–59.
13. R. A. Morano, "Managerial Counseling for Organizational Effectiveness," *Personnel Journal* 54 (September 1975): 494.
14. G. C. Patti, "Countdown on Hiring the Handicapped," *Personnel Journal* 57 (March 1978): 144.
15. Morano, "Managerial Counseling for Organizational Effectiveness."
16. E. L. Parke and C. Tausky, "The Mythology of Job Enrichment: Self-Actualization Revisited," *Personnel* 52 (September/October 1975): 12.
17. See D. Spiegel, "How NOT To Motivate," *Supervisory Management* 22 (November 1977), 13.
18. M. DePaul, "Workplace Safety Seen Demanding More than Drug-Free Workplace," *The Oil Daily,* November 1991, B7.
19. Bureau of National Affairs, *Counseling Policies and Programs for Employees with Problems,* ASPA-BNA Survey No. 34 (Washington, DC: Bureau of National Affairs, March 23, 1978), 1. Also see P. Stuart, "Investments in EAPs Pay Off," *Personnel*

Journal 72 (February 1993): 43–54; and J. Beilinson, "Are EAPs the Answer?" *Personnel* 68 (January 1991): 3.

20. Bureau of National Affairs, *Counseling Policies and Programs.*

21. "Ten Steps to a Near-Drug-Free Workplace," *Supervision* 54 (June 1993): 6.

22. V. Gibson, "Intervention Theater: The Point Hits Home," *HR Focus* 69 (August 1992): 15.

23. P. Stuart, "The Chemical Dependency Care Package," *Personnel Journal* 70 (June 1991): 94.

24. J. Hines, "Counseling the Problem Drinker at Work," *Personnel Executive* 1 (February 1982). Also see National Institute on Alcohol Abuse and Alcoholism, *Occupational Alcoholism: Problems, Programs, and Progress* (Washington, DC: NIAAA, 1973).

25. See R. W. Hollmann, "Beyond Contemporary Employee Assistance Programs," *Personnel Administrator* 27 (September 1981): 37–41.

26. B. Smith, "Compulsive Gamblers: In over Their Heads," *HR Focus* 69 (February 1992): 3. Also see J. Popkin and K. Hetter, "America's Gambling Craze," *U.S. News and World Report,* March 14, 1994, 43.

27. Ibid.

28. "How One State Counsels Its Habitual Bettors," *U.S. News & World Report,* January 28, 1980, 74.

29. Ibid. Also see S. Overman, "Addiction: Odds Are Gamblers Cost Companies," *HR Magazine,* April 1990, 50–53.

30. P. Stuart, "The Hidden Addiction," *Personnel Journal* 70 (November 1991): 104.

31. Concepts are adapted, in part, from B. Bugelski and A. Graziano, *The Handbook of Practical Psychology* (Englewood Cliffs, NJ: Prentice-Hall, 1980).

32. Ibid.

33. K. Davis, *Human Behavior at Work: Organizational Behavior,* 6th ed. (New York: McGraw-Hill, 1981), 454.

34. The discussion is based upon the work of R. J. Walsh, "Ten Basic Counseling Skills," *Supervisory Management* 22 (July 1977): 2–9.

35. K. M. Denkowski and G. C. Denkowski, "Client-Counselor Confidentiality: An Update of Rationale, Legal Status, and Implications," *Personnel and Guidance Journal* 60 (February 1982): 371.

36. Walsh, "Ten Basic Counseling Skills," 2–9.

The Golden Gate

"Everyone's got problems today," began Mike Wade. "If you don't have a problem, something's wrong with you. And I really question whether it is my responsibility to become involved in my employees' personal lives. Frankly, I don't have the time. When they ask me for advice about their personal problems, they usually don't take it. So why bother? Besides, I am too busy taking care of my own life without getting involved in theirs."

Mike Wade was a government employee working for a city in north-central California. He supervised a group of professional planners. In total 14 men and women—all college graduates—reported to Mike. As a group, they were responsible for land-use planning for their city.

"At times, I think half of my staff is either unhappy, crazy, or just plain weird. A couple of the guys are boozers. They either take long weekends every now and then, or they come to work hung over the day after partying. And I am pretty sure another—Michael—is supporting a coke habit. He's still functional but his work is going downhill. I'm going to have to talk with him one of these days soon. What he does outside of the office is not my concern. It's none of my business."

Mike reflected on the life styles of members of his group and mused that their styles were, indeed, varied. Probably would raise the eyebrows of the less liberal, he thought. But they were young and they would learn.

"I've got this one guy, Frank. We call him the 'Prophet.' He tries to convince the rest of us that the world is coming to an end, maybe tomorrow. He's unhappy most of the time. When he is around the others for very long, they start feeling blue. I usually have him working by himself."

"Then there is Mary Alice. She just goes berserk every now and then. Most of the time, she is fine. Pleasant. Does good work. Then, wham! Her behavior is 'off the wall.' Once she tried to run over some fellow at Westgate Shopping Mall. He walked in front of her car as she was parking and she chased him inside one of the stores. Fortunately, he didn't file a complaint. Just a few weeks ago, I forgot to say good morning to Mary Alice as we passed in the hall. I was thinking about something else. Later in the day, she came storming into my office, demanding to know why I didn't like her. I have never seen so many tears as she berated me for being so insensitive. The next day she was fine. Didn't even remember what happened the day before."

Mike paused and recalled an incident from his early years as a supervisor when he worked in San Francisco. "We had this very bright planner—Julie—who was a member of my group. She did a great job and was my favorite employee. Now and then she would get down for long periods and dropped hints that life just wasn't working out for her. It started after her divorce. Then her only child, a two-year-old daugh-ter, died. Her problems went on for several years although she always did her work.

"One day she stated she had found an answer to her problems. A couple of days later she didn't come to work. We learned that afternoon she'd jumped from the Golden Gate Bridge. The strange thing about it was that she seemed to be getting better. Why, the day before she died she had even bought a plane ticket to Hawaii, where she planned to spend her vacation. After that, I came to the conclusion I just didn't want to get involved in the personal problems of others. There's nothing I can really do to help them anyway."

There was another long pause, finally punctuated by the psychologist's encour-agement, "Go on, please."

Questions

1. When should a supervisor intervene in the personal problems of employees? What criteria would you use in making your decision?

2. Would you agree with the statement, "It is none of my business what my employees do in their personal lives as long as it does not affect their job per-formance"?

3. For the several employees of Mike Wade needing assistance, how would you have treated their problems through the counseling process?

4. What, if any, responsibility does Mike Wade share for the well-being of employees suffering from personal problems? The addicts? Mary Alice? Julie?

Case 16-2

How Do You Smell Relief?

Jim Bradford sat at his desk, shoulders slumped, and forehead cupped in the palm of his left hand as his elbow rested on the desk. It was midafternoon of a hot late-summer Friday. In front of him lay the open personnel file of a young man who had started recently—Harvey Shafer. He had talked to Harvey several times about prob-lems that he was creating, but to no avail.

He would talk to him again when Harvey returned before quitting time. Jim won-dered to himself what he should do. What should he say? How could he motivate Harvey to conform to the behavior of others?

Harvey joined the U.S. SCS (Soil and Conservation Service) staff two months ago. As he walked through the front door of the small district office located in a com-munity in eastern Nebraska, he passed office harmony on its way out. The federal Soil and Conservation Service did the work suggested by its name. It assisted farmers and ranchers with a variety of services directed toward preventing soil erosion, handled acreage allotments for government subsidy and soil bank programs, and assisted agricultural producers in obtaining funds for conservation practices. The customers of SCS were farmers and ranchers. Eastern Nebraska's economy was based upon agriculture. A substantial majority of the agriculture population could be considered politically conservative.

Harvey had graduated six months previously from a midwestern college where he had majored in agronomy. Harvey was very bright. He scored at the top of a Civil Service examination that brought him to Nebraska. Harvey could be described as an individualist, perhaps eccentric would be more accurate. Physically, he was a large young man. To say he wore his hair long was an understatement. It hung in locks and a few snarls below his shoulders. His presence was preceded by an odor suggesting Harvey needed a bath—make that two baths. He came to work the first day wearing a soiled T-shirt inscribed across the front with "Eat, drink, and be merry for tomorrow I will be in Utah." Other shirts carried mottos on sex, politics, and religion guaranteed to offend almost every group within the socio-economic-political spectrum residing in eastern Nebraska.

Harvey's work required him to travel with other SCS employees to farms and ranches in the area. He also met with farmers and ranchers in the SCS offices. A common complaint was "Harvey smelled."

The first complaints about Harvey began within an hour after his arrival. During the next two months, they were recorded from farmers, coworkers, and even the mayor of the community. In fairness to Harvey, though, it should be reported his work was competently performed. He just looked and "smelled" differently from everyone else. People seemed to worry about the length of his hair. While some found his T-shirts clever, other folks took offense and voiced their complaints with Harvey's boss. But the one problem everyone agreed on was Harvey's "fragrance."

"How do you smell relief?" one coworker wistfully asked a colleague.

"When you're upwind from Harvey," his friend replied.

Questions

1. Is the issue here one of discipline? Motivation? Explain.
2. How can Jim change Harvey's behavior to the desired form?
3. Is the length of Harvey's hair an issue? Why or why not? How about the T-shirts and absence of personal hygiene?
4. Any ideas toward explaining Harvey's behavior? How would knowledge of Harvey's behavior be useful in arriving at a solution?

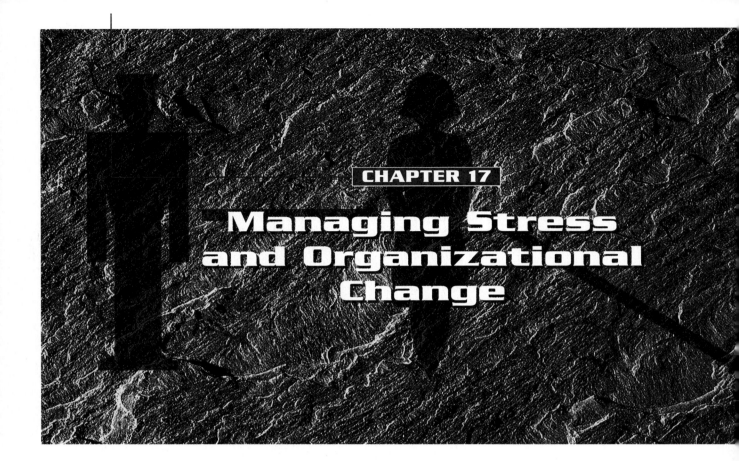

CHAPTER 17

Managing Stress and Organizational Change

● Following a loss of 45 to 3 to the Detroit Lions, Pittsburgh Steeler Coach Chuck Noll is quoted as saying, "As I was walking back here, I mulled over what the turning point of the game was. I decided it was the opening kickoff."[1]

LEARNING OBJECTIVES

1. Describe the phenomenon of job stress.
2. Indicate why not all forms of stress are viewed negatively.
3. Indicate the conditions that create stress.
4. Define the term *defense mechanism,* and explain the several types of behavior that can occur.
5. Give methods supervisors can apply to reduce stress.
6. Explain why people resist change and stages of the change reaction process.
7. Relate the supervisor's role in making changes including the principles of the change process.

"Ah, another day at the salt mines," Carla wistfully thought as she arrived at work, parking her two-year-old Taurus in the north lot. "I need to talk to Joe about his work. Something's eating at him. He's been irritable all week." Later in the morning, she had the opportunity to raise her concern as she walked by Joe's work station.

"Joe, what's the problem? You've been moody all week."

"I tell you Carla, it really makes me mad when I'm held up in completing my assemblies because the group over there," Joe pointed to a subassembly wiring section, "doesn't get their work over here in time. It makes me look bad. It's the fourth time this month it has happened. And the result is you jump on my case for being behind and it isn't my fault."

"My, but we're a bit cantankerous today, aren't we?" Carla responded, partly in chiding Joe and partly reflecting her own irritability. "If you're having a problem why didn't you come to me for help?"

"Humph. First, you didn't ask. Second, you have always been too busy, it seems. Third, you haven't exactly been cheerful yourself lately," Joe responded.

Job Stress

Each of us is like a spring:

> with different size and shape and tolerance levels. As long as you don't stretch a spring beyond its elastic limits, it bounces back when you let go. It gets bent out of shape, however, if stretched beyond its normal limits, and will snap if stretched far enough. So it is with people and stress; as long as we live within our individual elastic limits, stress can be invigorating and useful. But when we go beyond our capacity, we get "bent out of shape" and may need assistance to bounce back.[2]

We begin the chapter with a discussion of stress and its causes and methods for dealing with it. (See Figure 17-1.) The latter portion of the chapter examines organizational change and how supervisors can attempt to manage its impact upon their work groups.

The topic of stress has organizational importance for several reasons. First is the magnitude of its effect on workers. One study conducted by Northwestern National Life Insurance found that 46 percent of U.S. workers considered their jobs highly stressful. About one-third of American workers were considering quitting their jobs because of the amount of stress they were feeling.[3]

Second is the cost. It is estimated the costs of stress-related illnesses exceed $150 billion each year in the United States.[4] Workers who file stress-related claims against their employers are frequently away from work for longer periods of time than those with other forms of work-related injuries. Costs increase because of the length of time for rehabilitation and visits to psychiatrists. "In medical treatment and time lost, stress cases cost, on average, twice as much as other workplace injuries: more than $15,000 each."[5] (See box titled "Stressed Out?")

stress
A condition experienced whenever a person is confronted with a demand or challenge that threatens his or her ability to attain valued outcomes.

There's no universally accepted definition of the term *stress.* For our purposes, **stress** is experienced whenever a person is confronted with a demand or challenge that threatens his or her ability to attain valued outcomes.[6] A newer term used by stress experts is *rustout,* which can be as debilitating as burnout.[7]

Figure 17-1 How to Handle Stress

Source: Beetle Bailey, August 9, 1993, King Features Syndicate, Inc.

Stressed Out?

The number of stress-related workers' compensation claims has ballooned in states such as California that compensate for so-called "mental-mental" injuries. In these, an intangible (mental) injury results from an intangible (mental) cause, such as stress. California courts have awarded compensation to workers who just say they feel hurt. For example, a former cake decorator with Albertson's, a supermarket chain, won compensation in part because she said her supervisor had been "very curt" with her. He had told her to "get the lead out" and to "get your butt in high gear," and had reprimanded her for leaving cakes out of the freezer. She was distressed, sued, and won.[8]

The most common view of the relationship between stress and job performance is that performance is adversely affected by stress. Others hold that stress improves performance. The truth probably is found somewhere in the middle. Smaller amounts of stress are beneficial because they arouse people to perform. High levels, on the other hand, can lead to confusion and misdirected effort detracting from achievement. As in the situation of conflict, discussed in Chapter 12, the effective supervisor's intent is not to totally eliminate stressful events—which cannot be done in entirety—but rather to monitor and manage the environment in which stress occurs.

> Job stress can be thought of as an internal state of arousal which results when an individual sees his or her performance or behavior leading to positive or negative consequences or outcomes. Furthermore, the amount of stress will be related to positive or negative consequences or outcomes.[9]

In physics, radiation is measured in roentgens. It is unhealthy to accumulate too much radiation within a given period. Over time, though, radiation is dissipated from the body. Similarly, it is emotionally damaging to experience large doses of **emotional stress** within a given period of time. Those who do run the risk of emotionally "glowing in the dark." Sensitivity to our employees' personal lives as well as their working lives would show varying states of social transition events, which lead to emotional stress. Some individuals are enjoying periods of calm while others are adrift in turbulent waters and may be undergoing profound problems in their lives.

emotional stress
An unhealthy condition that occurs when a person is subjected to excessive social transition events leading to emotional overload.

Evidence or symptoms of excessive stress include insomnia, anxiety, irritability, fatigue, drug dependency, excessive appetite or loss of appetite, inability to concentrate, and a decline in the quantity or quality of work. Prolonged periods of stress can lead to more serious physical and mental disorders. The symptoms are red flags denoting more serious problems.

Generally, there is a correlation between the number and severity of stressful events occurring within a time period, such as one or two years, and a person's state of health. The more stress, the greater the incidence of illness. Life stress or emotional stress is measured by stress-inducing events, which could include the death of a family member, divorce, change in work duties, or even a holiday celebration. One instrument for measuring stress is the Holmes and Rahe Social Readjustment Rating Scale, shown in Figure 17-2.

When people accumulate large numbers of life-change units within a two-year period, the rate of illness increases. For example, it is estimated that about 90 percent of those accumulating 450 points become ill in the near future. The illness rate declines to about 66 percent with the accumulation of 300 points and

Figure 17-2 Social Readjustment Rating Scale

Life Event	Mean Value
1. Death of a spouse	100
2. Divorce	73
3. Marital separation from mate	65
4. Detention in jail or other institution	63
5. Death of a close family member	63
6. Major personal injury or illness	53
7. Marriage	50
8. Being fired at work	47
9. Marital reconciliation with mate	45
10. Retirement from work	45
11. Major change in the health or behavior of a family member	44
12. Pregnancy	40
13. Sexual difficulties	39
14. Gaining a new family member (e.g., through birth, adoption, oldster moving in, etc.)	39
15. Major business readjustment (e.g., merger, reorganization, bankruptcy, etc.)	39
16. Major change in financial state (e.g., a lot worse off or a lot better off than usual)	38
17. Death of a close friend	37
18. Changing to a different line of work	36
19. Major change in the number of arguments with spouse (e.g., either a lot more or a lot less than usual regarding child-rearing, personal habits, etc.)	35
20. Taking out a mortgage or loan for a major purchase (e.g., for a home, business, etc.)	31
21. Foreclosure on a mortgage or loan	30
22. Major change in responsibilities at work (e.g., promotion, demotion, lateral transfer)	29
23. Son or daughter leaving home (e.g., marriage, attending college, etc.)	29
24. Trouble with in-laws	29
25. Outstanding personal achievement	28
26. Wife beginning or ceasing work outside the home	26
27. Beginning or ceasing formal schooling	26
28. Major change in living conditions (e.g., building a new home, remodeling, deterioration of home or neighborhood)	25
29. Revision of personal habits (dress, manners, associations, etc.)	24
30. Trouble with the boss	23
31. Major change in working hours or conditions	20
32. Change in residence	20
33. Changing to a new school	20
34. Major change in usual type and/or amount of recreation	19
35. Major change in church activities (e.g., a lot more or a lot less than usual)	19
36. Major change in social activities (e.g., clubs, dancing, movies, visiting, etc.)	18
37. Taking out a mortgage or loan for a lesser purchase (e.g., for a car, TV, freezer, etc.)	17

Life Event	Mean Value
38. Major change in sleeping habits (a lot more or a lot less sleep, or change in part of day when asleep)	16
39. Major change in number of family get-togethers (e.g., a lot more or a lot less than usual)	15
40. Major change in eating habits (a lot more or a lot less food intake, or very different meal hours or surroundings)	15
41. Vacation	13
42. Christmas	12
43. Minor violations of the law (e.g., traffic tickets, jaywalking, disturbing the peace, etc.)	11

Source: Thomas H. Holmes and Richard H. Rahe, "The Social Readjustment Scale," *Journal of Psychosomatic Research* 11 (1967): 216.

drops to about 33 percent when only 150 points are accumulated. While not an infallible guide to predicting illness, still it makes sense that employees who encounter substantial adversity in brief periods are more prone to both illness and problems on their jobs.[10] The same applies to supervisors.

Causes of Stress

What causes stress? The principal sources of employee stress are (1) the characteristics found in the personal life of an employee, (2) the conditions present in the work environment, and (3) the situations occurring within the job itself.[11]

Simply being alive as the 21st century approaches is highly stressful. An effective supervisor is mindful of the stress employees bring to the workplace each day.

In the first instance, family problems or emotional experiences such as divorce, remarriage, or difficulties with children are responsible for stress. In the second case, working conditions can contribute to stress. Such stressful environmental factors can include noise, poor lighting, exhaust fumes, solvent and glue odors, and temperature variations. Sometimes, people become physically ill. (See box, "Office Stressors.")

Stress has a cascading effect when a person experiencing stress inadvertently influences others. This phenomenon is known as **assembly-line hysteria,** arising from a factory incident in Israel. Hysterical behavior is reflected in both a psychological and physical response of emotional excitability or fear and emotional stress. A person may become unconscious for a brief period of time. In many instances, physical irritants were not responsible for the illness. Rather, "the spread of psychogenic illness seems most likely when several people find themselves in a stressful situation with no customary way of coping with it."[12] One of the authors witnessed the event in class when a student experienced a convulsive attack from an epilepsy seizure and passed out. Subsequently, another member of the group fainted, and so on. It was time to dismiss the class before others were unconscious. (Who ever said a lecture was not stimulating?)

Then, there are **stress carriers,** whose behavior causes stress for others. "Some people are like Typhoid Mary. They never seem to suffer stress but readily create it in others."[13] They may occupy higher levels of management, transmitting their ailment to lower levels. "Supervisors with high energy levels and needs for achievement may be the worst offenders."[14] We may also call these folks *stress seekers* or *stress junkies.*[15]

Stress is not limited to large organizations. However, a distinguishing characteristic of complex organizations is their extensive differentiation of tasks. Many different types of work are performed in a myriad of departments. The structure of organizations reflects a variety of goals, varying degrees of formality, and different management styles. As a consequence, the probability of incurring stress increases with the growth in complexity of organizations.

Within the complex organizational environment, several major types of conditions are found that are stress-inducing, especially when organizational members are unable to attain their goals. They include competition for resources, task interdependence, jurisdictional ambiguity, communication barriers, individual traits, and miscellaneous factors.[16]

Competition for Resources. Resources are limited. Probably more than ever before in our lifetimes, the quantity and availability of resources is a major concern of managers and supervisors. The charge to us becomes: "Do more with your budget allocations, equipment, working space, supplies, support services, and personnel." (See box on page 352 titled "Don't Forget the Obvious.") The likelihood of stress arising from this competition increases with the scarcity of resources. The more restricted the supply relative to demand by the various groups, the greater the probability of stress and its intensity.

Task Interdependence. When groups are dependent upon the performance of others, the probability of stress arising increases, especially when the groups have different goals. Task interdependence takes different forms. A group may be dependent upon others or it may be a mutual dependency—a symbiotic relationship. Furthermore, the forms of dependency vary. They can include assistance in performing work, information, supplies, or something else required for the well-being of a group. Also, the greater the difference in goals between groups, the more opportunities for stress developing.

---

assembly-line hysteria
A phenomenon first noted in Israel in which a person experiencing stress inadvertently influences others to become stressed.

stress carriers
Persons whose behavior causes stress for others.

Office Stressors

A recent poll of company managers found that the following workplace characteristics generate consistently high levels of stress:

- Demands on time

- Excessive workload
- Dealing with organizational politics
- Responsibility for subordinates[17]

Jurisdictional Ambiguity.   Sometimes conflicts arise in determining who has the power or authority over performing an activity or function. In other words, who does what? Who should be doing what? If responsibilities overlap or there are gaps in responsibilities, conflicts leading to stress tend to increase. If work boundaries are not clearly defined, conflict can occur. In some organizations there is a natural competition among supervisors to extend their spheres of control leading to incorporating or duplicating operations of other supervisors.

Status Problems.   Time and resources are wasted when perceptions of status differences cause a group to react hostilely toward another, including withholding cooperation. Problems also arise when attempts by one group to improve its status are perceived as a threat to the status of others.

Communication Barriers.   Several types of communication problems found in organizations lead to conflict and stress. They include overloads of information, insufficient upward or downward communication, and confusion because messages were poorly designed or were distorted in transmission.

Individual Traits.   Personality traits can contribute to creating stress. For example, stress is greater when people are authoritarian, have low self-esteem, or are unable to compromise. At times, people hold to inflexible positions with agreement becoming increasingly difficult, if not impossible, to obtain.[18] In particular, those with overaggressive behavior or abrasive personalities either experience stress or create stressful conditions for others.

Miscellaneous Factors.   Finally, job-induced stress is created by a variety of other factors including the following:

- An unchallenging job, or feeling that personal talents are wasted
- Job insecurity or uncertainty about professional status
- Insufficient authority for the amount of job responsibility
- Too much work or working schedules that are too tight
- Role conflict when expectations from different roles (such as work values and personal values) are incompatible
- Pettiness of large organizations (too many policies and regulations that do not make sense or seem unnecessary at times)
- Deadlines[19]
- Supervisors, themselves, who fail to allow subordinates to share input, provide insufficient training, or are insensitive to employee needs.[20]

Individual Reactions to Stress

A forerunner of stress is frustration. **Frustration** occurs when a person is unable to satisfy some need or achieve some goal. Frustration leads to stress. The greater

frustration
A stressful condition occurring when a person is unable to satisfy some need or achieve some goal.

Don't Forget the Obvious

Managers who want to reduce stress should make sure workers have the tools and training they need to get jobs done. Says John Murray, a police bomb deactivator in Florida, "I'm lucky. I've got the best equipment and the best training. There are departments where all they used to give you was a mattress and a fishhook."[21]

the need or more important the goal, the more intense the frustration when it is not satisfied or attained.

Mature individuals will attempt to master frustrating situations by circumventing or removing the barrier obstructing their pursuit to achieve a goal, which may be other people, physical objects, or the personal limitations of the individual. You may, however, be supervising individuals who are immature.

When a person is unable to overcome the source of frustration, several outcomes are possible. One likely candidate is stress. Another is anger. **Anger** is an acquired emotion reflecting displeasure, developing over time into more emotional problems. Examples of anger include temper tantrums or screaming, habitual complaining or whining, and picking on other people.[22]

anger
An acquired emotion exhibited as a strong feeling of displeasure, developing over time into more emotional problems.

defense mechanism
A nonrational attempt to reduce tension and anxiety from needs that are not satisfied.

Defense Mechanisms.   A **defense mechanism** is a nonrational attempt to reduce tension and anxiety from needs that are not satisfied.[23] Through the implementation of a defense mechanism, an employee attempts to reduce the frustration that occurs when he or she is unable to achieve an important personal goal. Many human motives are accompanied by an awareness of both the effort to be expended and knowledge of the reasons behind the actions. Thus, a person's behavior is predictable. The individual is capable of describing feelings about why specific actions are taken. Purposive behavior and subjective experience result. "I know *what* I am doing and I know *why* I am doing it." Defense mechanisms, on the other hand, are comprised of subconscious motives and indirect expressions. People are not aware of their motives although their behavior may appear purposive (goal-directed). "Yet they themselves often vehemently deny the motive that would be inferred, or even report the opposite motivation."[24]

Figure 17-3 on page 354–355 presents the most common defensive responses to frustration. These forms of reaction to frustration or defense mechanisms are not always injurious either to the individual or the organization. In making an assessment of the potential harmful effects of defense mechanism behavior, the following criteria are suggested:

- *Problems created.* Is there any damage from the behavior? How is the individual injured? The organization?
- *Time dimension.* Is the behavior of recent origin or has it occurred for a longer period of time?
- *Severity of problems.* How serious are the problems? Have they become more acute over time?
- *Identity of the causes.* Can sources of the problems be identified with certainty? Or by speculation only?
- *Availability of a solution.* Are there practical alternatives available to solve the problem?

Women, Work, and Role Conflict

As more women have moved into the world of paid work, fears that holding a job would lead to divorce have not been supported. A 15-year study of 2,742 women found that age, education, wages, and attitudes toward work had no effect on divorce rates. However, divorce was pre-dicted by the number of hours spent on the job by married women. Apparently, high work involvement for women remains incompatible with husbands' expectations of wives and marriage.[25]

It could be a tricky endeavor to rid someone else of defense-mechanism behavior. Perhaps an "organization exorcist" is required. What appears simple on the surface can assume complex proportions because we lack sufficient infor-mation or background. Take, for example, a supervisor who has never been pro-moted beyond the first level of management. He then enthusiastically dedicates himself each year as the department's United Way chairman to be the most suc-cessful fund raiser in the organization. His perceived job inadequacy is offset by the fund-raising success. This behavior is a form of compensation.

A supervisor's capacity for changing undesired employee behavior is greatest where: (1) the supervisor knows with certainty the cause of the problem and (2) there is a practical solution. If an employee's behavior is harmful to the employee, to others, or to the organization, then something should be done. In many instances, though, the cause of the adjustive reaction taken is unknown— and the cause may originate outside the job sphere. In other instances, the defen-sive mechanism could be entirely internalized with little, if any, observable evidence of its presence. Take fantasies, for example—how do you know when a person is having one? We suspect we would be more than a little concerned in some cases if we actually knew the content of some fantasies. In extreme forms, they could resemble the mind-set of a cat who conveys appreciation to her food provider by purring while thinking, "If you were smaller, or I, larger, I would have you for lunch." Perhaps some things are better left unknown, as suggested in Figure 17-4.

Finally, in attempting to eliminate defense mechanism behavior without an adequate alternative for it, you could be introducing a condition of tension or anxiety that is painful for another person. To some extent, life is more pleasant (or less painful) because of people's ability to redefine reality in terms with which they can cope.

Supervisors should monitor the working environment to determine feelings and attitudes of employees and determine whether they are experiencing frus-trations and stress. When necessary, changes should be implemented in the environment to reduce incidents causing stress. Regardless of the strategies applied, supervisors should not bottle up frustration and anger. Such a practice could be dangerous. Rather, supervisors may implement more productive meth-ods for handling those who are less disturbed emotionally or mentally such as applying a catharsis technique as described below.

Catharsis.   **Catharsis** is a technique for relieving tension and anxiety by bring-ing a repressed problem to consciousness or out into the open. In one sense, it is the purifying or cleansing of emotions. Venting feelings can lead to a reduction of tension. Supervisors can provide catharsis through direct expression, socially sanctioned activities, displacement, and the grievance process.

catharsis
A technique for relieving tension and anxiety by bringing a repressed problem to consciousness or out into the open.

Figure 17-3 Defensive Response to Frustration

Adjustive Reactions	Psychological Processes	Illustrations
Flight or Withdrawal	Leaving the field in which frustration, anxiety, or conflict is experienced, either physically or psychologically	A salesperson whose big order falls through takes the rest of the day off; constant rebuff or rejection by bosses or coworkers pushes an older worker toward being a loner and ignoring what friendly gestures are made
Compensation	Individuals devote themselves to selective pursuits with increased vigor to make up for feelings of real or imagined inadequacy	Zealous, hard-working president of company's 25-Year Club who has never advanced beyond first-level management
Conversion	Emotional conflicts are expressed in muscular, sensory, or bodily symptoms of disability, malfunctioning, or pain	A disabling headache keeps a staff member off the job the day after a cherished project has been rejected
Displacement	Redirecting pent-up emotions toward persons, ideas, or objects other than the primary source of the emotion	Roughly rejecting a simple request from a subordinate after receiving a rebuff from the boss
Fantasy	Daydreaming or other forms of imaginative activity provide an escape from reality and [provide] the imagined satisfactions received from the activity	An employee's daydream of the day in a staff meeting when he/she corrects the boss's mistakes and is publicly acknowledged as the real leader of the working unit
Identification	Individuals enhance their self-esteem by patterning their own behavior after others, frequently internalizing the values and beliefs of others; also, vicariously sharing the glories or suffering the reversals of other individuals or groups	The "assistant-to" who takes on the vocabulary, mannerisms, or even pomposity of his/her boss
Rationalization	Justifying inconsistent or undesirable behavior, beliefs, statements, and motivations by giving acceptable explanations for them	Padding the expense account because "everybody else does it"
Reaction-Formation	Urges not acceptable to consciousness are repressed and in their place opposite attitudes or modes of behavior are expressed with considerable force	An employee who has not been promoted who overdoes the defense of his/her boss, vigorously upholding the company's policies
Regression	Individuals return to an earlier and less mature level of adjustment in the face of frustration	A supervisor who is blocked in some administrative pursuit busies himself/herself with clerical duties or technical details more appropriate for his/her subordinates
Repression	Completely excluding from consciousness those impulses, experiences, and feelings that are psychologically disturbing because they arouse a sense of guilt/anxiety	A subordinate "forgets" to tell the boss the circumstances of an embarrassing situation

Adjustive Reactions	Psychological Processes	Illustrations
Fixation	Maintaining a persistent nonadjustive reaction even though all the cues indicate the behavior will not cope with the problems	Persisting in carrying out an operational procedure long since declared by management to be uneconomical as a protest because the employee's opinion was not asked
Resignation, Apathy, and Boredom	Breaking psychological contact with the environment, withholding any sense of emotional or personal involvement	Employee who, receiving no reward, praise, or encouragement, no longer cares whether or not the job is done properly
Negativism	Active or passive resistance to something, often operating unconsciously	The supervisor who, having been unsuccessful in getting out of a committee assignment, picks apart every suggestion that anyone makes in the meetings
Projection	Individuals protect themselves from awareness of their own undesirable traits or unacceptable feelings by attributing them to others	Unsuccessful person who, deep down, would like to block the rise of others in the organization and who continually feels that others are out to "get him/her"

Source: Adapted from Elton B. McNeil, "Psychology and Aggression," *Journal of Conflict Resolution* 3, No. 3 (1959): 200–206 and 209–220.

In direct expression, employees are encouraged to let supervisors know how they feel. A supervisor may tell employees, "If something is bothering you, get it off your chest." This creates a verbal outlet, although there are risks that the aggrieved person will not stop at the talking stage but will act in a physical manner. (See box on page 357 titled, "How Do You Feel?")

Figure 17-4   Things Better Left Unsaid

Source: Garfield, 5/11/84. GARFIELD reprinted by permission of UFS, Inc.

Socially sanctioned activities such as sensitivity training and group therapy classes are methods for increasing awareness of the events or environments affecting one's behavior. Even competitive sports sponsored by the employer provide an outlet for reducing stress. There may be more merit to sponsoring a company bowling or basketball team than previously thought, along with the creation of recreational facilities on company property to encourage strenuous physical exercise. Many Japanese—and some U.S.—companies do just this.

Behavior directed toward some object other than the source of the problem is known as displacement. When the object is another person, the consequences usually are unpleasant. An example of displacement is when a supervisor's boss behaves in a hostile fashion toward the supervisor, and the supervisor responds with a similar treatment toward a member of the work group. The process continues as one party vents anger on another, who responds in a like manner.

The act of filing a grievance can be interpreted as taking a positive step toward correcting a problem. A procedure for systematically handling problems to provide justice is potentially a valuable outlet for frustration. Something is being done. We also anticipate that frustration is checked or reduced to some extent during the time required for the grievance to be settled.

In the next section, we examine the process of organizational change and its impact upon people including its stressful nature and how to deal with it most effectively.

Organizational Change

Social changes are found throughout our society and among the nations of the world. Last year's warring enemies are this year's allies, selling us their cars and television sets. Change is a fact of institutional life. On the one hand, change is a continuing threat to our sense of permanence and stability. On the other, change may lead us to a better future.

In a former era of this nation, big was beautiful, whether cars, sofas, or families. Today "Small is beautiful. Less is more." In the 1970s, those were trendy catch-phrases. In the 1980s they were becoming new principles of sound business management.[26] And "downsizing" continues unabated in the 1990s.

Innovation is a continuous part of our lives.

> A great obsession of Western industrialized civilization has been its preoccupation with newness. Driven by the furies of fickle technology, our consuming society flits from one new gadget to another—experiencing along the way the transition, uncertainty, and complexity of future shock. The ambiguity-borne stress that occurred only occasionally in the physical or cultural environment of earlier societies when they suffered some kind of cataclysm has become a constant stress in the contemporary world.[27]

With the threat of lost skills, lost jobs, diminished incomes, and a reduced sense of self-worth, many of us view change, at best, with ambivalence, as epitomized in the following scenario: "Congratulations, Murphy, on your suggestion of the month. You've won $100. As a result, we have eliminated 10 jobs. Unfortunately, one of them was yours."

How Do You Feel?

Sensitivity to what is causing personal problems is an important skill. Some people are not very perceptive to crises experienced by others. Av Weston of ABC news has coined a term for insensitive journalists. After witnessing a tragic fire on Christmas Eve, he observed what he was later to label "How Do You Feel?" journalism.

"[The fire] had wiped out an entire family except for the father who was away at the time. He stood there looking at the wreckage, which contained a gift-wrapped bicycle. The reporter jammed his microphone forward: 'Well sir, how do you feel?'
The man hit him."[28]

We are a nation of people and institutions in transition. In the pages ahead, our goal is to review how the change process affects the behavior of organizations and their employees, look at the several types of change occurring, suggest why people resist change, and indicate the role of supervisors in implementing planned change.

Change in Organizations

Thomas Bonoma and Gerald Zaltman describe **organization change** as

> a modification in the tasks, technology, structures, or people in an organization. This modification referred to is something that is new to the organization, and thus represents an innovation to that organization.[29]

organization change
A modification in the tasks, technology, structures, or people in an organization creating something that is new to the organization.

Change is the process of replacing or exchanging something, usually with something else within the same general category. In other words, the new different state or condition has some resemblance to that which preceded it. The automobile replaced the horse as a basic form of transportation. Transportation was not eliminated—just the method by which it was carried out. Similarly, the personal computer is replacing the typewriter as a mode of writing equipment. Change does not require a physical transformation. For example, values and attitudes change. Not all change, of course, is negative to individuals. Graduation from college, getting married, and being promoted are viewed as positive changes.

change
The process of replacing or exchanging something, usually with something else within the same general category.

Because change is a constant companion, our language possesses many words implying change, such as *remodel, diversify, convert, transform, alter, modify, expand, replace,* and *substitute,* to name a few. Verbally, at least, we are equipped for change. (See Chapter 1 for more about change.)

The nature of change also varies. Some changes are so small and insignificant that they go undetected, while others require deep personal adjustments to absorb. And some people are unable or unwilling to make the adjustments to change. Consider the following examples of change you may encounter during your working life:

- Introduction of radically new technology into an office or factory.
- Closing of a manufacturing plant or phasing out of a branch office where you work.
- Rapid expansion of operations including the number of employees working for you.

Robots continue to take over work once done by humans.

- Reassignment of members of your work group to another location in a separate building.
- Acquiring a new boss—one who exercises a very different style of leadership than your former one.
- Having your company acquired by another firm.

Yet, it seems that certain organizations are capable of introducing change using a proactive strategy with minimum upheaval while others have problems in "tying a new pair of corporate shoelaces." Why are some so successful while others fail? Chances are that the former understand the forces of change and have developed methods for dealing with change productively.

The process of change creates for many people a feeling of stress. It arises out of the uncertainty of what the future will be like and the possible personal harm it may bring. In other words, it upsets our zone of security.

The Zone of Security

zone of security
An individual's sense of security arising from stable working conditions and relationships with others that make a person's future more predictable.

Employees normally want to be successful in their jobs and to attain job security. Over time, an employee develops a **zone of security** reflecting stable working conditions and relationships with others. The zone is shaped by (1) the creation of comfortable working habits, (2) learning skills and how to follow procedures, (3) following the rules and policies of an organization, and (4) establishing reciprocal working relationships with people who warrant our trust.

The zone of security reduces feelings of uncertainty and makes a person's future more predictable. Job success and job security are fostered by the existence of the zone of security.[30] We seek to attain a condition known as **homeostasis,** which is a balance or harmony in our working lives. When our "security blanket" is changed or removed, we may experience a feeling of disequilibrium, an emotional imbalance or psychological instability. Both psychological as well as physiological problems can result. In our own ways, we attempt to avoid these problems by resisting change and reducing the amount of stress we experience.

homeostasis
A balance or harmony achieved in one's working life.

The Forces of Change

It is not mysterious why organizations implement changes. Clearly, managers make many innovations willingly because they view the outcomes as beneficial. In some manner, the new conditions or states created by change are superior to the former ones: lower unit costs, higher product quality, reduced risks, more customer value, better control. Still, in many instances, the process of change is painful to some of the persons affected by it because of a lost job, reduced status, or stress. Consequently, the process of change can produce a personal hurt that we would avoid—if only we could.

In many circumstances, change is mandated by forces or conditions supervisors cannot control as individuals. Even higher managers lack the capacity for holding back those forces originating outside of their organizations. Examples of internal and external environmental forces are found in Figure 17-5.

External Environment.   The external environment consists of several types of forces leading to change. These include economic, legal, political, social, cultural, and technological factors. For example, economic conditions create changes arising from competition, recessions, periods of rapid growth or decline, and high inflation rates. Failure to make successful adjustments can severely impair an organization's future operation or may even terminate its life. Legal and political forces found in law and actions of regulatory agencies exact changes. Social and cultural forces reshape value systems, attitudes, and institutions. Technological innovations produce advancements that, if not adopted, quickly create competitive inferiority for the laggards.

Internal Environment.   An organization's internal environment must adapt to the external forces. Consequently, new goals are formulated. Different organizational structures are created. People are moved around, sometimes asked to leave. The abilities, interests, and motivations of people may change. With rapid technological development, new skills are required. All of these dynamic factors require flexibility and the capacity to adjust and adapt to the new realities confronting organizations.[31] Still, in many instances, the process of making changes is frustrating and painful.

The Change Reaction Process

Somewhat predictably, the larger the number of resistance issues raised by employees, the greater the amount of personal stress they experience. Where change is perceived as a threat or unpleasant experience, workers undergo a number of negative emotional experiences as they internalize the meaning of the change and how it affects them personally. Workers go through several phases in the change process. Some never get through it. (See Figure 17-6 on

Figure 17-5 The Forces of Change

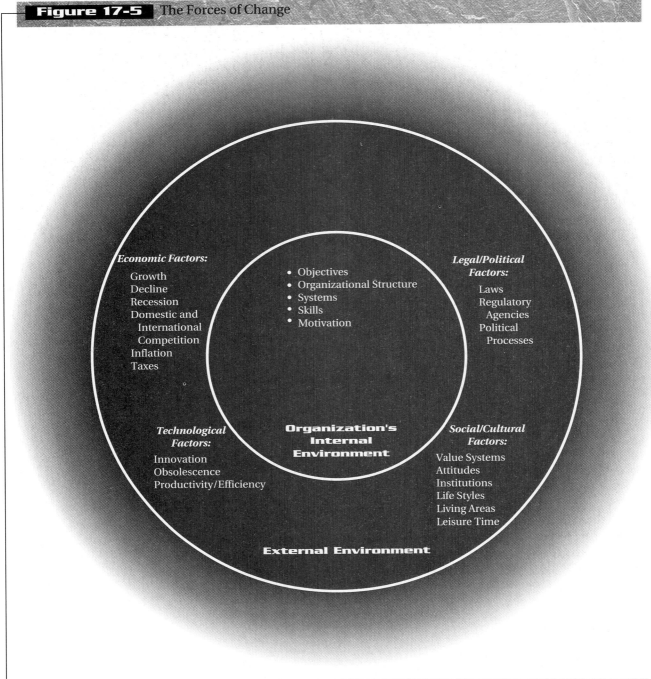

Economic Factors:

Growth
Decline
Recession
Domestic and
International
Competition
Inflation
Taxes

Legal/Political Factors:

Laws
Regulatory
Agencies
Political
Processes

- Objectives
- Organizational Structure
- Systems
- Skills
- Motivation

Organization's Internal Environment

Technological Factors:

Innovation
Obsolescence
Productivity/Efficiency

Social/Cultural Factors:

Value Systems
Attitudes
Institutions
Life Styles
Living Areas
Leisure Time

External Environment

page 361.) The first phase is an initial surprise or shock in learning about the change. The final phase is acceptance of the change. It should be apparent that the type of change we are describing is one with substantial significance to employees, thus excluding such issues as having one's office painted battleship

Figure 17-6 The Change Reaction Process

Phase	Emotional Response
1. Shock	The unexpected event produces anxiety and stress.
2. Disbelief	An initial refusal or reluctance to believe that "this is happening to me."
3. Guilt	The feeling that the individual is somehow responsible for what is happening. "It is my fault."
4. Projection	Placing the blame on someone else. "Management can't make up its mind and I suffer the consequences."
5. Rationalization	Becoming more comfortable with the idea of change. "Maybe it will work after all. Seems like an interesting plan."
6. Integration	Relating the various parts of the plan to a more comprehensive whole. "I think I see what they are trying to do and where my job is going to fit."
7. Acceptance	Viewing the change as satisfactory or favorable. "It's a better way of getting the job done and I think I am going to like it."

gray without being told in advance—still, to be on the safe side, previous consultation is advised.

An optimum change reaction should proceed rapidly through the first four dysfunctional phases. These phases represent the normal emotional responses when persons feel threatened. However, they block effective change. The fifth through seventh phases are considered functional. They represent adaptive behavior that is supportive of the change. Still, the methods of introducing change applied by higher management and supervisors will determine how rapidly and smoothly transitions take place and whether individuals ever proceed beyond the first four phases.

Principles of the Change Process

The Supervisor's Role

Planned change is well thought out before implementation begins. Objectives are clearly defined. Then, procedural steps are developed for achieving those objectives. A supervisor's role in the process varies from intensive involvement to a passive part. Sometimes, supervisors intentionally choose passive roles when they see no benefit from participation or they are busy with other matters. In addition, they may be antagonistic toward the change, view the effort as a futile exercise because their input is not instrumental in change decisions, or they see the change implemented successfully without their participation.[32]

In other circumstances, though, the supervisor should be involved in the change. As a link in the chain of command between their work team members and higher management, supervisors play an important role in communication and leadership. They should keep their subordinates informed about what is happening, train them to perform new tasks, and, through good leadership, provide motivation to see the process successfully completed.

The Principles of Change

Principles are basic truths. In this instance, they should serve as guidelines to management in implementing changes. A supervisor's ability to incorporate changes in a work group is made easier when the principles are followed. Most of them could be considered common sense.

- *Clearly state the purpose of the change.* Employees are curious about the "whys" of change. They may be skeptical about management's motives if, in the past, management has not been up-front with them. In most cases, employees should be informed about the purpose of the change. Explanations should be logical and complete, with no hidden agendas.

  Describe what the desired future will be like following the change. It may be useful to present a vivid picture of that future in specific terms, rather than explaining the goal in either complex or abstract terms. "Let me show you a picture—a schematic rendition—of what your office will look like and where you will be working in the new building," is more effective than, "Take my word for it, you'll like your new office."

- *Describe the payoff for the employee.* "What's in it for me?" Selfish? Probably. But if we want to enlist support, personal benefits to employees should result from the change they are asked to make. We should describe the benefits. However, if there are rewards for support, then there should be penalties for noncompliance. Describe the benefits and penalties. Unfortunately, today, many are forced to choose between two negatives—a little pain versus a lot of pain.

- *Encourage meaningful participation.* Participation should be legitimate, not a PR job. Participation improves communications because it helps people to be better informed. In some cases, we acquire information from workers that will improve our decision quality.

- *Communicate frequently.* When the change process covers a long time span, periodic progress reports are helpful. Explain the stages of change, indicating what employees can expect in the future. For example, during the early 1980s AT&T was ordered by a federal court to divest its telephone operating companies throughout the United States. AT&T conducted extensive communication with its employees informing them about their futures.[33]

- *Obtain support from informal leaders.* Enlist the support of informal leaders. Because of the influence informal leaders have within their groups, their support for change is important. Understanding group roles permits contacting individual members for support based upon the roles that they perform.

- *Prepare employees through training.* Change will be less stressful when those affected are prepared to perform their new jobs. Training is an important method not only for getting the future job done but also for instilling confidence in employees that they will be successful in attaining the new performance standards. Supervisors should emphasize the investment factor in training workers and the investment in the equipment or machinery they will be using. "Look, the company thinks you are important. They are spending $5,000 to train you to operate the new $1 million piece of equipment."

- *Concentrate on attaining good leadership.* Effective leadership is always important, but especially during periods of change. Supervisors, through their own self-confidence, can reassure others that survival is not only a distinct possibility but a certainty. "Maybe there's nothing to worry about. See how 'cool' our boss is."

- *Create a supportive organizational climate.* Most supervisors probably lack the resources, including authority or power, to make anything more than modest changes in an organization's climate. Within their work groups, however, they can attempt to create supportive group climates. Constrained by an organization's climate, a supervisor translates change into results in the most feasible manner available.

- *Consider the effects of change upon group culture.* One of the major results of change is its effect upon group culture. Status relationships are often altered. Task and social roles may be modified. Friendship relationships are impaired. All of these outcomes contribute to group culture shock during change. In these instances, the supervisor should assist during the change process by understanding the former relationships, how change affects those relationships, and the types of support employees require during transition.

In the remaining two chapters comprising Part 4, the focus of discussion shifts the supervisor's own personal needs for becoming more effective in managing a work team. These chapters are designed to give you many insights of appropriate strategies and skills to apply in various situations supervisors encounter in making decisions and handling problems. Part 4 gives methods which supervisors can apply to use their job time most effectively and provides guidance in career planning and development.

Later in the day, Carla had a few spare minutes. After finishing a production report in her office, she reflected on her brief conversation with Joe in the morning.

"I'm glad Joe can't count beyond three," Carla thought to herself—and just kidding, of course, as Joe was one of her most reliable and productive workers. With some serious consideration of the incident she realized there was more to it than met the eye, so to speak.

"Maybe there is some truth to what Joe was telling me. I have been very busy and my boss has put a lot of pressure on me lately. In fact, thinking about it, he blames me for things that are out of my control and I end up doing the same thing to members of my group," Carla decided.

"I'd better check to see if I have any more 'Joes' in my group, and I need to talk with the supervisor of the subassembly group—right away."

Summary: Focus on Skills

A person experiences job stress when he or she is confronted with a demand or challenge that threatens his or her ability to attain valued outcomes. Change is the process of replacing or exchanging something, usually with something else within the same general category.

Following are 11 suggestions to help supervisors manage stress and change within work teams and organizations:

1. Identify the symptoms of excessive stress including periods of insomnia, anxiety, irritability, fatigue, drug dependency, excessive appetite or loss of appetite, inability to concentrate, and a decline in the quantity or quality of work. If acute or prolonged in nature, they may indicate the presence of stress—or something more serious.

2. Realize that the sources of stress may occur within the personal life of an employee, in conditions found in the work environment, and within the job itself.

3. Consider the cascading effect of stress found in assembly-line hysteria and stress carriers.

4. Keep in mind that effective management of stress includes successful competition for resources, maintaining harmony where there is task interdependence, removing jurisdictional ambiguities, minimizing status conflicts, practicing open and honest communication, and understanding individual traits of workers.

5. Reduce stress by making jobs more challenging, utilizing the range of individuals' talents, providing appropriate balance of work, resolving role conflicts, avoiding too many policies and regulations, refraining from creating information overloads, and setting realistic deadlines.

6. Understand defense mechanism behavior, the types of adjustive reactions persons take, and the appropriate responses, if any, to each.

7. Use techniques such as catharsis to reduce frustrations.

8. Assume that the remainder of your working life will be filled with continuous changes and encourage all with whom you work to take proactive approaches to problem solving and forecasting.

9. Understand how both external and internal organization environments bring about changes.

10. Appreciate the zone of security employees follow when change is introduced affecting their working—and personal—lives.

11. Apply the principles of change to, as Captain Picard of the Starship Enterprise says, "Make it so." They include: clearly state the purpose of the change, describe the payoff for employees, encourage meaningful participation, communicate frequently, obtain support from informal leaders, prepare employees through training, concentrate on providing good leadership, create a supportive organizational (or work group) climate, and consider the effects of change upon group culture.

Review Questions

1. What is job stress? Are all forms of stress harmful? Explain.
2. Comment on the following: "Supervisors should attempt to manage stress within their work groups."
3. Indicate the more common symptoms of stress.
4. Give the major causes of stress.
5. What methods do employees utilize to reduce stress?
6. What is a defense mechanism? Under what circumstances are they harmful? Should supervisors attempt to eliminate defense mechanism behavior of employees? Explain.
7. What techniques are available to supervisors to reduce frustration and stress of employees?
8. What is organizational change? Why does it occur?
9. Give three types of change. How are they interrelated?
10. What is the zone of security?
11. Describe the stages of the change reaction process.

12. State the principles of change the supervisor can apply in assisting employees to adapt to change.

Notes

1. "Lions Devour Steelers," *Missoulian,* November 25, 1983.
2. J. E. Yates, "Managing Stress," *Management* 1 (September 1979): 13.
3. A. Farnham, "Who Beats Stress Best—And How," *Fortune,* October 7, 1991, 71.
4. See R. Maturi, "Stress *Can* Be Beaten," *Industry Week,* July 20, 1992, 23–28.
5. Farnham, "Who Beats Stress Best," 72.
6. J. E. McGrath, "Stress and Behavior in Organizations," in *Handbook of Industrial Psychology,* ed. M. D. Dunnette (Chicago, IL: Rand-McNally, 1976).
7. Farnham, "Who Beats Stress Best," 76.
8. Ibid., 71.
9. B. M. Meglino, "The Stress-Performance Controversy," *MSU Business Topics* 25 (Autumn 1977): 53.
10. See M. T. Matteson and J. M. Ivancevich, "The How, What and Way of Stress Management Training," *Personnel Journal* 61 (October 1982): 768–774. Also see R. D. Allen and others, "Occupational Stress and Perceived Organizational Effectiveness in Formal Groups," *Personnel Psychology* 35 (Summer 1982): 359–370.
11. B. M. Meglino, "Stress and Performance: Are They Always Incompatible?" *Supervisory Management* 22 (March 1977): 3.
12. M. J. Colligan and W. Stockton, "The Mystery of Assembly-Line Hysteria," *Psychology Today,* June 1978, 94.
13. L. L. Steinmetz and H. R. Todd, Jr., *Supervision: First Line Management,* 5th ed. (Homewood, IL: Irwin, 1992), 330.
14. Ibid.
15. J. S. Shepherd, "Manage the Five C's of Stress," *Personnel Journal* 69 (July 1990): 64.
16. The discussion is based upon K. N. Wexley and G. A. Yukl, *Organizational Behavior and Personnel Psychology* (Homewood, IL: Richard D. Irwin, 1977), 173–177.
17. "Rough Day at the Office," *U.S. News & World Report,* July 1988, 66.
18. Farnham, "Who Beats Stress Best," 82.
19. Yates, "Managing Stress," 14.
20. A. Nelson, "Supervisors Unwittingly Cause Work Place Stress," *Supervision* 51 (December 1990): 5–7.
21. Farnham, "Who Beats Stress Best," 82.
22. "Why You Get Angry—And What To Do About It," *U.S. News and World Report,* April 26, 1982, 74.
23. See T. W. Costello and S. S. Zalkind, *Psychology in Administration: A Research Orientation* (Englewood Cliffs, NJ: Prentice-Hall, 1963), 147.
24. B. Berelson and G. A. Steiner, *Human Behavior: An Inventory of Scientific Findings* (New York: Harcourt, Brace and World, 1964), 557–558.
25. V. Bozzi, "Love and Labor Lost," *Psychology Today,* April 16, 1988.
26. *The Wall Street Journal,* October 15, 1982.
27. W. Woodworth and R. Nelson, "Witch Doctors, Messianics, Sorcerers, and OD Consultants: Parallels and Paradigms," *Organizational Dynamics* 8 (Autumn 1979): 17.
28. W. L. MacDougall and D. R. Levine, "TV News Gets Bigger, But Is It Better?" *U.S. News & World Report,* February 21, 1983, 50.
29. T. V. Bonoma and G. Zaltman, *Psychology for Management* (Boston, MA: Kent Publishing Company, 1981), 299.
30. See L. W. Mealiea, "Employee Resistance to Change: A Learned Response Management Can Prevent," *Supervisory Management* 23 (January 1978), 18–19.
31. See J. C. Wofford, *Organizational Behavior: Foundation for Organizational Effectiveness* (Boston, MA: Kent Publishing Company, 1982), 397–398.
32. Bonoma and Zaltman, *Psychology for Management,* 300.
33. T. Payne, "Passage—Getting from Here to There During Change," *Supervision* 54 (May 1993): 11.

Hard Times

Hard times had fallen on the Mallory Corporation. The recent recession had reduced sales by 50 percent. The company had not shown a profit in over four years. Mallory manufactured fine furniture at the top end of the line. Typically, the company sales followed general economic trends such as disposable personal income and new home construction.

To survive, Frank Mallory, the owner and general manager, had decided to switch half of his production from hand-crafted furniture to less expensive, unfinished furniture. New equipment and manufacturing processes would be implemented. He foresaw a need for the same number of employees when economic conditions improved, although half of the workers would need to be retrained to operate the equipment.

Frank faced another dilemma. If he spoke honestly with his employees about his proposed 50 percent reduction in the work force, some, if not most, of his best people might leave to find work elsewhere. Skilled workers usually could locate jobs even in poor economic times because of their craftsmanship. They were always in demand. And several already were thinking about starting their own small furniture manufacturing companies.

Frank disliked the idea of not giving them a warning that close to 50 would probably be out of work by the end of the month. Then, there was the problem of who would be laid off first. Some of the old timers with the most seniority were not as good at their jobs as some of the younger workers. Another concern of Frank's was the families of workers. Although some had their husbands or wives working, others were the sole support of their households. If they were laid off, they faced severe financial hardships.

Economic conditions were forcing Frank to make a change. Something had to be done in the near future. But what should he do?

Questions

1. How can Mallory retain his most skilled workers? (The skills required for the unfinished furniture should be considered in your decision.)
2. Assuming the workers were nonunionized, what criteria would you use in making your decision about which employees to lay off first?
3. Is it possible to be fair to workers and, at the same time, to consider the well-being of the company? How are the two related?
4. Would it be fair to treat all employees equally?
5. How should layoffs be handled in the future, assuming Mallory survives the current economic problems?

East Side, West Side

"Sometimes when you try to be fair, what do you get for it? A kick in the 'you-know-where,'" Molly Jorgensen lamented to her boss. "When we had to move to other offices, we had a choice of several on either the east side of the building or over on the west side. The east side offices are nicer. Yet, they are less convenient to the other services here. The east offices are also more private. However, the ones on the west side are closer to the employee lounge and the opportunity to socialize is greater.

"So I told my staff they could make the decision about which ones we would take. They met after work last Monday to vote on the issue. My policy is majority rule. The vote turned out six to five to take the offices on the east side. Well, we no sooner moved than the complaints began from the minor-

ity group. What made matters even worse, one of the six changed his mind. But we were already moved and the other offices were taken by the mail room staff. I don't think anyone is happy with the decision."

"What are you going to do now?" asked Molly's boss.

"I don't know," Molly responded. "There's got to be an answer somewhere. But it hasn't come to me yet."

Questions

1. What went wrong? Is employee participation in decision making a good idea in this situation?

2. How would you have handled the situation initially?

3. What should Molly do now?

4. What other management lessons are illustrated by this case?

PART 4

Individual Considerations for the Supervisor

In Chapters 18 and 19, we examine the process of personal development and growth. First we look at improving the use of time, that is, methods supervisors can use for increasing their time effectiveness. Finally, we conclude our study of supervisory management with a presentation on career development.

CHAPTER 18

Using Time Effectively

● Not all meetings are created equal.[1]

Lynn Oppenheim

LEARNING OBJECTIVES

1. Understand the concept of time management, indicating why it is important to supervisors.
2. Show how a supervisor's time is controlled by three sources.
3. Explain the causes of procrastination.
4. Identify the major time wasters.
5. Describe methods you can apply to increase time effectiveness.
6. Perform a time analysis of work activities and know how to implement a plan to use time more effectively.

CHAPTER 18   Using Time Effectively

Time management is a serious study of how time is spent. The purpose for analyzing time and activities is to increase overall job effectiveness. In this chapter, we look at major time wasting activities encountered by the typical supervisor. Then, methods are presented for reallocating time effectiveness, including the maintenance of a daily time log. A procedure is demonstrated for reallocating time to more productive purposes.

CHAPTER 19   Career Planning and Development

Careers and career paths are the subject of Chapter 19. People follow either one of two career routes: passive or active career development. A development matrix is suggested for supervisors. It includes (1) technical and professional development, (2) interpersonal development, and (3) managerial and administrative development. Finally, the responsibilities of the individual and those of the organization are considered in the professional growth and development process.

"What a beautiful day," Carla thought as she drove down Evergreen Way to work at the Boeing aircraft plant in Everett, Washington. "I've been putting off for months finishing a plan for improving our unit's productivity. Because we're instituting a reengineering program the first of the year as a part of the company's TQM, I want to get a head start. But I need to find time to do some serious work on this. It seems that good intentions to complete the project just don't work out. Too many interruptions. Today's going to be different, though, and I'm going to spend the entire afternoon on this project."

Using Your Time More Productively

Peter Drucker observed, "Time is the scarcest resource and unless it is managed nothing else can be managed."[2]

Knowing how to use time effectively is one of the greatest assets a manager can possess. When things change quickly as they do today so that obsolescence is always just around the corner, the manager who squanders this precious resource is truly at a great disadvantage. Yet many managers allow themselves and their subordinates to behave in ways that waste a great deal of time.[3]

Estimates vary about the amount of time wasted, but for those forms of work in which machines do not dictate the pace, the amount of time wasted can be large. For example, it is estimated that most office workers—and their supervisors—could increase their productivity 20 to 40 percent by managing their time better.[4]

On occasions, we have asked supervisors if they have ever analyzed how they spend their time. Probably less than 5 percent have attempted a meaningful time analysis. Yet, on the job as in the classroom, some people seem to obtain more results from their use of time than do others. What is their secret? We suspect those using their time more effectively have made a conscientious effort to manage how they spend their time.

Although supervisors may have limited responsibilities for planning other than in the short term, most of them *can* make improvements in their personal management of time, a form of planning and organizing—self-discipline, if you will. In this chapter, we are continuing the change process discussed in the previous chapter. However, rather than change prescribed by higher management, our reallocation of how we spend time is self-determined. (See box titled "Compressing Time.")

Time management is a study of how time is spent for the purpose of increasing overall job effectiveness. An indirect, yet important, benefit of better time management is the freeing up of time that can be directed toward other job tasks or valuable life activity spheres of family involvement, community activities, and recreational pursuits.

Culturally, we view time differently. The Navajo consider the here and now and tend to discount a promise of something occurring in the future, while the Japanese view the long term in many decades and the Chinese, in centuries.

> As a rule, Americans think of time as a road or a ribbon stretching into the future, along which one progresses. The road has segments or compartments which are to be kept discrete ("one thing at a time"). People who cannot schedule time are looked down upon as impractical.[5]

Some individuals consider time as a commodity to be saved. Others view it as investment. Unfortunately, others live in a gray area in which time is seen as a sentence to be served and wait anxiously for the working—or studying—to end.

A major accomplishment of successful supervisors is their ability to manage their time and avoid time traps.[6] Each of us has 10,080 minutes each week to

time management
A study of how time is spent for the purpose of increasing overall job effectiveness.

Learn to manage time well or it will manage you! Effective time management and effective supervision go hand-in-hand.

Compressing Time

Time is an increasingly rare commodity. All of the "toys" we now have at our disposal—FAX machines, cellular phones, high-speed on-line computer systems—are invaluable in today's business world. Back in the fifties, when we were just beginning to envision these high-speed, labor-saving devices, we were concerned with how we would deal with all the leisure time we would have.

Unfortunately, no leisure time resulted. Instead, these marvelous machines force us to get work done in a shorter time. What we used to take a week to get done, we now do in a day. Our customers expect it, our bosses insist on it, and the competitive market demands it. Time is compressed.[7]

spend. No one has more, no one has less. How we consume this 10,080 minutes depends upon how wise we are as supervisors and leaders.

The value of time is directly related to the deadline by which a task must be accomplished and our ability to accomplish the task. Consequently, if the tasks performed are unimportant and there are no pressing deadlines for their completion, time has less value. But this does not accurately describe situations supervisors face continuously. Supervisors time is valuable. On the following pages, we will review how supervisors use their time; take a look at common time-wasting activities; and identify ways we can improve our time effectiveness, or the use of our time.

Influences on How Supervisors Spend Their Time

William Oncken and Donald Wass describe how a supervisor's time is controlled by three sources:[8]

1. *Boss-imposed time.* The boss exercises control over the time of a supervisor. The supervisor has to be responsive to the dictates of the boss. Failure to do so can bring about quickly applied penalties.
2. *System-imposed time.* Here, the supervisor must respond to the needs inherent within the organization or system. For example, requests from peers for assistance must be answered satisfactorily. To fail to do so will also bring about sanctions, although often less direct or not as rapidly imposed as in boss-imposed time.
3. *Self-imposed time.* Supervisors determine what they plan to do with self-imposed time. However, part of it may be consumed by subordinates. What remains is discretional in use. There are no direct organizational sanctions or penalties governing self-imposed time. Although it is the easiest segment of time to violate, it is also potentially the most productive area within which an increase in time effectiveness can be made. The supervisor controls this segment, although subordinates can exercise influence.[9]

How supervisors spend their time, then, is heavily influenced or controlled by others. Less independence is available than one might expect. In managing time, it would appear more realistic to change one's own behavior than that of the boss. Subordinates are another matter. Over the long run, one of the most effective means for improving time management is role modeling. If a supervisor's boss is a good time management role model, half the battle is won.[10]

Procrastination

Our management of time is also influenced by circumstances escaping our awareness but subconsciously affecting our behavior. Although poor scheduling may create inefficient use of time, a major problem arises from procrastination. (See Figure 18-1.) To **procrastinate** is to postpone or needlessly put off doing something until a future time. "Procrastination is not just a bad habit but a way of expressing internal conflict and protecting a vulnerable sense of self-esteem."[11] Procrastination may result from such causes as fear of failure, apprehension of being too successful, indifference arising from the routine or boredom of tasks, or resistance to authority exercised over us. Introspection would be valuable for identifying the underlying causes of our motives here. (See box titled "Procrastination.")

The fear of failure is manifested through delays. At the last minute, a project is completed. If the outcome was successful, we can fall back on the notion that we performed at an acceptable level and would have done even better with more time.

The fear of success is a more perplexing situation. It does not meet the test of reasonable behavior. For example, "I'm really depressed. I won the lottery." Yet, when considering what could happen as the result of success, some people move in the other direction. Promotions, transfers, fame, and adverse peer reactions are undesirable to them. They may say, "I don't want to move." "I don't want all that attention." Procrastination, in these areas, is viewed as a solution, not a problem. If a person puts off buying a lottery ticket, for example, he or she will not have to cope with the undesired effects of winning.

Many if not most jobs typically possess some boring features. We may perform those tasks last and avoid them, if possible. Thus, the chore-work is the last performed. Studying for an important examination, for example, probably has a high opportunity cost in terms of pursuits that would provide more short-run pleasures.

Finally, we may resist the authority others have over us. One of the ways in which we rebel is to delay carrying out some assigned tasks. Often, delays are per-

procrastinate
To postpone or needlessly put off doing something until a future time.

Figure 18-1 Procrastination

Source: Peanuts, 4/10/82. PEANUTS reprinted by permission of UFS, Inc.

Procrastination

Beth spends hours sorting through papers and straightening her desk rather than working on the report due the end of the week. Greg hides from his sales manager because he hasn't put together the sales figures his manager requested. Marjorie knows she should be sorting her records to prepare for filing her income tax return, but they are still piling up in a box.[12]

petrated because we are able to convince others that actions are not possible at this time.

A realistic approach to improving the use of time should consider, first, the organizationally imposed restraints and, second, the psychological implications. Consider the following methods for reducing the urge to procrastinate.

Steps to apply in breaking the procrastinating habit include (1) take the first step on the project that has been delayed, perhaps spending only 10 minutes initially and anticipating that by the end of this period personal involvement is beginning to develop; (2) apply the principle of tying a mental process to a physical action such as using a word processor to put your thoughts down; (3) do additional research to gather enough information to see the problem more clearly; (4) develop self-motivation by listing the advantages of completing the project and the disadvantages if it is not finished; (5) establish a realistic deadline for completion; and (6) persevere and if stuck in one part of the project turn to another stage.[13](See box on page 376 titled "Behavior Modification.")

Time-Wasting Activities

Time wasters come in a variety of forms. They consist of the occurrence of activities, events, and conditions producing few tangible outcomes or results of low value.[14]

time wasters
The occurrence of activities, events, and conditions producing few tangible outcomes or results of low value.

Obviously, not all supervisors work at desks, are interrupted by countless visitors, or are immersed in a sea of correspondence. Each organization is different, creating a unique working environment. What is a time waster for one person causes no problems for another. R. A. Mackenzie has identified 15 of the most frequently mentioned time-wasting activities or conditions managers face. These are listed in Figure 18-2. Although Mackenzie investigated high-level managers, his findings are also applicable to many supervisors. A full 75 percent of Mackenzie's time wasters are in the self-imposed time category. Mackenzie's scenario, developed over 20 years ago, is still valid today. (Refer to Chapter 2 for a discussion of the Pareto principle.)

Supervisors attribute their own wasted time to a variety of causes. Their bosses and organizations may waste their time through poor communication practices, too many meetings, and too much paperwork. Sometimes their bosses may be poor delegators, creating work bottlenecks. Or the reverse may be present where their bosses abdicate by delegating all of their work to their supervisors. In other instances, organizations fail to provide enough employees for the amount of work, hire untrained people or people with insufficient skills, or fail to provide adequate working facilities. However, the majority of time wasters cited by supervisors were self-caused. (See Figure 18-3.)

Behavior Modification

Try behavior modification to help break bad habits. For example, use a rubber band around your wrist. Whenever you do something as a habit you wish to break, give yourself several smart slaps with the rubber band. Either your habit will be broken or you will end up with a sore wrist.

Another technique with the imposing label *response costs contingency management* requires earning rights to do things. For example, when you should do something you find unpleasant, provide yourself with a reward after completing the unpalatable task.

Desensitizing is another behavior modification measure. Work up to the unpleasant event—for example, completing the writing of a speech you are going to make. Then, through a series of images, visualize elements of the scene, perhaps following a sequential order. For instance, begin by visualizing preparation of the speech and the topics you plan to cover. Visualize walking out on the stage before your audience. Visualize making your opening statements and, later, the questions you will be asked and your answers.[15]

Improving Your Time Effectiveness

Although dramatic 20 to 40 percent improvements in productivity may occur through better time management, in reality many solutions are neither simple in design nor easily implemented. Time management writers have developed an impressive array of strategies for tackling the problem, ranging from clever and ingenious to impractical and ludicrous. Strategies for conserving time for more effective use should not be counterproductive or unduly unpleasant. If our friends occasionally waste our time, we can terminate friendships, but the working environment is less pleasant because a support system has been removed.

Figure 18-2   Mackenzie's 15 Major Time Wasters

1. Telephone interruptions
2. Drop-in visitors
3. Meetings (scheduled and unscheduled)
4. Crises
5. Lack of objectives, priorities, and deadlines
6. Cluttered desk and personal disorganization
7. Ineffective delegation and involvement in routine and detail
8. Attempting too much at once and estimating time unrealistically
9. Lack of, or unclear, communication or instruction
10. Inadequate, inaccurate, or delayed information
11. Indecision and procrastination
12. Confused responsibility and authority
13. Inability to say "no"
14. Leaving tasks unfinished
15. Lack of self-discipline

Source: R. A. Mackenzie, *New Management Methods for You and Your Staff* (Chicago, IL: Dartnell, 1975), 75.

Figure 18-3 Examples of Time Wasters and Sources of Problems for Supervisors

The Time Wasters	Sources/Causes of Problems		
	Supervisor	Boss	Organization
Poor communication	■	■	■
Too many meetings or unproductive meetings	■	■	■
Insufficient information to make timely decisions	■	■	■
Too much paperwork or in-house reporting	—	■	■
Interruptions by visitors, colleagues, and employees	■	—	■
Inadequately trained employees	■	—	■
Noise	■	—	■
Telephone interruptions	■	—	■
Lack of delegation	■	■	—
Insufficient number of personnel, inefficient equipment, lack of facilities	—	—	■
Facilities scattered in different locations	—	—	■
Poor filing systems	■	—	—
Too many routine tasks	■	—	—
Procrastinating in crisis management	■	—	—
Cluttered desks	■	—	—
Coffee breaks too frequent or too long	■	—	—
Lack of work priorities	■	—	—
Making mistakes and redoing work	■	—	—
Lack of good organization	■	—	—
Failure to listen	■	—	—
Too many outside activities	■	—	—

We could do without coffee breaks and lunch periods, and work instead. But we enjoy our breaks and lunches and the people with whom they are shared.

On the other hand, a strategy to keep people out of the supervisor's office unless a crisis has struck is the "red geranium ploy" borrowed from a former television series, "The Waltons." When the children's parents wished to be alone in their house (without umpteen children or the grandparents), they placed a red geranium on the porch railing. Everyone knew that meant to stay out of the house. It is not only effective, but it retains the goodwill of others. Supervisors might get a red geranium for their office and display it in a visible place when they do not wish to be disturbed (see Figure 18-4). As an extension of nonverbal communication and the management of symbols, it is a superior method to erecting a "Keep Out" sign and is less unbecoming than screaming, "Get out. Can't you see I am busy?" Once people are trained to the meaning, the red geranium, when placed in its strategic location, conveys the message subtly and humanely. The office is also a more attractive place to work—if you like geraniums. Granted, your employees may talk about your eccentric behavior, but they may develop their own equally creative methods for handling interruptions.[16]

Figure 18-4 The Red Geranium, Visibly Displayed

How a supervisor attempts to improve the effectiveness of time use should be based upon (1) the practicality of the method (remember, time constraints may be boss- and system-imposed), (2) the amount of improvement in overall team operational effectiveness (rather than transferring your problem to someone else), (3) acceptance of the change by others, and (4) the psychological dimensions determining why people—including yourself—procrastinate.

We will review a few methods for improving time effectiveness. They zero in on the major areas where improvements could produce the largest benefits.

Strategies for Improving Time Use

Delegate.   The more routine tasks and recurring types of decisions should be delegated to subordinates for monitoring and decision making. (See Chapter 6, "Organizing Principles.") Notice how the use of policies and procedures enables us to delegate. One of the myths of delegation, though, is that it always saves the supervisor time. Why? First, it may be hard to find subordinates who have time to complete the additional tasks. Second, delegating to the wrong person will likely require more time than if the supervisor completed the task him- or herself.[17] Another potential problem is that subordinates may resent having bosses delegating only the "chores" to them, saving the most interesting tasks for themselves.[18]

Improve Job Content.   Through job analysis, the content of the supervisor's job may be improved. In larger organizations, technical assistance might be obtainable. A listing or weighting of tasks should identify those carrying the highest payoff. If there is insufficient time to do everything, then those tasks with the lowest payoff should not get done. However, it is not uncommon for individuals to undertake low-priority tasks first because they are more enjoyable or they are easier to perform. In starting a work day, allow a few minutes to do something that is especially enjoyable even if the activity is not a priority item. Here, the activity serves as a motivator for getting through the remaining work day.

Engage in Networking.   **Networking** is building relationships through exchange or sharing of information, ideas, or resources among individuals, both horizontally—on the same organizational level—and vertically, at higher or lower levels. Supervisors network by getting to know other persons, especially those outside their immediate work area responsibilities, and learning about their skills, interests, strengths, and weaknesses. Networking takes numerous and diverse forms. For example, supervisors learn about other persons by taking work breaks with them, sharing lunch, joining organizations either within or outside of their organization, or becoming an information vagabond. An **information vagabond** is any individual who informally obtains information from various sources, identifies the content of messages in terms of informational needs of others, and transmits information to them. When the practice is widespread, communication networks transcend the more traditional formal channels. Conceivably, a building custodian may share information with the company president—or vice versa. Consequently, when supervisors have problems or informational needs, they know where to go for assistance, thus saving time.[19]

networking
The building of relationships through exchange or sharing of information, ideas, or resources among individuals.

information vagabond
Any individual who informally obtains information from various sources, identifies the content of messages in terms of informational needs of others, and transmits information to them.

Control Access and Block Interruptions.   Changes in the work environment can save time. Blocking access to your work area from those who do not need to be there prevents unnecessary interruptions. Redesigning the layout of offices might include changing entryways, using furniture and cabinets to screen out distractions and provide greater privacy. Centralized telephone-answering systems channel calls and can block interruptions. Modify the open-door policy where the "door" is open, say, Tuesday and Thursday from 1:00 to 3:00 PM. Thus, the open door policy becomes more figurative than literal.[20]

Be Organized.   The components of being organized include having a plan to follow along with a schedule of what activities to follow and when. Have a place for everything because it generally takes longer to find something that has been misplaced.[21] Don't have a problem twice. That means not only having the proper resources available (equipment, tools, and supplies), but also making sure they are in operating order. In the era of high tech, don't overlook low-tech solutions. For some uses, an old-fashioned calendar is more effective than an elaborate electronic datebook.[22]

Limit Written Communication. "One of the peculiar things about the flow of paper on our desks is that it always increases —it never gets less."[23] With the advent of voice mail and e-mail, with computers and modems and scanners, the amount of written communication in many organizations has declined or taken an electronic form. Hallelujah! Paperwork often wastes time. Review reports, memos, and correspondence to determine if any can be eliminated. Why write a memo if you can talk to someone on the phone—other than as a form of self-protection? For some correspondence, use standard form letters, that is, a series of most common answers, ideally tucked away in your computer's memory. Never handle letters or memos more than once. Answers may be written on the letters or memos and returned without retyping a separate answer. And set a deadline for answering, such as by the end of the next working day. Have a good and convenient filing system that is periodically purged of outdated materials.

Along the same line, use more easily understood terms. Instead of the Defense Department's nomenclature of a "portable hand-held instrument inscriber," just say *pencil.* Finally, subordinates should be required to prepare written material in a format that permits a rapid conclusion to be reached and decisions made. When feasible, have them use a single-page executive summary at the beginning of the reports. (See box titled "The 25-Pound Report.")

Improve Meetings. If supervisors should institutionalize meetings with team members, they should also hold them at regular intervals at the same time and day of the week, maintain specific starting and ending times, use an agenda prepared and circulated in advance, show no mercy for those attending unprepared or arriving late, and have the person who talked the most at the preceding staff meeting take the notes at the next meeting. Develop methods for handling unwarranted meeting disruptions, including the disrupters themselves.[24] When possible, attend fewer meetings or send a subordinate stand-in.[25] Actually, formal meetings are usually required for only important decisions or issues.[26] Finally, keep a scorecard for evaluating the productivity and quality of meetings you conduct or have to attend. Figure 18-5 on page 382 represents a chart for tracking the value of a meeting. With a maximum of 100 points, each criterion is worth from 0 points (awful) to 10 points (outstanding). The supervisor's goal should be to increase the total value of such meetings.[27]

Increase the Amount and Effectiveness of Training. Perhaps one of the largest dividends in time management is providing additional training to employees whereby they can perform at higher levels with less supervision. Supervisors should consider cross training to increase flexibility in making work assignments and scheduling.

The 25-Pound Report

The incident is a Pentagon legend. On one of his first days as Secretary of Defense, Caspar W. Weinberger arrived at his desk to find a report giving the reasons for a single budget item. It was 2,916 pages long. Weinberger hit the roof, to the extent that his easygoing temper can fly. He called for an all-out war on the stultifying proliferation of paper and procedures throughout the department.[28]

Improve Personal Use of Time. There are numerous strategies for managing time. A few of the best are as follows:

1. Establish priorities for tasks.
2. Set realistic deadlines. (If you do not already use a sophisticated method to estimate how long it will take to complete a task, multiply the estimated time by two.)
3. It is more motivating to complete an entire task or project at one time than by bits and pieces over a longer time, with the following exception. Use the **Swiss cheese method of project management** for very long or complicated projects—"poke holes" in the project by completing small pieces, one at a time.
4. Learn how to say "no" to requests for your time when you are already busy (and when you can get away with it). Commonly, persons who already are acknowledged as very effective in performing their jobs are the first asked to undertake new assignments.
5. Never procrastinate.
6. Perform an audit of how you spend your time. Identify the most and least productive uses of time.
7. Realize that time management should incorporate not only the organizational requirements of "to have" and "to be" but also the personal needs dimension reflecting values. The "to have" means possessing something such as having your boss satisfied with your work or owning a new car. The "to be" implies the values to be achieved such as advancing to a more exciting job or becoming financially secure.[29]

Swiss cheese method of project management
Method for increasing motivation to complete an entire complicated task or project by completing small pieces, one at a time.

Finally, don't be the cause of inefficient time use by subordinates. Consider the following ways supervisors waste time of their team members: keeping them waiting for a decision or a meeting, giving poor instructions, or interrupting their work. "It might be helpful if we viewed appointments as contracts between people that ought to be honored as diligently as their written counterparts."[30]

Learn to say, "no." It's one of the most important and difficult time management skills of all.

A Model for Increasing Time Effectiveness

"Before you can manage time, you have to know what you're managing."[31] Supervisors should perform a periodic audit or inventory of how they spend their

Figure 18-5 Rating Your Meetings

| | | | | Rating | | | | | | |
| | Poor | | | | | | | | | Excellent |

	0	1	2	3	4	5	6	7	8	9	10
1. Starts on time?											
2. Has an adequate written agenda?											
3. Everyone present and prepared?											
4. Follows written agenda in order, without digression or backtracking?											
5. Leader encourages participation?											
6. Plenty of discussion of important points, without repetition?											
7. General agreement by end of meeting?											
8. Everyone clear regarding outcome of meeting, what each is to do as a result of meeting, and when he/she is to do it?											
9. Agenda completed?											
10. Ends on time?											

Keep completed scorecards as a record of your meeting experiences.

Source: Robert Moskowitz, *How to Organize Your Work and Your Life,* rev. ed. (New York: Doubleday, 1993), 110–111.

time. The audit provides a basis for analysis and preparation of a time management plan. An audit requires entering the amount of time consumed for each type of task or activity area during a given period such as one week. Several methods are available for measuring how a supervisor spends time. From the general to the specific, the approaches are (1) general activities, (2) functional, and (3) specific task or activity audits.

General Activity Analysis

This method is a simple means for measuring how time is spent. We use four categories:

- *Routine work.* Mechanically and regularly performed activities.
- *Normal work.* Basic supervisory functions comprising the majority of the workload; the day-to-day tasks involved in supervising.
- *Special work.* Nonrecurring assignments.
- *Creative planning.* Work designed to produce new methods or improvements in the work unit's operations.

Ideally, time is reallocated by delegating some of the routine work to subordinates while the creative work segment is increased.

Functional Analysis

Time is allocated to the individual supervisory functions of planning, organizing, staffing, directing, and controlling. If the supervisor also performs operative work (that is, the same work as members of the group supervised), a sixth category is included. Time effectiveness may be improved by reducing the operative work while increasing the time spent in the five functional areas. Functional analysis is primarily useful to obtain a general impression of how time is spent.

Activity or Task Analysis

The amount of time spent in each activity of a job is measured on a daily or weekly basis. An example of a daily activity **time log** is given in Figure 18-6. Common supervisory activities are included in this example, which is an actual listing of one supervisor's work activities. Those activities should be divided into sufficiently detailed tasks to identify meaningful time expenditures. For example, "communication" is probably too broad an activity for identifying which types of communication activities are most and least productive. Therefore, a more meaningful classification could be "reading and answering correspondence," "meeting with my boss," "holding staff meetings," and "counseling employees." The log should be maintained for an entire work week or several weeks.

time log
A method for recording activities performed and the amount of time spent performing them.

At the end of a week's recording of time by activities, the various activities are totaled. Figure 18-7 is an activity analysis and plan for improving time effectiveness. Instructions for completing the weekly summary in Section I of Figure 18-7 are as follows:

Column 1—Rate each activity in terms of its perceived worth. Those tasks producing the greatest results are considered "very important" and receive a 3; "important," 2; and "unimportant," 1.

Column 2—The weekly summary of time consumed by each activity is noted.

Column 3—The optimum or ideal amount of time the supervisor would like to spend for each activity is recorded in this column. For example, if 4 hours out of a 40-hour week are consumed in staff meetings, are these meetings producing 10 percent of the supervisor's total effectiveness? Also, are staff meetings the most important use for that time?

Column 4—The amount of reduction in time from the current level is indicated. For example, the supervisor may wish to reduce the amount of time spent in such activities as correspondence, attending committee meetings, preparing reports, making telephone calls, and meeting with the boss.

Column 5—Here, the amount of increase in time from the present level is entered. Our example reflects a desire to spend more time training new employees, scheduling work, planning, and being available for counseling employees.

Column 6—Present time effectiveness is computed by multiplying column 1 by column 3.

Column 7—A targeted time effectiveness is obtained by multiplying column 1 by column 3.

Section II of Figure 18-7 is concerned with a time effectiveness analysis in which the supervisor determines the improvements in the use of time to be

Figure 18-6 Daily Time Log

Instructions: List all of your work activities in which you spend a minimum of one-half hour during the week, although some of these activities may not be performed today, or you spent less than one-half hour on them. Then, record, at 15-minute intervals, how the time was spent. Total the day's results.

Job Activities	8–9	9–10	10–11	11–12	12–1	1–2	2–3	3–4	4–5	Total Hr Min
Giving employees instructions										
Reading & answering mail										
Meetings with my boss										
Training new employees										
Attending committee meetings										
Preparing reports										
Reviewing employees' work										
Receiving & making telephone calls										
Counseling employees										
Scheduling work										
"Creative" planning										
Deadtime: Coffee breaks										

Figure 18-7 Time Effectiveness Analysis

Section I: Weekly Time Log and Analysis

Instructions: Column 1: Rate each activity in terms of its perceived worth. Use a "3" for "very important," "2" for "important," and "1" for "unimportant." Column 2: Enter the total amounts of time for each activity from the daily time logs during the week. Column 3: Give your estimate of the optimum amount of time that should be spent for each activity. Column 4: Enter the amount of reduction in time, for each activity where such reduction is desired. Column 5: Enter the amount of increase in time for each activity where such increase is desired. Column 6: For each activity, multiply columns 1 and 2. Column 7: For each activity, multiply columns 1 and 3. Note: Columns 4 and 5 must be equal or you must adjust Column 3 for the next time period.

Job Activities	(1) Value of Activity 3, 2, 1	(2) Weekly Summary of Time	(3) Optimum Time to Spend	(4) Amount of Reduction	(5) Amount of Increase	(6) Current Effectiveness Rating (Col 1×2)	(7) Targeted Effectiveness Rating (Col 1×3)
Giving employees instructions	2	4	4			8	8
Reading & answering mail	1	4	2	2		4	2
Meetings with my boss	2	3	2	1		6	4
Training new employees	3	2	6		4	6	18
Attending committee meetings	1	4	2	2		4	2
Preparing reports	1	4	2	2		4	2
Reviewing employee's work	3	6	6			18	18
Receiving & making telephone calls	1	6	4	2		6	4
Counseling employees	3	1	2		1	3	6
Scheduling work	2	2	4		2	4	8
"Creative" planning	3	2	4		2	6	12
Deadtime · Coffee breaks	2	2	2			4	4
Total	– – –	40	40	– 9	+ 9	73	88

Section II: Time Effectiveness Analysis

A. To determine your present time effectiveness:

$$\frac{\textit{Current Effectiveness Rating (Total Column 6)}}{\textit{Weekly Summary of Time (Total Column 2)}} \div 3$$

$$\frac{73}{40} \div 3 = 61\%$$

B. To determine your targeted improvement in time effectiveness:

$$\frac{\textit{Targeted Effectiveness Rating (Total Column 7)}}{\textit{Optimum Time to Spend (Total Column 3)}} \div 3$$

$$\frac{88}{40} \div 3 = 73\%$$

C. To determine your percentage increase in time effectiveness:

$$\frac{\textit{Targeted Effectiveness "B" Above – Present Effectiveness "A" Above}}{\textit{Present Effectiveness "A" Above}}$$

$$\frac{12}{61} = 20\%$$

D. Conculsions:

   1. My most effective use of time is: _____

   _____

   2. My least effective use of time is: _____

   _____

Section III: Action Plan for Making Improvements

A. For each activity you plan to spend less time on, describe *how* you will accomplish the goal.

   1. The activity: _____

    The action(s) taken: _____

    _____

    _____

   2. (Repeat for each activity.)

B. For each activity you plan to spend more time on, describe *why* you think more time is needed and *how* you will accomplish the goal.

   1. The activity: _____

    The justification (why):q_____

    _____

    The action(s) taken: _____

    _____

    _____

   2. (Repeat for each activity.)

achieved by altering how time is allocated. The example indicates a 20 percent improvement in time effectiveness could be obtained by making reallocations of time among activities. It may be difficult to reduce time expenditures in the targeted reduction areas because they are system-imposed. In such circumstances, changes in the organization itself would be required, which may not be practical. For this reason, it is important to identify specific courses of action that are realistically available in reallocating time.

Section III of Figure 18-7 is an action plan outlining methods to be used to reallocate time. The plan is based upon an analysis of present time expenditures and the strategies for improving time effectiveness through reallocation of how time is spent. Identify tasks you are performing that could be eliminated entirely, reduced in scope, consolidated, or delegated to others. As an example, consider reducing correspondence time from four to two hours per week. A supervisor can make this reduction by developing routine letter responses for commonly used replies or by delegating more of this task to a secretary, if one has a secretary who has the time available. Or, the supervisor could use a computer, e-mail, or voice mail. Whatever the solutions chosen, they should be realistic.

Committing more time to certain tasks should be justified by the anticipated benefits to be received. The proposed increase in training time, for example, may be justified by such benefits as increased worker productivity, improved quality of work, and so forth.

Time audits should lead to establishing time effectiveness goals. Also, supervisors should apply time analysis to their subordinates. Are they spending their time on the most productive tasks? Time audits are applications of the reengineering concept. Periodic audits are required to determine improvements in the use of time. Initially, set a goal for reviewing every two or three months how time is spent. When improvements are large, the value of performing audits becomes apparent. What would a supervisor do with one or two additional days each week? In the final analysis, it's not so much how many hours a person works but rather how "smart" he or she works and the results obtained from those hours.

It was two hours after Carla's shift ended and she had not yet been able to find time to work on her special project. In spite of her good intentions, there had been continuous interruptions during the day and her schedule had slipped until only now was she completing her regular work. Ah, frustration!

As Carla drove away from the plant, she reviewed the events of her working day. "I've got to get a handle on this and get it done. I can't do it at home because the records I'm using are not to be removed from the plant and most are only accessible from the mainframe to my computer. What am I doing wrong?

"There were too many interruptions and some could have been prevented. Maybe my open door policy should be closed a bit. Some of the things could have been handled by my folks. Maybe I need to delegate more. Then there was almost an hour with Larry, my boss, who wasn't having a busy day and wanted to shoot the breeze—not many work matters, just talk. And when he wants to talk, he expects me to listen. I think tomorrow at my semi-monthly staff meeting with my group, I'll try to take care of some of these items. Then, it's off to the small east conference room—it has a PC and a door with an inside lock on it."

Summary: Focus on Skills

Time management seeks to identify how time can be used more productively. It is a form of planning and organizing. Improvements are made by analyzing how time is spent, establishing priorities, and developing strategies for eliminating wasted time. Time saved is reallocated to more productive activities.

Following are 20 suggestions to help supervisors to improve their time effectiveness:

1. Ascertain how work time is controlled by three sources: boss-imposed, system-imposed, and self-imposed.
2. If procrastination occurs, identify its causes.
3. Follow steps to stop procrastinating including: take the first step of completing a project, apply the principle of tying a mental process to a physical action, do additional research, develop self-motivation by listing advantages of completing the project and the disadvantages if it is not finished, establish a realistic deadline for completion, and if stuck in one stage move to another.
4. Apply behavior modification such as the rubber-band-around-the-wrist technique, rewards for project completions, and desensitizing.
5. Get a "red geranium."
6. Delegate.
7. Improve job content through such methods as job analysis and prioritizing tasks.
8. Engage in networking by building relationships with others outside of your work team.
9. Control access and block interruptions.
10. Be better organized by having a plan and schedule for activities, ensuring everything is in its place, and not having a problem twice.
11. Limit written communication and use language people understand.
12. Improve meetings by limiting their number, holding them at regular intervals at the same time and day of the week, maintaining a specific starting and ending time, using advance agendas circulated to those attending, controlling unwarranted interruptions, and using subordinate stand-ins for meetings.
13. Increase the amount of training of subordinates and use more effective training methods.
14. Establish priorities for tasks.
15. Set realistic deadlines.
16. Apply the "Swiss cheese" method for long and complicated projects.
17. Learn how to say "no."
18. Don't be the cause of inefficient time use by team members.
19. Perform a time audit to determine what are the most and least productive uses of time.
20. Develop and implement an action plan outlining methods to use in reallocating time.

Review Questions

1. What is the purpose of time management? What are its benefits?
2. A supervisor's time is controlled by three sources. What are they, and which one provides the supervisor with the greatest opportunity for improvement?
3. Why do people procrastinate? If you procrastinate, what are the causes?
4. Indicate six major time-wasters. Suggest solutions for overcoming the problems.
5. Describe the functional analysis of time and activity analysis. Why is activity analysis generally superior?
6. Describe the weekly time-log model with an illustration of its operations.
7. Using the examples in this chapter, maintain a time log for one week. Orient the log to your particular needs. What level of time effectiveness are you attaining, being realistic in your analysis?

Notes

1. L. Oppenheim, "Mastering the Meeting," *Chief Executive* (June 1991): 64.
2. P. F. Drucker, "How to Be an Effective Executive," *Nation's Business,* April 1961, 34.
3. M. F. Villere and M. M. LeBoeuf, "The TA Way to Stay on Top of Time," *Supervisory Management* 22 (February 1977): 9.
4. "How to Stop Wasting Time—Experts' Advice," *U.S. News and World Report,* January 25, 1982, 51.
5. E. T. Hall, *The Silent Language* (New York: Doubleday and Company, 1959), 15.
6. See R. A. Mackenzie, *The Time Trap* (New York: McGraw-Hill Book Company, 1975).
7. J. Menough, "Compressing Time," *Rubber World,* June 1991, 16.
8. W. Oncken and D. L. Wass, "Management of Time: Who's Got the Monkey," *Harvard Business Review* 52 (November-December 1974): 75–80.
9. Stein suggests that supervisors have other time commitments to deal with including staff time, vocational time, personal time, and career time. See F. J. Stein, "Finding Management Time," *Supervisory Management* 38 (February 1993): 7.
10. See A. W. Farrant, "Are You Wasting Your Time?" *Supervision* 39 (December 1977): 23–24.
11. J. B. Burka and L. Yuen, "Mind Games Procrastinators Play," *Psychology Today* 16 (January 1982): 32.
12. "Do It Now! Overcoming Procrastination," *Supervision* 54 (June 1993): 5.
13. "How to Stop Putting Off Till Tomorrow What You Really Should Be Doing Today," *Strategies for Business Owners* 20 (December 1990): 15–16. Also see J. Davidson, "Creative Procrastination," *Supervisory Management* 37 (October 1992): 9.
14. Many writers today use the term *time bandits* for time wasters. "Foil the Time Grabbers," *Executive Female* 15 (July–August 1992): 9.
15. S. S. Moramarco, "Stage Fright: What It Is and How to Beat It," *Supervisory Management* 22 (June 1977): 30–33.
16. Also see "Manage Your Time, Build Higher Profits," *Profit-Building Strategies for Business Owners* 22 (October 1992): 7.
17. L. Grensing, "Dispelling the Productivity Myths," *Security Management* 35 (December 1991): 18.
18. I. Masak, "Dare to Delegate," *CMA—The Management Accounting Magazine* 66 (October 1992): 6.
19. For more about networking see W. J. Rinke, "Networking Tips," *Training and Development* 46 (September 1992): 11.
20. R. Alexander, "Starving Out the Time Gobblers," *Supervisory Management* 38 (March 1993): 8.
21. "A Place for Everything," *Corporate Report—Kansas City* (May 1989): 15. Also see M. Dennis, "Organization is Crucial in the Management of Time," *Business Credit* 94 (October 1992): 27.
22. D. Schultz, "Improving Productivity in Management," *Journal of Property Management* 56 (July–August 1991): 31. Also see S. Silver, "The Zen of No Loose Ends," *Associate Management* 38 (September 1986): 22–25.
23. R. Wilkinson, "Eight Supervisory Tips," *Supervision* 52 (July 1991): 12.
24. D. Osburn, "Managing Meeting Disrupters," *Manage* 42 (May 1991): 8–36.
25. "Streamline Your Work Day!" *Practical Supervision,* July 1993, 3.
26. D. Brown, "Time-Saving Techniques," *Management Review* 80 (October 1991): 8.
27. R. Moskowitz, *How to Organize Your Work and Your Life,* rev. ed. (New York: Doubleday, 1993), 110–111.
28. "Weinberger: The Knife is Moving Sharply," *Time,* July 27, 1981, 10.
29. S. R. Phillips, "The New Time Management," *Training and Development Journal,* April 1988, 73–77.
30. T. Pollock, "A Personal File of Stimulating Ideas, Little-Known Facts and Daily Problem Solvers," *Supervision* 54 (February 1993): 24.
31. P. Patterson, "Effective Time Management Takes Diligence," *Institutional Distribution* 27 (July 1991): 108.

Case 18-1

Once upon a Time

Janice Johnson stared at the wall clock in her office—7:00 PM and she was still behind completing the monthly budget report which had to be finished before leaving for the day. To make matters worse, it was Friday evening. Everyone was gone except Herbert Worley, the custodian. Janice was principal of Grant Elementary School in Galena, Illinois. She supervised 20 teachers who taught from kindergarten through eighth grade students. She also was responsible for the vice-principal and four supporting staff personnel including two teacher's aides, a secretary, and the custodian, Herb.

At this moment, Janice was feeling very ambivalent about her job. For the past four years, she had been Grant's principal. For the previous six years, she had been a vice-principal at another elementary school in a community near Chicago, and prior to that, had taught in different elementary grades for six years. "If rising up the organizational ladder and becoming an administrator are so good, then why am I spending more and more time at work?" she thought. "I enjoy most of my job, but it is the constant interruptions and things that have to be done now that I don't like. I never seem to get anything finished. The work just stacks up. And the stacks seem to get higher and higher." She surveyed her office and her desk. Sure enough, the evidence was there. Several piles of paperwork were on her desk. They ranged from an inch or so of material, to one stack a foot in depth. "Darn," she thought.

"It seems everyone wants to talk to me or wants me to do something for them," Janice reflected on the day's activities. She had arrived at work a few minutes after seven this morning. The building's boiler was not functioning properly, so she called a repairperson. A few minutes later, one of her teachers called saying she was too ill to work and would not be coming to school today. Janice called four substitute teachers before locating one who was able (and willing) to fill in. During the day, there was a staff meeting with her faculty, a meeting with the county superintendent of education, a PTA group meeting, private meetings with three parents about their children's mischievous behavior, and so on.

Janice also worked on several reports, some overdue, attempting to complete them. The monthly supply requisition, student attendance report, and the budget report that was in front of her now were the most pressing ones. She also talked to several of her faculty individually and collectively during the day, covering such topics as how to maintain discipline in the eighth grade classroom, advising others about recent policy changes affecting their benefits, and counseling a young teacher about teaching methods. Janice even talked to Henry and Harriet (her fourth and sixth grade teachers) about their developing romance and what was proper behavior. They had been observed again hugging in the hallway. Janice recalled numerous telephone calls she had answered or made. Then there was the correspondence.

Herb Worley walked by her office and stopped at the door. "Working late again, Janice," he observed. "You've been doing a lot of that lately."

"Once upon a time, Herb, I could get out of here by five o'clock like everyone else. But things just seem to pile up on me," Janice said.

"Why Janice, you must have better things to do than be working here after seven. How old are you? I bet you must be about 38?"

Janice responded with a smile.

"As I was saying," Herb continued, "you are about the age of our last principal." Herb walked down the hall pushing his large dust mop.

Then Janice realized her predecessor was 38 when he was stricken by a heart attack that proved fatal. In fact, it was in this office and where she was sitting. Some said it was from overwork.

Questions

1. Who has the primary responsibility for the predicament Janice is experiencing?
2. What is the problem Janice is experiencing? Develop a plan of action to assist Janice in remedying this growing problem.

3. Why do people allow their work to expand, requiring them to spend more and more hours on the job?

4. What happens when people become overworked?

Case 18-2

Bosses

During the past half hour, six members of an informal group of staff supervisors had gathered in the student center cafeteria at Long Beach State University. It was 7:30 on a Friday morning. The customary meetings had begun several years ago. Each Friday morning, an hour before work began, they met in the campus cafeteria primarily to socialize, as they enjoyed one another's company. The group consisted of supervisory personnel from an assortment of staff support areas of the university including the admissions office, center for student development, physical plant, campus security, controller's office, and food service.

Although the meetings were very informal and filled with casual conversation, a lot of information was exchanged about what was going on at the university. This morning, the conversation turned to the subject of bosses after one of the group said she was experiencing a problem with her boss. The topic evidently stimulated others because they began sharing information about their past bosses who caused them problems. A sampling of their comments follows:

The incompetent: "I had a manager once who just didn't understand the work I was doing, let alone what my employees did. He didn't know our programs or procedures. Therefore, he was unable to represent us to the administration. Many times, he couldn't get the resources we needed while it seemed that other supervisors got their budgets approved. He also was unable to protect us from unnecessary hassles from above. He just seemed lost and wasn't on top of the job. As a result, I spent too much time fighting his battles."

The filter (or plug): "My boss wouldn't share information with me. I was left in the dark about what was going on. When my workers would ask questions, at times I couldn't give them the answers because my boss did not keep me informed. It made me look bad to my employees, especially when the grapevine had the information. When I could, I tried to access the grapevine or find other sources of information."

The nondelegator: "I had a boss who just would not delegate authority. As a result we were always having production delays and missing deadlines. Class schedules were late getting out. Students were frustrated about what courses were being offered the next term. I could crawl under a rock, at times."

The abdicator: "You should be so lucky. Mine delegated his entire job to me. I was overwhelmed with work. He didn't do anything. Just gave me all of his work. Talk about managing time. I managed mine and his both."

The grey ghost: "We had an administrator once who was known as the 'grey ghost.' He just seemed to disappear after coming to work. He was at work at the beginning of the day and at the very end, but during the day, no one could locate him. Often, we couldn't make decisions and had to wait until he showed up—if and when he did return to his office."

The MBP: "My boss was a first-class taskmaster at following policy and making sure that everyone else did also. Management by Policy (MBP), that was the standard order of the day. Policy conformity. Results seemed less important than the policy and procedural methods we had to follow. Now and then, we needed to 'bend' a policy to get something to work because either the policy didn't fit the situation or something had to be done right away. You could say, my boss was more interested in counting paper clips than obtaining tangible results."

It was a few minutes before eight o'clock as members of the group began leaving for their day's work. Only two remained as one said to the other, "If we had such poor bosses, how come all of us turned out to be such good bosses, ourselves?"

Questions

1. Explain how management practices illustrated in this case create problems for supervisors and waste their time.
2. Each of the examples of dysfunctional bosses illustrates waste of supervisors' time. Indicate how these supervisors could have attempted to reconcile the situations they experienced. In other words, how does boss-imposed time affect the ability of supervisors to manage their time?
3. It has been suggested that the ultimate management skill is being able to manage one's boss. How might this be done by the supervisors in this case, considering the types of bosses they have?

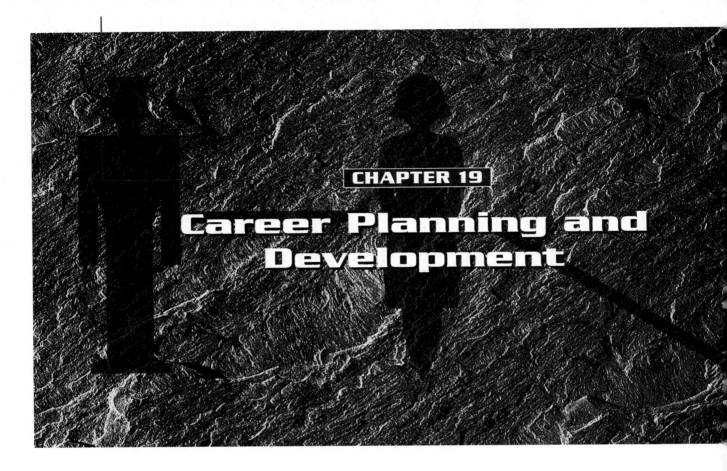

CHAPTER 19

Career Planning and Development

● Luck is where opportunity meets preparation.

Anonymous

1. Understand the concept of job satisfaction and its major components, intrinsic and extrinsic needs.
2. Explain the meaning of *career.*
3. Indicate why young people sometimes remain undecided about their vocational choices.
4. Indicate the meaning of career paths.
5. Describe why career paths are important to those who have them.
6. Distinguish between passive and active career development.
7. Discuss the shared nature of career development within organizations.
8. Understand the major strategies to follow in career management.

Carla was working in her small office at the Boeing plant. She was alone. The day had been particularly frustrating for Carla. With a full agenda of her daily assignments to carry out, throw in three or four unplanned events including one emergency, plus receiving the normal pressures from her boss to speed up a rush project, and a couple of complaints from members of her group, she once again kicked back with feet on her desk and proceeded to "beat up on herself." Adding to her frustration was the approaching annual appraisal from her boss.

"Am I really cut out for supervision and management? When I was offered this job, they gave me a functional job description. Any resemblance between reality and that description is purely accidental, coincidental, and more than a bit of fiction. It doesn't tell you the dynamics of what's going on here—people, stress, constant changes.

"But I enjoy my job and the people I work with. And the company has been good to me.

"Maybe I'm not supervisory material and should look for another kind of job. When I finished school, I made a plan for my career and set goals. Where I wanted to be and what I wanted to do. So far, I'm more or less on schedule."

Carla's reflections were interrupted by her boss, Larry, as he walked into her office with a serious expression. "Carla, at the end of your shift, I need to see you in my office. It's important. I'm in a hurry right now, but be there at three."

"What have I done now?" she wondered, with more than a bit of apprehension.

Bill Moyers once said, "It is not a certifiable fact, but more a statement of faith that each person is capable of being creative."[1] The implication is that people have the capacity to grow, change, and develop their talents to the extent they desire to grow. (See Figure 19-1.)

Professional growth can be measured several ways. For some, professional development means a career with periodic advancements, increasing job responsibilities, and the status conveyed by peers. Others see growth as maintaining professional skills in fields or occupations in which knowledge is rapidly changing.[2] It means keeping current. Most of us, though, want jobs and careers that permit a good measure of job satisfaction and the opportunity to make real contributions to our organizations.

In the pages ahead, we consider several topics including the importance of obtaining employment and job assignments that provide you with sufficient intrinsic value to make your working life more meaningful—or at least more interesting, challenging, or less stressful. To do this, we describe the concept of job satisfaction and how it is obtained in several dimensions. Finally, a career planning model is introduced for guidance in developing vocational interests into a life-long career.

Job Satisfaction

job satisfaction
The attitudes people have about their jobs.

Most people want jobs that are satisfying. **Job satisfaction** refers to the attitudes people have about their jobs. The United States and other industrialized nations have experienced a growing alienation of workers from their jobs and their employers. Gerald Susman, an organizational behavior professor, estimates that "25 percent of all U.S. workers . . . are unhappy in their jobs for one reason or another."[3]

Granted, many workers are alienated from their jobs. But their alienation is also found in other segments of their lives and is not solely reserved for their work and employment. Jeffrey Kane defines *work alienation* and its opposite, *work*

Figure 19-1 Some Careers Are Destined by Fate

Source: B.C. Cartoon, by permission of Johnny Hart and Creators Syndicate, Inc.

involvement, as "the extent to which one looks to work to provide the total amount of intrinsic fulfillment desired from life in general."[4] **Intrinsic fulfillment** means gratification of nonphysiological needs such as the "feelings one has in accomplishing something worthwhile." On the other hand, **extrinsic fulfillment** arises from such job elements as compensation, promotion, or the status attached to one's job. A person is, therefore, "completely work alienated when (intrinsic fulfillment) equals zero and completely work involved when it equals 100 percent."[5]

Kane believes that a person may not obtain rewards that produce intrinsic fulfillment from work; yet that person can continue working for extrinsic rewards obtained. In many cases, the job is not the focal point of the worker's life or even a source of great meaning. Rather, the job is an important vehicle by which a person enjoys other activities that bring satisfaction.

Work provides only one potential source of intrinsic rewards. Total intrinsic fulfillment from life is achieved from several sources—what Kane calls *activity spheres*. The other spheres include family, involvement in community affairs, and recreational activities. Thus, when considering all sources of fulfillment as totaling 100 percent, for most people substantially less than 100 percent of their intrinsic fulfillment will be obtained from work. In fact, "it is undoubtedly healthy for most persons to be work alienated to some degree."[6]

We can examine the degree of job satisfaction by either looking at the entire job or reviewing the individual components comprising that job. For example, the **global view of job satisfaction** encompasses all aspects of a person's job. It is the sum of all intrinsic and extrinsic elements that, combined, create the total job. Rarely have we encountered an employee who would rate his or her job as a "1" on a scale of 1 (low) to 10 (high).

The **component view of job satisfaction** considers the different job elements and the degrees of satisfaction derived from each. The major components of a job include the following:

- The nature of the work (intrinsic values)
- Coworker relationships
- Compensation received
- Promotional opportunities
- Quality of supervision received
- Working conditions (the physical environment, including safety)

While the global view is a macro perspective of the job, the component view is a micro treatment of individual elements. Typically, varying degrees of satisfaction are found for each job component. As one might expect, the relative importance of the components, themselves, varies from one individual to the next. For some of us, having interesting, challenging work is more important than pay—at least beyond some point. Others, facing personal financial crises, probably have the opposite opinion. This may be related to Maslow's hierarchy of human needs. (See Chapter 11.)

Figure 19-2 illustrates the two views of job satisfaction along with the relationship of the components to a person's life activity spheres. **Life activity spheres** are the relative distribution of an individual's intrinsic values into various categories including work, family, recreation, and community service. Diagram (a) portrays the interactions of the several job components, and (b) represents a distribution of components for a person who, in this illustration, places a relatively

intrinsic fulfillment
Gratification of nonphysiological needs such as the feelings one has in accomplishing something worthwhile.

extrinsic fulfillment
Gratification of needs arising from job elements such as compensation, promotion, or job status.

global view of job satisfaction
The sum of all intrinsic and extrinsic elements that create a person's total job.

component view of job satisfaction
Considers the different individual job elements and the degrees of satisfaction derived from each.

life activity spheres
The relative distribution of an individual's intrinsic values into various categories including work, family, recreation, and community service.

Figure 19-2   Views of Job Satisfaction and Work as a Life Activity Sphere

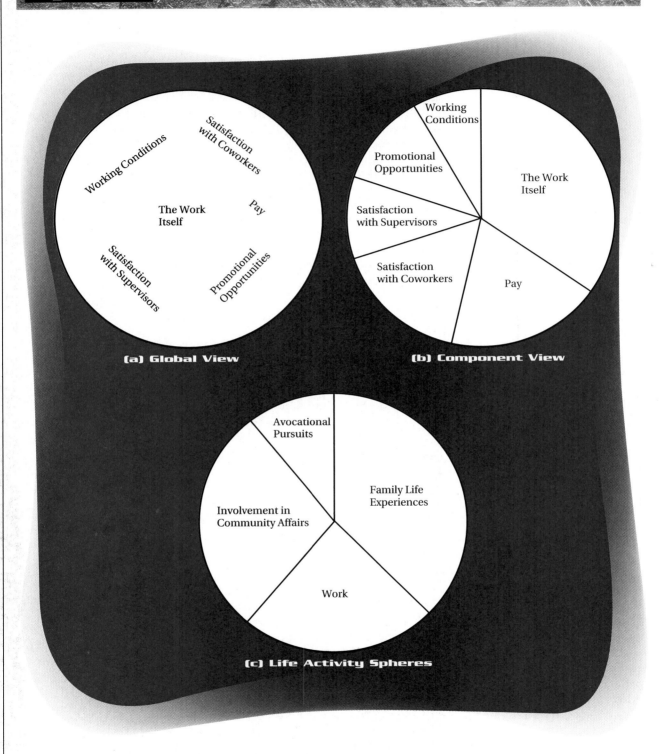

(a) Global View

(b) Component View

(c) Life Activity Spheres

high value on the intrinsic value of work and attaches less importance, in descending order, to obtaining satisfaction from coworker relationships, compensation, and so forth. Diagram (c) incorporates the worker's job as one activity sphere into the context of other life activity spheres. In this particular example, the worker seeks greater fulfillment from family experiences and less from other spheres, including her or his job.

Patricia Renwick and Edward Lawler confirmed there is a difference between what people consider important aspects of jobs and what actually brings them satisfaction. (See Figure 19-3.) In one study, people considered the "chance to do something that made them feel good about themselves" as the most important aspect of a job. However, in terms of producing job satisfaction, it managed to rank only in eighth place. While people thought the "friendliness of people they worked with" was not very important (ranked in 14th position out of 18), friendliness of coworkers produced the most satisfaction of all job aspects. Interestingly, "job freedom" was second in importance in producing job satisfaction, showing the importance of employee empowerment. At the bottom of

---

Figure 19-3   Importance of and Relative Satisfaction with Selected Aspects of Jobs

Aspect of Job	Ranked Importance	Ranked Satisfaction
Chances to do something that makes you feel good about yourself	1	8
Chances to accomplish something worthwhile	2	6
Chances to learn new things	3	10
Opportunity to develop your skills and abilities	4	12
The amount of freedom you have on your job	5	2
Chances you have to do things you do best	6	11
The resources you have to do your job	7	9
The respect you receive from the people you work with	8	3
The amount of information you get about your job performance	9	17
Your chances for taking part in making decisions	10	14
The amount of job security you have	11	5
Amount of pay you get	12	16
The way you are treated by the people you work with	13	4
The friendliness of people you work with	14	1
Amount of praise you get for a job well done	15	15
The amount of fringe benefits you get	16	7
Chances for getting a promotion	17	18
Physical surroundings of your job	18	13

Note: Data are based upon a systematic random sample drawn from 23,008 questionnaires readers returned.

Source: Patricia A. Renwick and Edward E. Lawler, "What You Really Want from Your Job," *Psychology Today* 11, No. 12 (May 1978), 56.

the list for producing satisfaction was "the chance of getting a promotion." We can conclude that people pursue several goals in their careers, which bring differing degrees of satisfaction.

Determining When It's Time for a Change

psychological traps
An unwillingness to break relationships that have been unproductive for a long period of time.

Sometimes, we become entangled in **psychological traps.** By that we mean an unwillingness to break relationships that have been unproductive for a long period of time. The "victim" maintains hope that personal goals will be realized within an organization in the future. Perhaps promises have been made, but do not materialize.[7] These may include promises of promotions or reassignments to jobs of greater interest. Sometimes these unfulfilled relationships are best severed. In other instances, one's job may no longer be interesting or capable of providing a minimum amount of intrinsic rewards. Today, many individuals make midlife career changes, often dramatic ones.[8] It is often very difficult to break away from a job or organization and leave behind the educational preparation and years of experience. Some of the fears that people experience in dealing with organizational change are probably also found in those workers contemplating career changes. (See Figure 19-4.)

Careers and Career Paths

career
The sequence of work-related positions occupied throughout a person's life.

A **career** is the sequence of work-related positions occupied throughout a person's life. A career encompasses those stages and transitions over time that reflect one's needs, motives, and aspirations as well as societal and organizational expectations and constraints.[9]

Where are you going and how will you arrive at your career destination? We don't mean within the next few weeks or months, but long-term career goals. How would you describe your career interests and the intrinsic areas that would bring you the greatest satisfaction, considering life activity spheres and the component and global views of jobs?[10]

Almost everyone has a career, whether it be working in a business or for nonprofit organizations or maintaining a family household. Household maintenance—managing a home and raising children—is a beautiful career and

---

Figure 19-4 One Does Not Treat a Career Change Lightly

Source: Peanuts, 7/20/84. PEANUTS reprinted by permission of UFS, Inc.

How to Succeed by Really Trying

Roger Staubach was a very successful professional quarterback for the Dallas Cowboys football team. The "pure challenge" of this athlete's work, no doubt, was an important career anchor.

In fact, Staubach's will to succeed and his ability to lead his teammates to come-from-behind victories earned him legendary status among football fans. In the course of his 11-year pro career, Staubach rallied the Cowboys from behind to win a record 23 times. In 14 of those games, the Cowboys trailed as late as the final two minutes of the game.[11]

---

those pursuing it often receive less acclaim than is warranted. Careers are a source of immense pleasure for many people. They never wish to retire. Yet, for others, retirement is viewed as an escape from prison with sentence served. For most of us, work is indispensable, partially because we need the income. Still, studies have indicated a substantial majority of wealthy individuals prefer working to lives of total leisure. Careers provide personal satisfaction by allowing us to utilize our skills and creativity. They also allow us to acquire new skills and knowledge, broadening our horizons. When successful, we will exit the world having made it a better place than when we entered. (See box titled "How to Succeed by Really Trying.")

Many people have difficulties in finding the right jobs, or keeping them once acquired, and they receive only a small measure of intrinsic satisfaction from their work. It is estimated "the average worker under 35 years of age goes on a job hunt every year and a half. Over 35, the average is once every three years."[12] In fact, "the average American worker can now expect to have eight different jobs over the course of her/his lifetime."[13] Making career choices even more complicated are the changing demands for skills. The occupation that is in high demand today may be out of vogue next year.[14]

Some concepts related to careers are career management, career planning, and career development. **Career management** is concerned with the process of developing a concept of one's self relative to work roles and being a competent employee.[15] **Career planning** is the process of creating actions required to progress along chosen pathways in organizations. **Career development** is the process whereby individuals identify and acquire transferable skills as they move along the management track. (See Chapter 1.) Some elaboration of these concepts is warranted.

Career Management

What motivates you when thinking about your future career? (Early retirement is not an acceptable response.) What turns you on? Off? Early in formulating their career, supervisors need to answer these questions. They need to define their career anchors. A **career anchor** is something that provides support or stability, just as anchors keep ships from drifting away. Career anchors keep the supervisor focused on his or her career objectives and those types of jobs perceived as providing satisfaction. In other words, job content is the critical factor in managing a career.

The concept of career anchoring was originated at the Massachusetts Institute of Technology by Professor Edgar Schein.[16] The Texas Instruments center for employee development, near Dallas, utilizes Schein's evaluation process with the following categories of anchors:

career management
The process of developing a concept of one's self relative to work roles and being a competent employee.

career planning
The process of generating action steps for individuals to progress along chosen pathways in work systems.

career development
The process whereby individuals identify and acquire transferable skills as they move along the management track.

A career anchor provides support and stability to an individual. Such anchors include technical or managerial challenge and lifestyle. Which of these anchors are important to you?

career anchor
Something that provides support or stability in the pursuit of a career, including obtaining job satisfaction from the content of jobs performed.

Technical/functional competence. Exercising skills in these areas provides a sense of identity. Greatest satisfaction comes from being able to apply these skills.

General managerial competence. Here, the goal is to have responsibility and accountability for total results. Although work is incorporated within the achievements of the organization, the success of one's employer is important.

Autonomy/independence. Flexibility of a job allowing one to determine how and when to work creates satisfaction. Being one's own boss as an entrepreneur in one's own business is another way to achieve autonomy.

Entrepreneurial creativity. The objective of achieving success is through creating one's own business. In the short run, employment with another organization may be necessary, but the goal is "going it alone" as quickly as possible.

Security/stability. The sense of success is achieved through permanent employment and the financial security it creates.

Service/dedication to a cause. Personal values guide the career into jobs contributing something of value to society or some segment thereof. Promotions or transfers may be sacrificed in this pursuit.

Pure challenge. Novelty, difficulty, and variety direct this job pursuit. Winning over the impossible situation has great importance. Easy achievement is rapidly seen as boring.

Life style. Job importance is dictated by how it corresponds with your desired life style. The job is a part of that life style. How you live, in total, encompassing a variety of intangibles, including *where* you live, influences your selection of employment.

Evaluation of these categories leads to identifying your career anchors and your personal values as they relate to developing your career strategies.[17]

Individuals achieving greater success with their careers generally engage in various career-related activities. Brian Kleiner suggests the following strategies for career management:[18]

- Develop and maintain basic career competencies.
- Know the formal criteria by which you will be judged.
- Know the informal criteria by which you will be judged.
- Develop alliances.
- Be a top-notch performer.
- Get an interim feedback report [on your performance].
- Become crucial to a boss who's clearly a "star on the rise."
- Look for ways to stand out from the pack.
- Train your replacement early [thus, making you replaceable in your current position as you move up within the organization].

- Keep your options open as much as possible.
- Periodically reassess your career.
- Leave the company at your convenience and on a good note.

That's career management. Career planning and development are less political.

Career Planning

Career management requires developing career plans. Why would a supervisor want to have a strategic plan?[19] A strategic long-range plan assists individuals in developing objectives and courses of direction in their lives. The strategic plan facilitates channeling activities toward some desired end result. In the meantime, one's strengths and weaknesses must be identified. The career plan reflects a vision of the future. Whereas career management requires identifying interests and activities and selecting those jobs perceived as creating satisfaction, career planning requires knowledge of projected job demand.

Planning your career, to some degree, should include the consideration of potential future demand for specific types of jobs. That is, is the job you are interested in going to have a growing or declining demand? In Figure 19-5, the estimated job demand, by occupational categories, is given for the period from 1990 to 2005. Figure 19-5 reflects forecasts by the U.S. Department of Labor, Bureau of Labor Statistics, as of spring 1992. Data are combined from 245 occupation subgroup clusters organized into 33 broad occupational categories. Selected for inclusion were those jobs possessing high projected growth rates and those with large numbers of persons currently employed. Note that while some of the jobs may require lower skills, many others are highly skilled. In addition, in each category there will be supervisors providing oversight.

Not all job categories can expect growth in the years ahead. Figure 19-6 on page 404 portrays those occupations that are projected to shrink in employment opportunities between 1990 and 2005.

A number of strategic job planning models exist. One that may be appropriate for supervisors is called *SWOT,* which means "identify your strengths, weaknesses, opportunities, and threats."[20] For example, what are your strengths? They could include your education, good health both physically and financially, a beneficial working relationship with your boss and team members, and your organization's good financial condition. Your weaknesses might be a lack in any of these areas. Similarly, analyze the other dimensions of SWOT, namely opportunities and threats arising from such factors as changing life styles and technology. Opportunities are found in expanding occupations while threats occur in those that are declining.

Career Indecision

Today, many persons face "casserole" careers, states Wendy Crisp, where "there is a growing trend among working people to combine several careers."[21] Several years ago, a man of about 45 came into the office of one of the authors. He sat down and said in a troubled voice, "I wonder what I will be when I grow up." After changing jobs several times, he still had not arrived at a career choice. And he felt guilty because his wife worked while he was, at that time, unemployed. He was still searching after 25 years, and that can hurt.

Figure 19-5	Projected Demand for Selected Occupations with Above-Average Growth, 1990–2005

Occupation Cluster	Estimated Employment 1990	Percent Increase in Employment 1990–2005	Numerical Increase in Employment 1990–2005
Executive, Administrative, and Managerial Occupations			
Accountants and auditors	985,000	34	340,000
General managers and top executives	3,086,000	19	598,000
Health services managers	257,000	42	108,000
Hotel managers and assistants	102,000	44	45,000
Management analysts and consultants	151,000	52	79,000
Marketing, advertising, and public relations managers	427,000	47	203,000
Computer, Mathematical, and Operations Research Occupations			
Computer systems analysts	463,000	79	366,000
Operations research analysts	57,000	73	42,000
Social and Recreation Workers			
Human services workers	145,000	71	103,000
Teachers, Librarians, and Counselors			
Kindergarten and elementary school teachers	1,521,000	23	350,000
Secondary school teachers	1,280,000	34	437,000
Health Assessment and Treating Occupations			
Physical therapists	88,000	76	67,000
Registered nurses	1,727,000	44	767,000
Respiratory therapists	60,000	52	31,000
Licensed practical nurses	644,000	42	269,000
Radiologic technologists	149,000	70	103,000
Technicians (except health)			
Computer programmers	565,000	56	317,000
Paralegals	90,000	85	77,000
Marketing and Sales			
Cashiers	2,633,000	26	685,000
Retail sales workers	4,754,000	29	1,381,000
Service sales reps	588,000	62	352,000
Travel agents	132,000	62	82,000
Administrative Support Occupations Including Clerical			
Clerical supervisors	1,218,000	22	263,000
Secretaries	3,576,000	15	540,000

Occupation Cluster	Estimated Employment 1990	Percent Increase in Employment 1990–2005	Numerical Increase in Employment 1990–2005
Service Occupations			
Correction officers	230,000	61	142,000
Guards	883,000	34	298,000
Food and Beverage Preparation and Service Occupations			
Chefs, cooks, and other kitchen workers	3,069,000	34	1,035,000
Food and beverage service workers	4,400,000	28	1,223,000
Health Service Occupations			
Medical assistants	165,000	74	122,000
Nursing aides and psychiatric aides	1,374,000	43	587,000
Personal Services and Cleaning Occupations			
Flight attendants	101,000	59	59,000
Gardeners/groundskeepers	874,000	40	348,000
Homemaker-home health services	391,000	88	343,000
Janitors and cleaners	3,007,000	18	555,000
Preschool workers	990,000	49	490,000
Transportation and Material Moving Occupations			
Truck drivers	2,701,000	24	659,000

Source: Adapted from U.S. Department of Labor, *The Job Outlook in Brief: 1990–2005* (Washington, DC: Bureau of Labor Statistics, Spring 1992, 12–41.

The search for the right job can be arduous for young people as well as older people. It is not uncommon to spend several years in college before arriving at a career decision. Some do not make career decisions until after leaving college. Paul Salomone has identified several reasons why young people are undecided about their vocational choices.[22] For example:

- Bright students who have not chosen a specific vocation may be delaying that choice because they are capable of doing many things and, therefore, have many more alternatives.
- Students may have a complex and creative outlook about the world of work.
- People change their vocational preferences in response to positive reinforcements from others, especially when the others are numerous and significant to the person concerned.
- Besides having many capabilities, some students have many varied interests or have interests that have not yet crystallized; their interests may continue to shift as new experiences occur.
- Students may recognize that they need more information about various occupations, job demand, educational requirements, and so on.

Figure 19-6	Projected Demand for Selected Occupations with Declining Employment Opportunities, 1990–2005

Occupation Cluster	Estimated Employment 1990	Percent Decrease in Employment 1990–2005	Numerical Decrease in Employment 1990–2005
Communication equipment mechanics	125,000	−38	−48,000
Precision assemblers	352,000	−33	−116,000
Private household workers	782,000	−29	−227,000
Armed forces jobs	2,036,000	−20	−411,000
Farm operators and managers	1,223,000	−16	−200,000
Line installers and cable splicers	232,000	−14	−32,000
Water transportation occupations	49,000	−13	−6,600
Metalworking and plastics-working machine operators	1,473,000	−8	−122,000
Bookkeeping, accounting, and auditing clerks	2,276,000	−6	−133,000
Bank tellers	517,000	−5	−264,000
Typists, word processors, and data entry keyers	1,448,000	−3	−46,000

Source: Adapted from U.S. Department of Labor, *The Job Outlook in Brief: 1990–2005* (Washington, DC: Bureau of Labor Statistics, Spring 1992), 12–41.

■ Students' recognition that there is a need for information about how to decide on a vocational choice may cause choice delay.

■ People's uncertainty about their vocational aspirations and goals and about the type of work environment in which they will prosper may cause hesitation about making a vocational choice.

■ Students may be uncertain about the economic practicality of a long-considered vocational goal and may wish to reconsider the plan.

All of these would seem valid reasons for delaying vocational choices. Once decisions are made, they are sometimes difficult to reverse, at least in the short run.

Career Paths

career paths
The routes of progression from one job to another, usually considered an advancement.

Career paths are the routes of progression from one job to another. Usually, they are considered an advancement. However, today we find an increasing number of people making lateral job choices.[23] (See box titled "Not Always Up, Sometimes Sideways.")

"The development of realistic career paths encompasses three underlying steps: (1) define work activities, (2) identify personal requirements, and (3) establish natural job families."[24] Once these steps have been identified, the next action is to establish your career goals. Your goals should be clearly stated, that is, specific or quantifiable. They should be reasonably attainable although set at a high performance level to provide greater motivation. Then, provide for flexibility in

Not Always Up, Sometimes Sideways

The quickest way to reach the corporate ladder's top rungs is not always by earning a straight line of promotions. Making strategic lateral moves is another way of working your way to the top.[25]

A lateral career move within a corporation can help a career. The employee should look for line positions that have a supportive boss, get a description of the position, evaluate the job offer carefully, and prepare by retraining.[26]

Lateral career movements are becoming the norm in the 1990s due to the proliferation of mergers, restructurings, and downsizings that limit vertical employee options.[27]

the event they require modification at a later date.[28] (See box titled "Career Flexibility.")

Career paths can be important both to employers and employees. Paths allow more career predictability. They provide a map of the progression of jobs individuals could anticipate following. Often, branch paths exist where individuals are not limited to only one route. Career paths are also useful in counseling employees in the development area. For example, a prerequisite for promotions is the acquisition of the necessary skills.[29]

Career Development

More than a few supervisory and management development programs fail to produce sought-after behavioral changes in the participants. Although these programs are successful for developing technical and job skills, they may overlook other important skills such as communication, developing teamwork, and leadership. Functionally, many are weak in preparing supervisors to direct and control.[30]

Passive versus Active Development

Presently, most successful large organizations have an interest in developing their supervisory personnel. They offer learning experiences through their supervisory training programs. Some of these programs are arranged with outside trainers. Generally, employers defray the developmental costs of such training. Other development opportunities include professional association memberships, seminars, and paid subscriptions to journals and trade magazines.

Professional development follows either a passive or an active route. **Passive development** requires relatively little interaction from an employee. Information is transmitted to the person without requiring any preparation, integration, analysis, or reporting. An example of passive development is attending a professional seminar. During attendance, the individual listens to lectures, may take a few notes, asks a few questions, and perhaps, participates during discussion periods. Some would indicate the majority of professional development is of the passive variety. Overall, passive learning is less effective than the active form of career development.[31]

Active development is exemplified by "hands-on" experiences. Coaching is one example of active development. Mentoring is another. In many cases, the coach is also an employee's boss. The coach shares information, gives counsel, and personally undertakes the development of a subordinate. Where the

passive development
Relatively little interaction is required from an employee in the professional development process.

active development
Hands-on experiences in the professional development process when an employee receives coaching or mentoring.

One of our students, a young woman majoring in business and science, planned to enter medical school upon graduation. That is, if she was accepted. In the event she was unsuccessful, she had a back-up plan. Namely, she would enter law school, where she planned to specialize in medical malpractice law.

assignments are varied and rigorous, this form of development can be very effective. In other situations, a subordinate stands in for the boss, thus acquiring on-the-job training. Either internal or external types of training sessions heavily oriented to techniques involving employee participation can be effective. The participation could include role playing, simulation exercises, and programmed instruction.

Regardless of the organization's response toward career planning assistance for its employees, a supervisor needs to create a career plan. Major components include, in addition to objectives, (1) a self-assessment of skills and weaknesses, (2) methods to follow for professional development and maintenance of skill levels, (3) networking with peers, and (4) identifying a mentor to provide insight into strengths and deficiencies.[32]

Development Areas

Supervisory development has importance not only to supervisors but also to their superiors and employers. For development to be effective, each needs to support the process. Development areas typically include enhancing technical/professional, interpersonal, and managerial/administrative skills. At the supervisor level of management, skill needs are more often found in the first two areas. However, development experiences may also incorporate the latter. Examples of topics treated in the development process include:[33]

- *Technical/professional.* This category covers the area of the business in which the employee works and includes knowledge, methods, and techniques, as well as the ability to use them.
- *Interpersonal.* Learning is directed toward understanding motivation, effectiveness of relationships with coworkers, sensitivity training, and communication skills.
- *Managerial/administrative.* Training includes understanding the complexities of an organization, goal setting, problem solving, and controlling.

Figure 19-7 outlines the content of a supervisory development program, including the designation of responsibilities among the supervisor, boss, and organization.

The Ginsburg Career-Planning Model

Lee Ginsburg has crafted a model for career planning. It is a straightforward, step-by-step consideration of criteria important to an individual in making career choices. Part of the exercise involves a self-appraisal of attitudes toward several job factors. In addition, an individual responds to a series of organizational climate statements to ascertain the degree of match between company climate and personal values.[34] (See Figure 19-8.)

An effective supervisor functions as a coach. He or she shares information, gives advice, and helps an employee to develop.

Supervision as an Occupation and Career

We have traveled a rather long road since commencing our journey in Chapter 1. You now have a better basis for understanding the importance of supervisors and supervisory work. As in almost any other occupation, you will discover a large variation in talent. There are effective supervisors, ineffective supervisors, and supervisors whose skills are between the two extremes. F. J. Roethlisberger in a 1945 article in the *Harvard Business Review* described the foreman as the "man in the middle." She or he is still in the middle today. That is the nature of a supervisor's job. With responsibilities to higher management and to members of the supervisor's work group, it is difficult to satisfy both groups at all times.

Over the long run, the job of a supervisor probably is best performed by following a course of moderation. It is what we could call the **"Goldilocks theory of management."** Supervisors should aspire toward a course of action that is neither "too hot" nor "too cold," but "just right." Think of how many situations call for a response that is "just right." So it is fitting that supervisors are the "people in the middle." They represent management to their subordinates and may represent their employees to higher management.

Learning about supervision is a continuing process. One of the best teachers, though, is observation. Observe the methods of successful and unsuccessful supervisors. Why are the successful supervisors so articulate in the practice of their craft, making it appear easy and even fun at times, while others are swept away in a vortex of continuing controversy, damaging those who have the misfortune to be in their paths?

Several contemporary issues are expanding in importance and may affect your career. Observation indicates that the changes discussed in the following paragraphs are particularly noteworthy.

First, the rate of technological innovation will accelerate. Technology is following a geometric curve while human adaptation to that technology proceeds in more of an arithmetic progression. Organizations and their members will be facing even more stress in the years ahead. The ability to lead employees into the future will increase in importance.

Productivity and efficiency will continue to increase in factories and offices through the United States and throughout the world as we move more and more to a global economy. While on the one hand more automation and robotics technology will reduce unit labor costs, on the other many employees will find their jobs enriched or enhanced by performing more of the total work of completing the finished product.

As a corollary, more emphasis will be placed on bottom-line accountability. More rational allocation of resources can be expected in organizations in the future, not only in businesses but also in nonprofit organizations. Supervisors will need more skills than ever before as they compete for resources and justify what they have done with the assets they have received. Analytical tools will become more important. So also will the ability to communicate assume greater importance.

Technology will render many skills and jobs obsolete. Retraining workers will become a priority concern, with much of the responsibility assigned to or assumed by business organizations. In Western European countries, such training responsibilities have been handled by corporations for many years.

As a part of the technological advance, communication systems will continue to improve, providing real-time data and information for making decisions. To

Goldilocks theory of management
Supervisors should attempt to be moderate in decision making to avoid extremes of action.

Figure 19-7 A Development Matrix for a First-Line Supervisor

Who Develops	How Development Occurs		
	Professional & Technical	**Interpersonal**	**Managerial & Administrative**
Company provides environment & resources	Company courses Outside seminars Tuition assistance Study time Job training Industry courses Recognition programs Company-paid memberships & subscriptions	Company courses Outside seminars Tuition assistance	Company reports Company meetings Company courses Industry courses Company-paid memberships & subscriptions Tuition assistance
Superior provides encouragement, opportunity & feedback	Encouragement to take advantage of above Job training Example Appraisal & feedback Job rotation Special projects Insistence on development plan	Encouragement to take advantage of above Job training Example Appraisal & feedback Job rotation Team assignments Special projects Insistence on development plan	Encouragement to take advantage of above Example Appraisal & feedback Job rotation Special projects Insistence on development plan
Employee acts	Night school Professional associations Reading Self-study Attendance at seminars Personal development plan The job itself	Toastmasters Night school Reading Self-study Attendance at seminars Personal development plan The job itself Observation of effective superiors	Seeking out company information, e.g., reading annual reports Alert attention at meetings Asking "What can I contribute?" Personal development plan The job itself Observation of effective supervisors

Source: Edward J. Mandt, "A Basic Model of Manager Development," *Personnel Journal* 58, No. 6 (June 1979): 399.

respond to customer needs, organizations will become more flexible in production methods. Long lead times, common in the past, will continue to shrink as the period between production and consumption is compressed.

The factory is being rediscovered as the heart of industrial organizations. Too often neglected in the past for more glamorous jobs, the production process will attract more college-educated people who discover job opportunities they

Figure 19-8 Ginsburg's Career Planning Model

Past Education and Experience

Using the example shown here, draw up an educational record for your planning exercises. List each school you have attended from high school on, identify those areas in which you scored highest and had the most interest, and also show which areas you liked least and scored lowest. By simply noting the areas of highest and lowest achievement, you are already isolating specific areas for future avoidance or cultivation.

Next, make up an occupational experience chart similar to the one you used to recount your educational activities. On this chart, list each job you have held, noting the company you worked for, the relative size of the firm (both in dollars and employees), your position in the company, your overall level of satisfaction, what you liked most and least about your job, and your major areas of responsibility. In all these items, be honest with yourself.

	School	Degree/Major	Courses of Most Interest and/or Highest Grades	Courses of Least Interest and/or Lowest Grades
Education				

These exercises are designed to help you; they are not evaluation forms for a merit increase.

Finally, after you have completed both the occupational experience and educational record charts, spend a few more minutes on a special skills chart. Identify any special areas of skill in which you have either proficiency or interest. These may be derived from hobbies, social activities, community interactions, or self-taught skills. Concentrate on those areas that would not show up in the occupational and educational charts. Try to be complete; remember you want to develop as complete a picture of yourself as possible.

The Importance of Self-appraisal

Now comes one of the most important—and most revealing—of your career planning exercises: a self-appraisal of your needs, interests, and values. Using the following series of checklists, begin your introspective examination by answering candidly the questions posed.

Personal needs. Ask yourself a couple of questions: What motivates me? What do I really want out of my job? (The answers to these questions are critical to the further development of your career plan.)

(continued)

Rank the following items from most to least important, as they apply to you. Be honest in your response. Rank your answers as you truly feel—not as you think they "should be," nor as you think others would rank them:

- Pay
- Status
- Peer recognition
- Hours of work
- Business reputation of company
- Job stability
- Benefit programs
- Coworkers
- Autonomy
- Opportunity for advancement
- New experiences
- Variety in tasks
- Achievement through risk
- Social reputation of company
- Working conditions

If you received a large sum of money from an unexpected source—such as an inheritance or lottery—what would you do with it? Answer:

_____

_____

_____

(Your answer to this question is very revealing; the way in which a person treats his or her money is indicative of an underlying need structure. For example, one who saves his money is often motivated by a need for security, whereas one who spends it on designer clothes and prestige cars is status-oriented. Large donations to charity indicate a strong social consciousness, and large expenditures on travel indicate a desire for new experiences or for exploration. Finally, an investor in the stock market is showing his or her need for speculation.)

Climate needs. What type of organization do you prefer? In what types of climate do you perform the best? Consider the many "climate" descriptions below, and check the *five* that are most important to you:

- Goal-directed
- Well-structured
- Conservative
- Risk-oriented
- Stable and traditional
- New and formative
- Size: _____
- Entrepreneurial
- Professional management
- Sales-oriented
- Production-oriented
- Financially oriented
- Creative
- Age of management
- Promotion pace
- Chain-of-command-oriented
- Loose and informal
- Urban location
- Rural location
- Pressurized atmosphere
- Steady and predictable
- Ever-changing direction
- Paternalistic
- Socially responsive
- Educationally oriented
- Research emphasis
- Systems emphasis
- Degree of supervision: _____
- Incentive opportunities
- Reputation

(This list is representative of the kinds of climate characteristics a career planner should consider. Remember that an individual's success depends to a great extent on the compatibility of his or her personality with the climate of the organization. If the fit is a poor or incompatible one, frustration on both sides is likely to result.)

Planning Aids: Tests and Reviews

Psychological testing. A professionally developed psychological testing program can be an invaluable aid in career decision making. It serves to identify strengths and weaknesses in such areas as the utilization of mental skills (including analytical abilities, judgment, reasoning, quantitative abilities, and creativity), personality (including such facets as independence, drive level, need for support, confidence, need hierarchy, and value scheme), organizational abilities (including planning, delegation, time management, decisiveness, and ability to maintain an overview), and leadership and interpersonal skills (including dominance, deference, empathy, assertiveness, and persuasive ability).

The results of such testing will serve to confirm areas of suspected weakness, to compare your strengths and weaknesses against those of others in a specified comparison group, and to yield valuable information about yet-unused abilities and skills. When desired, interest tests can provide a summary of your strongest and weakest occupational patterns. When testing is completed, professional counseling will help you interpret these findings and properly integrate them into your career decisions.

An Overview: Seeing Myself from a Career Perspective

My most important needs are:

These would be met in a climate characterized by:

Within this climate, I would prefer a role involving these types of responsibilities:

In the achievement of these duties, the following values must not be compromised if at all possible:

Based upon a review of our financial needs, the income potential of my desired career path should be:

	Minimum	*Desirable*
Start	_____	_____
5 years from now	_____	_____
10 years from now	_____	_____

Source: Lee R. Ginsburg, "Career Planning: Steps You Can Take for Yourself," *Supervisory Management* 22, No. 5 (May 1977): 4–8.

---

previously overlooked. With the rebirth of the factory, the line organization will grow in importance.

Greater equity will be found in the working environment as many organizations try harder to be fair. They are being pushed not only by government but also by the increasing power of minority groups and women. Compensation may be determined more on the relative contributions of employees.

The concept of Total Quality Management will be mastered by an increasing number of organizations. Consequently, customers will receive greater value and overall higher quality of service. Organizations unable or unwilling to respond will provide opportunities for new market entries as they are forced out of operation.

Employee empowerment will increase as evidence grows supporting the value of power-sharing in expanding employee motivation and achievement. Consequently, organization culture, overall, should be improved.

Greater cooperation between labor and management may be expected as both parties realize their symbiotic relationship is served most effectively through cooperation. A comment by Akio Morita, the cofounder of Sony, reflects an optimism about this cooperation. Morita "likes to tell his employees that the company is like a 'fate-sharing vessel.'"[35] We are all in the same boat.

At three o'clock, Carla entered Larry's office. "Shut the door Carla," he said with a very serious tone. "I've got some bad news for you. You're out as supervisor of your unit starting this next Monday. You are going to be replaced."

Carla's heart dropped three feet, four inches.

Then Larry continued with a smile, "The good news is that you have been promoted to take over my job. I'm moving on to the planning section in the Renton complex. Your work has been excellent. Sure, you screwed up now and then, but you learned from your mistakes and you are the best of my supervisors. You always kept a good perspective on the needs of the company and your workers."

Carla was speechless—not a common occurrence. Then Larry came over, shook her hand and said, "Congratulations. You are a very dedicated person and the company is fortunate to have you. I've really enjoyed working with you," were his final words as he gave her a hug.

Summary: Focus on Skills

Job satisfaction consists of the attitudes people have about their jobs. The organizational climate is created by the various conditions and working relationships confronting a member of an organization at any given time. Career planning and development are concerned with the sequence of work-related positions a person occupies through his or her life.

Following are 19 suggestions for increasing supervisors' skills in career planning and development, including selection of jobs and organizations as places to work:

1. Consider the relative value of the intrinsic and extrinsic rewards associated with both your job and the organization providing it.
2. Plan your career as one of your overall life activity spheres, allowing for a balance of intrinsic rewards based upon your personal interests.
3. Take an active role in planning and managing your career rather than drifting without goals.
4. Engage in a continuing series of activities to develop and maintain your basic career competencies.
5. Know the formal criteria by which you will be evaluated.
6. Know the informal criteria by which you will be evaluated.
7. Develop alliances within your organizations to provide support and information; network with your peers.
8. Always strive to be a top-notch performer.

9. Set your performance goals high to "stretch" in achieving them.
10. Establish quantitative goals for your performance.
11. Seek interim feedback reports about your performance.
12. Perform your own self-assessment of your strengths and weaknesses.
13. Obtain a mentor to provide insights into your strengths and weaknesses, guidance, and support.
14. Become crucial to a boss who is a "star on the rise."
15. Look for ways to stand out from other employees, but do so without offending them.
16. Train your replacement early, thus making you replaceable rather than irreplaceable.
17. Keep your job options open as much as possible.
18. If you leave your employer, do so at your convenience and on a positive basis of good feelings all around.
19. Where you have choices, seek active rather than passive methods of career development.

Review Questions

1. What is job satisfaction? Explain how intrinsic and extrinsic needs create job satisfaction.
2. Give the two major views of job satisfaction. How do they relate to a person's life activity spheres?
3. What is organizational climate? How does it affect job satisfaction? What is the value either to a job seeker or a supervisor in understanding the organization's climate?
4. What is a career?
5. Why are some young people indecisive about their careers? Is this bad?
6. What are career paths? Of what value are they?
7. Distinguish between passive and active career development methods. Which is superior? Why so?
8. What factors would you consider in planning your career? How would trade-offs enter the picture?
9. For your own use, apply the career planning model presented in this chapter. Prepare a chart of your career to date and your ultimate desired destination. Consider your short- and long-run goals, and refer to work activity and life spheres. To make your career plan realistic, consider the relative importance of the several job components and of the job itself to the broader spectrum of life activities.

Notes

1. B. Moyers, Public Broadcasting System, April 10, 1983.
2. R. Bookman, "Rousing the Creative Spirit," *Training and Development Journal* 42 (November 1988): 67–71.
3. "Why So Many Workers Lie Down on the Job," *U.S. News and World Report,* April 6, 1981, 71.
4. J. S. Kane, "Work Alienation and the Dynamics of Intrinsic Fulfillment," Ph.D. dissertation, University of Michigan, 1977, 3.
5. Ibid.
6. Ibid., 4. For an interesting collection of interviews of persons talking about their jobs, see Studs Terkel, *Working* (New York: Random House, 1972).
7. J. Z. Rubin, "Psychological Traps," *Psychology Today,* March 1981, 52.
8. J. Fierman, "Beating the Midlife Career Crisis," *Fortune,* September 6, 1993, 51–62.
9. M. London and S. A. Stumpf, *Managing Careers* (Reading, MA: Addison-Wesley Publishing Company, 1982), 4.
10. See E. Winninghoff, "Wishcraft: Using Teamwork to Reinvent Your Career," *Working Woman,* February 1992, 24.
11. A. G. Holziner, "How to Succeed by Really Trying," *Nation's Business* 80 (August 1992): 50.

12. T. J. Kosnik, "Aiming for the 'Right' Company: Choosing from Among Job Offers," *S.A.M. Advanced Management Journal,* Spring 1979, 45.

13. J. G. Collins, "Career Survival, 'Star Trek' Style," *Working Woman,* July 1993, 80.

14. P. M. Buhler, "Are You on Your Way to Becoming Obsolete?" *Supervision* 51 (May 1990): 14–16.

15. See A. Mayo, "A Framework for Career Management," *Personnel Management* 24 (February 1992): 36–39.

16. S. Overman, "Weighing Career Anchors," *HR Magazine* 38 (March 1993): 56.

17. Overman, "Weighing Career Anchors."

18. B. H. Kleiner, "Managing Your Career," *Supervisory Management* 25 (March 1980): 17–20.

19. See C. Boivie, "Planning for the Future . . . Your Future," *Journal of Systems Management* 44 (February 1993): 25.

20. A. J. Sunseri and D. B. Kosteva, "Strategic Planning Is Essential to Career Success," *Healthcare Financial Management* 46 (March 1992): 100.

21. W. E. Crisp, "Casserole Careers," *Executive Female* 15 (November–December 1992): 80.

22. P. R. Salomone, "Difficult Cases in Career Counseling: II—The Indecisive Client," *Personnel and Guidance Journal* 60 (April 1982): 497.

23. See S. I. Narcus and J. G. Friedland, "Fourteen Steps on a New Career Path," *HR Magazine* 28 (March 1993): 55.

24. London and Stumpf, *Managing Careers,* 138.

25. R. Wynn, "Which Way Is Up?" *Black Enterprise* 22 (June 1992): 65.

26. E. G. Wyer, "No Promotion in Sight? How to Move Ahead Anyway," *Executive Female* 15 (November–December 1992): 29.

27. K. Mattes, "Our Company Redesigns the Fast Track," *HR Focus* 69 (November 1992): 23.

28. A. R. Gaedeke, "Your Goal Standard," *Manager's Magazine* 66 (August 1991): 23.

29. Ibid.

30. T. A. Newberg, "Exercises for Better Management Development," *Personnel Journal* 60 (October 1980): 850–852.

31. R. F. Reilly, "Corporate Assistance in Professional Development," *Personnel Journal* 60 (February 1981): 125.

32. See F. Filipczak and M. Picard, "Seize the Coachable Moment," *Training* 30 (February 1993): 72.

33. E. J. Mandt, "A Basic Model of Manager Development," *Personnel Journal* 58 (June 1979): 396.

34. For an extensive treatment of career guidance and occupation selection see A. W. Clymer and E. McGregor, "Solving the Job Puzzle," *Occupational Outlook Quarterly* 36 (Fall 1992): 3–6, and A. W. Clymer and E. McGregor, "Matching Personal and Job Characteristics," *Occupational Outlook Quarterly* 36 (Fall 1992): 7–13.

35. L. Morrow, "All the Hazards and Threats of Success," *Time,* August 1, 1983, 20.

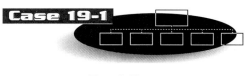

Case 19-1

David's

In 1958, Howard and Doris David opened a small restaurant in Cincinnati, Ohio, specializing in seafood dishes. In the period since then, David's has expanded from the one restaurant to over 100 located in 12 states in the Midwest. All of the restaurants are owned by the David family. In total, about 2,000 full- and part-time employees work for David's.

When asked about his philosophy of management development and higher education, Mr. David made the following comments:

"I guess I really don't believe higher education is necessary for the people who work in my restaurants, and that goes for my managers too.

"When I finished the eighth grade, I went to work in a small restaurant. That's where I got my real education—in doing things, not from books.

"We don't recruit managers from colleges. College graduates cost more than people without college educations, but they don't do any more. In fact, I am sure if we have any college graduates, they must work in accounting or data processing.

"All of our employees start at the bottom—washing dishes. Based on their ability, they have the same opportunities as anyone else for advancement in David's."

Questions

1. Do you agree with Mr. David's philosophy? Explain.
2. Explain the apparent success of David's without people possessing formal, or higher, education.
3. What is your opinion about the practice of starting every new employee as a dishwasher?
4. Would you be interested in working at David's? Why?

A Tale of Two Cities

Margo and Ralph Nicholson had been married for about two years. Both were starting their final years at college in Chicago. Both were management majors. Each made excellent grades. As graduation neared for them, they began job interviews with the school's placement center. As fate would determine, Margo was offered a junior management-trainee position with a large oil company headquartered in Los Angeles. It was her only job offer. Ralph also received only one offer—in New York City. Each wanted to accept her/his offer.

Questions

1. As an arbitrator, how would you handle this case and preserve the state of domestic tranquility?
2. How could Margo and Ralph resolve the difficulty?
3. What counsel would you give to couples when both partners have strong career aspirations?

Glossary

Abilene paradox A situation where everyone agrees with a decision that no one wants. (p. 212)

ability The actual capacity to carry out specific, job-related tasks. (p. 39)

acceptance rule Participative strategies should be used when acceptance of a decision by subordinates is important to the success of implementation. (p. 211)

accommodation A form of conflict management in which one party is willing to indulge the behavior of another. (p. 246)

active development Hands-on experiences in the professional development process when an employee receives coaching or mentoring. (p. 405)

active listening Provision of timely and appropriate feedback that improves the understanding between persons who are communicating. (p. 268)

administrative skills The ability to plan, organize, and control the work process. (p. 15)

adverse impact Occurs when an employment practice related to hiring, promoting, training, compensating, or terminating employees has a negative impact on an entire class of employees covered by equal opportunity legislation. (p. 54)

adverse treatment Involves intentional discrimination where a claim is made by an individual that an employer has committed illegal and intentional discrimination. (p. 55)

affirmative action Is a systematic attempt by employers to provide work-related opportunities to underrepresented groups. (p. 58)

affirmative action plans Documents describing the composition of a work force and outlining plans to increase underrepresented groups. (p. 59)

Age Discrimination in Employment Act of 1967 Makes it illegal to discriminate on the basis of age for individuals 40 years of age and older. (p. 52)

agency shop A union security arrangement in which all bargaining unit members must pay dues but do not have to join the union. (p. 74)

agenda An outline or plan for a meeting including a statement of the meeting's purpose and items to be discussed. (p. 211)

alternative dispute resolution Involves use of processes outside of the court system, such as mediators, arbitrators, in-house ombudspersons, and contractually prescribe grievance proceedings. (p. 49)

alternatives The types of actions that may be taken. (p. 202)

Americans with Disabilities Act of 1990 (ADA) Extends to all qualified persons with disabilities protection from discrimination in application, hiring, firing, promotion, compensation, training, or any other terms or conditions of employment. (p. 52)

analysis paralysis A state of inaction in decision making arising from over working a problem. (p. 207)

anger An acquired emotion exhibited as a strong feeling of displeasure, developing over time into more emotional problems. (p. 352)

anxiety A feeling of uneasiness or apprehension arising from an uncertainty about the future. In more serious cases, a person may experience a feeling of being upset, frequently accompanied by an undefined feeling that something bad will happen. (pp. 181, 333)

arbitration The use of a third party to resolve an issue based upon the merits of evidence introduced by each side. (p. 307)

arbitrator Functions as a judge in settling disputes and may or may not have authority to make decisions binding on both parties. (p. 80)

assembly-line hysteria A phenomenon first noted in Israel in which a person experiencing stress inadvertently influences others to become stressed. (p. 350)

associations Less formal collectives of employees that periodically meet and confer with management on a wide range of employment issues and negotiate employment contracts, but possess much less bargaining power than unions. (p. 68)

attitudinal restructuring The attempt to favorably influence the attitudes of participants toward one another by such actions as unilaterally conceding a point to give the other party evidence of good will. (p. 249)

attributional bias Occurs when people try to interpret a person or a situation based on available, sometimes incomplete or inaccurate information. (p. 151)

authority The right or power to command performance, require obedience, or make decisions. (p. 125)

authorization cards A minimum of 30 percent of employees must sign such cards indicating their desire to form a union to obtain approval of the National Labor Relations Board to conduct a representation election. (p. 78)

avoidance A form of conflict management in which one party evades or circumvents another. (p. 246)

bargaining units Composed of the specific group of employees a union must represent. Members of a bargaining unit are entitled to representation by the union even if they are not union members. (p. 73)

bases of power Leaders influence followers in many ways including sources of power that are legitimate, expert, referent, reward, and coercive. (p. 140)

BATNA (best alternative to a negotiated agreement) The most powerful and influential alternative one party has in negotiating with another to arrive at an agreement or solution to a problem. (p. 251)

behavior modification Contends that consequences of past behavior lead to, inhibit, or otherwise shape future behavior. (p. 233)

behavior observation scales (BOS) A graphic performance rating scale similar to BARS but requiring measurement of the frequency of occurrence of types of various job related behaviors. (p. 287)

behaviorally anchored rating scales (BARS) A graphic performance rating scale requiring behavioral assessment associated with a job. (p. 287)

benchmarking The continuous process of measuring products, services, and practices against the toughest competitors or those organizations recognized as industry leaders. (p. 103)

bona fide occupational qualification (BFOQ) Legal discrimination arising from predictors of job success based upon characteristics normally protected by law such as gender, race, religion, age, national origin, or disabled status. (p. 58)

bounded rationality model Consideration of alternatives is constrained by the limited capability of humans to assimilate and store data, thus causing decision makers to focus on only a few alternatives in making decisions. (p. 206)

boycott Union members refuse to use or purchase their employer's products. (p. 81)

brainstorming Generating ideas by permitting non-evaluative presentation of alternatives by group members to obtain as many ideas as possible for later evaluation. (pp. 14, 212)

broken record A communication technique in conflict resolution characterized by adhering to a position or response regardless of another person's attempt to change the subject. (p. 252)

budget A formal quantitative expression of management plans. (p. 106)

bureaucracy An organizational structure characterized by clear lines of responsibility and authority where communication, policies, procedures, and rules flow in a top-down manner from managers to employees. (p. 30)

cafeteria plans Compensation programs that allow employees to choose the mix of their benefits. (p. 173)

career The sequence of work-related positions occupied throughout a person's life. (p. 398)

career anchor Something that provides support or stability in the pursuit of a career, including obtaining job satisfaction from the content of jobs performed. (p. 399)

career development The processes whereby individuals identify and acquire transferable skills as they move along the management track. (pp. 10, 399)

career management The process of developing a concept of one's self relative to work roles and being a competent employee. (p. 399)

career paths The routes of progression from one job to another, usually considered an advancement. (p. 404)

career planning The process of generating action steps for individuals to progress along chosen pathways in work systems. (p. 399)

case law A body of law based upon precedent, that is, something that has occurred before that serves as a guide for future decisions. (p. 48)

catharsis A technique for relieving tension and anxiety by bringing a repressed problem to consciousness or out into the open. (p. 353)

central tendency errors Inaccurate evaluation of employees wherein all are consistently considered to be in the middle of a scale. (p. 291)

change The process of replacing or exchanging something, usually with something else within the same general category. (p. 357)

choice The right to choose among things or alternatives in making a decision. (p. 202)

Civil Rights Act of 1964 (Title VII) States that it is illegal for an employer with 15 or more employees in an industry affecting interstate commerce to discriminate on the basis of race, color, religion, sex, or national origin. (p. 50)

Civil Rights Act of 1991 Clarified the definition of "adverse impact" and its interpretation by the courts, requiring employers to prove the validity of their employment practices. (p. 54)

classroom training A form of training where employees go to a classroom to hear lectures, watch films, and do exercises. (p. 186)

closed office design Typically places a desk or other office furniture between people. (p. 273)

closed shop A form of union security that requires that employers hire only union members. (p. 74)

collaboration A form of conflict management in which all parties work together to find a solution. (p. 245)

collective bargaining The process of negotiation between management and a union to arrive at a contract and the process of administering an existing contract. (p. 68)

communication A process whereby symbols generated by people are received and responded to by other people. (p. 264)

communication rules Define the communication process to be used by group members. (p. 275)

comparable worth Providing equal pay for jobs of comparable value or worth. (p. 173)

compensation The pay and benefits employees receive such as vacation and sick leave, health insurance, and employer pension contributions. (p. 171)

competition A form of conflict management in which one party wins and the other loses. (p. 247)

complaint A verbal expression of a person's feelings reflecting pain, dissatisfaction, resentment, or discontent. (p. 301)

component view of job satisfaction Considers the different individual job elements and the degrees of satisfaction derived from each. (p. 395)

compromise A form of conflict management in which each party is willing to make concessions to arrive at a solution. (p. 247)

compulsive gambling A psychological addiction. (p. 332)

computer-assisted instruction Similar to programmed instruction except that computers are used to deliver training material and track employee progress. (p. 186)

conflict Situations when one party actually or potentially disrupts the goal-directed behavior of another party. (p. 244)

conflict management strategies Approaches to managing conflict situations based on assertiveness (behaviors intended to satisfy one's own concerns) and cooperativeness (behaviors intended to satisfy the concerns of others). (p. 245)

consensus decision making The process of finding a collective opinion wherein all group members are able to accept a group decision on the basis of logic and feasibility. (p. 213)

construct validity Exists to the extent a test or assessment accurately captures dimensions of an unobservable characteristic. (p. 57)

content validity Requires that the content of a test and the content of a job are logically matched. (p. 56)

contingency model A theory that leader effectiveness is determined by the fit between the leader's personality and the amount of situational control or predictability in the leadership situation. (p. 144)

contrast effect errors When comparisons between employees are not explicitly intended but still affect appraisal outcomes. (p. 290)

controlling The process of comparing results to objectives and taking corrective action when deviation from objectives occurs. (p. 105)

coordination A condition wherein harmonious actions result from individual and group efforts. (p. 132)

corrective counseling A form of counseling designed to identify conditions creating employee attitudes that cause undesirable behavior and disciplinary problems. (p. 328)

corrective justice The means by which employees who have been treated unfairly may seek and receive redress from the organization. (p. 300)

counseling A concentrated form of interpersonal communication with the purpose of assisting normal individuals in achieving their personal goals or function more effectively. (p. 324)

craft workers Employees in specific trades such as shoemaking or plumbing. (p. 72)

crime A public wrong committed by a person or organization against the state that violates a statute and implies a penalty to be levied. (p. 48)

criterion-related validity Predicts employee success (the criterion) on the basis of a performance measure (the predictor). (p. 56)

cross training Preparation of employees to perform more than one job. (p. 329)

cultural shock Describes the feelings a person may experience when placed in a foreign environment where friends and family are absent. (p. 181)

customer The recipient of a work team's output, either outside the organization or within the organization. (p. 36)

customer organization structure Satisfaction of different needs of specific customer groups determines the structure. (p. 121)

decertification The process of removing union representation through an election conducted by the National Labor Relations Board where a simple majority of bargaining unit members determines a union's continued representation. (p. 79)

decision A conscious choice of one alternative from a set of several alternatives. (p. 202)

decision making The process of making the selection of an alternative from several possible courses of action. (p. 202)

decision-making process A systematic process applied to making decisions, including definition of the problem or the goal to be attained through consideration of alternatives, selection of an alternative, implementation, and evaluation. (p. 204)

decision rules Procedural guidelines that direct, and tend to improve, a group decision-making process. (p. 212)

decision tree Illustrates the expected quantitative value of several possible alternatives and the probabilities of their occurrence. (p. 207)

defense mechanism A nonrational attempt to reduce tension and anxiety from needs that are not satisfied. (p. 352)

delegation A process of transferring authority from a member of management at a higher level to a person at a lower organizational level. (p. 125)

departmentation The process of creating organizational units of a manageable structure, composition of activities, and number of personnel. (p. 119)

deposition A statement given under oath to an opposing party's attorney. (p. 81)

depression A mental and emotional problem characterized by a dejected mood, dismal or dreary feeling, loss of motivation, and a feeling that few things are important and attempting to change things is useless. (p. 333)

developmental counseling A form of counseling used to assist employees in making the best use of their abilities in achieving their potential and to identify the goals and capabilities of those employees. (p. 329)

devil's advocate A method for countering groupthink when an individual argues against the group's preferred course of action. (p. 216)

differentiation The process of dividing the total amount of work that has to be performed into meaningful categories of tasks and workers. (p. 119)

directive counseling A form of counseling following a structured format or plan wherein the supervisor carries a substantial amount of the conversation by answering questions and giving advice. (p. 334)

dirty hands syndrome The belief of some higher level managers that supervisors should regularly participate in nonmanagement tasks. (p. 126)

discharge Permanent termination of an employee arising from disciplinary actions. (p. 312)

displaced workers Individuals who have lost their jobs in the manufacturing sector and are now working in the lower-paying service sector. (p. 19)

disposition A person's typical manner of behavior or way of acting in a given situation. (p. 327)

dissonance balancing Occurs when a person's image of something and the actual characteristics of that thing are rationalized when events do not go as well as planned. (p. 209)

distributive justice The impartial allocation of rewards and penalties based upon merit when each person's contribution to achieving organizational objectives is calculated in determining the appropriate distribution. (p. 300)

domino theory Untreated personal problems arising outside of the job have a tendency to spill over into the workplace. (p. 326)

due process Systematic, orderly procedures, including individuals' rights to raise objections to the charges and to be heard concerning actions pending against them. (p. 310)

effective leadership The ability to lead a highly productive work group. (p. 142)

effectiveness The capability of achieving organizational objectives. (p. 9)

efficiency Amount of production obtained based upon either a theoretical or practical limit of what can be obtained. (p. 8)

emotional stress An unhealthy condition that occurs when a person is subjected to excessive social transition events leading to emotional overload. (p. 346)

employee assistance programs (EAPs) Organization programs designed to help employees handle such problems as alcoholism, drug abuse, emotional illness, personal crises, and stress. (p. 331)

employee empowerment Expanding the power employees have over their jobs by increasing planning responsibilities, autonomy in making decisions, and so forth. (p. 230)

employee selection The process of hiring the right person for a job by screening the various jobs candidates through the use of tools such as application blanks, personal interviews, tests, and reference checks. (p. 162)

encapsulated development A situation in which employee expectations are raised through training and development activities, but the organization is not able to produce work opportunities for utilizing the new skills. (p. 330)

environmental factors Factors affecting performance that are outside the worker, over which the worker has little control. (p. 39)

Equal Employment Opportunity Commission (EEOC) The federal agency responsible for establishing guidelines to enforce Title VII of the Civil Rights Act of 1964 and investigating and resolving complaints of illegal discrimination. (p. 50)

Equal Pay Act of 1963 Makes it illegal to discriminate in pay based on gender. (p. 51)

equity theory Individuals compare the ratio of their own inputs to the outcomes to other's ratio of inputs to outcomes they receive. (p. 235)

ethics Is concerned with justifying behavior pertaining to questions of right and wrong; behavior is said to be ethical to the extent it is good or right for the larger community. (p. 15)

evaluation A review process of the outcome obtained from a decision. (p. 209)

evaluation criteria Standards against which to assess an employee's attributes, motivation, abilities, skills, knowledge, or behaviors. (p. 284)

exception principle Only exceptions to policies, rules, and procedures must be referred to higher management for action. (p. 129)

expectancy theory The force of motivation is a function of an individual's perception that effort will lead to a required level of performance (expectancy), the likelihood that performance will lead to an outcome (instrumentality), and the relative attractiveness of the outcome (valence). (p. 231)

external pay equity Pay and other compensation deemed fair by employees when comparing their jobs to comparable jobs in other organizations. (p. 172)

extinction Involves not reinforcing a pattern of behavior one is trying to reduce in another person. (p. 234)

extrinsic fulfillment Gratification of needs arising from job elements such as compensation, promotion, or job status. (p. 395)

feedback Occurs when information is transmitted back to other parts of a systematic process. (p. 11)

field of experience Factors and conditions influencing the communication process including perceptions, values, culture, attitudes, and opinions derived from previous experiences by the various communication participants. (p. 267)

fishbone diagram A statistical method that systematically assesses relationships between cause and effect. (p. 106)

flow chart A diagram that graphically depicts the sequence of steps in a process. (p. 107)

formal group A group composed of members brought together for the purpose of making decisions or solving problems, often a work group. (p. 274)

frustration A stressful condition occurring when a person is unable to satisfy some need or achieve some goal. (p. 351)

functional structure The most common form of organization structure based upon similarity of related jobs grouped together into units reflecting these similarities. (p. 120)

Gantt project planning chart Illustrates when the various stages of work must start to complete a project by the deadline. (p. 106)

geographic organization structure Organized by geographic territories, when facilities or markets are physically dispersed throughout the country or the entire world. (p. 120)

global view of job satisfaction The sum of all intrinsic and extrinsic elements that create a person's total job. (p. 395)

goal setting theory The process of setting specific and difficult, but achievable goals provides direction toward accomplishing a task and leads to high levels of motivation and performance. (p. 232)

Goldilocks theory of management Supervisors should attempt to be moderate in decision making to avoid extremes of action. (p. 407)

good faith bargaining Occurs when a party in a contract negotiation makes every reasonable effort to reach agreement with the opposing party. (p. 79)

grapevine The informal communication channel that connects the informal organization. (p. 276)

graphic rating scale A personal criteria appraisal instrument that describes employee performance by using adjectives, numbers, or descriptions of behaviors. (p. 285)

grievance A complaint that has not been solved or settled and is usually viewed as being more serious, often expressed in writing. (pp. 80, 302)

grievance procedure A prescribed series of actions between management and employees intended to resolve differences. (pp. 81, 314)

group cohesiveness The atmosphere of closeness that results in a group from common beliefs, attitudes, and goal directedness. (p. 253)

group communication Occurs when all members of a group are actively communicating within the context of the group. (p. 273)

group dynamics Reflect how interaction among individuals comprising a group affects the group decision-making process. (p. 216)

group objectives Goals set for an entire work team, effective with interdependent work groups in which it is impossible to separate individual effort or results within the team. (p. 293)

group polarization effect Occurs when group members shift toward either a risky or conservative decision creating a more extreme posture for the group as a whole. (p. 217)

groupthink Describes the breakdown in critical thinking that occurs within highly cohesive decision-making groups in which members strive for conformity. (p. 216)

halo effects Occur when a rater overgeneralizes from one aspect of an employee's performance to all other aspects of his or her performance. (p. 291)

Hawthorne effect When recognition influences people to perform at a higher level than they might otherwise, thus indicating that productivity is influenced by factors other than money or training. (p. 31)

heap reversal theory Suggests that when employees are promoted to supervisory positions from rank-and-file positions, they may experience anxiety due to their reversal in position from the top of one group (with their coworkers) to the bottom of another (management). (p. 6)

hierarchy of needs A vertical arrangement of needs with the most basic physiological needs at the first level and the most complex self-actualization needs at the highest level. (p. 226)

homeostasis A balance or harmony achieved in one's working life. (p. 359)

hot stove rule Discipline should be directed against the act rather than the person. (p. 311)

human relations school (of management) A school of thought emphasizing the importance of helping employees meet social and esteem needs associated with work. (p. 31)

human resource management A variety of organizational functions related to human resources including staffing, compensation, performance appraisal, worker safety, training and development, and, sometimes, labor relations. (p. 159)

human rights Actions are ethical only if they do not violate individual rights. (p. 16)

implementation The actions taken after making a decision, and followed by evaluation of the results obtained. (p. 209)

income statement A financial statement that depicts revenues, expenses, and profit or loss for a business enterprise over a period of time. (p. 28)

individual pay equity Employees' perceptions of fairness when comparing their individual pay and effort, education, training, and other inputs to a job with those of others in their organization. (p. 172)

industrial workers Persons employed in a general industry such as steel manufacturing or automobile production. (p. 72)

influence The ability to affect the thoughts and behavior of others. (p. 125)

informal organization The organization dynamics portraying the status, power, politics, friendship ties, and proximity of organization members; not represented by an organization chart. (p. 276)

information vagabond Any individual who informally obtains information from various sources, identifies the content of messages in terms of informational needs of others, and transmits information to them. (p. 379)

informational counseling A form of counseling involving exchange of ideas and information between the supervisor and employees or relating information necessary for workers to perform their jobs. (p. 329)

informational pickets Union members remain working but picket their employer and provide information supporting their position to people who pass by and to the media. (p. 81)

innovation The act of bringing something new into an established process or way of thinking. (p. 13)

instruction The transmission of information to a person performing work about the methods required for carrying out an order. (p. 190)

interdependent group A work group in which team members must rely on one another to attain a team goal. (p. 235)

internal pay equity Concerned with perceived fairness when employees compare compensation for their jobs with other comparable jobs within an organization. (p. 172)

interpersonal communication The communication between two people. (p. 266)

interviewing An information-gathering process wherein facts are obtained, usually through questioning the other person. (p. 324)

intrinsic fulfillment Gratification of nonphysiological needs such as the feelings one has in accomplishing something worthwhile. (p. 395)

ISO 9000 An international set of standards that provide a framework for showing customers how a firm tests products, trains employees, keeps records, and fixes defects. (p. 102)

job analysis The systematic investigation of a job in order to identify its essential characteristics and to translate these characteristics into a written job description. (p. 160)

job description Describes all work activities associated with a position. (p. 160)

job enrichment The process of increasing motivation factors in jobs by giving employees more control over their work. (p. 228)

job evaluation Method for quantifying the content of different jobs in terms of their relative value to the employer for the purpose of establishing wage and salary structures. (p. 173)

job redesign A part of the job characteristics model to increase motivation by adding skill variety, task identity, task significance, autonomy, and job feedback. (p. 228)

job rotation A form of cross training where employees are trained to do several jobs. (p. 186)

job satisfaction The attitudes people have about their jobs. (p. 394)

job specification Lists the minimum qualifications necessary to perform adequately in a specific position. (p. 160)

justice The impartial treatment of employees by organizations through maintaining conditions of fairness and equity. (p. 16)

kinesics Another term for body language that includes nonverbal cues such as eye contact, body posture, handshakes, facial expression, gestures, and body movement influencing the validity of the communication process. (p. 271)

KISS principle Acronym for designing communication messages stating: "keep it short and simple." (p. 269)

labor productivity Typically expressed in terms of the amount of production obtained per hour of labor. (p. 8)

labor unions Organizations of wage earners formed for the purpose of serving the collective interests of their members through the bargaining process with employers on such issues as employee compensation and working conditions. (p. 68)

Landrum-Griffin Act of 1959 Called the Labor-Management Reporting and Disclosure Act of 1959, it improved union internal affairs and governance by restricting illegal activities by union leaders and increased union member rights such as voting and dues paying. (p. 75)

leader decision theory Is concerned with the role and extent of follower participation in leader decision making; employees should participate if their contribution improves the quality of the decision and when follower acceptance of the decision is necessary. (p. 149)

leadership The process whereby an individual influences a group of followers to attain goals deemed important by the leader. (p. 140)

leniency errors Consistent and inaccurate evaluation of employees wherein all are considered near the top of a scale. (p. 291)

leveling Communication activity where two parties relate both negative as well as positive aspects about a job and themselves. (p. 170)

life activity spheres The relative distribution of an individual's intrinsic values into various categories including work, family, recreation, and community service. (p. 395)

line organization Creates products or services that are sold or distributed to customers or clients. (p. 127)

listening An accurate receipt and interpretation of communication wherein a person hears and pays attention to something or someone. (p. 274)

litigation The process of bringing forth a lawsuit, or claim for damages, in a court of law. (p. 19)

lockout Management locks the doors of a plant or office building keeping workers out of the workplace until they agree to contract terms. (p. 82)

malicious obedience A form of employee behavior occurring when an imprecise order or instruction is given, and the employee carries out the order or instructions literally to embarrass the supervisor. (p. 191)

management by objectives (MBO) A collaborative setting of goals between a supervisor and his or her superior and a determination of the criteria to be used for evaluating that supervisor's performance in achieving those goals. (p. 103)

management pyramid Consists of top, middle, and bottom management with supervisors occupying the bottom or first level of management. (p. 6)

managerial functions Activities performed outlining relationships between managerial inputs (planning, organizing, and staffing); transformation processes (directing); and outputs with feedback (controlling). (p. 11)

matrix structure A mixture of the functional organization structure and project management. (p. 122)

mediator A neutral third party who is skilled at helping opposing parties resolve differences but who has no authority to impose a solution. (p. 79)

mentor An individual who systematically develops a subordinate's abilities through intensive tutoring, coaching, and guidance. (p. 184)

model A representation of a real world event, process, object, or system. (p. 102)

moods A person's temporary state of mind or feelings. (p. 327)

motivation A psychological state that compels people to pursue or avoid certain activities or goals. (p. 39)

mum effect The tendency of subordinates to hesitate to pass bad or threatening news up the chain of command. (p. 276)

National Labor Relations Board (NLRB) Created by the Wagner Act of 1935, it is a federal government agency that polices unfair labor practices and oversees union elections. (p. 73)

need The lack of something requisite, desirable, or useful which, if met, will satisfy an individual. (p. 224)

need for achievement The need to exceed a performance standard such as a personal accomplishment. (p. 225)

negative reinforcement Occurs when a disliked condition is removed or avoided as a result of an individual's behavior. (p. 233)

negotiation jujitsu Applied in dealing with a difficult opponent by responding to a challenge through questions and requests for clarification rather than hostility. (p. 251)

networking The building of relationships through exchange or sharing information, ideas, or resources among individuals. (p. 379)

neurosis A very high anxiety level leading to difficulties in functioning. (p. 333)

noise Anything that detracts from the transmission quality of messages or anything that prevents the communication process from being completed. (p. 269)

nominal group technique (NGT) A form of "group" decision making in which the members do not interact directly, rather they record, rank, and vote on alternatives to arrive at the decision. (p. 215)

nondirective counseling A form of counseling wherein the supervisor functions in a supportive role as a listener. (p. 334)

nonprogrammed decisions Decisions that have not been made before or problems that have not been solved or treated satisfactorily. (p. 203)

nonpunitive discipline A method for bringing employee behavior into compliance through a process of counseling in which the employee's future conduct is emphasized. (p. 314)

norms Standards of behavior expected for an individual within a group. (p. 253)

Norris-LaGuardia Act of 1932 Permitted the formation of unions as legal entities and prohibited employers from requiring yellow dog contracts. (p. 72)

objective/goal Any value a person, firm, or organization desires to acquire, and in the acquisition process, is willing and able to make the necessary sacrifice of time, money, or effort. (pp. 99, 202)

Occupational Safety and Health Act of 1970 Act regulating safety and health conditions in most workplaces, excluding government, agricultural, and mining operations. (p. 170)

Occupational Safety and Health Administration (OSHA) A federal agency created by the Occupational Safety and Health Act of 1970 to establish safety and health standards and monitor compliance in the workplace. (p. 170)

ombudsperson A person appointed by senior management to investigate employee complaints, report findings, and make recommendations leading to equitable settlements of grievances. (p. 304)

on-the-job training (OJT) A form of training employees while they are doing the actual job or some parts of it. (p. 186)

open door policy When individuals are encouraged to bring their problems or concerns to their supervisor or managers. (p. 302)

open office design Typically has the desk and chairs aligned so that there are no physical barriers between those sitting in the office. (p. 273)

open shop A union security arrangement in which employees are free to determine whether they join the union and do not have to pay union dues if they decide not to join but are still represented by the union. (p. 74)

open system A type of system affected by external factors such as government regulation, new technology, and competition. (p. 12)

operant conditioning Behavior is changed through application of positive or negative reinforcement, punishment, or extinction. (p. 233)

operating budgets Project the amount of income to be received or expenses of a supervisor's unit during a given period such as a year, quarter, or month. (p. 106)

oral reprimand The first stage of the progressive disciplinary process when an employee is orally informed with precisely stated facts that an offense has occurred. (p. 312)

order A command to someone to do something or to refrain from doing something. (p. 190)

organization change A modification in the tasks, technology, structures, or people in an organization creating something that is new to the organization. (p. 357)

organization chart A symbolical illustration of organizational units and the formal authority relationships among personnel. (p. 120)

organization design A process of determining the division of work and establishing formal authority relationships among members of an organization. (p. 119)

organization structure The configuration of interpersonal and authority relationships within a work unit and among other organizational work units. (p. 118)

organizational culture The shared beliefs, values, language, history, rituals, and stories held by members of an organization. (p. 37)

organizational discipline A form of training to produce a desired type of behavior when deviations from the norm occur; the intent is to modify behavior. (p. 307)

organizational justice The impartial treatment of employees by organizations through maintaining conditions of fairness and equity. (p. 300)

organizing The function of creating the structure of working relationships, designing facility layouts, balancing workloads, and scheduling work to be performed. (p. 117)

orientation A process whereby a new employee is introduced to the organization and to the specific requirements of the job. (p. 180)

overlearning Consists of learning and practicing a task far beyond the point at which the task has been successfully learned. (p. 189)

paranoia A form of thinking disorder in which the individual experiences delusions, such as false beliefs of persecution or exaggerated personal importance (grandeur). (p. 333)

paraphrasing An active listening skill involving repeating back in your own words what you thought you heard the sender say. (p. 269)

Pareto chart A diagram used to determine priorities by identifying and distinguishing between the important events or activities and the unimportant ones. (p. 34)

Pareto principle Illustrates that often a few items, events, or people will comprise the majority of something, and vice versa. (p. 34)

parity principle The amount of formal authority should be commensurate with the amount of responsibility a supervisor possesses. (p. 128)

passive development Relatively little interaction is required from an employee in the professional development process. (p. 405)

path-goal theory A follower-driven theory of leadership that defines effective leadership in terms of leader behavior that enables followers to achieve satisfaction by accomplishing their goals. (p. 146)

patron A person who supports people in adjusting to their jobs and organizations by providing friendship and information about the organization and community. (p. 184)

pay adequacy A pay level that allows an employee to meet basic needs and to achieve a standard of living that is minimally acceptable to the employee. (p. 171)

pay equity Pay level that is fair. (p. 172)

pay-for-performance Compensation programs that tie pay raises or bonuses to employee performance. (p. 172)

peer evaluation A form of performance appraisal in which members of a work team evaluate each other's performance. (p. 292)

people skills The ability to get along with and to motivate individuals and work teams. (p. 15)

perception checking Verifying what you perceive to be the intent of another person's communication message. (p. 269)

performance The productivity and quality of individual or group output. (p. 8)

performance appraisal The periodic assessment of employee job performance and behavior. (p. 284)

performance criteria Evaluation standards based on employee behavior or output that are definable and observable. (p. 285)

performance review A periodic meeting between a supervisor and employee to discuss the employee's performance appraisal results. (p. 289)

performance standard Management's expectations of what persons should do in their jobs and how well they should perform. (p. 101)

person analysis The determination of training needs of individual employees. (p. 185)

personal criteria Evaluation standards based upon traits or innate characteristics of employees such as personality traits of dependability, loyalty, team play, and initiative. (p. 285)

plan A course of action designed to produce some specific result or outcome. (p. 95)

planning The process of determining what objectives to pursue and what activities to perform to achieve them. (p. 92)

policy A guideline consisting of a principle and a rule governing the behavior of employees in an organization. (p. 100)

positive reinforcement Occurs when an attractive consequence is presented to an individual as a result of behaving in the desired manner. (p. 233)

principled negotiation Deciding issues on their merits rather than through a haggling process. (p. 249)

problem When there is a difference in results obtained and what was targeted to be achieved in objectives. (p. 202)

problem-solving teams Having no decision making authority and serving in a fact-finding or advisory capacity, they concentrate on finding solutions to work-related problems. (p. 124)

procedure Specific method followed in performing a task or following a policy. (p. 101)

process or equipment organization structure Organization is based upon the major processes or types of equipment used in making products. (p. 122)

procrastinate To postpone or needlessly put off doing something until a future time. (p. 374)

product organization structure Shaped by the products or services produced, often used by firms having several types of products with different quality, image characteristics, or markets. (p. 120)

productivity The ratio of output (the results of production) to input (the various economic resources used to produce that output). (p. 8)

program A comprehensive plan that includes objectives to be attained, specification of resources required, and stages of work to be performed. (p. 95)

programmed decisions Types of problems or decisions repeatedly encountered with solutions codified into methods for handling them such as policies, procedures, work rules, performance standards, tolerance limits, and sets of decision rules. (p. 203)

programmed instruction A form of training where employees study standardized printed instructions and take tests after completing sections of the program. (p. 186)

progressive discipline The practice of increasing the severity of disciplinary penalties each time an employee is disciplined. (p. 312)

progressive-part training Involves training in gradually building steps with previous learning reviewed during each session before new tasks are learned. (p. 188)

proxemics The study of the way people use space. (p. 271)

psychological contract Expectations formed during the interviewing process by a job applicant and the employer about the other's future behavior if the applicant is hired. (p. 169)

psychological traps An unwillingness to break relationships that have been unproductive for a long period of time. (p. 398)

psychosis Consists of a large number of serious mental disorders where individuals have extreme distortions in how they think and perceive the world. (p. 333)

psychotherapy A longer and in greater depth process and analysis than counseling; concerned with reconstruction of the person and larger changes in personality structure. (p. 325)

punishment Occurs when an unpleasant consequence is delivered to a person after exhibiting an undesirable form of behavior. (p. 234)

pure-part training Involves teaching each of the parts separately, with a final session that puts the parts together. (p. 188)

quality The essential characteristics of something, typically measured in the degree of excellence, value, or worth. (p. 9)

quality circle A relatively small team of workers who meet periodically to find ways to improve the quality of work processes. (pp. 35, 124)

quality rule Participative strategies should be used when the supervisor needs information from group members to improve decision quality. (p. 211)

range of sensitivity The appropriate degree of awareness a supervisor should maintain of personal and job problems of employees. (p. 326)

rater errors A systematic recording of invalid impressions by a rater. (p. 290)

rationalization A process that compromises evaluation when decision makers attempt to cause outcomes to appear reasonable even though actual results suggest a different interpretation. (p. 209)

realistic job preview Occurs when the hiring organization arranges for a job candidate to experience the work environment before being employed. (p. 169)

recruitment The process of acquiring employees to fill job positions. (p. 161)

reengineering The search for and implementation of radical change in business core processes to achieve breakthrough results. (p. 104)

reliability Is the ability of a test to provide consistent results. (p. 56)

remedial counseling A form of counseling of employees whose performance is not up to par or whose behavior, such as careless work, disinterest in the job, or chronic absence or tardiness, is not acceptable to the organization. (p. 328)

reverse discrimination Occurs when a dominant group is excluded from employment or training opportunities because of affirmative action. (p. 59)

right-to-work laws Authorized by the Taft-Hartley Act, state laws permitting prohibition of union and agency shops. (p. 75)

role conflict occurs when expectations from different roles are incompatible. (p. 253)

role models Persons who by virtue of their position influence the behavior and performance of those around them. (p. 150)

roles Standards of behavior expected for individuals within a given position. (p. 253)

run chart A common TQM statistical tool that tracks trends. (p. 108)

scalar principle There is a chain of command within an organization, and authority flows from the top of the management hierarchy to the bottom. (p. 129)

schedule A plan specifying the sequence of work to be performed. (p. 131)

scheduling The process of specifying the activities of a plan, the sequence for performing these activities, the time frames for completion of each phase of work, and a deadline for accomplishment of the plan. (p. 131)

scientific management A management approach developed in the early 1900s that scientifically assesses the best methods for accomplishing work. (p. 29)

screening A process designed to eliminate from further consideration those persons who do not possess the minimum requirements set forth in the job specifications. (p. 164)

secondary boycott Union attempt to influence third parties such as suppliers and customers to refrain from conducting business with the employer; made illegal by the Taft-Hartley Act. (p. 81)

self-managing teams Well-trained and informed individuals working together as a group who manage their own work by setting goals, planning how goals will be accomplished, solving problems, making daily operating decisions, scheduling work, and hiring team members. (pp. 125, 210)

semiautonomous teams Led by a supervisor and extensively involved in day-to-day work team activities, they perform the functions of planning, organizing, and controlling and may participate in setting goals for their work units along with providing information or making operating decisions. (p. 125)

sender-receiver model A representation of the communication process with several elements or stages beginning with the encoding of messages by the sender, message transmission, decoding by the receiver, and response or feedback. (p. 266)

sensitivity audit A personal evaluation by an individual of the effects of her or his nonverbal behavior upon other persons. (p. 272)

severity errors Inaccurate evaluation of employees wherein all are consistently considered to be at the bottom of a scale. (p. 291)

sexual harassment Any unwelcomed sexual advances, requests for sexual favors, or other verbal or physical conduct of a sexual nature associated as a condition of employment, or that otherwise interferes with an employee's job performance. (p. 51)

silent grievers Persons having quiet grievances without overt expression of feelings of actual or imagined unfair treatment. (p. 305)

situational leadership A theory of leadership that states leaders should modify their behavior based on the maturity of followers. (p. 147)

social loafing Occurs when group members put in less effort believing their individual contributions cannot be assessed. (p. 216)

span of supervision The total number of people for whom a supervisor is responsible; the ideal span is the number that can be supervised effectively. (p. 130)

squeaky wheel Slang term implying an overly dominant team member who can compromise the quality of a group's decision by over-participation. (p. 216)

staff organization Assists the line and other staff units by providing specialized services, expertise, or control over activities when the staff possesses functional authority. (p. 127)

statutory law The collection of legislative branch writings consisting of rules or regulations covering a wide range of subjects affecting society. (p. 48)

stereotyping The classification of individual behavior made on the basis of a group standard; an oversimplified opinion or belief about someone often not supported by facts. (p. 151)

strategic planning A continuous, interactive process aimed at keeping an organization as a whole appropriately matched to its environment. (p. 95)

stress A condition experienced whenever a person is confronted with a demand or challenge that threatens his or her ability to attain valued outcomes. (p. 346)

stress carriers Persons whose behavior causes stress for others. (p. 350)

strike Union members voluntarily refuse to work. (p. 81)

substance addiction A physiological dependency condition that also has social and psychological consequences. (p. 332)

suggestion teams Having low team autonomy with little authority for making or implementing decisions, they make only recommendations. (p. 123)

superordinate goals Higher-order goals that transcend individual group differences and compel groups to work together to solve common problems. (p. 254)

supervision The first line of management that oversees efforts of workers for the purpose of accomplishing group and organizational objectives. (p. 6)

supportive communication techniques Methods for reducing defensiveness in communication by applying positive rather than negative messages. (p. 270)

suspension The disciplinary action of temporarily laying off an employee without pay. (p. 312)

Swiss cheese method of project management Method for increasing motivation to complete an entire complicated task or project by completing small pieces, one at a time. (p. 381)

system A flow of inputs, transformation processes, outputs, and feedback. (p. 11)

tactical planning Emphasizes current and short-term activities to achieve the objectives of strategic plans. (p. 95)

Taft-Hartley Act of 1947 Also, called the Labor-Management Relations Act of 1947, it reduced union excesses by defining employer and employee rights, outlawed closed shops, and permitted states to enact right-to-work laws. (p. 73)

task analysis The de_inition of tasks involved in performing a job; definition of knowledge, skills, and abilities required to perform the tasks; and development of training objectives. (p. 185)

task force Serving in a fact-finding or advisory capacity, a team of management and nonmanagement personnel who have been assigned to a specific problem or issue. (p. 124)

team Consists of two or more people who must coordinate their activities to accomplish a common goal; empowered to exchange information and participate in decision making. (p. 123)

team management A task-motivated leadership approach that includes the full participation of followers. (p. 144)

technical skills Job knowledge including knowledge of work processes of those in the supervisor's work group. (p. 15)

technology The practical application of human knowledge. (p. 17)

therapeutic counseling A form of counseling to diagnose personal problems and help employees, through trained third parties, overcome them or cope with them more successfully. (p. 331)

time log A method for recording activities performed and the amount of time spent performing them. (p. 383)

time management A study of how time is spent for the purpose of increasing overall job effectiveness. (p. 372)

time wasters The occurrence of activities, events, and conditions producing few tangible outcomes or results of low value. (p. 375)

tort A private or civil wrong committed by one party against another person or organization or to a person's property or reputation. (p. 49)

total quality management A management system used to assure the continuous improvement of an organization's ability to meet and exceed customer needs and expectations. (p. 33)

training Is a systematic attempt to change employee behavior through the learning process in order to improve performance. (p. 39)

training plan The integration of person and task analysis into a plan of action that includes specifying training objectives, training program design, times frames, and employees to be trained. (p. 186)

training program The portion of a training plan that actually delivers instruction or otherwise facilitates learning. (p. 186)

trait approach An erroneous belief that effective leaders possess a universal set of common characteristics such as intelligence or compassion. (p. 142)

two-factor theory Needs are satisfied by two types of factors: hygiene factors that are related to the work environment capable of reducing job dissatisfaction; and motivators that are intrinsic to work and an individual and can improve job satisfaction and motivation. (p. 227)

Uniform Guidelines on Employee Selection and Procedures Established in 1978, describe equal opportunity compliance requirements and include a discussion of validation procedures. (p. 56)

union organizing The process of forming a union in an organization. (p. 76)

union security The amount of control a union exerts over its membership, including the right to represent employees and collect dues from members of a bargaining unit. (p. 74)

union shop New employees must join the union within a specified period of time after being hired and must pay dues to the union local. (p. 74)

union steward An employee who has been appointed or elected by union members to investigate complaints against management by members of a bargaining unit. (p. 80)

unity of command A relationship established in organizations in which members know to whom they are accountable. (p. 129)

utilitarianism An act is ethical if its overall benefit to the greater community outweighs its cost. (p. 16)

validation Requires that actions consistently and accurately relate to characteristics of the job and focus on job performance. (p. 56)

validity Is the accuracy of a measurement or test whereby tests measure what they are supposed to and the results are true. (p. 55)

vestibule training A form of training involving employees practicing the work processes and tools in a separate training area called a vestibule. (p. 186)

Wagner Act of 1935 Also called the National Labor Relations Act of 1935, it required employers to bargain with unions in good faith and prohibited certain employer practices such as discriminating against union organizers. (p. 73)

want The recognition of a need. (p. 224)

whole training Involves covering demonstration, practice, and feedback in one training session. (p. 188)

work rule Specific statement governing the behavior of employees while on the job. (p. 100)

written reprimand The second step in progressive discipline wherein the alleged offense is committed to a written form and becomes a matter of record. (p. 312)

yellow dog contract Requires an employee to agree as a condition of employment not to join a union or engage in union organizing activity. (p. 72)

zone of security An individual's sense of security arising from stable working conditions and relationships with others that make a person's future more predictable. (p. 358)

Chapter 13
Page **270** PEANUTS reprinted by permission of UFS, Inc. Page **277** By permission of Johnny Hart and Creators Syndicate, Inc.

Chapter 14
Page **286** Drawing by Stevenson; © 1988 The New Yorker Magazine, Inc.

Chapter 15
Page **307** Alfred W. Travers, *Supervision: Techniques and New Dimensions.* Copyright © 1988, pp. 266-269. Adapted by permission of Prentice-Hall, Englewood Cliffs, New Jersey. Page **313** From Mondy, R. Wayne and Noe, Robert M., *Human Resource Management.* Copyright © 1993 by Allyn and Bacon. Reprinted by permission. Page **315** Adapted from Jonathan A. Segal, "Did the Marquisde Sade Design Your Discipline Program?" *HRM Magazine* 35 (September 1990): 90-95.

Chapter 16
Page **326** Reprinted, by permission of publisher, from *Management Review,* April 1982 © 1982. American Management Association, New York. All rights reserved. Page **336** Reprinted, by permission of publisher, from *Supervisory Management,* July 1977 © 1977. American Management Association, New York. All rights reserved.

Chapter 17
Page **346** Beetle Bailey, August 9, 1993, King Features Syndicate, Inc. Page **348** Reprinted with permission from Thomas H. Holmes and Richard H. Rahe, "The Social Readjustment Scale," *Journal of Psychosomatic Research* (Vol. 11, 1967), p. 216, Elsevier Science Ltd., Pergamon Imprint Oxford, England. Page **335** GARFIELD reprinted by permission of UFS, Inc. Page **354** Adapted from Elton B. McNeil, "Psychology and Aggression," *Journal of Conflict Resolution* (Vol. 3, No. 3, 1959), pp. 200–206 and 209–220.

Chapter 18
Page **374** PEANUTS reprinted by permission of UFS, Inc. Page **382** From *How to Organize Your Work and Life* by Robert Moskowitz. Copyright © 1981 by Robert Moskowitz. Used by permission of Doubleday, a division of Bantam Doubleday Dell Publishing Group, Inc.

Chapter 19
Page **394** By permission of Johnny Hart and Creators Syndicate, Inc. Page **397** Reprinted with permission from *Psychology Today Magazine,* Copyright © 1978 (Sussex Publishers, Inc.). Page **398** PEANUTS reprinted by permission of UFS, Inc. Page **409** Reprinted, by permission of publisher, from *Supervisory Management,* May 1977 © 1977. American Management Association, New York. All rights reserved.

Index